THE NEW COOKING
OF BRITAIN AND IRELAND

Gwenda L. Heyman.

THE NEW COOKING OF BRITAIN AND IRELAND

A Culinary Journey in Search of Regional Foods and Innovative Chefs

GWENDA L. HYMAN

JOHN WILEY & SONS, Inc.

New York • Chichester • Brisbane • Toronto • Singapore

Library of Congress Cataloging-in-Publication Data:

Hyman, Gwenda L., 1934–
   The new cooking of Britain and Ireland : a culinary journey in
search of regional foods and innovative chefs / Gwenda L. Hyman.
      p.   cm.
   Includes bibliographical references and index.
   ISBN 0-471-01279-3 (pbk. : acid-free paper)
   1. Gastronomy—History.   2. Food—Great Britain—History.
3. Cookery, British.   4. Restaurants—Great Britain—Directories.
5. Cooks—Great Britain.
   I. Title.
TX635.H94   1995
641.5941'09045—dc20   94-38479

Printed in the United States of America

10 9 8 7 6 5 4 3 2 1

To my daughter
Rebecca
who loves Clotted Cream

FOREWORD

Gwenda Hyman is a brave woman. Twenty years ago she would not have dared to write this book and no publisher would have touched it. Even today she writes in the face of an unyielding view of Britain as a gastronomic wilderness. We may be good at castles and cathedrals, history and heritage, moors and glens—but if it's food you're after, buy a ticket to Paris or Rome. Myths, like treacle, are sticky substances. They take time to lick. But with this book, the British dinner plate is beginning to be licked clean. The message is clear—fly to London, Edinburgh, or Dublin, stay a while—then drive into the countryside and you will discover places that will thrill even the most fastidious gastronome. To rewrite Mr. Bush's famous words (if I dare), don't read my lips, read these words. You will eat well in Britain.

It is not as if the British Isles have always offered travelers a mean table. In the eighteenth century this country was on a gastronomic high and was the envy of Europe. Many celebrated chefs of the time wrote books of considerable influence, including John Farley, the famous head chef of the London Tavern. His ideas were snatched eagerly by a number of enterprising Parisian restaurateurs after the French Revolution, and English eating houses—known popularly as *les tavernes anglaises*—became enormously fashionable well into the nineteenth century. Meanwhile, in Regency England, the great chef Carême introduced high society to haute cuisine, and for the next 170 years smart dining in this country was overtaken by the European tradition. Through Escoffier right up to the Roux brothers, our palates were seduced by a succession of French masters who captured the gastronomic high ground. Over the past two decades all this changed as an increasingly affluent and better educated middle class discovered the pleasures of eating out, inspired by an extraordinary growth in media interest, which presented food as an important aspect of modern lifestyle. Enterprising and clever young Brits learned from their European tutors and started to assert their own imaginations. They traveled, they read, they ate and, gradually, using the enormous variety of raw materials available to them, they adopted fresh ideas to create a diverse, dynamic, and new pioneering approach to cooking. Eclecticism is the word most commonly used to describe this movement. In fact, what we are seeing is a kind of gastronomic liberation, a movement that has at last broken away from the rigidity of the French and Italian pedigrees. Now soy, salsa, and filo have become as much a part of our culinary lexicon as mustard, gravy, and apple pie.

A quick glance at Britain's history will tell you that this extraordinary renaissance in the British kitchen is less a phenomenon and more an example of the British character. From the medieval crusades and throughout our history as seafarers and mercantile adventurers, we have been a nation of magpies, poachers and, above all, inventors. The result in today's kitchen is an energy and a variety in the repertoires of this new breed of chefs, the effects of which are spreading rapidly right across the country—from the grandest of country house hotels to the most modest of pubs.

I travel extensively in Europe and I now believe that we are a match for anything that you might find in France and Italy. Indeed, too often I have eaten some pretty dismal meals in these countries. There is an arrogance and a complacency creeping into many of their kitchens. That does not mean that it is no longer possible to eat well on the continent. But equally, it is no longer true that you will eat badly in Britain. What *is* exhilarating is the difference in approach and attitude: a new dynamic that compares with the gastronomic developments also evident in the United States. In my view, London and New York are arguably the two most exciting cities in the world for the sheer versatility and quality of their restaurants. And the pioneering energy of the culinary movement on the West Coast compares with the buzz of creativity you will find in many of the regions of these islands.

Gwenda Hyman's book will give you a taste of what we have to offer. It is a sumptuous feast of heritage trail and gastronomic journey. There can be no better way to enjoy the new cooking of Britain and Ireland.

Kit Chapman

Kit Chapman, M.B.E. is the proprietor of the Michelin Starred Castle at Taunton. His book, Great British Chefs, *first published in 1989, is available in paperback, and he is currently writing a second volume to be published in the autumn of 1995.*

CONTENTS

FOREWORD   vii

PREFACE   xi

INTRODUCTION   1

1 A HISTORY OF BRITISH FOOD   9

2 LONDON   31

3 The Southeast   77
Kent, East Sussex, West Sussex, Hampshire, and Surrey

4 THE WEST COUNTRY   113
Cornwall, Devon, Somerset, Dorset, Avon, and Wiltshire,

5 THE HEARTLAND   145
Gloucestershire, Warwickshire, Oxfordshire,
Buckinghamshire, Bedfordshire, Hertfordshire, and Berkshire

6 THE MIDLANDS   170
West Midlands, Hereford and Worcester, Shropshire, Cheshire,
Staffordshire, Derbyshire, Nottinghamshire, Leicestershire, and Northamptonshire

7 EAST ANGLIA   199
Essex, Suffolk, Cambridgeshire, Norfolk, and Lincolnshire

8 THE NORTH COUNTRY   218
Cleveland, Northumberland, Durham, Tyne and Wear, North Yorkshire, West Yorkshire,
South Yorkshire, Humberside, Cumbria, Lancashire, Greater Manchester, and Merseyside

9 WALES   256

South Glamorgan, Mid Glamorgan, West Glamorgan, Powys, Dyfed,
Gwynedd, and Clwyd

10 SCOTLAND   314

Borders, Dumfries and Galloway, Lothian, Strathclyde, Central, Fife, Tayside,
Grampian, Highlands, Western Isles, Outer Hebrides, and Northern Isles

11 NORTHERN IRELAND   356

Antrim, Londonderry, Tyrone, Fermanagh, Armagh, and Down

12 THE REPUBLIC OF IRELAND   367

Monaghan, Louth, Meath, Dublin, Wicklow, Kildare, Wexford, Kilkenny, Waterford,
Tipperary, Cork, Kerry, Limerick, Clare, Galway, Mayo, Sligo, and Donegal

GEOGRAPHICAL LIST OF CONTRIBUTING RESTAURANTS AND HOTELS   419

BIBLIOGRAPHY   425

RECIPE INDEX   427

SUBJECT INDEX   431

PREFACE

I have often been asked during my years in America writing about food, "How can you be a food writer—you're English!" with a quickly added "just joking" at the expression on my face. The sad thing is that they are **not** joking. Many people firmly believe that British food is terrrible. This book gives me a chance to address this misconception and try to change the faulty image.

The truth of the matter is very different. Nowhere in the world is the pasturage for rearing beef, lamb, and other livestock as lush and plentiful as in Britain and Ireland. We have been acclaimed for our excellent roasts and chops and superlative dairy products since time immemorial. The fertile land and terperate climate grow succulent vegetables and luscious juicy fruits. Game is abundant; fish—particularly in Ireland—is so plentiful that in some Irish rivers it is said salmon can be pulled from the water with the bare hands. Most people with even a tiny patch of land grow their own vegetables. My father and grandfather grew copious amounts of produce, from parsnips, potatoes, and cabbages to tomatoes, lettuce, green beans, and enormous squashes which we ate stuffed. Cherries, apples, and a variety of soft fruits also came from the garden. My father, who is ninety years old, still looks after his garden; in early spring his greenhouse is full of vegetable and strawberry plants.

My grandmother prepared mouthwatering, delicious meals on her coal black iron range in the tiny Hampshire village of Leckford on the River Test. Everything Grandmother used was fresh. Buying vegetables at the village shop, which stocked everything from buttonhooks to baking powder, was unheard of. We stayed often at Leckford, and my brother, Bob, and I used to fetch milk directly from the farmer at the end of the village. We carried two metal milk cans with wide bottoms and narrow necks and contrived to arrive early so we could watch the farmer milking the cows before he filled our cans with warm, foaming milk. English hedgerows are full of berries and hazelnuts in autumn and, when we were not messing about either in or on the River Test, we would take a basket and a hooked stick to pull the canes forward and set off to collect blackberries or nuts for grandmother's delicious pies and breads. One of our favorite things to do on summer mornings was to set off before dawn to gather button mushrooms. (New button mushrooms gleam white in the darkness, and finding them is child's play.)

An annual event I remember all too clearly was harvesting the wheat. All the men in the village, from the shopkeeper to the blacksmith, helped the local farmers bring in the crop. We children thronged behind to watch the tractor cut a swathe around the edge of the field, then another within that, and so on until a six-foot square of wheat was all that was left standing. The men, each with a sack in one hand, circled the standing wheat, and as the tractor cut through the last of it, all the rabbits that had retreated to the center of the protecting wheat fled outward. The men leaped into action, and within seconds there were enough rabbits in the sacks to make pies and stews for the whole village. Really all that good food needs is fresh ingredients and a good cook, and England, Ireland, Wales, and Scotland have some of the best of both.

So why has British food such a bad reputation? The answer is that for a while we had many cooks who, thinking that French food was elegant and therefore what people wanted, turned out fussy, oversauced food without the training or firsthand experience to know how to cook French dishes properly. This is no longer the case. For the last twenty years at least, British and Irish chefs are among the best trained in Europe, and many of them travel to Asia to learn the secrets of exotic cuisines firsthand.

In this book I have tried, through recipes from some of the best chefs and recipes for regional dishes, to bring you a taste of the new cooking of Britain and Ireland as well as the delightful traditional cooking that still prevails. It would be impossible to include every chef who deserves to be mentioned, or every area worth visiting for a meal. There are many more places to eat beautifully cooked food and scores more scenic spots to see than I have written about here. I hope this book will inspire you to travel through Britain and Ireland and find them.

Acknowledgments

First of all I want to thank all the chefs who were so enthusiastic about this book—for the wealth of recipes they sent me, and for sharing their passion for good fresh food. Their restaurants or hotels are listed in the Geographical List. I also want to give a special thanks to Kit Chapman of the Castle Hotel, Taunton, Somerset; Shaun Hill of The Merchant's House, Ludlow, Shropshire; Francis Coulson of Sharrow Bay Hotel on Lake Ullswater, Cumbria; and Paul Henderson of Gidleigh Park Hotel, Chagford, Devon, who have supported me throughout the writing and researching of this book. For generously lending me their cookbooks and not complaining about the length of time I kept them, I want to thank my friends Gaile Binzen, Eileen Binns, Olwen Woodier, Suzy Maroon, Rosalie Wilkinson, Anne Catherine Fallen, and Sandra Bosworth. Jack and Alice Angel gave me access to their enormous collection of British and Irish cookbooks, for which I thank them. Gilli Davies fed me regional Welsh dishes and gave me three of the books she has written on food, as did Shaun Hill, Gerry Galvin from Drimcong House, County Galway, and John and Sally McKenna of Estragon Press, County Cork. I am also indebted to John Alwyn-Jones, Marketing Director for Wales, British Tourist Authority, and Bedford Pace, Public Relations Director, British Tourist Authority, for their help. The most heartfelt thanks go to my husband, Charles Hyman, who with great humor plowed through all the regional steamed puddings, pies, and pastries we tested together and gave his unfailing support throughout, and I am especially grateful to my editor, Claire Thompson, for her patience and gentle guidance in the making of this book.

Gwenda Hyman

INTRODUCTION

Traditional British food is simple and hearty, as befits a nation with a sometimes raw climate, yet one temperate enough to grow copious amounts of succulent fruits and vegetables. The people of these islands are fond of their roasts of beef, lamb, and pork, and it is no secret that the best meats in the world are nurtured here. Part of the reason for this is excellent pasturage. The climate, warmed by the Gulf Stream and given to lots of misty rain showers, is perfect for growing green, nutritious grass, as well as a wealth of fresh produce. British and Irish home cooking has always been varied, and frequently delicious, despite its dubious reputation. It is in the genes of the British to be self-deprecating, and accepting criticism with a laugh or a shrug is part of their nature. But if you read the backgrounds of today's most celebrated chefs, more often than not there was someone, be it grandmother, mother, or father, who sparked a love of good food and an absorbing interest in preparing food early in their lives. One classic example of this is Philip Vickery, who cooks brilliantly at the Castle Hotel, Taunton, Somerset. Both his mother and grandmother were excellent cooks, and Phil became adept in the kitchen at a very early age. Home cooks often excel at pastry and puddings, especially warm and comforting in inclement weather.

As nations passionate about gardening, Britain and Ireland are noted for a prolification of backyard greenhouses, and people vie with each other for the first red tomato and the biggest squash in the street. Increasingly, home gardeners are growing their own vegetables wherever they have enough land, and when this is not possible, fresh herbs are grown in pots on balconies and kitchen windowsills. Supermarkets, too, are rising to the occasion and taking an active role in promoting the lesser known fruits and vegetables and other ingredients new to the general public—even going so far as to label the organically grown, and therefore sometimes not so attractive-looking, produce as having been chosen for taste rather than appearance. Supermarkets provide fresher vegetables in greater variety than were available twenty years ago. Sainsbury's, one of England's best supermarket chains, publishes a magazine that introduces its readers to unfamiliar produce and exotic ingredients and provides recipes to encourage their customers to try new foods. Splendid emporiums, such as Harrods Food Hall, have always inspired their clientele by stocking a wealth of fruits and vegetables, as well as hundreds of cheeses and every type of sausage, dried meat, smoked fish, wine, dairy product, and bakery goody known to man. Now Harvey Nichols and other London stores are opening their own food halls, but Harrods has been in the forefront alone in this for years.

British food has for too long had a reputation for bad cooking. Every country has restaurants that disappoint, and Britain and Ireland are no exceptions. Cooks who skimp on the quality of their ingredients, or simply slide into sloppy methods of preparation, exist in all countries. In Britain bad cooking was frequently a failed attempt to create French dishes without either the necessary ingredients or the requisite training; but in Britain and Ireland cooking has positively leaped out of its former doldrums. In all corners of the countries, chefs are making wonderful fare with free-range chickens, beef that knows no hormone additives or fertilized feed, robustly flavored local game from venison to quail, a multitude of traditionally made farmhouse cheeses, superb dairy products, and excellent locally grown fruits and vegetables.

Vegetables are no longer universally overcooked, watery, and limp but are crisp, vivid-hued, and packed with flavor. One chef, not too long ago, joked about overcooked vegetables, saying he gave up cooking because he had to rise at six in the morning to put the cabbage on to boil for lunch at noon! Happily this canard can now join the other myths about British food. Vegetables always have played more than just a supporting role on the menu in these islands, and advice on how to retain their flavors has not been lacking. For example, John Farley's *The London Art of Cookery*, first published in London in 1783, contains his observation on cooking vegetables: "Numbers of cooks spoil their garden stuffs by boiling them too much. All kinds of vegetables should have a little crispness, for if you boil them too much, you will deprive them of their sweetness and beauty." In people's homes it would be unthinkable not to have an assortment of vegetables to accompany the roast on Sundays—usually two kinds of potatoes, one roasted under the joint until brown, crisp, and soaked with meat juices, the other mashed with butter and cream or milk. Cauliflower, cabbage, or Brussels sprouts appear in season with regularity, and in the summer months squashes are served sauced or stuffed. Shaun Hill, chef-proprietor of the Merchant House, his restaurant in a sixteenth-century half-timbered building on Corve Street in Ludlow, advocates starting a meal with the best you have to offer while guests' palates are still fresh and receptive. He thinks the best is often the wonderful, locally grown vegetables available almost everywhere today and points out that clean, sharp tastes encourage you to eat. He serves these vegetables perfectly cooked as a first course with a handful of wild mushrooms, or he purées them to make robust or delicate soups.

Breakfast and Tea

One meal, a perennial favorite that has appeared on British tables for several hundred years, is a breakfast consisting of ham or bacon, eggs, sausage, fried bread, and fried tomatoes, with innumerable cups of tea, followed by buttered toast and marmalade. Marmalade, by the way, did not originate in Britain but in Portugal, where it was made from quince (called *marmelo*). It was imported to England in the fourteenth and fifteenth centuries until Britons started making their own, experimenting with various different fruits; oranges won the day. Bubble and squeak, made by frying leftover potatoes and cabbage or Brussels sprouts and sometimes sliced onions, is still a breakfast treat in many parts of Britain. (The cabbage "squeaks" as it is fried in the hot bacon fat.) Kippers—those delectable plump smoked herrings—are steeped in hot water, patted dry, and gently heated in butter. The best ones come from Northumberland, the Isle of Man, or Scotland and have not been dyed a startling gold but keep their original silvery shade. Dying kippers is against the law in the Isle of Man. Deviled kidneys and kedgeree—a dish of rice, minced Finnan haddie, hard-boiled eggs, cream, and curry spices—have a colonial Indian heritage. Finnan haddie (smoked haddock) hails from Findon in Scotland and is usually simmered in water or milk. These dishes, all once common on the breakfast table, are now more often eaten on leisurely country weekends, or for a light supper or high tea. In Scotland, Scotch Pancakes, made with a soft dough and cooked on the traditional griddle, are delicious hot or cold. In the West Country, eggs are baked in lidded ramekins, nestled on a bed of chopped ham, crab, or shrimp with herbs, or buttered asparagus tips and grated cheese, until just set. The variations on this theme are endless. Budget-minded travelers to these shores have long known that a person can subsist very well for the day on a traditional English breakfast and little else. Now that we are no longer wholly an agricultural nation working in the fresh air from sunup to sundown, our breakfasts have become less hearty. Replacing the traditional "fry up" are cold cereals, toast, an occasional egg, and, of course, oatmeal.

Oatmeal, a high-energy food and easy to digest, has sustained the folk of Britain and Ireland at breakfast for many centuries. People in Scotland still regularly eat oatmeal with cold milk and a little salt—often, curiously, while standing or walking about. The English eat their porridge with brown sugar and milk or cream. The Welsh prefer *siot*, an oatcake soaked in *brewis*—an oatmeal broth—and buttermilk. A forerunner of porridge, served for centuries, was frumenty, made by soaking wheat or barley in water and leaving it in a warm place for three days. The grains burst, forming a jellylike mass with the grain suspended in it. Frumenty, sweetened with honey, was eaten with hot milk. Yorkshire folk preferred their frumenty flavored with nutmeg and a pinch of salt.

Tea is very often preferred over coffee both in the morning and during the day. "Let's put the kettle on for a cuppa" is a phrase heard all over Britain and Ireland from early morning—the first cup is usually had between the sheets—to late at night. In offices and stores, an afternoon without a tea break would be unthinkable. Some visitors confuse afternoon tea with high tea, though the two serve quite different functions. Afternoon tea served at four o'clock started as a light pick-me-up between lunch and dinner, when in the nineteenth century it became fashionable to push back the dinner hour to around eight o'clock in the evening. Something was needed to bridge the long gap between meals, and afternoon tea filled the bill admirably. Tearooms in towns and villages all over Britain and Ireland provide a particularly welcome break when one is exhausted from shopping or museum hopping. One can count on being served warm scones, baked everywhere in these islands, with fruit preserves and clotted cream (the heavy, rich crust of cream skimmed from the top of a wide low pan of unpasteurized milk that has heated slowly over a very low flame in the cool dairy room all day). There may also be tiny sandwiches of cucumber, cress, chopped egg, or smoked salmon; toasted tea cakes (in the cool months); lemon curd; fruit jellies served with cream; shortbread; and one good satisfying Madeira cake or fruit cake. Continuous recourse to the scalding teapot is in order. High tea is more substantial, though possibly less caloric, and can be a substitute for dinner, especially for children. The food possibilities are endless—cold meats or cold raised pies, or hearty one-dish soups, followed by salad, curried prawns and rice, omelettes, egg and chips, any of the aforementioned robust breakfast dishes, and a cake or pudding. Again, innumerable cups of tea are served to "wash it all down."

Changing Times

The great traditional recipes of cooks who wrote many of the early cookery books are now being perused once again and updated. Among these are Hannah Glasse, Eliza Acton, and John Farley, whose dishes evolved before the easy availability of prepared and packaged foods. Using modern equipment to mix, chop, and purée makes these recipes far less time-consuming than they once were, and their emphasis on fresh, seasonal foods meshes perfectly with today's new approach to eating.

British chefs, too, have taken a fresh look at their own culinary heritage and started to experiment with traditional recipes, regional foods, and comforting foods from childhood. As they have honed their culinary skills, the demand for fresher and better ingredients to work with has grown. Market gardeners, producers, farmers, and fishermen all over Britain and Ireland have responded, and the number and variety of pristine fruits, vegetables, and farmhouse cheeses have increased beyond belief. New methods of raising cattle, sheep, and pigs have resulted in improved flavor, less fat, and better cuts of meat. The fishing industry has kept pace with a wider range of fish and delivers it to its destination with greater speed and efficiency. Today, locally grown herbs and edible flowers are to be had in abundance. It is clear that the freshest and best ingredients obtainable, coupled with the creative skill of chefs who enjoy innovation, are the only prerequisites for satisfying, delicious food. The British and Irish are now much more receptive to new ideas in restaurant cooking, as they have always been receptive to the cooking in foreign restaurants in London and other cities. Chinese, Indian, Middle Eastern, and Southeast Asian restaurants can be found in every small town. Vietnamese cuisine, based as it is on fresh fish, lean meat, fruits, vegetables, and a wealth of freshly picked leaves, is uniquely suited to the prevailing tastes inherent in the new cooking.

During the booming 1980s, many of the country houses of the landed gentry were bought and turned into sumptuous hotels where guests could luxuriate in the quiet calm of the country and be pampered in every way. Often the hotel owners were not themselves chefs but sought young, talented chefs from London establishments to run their country house kitchens. This gave chefs the opportunity to generate fresh ideas with a wealth of superb ingredients and to become well known in the process. One of the very best of the genre is the Castle Hotel on Castle Green in Taunton, Somerset. Another beautifully situated retreat, hidden in the depths of rural Devon near Chagford, is Gidleigh Park Hotel, where Michael Caines, the head chef, ably mans the kitchens. Francis Coulson, a superb chef, directs the Sharrow Bay Country House Hotel on Ullswater in Cumbria. John Tovey, at Miller Howe on Lake Windermere, is another great chef with a flair for the dramatic. Unfortunately, luxurious hotels have been the hardest hit by the recession. Sadly, some have had to close their doors. Upscale restaurants, too, in most areas of the country, even in big cities, have suffered the same fate.

On the brighter side, however, it is astonishing to eat in modestly priced restaurants and to find the cooking as good as it is. Fresh vegetables, steamed to perfection, often five or six different kinds, and frequently homegrown, are served with the main course. Tiny vegetable tartlets or miniature mousses also adorn the plates. Interesting salads, once a rarity outside of the cities, are much in evidence. Soups, seasoned with lively fresh herbs or oriental spices, wild mushrooms in flaky pastry purses, imaginative potato dishes, and pasta, perfectly cooked with sauces that include ingredients as unusual as beet greens or chard, spark the menus. This renaissance in restaurant and hotel cooking evident in the last two decades continues to spread throughout the countryside. Surprisingly, meatless dishes are also prevalent. The number of vegetarians is growing rapidly in Britain and Ireland—among the young, who don't want to eat any food that is factory farmed, and among older people, who are concerned with staying healthy. The percentage of non-meat-eaters is high enough for restaurateurs to need to cater to them with interesting vegetarian selections. Several restaurants now have an evening each week when only vegetarian dishes are prepared. One such is Melton's, located in the old Roman city of York, in North Yorkshire, where chef Michael Hjort cooks excellent, creative food. British chefs today are masters of their craft and have every reason to feel equal to their European counterparts. Increasingly, too, the general public has come to realize the profound pleasure to be had from a well-cooked, beautifully presented meal and to take advantage of the wealth of creative talent in their midst.

Pubs

Even pubs, those former bastions of the forlorn sausage roll and factory-produced steak and kidney pie, viewed with dread for generations, are beginning to serve fresh well-prepared dishes. Part of the reason for better pub food is that breweries, which own most of the pubs in Britain, take a percentage of the beer profits. Providing customers with food along with their pints is a way for the publican to improve his balance sheet. When breweries first took over the public houses, the quality of the beer started to slide. Delivered in huge, metal containers, beer had none of the individual flavors of brews aged in wooden barrels with varying ingredients and water from different locales. A wave of public protest spawned a search for good local ales, and microbreweries were born. Since at one time everyone brewed his own beer at home, individual differences in flavor are considered an added bonus.

British beer is almost always served at cellar temperature. If a colder brew is desired, ask for lager, but it won't have the same taste as regular beer. British brews take time to get used to and time to explore. Guinness stout, the full-bodied brew of Ireland that fortifies body and soul on a cold day, is the perfect complement to many foods indigenous to Ireland. Try Guinness with Dublin Bay prawns, farmhouse cheeses, and Irish soda bread, or briny, Galway oysters. Moran's of the Weir is a traditional pub which has oyster beds right on its doorstep that provide some of the best oysters in Ireland. Moran's is at Kilcolgan, on the Gort road out of Galway city.

Pubs can be found on almost every corner in Britain and Ireland. They are sociable places, where affable, congenial folk regularly get together. If getting to know the natives is on your agenda, this is the place to do so. Talking to strangers in a pub is perfectly acceptable, particularly in villages. People go to pubs to catch up on the local news and on each other, and to spend a convivial evening.

The people of these rather chilly islands are also passionate about wine. It is not an exaggeration to say that by and large they are more knowledgeable when it comes to wines—where they are grown and which years are the best—than the average French person. In addition to wine grown close to home on the Continent, wines from South Africa, North and South America, and the Antipodes are very well known in Britain. A direct result of this oenophilic fervency is the wine bar. You will find wine bars wherever you go, not only in London and other major cities, but in small towns in the Shires. They are wonderful places for learning about wine, since they serve everything from first-class vintages down to regular plonk, as vin ordinaire is known in Britain. The quality of the food found in wine bars is frequently above average, and the prices generally are reasonable. Like pubs, wine bars are well-patronized spots where whiling away an evening can be fun.

Cheeses and Puddings

Not so long ago, the cheeses known to most of the British public were bland, plastic wrapped, and suffered from being kept far too cold. (Very cold temperatures dry out the cheese and alter its flavor. If you have the time to shop frequently, it is best to buy only as much cheese as you will need for the next day or two, rather than to resort to storing cheese in the refrigerator.) In the past fifteen years the availability of farmhouse cheeses has improved dramatically through the efforts of a small group of retailers who literally went to the farms all over Britain and Ireland to search out cheesemakers and bring their products to market. In the forefront are Patrick Rance, and now his son, Hugh Rance, who have a fabulous cheese store in Streatley, Berkshire. They encouraged new cheesemakers to begin producing cheeses of every description from cow's, goat's, and sheep's milk, preferably from unpasteurized milk on the farm where the animal was milked. Mr. Rance buys homemade cheeses directly from the farmers who make them and stores them at just the right temperature and humidity until they reach their peak of perfection. Only then are they allowed to be sold. There is no single factor that defines the special character and flavor of a good farmhouse cheese. Rather it is a combination of fresh, high-quality milk straight from the farm and a strong desire to spend the time and effort to make a distinctive cheese. Knowledge of the traditional methods of cheesemaking is essential. The old ways seem to work far better than mass production when it comes to making farmhouse cheese. Though several delicious cheeses are made from pasteurized milk—Colston Bassett Stilton is one example, and others are the several traditional pasteurized Cheddars—most farmers make their cheeses from unpasteurized milk.

Comfort food, as it is quaintly called, is served widely nowadays. This brings back delicious, old-fashioned desserts— such as sticky toffee pudding, bread and butter pudding, and rice pudding—frequently made with the recipe revised to lower the fat content of the original. In Britain and Ireland puddings have always been much loved. We have been a nation of pudding eaters since Saxon times, and many puddings are world renowned. Who among us has not tasted Christmas pudding fragrant with dried fruits and brandy and gaily decorated with a sprig of holly? Six weeks before Christmas, housewives from John o'Groats to Lands End assemble the ingredients for this national dish—suet, eggs, sugar, brandy, nutmeg, allspice, dried fruits, and candied citron. Each child in the family takes a turn at stirring the Christmas pudding and with eyes closed makes a wish. A silver threepenny bit is stirred into the stiff batter, supposedly to bring good fortune to the lucky finder. Yorkshire Pudding, the perfect accompaniment to roast beef, rises in crisp pinnacles, lighter than a soufflé when properly made, quite unlike the leaden, yellow lump dreaded by boarding-school children. Many dishes have quaint names like rumpledethumps, cock-a-leekie, fat rascals, and spotted dick or spotted dog. The latter is a boiled suet pudding studded with raisins, which could possibly bring to mind the spotted coat of a Dalmatian. To add to the confusion, to a large part of Britain the word *pudding* is synonymous with dessert and is frequently not a pudding at all. The swing in new British cooking toward homegrown fruits and vegetables, farmhouse cheeses, fish straight from the sea, and a renewed interest in beans, grains, and fresh herbs is good news indeed. The most important adjunct to a really good meal, though, is the skill of the cook. In the seventeenth century Andrew Boorde said, "God may send a man good meat, but the devyll may send an evyll coke to destrue it."

1

A History of British Food

Lush green fields, abundant rainfall, and mild temperatures have brought immigrants to Britain's shores since prehistoric times. Stone Age farmers hunted deer, elk, wild ox, wild pig, and a variety of seabirds, as well as swans, geese, and eiderducks, for food. Feathers were prized almost as much as flesh. Sheep and pigs were bred for food, and dogs and cattle were domesticated. Wild game, mainly badger and hedgehog, were hung until soft enough to eat, as we still hang game to tenderize it today. Occasionally, with the help of the dogs, the hunters were able to nab a bear or a wolf. Salmon, sturgeon, and cod were roasted over glowing coals. Meat was chopped, mixed with herbs, and boiled in a gut casing, producing a sausage resembling Scotland's haggis. Cattle provided milk, cream, and butter, as well as meat. During the summer, butter encased in leather or wooden containers was buried in peat bogs for use in the winter months. It was called "bog butter." Plentiful but limited varieties of herbs added flavor. Crushed seeds of coriander, poppy, and mustard seasoned winter foods. Wild parsnips, carrots, and edible young leaves were collected for the cooking pot. Ale was brewed, and a drink similar to mead was concocted from honey and wheat.

Iron Age farmers grew wheat and rye and ground the grains for flour. Unleavened bread, covered with a cooking pot, was baked on the hot hearthstone. Yeast was as yet unknown. Grain was used for porridge and gruel, and flour mixed with the blood of slaughtered cattle was made into black puddings. Edible nuts and fruits were gathered in the autumn; crab apples were turned into a rough cider.

The **Romans**

Even before the Roman invasion, Britain mined jet, tin, and copper and exported wool, corn, and cattle in return for wine and herbs. The Romans arrived in force in A.D. 43, and they ruled Britain for almost 350 years. Romans built cities of stone linked by arrow-straight roads, and palaces with indoor plumbing beneath decorative mosaic-tiled floors. Much was learned by Britain from her conquerors, and important agricultural advances occurred under Roman rule. New crops, such as flax and oats, were cultivated and fruit trees were imported, as well as new flowers, lots of different vegetables, fruits, and nut-bearing trees. A great deal of wine was imported, and grapes for wine-making were planted in southern England. Even more important was the vinegar that resulted as the wine soured. Vinegar was in great demand for preserving foods, for adding savor to cooked dishes, and as a refreshing drink when greatly diluted with water. The Romans also introduced many new herbs, among them rosemary, sage, dill, thyme, and marjoram, as well as their favorite seasoning, called *garam* or *liquamen*. This early prepared sauce was made by fermenting anchovies, and other small fish, with salt in closed containers for months, just as Asian fish sauce is made today. Spices, especially black pepper, were imported from Southeast Asia and China. Highly flavored sweet sauces for game were made with damsons and dates or prunes. Raisins sweetened sauces for veal, dried figs flavored boiled hams, and honey was as ubiquitous in foods as *liquamen*.

Britons learned to enclose land to create game parks stocked with deer and wild boar for the table, and to keep their pigs in sties and fatten them on grain. They also learned to trap snails, feed them until they grew too stout for their shells, and cook them in oil flavored with wine and *liquamen*. Dormice and baby rabbits were cooked the same way.

The Romans wisely invited prominent Britons to their inner sanctums and included them at their ostentatious feasts. Roman dishes were decorated with pearls, amber, gold beads, and precious stones. Peacocks and swans, elaborately dressed, their feathers reattached, ornamented Roman tables. Britons were soon reclining on couches placed at three sides of a low table, as the Romans did. Slaves used the fourth side to wait on the guests. Food was eaten with the fingers and hands, which were rinsed between courses. Each person brought his own napkins to the feast. During the gargantuan meal guests were entertained by clowns, acrobats, musicians, and gladiators. Roman legions guarding Hadrian's Wall were also well fed. Remains indicate they ate a large amount of pork, beef when they could get it, and also a fair amount of lamb. Lowland farmers north of the Wall kept the fortress supplied with meat. Oyster shells are found in the thousands near Roman settlements.

The Saxons

By A.D. 400 the Romans were hounded from British shores by invading Saxons. Angles invaded in force at the end of the fifth century. These two Germanic tribes gave the people of Britain their name—Anglo-Saxons.

Saxon housewives were very skilled. They tended herb gardens, and in their stillrooms they made myriad preserves, cordials, wines, simple cosmetic lotions, and perfumed powders. Even love potions were not beyond their capabilities. Scented flowers and herbs, such as rosemary, thyme, sage, garlic, saffron, mint, and marigold, masked the tainted flavor of salted fish and meats. Marigold flowers enhanced dried legumes and dishes containing cheese and veal. Cowslips were grown for their pollen, which attracted bees; clove-scented pinks sweetened wines; and violets embellished puddings. The earliest puddings, which were savory, date to the Saxon era. Made from mixtures of meat, grain, and herbs, they were encased in the cleaned lining of a sheep's stomach and boiled. Haggis, a specialty of Scotland, is still made this way. Once the suet crust was invented, superceding the work-intensive stomach lining, puddings proliferated, and both savory and sweet puddings were found everywhere. One early sweet pudding, called Sussex Pond, survives to this day; it encloses a whole lemon within the suet crust. Recipes for sweet puddings, from simple treacle to glorious plum, are legion.

Saxons salted their hams to preserve them. Pigs were very economical, as the entire animal from ears to tail was eaten. Pigs foraged for themselves, cost practically nothing to raise, and were especially loved in the western regions of the south. In the east, sheep were preferred, as the animal supplied not only meat but wool for clothing and milk for cheese. In the west midland counties roast mutton has been served with red currant jelly since earliest times. East Anglia prefers the tart taste of barberry jelly, and the Welsh mountain lamb goes well with rowan jelly. Mutton is served with a hot sauce of creamed onions in southern counties, and mutton raised on the salt marshes goes well with a hot laver sauce made from that dark green seaweed growing on seawater-washed lands. At that period, and for centuries to come, livestock was slaughtered as the hay ran out with encroaching winter. All animals except pigs, milk animals, and breeding stock were killed, one after the other. The offal was eaten immediately, and the rest of the meat preserved for the coming lean months by salting or smoking. By winter's end those animals that were saved were drastically malnourished.

When beef became popular in Britain, lean winter beef were driven by herdsmen to lowland pastures, fattened up, and sold to the growing population of London. The Saxon aristocracy were delighted with the abundance of game in Britain, and hunting soon became a major sport. Though Saxons were careful not to kill kids, lamb, or calves, so that game would replenish itself, other hunters were not so disposed, and by the time the Normans invaded Britain in 1066, bears were extinct.

The Vikings

In the ninth century, Vikings—fierce, pagan warriors from Scandinavia—began vicious raids on Europe, the British Isles, and Russia. The long Viking warship, with a high stern and a high prow, was decorated with an animal hide. The wooden ship was carved and painted, wooden shields hung along its length, and its square sails were striped in vivid colors. It struck terror in the hearts of all who beheld it. The Viking Age lasted until the eleventh century, terminating with the establishment of the stalwart kingdoms of Norway, Sweden, and Denmark. Many Vikings, also called Norsemen, Northmen, or Danes, eventually settled in the countries they conquered. Danes, despite their terrifying aspects, were unexpectedly good farmers. They instituted improved agricultural techniques, as well as new culinary skills for the proper storage of dairy products, the fermenting of whey, techniques for pressing meat, and smoke-drying as a means of preserving and enhancing meat's flavor.

The Normans

In 1066, two hundred years after the Vikings had raided Britain and Ireland, the Normans arrived, the last invaders to conquer these islands. Within little more than one hundred years, they had subdued large stretches of Ireland's southern and eastern territories. The French-speaking Normans brought a European bias to the islands that influenced both language and cooking. For example, sheep's meat soon became "mutton" from the French word *"mouton."* Normans were great meat-eaters, preferring beef, mutton, veal, and tender, young goat's flesh to pork, which they considered fit only for the poor. They also took with enthusiasm to sausages and blood puddings. Unlike Saxons, who spared the knife when it came to very young animals, the Normans relished veal and kid. They too began hunting with a passion, but to the consternation of the farmers whose land they galloped through, the new laws enacted by the Normans forbade any redress to the farmer when his crops were destroyed by marauding wild animals. Norman kings considered all hunting lands to be for their personal use, and poachers were routinely blinded or otherwise brutalized until 1217 when the laws were mitigated. Returning hunters looked forward to their traditional reward—pies containing the liver and lights (lungs) of wild game. Hare and rabbits were plentiful, and these were allowed to be trapped by the poor. Wild boars in large numbers roamed the forests until the fifteenth century, providing the much-loved delicacy called brawn, made from the animal's head and traditionally served as part of the Christmas feast. The wild boar became extinct in the seventeenth century, but brawn-making continues, using tame boar or domestic pigs. An economical dish, brawn fed the inhabitants of large feudal estates that developed under Norman rule.

Land was the basis of wealth, and large manor houses, built on huge tracts of land that held a village, mill, smithy, and ample pasturage for livestock, were virtually self-sustaining. The household ate in huge raftered halls. The lord of the manor and his guests were seated at a separate table raised on a dais. A fire was built between the dais and the rest of the feudal retinue, who ate at tables on the far side of the glowing embers. The first tablecloths Britons had seen covered the upper table, and a deep overhang protected their legs from drafts and prying eyes. A huge silver or silver-gilt salt cellar graced the head table. The placement of smaller salt cellars on the lower tables coined the phrase "below the salt."

Large slices of stale bread, called trenchers, substituted for plates and were renewed between courses. It was customary for noblemen to give their trenchers to the poor after a meal, or feed them to their dogs. Trenchers were replaced with wooden boards with a depression in the middle for sauces by the fifteenth century. These bread slices gave us the word *trencherman*, meaning a hearty eater. Platters were used to hold stews, but roasted meats were carved into manageable pieces and distributed to diners on the point of the carving knife. Everyone brought his own knife and spoon to table, as earlier the Romans used their own personal napkins. Spoons were used for soupy sauces or broths, and dagger-type knives speared or cut meat; forks were found only in the kitchen, where they had been used as cooking implements for centuries. Eventually forks became commonplace in Italy, and from there Catherine de Medici took them to France in 1533, along with her pastry cooks, when she married François I. However, it was another three to four hundred years before the fork was accepted in England. At the end of each course, a *"Sotele"*—a carved sugar and lard sculpture on a particular theme—often jellied and sometimes gilded, was presented to a favored guest. The theme of the carving generally bore some subtle relationship to the person honored, and these elaborate structures were meant to be eaten. At the end of the meal, when the tables had been cleared of all the dishes, guests were served whole spices, wafers, and sweet wine. Entertainment was often clowns or mime.

The main meal of the day was eaten in late morning, around half past eleven, and a lesser meal at five o'clock in the evening. At this time the lord of the manor heard requests or complaints from members of his mini-kingdom. Complicated rules of comportment at table had to be learned by diners. For example, it was considered unseemly to drink from a communal cup when your mouth was full of food. Gargantuan feasts were served on state occasions. In attendance on the king was a nobleman who was His Majesty's cup bearer and taster. Quite often the nobleman was given the king's gold cup for his services. The diet of the poor at this time was still coarse dark bread, broth, and a bowl of curds or sometimes cheese. One cheese of ignominious fame made from whey was so hard it had to be soaked and then beaten with a hammer before it could be eaten.

A dish served frequently in the Middle Ages was frumenty, made from grains left to soak in water until they burst and formed a thick gelatinous mixture of a porridgelike consistency. This dish and bacon and beans are considered to be the oldest-known dishes in England. Frumenty, cooked with egg yolks, saffron, and almond milk into a stiff pudding, accompanied venison and other game dishes. Another stiff pudding, blamanger, entailed cooking rice in almond milk, mixing it with shredded chicken and sugar, and cooking it again until it formed a dense mass. Blamanger was served with almonds and anise seeds. Spicy sauces, many of them containing pounded nuts and bread crumbs well moistened with vinegar, were placed on the table for dunking fresh meat or game. These forerunners of the English steak sauces became extremely popular as they disguised the taste of tainted meat. Fish and meat were also pounded and mixed with a great deal of clove, ginger, and cinnamon, or pounded fruit. These mixtures were rolled into balls or wrapped in dough and fried. At each of three courses on the table of a wealthy medieval household, innumerable dishes were served. The first course offered fritters, meat pies, a fish or eel dish, a roast or large joint of boiled meat, and brewet—thin slices of meat doused in a highly flavored cinnamon sauce. The second course included roasts, freshwater fish, bacon broth, a stiff pudding, and highly flavored pies and pasties. The third course would bring more game, eels, fish, fritters, and frumenty. The meal finished with a jellied dish.

Eggs were used copiously in custards, sauces, and puddings, as a thickener in stews and soups, and for fritters, stuffings, and pancakes. Omelettes were much in evidence and frequently were made with cheese, as we do today. This dish was called fraysse, not omelette. The enormous number of eggs called for in medieval recipes is indicative of the small size of the medieval egg compared with our twentieth-century jumbo.

Fish and meat were basted over a spit or boiled in spiced or herbed broths and served with imaginative sauces. Whale and porpoise were served to dignitaries, and unbelievable numbers of oysters were consumed. Fruits were abundant and frequently cooked with spices.

Medieval Times

The first usable cookbook was written at the behest of Richard II, in the later part of the fourteenth century, by his chief cooks. It was called *The forme of Cury*. Later medieval cookbooks show that cooks were well versed in the use of innumerable spices, as well as verjuice (a liquid made from the juice of vegetables), and ale for flavoring. Almond milk was used ubiquitously to thicken or enrich sauces and desserts. Due to the influx of Flemish and Dutch gardeners fleeing persecution in the early fourteenth century, gardening became more interesting, as they introduced many varieties of fruits, flowers, and vegetables. Monasteries, and manor houses too, had their herb gardens and vineyards. Religious rules forbidding the eating of meat on Friday were strictly upheld. Fast days prescribed a diet of vegetables or grain only. Monks and nuns never ate meat, but the bread and water diet, as it was called, was not just bread and water. All types of cereal were allowed, and these were made into flavorful vegetable soups with barley, oatcakes with butter and cheese, dumplings filled with fruits, bread and butter puddings, and stewed fruits with cream, cheese, and wine. Fountains Abbey in Yorkshire, and many other monastic houses, produced excellent food. One of the monastery rules was that the Prior was required to eat with his guests, and it was in no way a hardship to do so. Food during Lent was plentiful, at least in comparison to present-day diets. Eating spiced fruit soups, thickened with rice flour and garnished with dried fruits, almonds, and dates, was considered fasting—the only prohibitions were meat and dairy products.

Bread thickened sauces and was added to custards in sufficient quantity that the custard could be served sliced. Cakes evolved first as a treat for children on bread-baking day, when a piece of dough would be set aside and kneaded with dried fruits, nuts, or caraway seeds. Gradually these small confections became more elaborate, and lightened with beaten eggs, they became cakes.

Fish was as vital as bread. Restrictions against eating eggs and dairy products during Lent forced people to rely on fish. For most people fish was herring, caught in the thousands by fishing fleets in the summer months. In winter, of course, salted herring was the order of the day, disguised with parsley sauce, except for the very rich, who had their pick of choice, fresh fish that included haddock, plaice, sturgeon, and mackerel. Crab and lobster from Scotland and Ireland were also plentiful. Yarmouth in East Anglia was a fishing center for herring. Fishermen came from as far away as Devon, Cornwall, and Sussex to catch and salt the copious, nutritious herring for use in the winter months. Salt fishermen had their own Guild separate from the stock fishermen who dealt only in fresh fish. The Worshipful Company of Fishmongers, still in existence today, began in 1536 as a merger of the stock fishermen's and salt fishermen's Guilds. Salt fish was soaked, then boiled and served with copious amounts of butter and mustard. It was also put into pies after it had been beaten and soaked; sometimes fruit was put in the pie along with the salt fish. Later herring, first soaked in brine, were smoked. In medieval times, seal and porpoise were also used to supplement the diet on fish days. People living far from the sea built and stocked ponds with fish, or kept fish in the millponds. Unfortunately, the water in stock ponds was inclined to stagnate, making the taste muddy or worse. Boiling the fish in wine or beer and water, and serving it with a sauce rich in herbs and spiced with vinegar, was a common way to alleviate this problem. Large country houses had several ponds and employed a man to look after them and keep the great house supplied continually with fish. Rivers too were fished, salmon being the most highly prized catch. Pickling was the favorite way to preserve the noble salmon.

For the clergy, there was no restriction against "two-legged" creatures—only against "four-legged"—so poultry of all kinds was eaten on fast days. Estates kept poultry yards which housed pheasants and partridge as well as chickens, ducks, and geese. Even in those far-off days, poultry was force-fed in order to take care of the needs of these vast households. Dovecotes were another source of food open to the rich. At feast times, medieval tables groaned with a surfeit of birds—gull, egret, heron, quail, snipe, plover, thrush, finch, and blackbird—and for table decoration, swan and bustard. The poor contented themselves with a chicken or two, for special occasions, preferring to keep hens for their nutritious, and therefore precious, eggs. Whenever possible a householder kept a cow to supplement the diet.

Cows, goats, and sheep were all milked until about the 1500s when farmers felt that as cow's milk was so much more abundant than sheep's or goat's milk, it was easier to rely on cows alone for milking. The prevailing view was that milk was fit only for children, the aged, and the sick. This belief did not extend to cooked milk, which made delightful custards to eat and possets and caudles to drink. Rich cream cheese was inevitably made into cheesecakes. Adults delighted in thick cream and curded cream but considered butter to be suitable only for young children, who ate it for breakfast and supper.

Everyone ate pottage—a broth or soup of meat or cereal with root vegetables, which were called pot herbs. A Lenten pottage for those who could afford it was leek thickened with ground almonds. Vegetables have always been looked upon with great favor by inhabitants of these islands, and until the mid-1500s over 120 different varieties of vegetable were readily available. This cornucopia declined steadily both in markets and in seed catalogs, but today fresh, homegrown produce is sought after with enthusiasm.

Pickled vegetables were popular in the Middle Ages, as were salads, splashed with vinegar and oil and decorated with small blossoms or petals.

Citrus fruit, lemons, and bitter oranges from Seville were imported in the early thirteenth century and were eaten either fresh or pickled. Raw fruits, except for wild fruits, had the reputation of causing stomach disorders and were not really appreciated until about the reign of Charles II, when one particular orange seller, Nell Gwyn, became forever famous as the king's mistress. Dried fruits also were imported for the wealthy, but the biggest luxury import was almonds, which were needed as thickeners in so many dishes from soup to nuts. The poor thickened their soups with oatmeal.

Rural folk dwelt in one-room cottages with a central fire built on a large hearthstone. Flour, from grains that they had grown and ground themselves, mixed with water, was baked on the hot hearthstone under a pot. Insignificant game, such as squirrels, hedgehogs, and small birds, was wrapped in clay and baked on the hearth. Cooking was done in earthenware pots placed among the embers. Richer people even owned a butter churn. In manor houses, deep fireplaces held enormous spits for roasting—some were large enough to hold a whole ox. At the king's Clarendon estate, the kitchen employed three spits of that size, turned by a kitchen boy who lived in the kitchen and slept on the floor. A winch allowed the huge cauldrons to be swung out of the fireplace for loading. These had the capacity to boil a week's worth of meals for the family at one time. Tightly lidded dishes were stacked on perforated wooden boards placed inside the cauldron. Hooks at the top suspended puddings wrapped in pudding cloths. Medieval kitchens were equipped with many items in use today—frying pans, pots, a chopping block, cleavers, sharp knives, mallet, tongs, and even a waffle iron for making wafers. Pots were scoured with sand and bunches of twigs. The dairy, which had to be cool, was separate from the house, as was the bakery. New cooking methods evolved gradually, and by the end of the 1400s, people were braising their meats.

One rather odd facet of medieval food was its bright colors and heavy scent. As many dishes as possible were fashioned in layers, each one a different color. Saffron provided yellow coloring, sandalwood red, turnsole purple, and parsley juice green. Most custards came in shades of red, rice puddings were at least two colors, and meat balls were often gilded. Sheets of gold were used at feast times. Yet even with all this luxurious and gilded food, the Middle Ages suffered horrendous famines that depopulated villages and left nobody to till the soil. From 1455 to 1485, the War of the Roses, between Lancaster and York, did incredible damage to crops and fields, forcing the people who remained to grub for food, trap what small animals they could, and eat plants gathered on marshland.

Drying foods, especially fish, had been a major method of food preservation for centuries. It was actually preferred over salting, especially for nonoily fish such as cod, ling, haddock, and pollack. The drawback was the wet English climate that necessitated drying foods indoors and required copious amounts of fuel. Wind was found to be almost as good for drying as heat. Foods, dried or salted, needed to be soaked for hours to soften, and methods evolved in medieval kitchens to absorb the pervasive salt taste, such as cooking dried peas, beans, or legumes with the salted meats. In the kitchens of noblemen or rich merchants spices and also fruits were used in abundance, to mask the salt flavor.

Crusaders reported seeing sugar on their journeys east. Imported to Britain in rather grubby blocks, it was so expensive that it was kept under lock and key, and then used mainly for medicinal purposes or in small amounts as one would a spice. The Arabs controlled the sugar trade until the seventeenth century.

Pepper was also imported at such great cost that rents were sometimes paid in peppercorns. Cinnamon, nutmeg, mace, cloves, cardamom, and ginger cost far more to buy in Britain than on the Continent, as all spices came through European markets before they reached London. Alarmed by the rising prices for pepper and other spices, several London merchants met to form a new company called the East India Company, that was chartered by Elizabeth I in 1600 for the monopoly of trade with the Eastern Hemisphere. The British East India Company eventually controlled India, Burma, Ceylon, Malaya, and its strategically placed island, Singapore. The British managed to grow nutmeg on Penang, a small island off the northern Malay peninsula. Soon European nations transplanted spices to their own colonies, effectively ending the monopoly on spice trading. Once this happened, the prices plummeted.

Vanilla came from seed pods of orchid plants that grew wild in Mexico, which was under Spanish domination at that time. The Aztecs used vanilla to flavor their foods and their drinking chocolate, which was unsweetened and mixed with water, not milk. Also from Mexico came cochineal, made from the dried bodies of tiny insects. It replaced all the red colorants formerly used in food preparation. Gradually brightly colored foods lost favor and even saffron from crocus plants, grown on the flat fields of East Anglia, was relegated to buns and seed cakes. Britain's West Indian colonies supplied indigenous allspice. Salt too was mined in Britain or made from evaporated seawater. Wars were fought over the control of the mining of salt, essential to the human diet, and beseiged armies conquered by cutting off the supply. Salt was still a British government–held monopoly in India when Mahatma Gandhi led his followers to the seashore at Dandi to make salt illegally in 1930.

Christopher Columbus's New World had none of the spices produced by the Spice Islands. Nevertheless, Columbus was responsible for a global change in eating habits by introducing new fruits, nuts, grains, vegetables, and flowering plants to Europe, and on subsequent voyages bringing to the

New World, primarily to sustain his troops, pigs, sheep, chickens, horses, and other goods unknown in the New World. The foods from the Americas, particularly potatoes and corn, were far more nutritious than the grains then being grown. Corn strengthened whole populations that until then were largely undernourished, living on a diet of black bread, whey, and cheese. The potato was not immediately accepted, despite the fact that it was believed to be an aphrodisiac. It was not until the English realized that white potatoes could be used for thickening in place of flour or bread crumbs that people started to make use of them. Eventually it was discovered that mealy potatoes, mashed with treacle and boiled water, made a good warm environment to feed yeast. A small piece of yeast and a pinch of sugar mixed into the warm potato mixture would, if left for a few days, provide enough raising power for a week's worth of baking. In Ireland people became dependent on the potato to the point where some were consuming ten pounds of potatoes per day. The population of Ireland tripled in less than one hundred years. When the potato blight devastated the plants and left no seed potatoes to nurture subsequent crops, hundreds of thousands of people died, and a million more emigrated to the United States.

A Global Exchange of Foods

The exchange of foods and other plants between the old and new worlds that were to change Britain's daily life the most were potatoes, tomatoes, chocolate, vanilla, tobacco, dahlias, marigolds, petunias, and most of all sugarcane. Sugar became more widely used when the closing of the monasteries saw an immediate decline in the availability of honey. Monks kept bees for beeswax to make the vast numbers of candles needed in their religious rituals, and honey was a significant by-product. Sugar refineries were built at various ports around the coast. By the early 1800s the per capita consumption of sugar had risen to over thirteen pounds—much of it used in preserving fruits, in marmalade and jams, in candy-making, and in iced baked goods. Sugar was even added to European wines. Beekeeping for the honey it produced continued for a while longer in rural areas, but gradually country folk too succumbed to sugar and honey lost the place it had held as the chief form of sweetening.

Wealthy people, and those who traveled abroad, were accustomed to foreign ingredients and so were quicker to accept the novel foods coming from the New World than the less sophisticated. In remoter parts of the British Isles—Scotland, Ireland, and mountainous areas of Wales—the older cooking habits lasted for centuries longer than in the south where kinder climates facilitated the growth of new plants from Mediterranean countries. As late as the eighteenth century on Scottish islands, the hide was yet to be removed from an animal prior to boiling. Cattle were still bled in the spring, and the blood cooked down until it could be fashioned into cakes. These cakes, with a handful of oatmeal and milk from their cows, sustained Highlanders living in remote northern parts of Scotland.

The Flemish introduced hops to Britain in the fifteenth century and showed how they could be added to ale to make beer. This idea took a long time to take hold, even though the hops acted as a mild preservative, giving beer better keeping qualities. Herbs and spices continued to occupy the time of the sixteenth-century housewife, who tended the herb garden just as assiduously as had the Saxon housewife. Now herbs had many more uses than culinary. Dried meadowsweet perfumed and freshened rooms, the juice of balm leaves augmented beeswax to rub on furniture, potpourri were filled with rose petals, and it was discovered that various herbs could help control household insects—tansy discouraged flies, and mint fleas. It was believed that angelica was effective against witches, and meadow rue against the plague. Rosemary's strong scent was employed in many ways. Branches of rosemary were burned on the hearth to sweeten the air, students wore a sprig of rosemary as an aide-memoire, ribbon-tied bunches of rosemary at funerals were buried with the coffin, and gilded bunches of rosemary ornamented bridal wreathes at weddings.

In the sixteenth century Queen Elizabeth reigned. Her subjects enjoyed the arts—music, poetry, painting, and the plays of Shakespeare and Marlowe. Many cookery books were written; Edward White was prolific and published a series of books. The diet at least of the upper classes had not changed substantially. Despite the suspicion with which raw fruit was regarded, melons, quince, apricot, red and black currants, pomegranates, and citrus fruits continued to be imported from Europe.

By the middle of the sixteenth century, turkey was a great favorite in the great stately homes of Britain. For entertaining and on important holidays turkey replaced the peacocks, swans, and herons formerly used for celebratory occasions. By the following century, turkey and geese were so sought after once the harvest season was over that large flocks of both birds were driven to London on foot. The journey took several weeks, and before the birds were fit for the table they had to be fattened up again. Sauces could still be very complicated mixtures of spices, citrus, and wine, but this gradually gave way to the simpler flavors of celery, onions, or oysters. Stuffings too lost their dizzying number of ingredients, and by the eighteenth century oyster stuffing and chestnut stuffings were favored, as they are to this day. Pottages or stews became simpler by the end of the seventeenth century. Queen Henrietta Maria, the French wife of Charles I, drank a plain chicken bouillon for her health every day. Birds of all sorts were baked into pies that were cooled and filled with melted butter poured into a hole in the top crust to preserve them longer. The famous pie from medieval times that begins with a small boned and seasoned bird, stuffed inside a bigger one, and continues in this manner until the largest bird, usually a turkey, is stuffed with all the other birds, continued to be made for celebratory occasions well into the eighteenth century. But for the most part, pastry crusts were dispensed with in favor of potted birds. Small birds were frequently served on toast, and very small birds were tucked into dumplings—now wasn't that a dainty dish to set before a king!

Eggs were plentiful and inexpensive in the fourteenth and fifteenth centuries. However, they were not allowed to be eaten during Lent. Custards had been known since Roman times, as had caudles, those spiced, sweet beverages made with eggs and wine and consumed both as a nightcap and again for breakfast. Eggs were also used in baking, but in the Middle Ages egg whites were thought to be unwholesome, and only the yolks were used in fillings for tarts, pies, or to bind stuffing mixtures. Eggs and bread crumbs were used to thicken dishes such as pottage until the end of the Elizabethan era when French-inspired dishes replaced them. Meats and fish were more often simmered in a court bouillon and served with a flavored sauce. A decade or two later, flour and hot lard were fried together to a paste, and some of the court bouillon was added to make a sauce. From then on most thickened gravies and sauces were made this way. At the same time thinner sauces, made with court bouillon, wine, and citrus juice flavored with herbs and spices, grew in popularity. Soon the more elegant soups began to be served as a first course ahead of fish or meat dishes and puddings and potatoes provided starch at meals.

Tudor Period

Manchet, made in flat rounds, was the best white bread made in Tudor times. It was found mostly on the tables of the rich—coarse dark bread being the order of the day for the lower classes. Manchet was thoroughly kneaded, sometimes with the help of a kneading machine. Unleavened bread was still made, though raising the heavy dense dough with ale balm and yeast were now more common. In northern and western areas of the country bread was made with barley—more readily available than wheat—and it was frequently mixed with rye, peas, and oats into a very hard and lumpy dark loaf. Baking was done on hot stones placed around the fire and covered with an inverted iron pot banked with hot ashes. The kitchen oven was not invented until late in the sixteenth century, though bread was baked commercially in bread ovens. The demand for the softer wheat bread spread quickly, and soon wheat was being shipped from the northern counties of East Anglia and Yorkshire to London. Once they had tasted the finer wheat loaves, even the poor disdained the dark, coarse bread. By the end of the 1600s flour and butter pastes were prevalent for thickening, and eventually rich pastry was used for tarts and pies. Slowly dried fruits, sweeteners, and icing were left out of meat pies, and meat was left out of mince pies and fruit pies.

The Great Salt continued to divide the nobleman's dining table. Tableware was now becoming a status symbol, as royal households and stately homes displayed their beautifully wrought silver and gold dishes in their dining rooms. Henry VIII's feasts were served on gold vessels that together filled twelve shelves. He used an implement with a spoon at one end and two prongs for spearing food at the other. Elizabeth I had forks but used them only for eating sweetmeats. Forks were highly decorative with handles of gold, silver, and crystal but still were not in regular use except as kitchen implements.

British food remained solid and substantial—roasts of beef and mutton, chickens, pork, game, hearty soups and stews, boiled vegetables swimming in butter, and warming puddings to keep out the raw British weather. Ale or tea with milk and sugar were the preferred drinks to wash down all this food. Tea, dubbed the China drink, gained in popularity as an everyday beverage in the middle of the 1600s. Before that time it was imported for its medicinal purposes.

In Hamburg, Germany, a yeast was cultivated that had better and more predictable raising properties. Demand in England for this new yeast soared, and within a decade or two almost 6,000 tons a year were being imported. Soon after the German, and later Dutch, yeast came on the market, England developed a raising powder that effectively did away with yeast for raising cakes and scones, except where a heavier yeasty dough was desired, as in hearty Hampshire lardy cakes, Yorkshire tea breads, and the Welsh Bara Brith.

People have often called the British a nation of bakers, and the list of regional country breads in these islands is indeed long, from the aforementioned breads to Hot Cross buns eaten on Good Friday, Bath buns, Whigs from Loughborough, Surrey bread, Yorkshire tea and breakfast breads, Newcastle bread, Drover's (sheepherder's) bread, London buns, Rosehampton rolls, and a wealth of Scottish baked goods—baps, bannocks, and petticoat tails—and delectable soda bread and fadge (potato cakes) from Ireland.

Seventeenth Century

By the early 1600s, West Country fishermen fished the waters off New England and Newfoundland. Their catch, air-dried or salted at sea, was generally sold to southern Catholic countries where it could be kept until needed, as England had lost its taste for salt fish. Shellfish, obtainable in large quantities from seaports, were beloved and affordable by rich and poor alike. Charles Dickens, two centuries later, spoke of the poor feasting on oysters in the streets of London. Crabs, lobsters, and smaller shellfish were frequently boiled in spiced water or a mixture of water, wine, or beer and eaten cold with vinegar and herbs. After the break with the Pope, fish days were no longer compulsory, and fish eating, with the exception of shellfish and salmon, declined. Stock ponds on larger estates were turned into ornamental water gardens. To this day, in many Catholic countries meat is preferred to fish, almost certainly because fish and penance on Fridays are synonymous.

In London, Billingsgate market, situated close to the port, was the place to buy fish then as it is now. In 1699 Parliament abolished tolls or taxes on the cargo boats and declared Billingsgate a free market. By the mid-1700s, it was found useful to pickle beef in vinegar to preserve it—especially for long sea voyages. Meat jelly was served embedded with pickled meats, and various small dishes of meat stewed in wine and water were cooled until they set before serving. Sweet foods—cakes, fruit tarts, marzipan treats, preserves, and jellies, often flavored with rose water—were eaten as a separate course at the end of the meal, or firmly set transparent, sweet jellies with various fruits, nuts, and dried or candied peels were unmolded and used as a decorative centerpiece for the table. Rose water eventually gave way to lemon juice as a flavoring.

The art of preserving meat in butter became very popular in the early seventeenth century. Pork, cooked with salt, spices, and wine for several hours then drained, was placed in a pot and covered completely with melted butter. Beef, fish, variety meats, and game were also preserved in this way. Later meat was chopped, mixed with plenty of butter, and weighted to force out the air. Once this method was perfected, two or more kinds of meat, such as veal and tongue, were layered with butter to give a marbled appearance to the sliced meat.

Meat eating was by no means universal throughout England. The diet of the poor was most likely to consist of bread, cheese, bacon, and cereal, with an occasional fish caught from local waters. Small game could be trapped in the forests to supplement the diet, but after the Dissolution of the Monasteries by Henry VIII, and the rush to acquire large tracts of land for private estates, surrounded by farmlands and forests, the poor found it harder to find game or poach much of it under the eagle eye of the estate gamekeepers. Landowners became rich as they developed their huge properties, and a prosperous and influential new class of people, known as the landed gentry, came into being. As this class sought more power and questioned the Divine Right of Kings to govern as arbitrarily as they wished, the Civil War (1642–1649) broke out, culminating in the execution of King Charles I.

Fruits and vegetables began to be enjoyed more often. At this time Dutch and Flemish gardeners, who settled in the flatlands of East Anglia and parts of southern Britain, established thriving market gardens close to country towns, trading carrots, spinach, turnips, parsnips, and dozens of other fresh vegetables and fruits. Soon market gardens were flourishing just outside London, using night soil as fertilizer. Gradually over the years the traders moved to Covent Garden, an area where there had once been a garden and orchard that supplied produce to Westminster's Convent of St. Peter

Fresh herbs lost some of their importance in late seventeenth-century kitchens, as fresh meat could now be eaten year-round. Since it was not yet as readily available in Scotland, the Scots frequently resorted to eating pigeons as a steady source of fresh meat. Transportation methods improved in the early 1700s so that fresh fish could be taken to inland towns in barrels of salt water. Oysters were plentiful and were eaten in large quantities. Salted meat and salted fish were no longer winter staples. Pudding had long taken the place of cereal pottage. By the 1740s roast beef and plum pudding were national dishes. Sauces made from pickled mushrooms, walnuts, and especially anchovies were in great demand. Sauces from Asia, such as soy sauce and most especially fermented fish sauce, which was not recognized as such, had created an appetite for piquant pickles and relishes to accompany meats. It was a short step before the sauces themselves were added to cooked dishes as seasonings, replacing mashed green herbs, and the wilder Stuart concoctions containing forty or more ingredients. Simple sauces of mustard, parsley, or anchovy appeared. But the ubiquitous melted butter sauce saw the widest use, most swimmingly on vegetables but frequently on every dish.

Beer and ale were undisputed as the nation's preferred beverages up until the middle of the 1700s, despite the availability of wines and spirits. A Royal Edict in 1637 forbade alehouses, taverns, and similar establishments to brew their own beer on the premises and ordered that beer be purchased from a common brewer. This did not stop housewives from brewing beer at home, but the price of fuel, when it grew scarce in the south, and the cost of brewing equipment did. Brewing continued in the west where fuel was easily obtainable, in barley-growing areas of northern England, and in Scotland. Hops were grown, as they are today, in Kent where the climate is mild. In colder climes herbs, such as sage and hyssop, were substituted for hops. Herbal ales were hailed as cures for various ailments or simply enjoyed as a spring tonic. Cider was introduced to southern England by the Normans and its use quickly spread northward. Cider could be made from either apples or pears. When only pears were used it was called perry.

In rural towns fruits were sold on the streets by costermongers and "orange wives" or displayed for sale at country fairs. Hybridized new fruits from the New World and established varieties in England yielded better varieties of raspberries, strawberries, and black and red currants. Melons came from France, and hothouses or conservatories on large estates experimented with growing grapes, peaches, and pineapples. Raw fruit finally received a clean bill of health from prevailing medical opinion. In Ireland the potato was eaten every day. Easier to grow than wheat, the potato had the added advantage of being grown underground. This frequently foiled marauding enemy soliders who were less likely to pillage fields where the crop was less visible.

Port and Madeira were consumed in quantity from the seventeenth century on. Spirits, often distilled at home, led to drunkenness. This was the case particularly among the poor on the streets of London throughout the 1800s, where gin mills were prevalent until increased taxation somewhat curbed the vice. Heavy drinking was not confined to the poor, of course, but was less obvious among wealthy landowners. Brandy or cognac and rum from Barbados were favorite tipples. In Scotland distilling of malt beverages was as rife as it was in Ireland.

The next great change in the diet of the people of Britain came about not through invasion but through two inventions that revolutionized agriculture. The first was the invention, in 1700 by Jethro Tull, of the seed drill. The drill enabled farmers to plant their seeds exactly where they wanted them, and all at the same depth, instead of scattering them on the ground for the waiting flocks of birds. Increase in the size of the crop was astonishing. The second innovation was crop rotation, the work of Viscount Townshend, who introduced this technique later in the same century. A manifold expansion in crops was immediate. At the same time better breeding methods and new strains of cattle escalated meat and milk production. For the first time farmers began to realize the value of their land, and this led inexorably to land enclosure. Many poor people were left homeless if their dwellings happened to be on land that belonged to a farmer. A further incentive to the farmer bent on realizing a profit from his herd was the selling price of cheese, which was much higher than milk. Enterprising farmers made cheese with their milk, which in turn impoverished the diet of the rural poor as milk became harder to find.

As these new developments were taking place in the countryside, discoveries along different lines were greatly changing urban areas. For example, it was found that coal could be smelted into iron. The steam engine was invented, and soon ironworks were flourishing alongside the burgeoning coal business. People from rural areas, eager for work, flocked to the growing towns of Birmingham and Manchester in the Midlands. Liverpool too saw an upsurge in prosperity as trade with other countries increased and Liverpool became the undisputed hub for weaving cotton goods. It was not long before cotton, woven in Liverpool, was worn by colonists and native populations alike in tropical areas of the world. With the boost in exports, Bristol became a thriving port, second only to London. Ships returned to port with their holds filled with sugar, coffee, tea, and wine. Rum was imported at Whitehaven, Cumbria, influencing the local cooks to invent rum butter, which took its place beside brandied butter as a sauce for the nation's Christmas plum pudding. By the eighteenth century the Scottish and the Irish had perfected the art of whisky making and even introduced it to North America. Cider was a favorite in the West Country.

During the eighteenth century, English soldiers and their families were very comfortably settled in India with their cooks, house servants, and nannies. Indian curries and chutneys—or something that approximated curries and chutneys—were to become popular in Britain and have so remained to this day. Mocha, the center for coffee production, was near Aden, a British colonial town, and coffee had long been known as a stimulant. Coffee traveled much the same journey as spices—the Dutch planted it in their colonies and eventually it reached the West Indies. It was particularly popular for breakfast in English country houses, as was chocolate. Coffeehouses sprang up to keep pace with people's interest in these new beverages from foreign parts. The first one opened in Oxford, and gradually coffeehouses became almost the same as men's clubs—frequented for companionship as much as for coffee. Later coffee and chocolate drinking were supplanted by tea drinking. Tea came from China and found its way to England, at first in small quantities, through the East India Trading Company in Malaya. Though expensive, its popularity was assured when it was taken up at Court. Later tea drinking among gentlewomen at their own fireside became all the rage. Thomas Twining opened a tea-drinking establishment for women in London in 1717. This spawned tea gardens in London where people of both sexes and all classes could go and drink China tea. A hundred years were to pass before tea was imported from India and then Ceylon. Once the tax on tea was lowered so that all could afford to buy it, it quickly became the national drink.

Eighteenth-century upper-class Britons amused themselves by taking the Grand Tour to well-established cultural watering holes on the Continent. Some of them also learned to appreciate the different cuisines they encountered. A certain amount of French influence on British cooking came about through the occupation of the French Normans, and in Scotland through the French connections of Mary, Queen of Scots. The landed gentry frequently dispatched their chefs to Paris to acquire a smattering of knowledge of French cuisine—but deep down it was felt a poor substitute for real British food.

The Industrial Revolution (late eighteenth to early nineteenth centuries) in Great Britain brought many advances in engineering and science, some of them relating directly to food. The steam engine made it possible for grains, tea, and other foods to be shipped in bulk. The invention of canning and freezing meant that meat could come to Britain from the vast meat-producing lands of Australia and America. British fishermen could also go further afield for their catch. The cod-filled waters off the coast of Newfoundland were one such spot, and dried cod became a staple food for returning fishermen. Scientific advances made it possible to detect impurities in food, and this led to regulation of food products. Alum to whiten bread, copper to add a brighter green to vegetables, and the adulteration of tea, beer, jams, and many other processed foods were banned by law. Louis Pasteur identified organisms that caused food to spoil, and Nicholas Appert invented a method of preserving foods by excluding air from the containers, which led to safe methods of bottling and canning fruits, vegetables, and meats. The new techniques for chilling foods, and increased production of canned goods from Australia, Asia, and North America, made a greater variety of foods available to more people at a cost they could afford.

Twentieth Century

Nevertheless, in the early 1900s farm laborers and their families had a very hard time of it. They were little more than slaves to the often wealthy farmers who paid hired hands only two or three shillings for backbreaking seventy-two-hour workweeks. The laborers' diets were appalling: apples, potatoes, swedes (rutagabas), and bread washed down with unsweetened tea without milk, as even skimmed milk was considered a luxury. The children particularly were always hungry. Families were large and a laborer's wage was often as low as ten shillings a week.

The railway was the most important link in bringing more palatable food into the ever-growing towns. For example, Aberdeen, with the advent of rapid transportation, could dress beef, sheep, and pigs and dispatch the carcasses overnight to London, and rail cars could carry far more goods at one time than loads hauled in carts by road. Soon milk too was coming in from the countryside, mechanically cooled, placed in metal churns, and sent by rail to city dwellers who no longer needed to rely on cow keepers in the city for milk. Filthy stalls, sickly, undernourished cattle, and milk carried through the streets in open pails—often diluted with water—had made it virtually impossible to buy good, clean milk. Overseas goods, such as tropical fruits and other delicacies, arriving at English ports increased dramati-

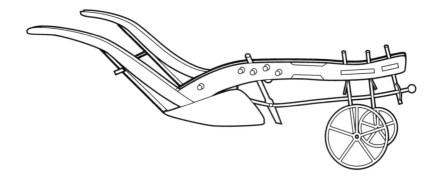

cally now that they could be sent with all due dispatch to their destinations by rail. The invention in the later 1800s of the iron range for cooking revolutionized cooking in the home. With an adjustable and economical heat source, more complicated recipes could be tackled without a large staff. This is turn induced publishers to put out cookbooks, some written by well-known chefs, such as *The London Art of Cookery* by John Farley. John Farley was principal cook at the famous London Tavern. One of the longest lasting, published in 1861, was Mrs. Isabella Beeton's *Book of Household Management*, with a quotation from Milton in the frontispiece reading, "Nothing lovelier can be found In Woman, than to study household good."

Taverns, or rather coaching inns, in the country were virtually farms situated on major highways, growing their own wheat or corn, fruit and vegetables, breeding livestock for the table, keeping bees for sweetening and beeswax for polishing furniture. The wife of the innkeeper needed to be proficient at many of the tasks written about in John Farley's book—making cheese and butter, curing ham and tongue, and making jellied and potted meats, such as brawn, so they would be ready for unexpected arrivals wanting a late supper. Housewives developed pie fillings that could be kept until needed for a quick dessert and made their own bottled sauces. Worcestershire Sauce and Yorkshire Relish were invented at coaching inns, and some of the better known regional foods owe their fame to coaching inns, among them Melton Mowbray Pie—a raised, jellied pork pie with a stiff crust. Cheese sold at the Bell Inn at Stilton, which stood on the Great North Road between London and York, became famous as Stilton cheese, though this cheese was made at a nearby village in Leicestershire and was never made at the village of Stilton. Authentic Stilton cheese, which is trademarked by the Stilton Cheesemakers Association, may only be made today in the counties of Leicestershire, Derbyshire, and Nottinghamshire.

By the early twentieth century vitamins and the components of food needed for good health were isolated, giving government and medicine the knowledge to promote good nutrition. It also eliminated the famines that periodically swept through the British Isles and Europe.

After World War I food in Britain become much more lively and interesting. This came about mainly through American hostesses in London who made it fashionable to cut the list of menu courses to three—as it is today—and began to entertain with much simpler dishes using really fresh ingredients. Mrs. Simpson was one of these new hostesses who captivated the then Prince of Wales. Wallis Simpson was extremely fastidious, impeccably dressed, and witty, and her food was delicious, novel, and amusing for her friends in London society. Everything had to be just so. She once sent back to the kitchen during dinner a dish containing a solitary tomato seed because the sauce should have been properly strained to eliminate seeds. She also upset the king's kitchen staff by ordering them to make American club sandwiches for the king and his guests at poolside. The staff rightly thought the king should be the only one to command their services. He told them that her wishes should be considered by them as though they were his own.

This new way of cooking and presenting food was taught by society hostesses to their cooks. Most women of that time did not cook themselves. With the advent of the second World War, this brief interest in great good food was forgotten. Rationing was severe in Britain, and the government took over the allocation of all food to everyone, and nourishment was its only function, an attitude that influenced cooking in Britain and Ireland for a very long time.

George Perry-Smith is perhaps the person most recognized for showing Great Britain the way to new and exciting cooking. In 1951 he opened a restaurant in Bath called The Hole in the Wall that served outstanding food. Greatly inspired by Elizabeth David's A *Book of Mediterranean Food*, published in 1950, his fare more than anyone's epitomized the new cooking that caught the imagination of young chefs. Perry-Smith's professional training was in teaching, and teach he did. A stream of his sous-chefs went on to open their own restaurants, notably Joyce Molyneux of The Carved Angel in Dartmouth, Devon. Gifted self-taught chefs, also spurred on by Elizabeth David's book on Mediterranean fare, began to open small restaurants in London catering to people venturesome enough to want to try dishes from these countries. Raymond Postgate, at about the same time in the 1950s, started a small club to collect and circulate personal reports on good restaurant experiences among its members. From this grew *The Good Food Guide*, edited by Tom Jaine, which is available in America as *The Best Restaurants of Great Britain* and is very useful to anyone looking for great restaurants and hotels with excellent chefs. As early as 1949, Francis Coulson opened the first country house hotel, with just a few bedrooms, at Sharrow Bay on the shores of Ullswater in the scenic Lake District. Excel-

ative cooking, unbridled enthusiasm, and a love of people assured the success of Sharrow Bay, which has grown over the years to its present splendor.

Another important influence on food in these islands was the proliferation of ethnic restaurants opened by the flood of immigrants to Britain in the 1960s. The highly spiced cuisines of India, China's Szechuan province, the Middle East, and more recently the sizzling hot cooking of Southeast Asia, became a source of inspiration for the new cooking of Britain and Ireland, and the light and lively flavors of ginger, lemon grass, cilantro, and chilies were quickly assimilated into the dishes of innovative chefs. An even greater influence, and a major source of expert training for young chefs in the 1960s, were the accomplished French chefs who arrived in London hotel and restaurant kitchens. Among them were the Roux brothers—Albert and Michel—Anton Mosimann, Raymond Blanc, and Michel Bourdin. In 1960, chef Ray Parkes opened a restaurant and introduced his clientele to the decorative style of cooking now called nouvelle cuisine at least a decade before that term was used in Britain.

In the seventies, Robert Carrier, an American actor-cum-writer and chef, persuaded the general public through his food articles and television program that cooking could be fun and eating a thoroughly enjoyable experience. Eventually he opened his own restaurant, Carrier's, in London's Camden Passage. There he experimented with ethnic foods, serving his entranced clientele complex and varied dishes from around the world. When in the 1970s photographs of artistically designed platters of spectacular and elegant nouvelle cuisine began to appear in magazines and in food sections of Sunday newspapers, the public's interest was aroused. Suddenly good food became a topic of conversation, and the great chefs who produced it became well known both in print and on television. Soon there were many new apprentices training in great London kitchens, but the boom in nouvelle cuisine's popularity was not to last. More and more restaurants whose chefs were not well trained and who used inferior ingredients turned out badly cooked imitations of this style of cooking. When dinner plates started arriving at the table with a few tastefully arranged vegetables on one side, a minuscule slice or two of sauce-splashed sea scallop or duck breast on the other, and acres of bare china in between, customers began to question whether they were getting their money's worth, especially when they left the table hungry.

A change was overdue. The increase in disposable income in the 1980s enabled people to travel abroad, and a greater awareness of interesting food and wine in France, Italy, Spain, and Greece began to assert itself. Knowledgeable middle-class restaurant-goers looked for better, more interesting cooking. The new discerning clientele encouraged restaurants to keep pace with their needs and spurred top chefs to create better and better dishes in healthy competition with one another.

2

LONDON

Romans laid out the first city streets of London in their usual formal grid pattern. The remains of these roads today are highways that led directly to major Roman towns outside the city limits. Linking these straight roads are ancient alley ways and narrow, twisting streets. Those with quaint names, such as Bread Street, Milk Street, and Fish Street, were lined with bakeries, fishmongers' stalls, and cow sheds, as well as goat pens and pig sties. Milk was hand-carried through the streets in open pails, and a little hot water was added to the pail before delivery to simulate warm, fresh, cow's milk. The Great Fire in 1666 leveled a great deal of the city. For three days after the fire stopped raging the ground where it had passed was still too hot to walk on. North of Cock Lane, Smithfield, where the fire stopped, houses that predate the Great Fire, though much restored, still stand. Charles II commissioned Christopher Wren and John Evelyn to rebuild London, and out of the ashes rose the glorious Wren churches. The City's streets were not enlarged after the fire but rebuilt to their former cramped dimensions. London grew in haphazard fashion with very little recourse to city planners, which is part of its charm. Blue plaques on houses tell of illustrious occupants who lived or died there. Surprises await around every corner. Apartment houses, called mansion flats, hotels, and department stores were built in the Edwardian era, changing the face of Piccadilly, Knightsbridge, and Kensington. Harrods huge department store took four years to build from 1901 to 1905, the Ritz Hotel was ready for guests by 1906, and Selfridges department store opened in 1908. London is a city of unending variety. It hides its glory in quaint out-of-the-way places—narrow alleyways between buildings on busy streets broaden into light-filled lanes

and courtyards containing exquisite houses, their mullioned windows graced by pristine lace curtains and neat flower-filled window boxes.

London is immense, and for the gastronomically inclined, eating in London is an astonishing and delectable adventure. Though there are restaurants galore in every borough, it will be necessary to search a bit for the places where you will eat like a king or queen. Popping into the nearest restaurant on the off chance that it will be a culinary highpoint is bound to cause disappointment sooner or later—just as it would in any city. If you will take the time to explore the best that London has to offer in hotel and restaurant cooking, you will eat very well indeed. Home-grown produce, succulent meats, fresh seafood, and unparalleled dairy products are second to none, and Britain and Ireland now have some of the most talented chefs in the world, creating innovative, satisfying dishes, which will lay to rest for all time the all too prevailing myth about bad food in these islands. Fruits, vegetables, and herbs were esteemed here even before the Romans brought scores of new herbs, flowers, and fruits with them from countries around the Mediterranean. Monks continued their apothecary or physic gardens during the Dark Ages, and in time every housewife in the land had her own plot growing herbs for remedies and for preserving and enhancing foods. Queen Elizabeth I started her day with a healthful tisane of herbs, as did many ladies of the land. London's chefs today are encouraging market gardeners to grow ever more unusual herbs and vegetables that are used in light, flavorful sauces, replacing the cloying mixtures that were once found everywhere. Flowers and petals too are enhancing salads, sorbets, and syrups.

Though London is packed with restaurants of every kind, from almost every ethnic group, not to mention tea shops, coffeehouses, wine bars, pubs, and cafés, nevertheless some districts of London will have more good eating places than others. Not to be neglected are the elegant restaurants in London's superb hotels—the Inn on the Park, Hamilton Place, the Dorchester, Park Lane, the Connaught, Carlos Place, the Savoy on The Strand, and the Ritz, on Piccadilly. In all of these establishments you will find not only first-class chefs and the best of food but super smooth service in opulent surroundings. Hotels like these are also great places for afternoon tea, and museums often have very good food. There are so many fine restaurants to explore in London that it is even more important to choose carefully if you have only a week or two to see and do what could easily take a lifetime.

Our culinary journey will take us from the western districts of Central London to the City, then over Tower Bridge to explore new development and old, south of the Thames. We will begin in Kensington and go on to Knightsbridge, Chelsea, Belgravia, Mayfair, St. James's, Westminster, Soho, Covent Garden, Bloomsbury, Hampstead, the City, Docklands, over Tower Bridge to Southwark, and then follow the river to Kew.

Kensington

Kensington is situated between Kensington Gardens and the River Thames. Aristocracy have lived here since the seventeenth century. Kensington became a royal borough when William III decided the mists from the Thames that shrouded his palace at Whitehall were bad for his health and purchased the Earl of Nottingham's Jacobean house in Kensington village. Christopher Wren was commissioned to improve the dwelling. Queen Anne built the Orangery to use as a "Summer Supper House." Try as she did, she was not able to get oranges to grow there. George I and George II also lived at Kensington Palace. It was at Kensington Palace that the Archbishop of Canterbury gave Princess Victoria the news that during the night she had become Queen of England. Today separate apartments in Kensington Palace house members of the royal family—Diana, Princess of Wales, and her two sons; Princess Margaret; and the families of cousins of Her Majesty the Queen. The palace is the focal point of Kensington. The Orangery, Kensington Palace, Kensington Gardens, is open for afternoon tea.

Orange Pudding with Caramel

4 oz. sugar (½ C.) for caramel
3   fresh oranges
1   lime
       grated zest of one orange
2 oz. sugar (¼ C.)
       pinch of salt
6   eggs
Garnish: thin slivers of candied orange peel

1. Place sugar in a small heavy-bottomed saucepan and melt over low heat. Increase heat, and stirring with a wooden spoon continue to cook until sugar has caramelized. Then quickly tip caramel into a one-quart mold and rotate to coat bottom and the lower part of the sides of mold.

2. Squeeze the juice from the citrus fruits into a small pan, add zest, sugar, and salt, and heat to dissolve sugar. Set aside. Preheat oven to 350°F (or gas mark 4).

3. Using a handheld electric beater, beat eggs until thick and pale colored, then slowly pour in juice mixture while continuing to beat. Pour into the mold.

4. Set mold in a baking dish and pour in enough hot water to come halfway up the sides. Place in the oven and cook for an hour or until custard has set. It will continue to cook for a few minutes after you have removed it from the oven.

5. Cool pudding and refrigerate until an hour before ready to serve. Run a thin knife around edge of pudding and invert onto a serving dish. Garnish with thin slivers of candied orange peel.

Serves 6

Kensington Gardens was the site of the Great Exhibition that Prince Albert organized in 1851. Near the site is the monument Queen Victoria had built in memory of her "blameless prince." Very elaborate, as Queen Victoria wanted, it was designed by Sir George Gilbert Scott. The frieze, which is really beautiful, contains reliefs of many of the talented, illustrious people who lived in Victoria's time. Kensington Church Street runs north from Kensington High Street to Notting Hill. This street is lined with some of the best restaurants in London. One of these is Clarke's, 124 Kensington Church Street, an attractive restaurant situated on two levels—the ground floor and the semi-basement—where diners can look into the kitchen. The chefs here are Sally Clarke, who is also the proprietor, and Elizabeth Payne.

Food is beautifully prepared, light and fresh with no cloying sauces. Another great place is Kensington Place, 201–205 Kensington Church Street, where chef Rowley Leigh's excellent cooking is modern and eclectic. At 20 Kensington Church Street, Church's Wine Bar is noted both for its wine and food. North of Kensington Gardens at 81 Holland Park, W11, is a restaurant called The Room at the Halcyon Hotel which serves great vegetarian food as well as British, French, and Asian dishes. Martin Hadde is the talented chef. His wife is a vegetarian, and each day there is an inspired set-price vegetarian menu with some very interesting dishes. Leading out of the semi-basement dining room is a pretty garden where you may choose to sit. The hotel has well-designed rooms in a former town house.

Wild Mushroom Ragout with Toast Points

1	oz.	dried porcini or morel mushrooms
4	oz.	shallots, minced
3	T.	unsalted butter
1	lb.	button mushrooms
1	T.	fresh tarragon or ½ t. crumbled dried tarragon
2	T.	flour
3	T.	medium-dry sherry
8	T.	sour cream or heavy cream (½ C.)
		fresh lemon juice to taste
2	T.	parsley, finely minced

1. Soak dried wild mushrooms for 30 minutes or until they are softened, then drain, reserving the soaking liquid for another use. Remove and discard any tough stems.

2. In a large skillet cook the shallots in butter over medium-low heat, stirring, until they are softened. Set aside.

3. Using a food processor finely chop the porcini or morel and the button mushrooms. Add mushrooms to the shallot mixture, and stir in the tarragon. Over medium-high heat, cook, stirring, until the liquid the mushrooms give off has evaporated.

4. Sprinkle in the flour and continue to cook, stirring, for 2 minutes. Remove from heat, and stir in the sherry. Carefully add the sour cream or heavy cream, stirring constantly. Add the lemon juice, seasoning to taste. Return to low heat and cook, stirring for 5 minutes or until it is thickened.

5. Sprinkle with parsley and serve on warmed plates with toast points. *Serves 6*

Leith's Restaurant, at 92 Kensington Park Road, W11, has recently been redecorated in a more contemporary style with softly tinted walls, huge mirrors, and light muslin blinds, while retaining the Victorian features of this sophisticated, former private house. The new design goes well with the head chef's cooking. Alex Floyd likes traditional-based dishes with defined, clean flavors. He was a finalist in the Young Chef and Roux Diner competitions and is a recipient of the Caterer and Hotelkeeper's Acorn Award. His favorite dishes are speedily cooked sea bass, turbot, brill, and scallops—much of which arrives glistening and spanking fresh from his native Scotland. At the other extreme, he loves to spend hours gently simmering flavorful casseroles of beef and venison. A recent dish of Ox Cheeks with braised celery served with mashed potatoes was superb—the meat was literally falling off the bones. There are three menus here: a vegetarian menu created with style and care, a menu that changes weekly, and another that changes with the seasons. A sensational dish is an appetizer of pigeon and foie gras. The foie gras is delicately cooked with a special sweet, fruity vinegar from Cabernet Sauvignon grapes. Alex Floyd came across this vinegar in Barcelona, and it is the perfect contrast to the slightly undercooked pigeon. Vegetarians make up 20 percent of the clientele here, and the vegetarian menu is a continuing challenge. Organic vegetables and herbs are grown especially for the restaurant in Gloucestershire by Prue Leith, the owner. In the hot summer months, Alex Floyd fills zucchini blossoms from the farm with chicken mousseline and serves then with a light curry sauce. One of his favorite suppliers is Mrs. Tee, who hunts up wild mushrooms in the countryside and arrives at Leith's with baskets brimming. Occasionally, in the autumn and winter months, Alex Floyd goes off to the countryside and shoots his own game. The recipe that Alex Floyd has contributed for this book follows.

Beer-Braised Casserole of Venison with Cabbage and Bacon Dumplings

3	lb.	venison haunch, diced
3	T.	oil
1	T.	concentrated tomato paste
4	oz.	flour (¾ C.)
20	fl.oz.	Guinness or dark beer (2½ C.)
20	fl.oz.	stock (2½ C.), made from the venison bones
1	lb.	button onions

Garnish with nicely shaped cooked root vegetables, such as carrots, swedes (rutabagas), parsnips, etc., and chopped parsley.

Marinade

1		lg. onion
2		carrots
1		leek
1		head of celery
1		sm. turnip
1		sprig of thyme
4		garlic cloves, crushed
20	fl.oz.	Guinness or dark beer (2½ C.)
10	fl.oz.	cherry beer (1¼ C.) (or other "sweet" beer)
10	fl.oz.	red wine (1¼ C.)
4	fl.oz.	port (½ C.)
12		juniper berries, crushed
12		black peppercorns, crushed
4		bay leaves

1. Roughly chop the onion, carrots, leek, celery, and turnip. Put all marinade ingredients into a heavy-bottomed pan and bring to a boil. Simmer for 20 minutes. Remove from heat and cool.

2. Pour the cool marinade over the diced venison and marinate for 24 hours. Remove venison from marinade and pat dry.

3. Place the oil in a very hot, heavy-bottomed, ovenproof pan. Heat until smoking, then thoroughly brown the venison in the oil.

4. Strain marinade, and reserve liquid. Add vegetables to the pan with venison and simmer gently for a few minutes. Stir in the tomato paste and cook for 10 minutes.

5. Preheat oven to 325°F (or gas mark 3). Add the flour and allow to cook for a further 10 minutes. Pour in the liquid left over from the marinade together with the beer and venison stock. Return to a boil and add the button onions, cover pan, and cook in the oven for 1½ to 2 hours (depending on the quality and tenderness of the meat). Season with salt and pepper.

6. Remove venison from casserole and place on a serving dish. Keep warm while you strain the sauce, and return it to the pan to reduce to a coating consistency. Then pour sauce over the meat, cover, and keep warm.

Dumplings

1	T.	vegetable oil
4	oz.	smoked, streaky bacon, cut into thin strips
8	oz.	cabbage, preferably Savoy, (1½ C.) shredded
4		slices white bread, diced into ¼-inch squares

4   egg yolks
4 oz. warm milk (½ C.), approximately
      salt, pepper, and nutmeg, to taste

7. Heat oil in a heavy-bottomed pan, add bacon, and cook for 5 to 6 minutes over moderate heat.

8. Add cabbage and cook gently for a few minutes. Remove from heat and cool.

9. Place bacon and cabbage in a bowl, add bread cubes and egg yolks, and knead until the mixture is beginning to bind together, then slowly add the warm milk, stirring until the mixture comes together. Season with salt, pepper, and a little grated nutmeg. Refrigerate, covered, for 2 hours to "rest."

10. Shape mixture into balls a bit smaller than a golf ball and gently blanch them for a minute in a little boiling salted water. Then place them carefully in the sauce in the covered casserole and reheat. Garnish, and serve piping hot.   *Serves 8*

Kensington and Notting Hill Gate to the north are blessed with a number of very good restaurants:

Julie's at 135 Portland Road, W11, cooks old-fashioned English dishes beautifully, and her Sunday brunch with typically British roasts and puddings is extremely popular. The restaurant is in the basement with a wine bar one floor up, and both have Victorian decor that complements the traditional food. Outside there is a garden for summer dining.

The restaurant 192 at 192 Kensington Park Road, W11, is a two-level establishment, again with a wine bar above and the comfortable busy restaurant below. Dan Evan's cooking is thoroughly modern British, which he executes with panache. His menu changes twice a day, and there is always something unexpected and exciting.

Launceston Place, 1A Launceston Place, Kensington, has wonderfully cooked traditional British food.

Downstairs at 190, 190 Queen Anne's Gate, SW7, is another restaurant started by Antony Worrall-Thompson. This one specializes in fish dishes with an elegant touch, such as smoked haddock with salmon carpaccio, but at very fair prices. Desserts are not to be bypassed.

Knightsbridge

Knightsbridge is also a very fashionable quarter of London, with beautiful shops and restaurants. Knightsbridge runs along the south side of Hyde Park. Here too is the headquarters of the Household Cavalry—the regiment that sits astride exquisitely groomed horses, wearing plumed helmets and gold breastplates on all-important state occasions as they accompany Her Majesty the Queen. Two wide streets lead from Knightsbridge—Brompton Road and Sloane Street. A very worthwhile place to stop and relax in the area is Patisserie Valerie, at 215 Brompton Road. Here are comfortable tables in the back or a marble-topped bar in front where you can watch the world go by. Afternoon tea is their forté, but light lunches are also served.

Harrods, the most famous department store in the world, is on Brompton Road. It is renowned for its Food Hall. If you can wrench your eyes from the dazzling array of foodstuffs, look up at the tiled ceiling made by Royal Doulton in about 1902. Harrods' cheese counter offers 500 cheeses—150 of them produced in Britain and Ireland. Vegetarian cheeses, such as Cornish Yarg, are made with vegetarian rennet instead of the usual calf's rennet. Welsh organic yogurt is available in the dairy case, and increasingly foods in the Food Hall are organically grown. String upon string of Italian and French sausages hang above one counter, where innumerable processed meats from around the globe are displayed, among them smoked wild venison, salt beef, roast beef, beef in aspic, MacSween's Scotch Haggis, roast hams, herbes de Provence ham, lamb, poussin, whole turkey, turkey breast, chicken en croute, duck in phyllo pastry, and beef biltong—a South African way of air-drying beef. In another case, bowls of beautifully made assorted sushi, decorated with gold and silver flowers, share space with bowls of caviar and truffled goose liver.

Feathered game birds hang above the poultry counter, and within it, tiny speckled quail eggs nestle next to gigantic goose eggs, sides of English bacon, and Scottish black puddings. One morning there were thirty-five varieties of fresh fish glistening beside ten varieties of shellfish and twelve of smoked fish. A wealth of Indian-prepared curries and chutneys, rice dishes, and naan and paratha—Indian breads—filled another counter. Pâtés smooth and coarse are displayed next to dozens of assorted pork pies—Britain's relished standby—not to mention Cornish pasties, quiches, and stunning-looking cocktail foods.

Gleaming local fruits and vegetables are beautifully arranged among their exotic cousins from all over the globe. The bakery counter, thronged with people, is near another display case filled with the most unusual and exquisitely decorated cakes—a wedding cake iced to look like the finest bridal lace, and birthday cakes for children, some doll-shaped, others molded to look like smart racing cars, and one designed to resemble a circus ring, topped with perfect edible clowns, three seals, and two tiny pink elephants.

Today Harrods is no longer the only department store in London with a well-stocked food hall. Selfridges and Harvey Nichols—known to the English as Harvey Nics—have opened their own. Selfridges is set up so that all purchases are paid for at one time before you leave the store, rather than paying for each item at a separate counter. Ethnic food shopping in London has also tripled in the last two years with high-quality Indian, Middle Eastern, European, and Asian markets scattered throughout the London boroughs.

Cabbage and Bell Pepper Salad with Almonds and Asian Noodles

2	medium-sized cabbages, chopped fairly finely
3	bunches scallions (1 C.), chopped
1	red bell pepper
1	yellow bell pepper
4 oz.	almonds (⅔ C.), slivered
4 oz.	pine nuts (⅔ C.)
2 T.	vegetable oil
10 oz.	package of dried, curled Asian noodles

Dressing

6 T.	sugar
12 fl.oz.	peanut oil (1½ C.)
3 T.	soya sauce
6 fl.oz.	rice vinegar (⅔ C.)
2 fl.oz.	fresh lime juice (¼ C.)

1. Toss cabbage, scallions, and bell peppers lightly together in a salad bowl.

2. Using a nonstick pan, toast almonds and pine nuts in vegetable oil until golden brown. Cool and add to the salad bowl.

3. Break noodles into small pieces and add to the salad bowl.

4. Whisk together salad dressing ingredients, pour over the salad, and toss well. Refrigerate for at least 4 hours before serving.

Serves 10 or more

Near Harrods, at 6 Basil Street, is Stockpot, a bargain of a restaurant with excellent, wholesome food, including regional specialties such as Lancashire Hot Pot. Desserts are comforting fruit-filled pies and puddings.

Farther along the Brompton Road is the Brompton Oratory. This magnificent church, built between 1880 and 1884, is the second biggest Catholic church in London. The richly embellished interior has a wealth of paintings, statues grace the side altars, and overhead the huge gilded dome is encircled by mosaic figures of the evangelists.

The world-renowned Victoria and Albert Museum is the next building of note on the Brompton Road. Essentially a teaching museum for design, here are vast collections of fine art and design from around the world. It is wise to decide ahead of time which areas interest you, because seeing it all at one time is impossible. Beyond the V & A are the impressive displays in the History Museum and the interesting objects and working models in the Science Museum.

On Prince Consort Road, nearby, is the Royal Albert Hall, where immensely popular Promenade Concerts, called Proms, are held for eight weeks every summer.

At 86 Brompton Road is the pretty restaurant Richoux that serves wonderful afternoon tea, as well as breakfasts and light meals.

A fine restaurant for lunch or dinner is Hilaire at 68 Old Brompton Road, where wide windows look out onto the street, giving you an opportunity to view the passing scene. The chef here is Bryan Webb—his father will probably greet you at the door—and the cooking is excellent, with eclectic ingredients and imaginatively reinvented British dishes. Don't pass up the rice pudding.

Shaw's Restaurant at 119 Old Brompton Road has a shorter menu at lunch featuring starters of warm salads of perfectly cooked scallops, or warm goat cheese salad on an artichoke heart, and a choice of four of five main courses with additional daily specials, such as risotto of exotic mushrooms with baby spinach, fresh Parmesan and asparagus, or monkfish with lentils and coriander. Frances Atkins is the chef, and her years spent in Scotland, where good venison, beef, and seafood are easily available, influence the longer dinner menu.

Off the Brompton Road is Beauchamp (pronounced Beecham) Place, a small street filled with unusual and sophisticated shops and boutiques that are well worth browsing. Wine bars and restaurants abound here too. Off Beauchamp Place is Walton Street, another attractive shopping street, where you will find Waltons Restaurant at number 121. Waltons has an extremely talented chef, Paul Hodgson, who has thrived there over the last four years. His very high standards reflect his training at the hands of the famous chef Robert Carrier. Waltons Restaurant is supplied on a daily basis with fresh produce and impeccable fish from Billingsgate Market. One of the delicious dishes Paul Hodgson has created is Seafood Sausage, made with the finest ingredients. His main course beef dish is outstanding, as is the calves liver. Dishes on the winter menu include Terrine of truffled foie gras with Sauterne jelly; Salad of Cornish scallops; Roast filet of Southdowns lamb; Breast of duck with orange sauce; and desserts such as Blackberry and apple charlotte; Dark bitter chocolate and praline terrine; Burnt English cream; and Treacle tart. One of the delights here is the attentive but not obtrusive staff. The restaurant has a bright, warm feeling. Yellow and gray silk draperies at the windows are repeated in the table decoration. There is also a smaller dining room, with bold red and yellow fabric wall and ceiling treatment, where private functions are held. Paul Hodgson has given us one of his favorite recipes to try.

Medallions of Prime Scottish Beef with Wild Mushrooms and a Dark Whisky Sauce

Sauce

1		onion
1		carrot
1		celery stick
1		sprig of thyme
1		sprig of rosemary
2	T.	oil
4	fl.oz.	red wine (½ C.)
2	fl.oz.	whisky (¼ C.)
40	fl.oz.	veal stock (5 C.)

1. Roughly chop the vegetables and herbs, and sauté in the oil in a heavy-bottomed saucepan.
2. Add red wine and whisky to the pan, then stir in the veal stock. Season and simmer until reduced by half.
3. Strain sauce and set aside.

Beef fillets and mushrooms

4	7-oz.	Scottish beef fillets
2	oz.	butter
1	lb.	fresh, wild mushrooms
2	fl.oz.	whisky (¼ C.)

4. Panfry steaks to medium rare in the butter. Add wild mushrooms to the pan and sauté for 2 minutes, then pour in the whisky and heat through.
5. To serve, reheat sauce, place beef fillet and mushrooms on a plate, and surround with sauce.   *Serves* 4

Brompton Road leads into Fulham Road, another haven of gastronomic delights. Fulham Road restaurant, at 257–259 Fulham Road, SW3, near Elm Park Gardens, is Stephen Bull's latest venture. His inventive Irish chef, Richard Corrigan, uses interesting ingredients, some of which are newcomers to this side of the Irish Sea. Fish dishes are plentiful here, as are the more unusual specialty meats. Homemade chocolates can be ordered with your coffee.

Bibendum, 81 Fulham Road, London, SW3, in the Michelin building, is possibly the best-known restaurant in London. Started by Sir Terence Conran, the chef is the incomparable Simon Hopkinson, who is justly famous for his wonderful, simple yet splendid cooking.

A pub, The White Horse, at Parsons Green, Fulham, has commendable food.

Sloane Street, named after Sir Hans Sloane (1660–1753), the court physician, collector, and antiquarian, leads down to Sloane Square, a lively place of shops and sidewalk cafés. In the square is the Royal Court Theatre—renowned for its avant-garde plays. From here the King's Road runs across Chelsea. This street is literally the King's Road. At one time it was a track that Charles II had paved to ease his frequent trips to Nell Gwyn's house in Fulham. The King's Road still has punk rockers and tawdry shops, though far fewer than before.

Chelsea

Chelsea is an attractive part of London, situated on the Thames, that retains its closely knit village community. Writers and artists live on its quiet streets, lined with elegant houses dating to the seventeenth, eighteenth, and nineteenth centuries. Anita Brookner, Sir David Frost, the Countess of Longford, and at one time her dizzyingly successful children lived in Chelsea. The painters Whistler, Turner, and Sargent lived here in their day, as did the writers Thomas Carlyle, Oscar Wilde, and Henry James. The air of antiquity, creativity, and grace gives Chelsea its quietly bohemian charm. It is a highly desirable residential neighborhood. Outside All Saints' Church overlooking the river is a statue of Sir Thomas More, erected in 1969. In the sixteenth century, Chelsea held the estate of Sir Thomas More—A *Man for All Seasons*—who made it plain that he thought Henry VIII's marriage to Anne Boleyn was illegal. King Henry's displeasure culminated in 1535 with More leaving his home by boat to sail downriver from Chelsea to the Tower of London, where he was beheaded. Eventually Anne Boleyn was to be executed at the same place. Henry VIII, as was his usual custom, annexed Thomas More's property and had a palace built for his children, Prince Edward and Princess Elizabeth, where they lived with their tutors.

Today the splendid Royal Hospital building is Chelsea's architectural masterpiece. Commissioned by King Charles II, Christopher Wren designed the hospital to house war veterans. The hospital's wide lawns and courtyard are a blaze of bloom in May when the Chelsea Flower Show is held here.

Wildly popular, the Flower Show is attended by every ardent gardener in the Isles. Members of the royal family are much in evidence. On one occasion, the Duke of Edinburgh picked up a hose and accidentally hosed down the Press! On the corner of Royal Hospital Road and the Chelsea Embankment is the Chelsea Physic Garden, with its entrance on Swan Walk. The statue standing in its center is Sir Hans Sloane, the court physician who gave land for the Physic Garden in 1676. These four acres of plants and trees comprise one of the oldest botanical gardens in the country.

The Canteen Restaurant at Unit G4, Harbour Yard, Chelsea Harbour, is owned by Michael Caine and Marco Pierre White, the supervising chef, and the kitchen is in the capable hands of Steve Terry. Squid ink risotto with calamari, grilled game, and lemon tart were very well done on a recent visit. Request a table by the window, if possible, so you can look out over the water.

Foxtrot Oscar, 79 Hospital Road, Chelsea, is a welcoming neighborhood restaurant with style. Food here is either typically British, as in steak and kidney pudding followed by trifle, or typically American with burgers and fries. The staff is friendly and the food honest and flavorful.

The Admiral Codington pub is well known for its good traditional British food—roasts at Sunday lunch—friendly ambience, and considerable collection of malt whiskys. Gaslights and wood paneling give the pub a wonderfully cozy Victorian air.

Stilton and Potato Tart

½ lb. ripe tomatoes, seeded and diced
1 t. salt
1 T. mustard
1 egg, lightly beaten
1 10-inch unbaked tart shell
4 oz. crumbled Stilton cheese (½ C.)
½ lb. russet potatoes (1½ C.), peeled and sliced ⅛" thick
1 med. onion, (⅔ C.) peeled and sliced ⅛" thick
 salt
 freshly ground pepper
1 T. minced fresh basil
2 T. olive oil

1. Preheat the oven to 425°F (or gas mark 7).

2. Place diced tomatoes in a strainer placed over a bowl and sprinkle with 1 tsp. salt. Set aside.

3. Mix the mustard and egg together and spread it in the bottom of the unbaked tart shell. Scatter the Stilton evenly onto the mustard mixture.

4. Arrange potato and onion slices in overlapping circles on top of the cheese. Season with salt and freshly ground pepper.

5. Gently toss the tomatoes with basil and olive oil, and scatter evenly over the potatoes and onions.

6. Bake in the middle of the oven for 30 minutes. Serve hot.

Serves 4

Belgravia

In Belgravia's spacious squares only residents have the key to the beautifully kept gardens, concealed behind trees and iron railings, in the center of the square. Vast parcels of land were given to Henry VIII's favorites, who grew rich on royal largesse and in later years hired architects to design luxurious town mansions and wide squares that contrast markedly with the narrow winding streets in the City. Today many of the mansions are occupied by upscale companies and art galleries.

On Motcomb Street, SW1, one of the little streets that honeycomb the area around Belgrave Square, is Motcombs, a delightful neighborhood restaurant reached down a flight of steps. There is also a good wine bar at street level that at lunchtime serves oysters, salads, and pies. The proprietor, Philip Lawless, offers impeccably cooked and generously sized fish dishes, as well as succulent oysters in many guises.

Nearby is Drones, at 1 Pont Street, started by David Niven, Jr., with childhood photos of many famous film stars decorating its walls. Its decor is bright and charming, and the menu has a long list of innovative fish dishes and super meats from Chateaubriand to burgers.

Mayfair

Mayfair got its name from the fair held here each May until the eighteenth century. Mayfair is one of the most desirable, wealthy areas of London. Elegant residences are built around the three main squares, Grosvenor, Berkeley, and Hanover. The streets follow the old grid pattern, and like Soho, the district has definite boundaries. Mayfair is bordered by Park Lane to the west, Oxford Street to the north, Regent Street to the east, and Piccadilly to the south. Park Lane still has some lovely houses, but many of these have made way for some of London's smart luxurious hotels. At the Oxford Street end of Park Lane is Marble Arch, brought from Buckingham Palace in the 1800s. Speakers Corner, where orators can climb on "soapboxes" and discourse to their hearts' content, is at Marble Arch. From the four main thoroughfares that enclose Mayfair many small streets, with interesting buildings, shops, and churches, lead to magnificent squares and the splendid houses in their centers. In Grosvenor Square is the U.S. Embassy, a huge gilded eagle over its doors. John Adams, the first American ambassador to the Court of St. James, lived at the corner of Duke and Brook Streets here. Grosvenor Square is the center of the huge estate of the Duke of Westminster, which was developed by Richard Grosvenor in the early eighteenth century. Blue plaques are numerous in this part of London. Curzon Street, running east to west across Mayfair, has some fine old houses among the towering commercial buildings. Just off Curzon Street is the delightful Shepherds Market, a quaint area of small shops and houses that has changed very little throughout its history. One of its major attractions is the old Bunch of Grapes pub, where people tend to congregate outside on benches and spend a convivial evening together. Mayfair's most famous street is Bond Street, now divided into Old and New Bond Street. Lovely shops sell antiques, jewelry, and expensive clothes. Sotheby's auction rooms and art dealers are well represented here. Gorgeous emporiums, such as Asprey's, display presents for the most princely pockets.

Piccadilly Circus has in its center a romantic pedestaled statue shooting an arrow from a curly bow, which has led to it being erroneously dubbed Eros. Piccadilly runs from the Circus to Hyde Park Corner. On the north side of the street not far from the Circus is the glorious Burlington Arcade that connects Piccadilly to Regent Street. Here are some of the most fashionable shops, and wonderful art objects to buy, in London. Farther along is the Royal Academy of Arts housed in Burlington House. On the south side is Fortnum and Mason—the grocer to Her Majesty the Queen—founded by a footman to Queen Anne, William Fortnum, and his landlord, Hugh Mason, who also had a stall in St. James's market. Above the doorway to the shop is a large ornate clock with a closed compartment on each side—one bearing an F and the other an M. On the hour the doors open and Mr. Fortnum and Mr. Mason emerge and bow to each other. Inside the luxurious emporium all is quiet elegance—shop assistants wear morning coats, and the floors are carpeted. As well as everything you ever hoped to find in the way of luxurious comestibles, there are three restaurants in the store, serving afternoon tea as well as full meals. Farther along is the Ritz Hotel, built by César Ritz in 1906, one of the most elegant hotels in London. Inside the lovely dining room is a ceiling painted to resemble the sky. Mirrored walls reflect gilded flowers and gorgeous chandeliers.

Fennel Soufflé

3		lg. heads of fennel
3		lg. eggs plus 2 extra whites
4	oz.	grated Parmesan cheese (1 C.)
3	oz.	Stilton cheese (¾ C.), crumbled
6	fl.oz.	light cream (⅔ C.)
1	t.	salt
½	t.	freshly ground pepper
		butter to grease soufflé dish
1	T.	fennel leaves, finely minced

1. Remove and discard tough fennel stalks and coarse or discolored outer ribs. Mince the youngest and freshest leaves. Set aside.

2. Slice tender fennel bulbs and cook in boiling salted water for 10 to 15 minutes. Drain, shaking colander gently to dry fennel.

3. Purée fennel in a food processor and pour into a mixing bowl. Beat into fennel purée the egg yolks, the Parmesan and Stilton cheeses, the cream, and seasonings.

4. Butter soufflé dish. Beat the five egg whites with an electric beater in a large bowl until they form stiff peaks. Preheat oven to 400°F (or gas mark 6).

5. Quickly mix one-fourth of egg whites with fennel mixture to lighten sauce, then gently fold in the rest of the egg whites. Immediately scrape into the soufflé dish, set on a baking sheet, and place in the center of the oven. Bake for 25–35 minutes. Serve immediately, sprinkled with minced fennel leaves. *Serves* 4

From here St. James's Street runs down to Pall Mall. On Piccadilly just past St. James's Street is the 53-acre expanse of Green Park, bordered by Constitution Hill on the far side. Piccadilly ends at the Wellington Arch, near Hyde Park Corner.

As you turn onto Park Lane you will come to the acclaimed Dorchester Hotel. Willi Elsener was appointed executive chef of the Dorchester's kitchens in March 1988. Trained at hotels in Switzerland, Willi Elsener was lucky enough to come to the Dorchester as deputy to Anton Mosimann, who provided him with an in-depth knowledge and understanding of the famous kitchens and restaurants here. During the refurbishment of the Dorchester, Willi Elsener, after his close involvement in planning the new kitchens, food areas, and Oriental restaurant, expanded his knowledge of both French and Oriental cuisine by working at the Ritz in Paris and attending a cookery course at the Thai Cookery School at the Oriental Hotel in Bangkok. Willi Elsener has enormous enthusiasm and respect for his profession, and a dedication to excellence and quality that has been recognized by the Automobile Association, which awarded the Terrace Restaurant three rosettes for 1993, following Egon Ronay's 1992 *Cellnet Guide to Hotels and Restaurants* award of two out of three stars.

Willi Elsener says, "My culinary philosophy is bound together with my philosophy of life. They are closely intertwined and cannot be separated from each other. Physical health and mental well-being are, to a large extent, dependent on what we eat; so, undoubtedly, we are what we eat! My philosophy is founded on three basic principles: Firstly, the value of tradition, secondly, a wealth of experience, and thirdly, the essential need for good nutrition with one constant and essential ingredient: freshness." Ingredients for the Dorchester restaurants are bought from home markets, France, and Hong Kong. Willi Elsener's two favorite dishes are baked escalope of sea bass filled with herbs and zest of limes, served with silver skin onions and strips of bacon and Chinese greens; and marinated glazed scallops served with an oriental salad.

The three restaurants at the Dorchester are the Terrace, which has the best in French cuisine with a light three-course menu and a three-course vegetarian menu. Some of the dishes on these two menus are a Small timbale and slices of Scotch lobster on a salad with marinated vegetables; Half-dozen Colchester oysters with caviar; Panfried goose liver on a salad of new potatoes with chervil and honey vinaigrette; Roasted quail with foie gras, caramelized raisins, and black mushrooms; Baked salmon parcel filled with a tomato and vegetable confit served with cardamom and pink grapefruit sauce; Fillet of lamb baked with a potato crust and Albany truffles; and Fillet of venison roasted with walnuts, chestnuts, and cabbage, with a sauce infused with dried mandarin peel. The Oriental serves a wide selection of dishes influenced by Chinese and Southeast Asian cooking, such as Jelly fish and mixed seafood marinated in sesame oil and chili bean sauce; Boiled prawns and chicken dumplings with ginger and spring onion sauce; Roasted Peking duck; Sliced chicken marinated in Shaoh Sing wine; Braised superior sharks' fin with brown sauce; Diced stir-fried beef with lemon grass and black pepper; Braised bamboo shoots and chinese mushroom in a spicy chili bean sauce and Braised E-fu noodles with crabmeat. The Grill Room, which "remains largely the same today as it was when the Dorchester opened in 1931," lists a wealth of traditional British dishes, such as Cock-a-leekie soup, Black pudding with warm potato and bacon salad, Roast Angus beef with Yorkshire pudding, Steak and kidney pudding, Cornish fisherman's pie, Dover sole, and a satisfying selection of puddings. Willi Elsener has contributed his recipe for panfried goat cheese salad.

Marinated Vegetable Salad with
Panfried Goat's Cheese in Sesame Oil Vinaigrette

1	t.	sesame seeds
½	t.	coriander leaves, finely chopped
½	t.	parsley, finely chopped
6–7	oz.	goat's cheese (preferably St. Maurice), cut into ½-inch-thick slices, 3 pieces each
1	T.	flour, for dusting cheese
1		egg, slightly whisked
1	T.	sesame oil

Sesame oil dressing

3–4	T.	sesame oil
½		garlic clove, peeled and crushed
2	oz.	red pepper (scant ½ C.), cut into fine strips
2	oz.	yellow pepper (scant ½ C.), cut into fine strips
1–2	T.	white wine
5	T.	chicken stock
1	t.	soya sauce, light
1		lime, juiced
2	t.	balsamic vinegar
3–4	T.	sunflower oil
		freshly ground pepper, salt

Garnish

1		spring onion, cut into fine strips
6		pieces of white chicory
1	oz.	mixed salad leaves (¼ C.)

1. To prepare dressing, heat 2 tablespoons sesame oil (from the 3–4 tablespoons) in a saucepan and add the crushed garlic.

2. Add the red and yellow peppers and sweat for one minute without coloring.

3. Add white wine and bring to a boil.

4. Add chicken stock, bring to a boil again, and simmer for 2 to 3 minutes. Remove from heat and add soya sauce, lime juice, and balsamic vinegar, stirring well.

5. Add remaining sesame oil and sunflower oil.

6. Season with salt and pepper, and set aside to cool.

Salad with goat's cheese

7. Preheat grill to highest setting and roast the sesame seeds on a baking sheet until golden brown. Allow to cool.

8. Mix herbs and sesame seeds together.

9. Spread the cheese slices on a tray and sprinkle herb mixture on top. Turn slices over and sprinkle remaining mixture on top. Set aside.

10. Remove peppers from dressing and mix with spring onions. Save the dressing.

11. Arrange three pieces of white chicory in a star shape on each plate. Set aside.

12. Dust the slices of cheese with flour and press lightly with your hand. Dip slices into the egg and remove.

13. Heat sesame oil in a nonstick pan and fry the slices of cheese gently on both side until golden brown.

14. Remove, place on kitchen paper, and set aside.

15. Mix the peppers and salad leaves together and arrange in the center of the chicory, then place the pieces of cheese between the chicory leaves.

16. Pour the dressing over the salad and serve.   *Serves 2*

Other superb restaurants to visit in Mayfair are: the Connaught, Carlos Place, W1, where chef Michel Bourdin cooks impeccable French and traditional English food. The setting is opulent, the dining room is paneled in mahogany, and the waiters wear tails.

Gary Rhodes at the Greenhouse, 27A Hay's Mews, London, W1, cooks the best of new innovative British food, ending with comforting desserts such as sticky toffee pudding and bread and butter pudding.

Langan's Brasserie, Stratton Street, W1, first became famous for its part-owner Michael Caine and now is applauded for its hundreds of great traditional dishes and the smoothness and friendliness of its service.

Mulligans at 13–14 Cork Street, W1, is as Irish as can be with traditional fare, such as Irish stew, washed down with pints of Guinness.

Zoe in St. Christopher's Place, W1, is part of the group of restaurants owned by Antony Worrall-Thompson. This is one of those restaurants where one level serves light fare and the other has elegant fine dining. The food too is split between hearty country fare—puddings and such like—and up-to-the-minute dishes made with flair and imagination.

Stephen Bull, 5–7 Blandford Street, W1, has a chef, Jon Bentham, who cooks inventive food, sometimes with a French, Italian, or Asian twist, using impeccable English ingredients. The restaurant has clean lines with little ornamentation. A few pictures hang on the walls. The attention is almost solely on the food here, and the menu is long. Dishes are attractively presented and cooked with flair and attention to detail.

Durrant's, George Street, W1, has an Italian chef cooking wonderful British food in a graceful Georgian house that was once a coaching inn. The hotel is furnished in top-notch antiques. Substantial meat dishes are wonderfully executed, from roast beef and leg of lamb to sweetbreads and steak and kidney pudding. Desserts are blissful.

The Guinea Grill, 26 Bruton Street, W1, near Berkeley Square, is housed in a converted garage. Here, before being seated you get to choose what you will eat from a delectable display of Scottish smoked salmon, steaks, and chops. Your choice is then grilled to perfection and brought to your table piping hot as you finish your last mouthful of first course, a brilliant way to manage a restaurant that is a little short on space.

The Ritz, Piccadilly, W1, has one of the most beautiful dining rooms in London with views over Green Park. Much of the food is typically French, but there are a substantial number of English traditional foods such as roasts and regional stews cooked by David Nicholls.

Green's Restaurant and Oyster Bar, 36 Duke Street, St. James's, concentrates on British traditional foods with an emphasis on fish, particularly kippers, smoked haddock, and shellfish such as lobster, crab, and Dublin Bay prawns, and of course oysters, which you can eat sitting at the oyster bar while Peter Manzi shucks them for you. He is a master at shucking oysters with a Galway Oyster Festival award to prove it.

Wilton's, 55 Jermyn Street, SW1, is known for fresh seafood delivered almost continuously throughout the day. The oyster bar here has the freshest and best. Wash them down with champagne, and finish your repast with a typically British sherry trifle.

Le Caprice, located just behind the Ritz Hotel at Arlington House, Arlington Street, SW1, has walls covered in David Bailey's photographs. Mark Hix is executive head chef, and the cooking is eclectic with many dishes prepared in the new imaginative British fashion—grilled goat's cheese, or fresh fish marinated in lime juice—which have great flair and appeal.

The Square, at 32 King Street, St. James's, is the winner of the Best Modern British Award for 1993. Here you will find sublime contemporary British cooking. The decor is smart and fun, and the service smooth.

Lanes Restaurant on the first floor at Inn on the Park, Hamilton Place, has the most magnificent buffet. This can serve as an appetizer with dinner, or on its own for a superb lunch. The green marble buffet is resplendent with huge, freshly grilled shrimp, salads of every stripe, cold meats, prosciutto, smoked salmon, smoked fishes other than salmon, roast meats, aspics, marinated vegetables, baby melons, and other wonderful fruits.

On a different scale but with considerable appeal is the Fountain restaurant in Fortnum and Mason, at 181 Piccadilly. Food here is as traditionally British as it can be, with hearty snacks such as Welsh rabbit or sandwiches, light meals featuring game pie and boiled hams, evening meals offering simple steaks and chops, and afternoon teas with all the scrumptious goodies you would expect in such an impeccable emporium. Afternoon tea at Fortnum and Mason, or at any of the better hotels or good patisseries, is a great way to take a break from sightseeing or museum-going.

At the West end of the Mall, overlooking an enormous statue of Queen Victoria on the circle outside the gates, is Buckingham Palace, the London residence of Her Majesty the Queen and the Duke of Edinburgh. Behind the palace is a 40-acre garden with a lake where the Queen holds her official birthday party in June. Buckingham House, as it was originally called, was built for the Duke of Buckingham in the eighteenth century and sold to George III who was looking for a new residence to escape "the dust trap" of St. James's. Renovated to palace status by George IV's architect, John Nash, who was also responsible for the ornate Brighton Pavilion, it has served all subsequent monarchs as the royal London residence. Today affairs of state, state banquets, and official receptions for visiting heads of state, weekly meetings with the prime minister, and investitures all take place at Buck House. At the opposite end of the Mall from Buckingham Palace is the Admiralty Arch, with three gateways, built as a memorial to Britain's longest-reigning monarch, Queen Victoria.

St. James's

St. James's is part of Royal London. St. James's Palace, between Green Park and the pretty water-filled St. James's Park, is named for the leper hospital that stood on this spot in the eleventh century. St. James's has served intermittently as a royal residence but went into eclipse when Queen Victoria decided to live in Buckingham Palace while in London. Princess Margaret lived at St. James's, and more recently it has become the London home of the present Prince of Wales. Inside the palace, the Chapel Royal still has the intertwined initials H and A, for Henry VIII and one of his unfortunate wives, Anne Boleyn. Nearby in front of Marlborough House is the exquisite Queen's Chapel, built for Henrietta Maria, wife of Charles I. The Queen Mother's London residence near the Mall, Clarence House, originally was built for the duke of Clarence, the then future king William IV. Good English roast beef is bound to be on the menu at several gentleman's clubs in the St. James's area.

Roast Beef with Green Peppercorn Sauce

1 beef tenderloin
1 T. olive oil
   freshly ground pepper
   salt
4 oz. brandy (¼ C.)

1. Preheat oven to 475°F (or gas mark 7). Coat the tenderloin with olive oil and season with salt and pepper.

2. Roast beef tenderloin on a rack in a roasting pan for 30–35 minutes (for medium rare) or to 150° F on a meat thermometer.

3. Remove from oven and let rest for 20 minutes, loosely covered with foil.

4. Meanwhile, skim fat from pan juices and discard. Pour brandy into roasting pan and bring to a boil, scraping up brown particles and deglazing the pan. Set aside.

Green peppercorn sauce

24 fl.oz. beef broth (3 C.)
3   shallots, finely minced
2 T. butter
2 T. flour
2 T. green peppercorns, drained
    pan juices from roast beef
1 T. fresh lemon juice
    freshly ground pepper
    salt
    parsley for garnishing

5. Bring beef broth to a boil and simmer over medium heat until reduced by one-third.

6. Sauté shallots for 4 to 5 minutes in butter. Stir in flour and cook for one minute. Add boiling broth and simmer for two minutes, stirring, until smooth. Stir in peppercorns, pan juices, lemon, and seasonings to taste.

7. To serve, slice beef, arrange on a large warmed serving platter, and garnish with parsley. Reheat gravy and pass separately.

Serves 6

Westminster

The Palace of Westminster, standing between the River Thames and West-minster Abbey, has long been Parliament's home. A palace has stood on this Thames-side site since the Danish king Canute lived here in the early 1000s and died in 1035. William the Conqueror lived at Westminster. His son, William Rufus, built Westminster Hall. All kings have summoned their parliaments to their royal residence. Parliament met here until Henry VIII moved his court to Whitehall Palace after a fire damaged Westminster in 1512. Parliament stayed on and has met here ever since.

When Oliver Cromwell came to power in the seventeenth century, he abolished the House of Lords and signed Charles I's death warrant. The House of Commons, meeting in St. Stephen's Chapel, refused to adjourn on Cromwell's command so he abolished the House of Commons too, only re-convening Parliament when short of funds. On Cromwell's death, the House of Commons invited Charles I's son to take the throne. Westminster was recon-structed after another fire in 1834.

For the Annual State Opening of Parliament, Her Majesty the Queen ar-rives in full panoply in the Irish State coach. The Queen sits on a gilded throne in the House of Lords and reads a speech going over the legislation that the government intends to put before Parliament in the coming ses-sion. The Queen, as a constitutional monarch, can consult, advise, and warn parliament, but not enforce her own opinions on government policy. Westminster Palace houses the Queen's Robing Room, the Princes Cham-ber, Lords Chambers, Lords Library, and the Royal Gallery, as well as the Central Lobby, Members Dining and Smoking Rooms, the Clock Tower, Vic-toria Tower, St. Stephen's Hall, and Westminster Hall. Members of each party sit on opposite sides of the house, facing one another—as they did on opposite sides of the central aisle when they convened in St. Stephen's Chapel. Two red lines on the carpet indicate where members should stand, and woe betide he or she who "oversteps the mark." Members can take visi-tors to tea in the palace.

The following recipe is an adaptation of the original Sticky Toffee Pud-ding recipe, created by Francis Coulson of Sharrow Bay Country House Hotel, Ullswater, Cumbria.

Sticky Toffee Pudding

---

    8 fl.oz. water (1 C.)
4–5 oz.   pitted dates (¾ C.), chopped
    3 oz.   unsalted butter (¾ stick)

6 oz.   sugar (¾ C.)
3   medium-sized eggs
7.5 oz.   flour (½ C.)
1 t.   vanilla essence
1 t.   baking soda

Sauce

8 fl.oz. heavy cream (1 C.)
6 oz.   dark brown sugar (⅔ C.)
¾ t.   molasses
3 T.   unsalted butter
½ t.   vanilla essence

1. Preheat oven to 350°F (or gas mark 4).
2. Bring water to a boil, add the dates, and let stand while you make the pudding.
3. Cream butter and sugar until light. Beat in eggs one at a time. Gently stir in flour. Add vanilla essence and set aside.
4. Add the baking soda to the dates and water and pour into pudding mixture, stirring to combine evenly.
5. Place in a well-buttered shallow 8-inch square pan and bake for 25–30 minutes or until set.
6. Meanwhile make the sauce by placing all ingredients in a small heavy-bottomed saucepan and slowly bringing to a boil while stirring. Pour a little of the sauce over the pudding to glaze the top and return to the oven for 30 seconds.
7. To serve cut in squares and pass remaining sauce separately.

Serves 6

Westminster Abbey is the most important church in the kingdom. All monarchs from William I to Queen Elizabeth II have been crowned here. Edward the Confessor rebuilt the Benedictine Abbey that once stood on this site. Henry III in 1245 began enlarging the abbey, and this work was to continue for another 100 years before completion. Henry VII's Chapel was added in the 1500s, and in the mid-eighteenth century Nicholas Hawksmoor embellished the west entrance with twin towers. The abbey is crammed with monuments to famous Britons—many memorials have been recently refurbished. Poets' Corner is one of the most interesting, honoring writers and composers. All the royal tombs are grouped in back of the High Altar. A pretty courtyard reached through an archway from the west front of the abbey, called Dean's Yard, provides a respite from the crowds inside. Here too is the entrance to the very interesting Cloisters used by monks for study and relaxation in the Middle Ages.

Soho

Soho, bounded by Oxford Street to the north, Charing Cross Road to the east, Regent Street to the west, and Leicester (pronounced Lester) Square to the south, has the air of an urban village. Leicester Square was in fact once a village green where people came to hang their washing to dry. Residents know one another in Soho. Every Sunday Soho waiters get together as a team to play football in Regent's Park. Surprisingly, the church originally owned the land that is now Soho. Following the Dissolution of the Monasteries, the land was annexed by Henry VIII and became part of his hunting grounds. The district's name came from the word "So-Ho," which at that time was a hunting cry. Subdivision followed the hunting grounds, and Soho was parceled off among the nobility. The Great Fire of London in the 1600s burned down so many homes that refugees from burned areas began congregating in Soho in the thousands, causing many of the wealthier occupants to move farther west. Lacemakers from France settled in Soho in 1685, bringing garlic, duck confit, ratatouille, and cassoulet to perfume the Soho air. By the mid-1700s artists, architects, doctors, and lawyers were occupying Soho's narrow streets. The last aristocrats were eventually scared west during the cholera epidemic of 1854. Though its former grandeur has disappeared along with the aristocrats, Soho square has a charm of its own. In the center of its garden is a delightful, tiny half-timbered cottage with a pointed roof and overhanging gables that looks as though it escaped from a fairy tale. Soho's street names evoke the trades, and sometimes the nationalities, of its first industrious immigrés—Brewer Street, Glassblower Street, Greek Street, and Dean Street. Italians came as cooks and waiters and then began establishing restaurants of their own. One of Napoleon's chefs is credited with starting the still much-frequented Wheelers at 19 Old Compton Street—known for its impeccable fish dishes. Italians were followed by Greeks and Germans. As early as 1903, 60 percent of Soho's inhabitants were not British-born. The latest ethnic group to arrive, the Chinese, cram Soho's ancient houses and have opened their own fragrant restaurants and Asian food markets.

Soho quickly became known for its great restaurants and at roughly the same time middle-class people in England began to entertain guests outside the home, something unheard-of until that time. Soho today is an area of fashionable restaurants, nightclubs, upscale wine bars, and Italian delicatessens. Young people congregate on the streets, and increasingly small tables and chairs are set out on the sidewalk in front of cafés, giving Soho a decidedly continental air. Soho is a small district with definite boundaries, as is Mayfair, unlike the more nebulous parts of town that seem to blend into one another. It is also fairly easy to find your way as it is one of the few

London areas where streets adhere to a grid pattern. Certain industries gravitate to one or two adjacent streets. Wardour Street is home to the film industry and Berwick Street has long had fruit and vegetable stalls. Despite the eclectic mix of cuisines in Soho, traditional English food is definitely coming into its own in London restaurants.

The Lexington, at 45 Lexington Street, W1, is a busy and much-loved local Soho restaurant. Mark Holmes is the head chef here now; previously he manned the kitchens at The Ivy and The Square restaurants. Mark Holmes's cooking is modern British. He says, "Over the past decade Britain has produced some great chefs. London particularly is thriving with good young chefs from all over the country coming to gain experience and bringing influences of their own to the capital." The Lexington is a relatively new restaurant, opened in 1992 by Martin Saxon and Harriet Arden. Menus here change daily according to which fresh ingredients are available. All the suppliers are in London. As well as the main restaurant menu, The Lexington has three private room menus. Dishes include Crusted cod with leeks and creamed mushrooms; Radicchio risotto; Char-grilled Provençale vegetables with balsamic vinegar; Rump of lamb with roasted globe artichokes; and Roast wood pigeon, spinach, and beetroot crisps. Desserts are comforting Burnt cream, Apple tart tatin, and Rhubarb compote with Jersey cream. British cheeses are served with walnut bread. The staff here is young and enthusiastic. Mark Holmes has contributed the following recipe for inclusion in this book.

Boiled Bacon, Mashed Potatoes, and Mushy Peas

1 small shoulder of bacon, boned, rolled and tied; reserve the uncooked bone

Court bouillon

2	med.	onions
2	lg.	carrots
1		celery stick
2	med.	leeks
10		coriander seeds
1		star anise
5		sprigs of thyme
1		bay leaf
10		peppercorns
4		garlic cloves

1. Completely cover the bacon with cold water and leave to soak for 24 hours, drain, and place in a saucepan large enough to easily hold the bacon and approximately 15 Imperial pints (about 17 U.S. pints) of fresh water.

2. Chop all the vegetables for the court bouillon and add to the bacon and water together with the remaining court bouillon ingredients. Bring to a boil and simmer for 1½ hours.

3. Remove the bacon. Strain the cooking liquid, discarding the vegetables and reserving 8 Imperial pints (10 U.S. pints) for the peas. Pour the rest of the liquid over the bacon so that it is just covered. Let rest 30 to 45 minutes while preparing the potatoes and peas.

Mash

7	lb.	potatoes, preferably Estima or similar, washed and peeled
		a good pinch of salt
8	oz.	butter
40	fl.oz.	milk (5 C.)
5	fl.oz.	heavy cream (½ C.)
1		bunch flat leaf parsley, finely chopped
		ground black pepper

4. Dice potatoes and run under cold water for 10 minutes. Place in a pan, cover with water, add the salt and bring to a boil. Simmer 5 to 10 minutes or until cooked.

5. Drain potatoes and pass them through a sieve. Heat butter and milk and gradually add to the potatoes, stirring constantly. At the last minute, add the cream and check the seasoning. Mix in the parsley just before serving.

Mushy Peas

1	lg.	carrot
1	lg.	onion
1		celery stick
1		leek
2		garlic cloves
3	oz.	butter
		the reserved bacon stock
½	lb.	dried split peas
1		sprig of mint
		salt and pepper to taste

6. To prepare peas, wash, peel, and chop all vegetables and sweat them in the butter.

7. In a separate pan, bring the bacon stock to a boil, add the peas, mint, and the uncooked bacon bone to the vegetables and

pour in 4 pints of the reserved stock. Cover pan and simmer for approximately 30 minutes or until cooked, adding more stock as necessary to keep the peas moist. Taste for seasoning.

8. To serve, place a scoop of potatoes on the plate. Place two slices of bacon on top of the potatoes, surround with sauce, and place peas to one side.

Serves 12

Chef's note: Leftover potatoes and peas can be made into "bubble and squeak" (fritters) and served with the bacon and some eggs the next day for breakfast or brunch. The remaining bacon can be used for sandwiches and cold cuts.

The Lindsay House on Romilly Street, W1, is one of a trio of restaurants that includes the English House and the English Garden. It is situated in the original sitting room of an elegant seventeenth-century house. The room is replendent with silk hangings and antiques, and is full of fresh flowers. The cooking is very English, but from an earlier century when meats were marinated in ale, game was served with fruits, and almonds were featured in many savory and sweet dishes. Cornish scallops and grilled breast of duckling are two of the chef's special dishes. The soufflés are a delight.

Among the best of Soho's restaurants, and with arguably the most innovative chef, is Antony Worrall-Thompson's Dell'Ugo at 56 Frith Street. Though the name—taken from a bottle of olive oil—is Italian, the food is decidedly eclectic. The ground-floor restaurant does not take reservations and serves light salads and other interesting fare. The upper floor is a wide spacious atrium. Here the restaurant is more formal, yet you can still choose among several dazzling dishes that are listed on the menu either as appetizers or as main courses, so it is not only nicely flexible but allows you to taste many delicious creations, such as radicchio and parmesan risotto with field mushrooms, roasted red bell pepper and anchovy spaghetti, mussels in a lentil broth with wilted greens, and crisp, crunchy chicken with garlic potatoes. One-pot dishes feature pulses and grains with chicken or duck confit and many other combinations. Breads are also superb. Though Mediterranean foods are prevalent, there are plenty of British, French, and Japanese dishes too. Go with friends and don't forget the caramelized rice pudding for dessert.

Alistair Little, nearby on Frith Street, also mixes a variety of cuisines with a brilliant style of his own. The restaurant is almost starkly furnished, the kitchen is visible from the dining room, and the emphasis is on the food, which is only right and proper as it is stunningly good.

Soho Soho, also on Frith Street, is a restaurant, café, bar, and rotisserie. It has a wonderful formal dining room upstairs and a wide open bustling restaurant downstairs where the food is very good—try the rotisserie chicken.

Tearooms abound in Soho—one of the best is Lascelles Old English Tea House at 2 Marlborough Court, Carnaby Street.

Almond Apricot Bars

1		egg yolk (save egg white for filling)
3	T.	buttermilk
10	oz.	flour (2 C.)
1½	oz.	whole wheat flour (not wholemeal) (¼ C.)
2	t.	baking powder
6	oz.	sugar (⅔ C.)
12	oz.	butter (1½ sticks)

Filling

6	oz.	blanched almonds (1¼ C.)
6	oz.	sifted confectioners sugar (1¼ C.)
1	t.	ground cardamom
½	t.	ground cinnamon
1		egg white
¼	t.	almond extract
2	T.	fresh lemon juice
4	T.	water

Glaze

7–8	oz.	apricot preserves (¾ C.)
½	lg.	lemon, juiced

Dough

1. In a small bowl beat together the egg yolk and buttermilk. Set aside.

2. Using a food processor, briefly whirl flours, baking powder, and sugar to fluff up and blend. Cut butter into pieces and add. Process until mixture resembles bread crumbs. Add yolk and buttermilk mixture and process to form a ball of dough.

3. Remove from processor and refrigerate dough wrapped in wax paper while you make almond filling and glaze.

Filling

4. Using food processor, coarsely chop almonds. Add confectioners sugar, cardamom, and cinnamon. Process briefly to mix. Add egg

white, almond extract, lemon juice, and water. Again process briefly. Set aside.

Glaze

5. Force preserves through a sieve into a small saucepan. Stir on low heat to soften preserves, mix in lemon juice, and heat to spreading consistency. Set aside.

6. Preheat oven to 350°F (or gas mark 4). Press dough to a uniform thickness into bottom of 13 × 9 × 2-inch ovenproof shallow pan.

7. Spread almond filling evenly over dough and bake for 40 minutes. Remove from oven and brush with apricot lemon glaze. Bake an additional 10 minutes. Remove from oven and cool in pan before cutting into bars.   *Yields* 20 *bars*

Covent Garden

A few minutes' walk from Soho is Covent Garden. These two vibrant areas are linked by their love of theater, restaurant dining, street musicians, jazz, and opera. However, they are completely dissimilar visually. Covent Garden was thoroughly renovated after the decision was taken to move the fruit, flower, and vegetable market to Nine Elms, south of the River Thames. Covent Garden is one of London's prettiest areas. Strict zoning laws prohibit the growth of sleaze, and in the last few years the number of new inhabitants moving into Covent Garden has risen dramatically. Opera and theater thrive as they have since the days when the orange seller, Nell Gwyn, turned to acting and then became the mistress of Charles II. Covent Garden's heyday as a fruit and vegetable market came when vegetables first became popular adjuncts to hearty meats and fish. Market gardens proved lucrative, especially near London. Eventually vegetable traders began to congregate around Covent Garden, an area where there had once been a garden and orchard that supplied produce to Westminster's convent of St. Peter. As Covent Garden, owned by the family of the Earls of Bedford, became more and more crowded with market gardeners, the earl turned the huge square into a piazza with porticos along two sides to shelter the traders. The next earl levied a toll from each trader who used the piazza to sell produce, and he earned a fortune in the process. Covent Garden until fairly recently was the main fruit, vegetable, and flower market in London, and had been since 1674. Traffic congestion around the area became untenable so the vast market was moved to south of the River Thames. Fortunately, after a long legal battle, the tenacious people who wanted to preserve the wide piazza and the market buildings won the day.

nately, after a long legal battle, the tenacious people who wanted to pre-serve the wide piazza and the market buildings won the day.

Mushrooms in Garlicky Tomato Sauce

2 oz.	olive oil (¼ C.)
¾ lb.	mushrooms, wiped and cut in thick slices
4 lg.	cloves of garlic, minced
1 T.	fresh lemon juice
½ t.	paprika
½	dried chili pepper crushed, seeds discarded
4 fl.oz.	homemade tomato sauce (½ C.)
3 T.	dry Spanish sherry
	salt and pepper to taste
2 T.	fresh minced cilantro

1. Heat oil over medium high heat in a frying pan, add mush-rooms and garlic, and cook for about 3 minutes.
2. Sprinkle with lemon juice. Add paprika and chili pepper and stir to coat mushrooms. Add tomato sauce, sherry, salt, and pepper and cook for 2 or 3 minutes longer.
3. Remove from heat and sprinkle with minced cilantro.

Serves 6 as an appetizer with toast points

The carefully restored market building is the heart of Covent Garden. Reopened in 1980, it now houses shops, restaurants, boutiques, wine bars, craft shops, and specialty food shops. Next to this on the south side is an in-formal bazaar, the Jubilee market, that sells flea-market goods, clothing, and toys. Crafts people bring their work to sell here at the weekend. St. Paul's Church, the parish church of Covent Garden, overlooks the central market, and its portico serves as a stage for outdoor entertainment as it has for the past three hundred years. Everything can be seen and heard here from jazz, juggling, and mime groups to fire eaters. The flower market building now holds the London Transport Museum, 39 Wellington Street, stuffed with an-cient vehicles and hands-on things for children to do. At 7 Russell Street is the Theatre Museum where exhibits cover the theater from Shakespeare's time until today. Here theater tickets for ongoing London shows can be pur-chased. There is also a pleasant café at 1E Tavistock Street.

Neal's Yard, a small street in Covent Garden, is particularly attractive and successful due to two enterprising men who each opened a business here—Paul Smith, one of Britain's foremost menswear designers, and Ter-

One shop not to be missed in Covent Garden is Neal's Yard Dairy, located at 9 Neal's Yard. Here Randolph Hodgson has a shop piled from floor to ceiling with different cheeses, both hard and soft, many of them blue, and some with the washed rind typical of Irish cheeses. Happily many more are ripening on shelves in his cool, humid cellar. Farmhouse cheeses are a thriving concern for farmers, restaurants, and dairy shops today, owing to the dedication of a handful of people who sought out dairy farmers, encouraged them to begin making these delectable fresh cheeses again, and bought and stored them until they reached the peak of perfection. Each cheese varies in taste from one milking to another depending sometimes only on which side of a field the cow browsed for her last meal. The shop also sells yogurt, double Jersey cream, crème fraîche, butter, milk, eggs, fruit cheeses, chutneys, mustards, olive oils, breads, oatcakes, and crackers, as well as a tome called *The Specialist Cheesemakers Directory* that you can use to go and visit the farmer who makes your favorite cheese. For people who experience difficulty in finding ingredients, there are several directories available listing the best purveyors of fresh foods, many of whom will happily mail items all over the country. Neal's Yard Wholefood Ltd., at 21–23 Shorts Gardens, is a great place to go for natural foods. They carry whole grain, additive-free and pesticide-free products, as well as raw honey, raw sugar, and all those good-for-you things.

The Ivy, 1 West Street, London, WC2, has been in existence on the same premises since the beginning of this century. The head chef, Desmond McDonald, has had a great deal of experience in many London restaurants, including the Ritz Hotel. The Ivy has earned a Michelin Red M. The menu is extensive. Some of the executive chef's favorite dishes are tripe and onions, dressed Cornish crab, and deep-fried cod with a minted pea purée. Skate with black butter, lemon, and capers is fresh and flavorful. Roasts and grills feature rack of lamb, and beef and Guinness sausages. Savouries and desserts list Champagne oysters, Scotch "woodcock," sticky toffee pudding, rice pudding with prunes and Armagnac, and a delightful pear and pistachio tart. The restaurant uses fresh fish and shellfish from the British Isles; small suppliers provide pristine vegetables, game, and farmhouse cheeses. Mark Hix, the executive chef, has contributed to this book his favorite recipe for Tripe and Onions.

Tripe and Onions

1½	lb.	honeycomb of ox tripe
1	lb.	white onions
1		garlic clove, crushed
2	T.	olive oil
2	T.	butter

1 T.	flour
6 fl.oz.	white wine (⅔ C.)
20 fl.oz.	chicken stock (2½ C.)
	salt and pepper
2 fl.oz.	heavy cream (¼ C.)
2 T.	chopped parsley

Suggested vegetable: mashed potatoes

1. Cut the ox tripe into 2-inch squares and place in a pan of cold water. Bring to a boil and refresh in cold water. Dry the tripe on paper towels.

2. Peel and slice the onions. Cook slowly over low heat with the garlic in the olive oil until very soft.

3. Add the pieces of tripe and the butter, stirring well.

4. Add the flour and cook over low heat for a few minutes. Slowly pour in the white wine and chicken stock, stirring constantly. Season with salt and pepper.

5. Bring to a boil, skim, and simmer for 1 to 1½ hours or until the tripe is tender.

6. Add the cream and chopped parsley just before serving, in separate bowls, accompanied by a good helping of mashed potatoes.

Serves 4–6

Rules, 35 Maiden Lane, WC2, was Lillie Langtry's favorite restaurant. It is typically gentleman's-club British in its Edwardian decor, and its menu lists all the traditional British foods of game, fish, steaks, and puddings.

Porters, at 17 Henrietta Street, WC2, also has an old-fashioned London decor much like a public house, and it features traditional favorites. It is known for its great pies—steak and kidney is mouthwatering—and for its steamed puddings served with custard sauce.

Le Café du Jardin, 28 Wellington Street, WC2, has its main restaurant in the basement, where as part of the decor a sizable and unusual steel bar is suspended from the ceiling. Tony Howarth, the chef, cooks interesting, appetizing, brasserie food that is very good. Frequented by theatergoers, the restaurant features a pianist in the evenings.

Crank's, in Covent Garden and at other locations throughout the city, is part of a chain of vegetarian restaurants that has very good nonmeat dishes. It is extremely popular, and you may have to wait for a table.

Spinach Timbales with Red Bell Pepper Sauce

2	lb.	fresh spinach, stalks removed
4	med.	red bell peppers
1	T.	raspberry vinegar
3	T.	butter
3	T.	flour
10	fl.oz.	milk (1¼ C.)
⅛	t.	nutmeg, grated
		salt and pepper, to taste
3		eggs
5	T.	heavy cream
2	T.	cognac

1. Wash spinach and spin dry. Place in a steamer over boiling water and simmer for 3 minutes. Drain and press out all the water. When cool, chop and set aside.

2. Roast red peppers under a broiler, and when they start to blister, remove to a paper bag for 15 minutes to steam.

3. Meanwhile, melt butter in a medium-sized heavy-bottomed pan, add flour and cook until foamy. Heat milk and add to the flour mixture, whisking with a wire whisk. Season with salt, pepper, and nutmeg and set aside to cool.

4. Peel and seed red peppers; cut two of the peppers into fine strips and arrange in the bottom of eight well-buttered, heat-proof ramekins. Cut up the remaining two peppers and place in a blender with a pinch of salt and pepper, and the raspberry vinegar. Blend until smooth, and put through a sieve. Stir into the pepper mixture 2 tablespoons of the sauce and half the heavy cream. Set aside. Preheat oven to 350°F (or gas mark 4).

5. Put the remaining sauce, the eggs, spinach, the remaining heavy cream, and the cognac in the blender and purée until smooth. Pour into ramekins and place in a baking dish. Pour in enough hot water to come halfway up the sides of the ramekins. Bake for 30 minutes or until a toothpick inserted in the center of the timbale comes out clean.

6. To serve, run a thin blade around the tops of the timbales and invert onto a warmed plate. Surround with pepper sauce and serve immediately.   *Yields 8 timbales*

The Lamb and Flag pub at 33 Rose Street, WC2, is a charming seventeenth-century pub serving good food and real ale. The scene here is upscale but friendly.

Sherlock Holmes, at 10 Northumberland Street, WC2, was frequented by the writer Arthur Conan Doyle. Memorabilia of Holmes can be seen in the bar area, and upstairs there is even a mock Sherlock Holmes study. Food here is very good.

Bloomsbury

Bloomsbury is the area north of Covent Garden made famous by a group of writers and artists who called themselves the Bloomsbury Group. Among this clique were Virginia Woolf, Bertrand Russell, Lytton Strachey, E. M. Forster, and others. Here too is the British Museum, an institute of learning that houses superb collections. The British Library is moving its 12 million books to a larger space in St. Pancras. A copy of every book published in London is in the collection, and the library must build two miles of new bookshelves each year to keep up with its ever-growing collection. Bloomsbury has some of the most spacious and lovely squares in London, their centers filled with quiet well-kept gardens. Bedford Square was laid out by Robert Adam from 1775 to 1783 for the fifth Duke of Bedford and is still looked after by the Bedford estate. Many of its graceful buildings today are occupied by publishing companies.

The Museum Street Café at 47 Museum Street, WC1, is an attractive and very good place to eat. It is a tiny restaurant serving a limited but perfectly cooked selection of British dishes, and an absolute haven after a morning spent in London's enthralling museums. At lunchtime the steaming bowls of soup and sandwiches on home-baked bread are just what the podiatrist ordered.

Grape Street is a good wine bar, near the British Museum, at 2 Grape Street, WC2, which serves excellent food as well as a good selection of wines, including some unusual ones not found everywhere else.

Hampstead

Farther north the terrain rises to Hampstead where the air is decidedly fresher, largely owing to Hampstead Heath's 800-acre swathe of grass, forest, walking trails, and lake. Hampstead, and its neighbor Highgate, though only four miles from the city center, have retained their village atmospheres more than any other rural area swallowed up by London. At one time Nell Gwyn lived at Lauderdale House in Highgate, not too far from Highgate Cemetery where Karl Marx is buried. Jack Straw's Castle is named for the executed leader of a group opposed to Sir Robert Hale's poll tax in 1381. Jack Straw is said to have hidden in the inn after defiantly burning down the Priory of St. John. Charles Dickens liked this inn. Dick Turpin, the dreaded highwayman, supped his ale at the ancient Spaniards Inn and Toll House on Hampstead Lane. The lovely eighteenth-century mansion, Kenwood, here on the Heath, owes its graceful facade to Robert Adam, who rebuilt Kenwood when Hampstead became popular as a spa. Londoners flocked to sample the waters and escape the city's fetid air. Kenwood, open to the public, displays paintings by Rembrandt, Vermeer, Gainsborough, Guardi, and Turner in its elegant rooms. Outdoor concerts are held here in the summer. Hampstead is a very desirable address and its pretty rows of eighteenth-century houses are home to many famous writers and artists seeking peace and quiet.

South of Covent Gaden is the Strand, once a "strand" or beach beside the Thames, and the main route between the City and the monarch's palace at Westminster. Today the Victoria Embankment is the closest road to the river. At one end of the Strand is the ornate Charing Cross railway station. An elaborate cross marks the spot outside where the coffin of Edward I's Queen Eleanor was set down on its way to Westminster Abbey for burial. A handful of Robert Adam's eighteenth-century townhouses still grace the Strand, and flower gardens, with statues of illustrious Britons, line the Victoria Embankment. Here too is Cleopatra's Needle, 1,000 years older than any other monument in London. Oridinally carved in 1450 B.C. for Thothmose III, it was presented to Britain in 1819 from Mohammed Ali, the viceroy of Egypt. The 180-ton, pink granite monolith was pulled by tugboats to its site beside the Thames, arriving sixty years after the presentation, partly because it was lost for a while en route when the tugboats' ropes brokes.

At the eastern end of the Strand stands Christopher Wren's pretty church of St. Clement Danes. The nursery rhyme "Oranges and lemons sang the bells of St. Clements" was inspired by its bells. Farther east is the many-turreted gothic building of the Law Courts and Temple Bar. This area holds the four beautiful Inns of Court—Lincoln's Inn, Gray's Inn, the Middle Temple, and the Inner Temple—surrounded by delightful, tree-filled gardens. Within the complex of "inns" is Staple Inn, one of the most beautiful restored black-and-white half-timbered buildings in London, complete with overhanging Elizabethan gables. Dr. Johnson lived for a while in one of its courts. These ancient tree-lined Inns of Court have been occupied since the fifteenth century or longer by lawyers qualified to practice at the bar. Lincoln's Inn's records date to 1292, and its fifteenth-century library holds the largest collection of law books in London.

The paneled dining room of the Savoy Grill, Strand, WC2, is frequented by the rich and powerful. Its menu is a balance of French and traditional British dishes. When dining at the Savoy Grill, it is possible to eat your first course before the theater and come back to finish the latter ones after the show, which is not only brilliant in its practicality but very considerate as well. Chef Anton Edelmann directs the kitchen of the River Restaurant at the Savoy, which overlooks the gardens and the River Thames. His menu caters well to vegetarians. Children also are welcomed, and families come often to the River Restaurant for Sunday lunch.

The City of London

Temple Bar at Fleet Street is the main gateway to the City of London, though traffic congestion forced Wren's gateway to be removed. Today a bronze griffin marks the spot. Fleet Street (the River Fleet now runs beneath the street through a pipe) was once the home of most major newspapers. These have now moved east to the newly refurbished Docklands area on the Isle of Dogs. The City of London is separate from London proper and has its own governing body. Far the oldest part of London, it rose on the site of the original Celtic settlement. The Romans made it their administrative center, and today it is the financial heart of Britain with the London Stock Exchange, the Royal Exchange, and the Bank of England in its midst. The 2,000-year-old city, covering 677 acres, has been rebuilt more than once, notably after the Great Fire of London in 1666 and again after the pounding it received from German warplanes during World War II.

Dr. Samuel Johnson's house in Gough Square, where in the 1750s he worked on his dictionary, is just off Fleet Street. Johnson and his friend and biographer Boswell often frequented the seventeenth-century pub the Cheshire Cheese, located in Wine Office Court, near Gough Square. Fleet Street ends at the Old Bailey, London's Central Criminal Court. Directly south of here near Blackfriars Bridge, at 174 Queen Victoria Street, EC4, is a great nineteenth-century pub in a decorative wedge-shaped building with a statue of a friar ornamenting the front. The inside is an extravaganza of Victoria glass screens, mosaic ceiling, wood carvings, bas-reliefs, and mother-of-pearl inlays.

St. Paul's Cathedral, originally built in medieval times, was destroyed by the Great Fire of London and rebuilt by Christopher Wren between 1675 and 1710. His body rests in the crypt. Around the great dome is the Whispering Gallery where you can clearly hear words spoken on the other side of the gallery 112 feet away.

To the north of St. Bartholomew's hospital, once a monastery dating to 1123, is the Smithfield meat market. It was a horse market until the Victorians prohibited the sale and slaughter of animals there because of the abhorrent smell. Smithfield market has been rebuilt once again in its 800-year history and reopened in 1963. North from St. Paul's is another refurbished area of London called the Barbican. The Barbican is home to the London Symphony orchestra; the Royal Shakespeare Company's two theaters are here; and the Barbican Art Center is unrivaled for its concerts, cinemas, art galleries, exhibition spaces, and its experimental theater, called the Little Pit.

The Quality Chop House, 94 Farringdon Road, EC1, is nearby. Charles Fontaine is responsible for the wonderful food served in this café, which looks decidedly run down from the outside. Pews like benches, which you sometimes have to share, separate the space into compartments. Delicious homemade sausages and smooth, buttery mashed potatoes are called Bangers and Mash on the menu, and you can even find that most British of repasts, egg and chips, but it will be cooked perfectly without the excess pool of grease. Charles Fontaine is renowned for his simply cooked good food. Everybody's favorites are his fish cakes, served on a bed of buttery vegetable. Comforting puddings or treacle tart with custard round out the meal.

Whittington's Wine Bar at 21 College Hill, EC4, located in the cellar, has unexpectedly creative food and a wide selection of European and Australian wines. Dick Whittington, the Lord Mayor of London, said to have traveled to London accompanied by his cat, is believed to have owned this building.

The Fox and Anchor at 115 Charterhouse Street in the City is also well known for its good food and ale.

The Guildhall on Basinghall Street, rebuilt many times, still has its original medieval walls. Home to the Corporation of London, the City's governing body, it also houses the various livery guilds of many London trades that were once extremely powerful. Now their functions are generally ceremonial, but members still support charities and schools, and only members of the guilds are allowed to vote in the lord mayor's election.

Just south of the financial center of the City is Leadenhall Market, ensconced in its marvelous, Classical-Revival arcade. A market has stood on this spot since the fourteenth century on the site of a former Roman basilica, parts of which were discovered in 1881 when the market was rebuilt. These treasures are now in the British Museum. The vaulted glass ceiling and the pilasters supporting it have all been refurbished to a sparkling freshness. Fishmongers, meat markets, and game and poultry sellers now share space with upscale restaurants, wine bars, and delicatessens selling bagels and a wealth of charcuterie and prepared foods.

Jellied eels is one of London's true regional dishes. Eels spawn in the River Thames that empties into the sea at Southend-on-Sea—London's closest seaside town. All along the strand at Southend-on-Sea, fishermen ply their plates of cockles, mussels, whelks, and jellied eels from small white fish stalls. However, it is not necessary to go that far to find London's specialty. East of Leadenhall Market on Gouleston Street, near the Aldgate underground station, Tubby Isaac's sells jellied eels from his fish stall to be eaten on the spot. Here you may spy a bowler-hatted gent, standing on the street, spooning up jellied eels, and if not that particularly London image, you will almost certainly see a Cockney or two—jellied eels are one of their oldest and fondest dishes.

To make jellied eels, first soak the cleaned eels in a good fish stock, spiced with whole peppercorns and a generous amount of vinegar—5 fl. oz. to a quart of stock. With a calf's foot and some fish bones make a jellied stock. Strain and season it well. Mix the jellied stock with a pint of the soaking liquid, and in this boil the eel chunks for at least an hour. Drain, reserving the stock, and skin and bone the eels. Place them in a serving dish. Strain and reduce the cooking liquid, adding a little more vinegar for flavor, and if necessary gelatin to ensure a good firm jelly. Pour this over the eels and chill before serving.

Near here on the River Thames is the famous fortress the Tower of London. In about 1078 William the Conqueror began building the White Tower at the southeast corner of the Roman wall that once encircled Londinium. Whitewashed by order of King Henry III in 1240, the White Tower, the original structure in the now much larger Tower of London, dwarfs the more recent walls and buildings that surround it. The White Tower stands near Tower Green, which resembles a shady village square. Here, on a spot out of sight of today's crowds, many influential prisoners were executed. Sir Walter Raleigh, sentenced to death by King James I in 1603, managed to live for thirteen years at the Tower in comparative luxury. He even had another floor built in his tower to accommodate his wife and son, and he grew tobacco in his tower garden. Though officially a royal palace, the last king to live here was Henry VII (1485–1509).

The famous Beefeaters wear stylish black garb, trimmed in red, emblazoned with a crown and the initials ER II across the breast. For occasions of state they wear ceremonial red and gold uniforms that weigh at least 15 pounds. The nickname "Beefeater" started in the 1600s when it was the responsibility of these loyal yeomen to taste the king's food for poison. Beefeaters today are senior noncommissioned officers who have served a minimum of 22 years and earned Long Service and Good Conduct Medals. One of their functions today is to be vastly knowledgeable tour guides. The foot-high black ravens who also patrol the grounds are literally beefeaters—strips of meat are part of their diet.

About 150 people make the Tower their home. Many of these are yeoman warders and their families who live in lodgings along one outer wall. If people living here expect to be out after midnight, they must ascertain the password for the day from the guardhouse in order to get back in. Also built into the outer wall is the beefeaters' pub, called the Yeoman Warders Club. There are still soldiers at the formidable Tower of London whose duty it is to protect the crown jewels. When on duty they stay in the Waterloo block. The jewels, which include several crowns embedded with enormous precious stones, are displayed behind very heavy glass and have been viewed by the public since the 1600s. A great part of the fascination of the crown jewels is the fact that every king and queen of England has worn them. Priceless, they are uninsured. They are stashed in the Waterloo block of the Tower complex, which is presently undergoing renovation—so check the opening hours before you try to see them.

East, along the wharf past Tower Bridge, is St. Katherine's Dock, another renovated area of shops, apartments, and offices. It also boasts a hotel and a spanking new marina. The Dickens Inn on St. Katherine's Dock serves hearty English food such as Lancashire hot pot and bubble and squeak. The rich and creamy rice pudding is a knockout. Many chefs in London's restaurants delight in cooking traditional dishes with the freshest of produce and the finest British ingredients obtainable. Fortunately this is getting easier to do as farmers, cheesemakers, market gardeners, fishermen, and butchers are realizing how great is the demand for the best they have to offer.

Grilled Herbed Spring Lamb Chops with Shiitake Mushrooms

8	double loin lamb chops, approximately 8 oz. each
2 t.	sea salt
20	black peppercorns
4 t.	dried oregano
2 t.	dried thyme
4	garlic cloves, peeled
1 lb.	shiitake mushrooms
6 T.	butter
6 T.	white wine
	tarragon or parsley sprigs for garnish

1. Using a mortar and pestle, crush salt, peppercorns, herbs, and garlic to a paste. Wipe lamb chops with damp paper towel and coat each chop on both sides with the herb paste.

2. Broil chops under preheated broiler for 6 or 7 minutes, depending on thickness; turn chops over and broil for 5 minutes longer for medium rare.

3. Meanwhile, cut out and discard woody stems of shiitake mushrooms. Clean gently with a mushroom brush or dampened towel and then slice.

4. Melt butter in a frying pan until hot and foamy; sauté mushroom slices in butter until tender—roughly 3 minutes—and stir in the white wine. Cook on high heat for one or two minutes. Remove to a warmed serving dish.

5. To serve, arrange lamb chops on heated serving platter, surround with shiitake mushrooms, and garnish with sprigs of tarragon or parsley.

Serves 8

Farther east is the Isle of Dogs, a teardrop-shaped peninsula formed by a deep bend in the River Thames. Shipping on the Isle of Dogs and at docks in the vicinity dates back to the days when Romans ruled London. Completely rebuilt from a partial wasteland, Docklands on the Isle of Dogs has 8.5 square miles (13.5 square kilometers) of new development that includes a brand new housing community, towering offices blocks where Fleet Street's major newspapers are newly ensconced, the London City Airport, and new light-rail transportation. Surprisingly, in the mist of all this high-tech stuff is a working farm complete with livestock and a riding stable, called Mudchute Farm.

New people, derisively called "yuppies" by longtime residents of the old river communities, are moving in in droves. Docker families who have been here for generations are none too pleased with the recent developments. The older residents dislike the new apartments where they have been relocated, finding them impersonal, even though living is easier with modern conveniences. Having run in and out of one another's houses all their lives, these Cockney families cannot understand why the new people lock their doors here, or why they buy one drink in a pub and then leave instead of staying to pass a convivial evening. Younger people are more optimistic, hoping the new development will make lots more jobs available to them.

London's teeming docks have fascinated writers for centuries. Daniel Defoe, Arthur Conan Doyle, Charles Dickens, and George Orwell have all chronicled the docks. In the Middle Ages, Geoffrey Chaucer was the commissioner of maintenance of the River Thames between Woolwich and Greenwich. The Museum of London has arranged that digs for early artifacts take place ahead of the bulldozers, so that as much as possible of the heritage of this historic part of London will be preserved. Roman remains of a jetty were discovered here, though most of the relics from this dig are now in the Museum of London. One artifact recovered is a flint knife dating to the Bronze Age. Porcelain collectors are ecstatic that the digs have located and affirmed the limehouse kiln site where copies of Chinese porcelain were fired in the mid-1700s.

The bustling Billingsgate Fish Market has been in Docklands since 1982, moved from its former site at Lower Thames Street in the City. The old Billingsgate Market since then has undergone a major face-lift. On the Isle of Dogs, fish is trucked in, rather than coming by boat, and from five to eight o'clock in the morning the market is thronged with both fish buyers and sellers. This is also the perfect spot for fantastic views of Greenwich Naval College that can be reached by a tunnel under the Thames.

Seafood Terrine with Salmon Caviar Sauce

1	lb.	fresh salmon fillet
4	T.	fresh lime juice
6	fl.oz.	fish stock or clam juice (⅔ C.)
12	oz.	fresh sole
4	oz.	sea scallops
2		whole eggs
1		egg white
4	lg.	limes, well-washed
8	fl.oz.	heavy cream (1 C.)
6	T.	minced fresh chives
		salt, pepper, and cayenne

1. Place 4 tablespoons of fresh lime juice in a bowl. Slice salmon lengthwise into thin strips and toss gently with lime juice. Marinate in refrigerator.

2. Pour fish stock or clam juice in a small pan and reduce over high heat to 2 tablespoonsful.

3. Roughly slice sole and scallops and place in a food processor with the eggs, egg white, ½ teaspoon of salt, ⅛ teaspoon of pepper (preferably white), and a pinch of cayenne pepper. Whirl in processor on off, scraping down sides for 2 to 3 minutes. Add to the mixture the juice of one large lime and process briefly to mix.

4. Place mousse in a medium-size bowl and refrigerate for half an hour.

5. Meanwhile, slice 2 limes paper thin and arrange slices in a design in the bottom of a loaf pan.

6. Set bowl of mousse onto a large pan of ice and beat in the heavy cream, one tablespoonful at a time, with a wooden spoon. Then beat in the reduced clam juice. Preheat oven to 325°F (or gas mark 3).

7. Spoon one-third of the mousse carefully on top of lime slices in loaf pan. Arrange decoratively over mousse half of the salmon strips and half of the minced chives.

8. Repeat layer, then cover strips with remaining mousse.

9. Place loaf pan into a larger baking pan and pour in hot water to a depth of 2 inches. Cook for 30 minutes or until firm when pressed. Cool. Chill for at least six hours.

10. Slice and serve with salmon caviar sauce.   *Serves 8–10*

Sauce

4 fl.oz. heavy cream (½ C.)
6 oz.   homemade mayonnaise (1 C.)
4 oz.   red salmon caviar   *Yields 2 cups*

1. Whip cream until it holds its shape in a spoon, and carefully mix with mayonnaise. Gently fold in salmon caviar.

2. Refrigerate until serving time. Slice and pass sauce separately.

The palatial buildings at Greenwich are an architectural treasure house, designed by most of the famous and talented architects of the day, including Inigo Jones, Wren, and Hawksmoor. Oddly enough, no monarch has ever lived at Greenwich, though Henry VIII was born here in 1491. Eventually the palace was turned into a naval hospital. Also at Greenwich is the exquisite Queen's House, originally intended for Anne of Denmark, who died before Inigo Jones finished the perfectly proportioned, gleaming white house.

Southwark

It is possible to walk across Tower Bridge on the upper walkway, 140 feet above the roadway. The walkway can be reached from an entrance in the north tower. From here can be seen spectacular views of the city and the Thames. On the south side of the river, at Shad Thames, SE1, Sir Terence Conran's Gastrodome at Butler's Wharf holds not only Le Pont de la Tour restaurant with its excellent, eclectic food but also a wine merchant, a prepared food deli and bakery, a brasserie/café, and a seafood bar. David Burke is the chef at Le Pont de la Tour, named for Tower Bridge, and tables here are at a premium. David Burke is from Ireland, so expect to find some Irish specialties on the menu. The restaurant with its superb riverside setting is designed to resemble a cruise ship.

The Butler's Wharf Chop House, in the Butler's Wharf Building, Shad Thames, SE1, has good traditional food with the emphasis on grilled meats. Also on Shad Thames is Butlers Grinders. Housed in an old warehouse since 1946, this company grinds spices on commission. Wafting through the air on grinding days are the agreeable aromas of cumin, mace, fenugreek, turmeric, cinnamon, and coriander.

During World War II this part of London saw some heavy bombing, but much of the debris has been cleared away and the place is looking up. The nearest renovated building to Tower Bridge is Hays Galleria, a shopping center with restaurants where you can get practically anything you want to eat—be it a full meal or just seafood with beer.

Opposite the Galleria, at 56–58 Tooley Street, SE1, is Antony Worrall-Thompson's newest restaurant, Café dell'Ugo. Housed in a former pub, the café in this barrel-shaped building is on two floors—downstairs the informal ambience is reminiscent of a wine bar, and menu selections are read from a blackboard. Upstairs there are porthole windows set in the nicely finished walls, and swagged tablecloths cover the restaurant's twenty tables. Choice is between roughly ten starters and ten main dishes, many of which are char-grilled. Vegetarians do very well here, and there are always dishes that are quite different than any at Antony Worrall-Thompson's other restaurants, to his credit.

The remains of the original Globe Theatre have been recently excavated in Southwark, and the theater is now under reconstruction. Next door is the Shakespeare Globe Museum. Southwark at one time was full of theaters, alehouses, and pits where cockerels, dogs, and other animals were baited for sport and gambling. They proliferated here particularly because Southwark was outside the legal jurisdiction of the city, and little was done to stop this. John Horniman, the man who first thought of putting tea in a tea bag, has a pub named after him here—The Horniman. One of the best

which are char-grilled. Vegetarians do very well here, and there are always dishes that are quite different than any at Antony Worrall-Thompson's other restaurants, to his credit.

The remains of the original Globe Theatre have been recently excavated in Southwark, and the theater is now under reconstruction. Next door is the Shakespeare Globe Museum. Southwark at one time was full of theaters, alehouses, and pits where cockerels, dogs, and other animals were baited for sport and gambling. They proliferated here particularly because Southwark was outside the legal jurisdiction of the city, and little was done to stop this. John Horniman, the man who first thought of putting tea in a tea bag, has a pub named after him here—The Horniman. One of the best preserved gothic churches in London, after Westminster Abbey, is Southwark Cathedral, located on this side of the Thames and presided over by the Bishop of Winchester, whose palace was on Clink Street. The only remaining vestige of this former glory is a single rose window set in part of a wall.

George Inn, located at 77 Borough High Street, SE, is not to be missed. Shakespeare's plays were performed in the George Inn's courtyard. Here a restaurant, real ale bar, and wine bar are located in the last remaining galleried inn in the city. This charming tavern has long white wooden terraces running across the front of the inn on the upper floors, festooned with hanging baskets of flowers. The main section of the inn, also painted white, has three stories of mullioned windows and above them half dormers look down from the roof. At one time many medieval inns stood on this street. Next door to the George was the Tabard Inn where pilgrims spent the night before starting their long walk to Canterbury. The inn is mentioned in *Little Dorrit*—Dickens was a regular patron of the George Inn, as he seems to have been of many of London's inns.

The south side of the Thames is where the new Covent Garden fruit, flower, and vegetable market was installed at Nine Elms, near Vauxhall Bridge, in 1974. The only pre-Reformation house left in London is on this side of the river, Lambeth Palace, the home of the Archbishop of Canterbury, who stays here when he is in London. The house was extensively renovated in 1829. Parts of this palace date to 1207. The gatehouse is fifteenth-century, and the chapel is even earlier. The garden, which is second in size only to the garden behind Buckingham Palace, has recently seen a great deal of renewal and loving attention.

Farther along the river is Rotherhithe, a town that boasts the seventeenth-century pub, the Mayflower, at 117 Rotherhithe Street, SE16. This old riverside inn is believed to be the spot where the Pilgrims set sail for America. The Mayflower has a terrace and excellent pub food.

Following the Thames as it winds west we come to Kew Gardens, home of the Royal Botanical Gardens—one of the foremost botanical gardens in

3

THE SOUTHEAST

The long southern and southeastern coastline of England, running from the Thames estuary to the Hampshire/Dorset border, comprises the counties of Kent, East and West Sussex, Surrey, and Hampshire, and the Isle of Wight. Surrey, north of West Sussex, borders the great metropolis of London. Though London has spread bedroom communities along the northern fringes of Surrey and Kent, the region is predominately rolling downlands, pretty villages, and rich agricultural areas. The North Downs is a ridge running from Guildford, Surrey, to the cliffs of Dover. The South Downs begin north of Chichester, West Sussex, and end at Beachy Head. The Weald, between the North and the South Downs, active first in iron mines and then in the cloth trade, now has flourishing hop fields and orchards awash with apple blossom in spring. Not surprisingly many recipes in southeast England are based on the bountiful apple.

The most important religious center in Britain, the cathedral city of Canterbury, is in the eastern region of this area. The Cinque Ports, Sandwich, Dover, Hythe, Romney, and Hastings, backed up by Rye and Winchelsea, situated on the vulnerable south coast closest to the European Continent, successfully defended England in medieval times from would-be invaders. Their wooden sailing ships are pictured on the seals of these towns. Hythe is still a fishing port today, keeping south coast restaurants supplied with fresh fish and shellfish.

Mussels in Creamy Herb Sauce

		generous pinch of saffron
2	T.	hot water
8	fl.oz.	dry white wine (1 C.)
2	lb.	mussels, scrubbed
2	T.	unsalted butter
3	sm.	shallots, minced
1		garlic clove, minced
12	fl.oz.	heavy cream (1½ C.)
2	T.	cognac
		Worcestershire sauce to taste
4	fl.oz.	fresh lemon juice (¼ C.)
1	t.	minced tarragon
1	t.	minced chervil
1	T.	minced Italian parsley

Garnish: parsley sprigs and lemon slices

1. Mix saffron with hot water and set aside to infuse.

2. In a large heavy-bottomed saucepan bring wine to a boil, reduce heat, and simmer for 3 minutes.

3. Add mussels, cover and steam, shaking pan once or twice, until opened, about 4 minutes. Using a slotted spoon, remove mussels from pan to a bowl, discarding any that are unopened. Reserve cooking liquid and remove mussels from shells. Set aside.

4. In a small pan, melt butter and gently cook garlic and shallots; do not brown. Add mussel liquid and reduce to about 4 fluid ounces or half a cup.

5. Stir in saffron and water, cream, cognac, Worcestershire sauce, and lemon juice, stirring constantly. Bring to a boil, stirring; reduce heat and simmer for 10 minutes.

6. Sprinkle in the minced herbs and continue to cook for a few seconds. Modify seasonings as needed.

7. Divide mussels between individual ramekins. Spoon over some sauce, garnish with parsley sprigs and lemon slices, and serve at once.   *Serves 4 or more as an appetizer*

The channel waters have receded over the years, and Rye, Winchelsea, and Sandwich are no longer lapped by the waves. Romney marsh has dried out, and New Romney is now an inland town. Nearby is the point of land famous for the large Dungeness crabs that are served dressed in their shells in fine restaurants in London.

Hot Crab Dip with Toast Points

1 lb.	softened fresh cream cheese
2 T.	sour cream or whipping cream
2 t.	prepared horseradish
4 T.	minced scallions
	a good pinch paprika
2 T.	minced fresh dill
	fresh ground pepper
2 T.	fresh lemon juice
1 lb.	fresh backfin crabmeat

1. Preheat oven to 350°F (or gas mark 4).

2. Beat together cream cheese, sour cream, and horseradish until smooth.

3. Add scallions, paprika, dill, pepper, and lemon juice and stir well. Gently fold in crabmeat.

4. Pour into a buttered soufflé dish and bake for 30 minutes or until bubbling hot. Serve immediately with toast points.

Yields 4½ cups

Kent

Kent is called the Garden of England and rightly so, as most of this county is richly fertile farmland and thriving fruit orchards. Conical oasthouses dot the Kent and Sussex landscapes. These quaint-looking structures are used for pressing the flower heads gathered from female hop plants, needed to flavor beer, before sending them to the breweries. Each year entire families escape London and come by train to Kent to pick hops in the fresh country air on "working holidays." Kent is famous for its excellent hops. Flemish farmers, who fled to England to avoid religious persecution, introduced the plant and by example taught the English to appreciate beer flavored with hops' unusual bitter taste. The new bitter beer, like the potato, was not an immediate success, but also like the potato, once hops were accepted the British made them their own. At one time every household made their own beer. Though it does not compare with some of the high-quality bottled beers available now, nevertheless it is fun occasionally to make your own beer, and it is simple to do. Hops and water are boiled together for half an hour, then strained over a good quantity of sugar. This is left to cool to lukewarm before yeast is added. The brew is left to ferment for five days, then bottled in well-washed bottles and securely capped.

During the centuries before coffee and tea were introduced to the British public, beer was the preferred drink with every meal, including breakfast. When tea supplanted beer as the national drink, concerns were raised that the loss of calories from beer would be detrimental to the diet and health of the poor. Milk was not taken with China tea at that time, and tea alone provided scant nutrients, if any.

Cakes originated on England's southern shores in regions where wheat was plentiful. Here when farmwomen mixed their bread dough, they set aside a piece to be kneaded with dried fruit and spices. This sweet treat was the beginning of cake-making. Before the advent of chemical raising agents, making cakes that were lighter in texture than regular bread dough was very hard work. Batter that was not yeast-raised needed somehow to have air incorporated into it before it would rise. One way to accomplish this was to beat a dozen or so egg whites until they were stiff and gently stir them into the batter. Beating that number of egg whites by hand was strenuous and time-consuming work, and folding them into a heavy batter or dough while retaining the air bubbles must have been a difficult task. Fortunately, in the late 1700s bicarbonate of soda came into use, and beaten egg whites as a way to raise cake batters and light bread doughs was discontinued.

Baked Cherry Chocolate Pudding

10 oz.	fresh cherries (2 C.), pitted
10 oz.	brown sugar (1¼ C.)
4 oz.	unsalted butter (1 stick), cut into bits
2½ oz.	slivered almonds (½ C.)
3½ oz.	unbleached white flour (⅔ C.)
6 T.	cocoa powder
1 t.	baking powder
¼ t.	almond essence
1 t.	vanilla essence
4 fl.oz.	plain yogurt (½ C.)
1 T.	kirschwasser
3	egg whites
	crème fraîche (optional)

1. Preheat oven to 350°F (or gas mark 4), and thoroughly butter a soufflé dish.

2. Toss the cherries with two tablespoons of the brown sugar and spread them evenly in the bottom of the soufflé dish.

3. Sprinkle the slivered almonds over the cherries, and set aside.

4. Sift together flour, cocoa, and baking powder.

5. Cream the remaining butter and sugar together and stir in the almond and vanilla essence and the kirschwasser.

6. Stir in alternately the flour mixture and yogurt, and mix well.

7. Beat the egg whites until stiff, and fold them gently into the chocolate mixture.

8. Spoon batter evenly over cherries. Bake for 15 minutes. Reduce heat to 325°F (or gas mark 3), and continue to bake for approximately 30 minutes longer. Cake tester should come out clean. Cool in the dish for 5 to 10 minutes.

9. To serve, invert pudding onto a warmed serving dish and serve warm with crème fraîche, if desired.   *Serves 8*

Dover, the most important of the Cinque Ports, is only twenty miles from Calais on France's northern coast. Dover Castle, built on the top of the famous white cliffs of Dover, rests on the foundations of a Saxon fort. In good weather the outline of the coast of France can be seen from the castle keep. This splendid castle, refortified continually through the centuries, has undoubtedly saved the Crown of England from her enemies on more than one occasion. Its stout walls have repelled repeated invasions. The fabulous white cliffs are the first glimpse of England to be seen from the sea. They seem to rise higher and higher above the horizon as the ship nears the coast. Romans led by Julius Caesar in 55 B.C. tried to land at Dover and were beaten back, only to land further along the coast at Deal. A 40-foot-tall Roman lighthouse still stands on the cliffs near Dover Castle, used now as a refuge for doves and pigeons. The Normans were the last invaders to attempt the channel crossing. Even Hitler thought better of it. During World War II, the Regency and Edwardian houses serenely facing the sea had deep cellars cut into the chalk cliff in back of the houses as refuge from bombs dropped from German aircraft on the return flights to Occupied France. Today ferries and hovercraft ply the waters between the two countries. The new Eurotunnel, affectionately dubbed the Chunnel, will cut travel time between London and Paris to three hours. Bookings on the passenger train can be arranged ahead of time. Enterprising rental car companies swap left-hand drive cars for right-hand drive cars at each end of the Chunnel.

The little town of Ashford grew in prosperity with the coming of the railways. Now it is a junction on the major M20, but it is still a peaceful place that holds regular cattle markets and has lovely eighteenth-century houses. Between Ashford and Canterbury on the A28 is the village of Wye. Thirty years ago the village doctor's house on Upper Bridge Street was converted into the Wife of Bath Restaurant, owned by John Morgan. Right in the conservation area of Wye, it is a great base for walkers wishing to explore the famous Pilgrims Way. Wye is home to an agricultural university, and students give the village a lively air. Stately homes, castles, and famous gardens are nearby, and the ports of Folkestone and Dover, not to mention the Channel tunnel, are within thirty minutes' drive. The former stables have been transformed into charming rooms with beautiful exposed beams, comfortable furnishings, and en suite facilities. The head chef, Robert Hymers, is enthusiastic about his suppliers, many of whom are so close he can order on a daily basis which, as he says, "is as fresh as you can get." Eggs, vegetables, soft fruits, orchard fruits, fresh herbs, milk, and cream all come directly from Ashford; game too is nearby. Robert Hymers is a New Zealander and he enjoys cooking with natural but robust herbs, spices, sundried tomatoes, saffron, and differently flavored oils. He is also happy with the wealth of farmhouses cheeses and wines available here. Some of his favorite dishes on his menu are Moule Marinière; Confit of duck; Lightly sautéd scallops with chervil on black noodles; Panfried Scotch beef in pepper oil; and Deep-fried king prawns in saffron batter with a curry and mango sauce. His menu changes every two weeks. Robert Hymers has given us his duck recipe for this book.

Duck Crepinette

2	lb.	duck meat
1	lb.	smoked bacon
1		shallot
½		fresh chili pepper
1		garlic clove
5		sage leaves, chopped
3	T.	parsley, chopped
2	T.	white wine
3	T.	bread crumbs
3		grindings of black pepper
		pinch of salt
¼	lb.	pig caul—a thin membrane veined with fat
3	T.	flour
1		egg plus 1 T. water, for wash
		bread crumbs
2	T.	olive oil
40	fl.oz.	duck stock (5 C.)
2	T.	green peppercorns

1. Mince the duck meat, bacon, shallot, chili pepper, and garlic. Remove any duck sinew and discard.

2. Place minced ingredients into a bowl, and mix in the sage, parsley, wine, bread crumbs, black pepper, and salt.

3. Shape into round patties about an inch thick and weighing 2–3 ounces each.

4. Wrap each one in enough pig caul to completely cover. Then lightly flour, dip in egg wash, and finally dip into bread crumbs. Preheat oven to 350°F (or gas mark 4).

5. Panfry in a hot pan with a little olive oil until brown, turn and brown the other side, then cook in the oven for about 10 to 12 minutes or until just cooked. Remove and keep hot.

6. Deglaze pan with duck stock, add a few green peppercorns, and reduce to form a sauce. Taste for seasoning.

7. To serve, pour sauce onto warm plates, place a crepinette on top, and garnish with vegetables of your choice.

Yields approximately 12 crepinettes

From Dover a Roman road passes through Canterbury on its way to Londinium. Ethelbert, king of Kent, was crowned at Canterbury in 597 by St. Augustine, who was the first to preach the Christian gospel in England. To this day Canterbury's city motto is "Hail, Mother of England." On Christmas Day 597, 10,000 people were baptized by St. Augustine. Six years later he became the first Archbishop of Canterbury, and he also instituted a bishopric at Rochester. Canterbury became a brilliant seat of learning and a magnet for scholars from all over Britain and the Continent. Marauding Danes burned down the cathedral in 1011, and the Normans started rebuilding it in 1070. From 1220 to 1538 Canterbury Cathedral contained one of Europe's most celebrated shrines to Thomas Becket, who was murdered while praying at the altar in 1170. Becket was beatified, and in 1420 over 100,000 pilgrims congregated in Canterbury on the anniversary of the saint's death. Footpaths crossing the downs—now part of the North Downs Way—were trodden by pilgrims walking toward Canterbury. Chaucer stayed at Canterbury (1360–1361) and *The Canterbury Tales* are a collection of stories told to beguile pilgrims on their long walk to the shrine. Canterbury is still partially surrounded by huge medieval walls that stand on Roman foundations. The city's Roman remains include part of a central heating system, a mosaic pavement, and the foundations of Britain's largest Roman theatre. German aircraft in World War II, trying to bomb Canterbury Cathedral in reprisal for the damage done to Cologne Cathedral, missed and suceeded only in destroying some nearby buildings. The University of Kent, opened in 1965, continues Canterbury's traditional role as a lively place of learning. Students and scholars throng the narrow streets. The ancient Hop Hoodening Festival has lately been rekindled with folk dancing and a Hop-Queen. It is held in September in the precincts of the Cathedral. Canterbury today is the seat of the Primate of All England.

Kentish Cob Nut and Artichoke Soup

8 oz.	shelled Kentish cob nuts (hazelnuts) (1½ C.)
1 lg.	onion, coarsely chopped
5	artichoke hearts, trimmed
OR	
1 10 oz.	package frozen artichokes
1	bay leaf
12 T.	butter
3 T.	Madeira wine
16–20 fl.oz.	chicken broth (4–5 C.)
4 t.	cornstarch
4 fl.oz.	white wine (½ C.)
½	red pepper

	salt and pepper
1 T.	minced fresh sage
10 fl.oz.	heavy cream (1¼ C.)
2–3 T.	finely minced parsley

1. Preheat oven to 350°F (or gas mark 4). Place nuts on a baking sheet in one layer and roast for 10 minutes, or more if necessary, until the skins are blistered and flaking. Remove from oven and wrap in kitchen towel to steam for 2 minutes. Rub briskly in towel to remove skins. Chop nuts finely and set aside.

2. Meanwhile defrost artichokes on paper towel.

3. Soften onion, artichokes, and bay leaf in butter without browning. Add the chopped nuts, half of the Madeira, and the chicken broth. Simmer, partially covered, for 30 minutes, stirring once or twice.

4. Meanwhile roast, skin, and purée the red pepper, season lightly with salt and pepper, and mix with 4 tablespoons of the heavy cream. Refrigerate.

5. Mix until smooth the white wine, remaining Madeira, and cornstarch. Stir briskly into the soup. Add the sage and simmer for another 10 minutes. Cool and pass through a sieve, pressing to extract as much of the vegetables as possible.

6. Return to pan and stir in remaining cream, bring slowly to a simmer, and cook for 2 minutes.

7. To serve: pour hot soup into bowls, add a ribbon of red pepper cream, and serve sprinkled with very finely minced parsley.

Serves 4–5

Near Hythe on the coast south of Canterbury is Lympne Castle, a fortified manor house that for 800 years was the seat of the archdeacons of Canterbury. Running from Hythe to Rye is the Royal Military Canal, built as a defense against the expected invasion of Napoleon, which failed to materialize. This part of England has seen all of Britain's invasions, and in its defense castles and martello towers have been constructed at strategic places all along the south coast. The three castles in the Deal and Dover area were built by Henry VIII, and the Thames estuary has long been fortified at Gravesend and Tilbury.

Just north of Canterbury is the old fishing town of Whitstable, renowned for over 2,000 years for its plump oysters. When Rome ruled Canterbury, Romans traveled north to Whitstable to eat the succulent bivalve. Britain's first passenger railway train in 1839 ran from Canterbury to Whitstable, a distance of six miles. Restaurants and ancient pubs in Whitstable serve plate after plate of oysters throughout the season.

Oysters with Dill Butter Sauce

2 doz. oysters
4 fl.oz. white wine (½ C.)
4 T. heavy cream
2 T. oyster liquid
4 oz. very cold unsalted butter (1 stick)
1 t. fresh lemon juice
1 t. fresh dill, minced
1 t. parsley, minced

1. Shuck the oysters, reserving 2 tablespoons of the oyster liquid. Set liquid aside. Place oysters on their bottom shells in one layer in a shallow heatproof dish—or two dishes, if necessary.

2. In a heavy-bottomed saucepan, boil wine and cream together until reduced to about 2 fluid ounces (¼ cup). Stir in oyster liquid and boil for 30 seconds longer. Preheat broiler until very hot.

3. Over very low heat, beat butter into the hot liquid in the saucepan bit by bit, whisking continuously, as you would to make a Hollandaise sauce.

4. Remove from heat and cool. Gently stir in the lemon juice and minced herbs. Refrigerate.

5. Grill the oysters just until their edges curl—about 4 minutes. Remove from grill and divide among four large heated plates. Top with a spoonful of sauce and serve immediately.   *Serves* 4

Farther west along the coast from Whitstable is Faversham, once a Roman port. This ancient and attractive town received its Royal Charter in 1352. At 80 Abbey Street is a timber and plaster house with an overhanging story that was once part of a Benedictine Abbey. The house belonged to the mayor, Richard Arden. He was murdered by his wife and her lover in 1559 after several unsuccessful attempts to kill him. The pair were caught and executed. In Market Place are several beautifully restored historic houses. One of these, the Guildhall, is Elizabethan. Faversham has a fine church and a Heritage Centre. Nearby, at Painter's Forstal, is Read's Restaurant, run by David and Rona Pitchford. They opened the restaurant seventeen years ago after teaching professional cookery in London. David's career included seven years at the Dorchester Hotel. He has won the Chef of the Year Award twice. The Pitchfords take advantage of fresh local and seasonal produce and are also supplied frequently by local fishermen and wine growers. The Pitchfords have shared with us several of their recipes. David Pitchford serves his Hot Montgomery Cheddar Soufflé with fresh asparagus and chive butter sauce, but he says it would go equally well with a tossed salad, or your own choice of garnish. He has also given us his recipe for a Parcel of New Season English Lamb Stuffed with a Maize-fed Chicken Mousse, which he serves with Dauphinoise potatoes and a miniature Ratatouille. One of David Pitchford's favorite desserts is Individual Raspberry Savarins with Eau-de-Vie Framboise Cream.

Hot Montgomery Cheddar Soufflé

	melted butter for cups
15 fl.oz.	warm milk (scant 2 C.)
	pinch of nutmeg
2 T.	onion
6 T.	butter
3 oz.	flour (scant ⅔ C.)
8 oz.	mature Cheddar cheese, finely grated (2 C.)
6	egg yolks (no. 2 size)
1 t.	English mustard
6	egg whites
	cream
	grated cheese

1. Butter eight straight-sided tea cups or mugs and prepare a bain-marie, which will be used to cook the soufflés in the oven.

2. Infuse the warm milk, nutmeg, and onion.

3. Melt the butter in a saucepan and add the flour, cooking gently for 2 minutes without coloring. Remove the onion and slowly add the infused milk, stirring continuously for one minute.

4. Remove from the heat and add the cheese one-third at a time, making sure the cheese is fully melted. Beat in the egg yolks and mustard. Preheat oven to 325°F (or gas mark 3).

5. Transfer sauce mixture to a large clean bowl. Beat the egg whites until stiff, then carefully add one-half at a time to the sauce. Fill the buttered cups two-thirds full, place them in the bain-marie, and cook in the oven for 20 minutes.

6. Remove cups from the bain-marie and allow to cool for one hour, then carefully remove the soufflés from the cups. Soufflés can be cling-wrapped and refrigerated for up to two days. When ready to serve, preheat oven to 475°F (or gas mark 9).

7. To serve, unwrap soufflés and place them upside down and well apart on a lightly greased baking sheet, as they will increase in size during the second cooking.

8. Brush the sides of the soufflés with cream and place a tablespoon of grated cheese on top. Cook for 7 minutes.   *Serves 8*

Beurre Blanc

20 fl.oz. fish stock (2½ C.)
2 T. chopped shallot
2 fl.oz. white wine (¼ C.)
2 fl.oz. double cream (¼ C.)
10 oz. unsalted butter, cut in small cubes (2½ sticks)
8 oz. tomatoes, skinned, seeded, and cut into diamonds (1⅔ C.)
1 bunch chives, finely chopped

1. In a small pan, reduce fish stock, shallots, and white wine to a syrup. Add double cream and lightly reduce.

2. Remove from heat and whisk in cold butter cubes, one piece at a time. Pass through a fine sieve and keep warm until needed.

3. Serve an appropriate amount of sauce with the soufflés, and garnish with tomato diamonds and chives.

Chef's note: We have served our soufflé with smoked haddock, fresh asparagus, and a chive butter sauce, but it will go very well with a tossed salad or the garnish of your choice.

Parcel of Lamb

1 short saddle of lamb
40 fl.oz. veal stock (5 C.)
8 oz. maize-fed chicken
8 fl.oz. heavy cream (1 C.)
4 sheets caul fat*
4 Dauphinoise potatoes
1 bunch rosemary

1. Bone the lamb and remove the sinew (or have your butcher do it and give you the bones). Brown the bones, add the veal stock, and simmer.

2. Cube chicken and whirl in the food processor with the cream to make a mousseline. Preheat oven to 425°F (or gas mark 7). Spread mousseline on lamb and roll up. Wrap in caul fat to make a parcel.

3. Roast in hot oven for 20 minutes per pound. Remove from oven and let rest for 10 minutes.

4. Slice and assemble on plate with Dauphinoise potatoes and ratatouille. Garnish with rosemary and serve.   *Serves* 4

*If unavailable at meat department, try an oriental market

Ratatouille

1		red pepper
1		green pepper
1		yellow pepper
1		zucchini
1		onion
1		eggplant
2	oz.	mushrooms (½ C.)
4	T.	olive oil
1		clove garlic
4	T.	tomato puree

1. Cut all vegetables into small dice.
2. Toss in olive oil flavored with the garlic.
3. Bind with tomato purée, correct seasoning, and serve.

Savarin Paste

8	oz.	strong flour (1½ C.)
¾	oz.	yeast
1	T.	sugar
4	fl.oz.	milk (½ C.), warmed
4	oz.	butter (1 stick), melted
4		eggs

1. Sift and warm the flour.
2. Dissolve yeast and sugar in warm milk until it froths.
3. Pour into well in the flour, stir in butter and beaten eggs, and beat mixture for 5 minutes.
4. Proof for 15 minutes, punch down, and pipe a ring of dough into 4 individual ovenproof molds. Let dough rise to top of mold. Preheat oven to 425°F (or gas mark 7).
5. Cook in hot oven for 15 minutes. Unmold to cool.   *Serves 4*

Soaking Syrup

8	oz.	sugar (1 C.)
1		cinnamon stick
6		coriander seeds

juice and zest of 1 lemon
1   bay leaf
20 fl.oz. water (2½ C.)

1. In a medium-sized saucepan, boil all ingredients together, cool, and strain.

1 oz.   eau de vie framboise
4 oz.   apricot glaze (½ C.)
10 fl.oz. heavy cream (1¼ C.)
2 oz.   castor sugar (¼ C.)
2   punnets of raspberries
10 fl.oz. raspberry coulis (1¼ C.)

2. Soak savarins in the syrup, and drain.
3. Sprinkle with half of the eau de vie framboise, and brush with apricot glaze.
4. Whip cream and add remaining eau de vie and castor sugar.
5. Fill the cavity with flavored cream, top with raspberries, and serve with coulis.

Farther east around the spit of Kentish coast are the holiday resorts of Margate, Broadstairs, Ramsgate, and Deal. These seaside towns became accessible to Londoners in search of fine sandy beaches when the railways got under way. Ramsgate is the hovercraft port linking England to France at Calais. Broadstairs was Charles Dickens's favorite vacation resort, primarily because of its calm peaceful atmosphere. He wrote *Nicholas Nickleby*, *The Old Curiosity Shop*, *Barnaby Rudge*, *David Copperfield*, and part of the *Pickwick Papers* in the fourteen years he spent writing at Fort House on the clifftop at Broadstairs. Fort House was the model for the clifftop dwelling in his novel *Bleak House*. He and his friend Wilkie Collins, who wrote the intriguing mystery *The Woman in White*, both stayed at Fort House. Broadstairs holds a Dickens Festival each year in June when townspeople dressed in Victorian costumes parade through the streets. Dickens, because of his *Christmas Carol*, is forever associated with the Christmas season.

Royal Family's Christmas Pudding

10 oz.   suet (2½ C.), grated
7–8 oz. golden raisins (1½ C.)
7–8 oz. dark raisins (1½ C.)
2 oz.   citron glacé (⅓ C.), minced

½ t.   allspice
¼ t.   freshly grated nutmeg
10 oz.   fine sugar (1¼ C.)
6 oz.   flour (1¼ C.)
½ t.   baking powder
14 oz.   fresh bread crumbs (4 C.)
4 lg.   eggs
4 fl.oz.   brandy (½ C.)
4 fl.oz.   milk (½ C.)
    organic holly sprig with berries
2 T.   brandy for flaming pudding when served

1. In a very large bowl, combine well the dry ingredients.

2. Beat the eggs until frothy. Whisk in the brandy and milk, then pour into the dry ingredients and mix well.

3. Cover and let sit for 12 hours, or overnight, in a cool place.

4. Coat the inside of a 2-quart pudding basin with butter, and spoon in the mixture. Place a circle of buttered waxed paper directly on the pudding.

5. Tent basin with a double sheet of foil, making sure there is enough room for the pudding to rise. Tie securely under basin lip with string, and lower carefully into a saucepan of boiling water that reaches halfway up the sides of the basin.

6. Cover saucepan with well-fitting lid and steam pudding for about 6 to 8 hours. You will need to replenish with *boiling* water as the level drops.

7. Remove basin, discard foil, and allow pudding to get quite cold. Wrap in cheesecloth, then foil, making sure it is airtight. Store in a cool place for at least 3 weeks or until needed.

8. To reheat, uncover pudding, put back in the pudding basin, and follow steps five to seven. Steam for 3 to 4 hours when reheating.

9. Invert pudding onto a warmed platter, and decorate with holly sprig. Pour brandy over pudding, ignite, and serve with hard sauce or custard sauce.   *Serves 8–10*

Britain's most beautiful castle is nearby in Kent. Leeds Castle, built originally by the Normans, is situated on two islands in a wide lake surrounded by a lovely landscaped park. The castle's romantic image is reflected in the lake water. Edward I gave Leeds Castle to his first wife and later to his second. Since then eight medieval queens have lived here. Another famous resident in 1740 was Lord Fairfax, who lived at Leeds Castle before emigrating to Virginia. In 1974 the castle became the property of the Leeds Castle Foundation and is now open to the public.

Avid gardeners flock from early spring to late autumn to Sissinghurst Palace, well known for its exquisite walled gardens, which were the passion of writer Victoria Sackville-West and her husband, Harold Nicolson. One of the most photographed is the White Garden. In the center of the grounds stands the tower where Vita Sackville-West wrote her books. This is also open to the public. When at the beginning of their marriage they bought Sissinghurst, an almost derelict Elizabethan mansion, the garden was little more than a wasteland. The work they put into it was prodigious. Vita Sackville-West wrote a gardening column for the *Observer* newspaper for 14 years, and the best of these informative articles have been collected into an illustrated book, *V. Sackville-West's Garden Book*.

On The Street in Sissinghurst is Rankins' restaurant, owned and run by Hugh and Leonora Rankin. This family restaurant has a mixture of French and English dishes. Among the latter are succulent roasts and English toffee ice cream served with caramel sauce. Hugh Rankin's cooking reflects the goodness of the fresh ingredients he buys for his kitchen from local suppliers—especially his wonderful seafood dishes served with butter sauce.

Near Sevenoaks is Knole, the biggest private house in England, set in a vast deer park. Victoria Sackville-West grew up at Knole. Owned originally by the Archbishops of Canterbury, this impressive pile passed to a cousin of Elizabeth I, Thomas Sackville, following the Dissolution of the Monasteries. Considerable remodeling was done by Sackville in the early sixteenth century. Since that time much of the house has remained unchanged. Intricate plasterwork ceilings, tapestries, paintings, porcelain, and vast Persian carpets can be seen at Knole. Most spectactular is a long gallery full of elaborately worked silver furniture

Tunbridge Wells—about thirteen miles from Knole—is a spa town that became such a favorite with visiting royalty that the crown prefixed the word "Royal" to its name. Queen Henrietta Maria, wife of Charles I, came to sample the waters in 1630, after the birth of the future Charles II. The iron-bearing spring was found in 1606 by Lord North. Tunbridge Wells is also famous for its colonnaded shopping street, The Pantiles, named for the baked tiles that paved the arcade. Thackeray House, on the Common at London Road, is privately owned and not open to the public. William Makepeace Thackeray wrote *The Luck of Barry Lyndon*, and *Vanity Fair*, among other works. A little farther north is Penshurst Castle, a fourteenth-century manor with its original timber roof still spanning the great hall. Originally owned by royalty, the manor was given in 1552 to the Sidney family. Fine china, silver, and furniture decorate the state rooms, and armor and family portraits are on display in the gallery. Walled gardens and a park surround the manor.

Northwest of Tunbridge Wells on the border with Surrey is Edenbridge, a small town on the River Eden. Ancient and picturesque houses line the old Roman road. At 87 High Street is Honours Mill restaurant, owned by the Goodhews. The food here is exceptionally well executed and the dining room with its low-raftered ceiling is charming. Not to be missed is Sussex Pond Pudding, known in Kent as Kentish Well Pudding.

Sussex Pond Pudding

7–8	oz.	flour (1½ C.)
1½	t.	baking powder
		pinch of salt
4	oz.	chopped beef suet (1 scant C.)
5	fl.oz.	approximately equal parts milk and water (½–⅔ C.)
6–7	oz.	unsalted butter (1½ sticks)
8	oz.	light brown sugar (1 C.)
1		lemon, scrubbed

1. In a large bowl lightly toss flour, baking powder, salt, and suet together. Make a well in the center and add the milk and water to form a dough that will roll out easily. Set aside just over one-quarter of the dough to make the lid. Roll out the larger ball of dough to fit pudding basin with an inch of overlap.

2. Cut the butter into pieces and place half the sugar and butter into the basin, top with the lemon, and finish with the remaining sugar and butter pieces.

3. Roll out remaining dough to fit top of basin and firmly pinch the edges together to form a tight seal. Cover with a circle of buttered waxed paper.

4. Form a loose-fitting circle of aluminum foil, by pleating the edges, large enough to cover the top and reach 2 inches of the way down the side of the dish. Tie securely with kitchen string. It is a good idea to make a handle of string across the top of the basin to facilitate removing the hot pudding basin from the boiling water.

5. Place pudding basin in a large pan of *boiling* water that reaches two-thirds of the way up the side of the basin. Keep water boiling for 3 hours or more, replenishing saucepan with boiling water as needed.

6. Turn off burner and carefully remove pudding from pan. Cut string and remove foil and waxed paper. Run a knife blade around edge of pudding to loosen, then place a shallow dish with at least 2-inch sides over pan and carefully invert pudding into dish.

7. Bring to the table and cut into wedges, spooning the delicious lemon, butter, and sugar sauce over each wedge. Divide the softened lemon among the helpings. *Serves 4–6*

About three miles from Edenbridge is the village of Hever where the fourteenth-century church has a brass of Thomas Boleyn—the father of Anne Boleyn, the second wife of Henry VIII. Anne Boleyn achieved fame by giving birth to the future Elizabeth I, and then by being beheaded in the Tower of London. Knowing what her fate would be, she remarked, "The king has been very good to me, he promoted me from a simple maid to be a marchioness. Then he raised me to be a queen. Now he will raise me to be a martyr." Anne Boleyn grew up in nearby Hever Castle. The castle was considerably altered by her family into a moated manor house in the fifteenth to sixteenth centuries. In 1903 the manor was bought by William Waldorf Astor, who proceeded at great expense to return the Castle to its original splendor and to build a Tudor-style village adjacent to Hever castle. He became a British subject and subsequently Viscount Astor of Hever.

East and West Sussex

Almost on the English Channel, near the border between Kent and East Sussex, is the strikingly picturesque town of Rye. Once a harbor, the town now stands on a marshy island, lapped by three rivers. The same fate befell Camber Castle just south of Rye; it too was stranded by the receding sea. Rye's cobbled streets are lined with many Elizabethan buildings. One such, the Mermaid Inn, in the eighteenth century became a favorite watering hole for smugglers. Legend has it that they sat at the inn's tables with loaded pistols beside them in open defiance of the Customs men. Lamb House, an eighteenth-century dwelling near the Mermaid, was the home of Henry James from 1898 until his death in 1916. Above the town is the belfry of St. Mary's Church that houses the oldest working clock in Britain, dating from the sixteenth century. At numbers 5 and 6 Landgate is the Landgate Bistro, a well-liked restaurant where chef Toni Ferguson-Lees cooks delicious and inventive dishes—his desserts are not to be missed.

A diverse and memorable number of puddings are part of the culinary legacy of Kent and East Sussex. The art of pudding making was introduced to England by the invading Saxons. Recipes with various fillings are legion. These include game; pork, apple, and onion; pork sausage; bacon; and steak and kidney. Sweet pudding recipes are even more numerous—Cabinet, Speech House, Snowdon, Yeomanry, Sussex Blanket, Plum, Gooseberry, Ginger, Queen of puddings, and Christmas pudding, to name a few. Puddings today are steamed in china basins, supplanting the earlier pudding cloths. Sussex and Kentish folk, however, say that puddings boiled in a cloth taste far better than those cooked in a basin. A pudding cloth should be of closely woven cotton fabric, soaked in water then wrung out and well floured. Placed over a colander, a suet crust lines the cloth and into this goes the filling. The cloth is pulled up and another piece of dough is placed on top of the first crust to form a lid and the edges pinched together. The cloth is tightly tied with string, and the whole "bag" is suspended in boiling water until the pudding is cooked. This can take two, three, or four hours, depending on the filling. Lighter puddings made without suet can be flavored with spices or dried fruit. Another popular method is to put two or three tablespoons of sweet fruit filling or golden syrup in the bottom of the pudding basin to form a sauce over the inverted pudding. Puddings are generally served with a thin vanilla custard sauce, but heavy cream, crème fraîche, or a wine sauce is also delectable.

West from Rye is the resort town of Hastings, one of the Cinque Ports. Near here William the Conqueror and well over 8,000 men perpetrated the last successful invasion of England. A historic battle took place further inland at Battle, where William and his men confronted Harold of Wessex and his Anglo-Saxon army. William ordered an abbey built on the spot where King Harold died, and the remains of Battle Abbey can still be seen. William built his first castle here in 1069. It is believed that in nearby Alfriston, monks from Battle Abbey built and maintained the present Star Inn. This structure is made of pale yellow plaster and ancient weathered timbers ornamented with carvings of beasts. Several of Alfriston's inns are medieval, including the George and the Market Cross. On the village green, called the Tye, is the fourteenth-century Clergy House—the first building bought in 1896 by the National Trust. Nicknamed Ye Olde Smugglers, the Market Cross Inn in the early 1800s was the meeting place of the Alfriston gang, headed by smuggler Stanton Collins. The gang lured an excise man to his death over a cliff, and the long arm of the law eventually transported Collins when he was caught for sheep stealing. Travelers have come to Alfriston since prehistoric times by the ancient ridgeway on which the village stands, crossing the River Cuckmere. Alfriston was first a Saxon settlement beside the river and then for a long period a thriving market town. Its Market Cross is the only one left standing in East Sussex. Gracing the square are houses, shops, and inns with well-preserved timber frames and fancy brickwork. St. Andrew's Church is known as the "Cathedral of the Downs" for its unusual beauty and cruciform shape. The marriage registry inside the church dates to 1504.

Normans changed forever the history of England and also its habits. Normans erected the huge fortresses at Dover, Lewes, Rochester, Bramber, and Pevensey, as well as cathedrals at Rochester and Chichester. Hastings was a very important town during the Middle Ages. The old part has narrow, winding streets and two lovely churches. Over the centuries the harbor silted up, and Hastings became a sleepy fishing village, waking only during the Regency period when sea air and bathing became fashionable.

Brighton, in West Sussex, at the foot of the South Downs, is a large resort made famous by Dr. Richard Russell, who wrote a book praising the
beneficial effects of bathing and fresh sea air. The small village once called
Brightelmstone, also known as "London by the Sea," as it has been called
in its 200-year history, became instantly popular in 1783 when George,
Prince of Wales, descended on Brighton with a circle of friends to bathe in
the sea and sample the air on the advice of the good doctor. In 1787 the
Prince of Wales bought a farmhouse here for his morganatic wife, Mrs.
Fitzherbert, and had architect Henry Holland turn it into a Royal Pavilion. In
1815 George, then Prince Regent, commissioned the famous architect John
Nash to further embellish the palace. Nash added several domes, pinnacles, minarets, and lacy porticoes to the ever more fabulous Royal Pavilion.
Now open to the public, the lavish interior is a sight to behold. The principal decorating theme is Chinese; hanging lanterns, Chinese ceramics, and
bamboo furniture are much in evidence. An opulent banqueting hall is
quite breathtaking. Reception rooms, filled with the original ornate furniture and ornaments, and a small bedroom, where Queen Victoria and
Prince Albert slept, can also be visited. Queen Victoria did not approve of
such opulence and sold the Royal Pavilion to the city.

Brighton is lively with entertainment for people of all tastes. Excellent
performances that often go on to the West End of London are held at the
Theatre Royal, established in 1807. In contrast, at the early eighteenth-
century Palace Pier are amusement machines from a bygone era, and stalls
selling small white plates of cockles, mussels, and whelks to be eaten on
the spot. Above the three miles of shingled beach are wide handsome es-
planades that boast magnificent, well-preserved Regency hotels with
sumptuous interiors. Brighton has museums, theaters, and an old quarter
called The Lanes where restored seventeenth-century fishermen's cottages
are now filled with antique shops. On King's Road is the Hospitality Inn,
which houses La Noblesse, a great restaurant excelling in the new British
cooking. The chef uses lots of vegetables, game, and fish with delicious
sauces and a terrific assortment of fresh cheeses. Langan's Bistro, an off-
shoot of Langan's Brasserie in London, serves uncomplicated food in a
well-run, bright, and charming restaurant at 1 Paston Place.

Visiting seaside resorts became the "in" thing to do because of the
Prince Regent's enthusiasm for healthly fresh air and sea bathing. Naturally
his courtiers and noblemen followed his example, and soon resorts proliferated all along the coast. Among them are Folkestone, Hythe, Hastings,
Bexhill-on-Sea, Eastbourne, and Worthing. Several of these retain their
original elegant Edwardian hotels. Near Worthing, at Sompting, is a most
unusual Saxon church with a gabled tower and shingled helm roof that are
the only ones remaining in England. Bognor Regis, a small quiet seaside

town, eight miles from Chichester, was made famous in 1929 when King George V was ordered by his doctor to rest here after an illness. When Bognor was again suggested as a curative resort, the king is reputed to have replied, "Bugger Bognor" and expired. Sir Richard Hotham turned Bognor from a fishing village to a resort with five miles of sandy beach in the 1700s. Hoping to attract royalty to Bognor, Sir Richard built some splendid houses near the seafront. He lived at Bognor until his death at Hotham Park House—now a woodland respite on a crowded day—and was buried at St. Mary Magdelene churchyard. Ancient headstones cluster around this lovely medieval church at South Bersted.

Glyndebourne, in East Sussex, was once a small opera house, seating 300, in the grounds of Sir George Christie, son of the founders of Glyndebourne. Extremely popular, the three-month opera season of world-class performances has been held since 1934 from May to August, though bookings are taken in March. Exquisite gardens surround the house, and protecting the gardens is that most English of devices, a ha-ha—a wide ditch aimed at keeping livestock from coming into the gardens and grazing amid the shrubs and flowerbeds. After the performance many people elect to picnic in the grounds. This year—1994—after a year of construction, Sir George Christie has had an impressive new Glyndebourne opera house built seating 1,200. Built into the hillside to minimize its size, it still looks imposing and, of course, rather alters the country house feeling that was a part of the pleasure of coming here. The new auditorium's interior is not ostentatious and carefully preserves the ambience of the former opera house.

Ten minutes from Glyndebourne by car, at Little Horsted, Uckfield, is Horsted House, an architecturally elegant building, embellished with turrets and towers, that was constructed in 1850 by the heir of a wealthy dyer, Francis Blanchard. The style of the house is neo-Gothic and resembles the patterned stone design of the House of Lords. Horsted has a splendid entranceway tiled with Minton tiles, and it has known some famous owners. In the 1960s Lord Rupert Neville, Treasurer to Prince Philip, Duke of Edinburgh, lived here. Naturally the royal family stayed here at that time on more than one occasion. In fact the Queen's Walk was built to enable Her Majesty to walk to nearby Little Horsted church undisturbed. Inside there is a library with a secret door that gives access to the former conservatory. Horsted has been remodeled and is now a country house hotel. Tennis courts and croquet on the lawn are outdoor activities available. Guests may choose to sleep in the Windsor suite used by Her Majesty or in the room formerly used by Prince Philip. Horsted has an indoor pool, part of which is surrounded by a garden area. The charming restaurant has lovely views over the grounds, and there is a first-class chef, Allan Garth, whose performance in the kitchen is not to be missed.

Another beautiful and interesting house to visit in the vicinity of Glyndebourne is Bateman's, the Jacobean house Rudyard Kipling elected to live in rather than his house at Rottingdean, where he was born. Kipling felt his Rottingdean home was too accessible to his overzealous fans. The house and walled garden, open to the public, are owned by the National Trust.

Chichester in West Sussex is a graceful old town with a Market Cross in the center of the city. This was given to Chichester by Bishop Edward Storey in 1501. Fifty feet high, and one of the finest examples in Britain, it stands at the axis of Chichester's four main streets. These streets cross at right angles, following the original Roman plan dating to the first century A.D. The building of Chichester Cathedral began in 1091 on the site of an ancient collegiate

church. Twice damaged by fire, the cathedral, nevertheless, is much as it was when finished during the twelfth to thirteenth centuries. Ships miles out to sea can see its 277-foot (84-meter) spire. Christianity came to Sussex in 681 when St. Wilfrid, a saint who was rather hard to get along with, was banished from the See of York, landed by ship at Selsey, and established a South Saxon diocese. A tiny seventh-century chapel dedicated to St. Wilfrid, where services are still held today, stands on a spit of land near Selsey. Many houses in Chichester are Georgian. Several beautiful examples, owned by former wealthy Chichester merchants, are on The Pallants and on West Street. Arguably the best equipped theater in the country was opened in 1962 here—the Chichester Festival Theatre. At 30A Southgate, on one of the four streets that begin at the Market Cross, is a good restaurant called Droveway, where Jonas Tester cooks excellent fish dishes.

Near Chichester are the remains of the biggest and most splendid Roman palace in England, Fishbourne Roman Palace. Built about A.D. 70 for Cogidubnus, patient excavation has revealed the whole north wing of the palace and much of the east and west wings. Elevated wooden walkways guide visitors to the most splendid parts of the excavation. Roman objects discovered during the dig are displayed in a separate museum on the grounds. The interesting garden grows only plants that were cultivated during the Roman occupation of Britain.

An excellent restaurant called the White Horse Inn can be found at Chilgrove, located in the pretty countryside between Chichester and Petersfield. Neil Rusbridger's fish dishes are superb. Desserts are delicious and homemade, and the White Horse boasts one of the longest wine lists to be found in West Sussex. Four miles north of Chichester is Goodwood House, the eighteenth-century mansion of the dukes of Richmond and Gordon. Built on the site of a former Royal hunting lodge, Goodwood is still associated with sporting events. In 1801, in the most beautiful setting imaginable on the grounds of the mansion, the third Duke of Richmond laid out Goodwood racecourse.

Mussels with Creamy Herb Sauce

		generous pinch of saffron
2	T.	hot water
8	fl.oz.	dry white wine (1 C.)
2	lb.	mussels, scrubbed
2	T.	unsalted butter
1		garlic clove, minced
3	sm.	shallots, minced

12 fl.oz. heavy cream (1½ C.)
 2 T.   cognac
           Worcestershire sauce to taste
 4 fl.oz. fresh lemon juice (¼ C.)
 1 t.   minced tarragon
 1 t.   minced chervil
 1 T.   minced Italian parsley
Garnish: parsley sprigs and lemon slices

1. Mix saffron with hot water and set aside to infuse.
2. In a large heavy-bottomed saucepan bring wine to a boil, reduce heat, and simmer for 3 minutes.
3. Add mussels, cover, and steam, shaking pan once or twice, until mussels have opened, about 4 minutes. Using a slotted spoon, remove mussels from pan to a bowl, discarding any that are unopened. Reserve cooking liquid and remove mussels from shells. Set aside.
4. In a small pan, melt butter and gently cook garlic and shallots; do not brown. Add mussel liquid and reduce to about 4 fluid ounces or half a cup.
5. Stir in saffron and water, cream, cognac, Worcestershire sauce, and lemon juice, stirring constantly. Bring to boil, stirring, reduce heat, and simmer for 10 minutes.
6. Sprinkle in the minced herbs and continue to cook for a few seconds. Correct seasoning.
7. Divide mussels between individual ramekins. Spoon over some sauce, garnish with parsley sprigs and lemon slices, and serve at once.   *Serves 4 or 5 as an appetizer*

Five miles from the estuary of the River Arun, guarding the country town of Arundel, is Arundel Castle, for 500 years the stronghold of the Dukes of Norfolk, who continue to live there today. Begun by Edward the Confessor, and extensively rebuilt in the eighteenth century, the castle contains a splendid library, rooms filled with fifteenth-century furniture, paintings by Van Dyck and others, and an armory. Next to the castle is a pretty village, whose main street climbs steeply up from the river. The Roman Catholic Cathedral, built in the late 1800s, was designed by Joseph Hansom who also invented Hansom cabs—London's distinctive, roomy taxis. Antique and book shops line the High Street, and a Museum of Curiosity holds stuffed animals and birds arranged in lifelike settings by Walter Potter, a naturalist and taxidermist.

Amberley, four miles north of Arundel, is an artist's paradise. The village is a graceful blend of different styles of houses and cottages, built with different materials—flint, tile, stone, and brick—some houses are thatched and some half-timbered. Attached to the old walls are names that indicate their advanced years—the Old Bakehouse, the Old Brewhouse, and the thatch-covered Old Malthouse. Rock plants, creepers, cascades of purple wisteria, saucer-sized clematis blooms, and climbing roses cling to ancient walls and eaves. The enchanting St. Michael's church is hidden at the end of a lane backed by the ancient walls of Amberley Castle that rise clifflike from the plain below. Last spring a wedding was taking place, and the bright young faces and fashionable clothes of the ushers and bridesmaids as they hurried to the church looked strangely out of place among such ancient dwellings. Inside the church are twelfth-century wall paintings, and the five bells in the tower have hung here since 1742. Within Amberley Castle's walls, in a beautifully manicured garden, stands a manor house hotel with several guest bedrooms. The dining room in the frescoed Great Hall, called the Queen's Room, serves very English, elegant, well-prepared meals. Nigel Boschetti is the chef.

Farther west is the utterly charming village of Bosham that sits on a little peninsula jutting out to sea. On the steep street leading from the harbor is a pub that on more than one occasion has had unknowing customers who parked their cars close to the harbor only to return later to find their cars afloat. Flooded streets are a commonplace in Bosham. When the tide goes out the exposed marshland is a delight for bird-watchers. Pretty cottages line the narrow streets. The ancient church and its lych-gate are especially lovely. The tower and chancel arch of Bosham's church are Saxon. King Harold, who fell at the Battle of Hastings, prayed here before embarking on a journey to France in 1064; the church is depicted in the Bayeux Tapestry. Legend told of the burial at Bosham of King Canute's daughter. Curiously, about a hundred years ago a stone coffin was found in the church of Saxon origin with the skeleton of a young child inside.

A much-loved and oft-visited treasure, 14 miles north of Chichester, is Petworth House. Originally built on the grounds of a thirteenth-century dwelling, where the chapel can still be seen, Petworth was rebuilt in the late 1600s and received several new additions in the 1800s. Turner was often a guest at Petworth House, and many of his paintings hang here, along with canvases by Gainsborough, Titian, Roger van der Weyden, Blake, and others. Carvings decorate the Grinling Gibbons room, and impressive sculptures are displayed in the north gallery. The extensive park was landscaped by Capability Brown. Ebernoe Horn Fair is celebrated each year at the Ebernoe Cricket ground near Petworth. A team from a neighboring village is challenged to a cricket match, and while this is taking place a horned sheep is roasted with its head protruding over the edge of the barbecue pit. Following the match, the players share the feast.

Marinated Lamb Roasted
with Rosemary and Red Wine Sauce

6–7	lb.	leg of lamb
2	T.	red wine vinegar
6		garlic cloves, sliced
2	T.	rosemary
2	t.	sea salt
2	t.	black peppercorns
4	fl.oz.	olive oil (½ C.)
2		lemons
12	fl.oz.	red wine (1½ C.)
8	fl.oz.	chicken stock (1 C.)

1. Trim lamb of fat, and rub with vinegar.

2. Cut small slits in lamb about 2 inches apart with sharp pointed knife and place a slice of garlic in each slit.

3. In a mortar and pestle make a paste of the rosemary leaves, salt, and peppercorns, and rub this into the lamb. Place in a large shallow dish.

4. Juice lemons and mix juice with olive oil. Pour mixture over lamb and marinate lamb overnight in the refrigerator, removing 2 hours before cooking time.

5. Preheat oven to 400°F (or gas mark 6). Place lamb in a roasting pan on a rack and roast for 10 to 15 minutes. Mix the red wine and chicken stock together and pour half of this into the roasting pan.

6. Lower heat to 350°F (or gas mark 4), and continue to roast for about an hour or an hour and a half, depending on your preference for pink or well-done lamb. Continue to add wine and stock to the pan as needed, basting occasionally.

7. Remove lamb to a warm platter and let rest for 10 minutes. Keep warm.

8. Degrease pan juices and strain. Season and serve separate.

Serves 6–8

On the road between Chichester and London are several very pleasant places to stop for a meal. At Lower Beeding, near Horsham, is a pub called Jeremy's at the Crabtree, where Jeremy Ashpool's cooking is greatly admired for its straightforward goodness. Here are excellent fish, roasts, vegetables, and English puddings. Farther north, on Dorking's West Street, is Partner's West Street, a half-timbered restaurant that serves inventive and elegant food. Dorking, close enough to London to house commuters, is a pretty town at the foot of the North Downs, surrounded by some lovely countryside. It is popular with walkers and hikers who scale Leith Hill's fairly strenuous trail to the summit with enthusiasm. The Pilgrim's Way is just north of Dorking.

Farther north, near East Grinstead in West Sussex, is an Elizabethan stone mansion, built in 1598, called Gravetye Manor. In 1884 the house and the thousand acres in which it stands were bought by William Robinson, one of the great gardeners of all time, who created the exquisite gardens that are his memorial today. Gravetye Manor, transformed into a magnificent hotel and country club by its present owner, Peter Herbert, has lovely oak paneling throughout the ground floor. The hotel is splendidly furnished, and the beautiful dining room, candlelit at dinner, has a huge log-burning fireplace. Stephen Morey, the chef at Gravetye, says they are blessed with over an acre of kitchen gardens where much of the fruit, vegetables, and flowers needed by the hotel are grown. Their extensive range of greenhouses produce fresh herbs, early crops of spinach, lettuce, and other delicate vegetables. Stephen Morey says they are always assured of beautiful eggs from their brood of over 150 free-range chickens. Gravetye deals with many local suppliers. Venison, pheasant, hare, and rabbit are all plentiful in West Sussex. Attesting to this are excellent Terrine of Local Game, Breast of Pheasant wrapped in Bacon, and Roast Breast of Wild Duck, all on current menus. Gravetye Manor's dessert menu offers a delicious Bakewell Tart served with ice cream that Stephen Morey says is one of his favorite dishes, as is the recipe for his excellent terrine that he shares with us here.

Chicken and Stilton Terrine with Walnuts

6	chicken breasts, skinned and boned
	pink salt
	port wine
12	Savoy cabbage leaves
8 oz.	walnuts (1⅔ C.)
8 oz.	Stilton, crumbled (2 C.)
	white pepper

1. Marinate the chicken breasts in pink salt and port wine overnight. Blanch the cabbage leaves and roll them out between two cloths to break all the fibres.

2. Season the Stilton with milled white pepper and sprinkle with port. Roast the walnuts and peel them, making sure that all the dry skin has been removed.

3. The next day, line the terrine mold with the blanched cabbage leaves. Place two of the chicken breasts in the bottom of the terrine, add some of the Stilton, and scatter walnuts on top. Repeat the layers until all the ingredients have been used. Preheat oven to 475°F (or gas mark 9).

4. Fold the cabbage leaves over the filling. Put the lid on and place in a water bath which must not exceed 200°F (or gas mark ¼), and cook in the oven for 45 minutes. Allow terrine to rest for 10 minutes before slicing.   *Serves 8*

Hampshire

In neighboring Hampshire is the cathedral city of Winchester, once King Alfred's capital. Saxon kings, and some of the early Norman kings, held court in both London and Winchester.

Winchester's cathedral, one of the longest in Europe, took 300 years to complete. Medieval walls surround the cathedral close, adjoining sixteenth-century half-timbered houses. Jane Austen, author of many novels, among them *Pride and Prejudice* and *Sense and Sensibility*, died in 1817 at Winchester in a house on College Street. Her tomb is in the cathedral, and her house at Chawton, northeast of the city, contains memorabilia of the writer's life and is open to the public. Winchester has innumerable ancient dwellings that date from the 1300s to the 1600s. St. Swithun, a ninth-century Bishop of Winchester, asked to be buried when the time came outside the cathedral where rain would fall on his grave. In 862 his wishes were followed, but nine years later his body was reinterred within the cathedral. Legend has it that this made the former bishop so furious that he caused a downpour that lasted for forty days. And ever since, if it rains on July 15, St. Swithun's Day, you can expect it to continue for the next forty. The River Itchen, known for its salmon and trout fishing, runs through the city of Winchester.

One of the most renowned trout and salmon fishing rivers in England, the River Test, flows from its source near Basingstoke in Hampshire, spreads to form the delightful water meadows near the village of Chilbolton, meanders through the pretty thatched village of Leckford with its ancient church and thriving fish hatchery, continues through the market town of Stockbridge, and passes Mottisfont Abbey, famous for its old roses planted in walled gardens, on its way to join the channel at Southampton Water.

Trout with Asparagus, Lemon, and Capers

2	brook trout, cleaned
	flour for dredging
	salt and pepper
	vegetable oil for frying
1 lb.	tender asparagus, trimmed
3 T.	fresh lemon juice
3 T.	capers, drained
3 T.	clarified butter
2 t.	snipped dill
	parsley sprigs for garnish

1. Dredge brook trout in seasoned flour, and fry over moderate heat in vegetable oil, turning once until cooked through—10 minutes for each inch of thickness. Remove to a warm serving dish.

2. Meanwhile steam asparagus until just tender and remove to a warm place.

3. In a small saucepan, heat the lemon juice, capers, and butter until hot. Season and mix in the snipped dill.

4. Pour the sauce over the trout—you may fillet them first if you wish—and serve immediately, garnished with parsley sprigs.

Serves 2

Near the source of the River Test is Stratfield Saye, a lovely mansion set in charming grounds, that was bought by the first Duke of Wellington in 1817 with money given him by the nation that idolized him because of his great victory at Waterloo. Memorabilia of the Iron Duke can be seen here, including paintings looted by Napoleon and recaptured by Wellington. Near the West Sussex/Hampshire border is Havant, crisscrossed with Roman roads. South of the town, near Emsworth, are the recently discovered remains of a Roman villa. At 36 North Street, Emsworth, is Spencers Restaurant, owned by Denis and Lesley Spencer. The Spencers prefer to use small local suppliers to buy fresh produce for their kitchen because Lesley Spencer feels small suppliers sometimes provide superior quality and service. Denis Spencer's menu changes frequently and features great vegetarian food as well as a tempting array of fish, game, poultry, and meat dishes. Some of these dishes are enlivened with oriental seasonings, Javanese nuts, and a judicious dollop of coconut milk. Don't miss the Baked Goat Cheese en Croute, the Grilled Fresh Salmon or Halibut with Vegetables, or the Steamed Hazelnut Sponge Pudding with Chocolate Sauce. This cozy restaurant has gas-lighting, antique paintings on the walls, and alcoves filled with books—it is a wonderful setting for a festive Christmas dinner. On a recent visit Denis Spencer divulged that there may be a musical, female ghost who sings on an upper floor of this delightful building. He has heard but not seen this phenomenon. In addition to his restaurant at Emsworth, Denis Spencer is head chef at Spencers at the Waterside, a restaurant at the Waterside Club situated on the top floor of the Port House in the prestigious Port Solent Marina. Spencers at the Waterside is one of Port Solent's greatest attractions. Here is Denis Spencer's delicious recipe for Scotch Salmon.

Marinated Scotch Salmon Salad

Marinade

4	fl.oz.	dry white wine (½ C.)
3	fl.oz.	white wine vinegar (⅓ C.)
2	fl.oz.	extra virgin olive oil (¼ C.)
		mixed herbs
		juice of ½ lemon
10		thinly sliced mushrooms
2		thinly sliced shallots
2	t.	wholegrain mustard
2	t.	castor sugar
1	T.	clear honey
		salt and pepper to taste
		mixed salad leaves
16		thin slices of Scotch salmon

1. Whisk all the marinade ingredients together 48 hours prior to serving the salmon.

2. Pour a little of the marinade onto a lipped tray and arrange the salmon on it, being careful not to overlap the slices. Pour over the remaining marinade to cover all the fish. Cover with a sheet of waxed paper and refrigerate for 24 hours.

3. To serve, arrange finely cut salad leaves around the inner edge of a dinner plate to form a nest, then lay 4 slices of salmon neatly in the middle of each plate. Spoon some of the marinade over the salmon and some over the salad nest. Serve immediately.

Serves 4

Portsmouth on the Hampshire coast is the home of the Royal Navy. Henry VII strengthened the sea walls and built the first dry dock at Portsmouth. His son, Henry VIII, continued to build and created the first royal dockyard. These fifteenth-century defensive walls embrace the harbor still. Countless naval heroes have lived at Portsmouth. Vice Admiral Viscount Nelson embarked from nearby Southsea beach on his last voyage on HMS *Victory*. Nelson's flagship at the Battle of Trafalgar can be seen at the Portsmouth docks, alongside the Tudor warship *Mary Rose*, sunk in 1545 and raised in 1982. Many famous literary figures have lived in Portsmouth— Arthur Conan Doyle, H. G. Wells, and, when he was a child, Rudyard Kipling. Charles Dickens and George Meredith were born here. Portchester Castle's stout walls, two miles west of the harbor, stand on land surrounded on three sides by the sea. Wide wooden stairs climb to upper floors, eventually leading to the ramparts, where there is a wide panorama of the hills to the north and the channel to the south. Within the castle grounds are a wide cricket green and a delightful church, both in use today.

The New Forest, in Hampshire, is a beautiful wooded area that attracts many holidaymakers. A royal hunting preserve from the time of William the Conqueror, today its 92,000 acres comprise the largest national parks and nature reserves in Britain. Foresters who dwell here have the right to gather wood or cut peat for fuel and to graze their animals. The New Forest ponies roam at will as they have for millennia. Well-mannered, small, and sturdy, the ponies are perfect for young riders, and many of them are exported for that purpose to the United States.

Near the pretty village of Lymington is the ancient ruin of Beaulieu Abbey, a former Cisterian house. On the property is the family home of the Montagus, Palace House, a beautiful sixteenth-century dwelling, set in 7,000 acres of manicured grounds. The upper drawing room in the palace, once the monastery's chapel, now displays a collection of early keyboard instruments. Crowds of people each year visit Beaulieu—pronounced Bewley— drawn by the ruins, the palace, and Lord Montagu's National Motor Museum, filled with vintage vehicles.

A former shipbuilding center, fed by the prodigious wealth of timber available from the New Forest, is on the estuary of the Beaulieu River at the ancient village of Bucklers Hard. Three of the many ships built here fought at the Battle of Trafalgar, including Nelson's *Agamemnon*. The main street at Bucklers Hard is much wider than normal to accommodate the logs used for shipbuilding that were rolled down to the water's edge. Eighteenth-century red brick houses face each other across the wide expanse.

The town of Romsey, situated on the banks of the River Test, grew around the abbey founded in A.D. 907 by Edward, son of Alfred the Great. The abbey's Norman church is all that is left today. A statue of former prime minister Lord Palmerston (1784–1865) stands in the Market Place. He was born and died at Broadlands House, an eighteenth-century mansion on the outskirts of Romsey. Broadlands, set in 400 acres of grounds beautifully landscaped by the master designer Capability Brown, was the home of the late Earl Mountbatten of Burma. Prince Charles and Princess Diana spent part of their honeymoon at Broadlands. At 21 Palmerston Street in Romsey is the Old Manor House restaurant, where the eclectic chef, Mauro Bregoli, cooks wonderful dishes from a wide range of international cuisines.

Southampton has seen many illustrious people come and go through its great seaport over the past 1,000 years. After the battle of Hastings, William, Duke of Normandy, ordered his ships to dock here; Richard the Lionheart left from here on his Crusades; and Edward III, in a fury after the French plundered the town in the 1300s, set forth eight years later to redress the damage and fought the successful Battle of Crécy. The *Mayflower* embarked from West Quay on her voyage to America. The same voyage is made today from Ocean Terminal by HMS *Queen Elizabeth* II. Though Southampton suffered from considerable bombing during World War II, many of her splendid old buildings remain. Tudor House has oak-paneled rooms of sixteenth-century furniture within its half-timbered walls. Mullioned windows and overhanging gables make this one of the best examples of its period in Southampton. In medieval times, wool was exported from Southampton. The fourteenth-century Wool House now holds the Maritime Museum and its extensive collection of model ships. The High Street in the city boasts some remarkably well-preserved taverns—the Red Lion is the oldest, dating from the twelfth century. To assuage hunger today you could not do better in the city than Brown's Brasserie, an outstanding restaurant at Frobisher House, Nelson Gate. Patricia Brown cooks wonderful food, and her menu covers a wide range of delicious dishes from oysters in a creamy sauce to fabulous desserts. Some of these take considerable expertise to execute—which Patricia Brown obviously has.

Alton, in Hampshire near Chawton, lies on a Bronze Age track that later became the Pilgrim's Way. Georgian houses border Alton's main street. In 1643 during the Civil War, Alton witnessed the struggle beween the Roundheads and Royalists when fighting continued even inside the parish church of St. Lawrence, ending with the Royalists' defeat. Musket balls are still imbedded in the walls that surround the church door.

Across the Solent from the coast of Hampshire is the diamond-shaped Isle of Wight. Sharp pinnacles of rock, called the Needles, jut out from the southwestern edge of the Isle. This protrusion was once part of a land bridge to the mainland. Queen Victoria and her husband, Prince Albert, built a villa that he designed on the Isle of Wight. Here with their nine children they enjoyed privacy hard to imagine elsewhere. The family ate breakfast to the sound of bagpipes and happily spent time in everyday pursuits, such as gardening. The royal couple thought it better to set their children a good example than to chastise them, and they remained a very close family. Queen Victoria and her eldest daughter, Vicky, kept up a correspondence almost daily for over forty years, until the time of Queen Victoria's death in 1901. Prince Albert died of typhoid in 1861, devastating the Queen, who never recovered from his loss and refused to wear anything but black for the rest of her life.

Cowes was made famous by Victoria's eldest son, Edward. The foremost yacht club in Britain is here; it houses the very formal Royal Yacht Squadron. The island has many seaside resorts with sheltered sandy beaches tucked among the dramatic cliffs. The center of the island is mostly rolling, fertile land devoted to agriculture. At Carisbrooke are a castle and a lovely Norman church. Poet Alfred, Lord Tennyson, lived at Farringford House for some thirty years and took his daily walks on Tennyson Down, named after him. Excursions and family-oriented entertainments abound on the Isle of Wight, and for the energetic there is a footpath that completely encircles the Isle along the cliff tops; many shorter trails wind inland over countryside that is reminiscent of Hampshire. A regional speciality of the Isle of Wight is doughnuts.

Surrey

East of Hampshire is the home county of Surrey. Guildford, the county town of Surrey, is the home of the University of Surrey, and a red brick Gothic-style cathedral on Stag Hill dominates the town. Building started in 1936, and it is one of only three Anglican cathedrals erected since the Reformation. Guildford's steep High Street runs down to the River Wey, a pretty waterway with locks built in 1653 and now used only for recreational boats. The houses on the High Street look mostly Georgian, but several have a Georgian facade fronting a building that dates to a much earlier period. One of these is the Guildhall, which conceals a Tudor building. This elegant hall has an overhanging balcony with tall windows, an elaborate clock dated 1683 that is turned so its face is visible as you walk along the street, and a graceful bell turret—its crowning glory. Inside is a set of measures given to Guildford by Elizabeth I. Further along is Abbot's Hospital, an almshouse used to this day, that was built in 1619 by George Abbot, Archbishop of Canterbury. An art gallery resides in Guildford House, built in 1660. Situated on a mound, in walking distance from the High Street, is the ruin of Guildford's twelfth-century castle. It is still possible to climb the

keep and be rewarded for your efforts with a good view. The castle museum contains memorabilia of Charles Dodson (Lewis Carroll), author of *Alice in Wonderland*, who died and is buried at Guildford. Good hiking trails start directly from the town, which is situated on the North Downs. The Pilgrim's Way passes just south of Guildford.

Richmond-on-Thames, Surrey, is famed for its maids of honor, small individual puff pastry tartlets. Henry VIII gave them their name after seeing Anne Boleyn's maids of honor eating these delicious pastries. The filling is an egg batter with ground almonds, flavored with orange flower water. Rose water and orange flower water were popular flavorings until the eighteenth century. The recipe, that has evolved over time, has acquired an additional ingredient, raspberry jam, and the orange flower water has been replaced with cinnamon or brandy. Richmond-on-Thames in Surrey and Richmond in Yorkshire both claim Maids of Honor as their own. Richmond-on-Thames received its name from Henry VII, who built a palace here and called it Rychemond after his Yorkshire holdings. Though little of the palace remains today, Richmond-on-Thames has Tudor houses and from the same period the parish church of St. Mary Magdalene. A very popular Sunday escape from the city at the weekend is Richmond Park. Comprising 2,470 acres, it is the biggest Royal Park and affords refuge for many species of wildlife, particularly deer. Several hunting lodges remain in Richmond Park, one of which, Thatched House Lodge, is a royal residence. The Maids of Honour tearoom at 288 Kew Road in Richmond is a very pleasant place to stop for rest and refreshment.

Kingston-on-Thames is a thriving market town with many half-timbered houses that stands across the river from Hampton Court Palace. Seven Saxon kings were crowned here during the tenth century, seated on the King's Stone. The Stone still stands in front of the Guildhall. Benthall's is a large, airy, and surprisingly elegant department store in the center of Kingston that has an excellent restaurant for lunches or for afternoon Devonshire cream teas.

Cardinal Wolsey built Hampton Court Palace in East Molesey, Surrey, as a country retreat for himself. Henry VIII, however, annexed the palace later. Henry spent a great deal of time and money making Hampton Court even more glorious. Jane Seymour gave birth to their son, Edward VI, at Hampton Court, dying from the effort two weeks later. Catherine Parr and Catherine Howard were married to the king at Hampton Court. William III had Christopher Wren make some improvement to the building during his reign, and the gardens in front of the palace windows were redesigned to remind the king of the Dutch gardens of his home at Het Loo. Lining the immense driveway to the bridge over the now dry moat are many "grace and favor" houses inhabited by royal permission. Over the years there have been ghost stories associated with some of these houses. One such tells of an unaccountable whirring noise coming from behind a wall in one of the houses. It was so persistent the wall was knocked down to try to solve the mystery. Found behind it seated at a spinning wheel was the skeleton of a female. A search for a draft of air that might have caused the wheel to spin proved fruitless. Perhaps an irate husband bricked up his faithless wife with her spinning wheel. Another ghost thought to be that of the unfortunate Anne Boleyn has been heard running from the chapel. Hampton Court's enclosed gardens behind the palace are truly lovely. Walkways border the planting beds, which are a riot of flowers in the summer months. In spring hundreds of daffodils bloom under the mighty trees. For the brave there is a mysterious maze of paths lined with dense, high hedges that all too often lead to a dead end. At least one person a week gets lost in the maze during the summer. Tennis was popular with the royals and one of England's earliest tennis courts can be seen here. The Long Water, filled with the Queen's swans, that stretches from the formal gardens into the Great Park, was once the setting for glittering musical parties held aboard the Royal barge. Herds of majestic antlered deer throng the Great Park today. Each year in July a flower show is held on the Long Water.

Runnymede, a small island in the middle of the Thames southeast of Windsor in Surrey, is where King John (1199–1216), under duress, signed the Magna Carta. A cupola beside the river commemorates this event which in effect resulted in the beginnings of the British Parliament and ensured the freedom that every Briton feels is his right. Drawn up by the powerful Barons of the Court of King John, the Magna Carta spelled out these rights and guaranteed the Freedom of the Church. This document ended the era when kings believed they had a God-given right to rule—imposing penalties, confiscating property, and behaving as they pleased. The document's final form was agreed upon by the king and the barons on June 15, 1215, at Runnymede. A reluctant King John signed the document about a week later. On a shady hillside just two hundred yards away is a simple slab memorial to John F. Kennedy. The acre of land that surrounds the memorial was ceded by Britain to America.

4

THE WEST COUNTRY

Cornwall's once inaccessible terrain provided a refuge for Celts fleeing the invading Saxons. Hardworking people, the Celts mined for tin and copper, tended cattle and sheep, and fished off the treacherous Cornish coast. Until the eighteenth century they spoke only their own Celtic tongue, and to this day some of them consider Cornwall a region separate from England and seek to revive the Celtic language. Cornwall throughout its history has been a place of mystery. Legends defined Cornwall—of fierce smugglers, of ships battered beneath towering cliffs, and of King Arthur and his knights. The region remained inaccessible until the mid-nineteenth century when Isambard Kingdom Brunel built a bridge spanning the River Tamar between Plymouth, Devon, and Saltash, Cornwall. This enabled railways to penetrate the little-known Celtic world. The bridge was fortuitous for the Cornish people as tin mining was just beginning to be less profitable, and fishing was about to be taken over by large trawling companies. Later a highway bridge joined Brunel's masterpiece and Cornwall's isolation was ended forever.

Cattle and dairy farmers thrive, and Cornwall's china clay is sought after by potteries and crafts people everywhere. But the true economic mainstay of the Cornish people, as it is for the West Country as a whole, is tourism. Summer months find picturesque fishing villages crowded with day-trippers and holidaymakers. Immensely popular is Clovelley on the Devon coast, where quaint, hilly, cobbled streets are lined with pretty cottages. Traffic is forbidden here, and donkeys carry your luggage on their backs down the steep, cobblestoned hill to your hotel. Polperro and Mousehole, on the south Cornish coast, and Ilfracombe, on Devon's Bideford Bay, are magnets that draw foreign as well as British tourists. Enticing hidden coves offer shelter and seclusion. Many resort towns, such as Newquay, have long sandy beaches. In the eighteenth century, Newquay—a thriving port—shipped her abundant dried fish to Spain and Italy. Westward Ho! in Devon, named after the novel by Charles Kingsley (1819–1875), has a three-mile-long sand beach that when the tide is out is almost as wide as it is long. Surfers are attracted to the rolling waves at Bude, and Padstow—a safe haven for fishing boats for over a thousand years—attracts yachtsmen. Warmed by the Gulf Stream, the climate is sunnier in the West Country than almost anywhere else in the British Isles. Palm trees grow in sheltered areas. The lack of industry in the West Country contributes to the freshness of its air and also to its relatively sparse population.

Tintagel's clifftop ruin on the windswept Cornish coast is associated with the legend of King Arthur. Here tales are told of a romantic castle built for Arthur and Guinevere. Merlin they say lived in a cave in the cliff. All that remains today are traces of a sixth-century monastery and a twelfth-century fortress built by the Earl of Cornwall.

The coastal villages of Newlyn, near Penzance, and Brixham in Devon are both thriving fishing ports with flourishing quayside fishmarkets, providing lobsters, crabs, and myriad fresh fish so vital to the success of good restaurants and hotels in the West Country. Brixham's colorful houses climb the steep hillside that overlooks the busy harbor. In the 1800s both ports were havens for painters. Newlyn has a museum displaying the paintings of its famous local artists.

Cornish Lobster Thermidor

1	lg.	lemon
1	T.	salt
2		very large (or 4 smaller) lobsters
½	lb.	fresh mushrooms, sliced
2	oz.	unsalted butter (half a stick)
		pinch of salt
4	fl.oz.	dry white wine (½ C.), if necessary
3	T.	flour
2	t.	Dijon mustard
2	t.	fresh tarragon, minced
		splash of hot pepper sauce, or pinch of cayenne pepper
1	T.	dry sherry

4 fl.oz. light cream (½ C.)
white pepper
grated Parmesan cheese

1. Squeeze lemon and pour 2 tablespoons of juice into a lobster pot with 3 inches of salted water. Bring to rolling boil, plunge in lobsters, cover, return to boil, and cook for 7 minutes.

2. Remove lobsters to large bowl, and when cool enough to handle, break lobsters apart over the bowl to catch the juices. Pull off and discard heads. Push lobster meat out of tails and discard vein. Crack claws, remove meat, and cut in cubes. (Alternatively, claw meat can be left whole and used to garnish finished dish, if desired.) Cube meat from lobster tails.

3. Sauté lobster meat in one tablespoon of butter for one minute. Place in large bowl. Cut membrane from front of tail shells and discard. Rinse shells and place in lightly buttered baking dish.

4. Strain juices into a small saucepan and boil over high heat until reduced to about 4 fluid ounces (½ cup). Meanwhile, in a small skillet over low heat, cook mushrooms in one tablespoonful each butter and lemon juice with a pinch of salt for 5 minutes.

5. Drain mushrooms and reserve juices to mix with reduced lobster liquid. There should be about 8 fluid ounces (1 cup) of liquid; if not, add some white wine. Add the mushrooms to the lobster meat.

6. In a saucepan over medium heat, melt remaining butter, stir in flour, and cook one minute. Add liquid and cook for 3 minutes until boiling and smooth. Stir in mustard, tarragon, hot pepper sauce or cayenne pepper, sherry, and light cream. Season to taste with white pepper.

7. Pour two-thirds of the sauce over lobster meat and mushrooms and toss gently. Fill shells with lobster, pour remaining sauce over shells, and sprinkle with Parmesan cheese. (May be prepared ahead until this point and refrigerated.)

8. Preheat the oven to 400°F (or gas mark 6), and bake the lobster dish for about 10 minutes, until flecked with brown. Serve garnished with lobster claws, if desired. *Serves* 4

Falmouth, one of the major holiday resorts on Cornwall's southwestern coast, was a thriving port in the days when merchant ships were under sail. It is situated on a magnificent harbor guarded by two castles, Pendennis and St. Mawes. Farther west, Penzance stands on Mount's Bay, its four miles (6.4 km) of sandy beach facing the island of Mount St. Michael's. Accessible by foot at low tide, a castle on the Mount incorporates the remains of a twelfth-century Benedictine monastery. Due to the mildness of the weather here, Penzance has some of the loveliest gardens in Britain—Morrab Gardens in town, and Trengwainton Gardens, owned by the National Trust, two miles (3.2 km) outside the town.

Bodmin, in the Fowey valley, is the county town of Cornwall, and it has Cornwall's largest parish church. Lanhydrock House, situated near the lake-dotted Bodmin Moor, is a splendid seventeenth-century country house that was rebuilt in the 1800s after a fire. Numerous and interesting rooms are on display—not only gracious reception rooms but servants' quarters too. A beautiful seventeenth-century plaster ceiling graces the unusually long gallery at Lanhydrock House. The coach house is also open to the public and has a fascinating collection of hundred-year-old vehicles. Woodland walks in the extensive grounds are numerous, and there are even places where picnicking is allowed.

Land's End, the farthest point west in England, is visited by most people who go to Cornwall, and more often than not they have their photographs taken teetering on the edge. Land's End can be reached by the cliff-top path that rings most of Cornwall.

Only twenty-eight miles (12.8 km) off the Cornish coast are the Scilly Isles (pronounced Silly Isles), though it can seem a lot farther than that if you choose to take the steamship across on a rough day. Today you can hop over by helicopter which takes barely twenty minutes. The Scilly Isles are famous for their flowers. The first signs of spring in London florist shops are bowls of fresh daffodils from the Isles. St. Mary's, the largest of the many islands that make up the Scillys, has pristine beaches, many of them deserted, which can be reached by boat. Boat rentals are particularly popular with ornithologists. The outer islands are a haven for seals, puffins, and dozens of bird species. In migration season the number of species swells from 130 to 300, making the Scillys a bird-watcher's paradise.

Two huge areas of the West Country are designated National Park lands—Exmoor to the north along the coasts of Somerset and Devon, and Dartmoor to the south. Exmoor's 170,000 acres, made famous by R. D. Blackmore's novel *Lorna Doone*, encompass villages, farmlands, forested ravines, barren ridges, and the famous wild ponies, descendants of the Stone Age horse. Dartmoor's 234,000 acres comprise bleak, wild moors covered with heather and bracken interspersed with mud-filled bogs. Strange granite outcroppings interrupt the skyline, and ponies roam among Bronze Age village remains. These hardy creatures forage for themselves during the summer, eating mostly grasses, heather, and gorse. When winter comes, the ponies are rounded up, tags attached to the ears of foals, and in order to keep the numbers manageable some of the ponies are sold.

On the coast south of the park is Plymouth, Devon, home of the Elizabethan naval heroes Sir Francis Drake and Sir Walter Raleigh. A statue of

Drake, who circumnavigated the globe, stands on Plymouth Hoe. When Drake was told by a lookout that the Spanish fleet had been sighted, he calmly continued his game of bowls on the Hoe. Only when the game was finished did he leave the Hoe and take his ship into battle to defeat the Spanish Armada. Plymouth is equally famous today for the voyage the Pilgrim Fathers made when they sailed from Plymouth, after stopping here for repairs to their ship. The steps in Sutton Harbour now bear the name "Mayflower," and there is a Mayflower Stone in New Street.

James Cook, the explorer and map maker, also sailed from Plymouth, in 1772. Plymouth boasts the largest naval dockyard in the United Kingdom at Devonport, founded in 1691. The city attracts holidaymakers both for its historical associations and as a convenient central base for touring Devon and Cornwall.

Farther along the south Devon coast, in upscale Dartmouth, known to many yachting enthusiasts, is one of Britain's finest restaurants. Given a 4-star rating for its excellent food by the *Good Food Guide* and honored by Michelin and many others, the Carved Angel, presided over by a huge wooden angel, owes its reputation to the creative cooking of proprietor Joyce Molyneux and Nick Coiley. The Carved Angel's situation on the River Dart ensures a plentiful supply of spanking fresh fish, and shellfish—especially Dart crab and lobster. Local suppliers bring poultry and game—in fact, practically all ingredients are local. The exciting flavors of the food here are achieved by judiciously combining different textures and tastes, such as elderflower with avocado, and orange with anchovy and olive. Desserts are sublime. Ice cream and sorbet owe their delicate tastes to scented geranium and rose petals gathered in Joyce Molyneux's garden. Joyce Molyneux is one of the many pupils trained by George Perry-Smith, the distinguished chef and teacher who has done more than anyone to promote the simple goodness of English food by the imaginative use of pristine ingredients in dishes he cooked at his restaurant in Bath, The Hole in the Wall.

Driving from Dartmouth along the coast through the attractive fishing port of Brixham and on to Torquay, you will come to the Mulberry Room Restaurant, at number 1 Scarborough Road. The restaurant occupies the ground floor of a Victorian terraced house in a neighborhood away from the town center. In summer French windows open to a flowery patio that reflects the soft, pastel colors of the table linens inside. The restaurant has a light, airy feel to it in summer, and in winter a log fire burns in the Victoria fireplace. Lesley Cooper, the chef proprietor of the Mulberry Room, is an excellent cook and loves robust flavors, such as sun-dried tomatoes, olives, herbs, and smoked fish and poultry. Bouillabaisse is one of her favorite dishes. Her suppliers are local, enabling her to change her menus twice weekly. Dishes from a recent menu are Pheasant and chestnut soup; Terrine of vegetables with homemade pickles; Stuffed mushrooms with pine nuts; Roast monkfish with Becks bitter ale sauce; Braised sirloin of beef with onion bay sauce; Chilled lemon soufflé; and Honey and fromage frais pie. Vegetarians are well catered to here, for Lesley Cooper is concerned that her dishes be healthy as well as delicious. Her recipe for spanking fresh herring follows.

Grilled Herring with Rhubarb and Allspice

1 lb.	rhubarb
4 oz.	brown sugar (½ C.)
	olive oil
1	onion, peeled and finely chopped
	ground allspice
4 lg.	filleted herring, each weighing 8 ounces
	salt and pepper

1. Preheat grill for 15 minutes.
2. Trim rhubarb and cut into 1-inch pieces. In a medium saucepan, stew the rhubarb, sugar, and 2 tablespoons of water until very tender.
3. Meanwhile, drizzle a little olive oil into a frying pan, heat oil, and stir in the chopped onion and allspice. Cook gently until onion just begins to brown. Remove from heat and stir onion into the cooked rhubarb.
4. Open out each herring fillet, season with salt and pepper, and spread with a layer of rhubarb sauce. Make two diagonal cuts on each side of the fish. Place herring on a lightly oiled grill pan and grill for about 5 minutes on each side or until the flesh is opaque.
5. Serve herring accompanied by additional rhubarb sauce. This dish is particularly good served with a tossed green salad.

Serves 4

Above Torquay near Teignmouth is Powderham Castle, where the original building was completed in 1390. The castle was considerably modified and restored in the eighteenth and nineteenth centuries to repair damage to the castle during the Civil War. The interior has gracious period furniture, paintings, and porcelain. The eighteenth-century stucco work and the music room are by James Wyatt. From the deer park there are fine views over the Exe estuary. There is a café and a gift shop, and picnicking in the deer park is encouraged.

So much of the West Country is surrounded by sea that fish, particularly hake, halibut, haddock, and turbot, are plentiful. Simple butter sauces that don't mask the flavor are best with this gleaming fresh fish. Butter and lemon are replacing the three typically English sauces—parsley, egg, and mustard—that used to accompany all fish with the exception of mackerel. Mackerel's strong flavor needs a more robust accompaniment, such as red currant or gooseberry sauce. The noble salmon has flesh of such delicacy that it needs only butter, with a little lemon or fresh herbs when served hot, or dill and cucumber when cold. A bowl of Hollandaise sauce is a rich and magnificent treat with salmon for festive occasions.

Sole Fillets with Apple, Cider, and Cream Sauce

1½ lb.		sole fillets
		sprigs of fresh tarragon
2	T.	red onion, diced
1		ripe tomato, seeded and diced
1		small tart apple, peeled, cored, and diced
		butter
8	fl.oz.	fish stock or clam juice (1 C.)
6	fl.oz.	sparkling cider (preferably Somerset) (1 C.)
2	fl.oz.	heavy cream (¼ C.)
1		egg yolk
		salt and pepper
1	t.	prepared Dijon mustard
3	T.	Calvados or apple brandy

1. Place fillets underside up, place tarragon sprig on one end of fish, and roll up; or if large, fold in two. Preheat oven to 350°F (or gas mark 4).

2. Scatter red onion, tomato, and apple evenly in bottom of buttered, heatproof shallow serving dish, large enough to hold sole rolls in one layer.

3. Place sole on top of vegetables and pour in the fish stock or clam juice and the cider. Cover with buttered waxed paper, cut to fit dish.

4. Bake in oven for 10 to 12 minutes or until sole are just cooked through. Remove sole and drained vegetables to a serving platter and keep warm. Reserve juices.

5. Meanwhile, beat together cream and egg yolk. Set aside.

6. Pour juices into a small saucepan and boil down to roughly half the amount. Season with salt and pepper. Remove from heat and beat in the cream and egg yolk.

7. Reheat slowly; do not allow to boil; when very hot add the mustard and Calvados or brandy and pour over fish. Serve immediately.

Serves 6

An equally luxurious product of Cornwall and Devon is clotted cream, made by filling a very wide, low, heat-proof pan with milk straight from the cow, and leaving it for hours over the very lowest flame until the thick, yellow cream rises to the top. Watching the farmer's wife skimming this luscious creamy crust from the milk, one afternoon at summer's end, was a revelation. The freshly clotted cream was so solid that a ladleful dolloped onto a sheet or two of waxed paper could be transported safely by simply pulling up the four corners to form a paper sack. Traditionally, this luscious cream is served with warm scones and a pot of strawberry jam for afternoon tea. But, of course, it is perfectly delicious with pies, tarts, and puddings. Bakeries in the West Country sell freshly made doughnuts, shaped like hot dog rolls, split lengthwise and filled with clotted cream. The trick is to be able to wait until the doughnut is cool enough that the clotted cream stays put!

Cream cheese is another product made in the farmhouse dairy, though it cannot be made with homogenized milk. With milk fresh from the cow the procedure is fairly simple, involving only a cheesecloth for draining the whey and a weighted board for pressing the moisture from the curds. Homogenized milk and ordinary kitchen utensils can be used to make cottage cheese, and if you have a little leftover yogurt to use as a starter, yogurt too is a snap to make.

Summer Pudding with Clotted Cream

8   slices of good homemade white bread, crusts removed
20 oz. assorted ripe berries—raspberries, blackberries, and
          strawberries (4 C.)
5 oz. red currants* (1 C.)
4 oz. sugar (½ C.)
3 T.   fruit-based liqueur
2 T.   brandy
*If red currants are not available, substitute more raspberries

1. Using a medium-sized bowl with straight sides, cut a circle of bread to fit the bottom of the bowl, then cut wedge shapes to completely line the sides of the bowl, and finally 2 half-circles to fit the top.

2. Place the fruit, sugar, liqueur, and brandy in a saucepan and heat gently until sugar is dissolved. Pour into bread-lined bowl and position the top slices of bread to completely cover fruit.

3. Place a plate, slightly smaller than the rim of the bowl, directly on the bread, and place a one-pound weight on top. Refrigerate for at least 8 hours.

4. Remove weight and plate and invert the pudding onto a serving dish. Serve with clotted cream.   *Serves 4–6*

In most parts of the British Isles, though not in Scotland, public footpaths crisscross the countryside. These footpaths, originally the shortest route to the church, or the river, or the next village, have been rights-of-way for the general public for centuries. Some of them started as coffin routes, for carrying the deceased from home to graveyard. Wide stone benches are still found at intervals along the path, where pallbearers could set down the coffin and rest awhile. Public footpaths often traverse private property, which owners tolerate as long as no damage is done to crops and gates are securely refastened to safeguard livestock. A public footpath runs along the top of the cliffs from Poole, Dorset, on the south coast of the West Country peninsula, to Minehead, Somerset, on the north. In some places the sea directly below pounds the cliffs with tremendous force. Although some stretches involve a fairly arduous climb, the walk is popular not only with stout-booted hikers but also with day-trippers who plow cheerfully ahead in flimsy summer sandals.

Chagford, a charming Devon village, with interesting shops and good pubs, is two miles (3.2 km) from Gidleigh Park. This handsome mock-Tudor country house hotel is set in forty acres of magnificent and secluded grounds on the North Teign River, within the Dartmoor National Park. Paul and Kay Henderson, the American owners, have brought Gidleigh Park to the peak of perfection inside and out through dedicated hard work. Gidleigh Park has won many awards and accolades from major guides, including *Egon Ronay*, *Michelin*, *Good Hotel*, and *Good Food Guide*. One and a half miles (2.4 km) from the nearest road, Gidleigh Park is peaceful and very quiet. The splendid gardens restored under the direction of head gardener Keith

Mansfield are famous. One of the most spectactular features of the grounds is the water garden, which was rebuilt and planted in 1986. There is a pavilion in the grounds reached by a charming footbridge over the Teign which can accommodate two, three, or four people comfortably. Manicured croquet lawns are nearby. The house has two suites and twelve bedrooms individually furnished with antiques and English fabrics. Each has a private bathroom and all amenities expected of such a highly rated country house hotel. The public rooms are spacious with splendid views, fresh flowers in every room, and a log fire every day of the year. The dining room is paneled with views over the grounds from the mullioned windows. Everything served here is made from the best produce available in Britain. Wines are chosen by Paul Henderson, and the list alone has won many awards. Head chef Michael Caines's menu has a Terrine of duck foie gras with Madeira jelly; Langousine marinière and a salad of leek confit; Bresaola and provençale vegetables and Parmesan; Lobster fricassé with herbs; Calf's sweetbreads, risotto, sautéed foie gras, and asparagus; Beef fillet and roast shallots with red wine sauce; and desserts that include Pear crèpe soufflé; Crystallized apples with green apple sorbet; and a plate of caramel desserts—this is but a fraction of the possibilities. Paul Henderson has given his permission to include the following recipe.

Crab Ravioli

1	lg.	crab
		coriander seeds
		white peppercorns
6	oz.	(scant) scallops
1		egg yolk
4	fl.oz.	cream (½ C.)
6	oz.	brown crab meat for purée
		salt, cayenne pepper
1	lb.	(generous) white crab meat
1	oz.	fresh ginger (scant two T.), very finely shredded
½		lemon, juiced
½	lb.	ravioli paste (see recipe below)

Garnish

slivers of ginger
julienne of coriander
pink grapefruit segments

1. Cook the crab with coriander and white peppercorns for about 20 minutes from the moment it boils, and allow to cool.

2. Once cooled, take out and separate the white and brown meat, keeping the carcass for sauce.

3. In a food processor, blend the scallops to a fine mousse, add the egg yolks and half the cream, then pass through a fine sieve.

4. Separately blend brown crab meat and pass through a sieve.

5. Over ice, combine the brown crab and scallop mousses, and then carefully add the rest of the cream. Season lightly and let rest for 5 minutes.

6. Add the white crab meat and shredded ginger, season with cayenne and lemon juice, and refrigerate.

7. Place five ravioli around the plate, add sauce, garnish, and serve.   *Serves 2*

Ravioli paste

2 t.   water
2 t.   olive oil
1   packet of saffron powder
1   egg
3   egg yolks
4 oz.   plain flour (¾ C.)

1. Put the water, olive oil, and saffron in a casserole and boil for 30 seconds, remove and cool.

2. Add the infusion of saffron to the eggs, and then to the flour. Mix by hand, then leave until used.

3. Roll out the pasta, preferably through a pasta machine on the finest grade. Cut into 10-cm circles and rest.

4. Pass the circles through the finest roller again one at a time (if you do more it will dry out.)

5. Place half a tablespoon of crab mix on each circle of pasta and form ravioli. Place on floured cling film.

6. Cook in simmering water for 6 minutes and drain on a cloth.

Sauce

5 oz.	(scant) shallots, peeled
1¾ oz.	ginger (3 T.), minced
3½ oz.	lemon grass (5 T.) (inner stalk)
	olive oil
¼ oz.	peppercorns (1½ t.)
¼ oz.	coriander seeds (1½ t.)

    6. oz.   (scant) brown crab meat
    1   crab carcass broken into small pieces
    16 fl.oz. water (2 C.)
    24 fl.oz. vegetable nage (stock) (3 C.); see recipe

To finish

    dash of cream
    6 oz. butter (1¼ sticks)
    salt, pepper
    lemon juice

   1. Sweat the shallots, ginger, and lemon grass in olve oil for 5 minutes. Add the peppercorns and coriander seeds and sweat another 2 minutes.
   2. Add the brown crab meat and crab carcass and sweat for another 2 minutes.
   3. Add the water and vegetable nage, and cook carefully for 20 minutes. Pass through a fine sieve and set aside.
   4. Reduce stock if necessary for flavor.
   5. Add cream, then butter, whisking continuously; season, then add lemon juice.

Vegetable nage (stock)—2 quarts

    4 onions
    4 leeks
    10 carrots
    1 celery
    16 garlic cloves
    6 star anise
    2 pinches ground white pepper
    1 bay leaf
    24 pink peppercorns
    1 bottle dry white wine
    4 sprigs thyme
    4 sprigs tarragon
    6 sprigs chervil
    2 sprigs coriander

   1. Peel, wash, and cut the vegetables in ½-inch dice. Put all vegetables, unpeeled, and crushed garlic, anise, ground pepper, bay leaf, and peppercorns in a stainless steel saucepan and cover with cold water.

2. Bring to a boil until the vegetables are cooked. Add white wine and bring back to a boil. Remove from heat; add thyme, tarragon, chervil, and coriander.

3. Let it infuse for about 6 hours before using.

Exeter, Devon's cathedral city, was once the walled Roman city of Isca Dumnoniorum, built on the site of an early Roman fortress. Parts of its Roman heritage are still visible. Since that time Saxons, Danes, and Normans have left their mark on Exeter. Exeter Cathedral has also gone through periods of rebirth. Started as so many British cathedrals were by the Normans, the cathedral was rebuilt to its present dimensions from 1270 to 1360. Two Norman towers attest to its long history. Exeter was badly bombed during World War II, but much of the ancient city survives. A fine collection of old vessels can be seen in the Floating Exhibition, part of the Maritime Museum, in the Exeter Ship Canal. One of these beautiful boats was used in the film A *Man for All Seasons*.

Tiverton Castle, between Exeter and Taunton, was built in 1106 by the first Earl of Devon, but two towers are all that remain. The huge gatehouse is from the fourteenth century. Inside there are period furnishings and a collection of clocks. In the town of Tiverton is an old school, Blundell's, built in 1604 by Peter Blundell—a description of this building is in R. D. Blackmore's novel *Lorna Doone*. Among the treasures in the Church of St. Peter are splendid ship carvings, and a candelabra and organ that date to the seventeenth century.

This cake, or bread, is an updated version of the Saffron Cake that was made before the advent of baking powder in the West Country. It makes an excellent tea bread or breakfast bread.

Devon *or* Cornish Saffron Cake

	a lavish pinch of saffron
2 T.	warm water for soaking saffron
1 lb.	unbleached white flour
1 ½	packages rapid-rise dry yeast
4 oz.	sugar (½ C.)
1 t.	mixed spices—cinnamon, nutmeg, allspice
	pinch salt
6 oz.	unsalted butter (¾ stick)
6 oz.	mixed dried fruit and nuts, either golden raisins and almonds, dates and hazelnuts, or dried cherries and walnuts (1 ¼ C.)

grated zest from 1 lemon or 1 orange

6–7 fl.oz.   milk (⅔ C. or more), heated to very warm (125–130°F)

1. Soak saffron in warm water for at least 6 hours.

2. In a large bowl place flour, yeast, sugar, spices, and salt and stir with a wire whisk to aerate.

3. Cut in butter until crumbly and stir in dried fruit, nuts, and lemon zest.

4. Make a well in the center of the mixture and pour in the very warm milk and the saffron, mixing to form a soft dough. Add a little more warm milk if necessary.

5. Place dough in an oiled bowl, cover, and leave in a warm place until doubled in bulk—about one hour.

6. Punch down and fold into a rectangular shape. Place in buttered 9" × 5" loaf pan and let rise again in a warm place for 45 minutes, or until cake is well above top of loaf pan. Meanwhile preheat oven to 375°F (or gas mark 5).

7. Bake for 35–40 minutes. Watch for burning, and if necessary tent with foil. Remove to cake rack to cool.

Chef's note: This makes an excellent breakfast bread.

Between Exeter and Bideford twelve miles (19.3 km) southeast of Great Torrington is the interesting village of Winkleigh, which was occupied first by Saxons and later by Normans. William the Conqueror gave Winkleigh to his wife, Mathilda, and shortly afterward two manor houses were built here. One of these was renovated extensively in the eighteenth century and is now a private house. All Saints' Church dates mainly to the fourteenth and fifteenth centuries with some later renovation. It has fine wagon roofs supported by seventy carved angels and many interesting bosses including one thought to represent Catherine of Aragon. Church house, built in 1535, has been converted into two dwellings. Many fine seventeenth- and eighteenth-century cottages are still to be seen on Vine Street, and the ancient almshouse founded in 1681 is from roughly the same period. The housing of the village pump and water trough on Fore Street commemorates William IV. On Castle Street at the sign of the owl is the wide-windowed restaurant Popham's, a charming, tiny establishment open for lunch and morning coffee, where homemade dishes are cooked right before your eyes with enormous enthusiasm and joie de vivre by Melvyn Popham. The atmosphere is warm and friendly. Melvyn Popham's dedication to fine cooking, combined with the freshest Devon ingredients, creates light, innovative dishes that few can resist. It is essential to book for lunch—noon to three o'clock—while dishes are still available. Some dishes on the menu include Fresh asparagus and smoked salmon; Salmon baked in pastry with currants and ginger served with Hollandaise Sauce; Breast of chicken stuffed with leeks, grapes, and watercress; Chestnut and orange roulade; and Walnut and Drambuie charlotte with vanilla sauce. Melvyn Popham says that people have been known to request a bowl of his renowned sticky toffee pudding for breakfast! Delicious quiches and home-baked cakes are served with a bottomless cup of morning coffee. Popham's is unlicensed, so bring your own bottle if you want to—there's no corkage charge. Here are two of Melvyn Popham's favorite recipes that he has contributed to this book.

Avocado Salad with Hot Smoked Bacon

	assorted salad greens
2	red grapes
2	green grapes
½	ripe avocado, cut into bite-sized pieces
1 T.	tomato, seeded and chopped
2	streaky rashers of smoked bacon, chopped small

Dressing

2 T.	walnut oil
1½ T.	ground nut oil
1 T.	sherry vinegar
½ t.	mustard
	salt and pepper, to taste

1. Mix salad dressing ingredients in a jar, and shake well before using.

2. Arrange assorted salad leaves in center of plate. Top with sliced grapes, followed by avocado pieces, then tomato. Drizzle dressing over the salad.

3. In a nonstick pan quickly fry the bacon until crisp, stirring all the time. Spoon over the salad and serve immediately.   *Serves* 1

Marinated Duck Breast with Plum Sauce

4   duck breasts

Marinade

3 T. clear honey
2 T. sherry vinegar
1 T. soy sauce
1 t. fresh ginger, grated

1. Mix marinade ingredients together in a dish large enough to hold the duck breasts.
2. Prick the duck breasts all over and place in the marinade. Cover with film and refrigerate overnight.
3. Preheat oven to 400°F (or gas mark 6). Place duck on a wire rack over a roasting pan. Cook for 17–20 minutes for pink meat. Leave to rest for 5 minutes.
4. Cut duck breast into thick slices and arrange on warm plates with vegetables of your choice and plum sauce, OR serve on a bed of assorted salad greens with fresh asparagus.

Plum sauce

1¼ lb. plums
4 oz. castor sugar (½ C.)
1 T. red wine vinegar
3 T. water

1. Place ingredients in saucepan and simmer to a pulp.
2. Press through a sieve and keep warm.

Barnstaple has a rich history and has many fine buildings to visit. A twisted wooden spire that has since been covered in lead tops the Parish church that dated to 1318. Since Norman times Barnstaple has been an inland port, and the Long Bridge spanning the River Taw was built in 1273. Medieval fireplaces and paneling grace the fifteenth-century Three Tuns Tavern, and two almshouses date from the 1600s. Parts of St. Anne's Chapel Museum are mid-fifteenth century, but the crypt predates this considerably. The building was once a grammar school. John Gay, who wrote *The Beggar's Opera*, went to school there.

East of Barnstaple at East Buckland is the Lower Pitt Restaurant, owned by Suzanne and Jerome Lyons. Although it is called simply a restaurant, in fact there are three comfortably furnished double rooms of great character for overnight guests. The light-filled dining room overlooks the extensive grounds surrounding the Lyons's sixteenth-century house. The relaxing ambience in the dining room is enhanced by hanging ferns, soft green napery, and crisp white tablecloths. A log fire crackles in the cozy lounge bar on winter evenings. The Lower Pitt restaurant has been mentioned in several guides, including the *Good Food Guide* and *Egon Ronay*. Herbs and vegetables, from broad beans in early summer to artichokes and parsnips in winter, are grown by Jerome Lyons in his two-acre garden. Five fresh vegetable dishes accompany each entrée. Meat of exceptionally high quality is available in this part of Devon. Suzanne Lyons says that although her recipes are gleaned from all over the world, her ingredients are strictly local. The menu features Sesame chicken with mushrooms; Fresh prawns sautéd with mushrooms and cashew nuts; Local mussels grilled with garlic butter; Escalope of Salmon with salsa verde; Spinach roulade filled with cream cheese and herbs; and Boeuf Stroganoff. A selection of desserts includes Gâteau Lyonnaise with chocolate and chestnuts; or Pavlova filled with fresh fruit and cream. Fresh farmhouse cheeses come from Devon farms. Suzanne Lyons has contributed the following recipe for this book.

Venison Steaks in Cumberland Sauce

2 6-oz.	haunch steaks of venison
1 t.	red currant jelly
2 T.	Port wine
2 T.	orange juice, freshly squeezed
	watercress for garnish

Marinade

5 fl.oz.	sherry vinegar (scant ²/₃ C.)
10 fl.oz.	grapeseed oil (1¼ C.)
1	shallot, minced
	rosemary sprig
	salt and pepper

1. Thoroughly mix marinade ingredients, and marinate the venison steaks overnight.

2. When ready to cook, drain steaks. Heat pan to very hot, and sear steaks on both sides. Continue to cook for 10 minutes or until cooked. Remove from pan and keep warm.

3. Using the same pan, stir in the red currant jelly, Port wine, and orange juice. Reduce over high heat until thickened, and pour over steaks.

4. Garnish with watercress and serve immediately.   *Serves 2*

North of Devon is the beautiful apple blossom-washed county of Somerset. Cider is one of Somerset's major industries. Apples were first introduced by the Druids. New varieties of crisp cider apples were brought to England later by the Romans, and lastly by the Normans. Today Kingston Black, Dabinett, Sweet Coppin, Brown's Apple, and Yarlington Mill are used to make cider, and the high sugar content of these particular varieties gives West Country cider its deep strong flavor. Alcohol is produced by natural yeasts within the fruit. In farmhouses the cider is often fermented directly after crushing in wooden barrels. Unprocessed cider is called "Scrumpy" and has been since time immemorial. Traditionally, farm laborers' wages were made up in part by gallons of cider. Mulled cider is a delicious warming drink on a bitter night. Around Taunton the heady smell during cider-making season perfumes the whole town, as hundreds of tons of apples grown in the Vale of Taunton and the Quantock Hills are crushed. The season lasts from September when the apples ripen to the end of the year. English hard cider is dry and clear, and it often has an alcohol content as high as 8 percent. Merrydown Cider is so strong that the company now markets it as a wine. Taunton, the principal town in Somerset, is mentioned in the *Anglo-Saxon Chronicle* that dates to A.D. 722.

Cheese making in Somerset's Mendip Hills was recorded as early as the eleventh century. As the soil here is responsible for the taste of Mendip Hill cheeses, rather than the breed of cow producing the milk, it was almost certainly cheese with a cheddar taste that was made so long ago. Cheddar cheese has been popular since Elizabethan times. Possibly the best-known English cheese in the world, you can find cheddar in any country where cheese is eaten. Its taste is not affected by travel, as the cheddaring process requires the curds to be stacked, which forms cheese with a good firm consistency. Strong and rich with a pleasing texture, this fine cheese is also made now in Devon, Cornwall, Avon, and Hereford. As the individual character and taste of cheddar cheese comes from the type of soil the pastures thrive on, this means that wherever this same soil is found cheddar cheese can be produced successfully. Summer is the ideal time to make cheddar when the grass is thick and full of flavor. Unpasteurized milk cheddar, matured for up to twelve months, is made today by the Cheddar Gorge Cheese Company at Cheddar Gorge. As with Cheshire cheese, cheddar's flavor is enhanced by toasting. Wells Stores carry many of the farmhouse cheeses made in Somerset, which include Double Gloucester, Leicester, Coleford

Blue, Somerset Brie, and Caerphilly, as well as cream cheese and cottage cheese. A Ploughman's lunch, famous in pubs throughout Engand, consists of a slab of cheddar, preferably farmhouse, a crusty roll of homebaked bread, and a pickled onion—although sadly the mouth-puckering pickled onion is being replaced lately by a dark dollop of a rather sweet store-bought pickle. A pint of good English ale or beer, fragrant with hops, is the perfect accompaniment to a Ploughman's lunch.

In Taunton on Castle Green is the Castle Hotel, which for two generations has been owned by the Chapman family. The hotel is presently run by Kit Chapman, who is vastly knowledgeable about food. Kit Chapman appears often on television extolling great good food and is presently writing another book all about food and chefs, called *Great British Chefs*. No English hotel has won more praise, more laurels, more consistently, than the Castle Hotel. One of Britain's most celebrated privately owned establishments, the Castle is a perfect place for a weekend of good food and wine, and great comfort in civilized surroundings. Here are thirty-three bedrooms and five suites, each differently decorated and furnished. Tapestries adorn the walls of the wide staircase. The Castle Hotel is intimately connected with Taunton Castle, which is the earliest English fortress by at least two hundred years to have any written historical record. The site of the hotel has probably been that of a castle for over twelve hundred years and once formed part of the ancient Taunton Castle, built (probably of wood) in A.D. 710 by Ina, king of Wessex. This is recorded in the *Anglo-Saxon Chronicle*, the earliest history in any modern language. Taunton and the castle were burnt to the ground by the Danes in 1001, but fifty years later both were flourishing once more, and before 1066 a third castle was in existence. In 1127 a Norman castle is mentioned built by the Bishops of Winchester. In June 1685, the Duke of Monmouth, illegitimate son of Charles II, arrived at Taunton and was proclaimed King on June 20. Later "Monmouth's officers were heard roystering at the Castle Inn." A few months later, the Bloody Assize of Judge Jeffries, who sentenced over five hundred people to death, was held in the great hall of the castle, and many of Monmouth's men were executed in the streets of Taunton. The castle was later dismantled, and part of it became a hostel which for the past three hundred years has been a hotel. Much of the interior of the hotel as it exists today is really medieval. Indeed, some of the bedrooms stand on the old gateway, once the porter's "lodge." In the eighteenth and nineteenth centuries, the hotel provided elaborate facilities for travelers. The Bath coach and the Exeter coach left the hotel every day. The starting of a coach was one of the great events of the day. "You would see the tradesmen at their shop doors, with their aprons and straw hats, taking the greatest interest in changing and putting to. The horn would blow and off they would go, and all was quiet again."

The Somerset County Museum, with archaeological finds including a Roman mosaic, is housed in the castle. Part of the original moat, dating to 1160, is exposed in the Castle Hotel's pretty Norman garden. The secluded west front of the hotel, set in its own courtyard, is totally festooned in possibly the most magnificent wisteria, about 150 years old, in Great Britain. Functions of all kinds are held in the Monmouth Room and the Moat Room. Music weekends are held here three times a year, as are theater weekends in conjunction with the Brewhouse Theatre.

The dining room in the Castle Hotel is L-shaped with dusty pink table coverings topped with crisp white linen tablecloths. Elegant dusty pink and green striped curtains enhance the enormous windows. Outside in the spring these windows are covered with the heavy, nodding wisteria blossoms. The vine has to be trimmed back every autumn to keep the windows clear. The flower-filled dining room is warm and welcoming yet extremely elegant. Philip Vickery's cooking is out of this world. It is deceptively simple—in fact it is deliberately simple—and the ingredients so fresh and true to taste that it ends up being the best food you ever ate. A dish of grilled baby Dover sole with lemon basil butter eaten at dinner on a recent trip was superb, and the handsome, vibrant vegetables were cooked to perfection. Phil Vickery was appointed head chef at the Castle in October 1990, after two spells at Gravetye Manor and a year with Ian McAndrew at Restaurant 74 in Canterbury. Cooking has been a passion with Phil Vickery from an early age. His origins are Lancastrian, and both his mother and grandmother are excellent cooks. He has about six chefs working under him in the kitchen. Most of the ingredients he works with come from suppliers based in Somerset, and he says that the consistent quality and freshness of the local produce at the Castle Hotel makes cooking today a tremendous pleasure. The Castle Hotel has a Michelin Star and is rated among the top forty hotels in Britain.

Phil Vickery's major specialties include Potted game with spiced pears, Baked crab tart, Spiced lamb pie, Salad of braised ham hocks with English mustard and shallots, Honey-glazed collar of bacon with Madeira sauce and creamed potatoes, Beef stew with carrots and savory dumplings, Steamed steak and kidney pudding, Braised shoulder of lamb, Braised duck with lentils and creamed potatoes, and Seared wild salmon with a spice crust and spring onion crème fraîche, to name a few. Some of the wonderful desserts are Diplomat pudding, Bitter chocolate leaves with lime crème fraîche and syrup, Summer pudding, and Almond blancmange with rose petal syrup. Phil Vickery and Kit Chapman have kindly contributed the following two recipes to this book.

Steamed Sea Bass with Saffron Potato and Roast Garlic

1	3–4 lb.	bass, scaled and filleted
20		garlic cloves
20		cherry tomatoes
2	lb.	potatoes—preferably Marfona, Romano, Wilja
10	fl.oz.	whipping cream (1¼ C.)
2	oz.	butter (½ stick)
		a pinch of saffron, dissolved in 1 t. of boiling water
1	sm.	bunch of fresh crisp sorrel
20	fl.oz.	well-flavored fish stock (2½ C.)
		olive oil

1. Remove any bones from the fillet using tweezers, then turn over the fillet and using a sharp knife make four or five small incisions across the skin. This stops the skin curling up when it is steamed. Store fish in refrigerator.

2. Scrape off the outer, dry skins of garlic and trim off the root end. Blanch in boiling salted water until they can be pierced with a knife easily. Set aside.

3. Make a small cross on the top of each tomato, place on a baking sheet, butter, and season well.

4. Wash, peel, and boil the potatoes until you can pass a knife through without any resistance whatsoever—this is very important. Once they are cooked, pass through a ricer or food mill, and add a little of the cream, butter, and saffron liquid. Check the seasoning and keep warm.

5. Pick over the sorrel, remove stalks, and tear into small pieces. Place in a small saucepan with the fish stock and reduce until thick and syrupy; pour in the remaining cream and reduce again until a sauce consistency is reached. Check the seasoning and keep warm.

6. Butter four small pieces of foil and place a bass fillet on each, season well, and steam the fish, making sure the water does not boil too rapidly or you will overcook the delicate flesh. Steam for approximately 4 minutes and keep checking for doneness.

7. Grill the tomatoes, and gently fry the garlic cloves in the olive oil until they are browned all over.

8. To serve, place the creamed potatoes on the plate and decorate the edge with a knife. Place the bass on top, arrange the garlic and tomatoes around the plate, and spoon over a little of the sauce. This dish goes well with a bowl of buttered spinach. *Serves* 4

Baked Egg Custard Tart with Nutmeg Ice Cream

6	egg yolks
1 t.	cornstarch
2 oz.	castor sugar (¼ C.)
16 fl.oz.	whipping cream (2 C.)
	a dash of rose water
1	6-inch sweet pastry flan case, baked blind
	ground nutmeg to taste

Garnish

	nutmeg ice cream
16 fl.oz.	black currant sauce (2 C.)

1. Preheat the oven to 325°F (or gas mark 3). Whisk the egg yolks, cornstarch, and castor sugar together, and pour on the boiling cream. Mix thoroughly and pass through a fine sieve. Stir in the rose water.

2. Pour into the prepared pastry case and sprinkle with a little ground nutmeg. Bake for approximately 40 minutes. Be careful not to cook the custard too quickly, as this will cause it to curdle.

3. Remove from the oven and cool. Place in the refrigerator and chill overnight.

4. Serve with nutmeg ice cream and black currant sauce.

Serves 6

The River Tone runs through the town of Taunton, and along its banks beautiful flowered walks beckon from the city center. Drive out into the open countryside around Taunton and you will see pretty thatched roof cottages and half-timbered pubs. The gently undulating Quantock Hills enfold picturesque villages in wooded valleys. In spring the slopes of the Blackdown Hills are awash with apple blossom. Near Minehead on the northern coast of Somerset is the ancient village of Dunster. Lining its cobbled sidewalks are quaint cottages with sparkling mullioned windows. Notable oddly shaped chimneys may have been a legacy of Flemish immigrants. Near the restored water mill, powered by the River Avill, are very pretty cottages washed in soft pastel colors, their walls draped with clematis and wisteria, surrounded by lovingly tended gardens. On the hill above the village is Dunster Castle. A massive stronghold built by the Normans, it was bought in 1376 by Lady Elizabeth Luttrell, whose family lived in it for six hundred years. It now belongs to the National Trust. The interior is full of lovely furniture and tapestries. Don't miss the seventeenth-century plasterwork ceiling in the dining room and above the staircase. The balustrade here is

carved with huntsmen, hounds, and stags. Walking from room to room the feeling is so strong that the castle is still inhabited that you expect to see an open book or a piece of half-finished embroidery left on a chair. The terraced walks and garden command fine views of Exmoor, the Quantock Hills, and the Bristol Channel. Dunster holds a County Fair in July each year, and on the first Friday and Saturday of December the houses are illuminated by candles, and villagers dance in the streets.

Wine was grown in England since before the Roman invasion. The monks at Glastonbury tended a vine given them by the king long before the Norman conquest in 1066. The Dissolution of the Monasteries also saw the destruction of monastic vineyards, and wine growing stopped until very recently. Happily, English vineyards flourish again all over the south of England, and their numbers continue to increase. The varieties of grapes produce white wines similar to German whites. Somerset white wines have won many awards and competitions. The wine has a strong fruity bouquet yet is light and fresh on the palate. Red wine needs mature vines, situated in an especially sunny spot, to produce an acceptable red. You can visit the vineyards to watch wine production, and at a few of these it is possible to buy a bottle to take with you.

There are ancient remains aplenty in the West Country—hill forts, stone circles, standing stones, and enormous chalk figures cut into the cliffs, as well as Bronze Age villages and huge earthen burial mounds, called barrows. Glastonbury, in Somerset, has several legends; one is that St. Joseph of Arimethea built the first Christian church here. Another says Glastonbury was King Arthur's Isle of Avalon. Glastonbury Abbey, built in the eighth century, was a pilgrimage site and a center of learning in the Middle Ages. Standing now are only the abbot's kitchen and parts of the chapel.

Between Glastonbury and the Mendip Hills to the north is the charming cathedral town of Wells. Wells is England's smallest city yet has one of its most magnificent cathedrals. Ina, king of Wessex from A.D. 688 to 726, started religious traditions in Wells by building a shrine here in the eighth century. The fabulous cathedral we see rose in the late 1100s, after the bishop of Bath decided to move with his retinue to Wells. At one time stone saints, prophets, and angels decorated the west front of the cathedral. Unfortunately, many of these were destroyed by pious seventeenth-century Pilgrims. Wells's astronomical clock crafted in 1392 still runs, and each quarter hour its knights joust above the city. One of the largest and oldest astronomical clocks ever built, it is world famous. Possibly the most resplendent fortified bishop's palace in England lies south of the cathedral. The crenelated fortress, encircled by a moat, sits in broad parklands. Inside are a splendid library, a pillared refectory, a huge banqueting hall, and a chapel. At one time the bishop in residence, his family, and household retainers held private daily services in the chapel. Sadly, as with many of the vast palaces and manors in England, the main part of the structure is now used for offices, and the bishop and his family live in a remodeled wing, swapping splendor for comfort and convenience. From the marketplace a medieval gateway, called the Bishop's Eye, beckons visitors to the palace. Well-fed swans floating on the moat occasionally ring the bell attached to the bridge to announce that they want to be fed. The swans inherited this curious trick from their forebears, who were taught to ring the bell for food by a bishop's daughter in the days of Queen Victoria. Behind the sixteenth-century Crown Hotel is the yard where William Penn (1644–1718), a Quaker, preached the gospel to a throng of citizens and was arrested. He was the founder of the state of Pennsylvania in America.

The county of Dorset to the east of Somerset is Thomas Hardy country. Hardy began writing his novels here in 1860 and used the county town of Dorchester as the setting for his work *The Mayor of Casterbridge*. Other famous Hardy books are *Tess of the d'Urbervilles* and *Jude the Obscure*. The latter book was burned by an irate bishop. Hardy seemed unconcerned, attributing the bishop's action to chagrin "presumably, at not being able to burn me." The County Museum has a Thomas Hardy Memorial room with a reconstruction of his study, and documents relating to his life and work. Near Dorchester is Dorset's Maiden Castle, a massive fortification of ramparts and ditches covering 115 acres. The finest earthwork in the British Isles, it reveals evidence of a Neolithic village dating from 2000 B.C. and an Iron Age village from 300 B.C. The 2,000-year-old Cerne Giant, a Celtic god of fertility and the hunt, still draws childless couples to his Dorsetshire hillside. The giant's outline is cut through the turf to expose the white chalk beneath. Kept neatly clipped by the Cerne Abbas villagers, the 180-foot figure is scrubbed clean every seven years. At the foot of the hill are the remains of a tenth-century Benedictine abbey, which has the guest house, a barn, and a three-story abbot's porch still standing. The village of half-timbered houses and thatched cottages is clustered around the abbey site.

Dorset's blue-veined cheese, Blue Vinney, though famous and sought after, is sometimes made from skimmed milk and can be on the dry side. A farmhouse Blue Vinney made from unpasteurized milk, matured for about three months, is available at Harrods in London as well as at Wells Stores in Streatley and Henley. Many of Dorset's wonderful farmhouse cheeses are sold at shops in Poole. In the Bridport area 56-pound cylinders of cheddar are made.

Dorset Apple Tea Cake

8	oz.	flour (1²⁄₃ C.)
2	t.	baking powder
½	t.	allspice, freshly ground (optional)
		pinch of salt
4	T.	lard
2	oz.	butter (½ stick)
4	oz.	sugar (½ C.)
2	oz.	currants or raisins (⅓ C.) (optional)
½	t.	grated lemon zest
3		apples, peeled, cored, and chopped
3–4	fl.oz.	milk (scant ½ C.)

1. With a wire whisk stir together the flour, baking powder, allspice, and salt.

2. Rub the lard and butter into the flour until crumbly.

3. Lightly stir in the sugar, currants or raisins, lemon zest, and apples. Add enough milk to hold the dough together. Preheat oven to 350°F (or gas mark 4).

4. On a lightly floured board, pat the dough into a circle about ³/₄-inch in thickness, or place the dough into a 9-inch straight-sided well-buttered baking dish, and pat dough to fit dish. Bake for 50–60 minutes. Cool tea cake and serve in wedges, split and buttered.

Serves 6–8

Bath, in the county of Avon, has drawn people to its three therapeutic hot springs for over two thousand years. The Romans built ornate baths over the warm spring waters that well up at a rate of 250,000 gallons per day, beneath what is now the city of Bath. Dedicated to the Roman goddess Minerva and the ancient Celtic god Sul, the Roman settlement was known as Aquae Sulis. Centuries after the Roman legions departed, in 1727, a remarkably well preserved golden-bronzed head of Minerva was unearthed near the baths. This can be seen at the museum next to the Roman baths. The excavation of the baths was completed in the late 1800s. Richard (Beau) Nash (1674–1762)—a very fashionable dandy—brought order and grace to Bath, and the city's heyday revolved around the famous Pump Room and the Assembly Rooms—the social center of Bath. Rebuilt since then, today the Pump Room holds a spacious restaurant where mineral spring waters and Bath buns are served.

Bath buns became famous during Bath's fashionable spa days. The sugar-coated buns, made from a yeast dough enriched with egg yolks and perfumed with saffron, are liberally sprinkled with caraway seeds and candied citrus peel. They are at their most delicious fresh from the oven. Sally Lunn is said to have lived in Bath in the eighteenth century, selling Bath buns and Sally Lunns, the soft cakelike bread that bears her name, in the streets of Bath. Yorkshire tea cakes and Chelsea buns from London are made with a similar dough, studded with currants but minus the egg yolks. Hot cross buns, eaten all over Britain and Ireland on Good Friday, are made from dough enriched with mixed spices. Before baking, a cross is made in the dough either with the back of a knife or by pressing two crossed strips of pastry dough or strips of candied peel into the top of the bun. Most buns and tea cakes are served split, preferably straight from the oven, and slathered with fresh butter. Made to be toasted before eating are crumpets. A yeast batter, poured into special crumpet rings, is placed on a griddle or in a frying pan and cooked on top of the stove. This produces a round flat shape with a lightly browned bottom and a top riddled with holes formed by the escaping steam—expressly to be filled with melting knobs of butter! Crumpets are much loved in Britain, especially on cold winter days. Then the smell of fragrant breads toasting before the fire, and scalding tea steeping in a pot, can really lift the spirits.

Bath is also renowned for its beautiful Royal Crescent, a sweep of houses graced with Ionic columns, built in the honey-colored stone indigenous to the area. The two center houses in the Palladian crescent are occupied by the Royal Crescent Hotel—only two tubs of greenery outside the front door give away the fact that it is not a private house. Famous people who have lived or died in Bath, among them Thomas Gainsborough, Lord Nelson, and John Wesley, the founder of Methodism, have historic plaques attached to their houses, as does Sally Lunn's house. On the other side of town the Priory Hotel, sitting in its own pretty garden, has twenty-one antique-filled rooms and a very good chef, Michael Collom. Recently Chris Chown, an imaginative and excellent chef whose country house Plas Bodegros has won numerous accolades in Wales, has bought The Hole in the Wall restaurant at 16 George Street. The restaurant opened on Easter weekend of 1993 and is doing very well. Bath remains a fashionable place for shoppers who come here from the surrounding counties, as well as for its over 80,000 inhabitants. Shops line the Pulteney Bridge that spans the River Avon.

Nearby Bristol on the mouth of the River Avon has been a thriving port since the tenth century. World War II devastated much of Bristol, but many treasures remain including the Theatre Royal, St. Mary Redcliffe Church built in the 1300s, and many old almshouses, inns, and ancient docks. Bristol's Cathedral on College Green began as the church of a Benedictine monastery in 1140 and became a Cathedral in 1542. Much of the original twelfth-century monastery remains. In 1552 the Society of Merchant Venturers was founded in Bristol to establish trade routes between Britain and America. Expansion of the routes brought wines, cocoa beans, and tobacco to Bristol in exchange for wool and leather. Sailors returning from the West Indies introduced rum and ginger to Bristol's citizens.

Regency crescents and Georgian terraces add elegance to the city. Bristol is known as England's Gateway to the World, and many Englishmen sailed from here to settle in America; Isambard Kingdom Brunel's great steamships, the *Great Western* and the *Great Britain*, were built here. The Clifton suspension bridge he designed was completed five years after his death in 1864. Just over one hundred years later, at the British Aerospace works at Filton, Bristol, the Anglo-French Concorde supersonic passenger aircraft was assembled. In January 1976, traveling at nearly one and three-quarters the speed of sound, it began regular commercial service. Bristol today is a lively university town, its harbor gay with recreational boats, its streets filled with well-stocked stores and a great many arts and craft centers.

Harvey's of Bristol has a restaurant at 12 Denmark Street, called Harveys, recently renovated, that serves well-cooked, flavorful modern British food. The creative chef, Ramon Farthing, has a sure hand with the fresh fish available in this city on the water. Desserts are scrumptious. Vegetarians are also well catered to at Harveys.

Lettonie is a Michelin-starred restaurant on the downs outside Bristol at 9 Druid Hill, Stoke Bishop. Though the restaurant decor is simple, smart dress is preferred, and children are welcome here. Martin Blunos is the chef, and he has a masterly hand with every dish he cooks. Modern and traditional British food—sweetbreads wrapped in bacon, nettle tartlets, and perfectly cooked lamb—is definitely worth a detour.

Wiltshire has a reputation—long held—for its excellent methods in curing bacon. Bacon is a totally British dish made with the carcass of the estimable pig. Although Europeans cure ham—the hind leg—they eat the carcass fresh. Salt was the most common means of curing bacon, a task usually performed by the farmer's wife until the advent of curing shops. Individual recipes for curing ham developed in separate regions of the country—some folk added juniper berries, or apple pulp left over from the cider press—but the common-to-all pickling ingredients were salt, saltpeter to give it a nice rosy color, vinegar, brown sugar or black treacle, and stout—a dark heavy ale. After steeping in this brew for several days, the hams often would be hung in the rafters to dry. If smoked ham was wanted, it was usually suspended in the fireplace chimney. Hams in coastal areas where seaweed was free and plentiful were smoked over seaweed fires. If the farmer had a barn, that was the place hams and bacon were hung to mature; if not, it was back to the kitchen rafters. Ham is eaten often at high tea and for breakfast. Cooking the ham was almost as complicated as curing it had been in the first place. The same kinds of ingredients were used for both, namely brown sugar, treacle or molasses, and beer, with added flavor and nutrition coming from onions and root vegetables that simmered with the meat. Once cooked it was left to steep in this fortifying liquid for at least twelve hours. Wiltshire's prowess at curing ham and bacon became renowned to the point where not only local pigs were cured there but droves of pigs were brought in from abroad, particularly from Ireland. A common sight and sound was the squealing of pigs being herded along the roads between the ports and the curing plants. Having lost a pound or two from all that walking and squealing, they usually needed to be fattened up again for a day or two prior to curing. Chippenham in Wiltshire cures their ham by air-drying and then slathers them with molasses and spices. Chippenham was a thriving trading center for many centuries. Old roads from all four points of the compass converge on Chippenham. Elegant sixteenth-, seventeenth-, and eighteenth-century buildings grace the old town. Here are fine churches, a museum, and an interesting ancient arched bridge. Chippenham still holds a major cattle market.

Stonehenge, situated on Salisbury Plain in Wiltshire, is known all the world over, even though a similar circle in Avebury is both older and larger. Towering mammoth slabs of stone topped with huge lintels form the large circle at Stonehenge, provoking questions about how and why it was built that remain largely unanswered. Now that Druid summer solstice celebrations are held at Stonehenge in June each year, the gigantic circle of stones is associated in some people's minds with Druids, though Stonehenge was erected long before Druids settled in Britain. The original Druids worshipped not in stone circles but in oak forests. Druid priests used golden shears to clip mistletoe from the treetops at their winter festival, believing it would bring them good fortune.

Salisbury Cathedral was started in 1220 and took forty years to build. Only its 404-foot-high spire, the tallest in England, was added later in 1334. The glorious west front has niches filled with statues of the saints and is unchanged since the day it was finished. Unlike most cathedrals that were altered or added to over many centuries, Salisbury Cathedral was conceived and built as a whole and remains unaltered. The wall and medieval gateways erected in the fourteenth century to enclose the cathedral and houses built on the cathedral complex still survive. One of the three original copies of the Magna Carta has been kept in the cathedral library since 1225—except for the years during World War II when it was hidden for safekeeping. The Magna Carta is Salisbury Cathedral's most important treasure.

Castle Combe was voted the prettiest village in England in 1962. The seventeenth-century cottages and houses are built with softly glowing, golden limestone from the Cotswold Hills. The village is situated in a deep valley near Chippenham, and the chattering Bybrook River runs through the village. St. Andrew's Church—also built in Cotswold stone—has been sumptuously decorated by the cloth merchants who made their fortunes in the wool trade. A wool market was held regularly at Castle Combe on the site of the covered market cross that was erected in the fifteenth century. Not long after Castle Combe became known as the prettiest village in England, Hollywood directors and stars descended upon the village in droves, built a harbor and jetty alongside the Bybrook to resemble a seaport, and began filming Dr. *Doolittle*. Visitors, and in the summer there are many, must now leave their cars at the village parking lot at the top of the hill and visit the village on foot—not a bad concession, and good for photographers who do not relish cars in their pictures.

Britain's luxurious country houses, about which so much has been written in fiction and in fact, were not simply country retreats from the bustle of the city from Friday to Monday. In their heyday, the power of the owner was tied to the amount of land surrounding his country house, the number of villages on that land, and even more importantly, the number of people living in these villages. The villagers to a man owed their livelihood and therefore their allegiance to the landowner. If necessary, and in earlier more turbulent days it was indeed necessary, the villagers would fight to protect their lords and masters. When the time came, they could be counted on to vote in local parliamentary elections exactly as they were told to vote by the landowner. The larger the holding, therefore, the more powerful the landowner. Until 1872 voting was public, and villagers were few who would risk eviction by not voting the way his Lordship expected. Often the fortunes of members of Parliament fell within the landowner's jurisdiction. Country estate owners ran their neighborhoods as they chose, and through their connections they had great influence in the running of the country and in foreign affairs.

These opulently furnished, splendid palaces, filled with awesome works of art, well-endowed libraries, galleries, music rooms, and reception rooms, were worth untold amounts of money. Suites of rooms, sumptuously decorated and furnished, were kept in pristine readiness in case the reigning monarch should come to stay. This was not so unlikely as it sounds; journeys were long and stopping at the local coaching inn was unthinkable. Elizabeth I, with her entourage, on more than one occasion was a guest who stayed long enough to bankrupt her hosts. Queen Victoria, who hated ostentation, was instrumental in bringing a little restraint to the usual opulence displayed on her visits by coming down to dinner dressed in a simple velvet dress, unadorned save for a sprig of heather tucked in her hair. The contrast to her hostess, loaded down with the family heirlooms, was marked. In no time fashions changed. Opulence was out and quiet elegance in. Eventually, and no doubt thankfully, the glittering grandeur of earls and lords of earlier times changed to the present-day style of landed gentry, who have taken to comfortable, moth-eaten tweeds and leather-patched old jackets with enthusiasm.

Several hundred country houses were demolished between 1920 and 1955. Others were refurbished as conference centers, schools, hotels, or company headquarters. Even more of these splendid mansions and historic sites have been handed over to the National Trust, usually with their original contents and a considerable endowment to boot. The Trust looks after the upkeep of the property and opens its doors to the public. Sometimes the original owners continue to live privately in part of the house as tenants of the Trust.

Near Frome, Somerset, the Longleat estate, which is actually over the county border in Wiltshire, is owned by Lord Christopher Thynne's father, the sixth Marquess of Bath. At one time the Elizabethan mansion was a thirteenth-century Augustinian priory. The huge house, nestled in a hollow beside a lake, reached by a mile-long driveway, was completed in 1580. The house contains very grand furniture and portraits. The vast library begun by Sir John Thynne, who built the house, contains over thirty thousand volumes. Walls in the state dining room are covered in goat leather tooled in Cordoba around 1620. The dining table's silver centerpiece, weighing nearly sixty-three pounds, was made by Garrard in 1837. Capability Brown, England's most revered gardener, landscaped the grounds in about 1760. In 1949 Longleat was the first privately owned mansion to become a commercial venture devoted solely to attracting visitors to the estate to help defray the astronomical costs and taxes levied on the owners. Today you can rent a boat and cruise the lake, visit a safari park, lose yourself in a maze, ride a miniature railway, and refresh yourself at a restaurant or café.

Britain's six Channel Isles are situated much closer to the coast of France than to England. Nevertheless, they have given their allegiance to England for at least seven hundred years. The two largest islands are Guernsey and Jersey. Holidaymakers from Britain throng here for the mild climate and superb beaches, but also to take advantage of tax-free accommodations and shopping. There is no VAT (Value Added Tax) in the Channel Islands. Jersey's churches and houses have a rosy hue from the pink granite used for building on this island. Some of the islands have remains of German fortifications. During World War II, Britain evacuated most of the islanders for safety, and in their wake the German army moved in. Using slave labor, the Germans built a large underground hospital and other installations. Some of these have been renovated into shops, beach houses, and restaurants. The islands of Alderney, Jersey, and Guernsey give their names to breeds of cattle that are justly famous for the rich milk they provide, which is often made into even richer clotted cream.

Burnt Cream with Raspberries

2		baskets of ripe raspberries
6		egg yolks
3		egg whites
6	oz.	sugar (⅔ C.)
3	T.	cornstarch
16	fl.oz.	light cream (2 C.)
8	fl.oz.	whipping cream (1 C.)
½	t.	vanilla essence
¼	t.	almond essence
6	oz.	castor sugar (⅔ C.)

1. Using a food processor, whisk egg yolks, egg whites, sugar, and cornstarch.

2. Heat the light cream and whipping cream until just beginning to simmer.

3. Pour hot liquid slowly into food processor while motor is running. Pour into a bain-marie, add vanilla and almond essence, and stir over boiling water until custard thickens—about 7 minutes.

4. Chill custard, stirring occasionally, until it is thick but not too firm to pour.

5. Divide raspberries among six 4-inch wide, heatproof ramekins, saving some of the best ones for garnishing. Fill ramekins almost to the rim with custard and return to the refrigerator for at least 6 hours.

6. Preheat broiler. Sprinkle custard with a thick layer of castor sugar and broil until golden brown. Refrigerate until ready to serve and garnish with remaining raspberries.   *Serves* 6

5

THE HEARTLAND

The Heart of England has not only some of the prettiest scenery in the country but also holds one of Britain's best-loved beauty spots, the Cotswold villages. The Cotswold villages are best visited on foot, as many lovely parts of the area are not accessible to motor vehicles. A much better appreciation can be had of the Cotswolds' breathtakingly beautiful villages by walking on the Cotswold Way Paths, an ancient footpath that stretches 95 miles (153 km) to the town of Bath. The Cotswold Hills afford an impressive backdrop to the beautiful medieval villages. Although at the highest level they reach only 1,000 feet (300 meters) above sea level, they are hilly enough to provide magnificent views. For centuries these lovely hills, formed by a 640-square-mile limestone escarpment running diagonally south of the Vale of Evesham, have provided pale, yellow limestone for building. A golden stone of such beauty, it was used to construct Oxford Colleges. The honey-colored stone also lends a warm, golden glow to the cottages and shops lining the village streets. The porous limestone holds water and is responsible too for the glorious green pastures where sheep and cattle have been reared for centuries. Wool from thousands of sheep brought prosperity to the Cotswold villages in Tudor times and again during the Industrial Revolution, when wool was needed to keep pace with cloth-weaving mills. Famous wool churches in some villages, built with the vast fortunes accumulated by the thriving wool merchants, glow both outside and in with rich ornamentation. Particularly impressive are the church and the Woolstaplers Hall in the village of Chipping Campden, where steep tiled roofs and tall gabled houses, as well as the shops on the High Street, are typical of Cotswold architecture. The Hall was built to house a rich wool merchant and his family in the fourteenth century. Many handsome buildings, including the old Almshouses and the Market Hall, have been carefully preserved. The church at Fairford still has its original fifteenth-century stained glass windows. Five miles north of Fairford is Bibury, a perfect jewel of a village on the wide, rippling River Coln. Trout can be seen in its clear, shallow water. Arlington Row holds some of the loveliest gabled cottages, with high-pitched roofs, in this scenic region. These houses were used in the fourteenth century to pen sheep before being converted to cottages to house workers from the Arlington Mill. Grinding stones still crush corn in the mill, which is now a museum, displaying fine Arts and Crafts furniture. William Morris, famous for his textile designs, was greatly attracted to the beauty of Bibury. Another village not to be missed is Broadway—across the county border in Hereford and Worcester. Broadway has beautiful Georgian, Stuart, and Tudor buildings. Here is the ancient church of St. John's and the church of Saints Peter and Paul. The Lygon Arms Hotel, which has sixty-four beautifully appointed bedrooms, is the most elegant hostelry in the vicinity. Broadway has several excellent restaurants. Picturesque place names abound in the Cotswolds—Upper Swell, Lower Swell, Wotton-under Edge, Upper Slaughter and Lower Slaughter, and Moreton-in-Marsh. Moreton-in-Marsh, whose main thoroughfare is part of the old Roman Fosse Way, has dignified stone houses, and a seventeenth-century curfew bell still hanging in the ancient tower. Nearby is Sezincote, a fanciful nineteenth-century Indian-style house, with a vast copper onion dome on the roof, said to have inspired the architect of the Brighton Pavilion. Not surprisingly, a wealthy former colonial from India built the estate. The house is surrounded by an oriental water garden and has a bridge flanked by two Brahman bulls. Burford village, about twenty miles from Cheltenham, has a delightful mix of stone and timber framed houses on streets that wind down to the Windrush River and over a medieval bridge spanning this tributary of the River Thames. Some of the ancient bridges are furrowed to make it easier for counting sheep for toll charges. The Norman church has an elegant fifteenth-century spire, a museum, and many antique shops to browse through.

Between Burford and Cheltenham, near the River Leach that meanders among the wolds, is Northleach, a pretty village of less than 2,000 people. A magnificent and most unusual church here is embellished with a porch that reaches to the second story, and a statue of the Virgin Mary beneath a canopy. On Market Place is Wicken's, Christopher and Joanna Wickens delightful restaurant, specializing in modern English cooking. Parts of the building that houses the restaurant date from 1643. The Wickens have created a warm, intimate setting by using subtle lighting and keeping the exposed stone walls and low ceilings. The majority of their fresh food suppliers are in Gloucestershire, including some excellent, fruit-packed wines from Crickley Windward and Three Choirs—both small modern wineries. Their menu changes often, depending on the seasonal ingredients available each day. Dishes that have received accolades from their clientele are English spiced beef on a bed of homegrown lettuces; Warm lentil and leek terrine with a salsa verde; Salad of barleyed white pudding drizzled with mustard dressing; Roast partridge with sherry gravy, parsnip purée, and red cabbage; Char-grilled Cotswold spring lamb cutlets, pea and mint sauce; Phyllo-wrapped pumpkin parcels on a blackberry coulis; and Semifreddo of chocolate and black cherries. The recipe that Christopher and Joanna Wickens have sent us has ingredients that are gathered from fields and gardens around Northleach.

Cotswold Rabbit in Yogurt

2	small rabbits
10 fl.oz.	natural yogurt (1¼ C.)
1	lemon, zest and juice
1	pinch of ground cumin
1	pinch of turmeric
1	small bunch of fresh thyme
	salt and ground pepper to taste
	toasted pumpkin seeds

1. Cut rabbit meat—using only the tenderest meat from the saddle and legs—into small cubes. Reserve remaining meat for casseroles or pâté.

2. Mix the remaining ingredients thoroughly, except for the pumpkin seeds, and toss the cubed rabbit in the yogurt marinade and leave for at least 4 hours or overnight.

3. Preheat grill, and cook rabbit, turning regularly, until well browned.

4. To serve, sprinkle with toasted pumpkin seeds, and accompany with a fresh green salad or vegetables, with fresh granary bread to mop up the juices.   *Serves* 4

Suggested wine: Three Choirs Seyval/Reichensteiner 1990—a steely dry Gloucestershire wine winner of a Gold Medal at VINEXPO 1993 held in Bordeaux

At Stow-on-the-Wold, the highest town in the Cotswold Hills, sixteenth- and seventeenth-century buildings house antique shops filled with elegant furniture, silver, china, and jewelry. The size of the market square in

this prosperous town attests to the days when important medieval sheep markets were held here. Fairs are still held here four times a year. The square has a market cross and wooden stocks, a reminder of the time when people, for relatively mild offenses, could be clapped into the stocks for days on end, at the mercy of gleeful street urchins.

Bourton-on-the-Water is a village within a village, which has constructed a perfect model of itself where you can walk around on miniature narrow streets among knee-high houses. Perfect tiny trees, lawns, a replica of the church, and the Windrush River with its own wee waterwheel enchant visitors. The village of Winchcombe boasts the romantic ruins of a Benedictine abbey, destroyed during the Dissolution of the Monasteries. Groups of ancient almshouses date to the sixteenth and eighteenth centuries. Nearby is the fifteenth-century Sudeley Castle, set in a lovely Elizabethan garden. The castle was home to Katherine Parr, the sixth wife of Henry VIII, and after his death she married Thomas Seymour at Sudeley Castle. Jane Grey stayed for a time at the castle, and Elizabeth I was a frequent visitor. The castle is open to the public, and on its ancient walls can be seen paintings by Constable, Rubens, and Van Dyke. Here too is a falconry display and a huge collection of antique toys.

Running across the tops of the Cotswold hills en route to Norfolk is the Icknield Way, a prehistoric track that dates to the Bronze Age. A similar prehistoric track, the Ridgeway, crosses the Berkshire Downs. These tracks are thought to have been direct lines between ancient religious sites. Many of the Roman roads that linked Britain's towns during their occupation have been paved over and are in use today. The Roman Watling Street is now the main roadway between London and Holyhead.

To the east are the Chiltern Hills. These hills, unlike the Cotswolds, are chalk-based, very soft, and not suitable for building. The material used for building here is flint. Warwickshire's cottage roofs are thatched, and those of the Cotswolds are generally slate. The style of architecture among the counties in the region is also quite dissimilar. Thatch is more commonly found in Warwickshire because the soil is too soft and chalky to yield good roofing material. Thatch can last for twenty years or more if looked after properly. Fine wire netting covers the finished thatch to guard against high winds and to deter small wildlife from nesting in it. Cottagers swear by thatch, as its insulating properties keep heat in and noise out. Thatch also adds immeasurably to the quaintness of these pretty cottages. Unfortunately, the cost of thatched roofs keeps rising as mechanical harvesting equipment and over-fertilization have undermined the strength of the wheat stalks needed for thatch in this part of England. East Anglians use rushes or reeds, which grow on the Norfolk marshes, for thatching. The land is drained at the beginning of summer to allow the rushes to dry out completely before harvesting. Reed-thatched roofs have four times the life span of wheat stalk roofs. Reeds have been sought after in Britain since before the Middle Ages, both for floor covering in churches and manor houses and for lighting. Tubular rushes, soaked in tallow and fixed with pincers to a block of wood, provided hours of illumination on dark winter evenings. Each household needed thousands of them to last through the winter, and the whole family, including children, spent many autumn hours gathering rushes.

Some of the foremost castles, palaces, manors, country houses, and their spectacular gardens and parklands are located in the Heartland of England. Warwickshire has a splendid castle standing on a cliff overlooking the River Avon. Built on the site of an Anglo-Saxon fort, Warwick castle was given by William the Conqueror to the first earl of Warwick as a reward for loyalty. Its rather grim exterior of lookout towers and battlements belies the beauty of its lavishly furnished state rooms, dominated by the spectacular great hall with its floor of red and white marble from Venice. Oliver Cromwell's death mask is in the great hall, and a helmet belonging to him is in the armory. Gracious drawing rooms and bedrooms, opulently furnished, are filled with interesting objets d'art. The earls of Warwick held their family property for nine hundred years until its upkeep became so prohibitively expensive that it was sold to Madame Tussaud's, the famed London waxwork museum. Now the rooms are rather spookily peopled with wax likenesses of recognizable former members of the nobility.

The medieval walled town of Warwick on the River Avon was almost burned to the ground in 1694. Gabled, half-timbered structures that escaped the inferno stand alongside Queen Anne houses built in the aftermath of the fire. The Lord Leycester hospital, founded by Robert Dudley, Earl of Leicester, in 1571, consists of a number of buildings, dating from the twelfth to the sixteenth centuries, and fortunately these survived the blaze. At different periods the buildings have been used as a guildhall, council chamber, and grammar school. The exterior is of Elizabethan gables and half-timbered walls with a very attractive overhanging gallery. The hospital's chapel, founded in 1123, is above the original medieval West Gate. The East Gate, dating from the 1400s, is at the other end of the High Street. Ancient stocks can be seen in the Market Hall, and grisly dungeons are occasionally open to the public through the courtroom in Shire Hall.

Warwickshire's Vale of Evesham has acres of market gardens justly famous for their delicious vegetables and fruits, particularly plums. In spring the Vale is awash in apple and plum blossom, and in fall roadside stands sell piles of fresh fruit, cider, and homemade preserves. To the west are the lovely valleys of the River Severn and the River Wye, and beyond these the border with Wales and Offa's great dike. In these river valleys are the historic cathedral towns of Gloucester, Worcester, Hereford, and Shrewsbury, as well as two important spa towns, Malvern and Cheltenham. The ruined Tintern Abbey is on the banks of the Wye River. Between the Wye and the Severn Rivers is the Forest of Dean. The "foresters"—inhabitants of the Forest—still have certain rights regarding the collection of fallen tree limbs and the foraging of domestic animals for food. The remains of iron- and coal-working sites are still to be seen at Cinderford, and the rituals of charcoal burners demonstrated at the craft museum. The Dean Forest Railway takes passengers aboard for a four-mile run on the remaining section of track. People come to the Forest to see the gothic castle, the caverns at Clearwell, and the many historic village churches, and also to walk the miles of woodland trails.

The city of Gloucester in the time of the Romans was a fortified port on the Severn River, built for the invasion of Wales. During the Middle Ages the Severn port was eclipsed by the port of Bristol on the Avon. A canal connecting Gloucester with the mouth of the Severn was built in the eighteenth century, and new warehouses sprang up along Gloucester's docks—several of which are still in use. Gloucester today is an inland port and a thriving commercial city, best known for its magnificent cathedral. The cathedral's core is Norman, built between 1089 and 1260, and consecrated on July 15, 1100. It is one of the most beautiful buildings in Britain. The exquisite fan-vaulted cloisters were a model for St. George's Chapel, Windsor. The choir is overlooked by the east window—a memorial to the men who died in the Battle of Crécy in 1346. The largest stained glass window in Britain, it depicts the Coronation of the Virgin.

Gloucestershire had half a million head of sheep in the sixteenth century. The sheep and the large tracts of grazing land were owned by the monasteries who became immensely rich by exporting fleece to the Continent. Henry VIII's Dissolution of the Monasteries, and the confiscation of their land, contributed to the rise in sugar consumption in England. The tons of honey used for sweetening, from acres of beehives kept on monastery grounds before the Dissolution, were no longer produced. Primarily the hives were there to provide the monks with sufficient beeswax to make the thousands of candles needed for their church services. Vast amounts of honey were distributed and sold throughout the country by the monks. People soon demanded sugar, which played a part in the Portuguese decision to use slaves as the labor force on their sugar plantations in Brazil and Africa.

Gloucester's rich, buttery, Double Gloucester is a hard cheese with a deep, mellow flavor. It is much in demand both for the cheese board and for cooking. The name Double Gloucester is thought to have originated because Double Gloucester takes two milkings to make, either the morning and evening milk of the same day, or the evening milk kept overnight and added to the next morning's batch. Single Gloucester is produced from skimmed milk. Gloucester cheeses are said to be wheel-shaped with a hard rind, due to the custom of rolling the cheeses down Cotswold slopes—as the Swiss do Gruyère—possibly because it is a lot easier than carrying them. In any event the custom is observed on Whit Monday—a Bank Holiday—when four cheeses are rolled down Cooper's Hill near Gloucester, followed in hot pursuit by whoever feels up to it. Cheese fairs were numerous and held often in the eighteenth century. The Barton Fair held in Gloucester on Michaelmas was one of the most important. Many of the huge wheels of cheese were bought for export—some going to the United States. Gloucester has been exporting cheese since the eighth century. A Gloucester Cheese-rolling ceremony is held on the first Sunday in May in Randiwick near Stroud.

Mushroom Caps with
Cashews and Double Gloucester Cheese

2	T.	olive oil
4	oz.	shallots, finely minced
1		garlic clove, finely chopped
2		mushroom caps, finely chopped
1	T.	tarragon, chopped
4	T.	cashews, unsalted, chopped
3	oz.	Double Gloucester cheese, (¾ C.) grated
2	T.	fresh bread crumbs
		salt and pepper
8		medium-large mushroom caps
½		lemon, juiced
2	T.	butter

1. Heat the olive oil and in it sauté over medium-high heat the shallots and garlic until soft but not brown.

2. Add the chopped mushrooms and stir to soften for 2 or 3 minutes. Cool mixture.

3. In a medium-sized bowl, toss together the cashews, tarragon, cheese, and bread crumbs, then stir in the shallot mixture and season with salt and pepper. Preheat oven to 350°F (or gas mark 4).

4. If the mixture is too dry to bind together, add a little cream. Brush clean the 8 mushroom caps, remove and discard stems, and dip caps in lemon juice.

5. Mound stuffing in the 8 caps and place them in a single layer in a buttered heat-proof dish. Dot caps with butter and bake for 10–15 minutes. Serve hot. *Yields 8 stuffed mushrooms*

Gloucester is another of the many English counties famed for its gingerbread. Mustard sauce is also associated with Gloucester. Made with a simple white sauce enriched with heavy cream, both the hot, powdered English mustard and the prepared Dijon mustard are added to the sauce, which is then finished with a little distilled white vinegar.

Halibut Steaks with Mustard Dill Sauce

1		halibut steak 1 inch thick
2		shallots, sliced

```
4  fl.oz.   white wine (½ C.)
4  fl.oz.   fish stock (½ C.)
           pinch of salt
1  T.      prepared mustard, Creole or Dijon
2  T.      fresh lemon juice
1  T.      minced dill
3–4  T.    heavy cream
           freshly ground pepper
           dill sprigs for garnish
```

1. Preheat oven to 375°F (or gas mark 5).

2. Wipe halibut steak. Sprinkle shallots in a heat-proof dish just large enough to hold fish. Place fish on shallots, and pour over the white wine and fish stock. Season with salt and cover with buttered wax paper.

3. Bake for 15 minutes or until just cooked through. Remove fish to a serving dish and keep warm. Strain juices from baking dish into a small pan and reduce to 4 tablespoons.

4. Stir in mustard, lemon juice, and dill. Simmer for one minute and then remove from heat and briskly stir in heavy cream. Season with pepper.

5. Pour over fish and serve garnished with dill sprigs.   *Serves* 4

A few miles east of Gloucester is Cheltenham. Cheltenham was once a sleepy Cotswold village that, upon discovery of restorative mineral springs in the eighteenth century, became a fashionable Regency spa. Several more springs were uncovered, prompting the construction of the impressive Pittville Pump Room. When the duke of Wellington declared himself cured of a liver ailment by the spring waters, Cheltenham's reputation was made. Cheltenham today is also renowned for its festivals of music and literature, its Cricket Festival, and the Cheltenham Gold Cup steeplechase.

South of Cheltenham is Cirencester, once a Roman administrative center. Cirencester was second only to London in its crucial importance to the occupation force. Several major Roman roads, including the Fosse Way, intersect here. Cirencester grew rich on the lucrative wool trade when it became the largest wool market in England during the Middle Ages. The small church of St. John the Baptist that the Normans built on the Market Place was enlarged almost to cathedral size by wealthy wool merchants, and today it is the architectural glory of Cirencester.

Berkeley Castle, built in 1153, is astonishingly well preserved, with a Norman keep, splendidly furnished state rooms, filled with tapestries and paintings, a fine great hall, and a dungeon where in 1327 Edward II was murdered with exquisite cruelty by his wife and her lover, Mortimer. In the fullness of time, Edward III had Mortimer executed and his mother, the queen, imprisoned for life.

A village visited by hundreds of tourists every year in the Heart of England is Stratford-upon-Avon, William Shakespeare's birthplace, lying in Warwickshire's beautiful Vale of Evesham. It is fitting that Britain's best-known writer was born in England's Heartland. Shakespeare was educated at Stratford's free grammar school. He married Anne Hathaway in 1582 and taught school for a while. Later he left Stratford for London, where he acted and wrote his major works, both tragedies and comedies. Shakespeare's output was prodigious; as well as thirty-seven plays, he wrote sonnets, poems, and several works dedicated to his patron, the earl of Southampton. He returned to Stratford-upon-Avon for the six years preceding his death in 1616, and he is buried in Stratford Church. On the edge of Stratford, in the village of Shottery, is Anne Hathaway's cottage, where Will is said to have courted Anne. The Shakespeare Theatre Season, featuring world-renowned players, performs from July 27 to August 15.

Fifteen miles southeast of Stratford is the village of Banbury, which dates from Saxon times and is famous for its Cross, built in 1859 to replace the one destroyed by Puritans in 1602. Banbury's medieval church was rebuilt in the eighteenth century and has an unusual copper cupola. Jonathan Swift appropriated the name Gulliver for his book *Gulliver's Travels* from a tombstone that caught his eye in the churchyard. An Oxfordshire specialty, Banbury cakes, baked in the village, are ovals of flaky pastry filled with dried currants, butter, brandy, nutmeg, cinnamon, and bread crumbs. After baking they are brushed with beaten egg white, dusted with castor sugar, and baked for a minute or two longer. The recipe for Banbury cakes differs little from Lancashire's Eccles cakes except for the shape—the latter are round—and for the addition of candied peel to the filling in Eccles cakes. (See Eccles cakes recipe in North Country chapter.) Children in Britain are very familiar with the name Banbury, partly for its delectable cakes but also for the nursery rhyme that most children know by heart.

> Ride a cock-horse to Banbury Cross,
> To see a fine lady upon a white horse;
> With rings on her fingers and bells on her toes,
> She shall have music wherever she goes.

The River Cherwell (pronounced Charwell) links Banbury with the university town of Oxford. Here the Cherwell flows into the River Thames, though during its journey through Oxford, the river is not called the River Thames but the River Isis. Where the two rivers meet rise the spires of the thirty-five independent colleges that make up Oxford University. Built over the years from the thirteenth century to the twentieth century, each college has a different architectural style. A fantastic, all-encompassing view over the spires, domes, and pinnacles of the colleges can be had from Boar's Head Hill. Many of the colleges are built from the same golden-hued stone as the Cotswold villages. Oxford is the second oldest university in Europe—only the Sorbonne is older. Oxford colleges are best explored on foot, or one can join the students and ride a bicycle. Magdalen College has stunning cloisters and behind these is a deer park, called Grove, where the beautiful Water Walks follow streams which meander here and there in this lovely pastoral setting. Facing Magdalen across the High Street is the University Botanic Garden, which blazes with old roses throughout the summer and early autumn.

Oxford's covered market, stretching an entire block between Market and High Streets, once was dedicated solely to the sale of meat and held forty butchers' stalls. Today only eleven are manned by butchers, but these are still enough to make the Oxford market a must for most carnivores. The present wood and iron market was built in 1773 on the same site as the former meat market, mainly with the idea of hiding the gory sight of so much butchered meat and entrails from the public gaze. Sometimes the aisles still have a faintly gruesome look with carcasses—from fully grown deer to small game birds—swinging from hooks above the stalls. The remaining fifty or so stalls feature fresh fruits and vegetables, delectable pastries, handmade pastas, farmhouse cheeses, Loch Fyne oysters and Arbroath smokies from Scotland, as well as jellied eels and kippers. The university is, of course, the market's best customer, as it has been for centuries.

Roast Loin of Pork with Apple Stuffing

4 lb.	boned pork loin
1	lemon, juice and zest
3	cooking apples, peeled and sliced thinly
2	whole cloves
½ t.	freshly ground cloves
	salt and pepper
3 T.	olive oil
20 fl.oz.	cider (2½ C.), preferably pale sparkling cider

1. Rub pork all over with lemon juice.

2. Toss sliced apples with lemon zest, add whole cloves, and layer apples on one inner side of the pork loin. Roll loin into a neat shape; tie with kitchen string and, if necesssary, skewers, to completely enclose apples. Preheat oven to 425°F (or gas mark 7).

3. Rub pork roll with salt, pepper, and ground cloves. Place in a roasting pan, pour oil over meat, and roast for 20 minutes. Lower heat to 325°F (or gas mark 3) and cook for another 1½ to 2 hours, basting with cider frequently during cooking.

4. Remove meat from pan and let rest in a warm place while you make the gravy.

5. Skim fat from pan juices, season juices, and bring to a boil, scraping the pan. Serve hot with the sliced pork roll.   *Serves 6*

The Oxford canal is very popular with boaters. It is probably used by more people than any other. It wends its way for almost eighty miles through the charming villages, woods, and fields of this storybook countryside. During the Industrial Revolution, 4,000 canals carried as much as 35 million tons of cargo each year from industrial cities to the estuaries of the Thames, Severn, Mersey, and Trent. Now, thanks to the Inland Waterways Association, formed after World War II, 2,500 miles of canals have been repaired, mostly by volunteers, and are now navigable. Extremely popular, they afford immense enjoyment and relaxation to hundreds of thousands of holidaymakers, boaters, and fishermen every year.

Some eight miles north of Oxford is Blenheim Palace, built by Sir John Vanburgh in 1704, home to the Dukes of Marlborough and birthplace in 1874 of Winston Churchill. It is the finest example of baroque architecture in England, and the largest. A vast collection of portraits, furniture, paintings, sculpture, and exquisite tapestries can be seen in the state rooms and the library. The park, which covers 2,000 acres, was landscaped by Capability Brown in 1760.

South of Oxford, Dorchester-on-Thame, situated a half-mile from where the Thame flows into the River Thames, was once a cathedral city with a diocese that stretched to Yorkshire. The cathedral was built by the Saxons in 634. Norman conquerors built the Augustinian Dorchester Abbey on the same site as the former cathedral. This same abbey church of St. Peter and St. Paul, with thirteenth- and fourteenth-century additions, is the village church today. A huge oak lych-gate erected in 1852 guards the entrance to the churchyard. Opposite the gate is a fifteenth-century gabled hotel with an overhanging upper story thought to be part of the original abbey buildings. Half-timbered houses and a seventeenth-century coaching inn flank the cobbled High Street, and along the interesting side streets there are several seventeenth-century thatched cottages.

A few miles south of Dorchester is the village of Moulsford-on-Thames. The Beetle and Wedge Hotel on Ferry Road, right on the River Thames, has a cozy beamed-ceiling Boathouse for winter dining, and in the summer, weather permitting, you can elect to eat in the Water Garden. Richard Smith says, "There is still an enormous job to be done in improving the quality and supply of ingredients and encouraging producers to produce for the specialist markets rather than producing for the supermarket trade." Richard Smith says his produce comes from two suppliers—one who buys locally whenever possible, and the other who buys at open markets in London, which means the produce comes from all over the world. Meats are the best that are available—this could be Scottish beef, Devon lamb, Dutch veal, and occasionally English veal. Wonderful fish, crabs, and scallops come directly from Cornwall and also from the south coast. Richard's idea of a really enjoyable meal would be scallops on a bed of glazed vegetables, half-pheasant with cream, cognac, and button onions served with rösti (a Swiss potato cake) and spinach, followed by an apple suet pudding with real custard. His menu features Artichoke heart with wild mushrooms and Hollandaise; Sautéed squid, scallops, black noodles, and shellfish sauce; Irish oysters; Brown shrimp with garlic mayonnaise; Sautéed foie gras with caramelized onions and Gewürztraminer; Suprème of duck with apples and Calvados; Grilled fillet of beef, wild mushrooms, and armagnac; Fillet of sea bass with asparagus tips and sweet red pepper sauce; and Red mullet with fennel and herb butter sauce. Desserts include raspberry cheesecake; Hot Cointreau soufflé with raspberry sauce; Hot apple and raspberry crumble with cream and ice cream; and farmhouse cheese. Richard Smith has given us permission to include the following recipes from the the Beetle and Wedge Hotel.

Ratatouille with Parmesan Shavings and Pine Nuts

2		red bell peppers
1		green bell pepper
2		medium large onions
3		zucchini
2		medium eggplants
5	fl.oz.	olive oil (½ C. + 2 T.)
1–2		garlic cloves, minced
		black pepper, freshly ground, to taste
		salt
16–20	fl.oz.	tomatoes (2–2½ C.), peeled, seeded, and roughly diced
2	T.	basil chopped

Garnish

Parmesan curls
pine nuts, sautéed in olive oil

1. Seed and core the peppers, cut into ½-inch dice the peppers, onions, zucchini, and eggplants.
2. Pour the olive oil into a heavy-bottomed large saucepan and heat to smoking. Add the onion and stir with a wooden spoon just until it begins to cook.
3. Add the garlic and the remaining vegetables, except for the tomatoes, sprinkle with pepper and a little salt, and cook on the highest possible heat for 5–10 minutes or until vegetables are just cooked.
4. Add the tomatoes, cook for a further minute or two, and remove pan from heat. Stir in basil.
5. Shave curls from a block of Parmesan cheese.
6. Serve ratatouille garnished with cheese curls and pine nuts.

Serves 4–6

Poached Chicken with Creamy Mashed Potatoes

3–4	lb.	chicken, preferably free-range
24	sm.	shallots
3	T.	garlic chopped
		white wine or chicken stock

Any of the assorted cooked vegetables to serve with chicken

onions or shallots
fennel
leeks
small baby carrots
celeriac, either as main vegetable or mixed with others

Potatoes

4		large, floury potatoes
6	T.	butter
5	fl.oz.	hot milk (½ C. + 2 T.)
		salt and pepper, to taste

1. Remove skin and joints that are not required from chicken.
2. Place chicken in large heavy-bottomed pan and add shallots and garlic. Cover with a mixture of water and white wine, or water and chicken stock, or water, chicken stock, and white wine.

3. Cover pan and bring slowly to a boil. Simmer for one hour. Meanwhile prepare and steam or boil the vegetables to accompany chicken.

4. Peel and rinse potatoes, then cut each potato into four pieces.

5. Boil until completely cooked. Drain, and if still wet put them in the oven for a few seconds.

6. Whisk in butter and hot milk. Season lightly—potatoes should taste creamy, with a buttery aftertaste. Serve immediately.

Serves 4

To the west is the remarkable village of Uffington, near Faringdon, Oxfordshire, where the outline of a huge animal, resembling a horse, was cut into the chalk downs below the Iron Age battlements of Uffington Castle. Estimates date the White Horse from the first century B.C., and it may be a cult figure connected with Epona, Celtic goddess of the horse. The White Horse is 400 feet (122 meters) across, and nobody knows for sure who cut it or when. Except for one or two newer houses, the village of Uffington is built entirely of chalk. The village church of St. Mary dates to the thirteenth century. Dragon Hill, just below the White Horse, is believed to be where St. George—the patron saint of England—slew the Dragon.

To the east of Oxfordshire is Buckinghamshire, famed for its Aylesbury ducklings. Buckingham, on the River Ouse, was the shire town until a fire almost completely destroyed it in the eighteenth century. Buckingham's oldest building now is the chantry chapel on Market Hill, which was rebuilt in 1475 and restored again in 1875. It is still in use for town meetings. Catherine of Aragon, in 1514, and Charles I both stayed at Castle House nearby. Two miles from Buckingham is Stowe House, once the country house of the dukes of Buckingham and Chandos and now a public school. The splendid gardens were looked after by the head gardener, Capability Brown, before he became the foremost gardener and landscape designer in the history of England.

After the narrow escape from the fire, the county government repaired to the town of Aylesbury, about fifty miles southeast of Banbury. Aylesbury ducklings are acknowledged by chefs from all over Britain as being exceptionally well flavored. Shaun Hill, in his book *Shaun Hill's Gidleigh Park Cookery Book*, says, "Never confuse the Aylesbury or Chinese variety of ducks with Barbary or other lean ducks. The native variety has delicious skin, a small but tender layer of pale meat, and quite a lot of fat. It suits roasting and steaming." The following Aylesbury duckling recipe from his book is reprinted here with permission from Shaun Hill.

Aylesbury Duckling, Steamed and Crisp-fried, and Served with Salad

1 × 6 lb.   Aylesbury duckling
         salt and freshly ground black pepper
4 T.   peanut oil

Cassis dressing

1 T.   white wine vinegar
1 t.   crème de Cassis
5 T.   olive oil
     salt and pepper

Salad

1 frisée lettuce
4 small bunches corn salad (mâche)
1 lollo rosso
4 spring onions

The duck

1. Take out the wishbone. This forms an arch around the base of the bird's neck, which you can feel if you run your finger around it. Remove it by lifting back the flap of neck skin to expose the meat and then cutting the bone out. It is easier to dismantle the duck after steaming if the wishbone it out.

2. Mill plenty of salt and black pepper over the bird, wrap in foil, and steam for 1½ hours. Use a steamer or a large covered saucepan with a little water in the bottom, in which case you will need to rest the duck on a grid to keep it clear of the water. You will also have to check the water level periodically lest it run dry.

3. Unwrap the foil and pour the clear cooking juices into a container for use in the dressing.

The cassis dressing

4. Mix the vinegar, Cassis, and a tablespoon of the duck's cooking juices (keep the rest of this—it freezes well and is useful for sauces or soup). Whisk in the olive oil, and season with salt and pepper.

The sweetness of the Cassis should be "balanced" by the vinegar. The cooking juices from the duck dilute the dressing so that it remains an emulsion - not separating back into components.

The salad

    5. Wash the lettuces in plenty of cold water. Shake dry and separate into leaves. Trim the spring onions.

To complete

    6. Cut the duck into four joints: two legs and thighs and two breasts. Try not to tear the skin, which will be quite fragile.

    7. Heat the peanut oil in a frying pan. Fry the duck pieces skin side down until they are crisp and brown. Lift them onto kitchen paper to drain for a few seconds.

    8. Place the salads around the edges of four cold plates, dipping each leaf briefly into a saucer of the dressing. Leftover dressing can be poured into the center of each plate. Season the salad with a little salt, and put a piece of crisp hot duck into the middle of it. Serve straightaway—the salad will wilt if you wait. *Serves* 4

Aylesbury has many well-preserved historic areas and several ancient inns, such as the King's Head in the Market Square, whose parlor window contains fragments of fifteenth-century glass depicting the coat of arms of Henry VI and his wife Margaret of Anjou. The twice weekly livestock market has been held since 1204 in the broad cobblestoned square overlooked by a centrally placed Victorian Gothic clock tower. St. Mary's Church also dates from the thirteenth century. The wife and three children of Sir Henry Lee, an ancestor of Robert E. Lee, the American Civil War general, are commemorated by an alabaster monument in the church with an inscription asking that crimson flowers be placed on Lady Lee's tomb. Her wish continues to be fulfilled, as it has since her death in 1584.

    The chalky soil of this region is ideal for growing beech, and magnificent stands of these trees cloak the Chiltern Hills that cut across the southeast regions of Buckinghamshire, Oxfordshire, and Hertfordshire. High Wycombe at the foot of the Chiltern Hills is a charming town with an eighteenth-century Guildhall. It also has an interesting Chair Museum commemorating the town's most notable industry. Nearby is Hughenden Manor, built in the eighteenth century, and home to Benjamin Disraeli, Queen Victoria's prime minister. West Wycombe is three miles northwest of High Wycombe. It has exceptional houses dating from the fifteenth to the eigthteenth centuries. West Wycombe Park is a Palladian mansion with painted ceiling, mirrors, fine furniture, and paintings. The beautifully landscaped grounds are embellished with classical temples.

    Northeast of High Wycombe is Chalfont St. Giles, where the blind poet Milton lived for a while in 1665 to escape the Great Plague. The houses grouped around the village green are half-timbered and the church is reached through an arch set in a row of gabled houses built in the sixteenth century. The village has great charm. Nearby is Jordans where William Penn was buried in the cemetery of the Quaker Meetinghouse.

Bedfordshire's best-known regional food—and many shires seem to have a baked goody of one kind or another—are whigs. These plain yeast buns are also made at Hawkshead, Cumbria. Slightly richer whigs are made in Bath. To make them, take a good bit of butter, rub it into flour, season with salt, and mix with dissolved yeast and warm cream. After the dough has risen, nutmeg, mace, cloves, caraway seeds, and sugar are kneaded in and the dough rolled out into flat cakes. A cross-shaped indentation is cut into the top, for ease in dividing the cakes, before baking in a hot oven.

Each shire has a regional specialty of one kind or another. In Bedford it is pears, or wardens as they are still sometimes called, that enterprising hawkers used to sell on Bedfordshire streets already poached in a sweet red wine sauce—an early prepared food.

Poached Pears in Red Sweet Wine

6	heavy pears
20 fl.oz.	red wine (2½ C.)
4	whole cloves
2	allspice berries
1-inch	stick of cinnamon (do not use ground cinnamon)
10 oz.	sugar (1¼ C.)
12 fl.oz.	heavy cream (1½ C.), optional

1. Peel pears and core through the blossom end so that pears can be stood upright in a serving dish.

2. In a pan big enough to hold pears in one layer, combine wine, cloves, allspice berries, cinnamon, and sugar. Add 8 fluid ounces of water and bring to a boil. Add pears, and if there is not sufficient liquid to barely cover pears add more water. Simmer pears, basting, for 15 minutes. Turn pears over and continue to cook for another 10 minutes.

3. Remove pears and stand them upright in a deep serving dish.

4. Boil wine mixture until reduced to a syrupy consistency. Pour over pears and serve warm with cream, if desired.   *Serves 6*

Of prime importance to Bedfordshire's acres of market gardens is its fertile black soil, growing succulent vegetables and fruits, as well as verdant pastures that nourish Bedfordshire's flocks of sheep. Harvest festivals and fairs all over Britain and Ireland are still held today without fail. At the harvest festival church service the altar is a cornucopia of autumnal fruits, vegetables, and flowers. The most pleasing sight is the upright sheaf of golden wheat that glows when the sun touches it. Fairs with their stalls, games, competitions, and general hilarity are great fun to attend.

Fennel, Carrots, and Snow Peas in Lemon Sauce

3	medium-sized fennel bulbs
1 T.	minced fennel leaves
1 lb.	snow peas (3 C.)
12 fl.oz.	vegetable broth (1½ C.)
	pinch of sugar
¼ t.	salt
1 lb.	baby carrots (3 C.), cut into 2-inch lengths
2 lg.	eggs
	juice of one lemon
	freshly ground black pepper, to taste

1. Trim and quarter fennel bulbs and mince a tablespoon of tender leaves.

2. Cook the fennel quarters, covered, in a little boiling water until tender—about 10 minutes. For the last 20 seconds of cooking time, drop in the snow peas.

3. In a large saucepan, bring the vegetable broth to a boil, add the sugar, salt, and carrots, and simmer, covered, until barely tender—about 7 minutes.

4. Remove vegetables with a slotted spoon to serving dish and keep warm.

5. Strain broth and reduce to one cup. Set aside.

6. Beat eggs for one minute, and while continuing to beat add lemon juice a little at a time. Beat in broth and cook in the top of a double boiler over simmering water for 2 or 3 minutes, stirring until slightly thickened. Add black pepper to taste.

7. Add minced fennel leaves and pour over vegetables. Serve at once. *Serves 6*

East of Bedfordshire's Chiltern Hills is Luton Hoo, built in 1767 for the third Earl of Bute by Robert Adam and rebuilt after a terrible fire in 1843. It is renowned for its elegant exterior and its magnificent art collection, many treasures, and mementoes of the Russian Royal Family that include Fabergé jewels. Capability Brown designed the 1,500-acre parklands.

John Bunyan, author among other works of *The Pilgrim's Progress*, was born in Bedfordshire, near Elstow, in 1628. A Nonconformist preacher, he was later imprisoned in Bedford. Buried in London, he is commemorated in Westminster Abbey.

Six miles from the old market town of Leighton Buzzard, which prospered because of its proximity to the Grand Union Canal, is the Victorian village of Woburn. The original Woburn Abbey was destroyed during the Dissolution. The present magnificent palace, built by Henry Flitcroft and Inigo Jones in the 1700s, has been the home of the dukes of Bedford for three hundred years. Fourteen state apartments include a room occupied by Charles I and Queen Henrietta Maria in 1636. The art collection is fabulous, and the gardens are lovely. Events are organized on a grand scale in the 3,000-acre deer park, where you will find a model village, an antique center, restaurants, and a pottery. The Woburn Wild Animal Kingdom and Leisure Park has rhino, giraffes, lions, tigers, and bears.

Ampthill, Bedfordshire, has many fine extensively restored Georgian houses in the town center. A cross in Ampthill Park marks the site of the fifteenth-century castle where Henry VIII sent his wife, Catherine of Aragon, to await the divorce that caused the break with Rome.

Berkhamsted, thirteen miles east of Aylesbury, is associated with many venerable historic figures and several modern-day esteemed writers. In 1066 William the Conqueror was offered the throne of England at Berkhamstead by the Saxon leaders he had beaten in battle. True to form,

William ordered the construction of a mighty castle nearby in the Chiltern Valley that was well liked by the king and his courtiers and continued to be so over many centuries. Supplying the needs of the castle turned the village into a busy thriving market town. Edward III's son, the Black Prince, who predeceased his father following an infection he picked up in battle, came to stay in the castle in the valley whenever he could. Today the most important large buildings in Berkhamsted on Castle Street are the Berkhamsted School, which has Victorian additions over a Tudor foundation, and the parish Church of St. Peter, which has a stained glass window in memoriam to the poet and hymn writer William Cowper, born here at the Old Rectory in 1731. Graham Greene, whose father was headmaster of Berkhamsted School, also lived in this 900-year-old town. Today Berkhamsted, bisected by a wide Roman road called Akeman Street, still holds a market on the side of this Roman road.

St. Albans, Hertfordshire, one of the largest Roman towns in Britain, was called Verulamium by the Romans. Surviving from Roman times is a heating system for a suite of baths in Verulamium Park, as well as mosaics, coins, jewelry, and household objects. The Roman theater here is the only one discovered so far to have a stage rather than an amphitheater. A story attached to the town's name tells of a Roman soldier, called Alban, who was executed here for hiding a Christian priest. Alban became the first Christian martyr, and after the Romans left, the Saxons built an abbey on the execution site. Over the intervening centuries, the abbey was rebuilt by the Normans. However, during Henry VIII's Dissolution of the Monasteries all but the Abbey Church and a gatehouse were destroyed. The gatehouse, once the main entryway to the monastery, is an impressive size and until 1868 served as the town jail. St. Michael's Church has its original Saxon nave, and the clock tower that soars to 77 feet (23.5 meters) has a curfew bell that dates to 1335. Medieval streets, and the oldest inhabited licensed medieval house in England, which was once a fishing lodge for the monks, are here.

Nine miles north of St. Albans in Ayot St. Lawrence is the house where George Bernard Shaw lived and wrote. His desk is undisturbed and in the hall is the rather odd machine on which the playwright exercised. Also in Hertfordshire is Hatfield House, a magnificent Jacobean mansion, originally built for Henry VIII in 1497 to house his children. Here are many mementos of Queen Elizabeth I, who spent a great deal of her childhood at Hatfield. The residence passed to Robert Cecil, first earl of Salisbury, and the major portion of the house was rebuilt. A little of the original residence remains, however, and the furnishings are wonderful to see.

Burnham Beeches, a 600-acre forested region of Buckinghamshire, attracts walkers from all over Britain. Beeches predominate, but oak, birch, yew, maple, and willow grow here too. Shiny dark beech leaves turn a rich, reddish brown in the fall, and in the spring rhododendrons display frothy pink, white, and purple blooms and the willows show their first shoots of tender green. Charcoal burners once inhabited these woods. Constant cropping of the trees to fuel the burners stunted their growth, and now the more wizened elderly specimens have taken on weird and wonderful shapes. Nearby is Stoke Poges, the large village where Thomas Gray often came to visit his mother, who lived here with her sister. Gray finished his poem "Elegy in a Country Churchyard" at Stoke Poges in 1750. The poem was inspired by the death of a friend he had made at Eton College. Gray wrote the lines inscribed on his mother's tombstone and is buried with her.

Olney, in Buckinghamshire, eleven miles from the border withNorthampton, has been renowned for three reasons, its lace making, its pancake race, and for William Cowper, the poet, who between 1767 and 1786 wrote several poems and the 300 Olney Hymns for which he is famous. Cowper and the eighteenth-century slave trader turned pastor John Newton collaborated on the Hymns. The Georgian house where he lived and wrote is now the Cowper and Newton Museum. Eighteenth-century bow front windows, a big fourteenth-century church, and handsome Georgian doorways along the wide High Street add dignity to this charming riverside town. The Market Place has a three-sided green and a memorial to the men lost in the two World Wars. Antique shops and coffeehouses line Market Place. From here to the church a pancake race is held every Shrove Tuesday. The prize for winning the race, while successfully tossing and catching a pancake from a frying pan, is a prayer book and a kiss from the sexton. The race has been held since 1445.

Shrove Tuesday Pancakes

1	lg.	egg
2½	oz.	flour (½ C.)
		pinch of salt
		pinch of sugar
4	fl.oz.	milk (½ C.)
		butter or oil for frying
		juice of one large lemon
2	oz.	fine sugar (¼ C.)

1. Beat the egg until frothy with an electric beater; continuing to beat, add the flour, salt, and sugar bit by bit.
2. When the mixture is smooth, slowly pour in the milk.

3. Heat a little butter or oil in a 6-inch frying pan until quite hot and pour in enough batter to thinly cover the pan. As soon as the top looks set, flip pancake over and brown other side.

4. Serve piping hot with a squirt of lemon and a sprinkling of fine sugar. Traditionally these are rolled up and dusted with more sugar.

Yields 6 pancakes

Reading, on the River Kennet, had twenty-eight households at the time of the Domesday Book. In 1121 Henry I built first a great abbey in Reading and then a nearby castle. The wool trade helped establish Reading as an important county town with many fine churches. The thirteenth-century gatehouse is all that remains of the abbey. Jane Austen attended school for a while in the gatehouse here, and Oscar Wilde was locked up for two years in the Old Prison down by the river. Reading is known for its biscuit making, brewing, and the production of seeds for horticulture. Judge Geoffrey Goldsmith, who lives in Reading, said that today the lovely limestone from the Cotswold Hills is being used to repair St. George's Hall, Windsor Castle, after the distastrous fire that damaged it so badly in 1993. The heavy limestone blocks are brought as far as Reading on the ancient narrow waterway—the Kennet and Avon canal—just as most goods traveled before the advent of the railway. From Reading the limestone is taken by road to Windsor Castle.

Nearby Mapledurham, an unspoiled delightful village, has a working mill, and many ancient houses. Mapledurham House, the charming home of the Blount family since 1588, has a large park that runs down to the banks of the River Thames.

Marlow, on the River Thames, is set between a foaming weir and wooded hills. A major attraction is the splendid suspension bridge spanning the river here. In town, the Old Parsonage and adjoining Deanery were once part of a fine fourteenth-century house that boasts beautifully paneled rooms and decorative windows. From 1817 to 1818 the poet Shelley lived and wrote *The Revolt of Islam* at Marlow, while his wife, Mary Wollstonecraft, wrote *Frankenstein*. T. S. Eliot also made Marlow his home for a period following World War I. At Marlow, situated in a glorious location by Marlow Bridge, is the Compleat Angler Hotel, Marlow Bridge, Bisham Road. Izaak Walton wrote his perennially popular book on fishing at Marlow. The hotel has forty-six well-designed, comfortable bedrooms. Each one is named for a particular trout fly. Dinner is served by candlelight, and the dining room has a wonderful view down the river. Food is marvelous as one would expect from a first-class four-star hotel.

Six miles from Marlow at Bray is the Waterside Inn on Ferry Road. The superb French restaurant here is under the direction of Michel Roux—a superb chef who has trained a raft of young chefs who have gone on to perpetuate his magic in many of Britain's finest establishments. The cooking is classical French, using the finest and freshest ingredients, but with sauces that are lighter than their French counterparts. The Waterside Inn has six bedrooms and a lovely small garden by the river.

In Berkshire's village of Streatley, on the Thames near the town of Goring, is the cheese shop of Patrick Rance, a pioneer in searching out and promoting farmhouse cheeses all across the country. He rekindled the public's interest and appreciation of these superb cheeses made from cow's, sheep's, and goat's milk. At last count, in his shop Patrick Rance was carrying over two hundred of these dewy fresh cheeses, which he refuses to sell until the customer has tasted a sliver of cheese to be sure that it is exactly right for his needs. The shop is now run by his son, Hugh Rance.

Windsor Castle, a great Norman fortress, is a favorite residence of Queen Elizabeth and Prince Philip. Situated on the River Thames in Berkshire, the park surrounding Windsor Castle is the site of the Royal Windsor Horse Show held each year. Prince Philip drives his own horse and carriage in the International Driving Grand Prix; Prince Charles played yearly for the Royal Windsor Polo Cup; and Princess Anne, the Princess Royal, has ridden in the Olympics. Windsor became a royal residence in the time of Henry I, who reigned from 1100 to 1135. Henry II began building the Round Tower in 1165, and the building was continued under successive monarchs. The walls of Windsor Castle enclose almost thirteen acres of land today. St. George's Chapel, built mainly by Edward IV, is one of the finest examples of church building of its period. The state apartments, which can be closed at short notice as they are used frequently by the royal family, contain a veritable treasure-house of paintings, furnishings, arms and armor, china and glass, tapestries, and royal trappings. Queen Mary's dollhouse, given her by the nation in 1923, is displayed here. It is charming, with miniature books, some handwritten by their authors, and tiny bottles of wine in the cellars, and all the miniaturized plumbing and lighting systems actually work. The Doll's House is a delight.

For racing enthusiasts, Royal Ascot is the focal point of the season. Held in mid-June, the four-day race meet is attended by the royal family, every noble who is able, and non-nobles who can afford it. Each day of the event, the open-topped royal carriages, drawn by four horses, roll down the course, and the royal family and their guests enter the glassed-in royal box in the Royal Enclosure, around which stroll the formally dressed ticket holders. It is necessary to apply for tickets weeks before the race meet. For women dresses and hats are de rigueur, and for men morning suits and top hats. Queen Elizabeth, a racing devotée and owner of several racehorses, attends Ascot each year looking very happy and enthusiastic as she does at the Grand National, Newmarket, and the world-famous Derby that is held in early June on Epsom Downs in Surrey.

Across Windsor Bridge is Eton College, founded by Henry VI in 1440. Eton is the most renowned boys' public school in England, and during school holidays it is possible to visit the exquisite chapel and the museum of Eton life.

In July at Henley-on-Thames is held the Royal Henley regatta where, over a four-day period, oarsmen from all over the world compete on the river. People from all strata of society throng the banks, some equipped with elegant picnic baskets; the band of the Grenadier Guards plays rousing music; and launches or rowing boats full of spectators, sporting silk parasols and usually with a champagne glass in hand, get as close as they can to the action.

Champagne Cocktail

		rind of ½ lemon; use zester for attractive strips
1		sugar lump
2		dashes of bitters
6	fl.oz.	chilled champagne (⅔ C.)

1. Stir all ingredients gently together.
2. Serve in chilled glass.   *Serves one*

6

THE MIDLANDS

The once predominantly green counties that make up the Midlands in the central part of England became the pulsing heart of the Industrial Revolution, and by 1850 they were coated with heavy soot. Coal smoke from iron smelting works, mills, and potteries blackened the air. Vast numbers of potteries worked day and night, among them Wedgwood, Royal Doulton, and Spode, to make lovely dinner services and graceful ceramic figurines prized by collectors the world over. The coal industry fouled the rivers, scarred the surrounding hills, and forced children as young as ten years of age to work in the mines. The Industrial Revolution caused immense damage to the area around Coventry, Stoke-on-Trent, Nottingham, Corby, Wolverhampton, Birmingham, and other cities. England was the first country in the world to begin industrializing and learned from bitter experience the downside of her booming industries.

Deforestation of Britain's wooded hills was caused by sheep farmers who cleared the woods, overgrazed the land, and moved on to repeat the devastation in new pastures. Soon the huge loads of timber needed to build props to shore up the mines came predominately from Scandinavian forests. The blockade of Britain during the First World War almost paralyzed British industry. This painful lesson made reforestation a priority. As young, healthy trees grew in newly green pastures, small towns and villages came back to the once bare hills. Today Britain provides timber for exportation. Regeneration is not feasible in mountainous areas cleared as long ago as the Roman era, where soil is shallow. The short growing season and frequent rain showers, coupled with poor drainage, cause plant life to rot in the wet, acidic soil, forming peat bogs.

170

The notorious "Black Country" spewed industrial smoke from its factories for years on end, but it is now energetically refurbishing its land and its image. Electricity drives the automobile plants in Cheshire and chocolate factories in Birmingham today, and it has become England's second largest city. A. E. Housman was born at Bromsgrove, near Birmingham, and went to school there. One of the pleasures of a visit to Birmingham is the wealth of Victorian pubs in the city where Brummies, as they call themselves, can congregate in the evening. Beautifully patterned glass screens separate the public bar from the saloon bar in older pubs and is repeated in the heavy glass entrance doors. The word Brummy comes from a rather derogatory reference, "Brummagen," used to describe the city when cheap and shoddy goods were manufactured in the 1800s. The counties surrounding the industrial areas are frequently an oasis of green. Birmingham is ringed by eight pastoral counties where small market towns with impressive churches, villages of golden limestone, and lively coastal resorts offer respite from the great urban centers. Wealthy landowners in vast ancestral homes contrive to keep the countryside in the region green and leafy. Close by are Hardwick Hall, designed for Bess of Hardwick in the sixteenth century; Kedleston Hall, a Palladian mansion set in a classical park built for Baron Scarsdale, whose family has occupied this house since the twelfth century; and Longshaw, with sixteen hundred acres of moors and woodland. Many of these palatial estates, faced with the astronomical costs entailed in their upkeep, welcome hundreds of paying visitors each summer to help defray their expenses.

A recreational benefit from the Industrial Revolution is mile upon mile of canals and navigable waterways built to transport goods. Their original use replaced by the railways, they suffered from years of neglect but now have been restored and offer opportunities for a growing number of city dwellers to ply hundreds of miles of waterways in sailboats or leisurely cabin cruisers. These colorful narrow boats travel no faster than four miles an hour. Birmingham alone has more miles of canals within its city limits than Venice. Dignified Victorian public buildings, museums, and art collections, second only to London, are also legacies of the Industrial Revolution. Urban renewal in many city centers has created a tree-lined oasis of small restaurants and shops.

Near Wolverhampton in the West Midlands, and open to visitors, are two beautiful, historic manor houses, Moseley Old Hall and Wightwick Manor. The former, an Elizabethan house laced with secret passages and priest holes, was a refuge for Charles I after his defeat at the Battle of Worcester. The garden is a delight—planted only with flowers and shrubs that grew in Elizabethan England. Wightwick Manor, a Jacobean-style manor house built in 1887, is also set in beautifully tended gardens. The interior of the manor has glowing stained glass windows, pre-Raphelite works of art, and William Morris textiles and tapestries.

The city of Worcester is known for its fine china and its exquisite glove making, a thriving industry here since the thirteenth century. Worcester's enormous cathedral, built beside the River Severn, soars above the city. Originally founded as a Saxon monastery in 983 to house the relics of saints, Henry VII added an intricately carved chapel in 1504 as a memorial to his son Arthur, who died at Ludlow. The cathedral is also the burial place of King John. Every third year, Europe's oldest music festival, the Three Choirs Festival, is held in a cathedral setting. The center of the city has many medieval buildings. Perhaps Worcestershire Sauce is Worcester's most famous product. Its name is forever commemorated on bottles of Lee and Perrin's sauce, familiar to cooks for flavoring practically any savory dish, not to mention the famed Bloody Mary. Two of the sauce's more potent ingredients—anchovies and tamarind—are used extensively as flavorings in Asian cooking. The site of the first Lee and Perrins sauce factory is on the Midland Road. The Dyson Perrins Museum contains the finest collection of Worcester porcelain in the world. Boat excursions on the river and along the Worcester-Birmingham canal glide through some very pretty countryside. Sir Edward Elgar (1857–1934) was born at Broadheath, four miles from Worcester. His house, now a museum, contains musical scores, personal memorabilia, and photographs.

Sixteen miles southeast of Worcester on the River Avon is Evesham, named for Eove, a young man who saw a vision of the Virgin Mary. An abbey was built to commemorate his religious experience in 714. Simon de Montfort, a heroic soldier who was killed at the Battle of Evesham in 1265, is interred in the abbey. The bell tower dates from 1533, and the old abbey gardens with twin churches are worth a visit. Here too is a well-run, very interesting rural museum called the Almonry Museum. Evesham today is a busy, prosperous, market town, surrounded by the fertile Vale of Evesham. This rich soil provides the hotel and restaurants in the area with much of their fruits and vegetables. The asparagus grown here is renowned for its excellence. Plum and cider apple orchards thrive, perfuming the air in spring.

Asparagus Stilton Crèpes with Hollandaise Sauce

Batter

	pinch of saffron, soaked in 2 T. hot water
8 fl.oz.	milk (1 C.)
4 fl.oz.	flour (¾ C.)
	pinch of salt
2	eggs

1. Process all ingredients until smooth, leave for 10 minutes to rest, and process again. Or beat ingredients together by hand.

Filling

1½ lb.	fresh thin asparagus
	butter for frying crèpes
6 oz.	crumbled Stilton cheese (1½ C.)
	pepper and salt to taste

2. Snap off tougher ends of asparagus stems, if any. Cut asparagus in 6-inch lengths and steam until just tender. Set aside.

3. Using a 6-inch frying pan, heat a little butter in pan, then ladle in enough batter to thinly cover bottom of pan and cook until browned and set. Repeat with remaining batter. Stack crèpes and keep warm.

4. Preheat oven to 425°F (or gas mark 7).

5. One at a time place a little crumbled Stilton on half of each crèpe, add a small stack of asparagus, and season. Fold over and place in a heat-proof shallow dish. Repeat with remaining ingredients.

6. Heat in oven for 10–15 minutes, then serve with Hollandaise sauce. *Serves 4*

Near the Avon in Evesham, in Cooper's Lane, off Waterside, is the Evesham Hotel. A 180-year-old cedar of Lebanon overlooks the Cedar Restaurant here. The hotel has been privately owned and managed by the friendly, humorous Jenkinson family since the mid-1970s. This is a perfect place to stay while visiting the Vale of Evesham, the nearby Cotswold villages, Warwick Castle, or Stratford-on-Avon, to name a few of the famous places in the vicinity. Ian Mann, head chef at the Evesham Hotel, says that all their fish arrive directly from Cornwall, and fresh meat and game come from local suppliers. Exotic ingredients are purchased through various specialists. Ian Mann's menu reflects the wealth of fresh ingredients grown in the Vale. Some of the dishes on his menu are Wild mushroom tart with garlic butter; Market-fresh soup of the day; Smoked salmon and marinated gravad lax; Game soup with wild mushrooms, tarragon, and chestnuts; Grilled Dover Sole; Chicken Macaire (a chicken leg stuffed with Stilton, wrapped in bacon and roasted, served cold on an exotic salad); Deviled Crab; and Poached turbot on a leek sauce with Jerusalem artichokes perfumed with saffron. Ian Mann has kindly contributed the following recipe.

Harmer Galette

---

8 oz. potatoes (1⅔ C.), peeled and thinly sliced
      oil for frying
4 oz. onion (¾ C.), sliced
6 oz. mushrooms (1¼ C.), any variety you wish
2 T. soy sauce
1 T. toasted dark sesame oil
1 t. fresh ginger, chopped
1 t. fresh garlic, chopped
1 t. honey or maple syrup
1 T. wine vinegar
      sea salt
      freshly ground black pepper

1. Preheat oven to 375–400°F (or gas mark 5–6).
2. Deep-fry the slices of potato until light brown. Drain on paper towels. Sauté the onions until soft, add the mushrooms, and cook for 2 to 3 minutes.
3. Using two 6-inch-wide ovenproof dishes, cover the bottom of the dishes with sliced potatoes and divide the onion and mushroom mixture between the two dishes. Arrange overlapping slices of potato in a circular pattern to completely cover the vegetables.

4. Mix the remaining ingredients, and pour them over the vegetables. Season with sea salt and freshly ground black pepper.

5. Bake for 15 minutes. Serve hot with a green salad, or use to accompany grilled pork or lamb chops. *Serves* 2

Regional specialties in Hereford and Worcester are rich Pax cakes eaten at Easter and meat and apple tarts which were once part of May Day celebrations. Hereford is justly famous for its hop growing and vies with the West Country in cider making. Hereford and Worcester share a border with Wales, and today most of the wine grown in Wales is bottled in Hereford. One succulent benefit from Hereford cider orchards is Trelough duck. Flocks of them live in the orchards and forage on windfalls. Their diet of cider apples accounts for the distinctive flavor of these prized ducks. English hard cider, unlike the darker, opaque American cider, can contain as much as 8 percent alcohol.

Romans first introduced apples to England. Now apples of many varieties are abundant. Cider apples, such as Redstreak, Sweet Coppin, and Kingston Black, differ from dessert apples in that they have the acid pulp and sweet juice necessary to produce cider's strong, crisp taste. Somerset, Devon, Hereford, and Worcester have the largest cider apple orchards. During the last three months of the year, when cider making is in full swing, the smell of crushed apples in cider towns such as Taunton is heady. An old Pagan custom of wassailing cider apple trees is alive and well in the small town of Street in Somerset. On January 17 the inhabitants of Street sing an invocation beneath an apple tree to ensure that the trees will bear well in the following spring. At the same time, a wassail cup is passed from hand to hand, filled with the year's homemade cider laced with gin.

Cranberry Apple Pie

4	oz.	brown sugar (½ C.)
2	T.	maple syrup
1	lb.	cranberries (3 C.), rinsed
1		tart apple, peeled and chopped
2	oz.	hazelnuts (⅓ C.)
6	T.	unsalted butter (¾ stick)
4	oz.	granulated sugar (½ C.)
1		egg
2½	oz.	flour (½ C.)
		crème fraîche or heavy cream (optional)

1. Preheat oven to 350°F (or gas mark 4).
2. Mix together brown sugar and maple syrup in a bowl large enough to hold the cranberries. Stir in cranberries and apple and toss until well coated with sugar and syrup.
3. Spread fruit mixture evenly in a 9-inch buttered pie dish.
4. Grind hazelnuts in a blender and set aside.
5. Beat butter and granulated sugar until fluffy. Beat in egg and flour and all but one tablespoon of the ground hazelnuts. This step can be done in a food processor.
6. Spoon batter over fruit and smooth with a spatula.
7. Bake for 45–55 minutes. Sprinkle with remaining ground hazelnuts and bake one more minute. Serve with crème fraîche or heavy cream, if desired. *Serves 6–8*

The tranquil area between the Welsh border and Birmingham is virtually undiscovered and completely unspoiled. The superb medieval town of Ludlow, once the capital of the Welsh Marches, grew up around the Norman castle that now sits on a rise overlooking the River Teme. In 1085, Roger de Lacy started building Ludlow Castle, an impressive sandstone fortress, on the restive border with Wales. Embellished to palace status in the thirteenth and fourteenth centuries, Ludlow Castle in 1326 was owned by Roger Mortimer, who helped his mistress, Queen Isabella, to murder her husband, King Edward II, and place her son on the throne. For a while the country was virtually ruled from Ludlow Castle. Though mostly a ruin today—only the circular Norman chapel and the Gothic state rooms in the castle can be visited—the town has remained much as it always was. Old buildings on Ludlow's charming streets encompass Tudor, Queen Anne, and Regency houses. A splendid black and white timbered coaching inn, the Angel Hotel, stands on Broad Street. Another inn, the elaborate half-timbered fifteenth-century Feathers Hotel, has lovely embossed ceilings and carved paneling. Here too is the thirteenth-century Readers House and the ancient Hoyser's Almshouse built in the eighteenth century. The Church of St. Lawrence, its original 135-foot tower still dominating the town, was begun in the twelfth century. In the nineteenth century the church was restored by Sir Gilbert Scott and Sir Arthur Blomfield. Ludlow's Butter Cross has stood here since 1743.

The timber-framed, sixteenth-century Merchant House on Lower Corve Street now houses Shaun Hill's new restaurant. Shaun Hill is a Master Chef of Great Britain and one of the first British members elected to the Académie Culinaire de France. Shaun Hill says the emphasis will be on the wealth of wonderful ingredients, particularly produce, available in this part of England. For many years Shaun Hill was chef at Gidleigh Park Hotel in

Chagford, Devon, and he has given us permission to reprint the following recipes from his book, *Shaun Hill's Gidleigh Park Cookery Book*.

The first dish needs no sauce but goes extremely well with a creamy potato dish like Gratin de Jabron, which follows. A small amount of fat left on the bones will sweeten the meat and heighten its lamb flavor. Lamb is available year-round but is at its best in early summer, and this is better than new season's lamb, which is overrated, and vastly superior to milk-fed lamb, which is virtually tasteless.

Rack of Lamb with Parsley

1 pair best ends of lamb
    salt and freshly ground black pepper
2 T. Dijon mustard

Stuffing

4 oz. unsalted butter (1 stick)
4 shallots, peeled and chopped
    bunch of parsley, chopped
8 oz. fresh bread crumbs (2¼ C.)
    salt and pepper

The meat

Good butchery will make carving the finished joint much easier. Ask the butcher when he splits the best end into two racks to chop either side of the chine bone rather than through it.

    1. Lift off the outer layer of skin and fat. It comes away easily and in one piece. The eye of meat will now be exposed but covered in a white gristly membrane. Take a sharp knife and remove this. Chop down the cutlet bones so they extend no more than 3 inches (7.5 cm) from the eye of the meat.

    2. Season with salt and pepper. Preheat oven to 425°F (or gas mark 7).

The stuffing

    3. Melt the butter in a saucepan. When it has melted, but before it colors, add the shallots, then the parsley and bread crumbs.

    4. Season with some salt and pepper and stir together to form a stuffing.

To complete

    5. Sear the meat in a hot pan, then roast in the preheated oven for 7 minutes.

    6. Preheat the broiler. Brush the racks with mustard, then pack the parsley stuffing over them.

    7. Brown under the hot grill. Carve into cutlets and serve.

Serves 4

Gratin de Jabron

This is the best *gratin dauphinoise* potato I have tasted and was a regular accompaniment to rack of lamb and rib of beef at the Capital Hotel in London when I worked there. It came via Pierre Gleize, an early adviser to the Capital, who owns and cooks at La Bonne Etape in southeastern France. The dish is a course on its own. It is creamy and garlicky and yet doesn't lose the flavor of potato. If you have a choice, use potatoes that aren't too floury. They will hold together better when cooked.

I have split the recipe into two stages because that is how I cook it, preparing most of the dish in advance. You may, of course, proceed directly from the first to the second stage if you prefer. The grated cheese is optional, and I now use it less often, especially when the gratin is to partner meat.

Stage 1

    2 lb. maincrop potatoes
    6 oz. unsalted butter (1½ sticks)
    3   garlic cloves, peeled and crushed
           salt and freshly ground black pepper

Stage 2

    10 fl.oz. milk (1¼ C.)
    10 fl.oz. heavy cream (1¼ C.)
    2 oz.   hard cheese (½ C.), preferably Cheddar or Gruyère, grated

Stage 1 (up to one day in advance)

    1. Wash and sort the potatoes. You are going to boil them in their skins so it will be an advantage if they are approximately the same size.

    2. Boil the potatoes until they are just cooked, perhaps even a fraction underdone, and drain the water. Peel off the skin and then cut the potatoes into thickish—¼-inch (6-mm)—slices.

3. Melt the butter with the crushed garlic in a frying pan. Unless you have a really big pan you will probably need to do this exercise two or three times in a smaller one. When the butter is melted, and mixed with the garlic but not yet hot or sizzling, add the potatoes and toss them. The object is to coat the potato slices with the garlic butter, not to fry them. Season with salt and pepper and then spoon them into a container until needed.

Stage 2 (20 minutes before you eat)

4. Spread the potato on a pie dish about one inch (2.5 cm) deep. Pour on the milk and cream. Sprinkle the cheese on top.

5. Bake at 350°F (or gas mark 4) for 20 minutes.   *Serves* 4

Shrewsbury, the county town of Shropshire, has fine black and white, half-timbered buildings, making this one of the best-preserved Tudor towns in England. A particularly fine example is the Abbot's House in Butcher Row, built in 1450. The present castle dates to about 1300 but was first erected at the time of the Norman conquest, around 1080. Stephen beseiged the castle, killing the entire garrison, in 1138. The king of Wales, David, was executed in the castle courtyard by order of Edward I in 1283. Two famous men have strong ties to Shrewsbury—Clive of India—Robert Clive (1725–1774), whose eighteenth-century Georgian town house has a great collection of Shropshire pottery and porcelain, was mayor here in 1762 and Shrewsbury's Member of Parliament from 1761 until his death. The other, Charles Darwin (1809–1882), was born and educated in Shrewsbury. The late eighteenth-century church, St. Chad's, in St. Chad's Terrace is a rare example of a round church, and St. Mary's Church is Norman and has splendid stained glass windows.

Shrewsbury cakes, a Shropshire regional delicacy, are small pastries almost identical to Lancashire's Eccles cakes (see recipe in North Country section), except that the Shropshire version has chopped mint leaves in the filling. Another specialty is the excellent fidget pie—ham or bacon layered with potatoes and apples—its jellied stock is poured into the pie dish with the filling before baking. Aspics—jellied stocks—are held in high esteem. When cooled and set, they hold the filling neatly in place when the pie is sliced. Shrewsbury is famous for Simnel cake, a festive cake eaten on Mothering Sunday, the fourth Sunday in Lent, or at Easter. Mothering Sunday originally was a day set aside to remember Mother Church, rather than mothers in general, but Mother's Day as we know it is definitely here to stay. Simnel cake is spicy and filled with dried fruits, candied peel, and at least half a dozen eggs. A round of marzipan separates the cake's layers, and another round of marzipan decorates the top. Eleven (some sources say twelve) small balls of marzipan are arranged around the rim of the cake.

One story says that the balls represent Christ's disciples, with the exception of Judas Iscariot. The cake could well have originated in Greece, where a similar one with twelve balls is made to honor the gods on Mount Olympus. Simnel cake traditionally was given to live-in maids to take home to their mothers on Mothering Sunday. Gladys Mann, in her cookbook *Good Food from Old England*, writes that the marzipan balls represent the eleven months of the year when the young women were apart from their mothers. Shrewsbury's most famous regional specialty is Shrewsbury biscuits (crackers)—a pale biscuit made with rice flour, wheat flour, and grated lemon peel—that pairs well with local farmhouse cheeses.

Special soul cakes, made with butter, eggs, milk, flour, yeast, and spices, are still baked by country bakers in Shropshire. Soul cakes are sent on November 2, All Soul's Day, to families who have suffered a bereavement during the year, and church services are held to pray for the souls of the dead. At one time souling became an excuse for children to beg sweetmeats by going door to door and singing this ancient ditty:

> Soul, soul, for a soul cake;
> Pray you good mistress, a soul cake.
> An apple, a pear, a plum or a cherry,
> Any good thing to make us all merry!

Halloween in the United States, where children dress up in imaginative costumes and go from house to house crying, "Trick or treat?" on October 31, has its origins here.

Shropshire's fishermen on the River Severn ply the waters in their traditional handcrafted coracles. These boats, light enough for fishermen to carry them down to the water on their backs, are fashioned of wooden laths covered in waterproofed canvas. Their design has not altered in two thousand years.

Cheshire is predominately a quiet pastoral county, dotted with half-timbered, black and white houses. This type of architecture is called "magpie." One of the most famous examples is the magnificent old house Little Morton Hall, near Congleton. Built between 1559 and 1589, it is adorned with beautiful Elizabethan plasterwork ceilings, carved gables, a great hall, and a chapel. In the grounds is an Elizabethan knot garden.

Chester, Cheshire's county seat, is a dignified and prosperous town. Glorious half-timbered houses line its ancient streets, and medieval, galleried arcades protect the inhabitants from sudden rain showers. Reached by short flights of steps, the galleries for centuries have furnished carriage- and cart-free shopping for its citizens. Chester is the best-preserved walled city in England; you can walk for two miles atop the walls seeing on the one side rolling green countryside and on the other, half-timbered shops on balustraded walkways, called the Rows. Chester was settled by the Romans in the first century A.D., on a strategic crossroads between northern England and Wales, and here the Romans constructed the largest amphitheater in Britain that has been discovered to date, just east of Newgate. William the Conqueror sacked the town in 1069, gave it to Hugh of Avranches to administer, and made him the first Earl of Chester. In the 1300s additional towers were added to the city walls, and within them buildings grew on top of the old Roman remains. Located within the city walls is Eastgate, built in the tenth century and reconstructed in the late nineteenth century. Eastgate is embellished with a fine Victorian clock. The cathedral, built on the site of a former Benedictine monastery, has intricately carved choir stalls that date from the late fourteenth century. The Chester mystery plays are performed every five years on a site within the city walls.

Cheshire is world famous for its distinctive and delectable cheese. Cheshire cheese is impossible to reproduce outside of Cheshire. Efforts to duplicate it in other regions of the country have failed to produce Cheshire's silky, crumbly texture and its nutty, slightly salty, flavor. The rich taste of Cheshire is enhanced by toasting. Tinted Cheshire cheese has an orange hue; untinted ranges from yellow to white. Blue Cheshire cheese is a special treat and rather expensive, as it is still more difficult to find than regular cheese. The reason for its scarcity is simply that the cheese turns blue by accident. Perhaps the blue mold has to do with the humidity or the temperature at which the cheese is stored while maturing, but the crumbly texture of regular Cheshire turns buttery and smooth in the blue version, and the mold lends its characteristic sharp, pungent taste to the normally nutty-flavored cheese. Cheshire cheese, blue Cheshire when available, traditional Derby, Leicester, and a host of other Midland cheeses are made locally now and can be purchased directly from the farmhouse.

Spinach and Blue Cheshire Cheese Tart

		pastry for 9-inch pie plate
6	oz.	tightly packed spinach (4 C.), stems removed
3–4	T.	light cream
		salt, pepper, and grated nutmeg, to taste
4	lg.	eggs
2	t.	Dijon mustard
1	oz.	bread crumbs (½ C.), toasted
8	oz.	sour cream (1 C.)
2	T.	snipped fresh chives
4	oz.	blue Cheshire (1 C.), crumbled
1	oz.	pine nuts (¼ C.)

1. Preheat oven to 375°F (or gas mark 5).
2. Steam spinach briefly until wilted. Drain and press to exude liquid. When cool enough to handle, chop, return to pan, and heat gently with cream, seasoning, and nutmeg. Set aside.
3. Break eggs into a bowl. Take one tablespoon of egg white and place in small bowl. Brush inside of pastry case with egg white. When dry, brush case with Dijon mustard. Sprinkle toasted bread crumbs in pastry case and top with spinach, spread in an even layer.
4. Beat eggs with sour cream and chives. Stir in blue cheese, season, and pour over spinach in tart shell. Sprinkle with pine nuts.
5. Bake for 35–40 minutes or until set. Serve warm.   *Serves 6–8*

Stafford's streets conform to the original medieval pattern. It has many half-timbered houses, one of which, High House, gave sanctuary to Charles I and Prince Rupert in 1642. Isaak Walton (1593–1683), author of *The Compleat Angler*, was christened here at the church of St. Mary. At Shallowford, northwest of the town in the cottage where he once lived, is a small museum dedicated to Walton. The Midlands are home to many of England's poets and writers. D. H. Lawrence—*Sons and Lovers* and *Women in Love*—was born at Eastwood, a small mining town in Nottinghamshire, and educated at Nottingham. His father was a miner. Lawrence's book *Lady Chatterley's Lover*, written in 1928, was considered scandalous when it was first printed. Partly because of this he and his wife, Frieda, spent most of their lives abroad. Lichfield, in Staffordshire, was Samuel Johnson's native town. He was born above his father's bookshop. Near Stafford is Shugborough, the fabulous country seat of the earls of Lichfield. This neoclassical building contains fabulous collections of porcelain, silver, furniture, and paintings. The Staffordshire County Museum is quartered here, and a Doric Temple and a Chinese dwelling are features of the spacious grounds. Lord Lichfield, the renowned photographer, lives at Shugborough. A cousin of Her Majesty the Queen, he has taken many royal portraits and captures on film the royal family's christenings and weddings. Staffordshire's regional culinary claim to fame is yeomanry pudding, a confection similar to Bakewell tart, made from raspberry jam, beaten eggs, and ground almonds.

Midland folk have a passion for sporting events of all kinds, but the one that causes the most heated discussions of pros and cons is fox hunting. Fox hunting is well entrenched in the Midlands. Everyone who is able to do so follows the hunt, if not astride a horse then on a bicycle or by car. The topic of the day is more likely to be hunting news than the weather—Britain's perennial preoccupation. Fox hunting is an expensive hobby. Only the very wealthy can afford the upkeep of a string of hunters and a pack of hounds, not to mention the trappings of meets, hunt parties, and those elegant pink coats. Artificial coverts of gorse are planted to encourage foxes to make their dens in hunt counties. Although a lot is heard about the growing antihunt movement in Britain, hunting is so thoroughly entrenched in the lives of the British and Irish that the sport shows no sign of dying out.

The city of Coventry in the West Midlands dates to Anglo-Saxon times. In 1083 Leofric, Earl of Mercia, built a Benedictine monastery here and began the development of Coventry's thriving wool center. Leofric's famous wife, Lady Godiva, asked him to reduce the taxes the people of Coventry had to pay. His reply that she would ride naked through the streets before he did any such thing is the basis for the legend of Lady Godiva. The legend is that she asked the townspeople to close their shutters, then rode naked through the town. The earl reduced the taxes. The tale has been added to through the centuries to include Peeping Tom, who peeped through the shutters and was blinded by the sight. On the clock situated above Hertford Street, the figures of Lady Godiva and Peeping Tom appear every hour, ensuring that the legend will live on. A modern statue of Lady Godiva, astride her horse, stands in Broadgate.

Coventry Godcakes

Traditionally given to children in Warwickshire by their godparents on New Year's Eve.

          puff pastry, either homemade or store-bought
½   jar of mincemeat
1 T. lemon juice or rum
1   egg white, beaten until frothy
          castor sugar

1. Preheat oven to 375°F (or gas mark 5).

2. Roll out the pastry on a lightly floured board, following package directions, if applicable, to a rectangle that is about ⅛-inch thick.

3. Cut pastry into 5-inch squares and moisten edges with water or milk.

4. Mix mincemeat with lemon juice or rum and place a dollop of mincemeat on one half of each square.

5. Fold to make a triangle and seal edges. Make two slits in the top of the pastry, brush with egg white, and sprinkle lightly with castor sugar.

6. Bake for 12–15 minutes. Remove to rack to cool.

Yields roughly 8–12 pastries

Coventry refused entry to Charles I in 1642, and to avenge his father, Charles II in 1660 ordered the city to dismantle its city walls. Twelve city gates were left standing after the order was carried out, and two of these stand today. The central area of Coventry is closed to automobiles and is resplendent with tree-filled parks. Most of the bicycle, sewing machine, and automobile factories are outside the city. The modern cathedral, built beside the ruins of original St. Michael's Cathedral, attests to the bravery of the people of Coventry during World War II. On November 14, 1940, forty acres of the city center were leveled in one air raid. The spire and blackened outer walls of the original building are linked to the new cathedral, forming the entrance. The interior is filled with golden light from the many beautiful stained-glass windows. Coventry is surrounded on three sides by the wooded countryside of Warwickshire.

In Derbyshire, Melton Mowbray's busy shopping streets have more than their share of butcher shops, their display cases bursting with delectable sausages, black puddings, and white puddings. It is not uncommon for butchers to hang rows of fur-clad rabbits outside their shops. Rabbits need to be hung anyway for a day or two, but the main reason they are displayed outside is that rabbits cannot be sold inside a shop nowadays unless they are skinned and wrapped in plastic. Hare is another animal that has been a part of the diet of these islands for centuries and is often made into a rich, gamy soup. A time-honored way to prepare hare is "jugged." Mature rabbits too can be cooked in this fashion. The hare, seasoned with salt and pepper, is put into a large stoneware jug, or a lidded casserole, with an onion and some herbs and simmered, closely covered, for about three hours or until cooked. The pan juices, seasoned with a little anchovy paste, are mixed with the hare's blood to make a thick sauce. A spoonful of vinegar is added to the sauce to prevent clotting.

Much in evidence in the shops of Melton Mowbray are the famous raised pies and crusty rounds of Stilton cheese. Curiously, the manufacture of Stilton cheese here is responsible for the distinctive flavor of Melton Mowbray pie. Whey left over from making Stilton is fed to local pigs whose destiny it is to be made into a raised pie. The whey gives a special flavor to the meat. Pork pies are popular everywhere, but on the Midlander's table they are a mainstay. The raised crust is made with a very firm, hot water pastry that is coaxed upward around a heavy wooden mold until it reaches its impressive height. The filling is made from diced pork, mixed with salt, pepper, and anchovy essence. Once the filling is firmly packed, the top crust positioned, and the edges securely pinched together, a pastry rose is put in place over a hole cut in the center of the top crust. Pastry leaves decorate the pie. An egg wash gives the characteristic glossy brown color of this famous robust regional dish. Sometimes a strip of parchment paper is wound tightly around the pie to help support the crust at the beginning of the three-hour baking period. Meanwhile, a rich jellied stock is made from the pig's feet, and as soon as the pie is removed from the oven, the jellied stock is poured into the hole beneath the rose to become, as it cools, a lovely aspic around the meat. Recipes abound for sturdy, flavorful meat and poultry pies.

Veal, Chicken, and Ham Pie

		shortcrust pastry for 10-inch pie
2		whole chicken breasts, boned and skinned
4		chicken thighs, boned and skinned
2		thick veal chops, boned
		salt and pepper to taste
2	T.	lemon juice
3	T.	butter
3		shallots, minced
4	T.	fresh parsley, minced
1	T.	fresh summer savory, minced
⅓	lb.	ham, sliced but not too thinly
3		eggs, hard boiled
12	fl.oz.	richly flavored chicken broth (1½ C.)
1		egg beaten with 1 T. water (egg glaze)
1		sheet of gelatin

1. Cut chicken into large pieces. Dice veal into ¼-inch cubes. Toss chicken and veal separately in lemon juice and pepper. Salt lightly and set aside.

2. Over medium heat, melt butter and sauté shallots for 2–3 minutes. Stir in parsley and summer savory. Set aside to cool. Preheat oven to 350°F (or gas mark 4).

3. Line a 10-inch pie plate with half of the sliced ham, sprinkle evenly with cubed veal, then spread shallot mixture evenly over veal.

4. Position the hard-boiled eggs so that they will slice crosswise when the pie is sliced. Cover with remaining ham, followed by the thigh meat, then the breast meat. Pour on 4 fluid ounces (½ C.) of the chicken broth.

5. Roll out the pastry. Moisten rim of pie plate and cover with a strip of pastry. Moisten strip and position pie crust over it, crimping edges to seal. Cut a one-inch hole in the center of pie crust. Decorate with pastry leaves.

6. Brush pie with egg glaze and bake for 1¼ hours.

7. Heat remaining chicken broth, stir in gelatin until dissolved, and pour as much as the pie will hold into the hole in the pie crust. Cool, then refrigerate. Serve with a green salad.   *Serves* 10

Stilton, renowned in all corners of the globe, is possibly England's best-known cheese. Stilton comes in hefty sixteen-pound (7.25-kilo) rounds, roughly ten inches high and seven inches wide. The texture is creamy—especially near the center where most of the blue veins are concentrated. Its outer crust, which forms naturally, is somewhat pitted and pale brown. The rich mellow taste, sharpened by the blue mold, is unforgettable. Baby Stiltons, popular as Christmas presents, are identical in quality and appearance but weigh closer to five pounds. Stilton is a registered trademark, and the Stilton Cheesemakers Association have specified since 1910 that Stilton may be made only in Leicestershire, Derbyshire, and Nottinghamshire, assuring that the high quality of the cheese will remain consistent over the years. The unfortunate habit of scooping out the soft, moist center of the round with a spoon is prevalent, and yet it ruins the cheese by causing the remainder to dry out. Stilton should be sliced carefully through the round, and the slice cut in wedges. Traditionally, once the ladies have withdrawn after dinner to what was once called the "withdrawing" room, Stilton was served with walnuts and port. Nowadays the preference for men and women is red wine and bread with a good crust.

Oddly enough, Stilton cheese has never been made in the eponymous village. Once upon a time the village was a busy coaching stop where people looked forward to a respite from the bouncing, swaying coach and a well-earned rest at Stilton's hospitable Bell Inn. Farmers from surrounding villages made good use of busy coaching inns to sell farmhouse victuals to the proprietor. The crusted, delectable cheese was one of these, and over time it was dubbed Stilton. One coaching customer, Daniel Defoe, described Stilton in 1722 as being "brought to the table with the mites and maggots round it so thick that they bring a spoon for you to eat the mites with, as you do the cheese." Now that the maggots are no longer served with it, the spoon is unnecessary. Derbyshire produces another great-tasting, buttery, white cheese with an open texture called Derby. Its cousin, Sage Derby, has a singular streak of green running through it. The juice of crushed sage leaves creates the streak and gives it a fragrant herbal taste. Sage Derby is eaten mostly at Christmas—perhaps because green is such an appropriate color at that time of year.

Poached Chicken with Sun-dried Tomato Sauce

8	sun-dried tomatoes packed in olive oil, sliced
8	Roman tomatoes, peeled, seeded, and diced
4 fl.oz.	heavy cream (½ C.)

2		shallots, sliced
6	fl.oz.	chicken broth (⅔ C.)
4		chicken breast halves, skinned and boned
1½	lb.	spinach, stems removed
2	T.	olive oil
		salt and pepper, to taste
6	T.	pine nuts, toasted

1. Drain sun-dried tomatoes and slice thinly. Place diced tomatoes and a little water in heavy-bottomed saucepan. Add sun-dried tomatoes and simmer until soft. Cool. Using a food processor, purée tomato mixture. Return to saucepan and stir in the heavy cream. Set aside.

2. Place shallots and chicken broth in a frying pan large enough to hold the chicken breasts in one layer. Bring to a boil. Slide in chicken breasts, cover, and poach until just cooked through. Set aside and keep warm.

3. Steam spinach briefly until wilted. Drain, pressing to exude water. Using the same saucepan, heat olive oil, gently stir-fry spinach for a few minutes, and season to taste.

4. To serve: divide spinach between four warmed plates. Slice chicken breasts and overlap slices attractively beside spinach. Scatter pine nuts on spinach and spoon ribbons of sauce over chicken. Serve immediately.   *Serves* 4

Bakewell is situated in a valley below the Peak District hills. In Roman times Bakewell had twelve wells producing pure, iron-rich water at a constant temperature of fifty-nine degrees Fahrenheit, and to this day Bakewell performs the well-blessing ceremony that dates to pagan times. Each July the wells, which have long since dried up or been filled in, are decorated as they have been for centuries with flower petals and leaves. The ancient Bath House at Bakewell, built in 1697, is open to the public.

Five miles north of Bakewell is the pleasant village of Eyam, made famous by the courage of its rector, William Mompesson, and the three hundred fifty villagers who lived there in the seventeenth century. In 1665 bubonic plague raged in London. Eyam's tailor, George Vicars, received a box of clothing from London that was contaminated with plague germs. When he sickened and died, Mompesson persuaded his terrified flock that staying in their village, rather than fleeing, would halt the spread of the disease to other villages. Out of the three hundred fifty villagers, two hundred fifty died, including Mompesson's wife. Plague Cottage is the home of George Vicars. Mompesson's church and the graveyard where whole families are buried are behind the cottage. It was generally believed that bubonic plague could be

spread through contaminated well water. Wells have always been very important, especially in rural areas, and to this day in many parts of the country
well-blessing or well-dressing ceremonies are held annually. Tissington in
Derbyshire has reason to be very proud of their five wells. Not only are they
dependable and continue to supply the town with water even through periods of drought, but during the formidable plague days the well water remained pure and the people of Tissington were spared. Huge areas of
Derbyshire were decimated. Bubonic plague killed thousands. In pagan
times, spirits were thought to reside in wells, and this was possibly the reason for the elaborate ceremony. Be that as it may, every year in the month of
May Tissington holds a well-dressing ceremony that entails making decorative plaques using flowers, leaves, and other natural objects pressed into soft
clay. These and and appropriate religious texts are suspended over the well.

Chatsworth House, located in the Peak District of Derbyshire and
known as the Palace of the Peak, is the domain of the dukes of Devonshire.
This magnificient house was built by Talman from the late seventeenth century to the early eighteenth century, replacing the Elizabethan home of
Bess of Hardwick, built on the same site. Dukes of Devonshire have lived
there ever since. The state rooms, where over the centuries royalty slept,
have beautifully painted walls and ceilings, superb furniture, and an incomparable art collection. The library holds 18,000 volumes, as well as prints
and manuscripts. Chatsworth's immense dining room alone could hold
eight normal-sized houses. The gardens were laid out by Capability Brown,
the foremost gardener and designer of his day. They contain cascades, an
aqueduct, and the highest gravity-fed fountain in the world. A farmyard and
an adventure playground are here too for children.

Derbyshire is well endowed with historic properties open to the public.
Haddon Hall is a medieval mansion that has been altered very little. It is
built around two courtyards on a bluff, overlooking the river. The oak-paneled
banqueting hall and minstrel gallery date to 1350. Windows with heraldic designs glow in the long gallery where interesting furniture, tapestries, and
paintings are on display. The old kitchens still have medieval ovens, huge
fireplaces, and ancient utensils. The chapel was built in the eleventh century.

To the northwest is the Peak District National Park—possibly the Midlands' most sparsely populated area. The Pennine Way starts in the Derbyshire section of the National Park. Bordered by Manchester to the west,
and the mill towns of Huddersfield, Halifax, and Bradford to the east, the
Pennine Way winds across parts of Yorkshire's beautiful limestone dales
and through the spectacular heather-clad countryside, written about so
skillfully in the novels of the Brontë family, particularly Charlotte Brontë's
Jane Eyre. The path follows Hadrian's Wall for a short time before heading
up through forested Northumberland along the Cheviot Hills to end at Kirk
Yetholm, north of the Scottish border. One of the most rigorous footpaths

in England, the Pennine Way winds for 270 miles through desolate terrain among the mountain tops of the Pennine Chain, called the backbone of England. Britain is known for the many long, generally well-maintained footpaths that crisscross the land. Signposted "Public Footpath," they are just that—open to the public even though they may cross private property. The rules are to do no damage, to close gates behind you, to keep to the footpaths, and to walk single file around crops. The Peak District National Park is not nationally owned land. Still in private hands, it is therefore not preserved by the government as a park. In much the same fashion as "Public Footpaths," the "Parks" are regions of particular beauty, or of environmental importance, where recreational activities are safeguarded for the use of the public, as well as other uses such as farming or peat-digging. Stout boots, waterproof gear, warm clothing, maps, and a compass are essential for any part of the Pennine Way. Hadrian's Wall, about twelve miles from the Scottish border, is well known as the northernmost border of the Roman Empire in England, built to protect the land from raid by the Picts. Other historic places visible from the Pennine Way are vestiges of Iron Age forts, Anglo-Saxon villages, ruins of the powerful and wealthy abbeys that owned most of the land in Yorkshire and beyond, and the many castles built to keep the marauding Scots at bay.

A welcome relief on a wet day is the Derbyshire village of Bakewell, whose famous regional specialty, Bakewell tart, or Bakewell pudding, as some insist it be called, comprises a pastry case spread with a layer of strawberry or raspberry jam, covered with an almond filling, and baked until golden brown. People from Bakewell, however, insist that the confection was created accidentally when a cook at the Rutland Arms Hotel mistakenly spread an egg mixture on top of jam in an open tart shell. Whatever the true story, the end result is delicious. The Old Original Bakewell Pudding Shop welcomes visitors to sample not only Bakewell puddings but their entire wide selection of fine baked goods.

Almond Tart

9-inch pastry shell

- 5 oz. flour (1 C.)
  pinch of salt
- 2 T. sugar
  strip of lemon zest, slivered
- 4 oz. unsalted butter (1 stick), cut in pieces
- 2 T. fresh lemon juice

1. Preheat oven to 400°F (or gas mark 6).

2. In a food processor, combine flour, salt, sugar, and lemon zest. Add butter and pulse on and off briefly, then add lemon juice and pulse on and off until dough forms a loose ball. Remove from food processor, dust with flour, and refrigerate for 30 minutes.

3. Either roll out pastry on a floured board, or press dough into a 9-inch tart pan with a removable bottom. Prick shell all over with a fork. Freeze for 15 minutes. Bake on the lower shelf of the oven for 10 minutes, pricking any bubbles that may arise. Remove to a rack to cool.

Filling

2½	oz.	blanched whole almonds (½ C.)
		a splash of almond extract
1	t.	vanilla OR 1 T. Amaretto liqueur
2		eggs
2½	oz.	sugar (⅓ C.)
4	oz.	unsalted butter (½ C.), softened
2	T.	flour
½	t.	baking powder
6	oz.	raspberry preserves (⅔ C.)
1½	oz.	slivered almonds (¼ C.)

4. Using a nut grinder or a food processor, grind the whole almonds. Do not over-grind, as the oil will separate from the nuts and cause lumping. Stir or shake to aerate. Add to the processor, and whirl for a few seconds, the almond extract, the vanilla or liqueur, the eggs, and the sugar. Add the butter in spoonfuls, followed by the flour and baking powder, and combine well.

5. Preheat oven to 375°F (or gas mark 5).

6. Warm the raspberry preserves, force them through a sieve, discarding pits, and generously coat the inside of the pastry shell.

7. Pour in the almond filling, sprinkle with the slivered almonds, and bake on the middle shelf of the oven for 25–30 minutes.

8. Serve at room temperature.   *Serves 8–10*

To the east is the county of Nottinghamshire and the city of Nottingham, the county town. Nottingham's regional specialty is the heavenly confection brandy snaps. These are made with a lacy butter cookie, flavored with ginger and brandy, that is removed from the cookie sheet while still warm enough to be malleable. Curved around a buttered dowel or wooden spoon handle until stiffened, the funnel-shaped brandy snap is traditionally filled with whipped cream. The filling for the following recipe for brandy snaps is lighter, but purists can substitute heavy cream for the frozen yogurt, if they wish.

Brandy Snaps

4 oz. dark brown sugar (½ C.)
4 oz. golden syrup (½ C.)
4 oz. butter (1 stick), plus extra for baking sheets
4 oz. flour (¾ C.)
1½ t. ground ginger
⅛ t. salt
3 t. brandy
1 pt. frozen yogurt, vanilla or lemon
crystallized ginger, chopped (optional)
fresh berries for garnish (blueberries go well with lemon
yogurt)

1. Preheat oven to 400°F (or gas mark 6). In a medium-sized mixing bowl stir together golden syrup and dark brown sugar. Melt butter until hot but not boiling and stir into syrup mixture until smooth.

2. Sift together flour, ground ginger, and salt, and beat into sugar mixture. Stir in brandy.

3. Lavishly butter baking sheets, and drop mixture 2 teaspoons at a time onto baking sheet. Mixture will melt completely and spread out, so place them well apart—four or five per sheet.

4. Bake for 5–7 minutes until dark golden color.

5. Allow to cool for a few seconds. They will still be very hot, so carefully but quickly position each brandy snap over a muffin cup of a nonstick muffin pan and press down to shape baskets, using a flat wooden dowel 1½-inch wide. (The implement used to push vegetables into an electric juicer is ideal.)

6. As soon as they harden remove baskets from muffin cups. Cool completely and store in airtight containers.

7. To serve, gently fill baskets with frozen yogurt, sprinkle with crystallized ginger, if using, and decorate with berries.

Yields about 2 dozen brandy snap baskets

Nottingham Castle and Sherwood Forest will be forever linked with the legend of the wicked Sheriff of Nottingham and Robin Hood and his Merry Men, who stole from the rich to give to the poor. The castle is built on a rock that the townspeople firmly believe is the very rock that Robin scaled when he breached the castle. Edward III and Edward IV both have connections with Nottingham Castle, Richard III set off from the stronghold in 1485 to his defeat on Bosworth Field, and in 1642 Charles I fled from his rebellious parliament to take refuge within its massive walls. Outside these is a bronze statue of Robin Hood. The castle today holds a museum and art gallery. Nottingham has a wealth of museums, as well as a university and many elaborately decorated buildings. The oldest settlement is on the site of the Lace Market, which has been a flourishing commerical center under Anglo-Saxon, Danish, and Norman jurisdiction. Nottingham is still renowned for its lace making, as well as for the manufacture of Raleigh bicycles and Players cigarettes. The first Boots the Chemists was opened on Goosegate in Nottingham in the late 1800s by Jesse Boot. Today Boots is Britain's biggest chain of chemist shops. A branch of this excellent company will be found in every town in England. Nottingham is also home to three major sporting clubs, inaugurated in the 1800s. Each year in October Nottingham holds its famous Goose Fair—an enormous glittering carnival whose origins go back to the Middle Ages.

Near to Sherwood Forest is the small market town of Southwell, famous for its twelfth- to fourteenth-century cathedral. In 1646 Charles I stayed in Southwell before his surrender to the Scots. Cardinal Wolsey spent his remaining years here. Nearby are the ruins of Newstead Abbey, originally an Augustinian priory founded in 1170, commandeered by Henry VIII following the Dissolution of the Monasteries. Built on the grounds of Newstead Abbey is the grand country house of George Gordon, Lord Byron, the colorful poet who is said to have hated Southwell and wished that it would be swallowed by an earthquake! The house is surrounded with over 300 acres of gardens and lakes. Lord Byron loved Homestead and spent a great deal of time there with his menagerie of beloved animals, filling the monk's mortuary on the property to create a bathing pool for himself and his dog Boatswain. Lord Byron sold the property in 1817 to pay his escalating debts. Owned now by the city of Nottingham, Newstead is a treasure-house of Byron memorabilia.

The vivid orange Leicester is one among the many tinted cheeses whose brilliant color give a rich hue to cheese dishes, assuring their continued high regard in the kitchen. Leicester cheese is not made in Leicester but in Melton Mowbray, Derbyshire. Good farmhouse Leicester cheeses can be found on farms in Cheshire, in Clwyd, Wales, in several places in Lancashire, and in North Cadbury in Somerset.

The medieval town of Leicester is the county seat on the River Soar with a cathedral and a university. Leicester's best-known landmark is the Victorian clock tower in the city's center. Formerly a castle built by William I guarded Leicester, but all that remains today is a mound in the beautiful castle gardens. Many buildings of interest here date from the Middle Ages to the eighteenth century. The Guildhall, once the medieval council chambers, is a wonderful black and white half-timbered building with small mullioned windowpanes. One mile north of the city is the former site of an Augustinian abbey where Cardinal Wolsey died in 1530. A slab marks the presumed site of his grave. Cardinal Wolsey built the magnificent Hampton Court Palace on the River Thames just south of London, which Henry VIII so admired that Wolsey thought it prudent to make the monarch a present of it. Leicester's hosiery and footwear factories are still important industries, although engineering is the biggest employer today. Interestingly, Leicester's streets are filled with dark-eyed handsome people—the women wearing bright saris, elegant sandals, and tinkling bracelets. About one-fifth of Leicester's inhabitants are Indians, who came here looking for work after World War II. Shops full of colorful fabrics or fragrant spices and delicious breads, hot from the griddle, cater to the Indian population. Marriages are still arranged for young people by their parents, but with each new generation the traditional customs weaken.

Spiced Shrimp with Coriander

1½	lb.	large fresh shrimp
1½	t.	cumin seed, freshly ground
2	t.	coriander seed, freshly ground
1	t.	fennel seed, freshly ground
½	t.	ground turmeric
3	T.	butter
1		garlic clove, minced
1		1-inch-thick slice of ginger, shredded
1		jalapeño pepper, seeded and sliced, or other medium hot small pepper (wear rubber gloves)
6		Roman tomatoes, peeled, seeded, and chopped
4	fl.oz.	clam juice or fish stock (½ C.)
½	t.	salt
3	T.	fresh lime juice
3	fl.oz.	crème fraîche (⅓ C.)
1	T.	whole cilantro leaves

1. Shell shrimp, devein, rinse, and refrigerate until needed.

2. Sauté the cumin, coriander, fennel, and turmeric in butter over medium heat for 2 minutes.

3. Add garlic, shredded ginger, and jalapeño pepper and cook, stirring for one minute longer.

4. Stir in the chopped tomatoes, clam juice or fish stock, and salt. Bring to a boil, lower heat, and simmer, partially covered, for 20 minutes, stirring occasionally.

5. Stir in lime juice. Return to a simmer, stir in shrimp, and continue to cook until shrimp is opaque. Remove from heat and place

shrimp in serving dish. Keep warm. Still off the heat, stir in the crème fraîche little by little. Reheat sauce over low heat, stirring constantly and making sure sauce does not come to a boil. At the last minute, stir in the cilantro leaves. Pour sauce over shrimp and serve with rice.

Serves 4

The countryside around Leicester has many beautiful churches. One of the most splendid, Twycross village church, has glorious stained glass windows made predominantly of the luminous Chartres blue. Originally the windows were a present from France to the English king at the time of the French Revolution, sent for safekeeping. When the French decided they wanted the windows returned at the end of World War II and offered to buy them for half a million pounds, naturally there was great resistance from the villagers. The windows at present remain in Twycross Church.

Northampton is known for its shoe industries, which sadly are now diminishing because of the increased importation of cheaply made footwear. In the 1200s King John bought a pair of boots at Northampton. In their heyday during World War II Northampton shod all the men and women in the armed forces. Benjamin Franklin's ancestors hailed from the village of Ecton, Northamptonshire, where for centuries they had been blacksmiths before emigrating to America in the late 1600s. Near Kettering, Northamptonshire, is Boughton House, home of the duke of Buccleuch and Queensbury. The house was originally a monastic dwelling that has been enlarged around seven courtyards. It contains a truly exceptional collection of Louis XIV and XV furniture, as well as paintings, tapestries, and a world-famous armory.

Ten miles south of Northampton in the tranquil village of Paulersbury is the Vine House Hotel and Restaurant. Built over three hundred years ago out of local limestone, Vine House and its adjoining residence, Vine Cottage, were converted in 1985 to a country hotel and restaurant by Julie and Marcus Springett. While all modern amenities were installed, great care was taken to preserve the original features, character, and charm of this delightful building. Marcus and Julie Springett bought Vine House in 1991. Six individually decorated bedrooms, one with a four-poster bed, all have private bathrooms. Active pursuits are plentiful—golf, riding, fishing, shooting, and, by prior arrangement, hunting. In the surrounding area are historic houses, castles, and gardens to visit. Marcus Springett is passionate about British food. His menu has a typically English Fresh pea soup; Pressed leeks topped with a quenelle of smooth chicken; Crab and mussel stew; Home-smoked salmon and smoked salmon sausage with tarragon sauce; Fillets of Dover sole stuffed with scallop mousse and steamed with a truffle butter sauce; and Fillet of beef topped with goat cheese and garlic butter. Desserts sparkle—Raspberry tart with honey and brown bread ice cream; and Rich dark chocolate terrine with chilled vanilla pod custard, coconut ice cream, and fresh fruit, to name but two. Near the hotel is a pick-your-own vegetable farm with perfectly ripe baby green beans, gooseberries, raspberries, strawberries, loganberries, and black and red currants that the Springetts put to good use. From Bedford a vegetable supplier provides many unusual vegetables and herbs for the kitchen. In the next village the soil is perfect for asparagus, and their friend, Mr. Wells, grows bundles of it for Vine House. A woman in the same village supplies organically grown carrots, rhubarb, Swiss chard, peppers, zucchinis, and cabbage. Game is supplied by a man in Northampton who shoots his own, and he also keeps them stocked with oak chips for their smoker. Meat comes from Leighton Buzzard and fish directly from markets in London. To supplement all this they grow produce and herbs in their own garden, and in the nearest field they pick wild sorrel, wild watercress, and tender nettle tops for soup. Marcus Springett has given us two of his recipes for the book. One of these comes from his Aunt Holda.

Aunt Holda's Recipe for Traditional Rissoles of Venison with Sautéed Potatoes and Red Wine Sauce

Rissoles

2		garlic cloves, chopped
1		shallot, chopped
1	oz.	butter
7	oz.	venison steak, cubed
4	oz.	pork fat (²/₃ C.)
1 ½	oz.	bread (approximately 2 slices, crusts removed) soaked in water and squeezed dry
1		bay leaf
³/₄	t.	rosemary, chopped
³/₄	t.	sage, chopped
		pinch of ground allspice
³/₄	t.	salt
¼	t.	ground pepper
½	t.	herbes de Provence
1		egg, whisked

1. Sweat the garlic and shallots in butter, and set aside to cool.

2. Mix all the ingredients except the egg together and pass through a fine blade of a mincer. Add the egg and mix well.

3. Make two patties and chill in the refrigerator until ready to cook.

Sautéed potatoes

  1 lg. potato
  ½ t. oil
          salt and pepper, to taste

4. Boil the potato in its skin in heavily salted water until tender. Refresh and cut into slices 3 inches wide.

5. Heat the oil in a nonstick pan, season potatoes well, and fry on both sides until golden.

Creamed onion

  4 oz.   onion (¾ C.), peeled and sliced
  ½   garlic clove
  5 fl.oz. milk (⅔ C.)
           salt and pepper
  2 fl.oz. heavy cream (¼ C.)
  1 t.   chopped chives

6. Put the onion, garlic, milk, and seasoning into a pan and simmer gently until soft. Strain through a sieve and drain for 2 minutes.

7. Pour the cream into a liquidizer, add the strained onion, and blend for one minute. Pour into a bowl, check for seasoning, and keep warm. Just before serving, scatter chives over bowl.

Red wine sauce

  3   shallots, chopped
  3 fl.oz. red wine (⅓ C.)
  2 T.   Port
  1   bay leaf
           sprig of thyme
           small sprig of rosemary
  ½   garlic clove
  4 fl.oz. veal or venison stock (½ C.)
  1 t.   butter
           salt and pepper
  2 T.   vegetable oil

8. Put all the ingredients except the stock, butter, vegetable oil, and seasoning into a saucepan and reduce to a syrup consistency.

9. Add the stock and return to a boil. Reduce the sauce by half and then strain through a fine sieve. Whisk in the butter and season to taste. Keep warm.

10. Preheat the oven to 450°F (or gas mark 8). Form the two patties into four rissoles. Heat the oil in a frying pan. Flour the rissole and fry on both sides. Place in the oven for 6 minutes.

11. To serve, stir the chives into the creamed onion. Place the sautéed potatoes in the middle of each plate with two rissoles on top. Pour the red wine sauce over and top each rissole with a spoonful of creamed onion. *Serves 2*

Red Summer Fruit Marinated in Rose Petal Syrup with Melon Sorbet

Rose petal syrup

10 fl.oz.	red wine (1 ¼ C.)
1	vanilla pod, split
	sugar—sweeten to taste
½ t.	cornstarch
1 T.	red wine
8 oz.	lightly scented rose petals
12 oz.	mixed red fruit (2½ C.), e.g., halved strawberries, raspberries, cherries, red currants, black currants, or blackberries

1. Boil together the 10 ounces of wine, vanilla pod, and sugar.

2. Blend the cornstarch with the tablespoon of wine and add to the pan. Boil again for 2 minutes. Pour the liquid onto the rose petals, cover, and marinate overnight.

3. The next day, pour through a fine sieve, pressing to extract all the juices.

4. Wash the fruits carefully and add to the marinade. Chill for 3–4 hours.

Melon sorbet

10 fl.oz.	syrup (1 ¼ C.)
10 fl.oz.	melon pulp (2 C.)—preferably Chantrase

5. Liquidize together syrup and melon pulp and pass through a fine sieve. Process through an ice cream machine.

Baskets

> 2 oz. plain flour (⅓ C.)
> 2 oz. icing sugar (⅓ C.) (confectioners sugar)
> 2 oz. butter (½ stick), melted
> 1   egg white
>   mint sprigs for garnish

6. Preheat oven to 375°F (or gas mark 5).

7. Sift the flour and icing sugar and add the butter and egg white. Whisk until homogenized and chill for 15 minutes.

8. Spread 1½ teaspoons of mixture into rounds 3–4 inches wide on an oiled nonstick baking sheet, and bake for 4–5 minutes.

9. Remove from the oven and press the rounds into bun tins to make them into basket shapes.

10. To serve, divide the fruit between four plates and place a basket, filled with sorbet, in the center. Decorate with a sprig of mint.

Serves 4

7

EAST ANGLIA

Romans, Saxons, Vikings, and Normans successively conquered the flat expanses of East Anglia. At one time this watery region held the great kingdom of the East Angles, later divided into the smaller kingdoms of north (Norfolk) and south (Suffolk). Cambridge and the Fens were ruled by the Middle Angles. The kingdom of the East Angles was established in Essex after the retreat of the Roman Legions. A Saxon village that was abandoned in about A.D. 650 has been reconstructed at West Stow in Suffolk. Three structures have been built—a communal hall and two thatched oak houses. East Anglia, with much of its land surrounded on three sides by water, is a region set apart from the rest of Britain. Parts of East Anglia are hauntingly remote. The back-to-back houses, soot, and polluted waters of the Industrial Revolution bypassed East Anglia, as did the bombs of World War II, allowing East Anglia to preserve undisturbed a great deal of her architectural history. There is even a Stone Age flint factory with labyrinthine pits and shafts that can still be visited near Thetford at Grimes Graves. The seventh century saw the spread of Christianity among East Anglians and the building of monasteries and churches was zealously undertaken. By the Middle Ages, East Anglia was the most densely populated part of England. For seven hundred years the wool trade brought prosperity to the region. Wool cloth, spun by Flemish weavers, was traded throughout the world and made the names Kersey, Worsted, and Lindsay household words. Handsome houses that once belonged to rich wool merchants are much in evidence, many of them turned into inns or museums. Here are some of the best-endowed churches in the country, adorned by the riches of grateful merchants.

East Anglia is known for many wonderful foods, including crab, samphire, ginger beer, harvest cakes, boiled beef and carrots with dumplings, Queens pudding, oysters, fish soup, apple dishes, and foods scented with saffron.

Norfolk Harvest Cakes

2 oz. butter (¼ C.), at room temperature
3 oz. sugar (⅓ C.)
1 lg. egg
6 oz. flour (1 C. + 2 T.)
1 t. baking powder
2 oz. crystallized ginger (¼ C.), chopped

1. Preheat oven to 400°F (or gas mark 6). Cream the butter and sugar until light and fluffy.
2. Lightly beat the egg and add to the creamed ingredients.
3. Sift the flour with the baking powder and add to the mixture with the crystallized ginger.
4. Butter small muffin cups or cake tins and spoon in the mixture. Bake for about 20 minutes.

The southernmost county in East Anglia is Essex. Its coastal region close to London has the lively seaside towns of Southend-on-Sea, Clacton-on-Sea, and Dovercourt, where cheerful London accents can be heard. Other stretches of the Essex coastline are wild and remote—the haunt of bird-watchers. The medieval walled port city of Harwich was home to the captain of the *Mayflower*, Christopher Jones, whose ship the Pilgrim Fathers sailed to America in 1620. Today ferryboats ply the waters of Harwich en route to Holland, Hamburg, and Esbjerg. Fishermen daily haul their boats up onto the pebbly beach at Aldeburgh, a quiet coastal resort. Aldeburgh men sailed with Sir Francis Drake in the ships *Greyhound* and *Pelican*, built here in the days before the lower reaches of the river silted up. It is still a haven for yachtsmen. George Crabbe, who was born in Aldeburgh, wrote the narrative poem *The Borough* in the mid-eighteenth century, and it was later adapted by Benjamin Britten as his famous opera *Peter Grimes*. Britten and the singer Peter Pears founded the annual Aldeburgh Festival, the largest music festival in England, which attracts music lovers from around the globe. Festival events are held in the Snape Maltings, the fifteenth-century church of St. Peter and St. Paul, and the Jubilee Hall. Not to be missed is the Aldeburgh Moot Hall, a glorious four-hundred-year-old half-timbered building used still for council meetings, which houses the town museum.

Inland from Aldeburgh is Framlingham, an old market town, where an interesting twelfth-century castle with a uniform curtain wall and square towers was constructed before square towers were replaced by round ones. In the seventeenth century the castle was bequeathed to Pembroke College, Cambridge, and a Poor House, which is still in existence, was built there.

The sea continues to encroach upon East Anglia's coastlands. At Dunwich the sea has buried the medieval town beneath the waves. Hundreds of houses and churches were washed away in one night. When the weather is stormy, nearby villagers claim to hear the church bells ringing below the surface of the sea. Not only towns but farmlands are gradually being lost to the waves.

Colchester has had settlements since the fifth century B.C.—the oldest recorded history in England. The Romans established a major colony at Colchester (Camulodunum). The last major, bloody battle waged against them was by Boadicea, queen of the Iceni tribe from East Anglia who, attempting to defend her kingdom from the Romans, was flogged and her daughters raped. In retaliation Boadicea and her army massacred Roman occupants of Colchester and went on to sack London and St. Albans. During the Roman counterattack Queen Boadicea took poison rather than be captured. The Romans proceeded to lay waste to the rebels' lands, finally subduing most of southern England. Roman remains here include mosaics, temples, and parts of the walls that girdled the city. When the Normans built here they used Roman bricks. Romans, who amplified our larders with many new foods, found the Colchester oyster on England's eastern shore exactly to their liking. To this day Colchester celebrates its famous oyster at an annual Oyster Feast.

Oyster Stew

```
 8 fl.oz.  milk (1 C.)
 8 fl.oz.  cream (1 C.)
 2 oz.     butter (¼ C.)
16 oz.     oysters (2 C.), shucked and juices reserved
           freshly ground black pepper, to taste
 1 T.      snipped dill
```

1. Put milk and cream into top of a double boiler, over boiling water, and heat until beginning to steam.

2. Meanwhile melt butter over moderate heat in a frying pan until hot. Add oysters, and as soon as their edges begin to curl pour them and the butter into the milk mixture.

3. Immediately season to taste and add snipped dill.

4. Serve at once in heated bowls. *Serves 4*

Quiet inland villages attract another sort of tourist, especially in the area where Essex borders Suffolk, for this is Constable (1776–1873) country. John Constable was born in the village of East Bergholt. His father was the mill owner at Flatford on the River Stour. Constable's paintings "The Hay Wain," "Flatford Mill," and "Willy Lott's Cottage" at Flatford have made this part of East Anglia famous. Boat rentals are easy to find in this flat water-laced land, and the best way to approach the mill at Flatford and see it at its romantic best is by boat. Nearby in the village of Dedham on Brook Street, Fountain House, a charming guest house filled with paintings, will give you a warm welcome. Run by James and Wendy Anne Sarton, the house has an oak-beamed dining room overlooking a lovely garden. Here the pristine vegetables are a delight. Wendy Anne Sarton cooks straightforward British dishes, such as succulent roast beef, deviled kidneys, and melt-in-the-mouth puddings.

Just north of the River Stour as it flows westward is Stoke-by-Nayland. The tall tower of its fifteenth-century church is a local landmark visible for miles. Constable painted a canvas of Stoke-by-Nayland church and was so taken with the flint and brick tower that he painted it into several other landscapes whether it belonged there or not. An old pub, called the Angel Inn, on the village main street has been renovated into a comfortable inn. The kitchen, under Mark Johnson, draws accolades and knowledgeable diners. Fresh fish and vegetarian dishes are always available, and great flair is shown in his oriental seafood parcels, rabbit terrine with Cumberland sauce, and spectacular fruit desserts.

Suffolk has some of the prettiest villages in East Anglia. Lavenham, Hadleigh, and Kersey are renowned for their exquisite sixteenth-century houses, built by wealthy mill owners. Flint built the cottages of East Anglia. Flint set directly into mortar was sometimes surrounded by bricks for added durability. Pargeting—an elaborate sixteenth-century relief plaster modeling—adds curlicues and leaf designs to house fronts. Many cottages in East Anglia are half-timbered, but the plasterwork between the timbers is often colored in soft pastel shades rather than the more usual plain white.

Wool was so important to the economy of England that in the Middle Ages Edward III decreed that the Lord High Chancellor should sit on a woolsack in the House of Lords, a tradition upheld to this day. Lavenham in the sixteenth century was one of the wealthiest towns in England and one of the most beautiful. Lavenham's modern inhabitants, justly proud of their lovely village, decided to bury their telephone lines so the look of the village was more in keeping with its Tudor heritage. Lavenham's church of St. Peter and St. Paul is a triumph of medieval architecture, and the detailed work of the stone masons and wood carvers is spectacular. Many of these tiny villages have richly endowed churches and roomy comfortable inns that once were the elegant homes of wool merchants. Unfortunately prosperity in East Anglia lasted only until the Industrial Revolution. Faster and cheaper methods of production in the Midlands saw a rapid decline in East Anglia's wool trade. Poverty was such that villagers did not have enough funds to tear down old buildings or even renovate them. This was a blessing in disguise as the villages stayed untouched, enabling their unique history to be enjoyed today. During the reign of Henry VIII, the Dissolution of the Monasteries put pay to the charitable contributions given by monks that were for some of the poor their only means of support. The Dissolution started with one thousand one hundred forty-eight of the wealthiest religious houses being annexed by the king and divided among his heirs. As the Dissolution continued the homeless monks and priests swelled the number of the poor.

Ipswich, the county town of Suffolk, is an ancient port on the Orwell estuary. Ipswich was very prosperous as a wool port in the 1500s. Cardinal Wolsey, who built Hampton Court Palace, was born here and founded a college in 1526. Only the Wolsey Gateway remains. In the Wolsey Memorial Art Gallery are paintings by Gainsborough and Constable. One of the oldest towns in England, Ipswich dates back to the tenth century. Despite rebuilding in the nineteenth century, there are still many fine medieval churches here, and today Ipswich is again a thriving port.

Further along the River Stour is Sudbury, another town well worth visiting, particularly for Americans, as William Dawes was born in Sudbury. The lantern in the tower of Old North Church in Boston that alerted Paul Revere was placed there by William Dawes. East Anglia's lovely landscapes and wide skies have inspired many painters, among them Thomas Gainsborough, who was born here. A museum celebrating the painter's life and work is now on display in his house.

Thaxted grew from a Saxon village into one of the richest communities in Essex through its wool and cutlery trade during the Middle Ages. The town's prosperity equipped the parishioners to build a beautiful and spacious cruciform church with an unusually high spire that towers one hundred eighty feet above the town. The regional dish best known in Essex and also in nearby London is boiled beef, and the dumplings that accompany the meat are a regional specialty in their own right.

Essex Boiled Beef and Carrots with Dumplings

2	lb.	salted silverside of beef
6		cloves
1	lg.	onion
1	lg.	celery stick
1		parsley sprig
8		young whole carrots
1		bay leaf

1. Cover beef with cold water and soak for 8 to 12 hours, changing water frequently to eliminate as much salt as possible. Drain. Place in a saucepan and cover with fresh water. Slowly bring to a boil, removing scum as it rises to the surface.

2. Press cloves into onion and add to the saucepan with the celery and the parsley. Lower the heat, cover pan, and simmer very gently at lowest possible setting for 1½ hours.

3. Add carrots and bay leaf and continue to simmer for a further 1–1½ hours or until meat is tender.

Dumplings

4	oz.	flour (¾ C.)
2	oz.	suet (⅓ C.), finely shredded
		enough buttermilk to form a dough

4. Mix together the flour and suet. Make a well in the center and stir in the buttermilk to form a dough.

5. Dip your hands in flour and roll dough into small balls.

6. When beef is cooked, remove to a serving dish and keep warm. Discard bay leaf, siphon off a pint of the cooking liquid, and reduce to make a light sauce to serve with the meat.

7. Meanwhile bring the remaining broth to a simmer and carefully add the dumplings. Replace lid and cook for 20 minutes.

8. Serve beef on a warm platter, surrounded by carrots and dumplings, and pass the sauce separately.   *Serves 4*

Saffron Walden was know as "Waledana" among the ancient Britons. "Saffron" was added to Walden's name for the expensive spice that was the town's most important industry from the time of Edward III to the late eighteenth century. Saffron is the costliest spice in the world. Eighty thousand pale purple crocuses are needed to make one pound of saffron, and the painstaking, backbreaking labor involved in harvesting the tiny stigmas is extraordinary. Crocuses must not be allowed to wilt in the heat or be attacked by insects, so they must be picked the minute they bloom, and dawn is the best time to harvest the three minute stigmas in each flower. In Spain, which produces the most saffron, whole families travel to the crocus field to help with the crop, as people once did at hop-gathering time in Kent. Saffron Walden's Church of St. Mary the Virgin is possibly the finest in Essex, and it may well have been built with proceeds from the tiny purple crocus. A burial ground here dates to Saxon times, and a twelfth-century Norman keep still exists. Nearby one of the most important earth mazes—a series of circular trenches—can be visited.

Sea Bass with Tomatoes, Saffron Sauce, and Spinach Mousse

    4 fillets of sea bass
    4 tomatoes
       juice of 1 lemon

Mousse

    6 oz. spinach (4 C., tightly packed)
    1   egg and 1 egg yolk
           salt, pepper, and nutmeg, to taste

Sauce

              pinch of saffron threads
    5 fl.oz. white wine (scant ⅔ C.)
    10 fl.oz. fish stock (1¼ C.)
    ½   red onion, chopped
    5 fl.oz. heavy cream (1¼ C.)
               salt and pepper

   1. Wipe the fish with dampened paper towel and refrigerate. Peel, seed, and dice the tomatoes. Set aside.
   2. Blanch the spinach in boiling water, then refresh under cold water. Drain, and squeeze out the remaining water. Finely chop spinach or whirl briefly in the food processor. Preheat the oven to 325°F (or gas mark 3).
   3. Whisk together the eggs, thoroughly stir in the spinach, and season to taste with salt, pepper, and grated nutmeg. Pour into four buttered ramekins and bake in a bain-marie for 30 minutes. Leave in a warm place until ready to serve.

4. Soak the saffron in hot water for 10 minutes. Meanwhile, place wine, stock, and the chopped onion in a saucepan and reduce. Add the cream and put sauce through a sieve. Stir in the saffron liquid and season.

5. Place fish in one layer in a shallow heat-proof dish and sprinkle with salt and lemon juice. Cover with buttered waxed paper and bake for 10 minutes.

6. Gently reheat sauce but do not boil. Pool sauce on each heated plate and top with a fillet of fish. Invert the spinach mousse to one side of fillet and a small mound of diced tomatoes on the other.

Serves 4

Northwest of Saffron Walden is the city of Cambridge. Cambridge University was originally founded in the thirteenth century by Franciscan, Carmelite, and Dominican monks. Following a disagreement at Oxford University, a group of students left and went to live in Cambridge. Seventy years later Cambridge University came into its own when the Bishop of Ely in 1281 opened the first college, Peterhouse. Henry VI founded King's College in 1441. King's Chapel, a separate building, has elegant fan vaulting and spectacular stained glass windows. Next to Peterhouse is the Fitzwilliam Museum, which has a fantastic collection of paintings and manuscripts—among these are works by Titian, Rembrandt, and Turner. The university today is a federation of thirty-one colleges, most of them dating from the Middle Ages. The myriad architectural styles encompass Norman, Tudor, Elizabethan, Georgian, and Victorian buildings, as well as the thoroughly modern Churchill College, which was completed in 1968. One of the best ways to see the colleges, and definitely the most leisurely, is to hire a punt and drift down the "backs" on the Cam River that flows behind the colleges. Another is to rent a bicycle to take you where cars cannot.

The Fenland facing the Wash between Lincolnshire and Cambridgeshire is a unique watery world that at one time was flooded each winter and used as grazing land in the summer. The Romans made attempts to drain the Fens. By building canals linking the natural waterways, they improved communications and made it possible to go by water from the Fens all the way to the city of York. Cereal growing and sheep rearing were extensively practiced, grain being exported to Europe from Dunwich, Yarmouth, and Brancaster. There were potteries in the Nene valley. East Anglia was fertile, industrial, and prosperous. East Anglia is rich in game. A specialty of this area is jugged rabbit, made originally in a jug or pitcher that before home ovens was stood in a pot of boiling water on top of the stove.

The Isle of Ely in Cambridgeshire was once a real island surrounded by marshy waters. The marsh today is fertile farmlands. Hereward the Wake established a stronghold on the Isle of Ely in 1070 and managed to hold the

town against the Normans for several months. The East Anglian hero was forced to surrender when the Normans finally managed to blockade the town. In many parts of England during the Norman era great castles were built at strategic points, such as Orford, Framingham, Norwich, and Castle Rising. Cathedrals erected at Ely, Norwich, and Peterborough during the same era are a great tribute to the Norman builders. Peterborough has one of Britain's finest Norman cathedrals. Ely Cathedral is one of the world's earliest. Its construction began in 1083 and was not completed until 1351. Over the intervening centuries both Ely and Norwich have been made larger and embellished. Ely is a good base for visitors interested in seeing East Anglia and the Fens.

Southeast of Ely is Newmarket. James I—the first king to rule Scotland and England—introduced horse racing to the English here, and races have been held ever since at Newmarket Heath. King James's grandson, Charles II, loved racing and actually rode at a race meet on more than one occasion. The racecourse, Rowley Mile, was named for King Charles's horse Old Rowley. He also installed his mistress, Nell Gwyn, at 5 Palace Street, Newmarket, while visiting. Since that time Newmarket has become the undisputed capital of horse racing, with dozens of stud farms, training stables, and auction houses—the most well known being Tattersalls. The famous Jockey Club, which governs English racing, is here at Newmarket.

Bury St. Edmunds, the cathedral city built in the twelfth century, is the burial place of Edmund, who was king of East Anglia from 855. King Edmund refused to give in to the Danes and was brutally slaughtered in 870. The king was first buried at Diss. When miracles began to be attributed to King Edmund, he was canonized and his martyred body removed to the Saxon monastery at Beodericsworth. The name of the town was changed to St. Edmunds Bury, which evolved to Bury St. Edmunds. The town has many fine historic buildings and an art gallery designed by Robert Adam where concerts are held. Nearby is Ickworth, a splendid Palladian mansion, beautifully furnished with Regency and eighteenth-century pieces.

Norwich, England's second largest city, is dominated by the spire of a medieval cathedral that was started in 1094. The stone to build the cathedral was shipped to England from Normandy and brought up the River Wensum. Norwich was originally a Saxon settlement built over a thousand years ago. Norwich castle also is Norman and has a marvelous keep. Located inside the castle is the large civic museum. Displays of archeological finds, silver, porcelain, and paintings, as well as a small aquarium, are here. For centuries Norwich has been the market center for most of East Anglia. A Georgian square in the city, called Tombland, gets its name from *toom*, a Saxon word meaning open-air market. The original Bishops Palace is now part of a celebrated boys' school, King Edward VI School; one of its famous pupils was Lord Nelson.

Adlard's at 79 Upper St. Giles Street, Norwich, is an elegant restaurant with walls covered in gorgeous green suede. Acclaimed as the County Restaurant of the Year, Adlard's has a number four rating in the *Good Food Guide*. David Adlard trained at the Connaught Hotel in London under master chef Michel Bourdin. David Adlard takes enormous pains to make sure that everything that comes out of his kitchen is as perfect as it can possibly be. He excels at producing lovingly simmered stocks for his flavorful sauces, and his cooking has won him a Michelin Star. Salad and salad flowers are grown in David and Mary Adlard's garden, fish comes straight from boats docking thirty miles (48 kilometers) away at Lowestoft. Wild mushrooms, quail eggs, fruits in season, and organic vegetables in summer are all local. The Adlards create a relaxing ambience with crisp, white tablecloths over floor-length dark green undercloths, candles, lamps, beautiful heavy glassware, and masses of fresh flowers. Waiters are bright and friendly but never intimidating. David Adlard's two pet peeves are waiters who hover, and having his wine bottle placed out of reach when he is having dinner. You won't find hovering waiters, and nobody will hide your wine bottle at Adlard's; it will be right there on your table. David Adlard is very keen on his wine list, and you are assured of a very catholic choice of European and American wines. Here are a few of the wonderful dishes on David Adlard's menu: Puff pillow of wild mushrooms, Madeira sauce; Char-grilled smoked salmon with tartlet of quail's eggs, beurre blanc sauce; Rack of English lamb with pesto crust, gratin Dauphinois, and a tart of ratatouille; Breast of Lunesdale duck with warm beet and spinach ragout and Ravioli of confit of its leg with gratin Dauphinois; Turbot in a red pepper coulis with grilled Mediterranean vegetables and braised fennel; and a Caramelized pear and mascarpone cheesecake; Mocha parfait with almond tuile and mint anglaise.

David Adlard's recipe for Seafood with Sauce Bourguignonne and Winter Vegetables follows. He says the amount of fish, winter vegetables, and croutons depends on the number of people you want to serve. He also says to select prime fresh seafood, preferably local. David Adlard uses monkfish, Dover sole, turbot, and mussels for his recipe.

Seafood with Sauce Bourguignonne and Winter Vegetables

Sauce bourguignonne

2		flat fish bones and trimmings
1½	T.	olive oil
½		carrot, chopped
½		onion, chopped
½		leek, chopped
½		stalk celery, chopped
1		clove of garlic
1	t.	tomato purée
½	sm.	bay leaf
2		stalks of parsley
½		sprig of thyme
5	fl.oz.	red wine (⅔ C.)
40	fl.oz.	good chicken stock (5 C.)
10	fl.oz.	fish stock (1¼ C.)
2	oz.	unsalted butter (½ stick)
2	T.	chopped chives (optional)

1. Chop the fish bones finely and cook in oil until brown all over.

2. Remove the bones and add the vegetables and garlic. Cook until golden. Add tomato purée and cook, stirring, for 3 minutes.

3. Add fish bones, herbs, and wine and reduce slowly until the pan is almost dry.

4. Add the two stocks and cook slowly for about 45 minutes. Pass through a sieve.

5. Reduce to the correct consistency and taste. Check the seasoning. Add a little bit of arrowroot if you think the sauce is a little thin.

6. Before serving, whisk in the unsalted butter.

Fish

2 lb. monkfish fillet
1 lb. turbot, boned
1 lb. Dover sole, boned
5 lb. mussels, scrubbed

7. Cut up the fish into small, elegant pieces.

8. Steam the mussels separately, removing them with tongs as soon as the shells open. Discard any that do not open. Steam the fish, taking care as some fish cook quicker than others. We start with monkfish and finish with Dover sole.

9. Drain the fish and pile in the middle of your hot plate or soup bowl.

10. Pour the sauce on top and sprinkle the winter vegetables and croutons over it. Finish with chopped chives, if you like.

Winter vegetables

¼ head savoy cabbage
3   parsnips
3   turnips
1 knob celeriac
3   celery stalks

11. Cut into small pleasing shapes: triangles, balls, matchsticks, etc.

12. Cook individually in plenty of salted water. When cooked "al dente," drain, refresh, and season again.

Croutons

7 slices stale white bread
4 T.   olive oil

13. Cut stale white bread into ¼-inch squares. Sauté in olive oil until golden brown.   *Serves* 10

Norfolk's Great Yarmouth was once a thriving port where fishing boats fetched in hundreds of pounds of herrings. It earned the title "Great" in 1272 when Henry III granted the town a charter. Great Yarmouth is a popular starting point for tours of the Norfolk Broads—inland waterways that cover a two hundred-mile area and link over thirty lakes. Visitors to this chain of lakes can hire a craft at either Wroxham or Horning (both villages are on the River Bure). The waterways were formed in the Middle Ages by turf cutters slicing ever deeper for peat needed to fuel fires. Boating on the Norfolk Broads attracts increasing numbers of yachtsmen. The land is so flat that the waterways are not always visible, and you will see sails moving that appear to be sailing through the fields. From the water you will catch sight of church spires, an occasional windmill, and many unusual species of bird life. England's largest butterfly, the swallowtail, makes its home in the reeds here. For the dedicated bird-watcher, winter is probably the best time to come, but the average sailing or cruising holidaymaker comes with the sun. Jetties at the water's edge once were used for unloading cargo, as most supplies then came by water. There is some concern among environmentalists that so many boats—some ten thousand a year—could be detrimental to the waterway's wildlife, and the disappearance of plant life from the water is causing even more anxiety, especially since the exact cause has not been identified.

Farther north along the shore from the Norfolk Broads is Cromer, an ancient town whose old narrow streets weave a web around the fourteenth-century Church of St. Peter and St. Paul and continue down to the shore. Cromer is justly famous for its excellent crab, and the old town is the center of Norfolk's crabbing industry. A new town has grown up around the old, to service the holidaymakers who vacation on Cromer's long sandy beaches. This deep sand, beloved by children for making sand castles and by sunbathers, is a peril to the fishermen. Offshore is a treacherous sandbank, called the Devil's Throat, that has caused trouble for the fishing boats for centuries.

Crab Salad

1	lb.	lump crab meat
2		ripe tomatoes, diced
1		jalapeño pepper, seeded and minced (use rubber gloves)
3	T.	minced fresh coriander
5	T.	fresh lime juice
3	T.	extra virgin olive oil
		salt and freshly ground pepper, to taste
1	lg.	ripe avocado

1. Combine all ingredients except avocado in a salad bowl and refrigerate.

2. Take salad out of refrigerator at least 30 minutes before serving, to take off the chill. At the last minute, peel and cube avocado and gently fold into salad.   *Serves 4, or 6 as an appetizer*

Also on this northern stretch of coast is Wells-next-the-Sea, where flint cottages and Georgian houses add grace to this old-fashioned fishing port. In the harbor are shrimp and whelk boats, both crustaceans much loved by holidaymakers, who buy small plates of them from seaside stalls as snacks.

Fettuccine with Mussels and Anchovies

3	lb.	rope mussels
8	fl.oz.	fish stock (1 C.)
4	fl.oz.	dry white wine (½ C.)
2		shallots, minced
2		sprigs of fresh thyme
3	T.	extra virgin olive oil
3		garlic cloves, minced
4		anchovy fillets, rinsed and thinly sliced
2	T.	lemon juice
12	oz.	fettuccine
6	lg.	basil leaves, thinly shredded

1. Scrub the mussels and put into a saucepan with a tight-fitting lid. Add the fish stock, white wine, minced shallots, and the sprigs of thyme. Cover and boil vigorously until the mussels open—2 to 3 minutes.

2. Remove mussels from shell, discarding any that do not open, and set aside.

3. Strain mussel cooking liquid and reduce to concentrate flavors. Set aside 8 fluid ounces (½ cup). Cool and freeze the remainder for another dish.

4. Heat olive oil in a medium-sized saucepan and gently sauté garlic for 2 minutes. Add anchovies and continue to cook for one more minute. Stir in mussel stock and lemon juice, and remove from heat.

5. Cook fettuccine, drain, and keep warm.

6. Reheat anchovy mixture, add mussels to heat through, and pour over fettuccine. Garnish with basil strips and serve immediately.

Serves 3–4

Moorings, at 6 Freeman Street, Wells-next-the-Sea, is an informal, friendly restaurant owned by Bernard and Carla Phillips. Carla Phillips is a dedicated cook who makes her own pickles and chutneys and also smokes chicken and fish for the restaurant. Suppliers are local, and there is succulent shellfish straight from the sea in summer and well-hung game in winter. Fruits and vegetables are pristine. The food here is inventive, satisfying, and reliable.

Nearby is Walsingham, where a vision of the Virgin Mary turned this small town into the most important pilgrimage site in England until the Dissolution. Between Walsingham and Wells-on-the-Sea is Holkham Hall, planned and built in the eighteenth century by Thomas Coke, Earl of Leicester. His family lives here still. The outside is austere in contrast to the luxurious interior, where visitors will see grand state rooms, decorative ceilings, a collection of classical art treasures, and fine paintings.

Norfolk Pheasant in Cider

1		plump pheasant, drawn and trussed
2	T.	lemon juice
4	T.	butter, for sautéing
2		slices of streaky bacon, chopped
1	sm.	onion, chopped
10	fl.oz.	sparkling cider (1¼ C.)
5	fl.oz.	chicken stock (scant ⅔ C.)
2		eating apples
		salt and pepper to taste

Garnish: well-shaped root vegetables and steamed new potatoes

1. Rub pheasant with lemon juice. Set aside.
2. Melt butter in frying pan and sauté chopped bacon and onion. Pour into a heavy, lidded ovenproof casserole, and place pheasant onto layer of onion and bacon. Preheat oven to 325°F (or gas mark 3).
3. Pour in cider and stock and bring to a boil over medium heat. Cover closely and bake for 30 minutes.
4. Meanwhile peel and core apples and quarter them. Remove lid and carefully put apples into casserole around pheasant. Season well, cover, and bake for a further 30 minutes or until pheasant is tender.
5. Remove pheasant to a warm dish to rest for 5 minutes and surround with root vegetables and steamed potatoes. Reduce the cooking liquid to a sauce consistency and serve separately.

Serves 4

The place that attracts more tourists than any other in the area is Sandringham House, situated eight miles (13 km) north of King's Lynn, a summer retreat for the royal family. In 1861 Edward VII bought Sandringham House and seven thousand acres of gardens, which today are open to the public except when a member of the royal family is in residence. King's Lynn on the River Great Ouse, rich in medieval architecture, is a busy port with ferry links to the Continent. Once part of the property of the bishops of Norwich, Bishop's Lynn, as it was then called, was renamed King's Lynn when the property was seized by Henry VIII. King's Lynn has several ancient buildings; two of the most impressive are the Trinity Guildhall and Town Hall. Each is constructed with an eye-catching checkered design. The town's prosperity during the fourteenth century is reflected in the elegant houses built by rich merchants. George Vancouver, born here in 1757, navigated the west coast of America in 1791 and gave his name to the island and the city of Vancouver. In 1204, when King John awarded the town its charter, King's Lynn was not nearly so far inland as it is today. Hundreds of thousands of acres have been reclaimed in the intervening seven centuries.

Cornelius Vermeyden, a Dutch engineer, created the New Bedford River in the seventeenth century, straightened the winding River Great Ouse, and made channels between the two so that the overflow from the Great Ouse could empty safely into the Wash. Vermeyden's work was sabotaged regularly by the people living on the Fens who did not relish change. Eventually the work was carried out by Dutch prisoners. At that time hundreds of windmills were used to drain the Fens, but nowadays the work is done by electric pumping systems. Crisscrossed today with hundreds of drainage projects that control the annual inundation, the Fens are without doubt England's richest farmlands. Crops grown on the reclaimed land are sugar beets, barley, potatoes, and acres and acres of flowers. Trees, planted in straight lines across the boundless expanse of flat land, act as windbreaks. The soil is peat black, but peat soil has disadvantages; it is very lightweight, and in dry summers peat soil can easily be swirled into dust storms, called Fen blows, which are strong enough to take away not only the top soil but seeds too. Fen blows add to the natural shrinkage of the Fenland, causing inundation to recur.

Fenland Apple Dumplings

1	lb.	shortcrust pastry, purchased or homemade
6	T.	apricot preserves
6	lg.	unblemished eating apples
6	t.	butter
6	t.	dark brown sugar
6		cloves

1. Roll out the pastry and cut into 6 squares, each roughly 6 inches across. Place a tablespoon of apricot preserves in the center of each square.

2. Peel and core the apples. Divide the butter and brown sugar among the apples and push down into the core cavity. Place a clove on top of the butter and sugar.

3. Place each apple on top of the dollop of preserves, and pull the pastry up to almost enclose the apple—leave a small space open at the top for steam to escape. Preheat oven to 375°F (or gas mark 5).

4. Lightly grease a baking sheet, place apples on the sheet, and cook for about 30 minutes or until golden brown.

5. Cool apples a little before serving with a custard sauce or heavy cream.   *Serves* 6

Charles Kingsley, poet and author of *The Water Babies* (1863) and rector of Eversley church in Hampshire, was once a student at Cambridge in East Anglia and in later years became a teacher there. Kingsley, captivated by the vast flat expanses around him, wrote the following words describing the fens:

> They have a beauty of their own, these great fens, even now, when they are dyked and drained, tilled and fenced—a beauty as of the sea, of boundless expanse and freedom.

Stamford was the capital of the Fens under the Danes. It is one of the finest medieval towns in Europe and was recorded in the Domesday Book as a market town. Well endowed with Tudor and Georgian houses, Stamford has a well-preserved fifteenth-century almshouse, and six of its seventeen medieval churches remain. One of these, St. Martin's, holds the tomb of Lord Burghley, treasurer to Elizabeth I and the builder of nearby Burghley House. Much of Stamford was destroyed by the Lancastrians, and the beauty of its seventeenth- and eighteenth-century buildings is largely due to its indigenous limestone and to the great architects Robert Adams, Inigo Jones, and John Thorpe, who lived in the vicinity of this medieval beauty.

Burghley House, which took over thirty years to build, is one of the finest Elizabethan houses in England. It was begun by Sir William Cecil, one of the queen's ministers, who in due course became Lord Burghley and Lord High Treasurer of England. For four hundred years Burghley House has been the home of the Cecil and Exeter families. The house is built around a courtyard and is embellished at every corner by towers and turrets. The state rooms have painted ceilings, silver fireplaces, and over 700 art treasures, as well as tapestries and exquisite furniture.

Grantham, a prosperous market town, is the administrative center of a huge, rich agricultural area. Built on a limestone plateau on the banks of the River Witham, Grantham has a fourteenth-century parish church, St. Wulfrum's, with a beautiful spire. Opposite the church is a fifteenth-century school where Sir Isaac Newton was a pupil. Oliver Cromwell made Grantham his chief base of operations. The fourteenth-century Angel Inn saw the signing of the duke of Buckingham's death warrant by Richard III. Grantham House is also of the fourteenth century. The daughter of Henry VII, Princess Margaret, stopped here on her journey north to marry James IV of Scotland. In Castlegate the sign of the Beehive Inn is an actual working beehive. Lady Margaret Thatcher, the first woman prime minister of England, was born at Grantham. Seven miles (11 kilometers) southwest of the town is the fabulous Belvoir Castle, home of the dukes of Rutland since Henry VIII's reign. In about 1800 James Wyatt rebuilt the house into a romantic Gothic-style castle. Following a fire, the duchess of Rutland had Wyatt's sons, Matthew and Benjamin, rebuild and redecorate the house in the fanciful French rococo style. A life-size statue of the duchess stands in the extravagant Elizabeth Saloon in the east tower.

Lincolnshire has rich agricultural lowland, called Marshlands, reclaimed from the north sea in the area around the Wash. Flowering bulbs planted in the lowlands are a breathtaking sight in spring as ten thousand acres of daffodils, lilies, and hundreds of tulips, planted by color in wide swathes, raise their faces to the sun. Spring flowers are gathered and shipped to many places, including the United States, though most of these flowers are grown primarily for their bulbs rather than for their blossoms.

Situated just north of the Wash in Lincolnshire is Boston, a town laced with man-made waterways—the delight of fishermen and boating enthusiasts. Boston's soaring medieval tower, nicknamed the Stump, has been a landmark for sailors since its inception in the fourteenth century. In the seventh century St. Botolph founded a monastery on what was then Fenland. In Boston's Guildhall are the prison cells where the Pilgrim Fathers were incarcerated in 1607 after their attempt to sail to the New World was thwarted by the betrayal of the Dutch captain. Thirteen years were to pass, most of it spent in Holland, before the Pilgrim Fathers were able to join other Pilgrims for the voyage aboard the *Mayflower*. It is not unusual to see the Stars and Stripes flying beside the Union Jack in Boston, so close is their tie to America. Further north Lincolnshire's undulating Wolds, bordering the sea, are an area of natural scenic beauty, interlaced with rounded chalk hills, quiet villages, tiny market towns, and wooded valleys. Sheep and cattle graze the Wolds, and sheep markets can be seen in some small towns, such as Louth. The Viking Way—a trail used by the invading Norsemen in the ninth century—swings southward through the Wolds.

England's Victorian poet laureate Alfred, Lord Tennyson, was born at Somersby, near the cathedral town of Lincoln, in 1809. The Usher Gallery on Lindum Road has a collection of memorabilia that include Tennyson's

pens, pipes, and hats, as well as the Usher collection of watches, minia-
tures, and enamels and fine paintings. Lincoln is built on the slope of a
high limestone plateau, on the banks of the River Witham. The highest part
of the town, and the oldest, is north of the river and holds the castle and
the triple-towered cathedral, which was started in 1083. A fire and an earthquake in the twelfth century destroyed much of the cathedral. The famous
octagonal tower was constructed in the fourteenth century following the
destruction of the original Norman tower. A wealth of medieval buildings
fill the area near the cathedral, and splendid sixteenth-century timber-
framed houses line Steep Hill as it descends from Castle Square.

8

THE NORTH
COUNTRY

People living in England's northern region differ not only in the way they view the world but also in their speech. Their vowel sounds and vocabulary are markedly dissimilar to those of their southern cousins. For example, small lanes or alleyways in the north country can be called snickets, wyndes, lonnens, or ginnels, depending on the valley or county the speaker calls home. Perhaps these differences can be attributed to invading tribes and nations that conquered northern areas of Britain at a particular period in history, namely Romans, Angles, Vikings, and Normans. The Vikings controlled a diagonal tract of land, called Danelaw, that stretched from Merseyside on the western shore to London's port in the east. The inhabitants of communities living within the Danelaw tract have difficulty understanding those who lived outside it. Children from villages only six miles apart called one another "foreigners" because their vowels and nouns were so different that they found each other incomprehensible. Despite these difficulties, all Northerners have one firmly ingrained idea in common, namely, that people from the south of England are snobbish, haughty, not as hardworking, and nowhere near as friendly as northern folks. This belief is especially entrenched in northerners who have never set foot in the south. People from the south, on the other hand, often think that the north of England is one of unrelieved industrial blight. They too could not be more wrong. Despite coal and shipbuilding yards in Tyne and Wear and along the Tees estuary, an area where swarms of people from Scotland, Ireland, and the West Country came in the 1900s looking for work, Northumbria has some of the most unsullied,

tranquil, and beautiful scenery in Britain. Stretching from Yorkshire to the border with Scotland, Northumbria's rugged Pennine Chain and Cumbria's high rocky fells in the west contrast with the long, sandy North Sea beaches in the east. Redcar, a resort town with its own racecourse, is one of many lively holiday retreats enjoyed by people from the industrial hubs of Middlesbrough, Stockton-on-Tees, and Darlington.

As well as splendid scenery, cultural pursuits are many and varied in the northern shires. Near the small stone market town of Barnard Castle, now a twelfth-century ruin, about fifteen miles west of Darlington, is the superb Bowes Museum. Here splendid art collections include paintings by Goya and El Greco. Farther north is Raby Castle—its brooding towers surrounded by 250 acres of parkland. The border area, liberally strewn with castles, monasteries, and priories, also has fortified houses knows as "pele" towers in both Northumbria and Scotland, built to shelter people and their livestock during the Border raids. In many villages fortified vicarages had enough room to shelter all the parishioners on upper floors of the house and all the animals on the ground floor. Intense fighting between Scotland and England necessitated the reinforcement of whole villages and towns. Alnwick, just north of Newcastle, is a fortified town and today boasts the best-preserved medieval fortress in Britain. Alnwick Castle, home to the dukes of Northumberland, has stone sentries on its north-facing battlements to fool invading Scots. Relentless skirmishing between Scotland and England forced Berwick on Tweed, a fortress town, to change allegiance thirteen times between 1147 and 1482.

On Northumbria's northern coast, overlooking the cliffs, is the dramatic ruin of Dunstanburgh Castle. The nearby town of Bamburgh was once the capitol of a Saxon king. Perched high on a rock is the striking Bamburgh Castle, which is still inhabited. The castle has a fine tapestry and weapons collection, and from its battlements it is sometimes possible to glimpse the Farne Islands to the north, settled in the sixth century by Irish missionaries. Peace has now come to the Borderlands, and today every February 14 people from both sides of the border get together to take part in the ancient ceremony of blessing the fishing nets, which heralds the start of the fishing season.

Baked Salmon Steaks with Dill and Cashew Nuts

4		salmon steaks about 1-inch thick
3	T.	lemon juice
		salt and pepper
2	T.	minced fresh dill
2	T.	shallots, chopped
4	fl.oz.	dry white wine (½ C.)
3	oz.	cashew nuts (⅔ C.), unsalted, coarsely chopped
4	T.	butter

Garnish: fresh dill sprigs, parsley sprigs, and ripe tomatoes, seeded and chopped

1. Pat salmon steaks dry and rub well with 2 tablespoons of lemon juice. Season and place in a shallow heat-proof pan. Preheat oven to 350°F (or gas mark 4).

2. Sprinkle minced dill and chopped shallots over fish, and pour wine carefully over the salmon.

3. Cover lightly with foil or waxed paper and cook for 20–25 minutes, depending on the thickness of the fish.

4. Meanwhile heat butter in a small frying pan and gently sauté cashews until beginning to brown. Season and add the remaining lemon juice. Set aside.

5. Remove salmon steaks to heated plates and keep warm. Pour juices into a pan and reduce to 4 tablespoons. Pour over fish.

6. Spoon cashews over fish and garnish plate with sprigs of herbs and a small pile of tomato concassée. Serve immediately.

Serves 4

Resorts edge the sandy North Sea coast of Northumbria from Berwick-upon-Tweed, just south of the Scottish border, along the towering cliffs of Yorkshire to Humberside's Cleethorpes. A May Fair is held at Berwick-upon-Tweed on the last Friday of the month. The fair's origins are lost in medieval mists of time, but it is known to have been well attended at least as far back as 1302. Alnwick, Hawkshead, and many other towns hold similar fairs. These festive occasions, which today have coconut shies, morris dancers, and puppet shows, can be traced to days when pagan rites were held in spring and summer to ward off evil spirits and to pay homage to powerful fertility gods. The May Day Feast was important, heralding as it did the fertile summer months, renewal, and growth. Milk dishes are considered appropriate for this celebration and custard tarts or syllabub—a creamy custard—were always part of the feast on May Day in Northumbria. Men participate still in the Flaming Tar ceremony on New Year's Eve. This requires each man to carry a lighted tar barrel on his head while marching through the dark streets to the town bonfire, where he then hurls the barrel into the flames.

Another regional specialty of Northumbria called Singin' Hinny is a simply a dinner plate-sized scone, served warm and eaten with enthusiasm for tea, either at four in the afternoon or at high tea in the early evening.

Durham is famous for its university, its castle, and its Romanesque cathedral. These three edifices—an impressive sight—sit in a row on a high wooded peninsula that towers above the River Wear. Durham Cathedral, built in the eleventh century, is the finest Norman cathedral in western Europe. Until 1836 the princely bishops of Durham governed as they wished within their own diocese—even minting their own coins. The original wooden cathedral was built by monks who fled the Holy Isle, carrying the body of St. Cuthbert to a place of safekeeping. They chose the impregnable site above the river to house the saint's remains. The Holy Isle, or Lindisfarne, is one of twenty-six tiny Farne Islands situated four and a half miles off the coast of Northumbria. The Farnes have been a holy site and place of pilgrimage since the earliest days of Christianity in Britain. St. Aidan and St. Cuthbert traveled to the islands in the seventh century. From 793 the monasteries were sacked repeatedly by Viking hordes. A fourteenth-century chapel still stands on Inner Farne, and on Lindisfarne's highest point is a sixteenth-century castle built to guard the harbor. The islands are now an important nature reserve visited by botanists and bird-watchers.

At one time all churches were sanctuaries for fugitives from justice, many of whom in those turbulent days were not necessarily criminals. As soon as the fugitive grasped the knocker on the church door, he was considered beyond the reach of the law, as long as he promised to leave the country within nine days. Dressed in the traditional white robe and carrying a cross, the fugitive went unmolested by the law down to the nearest dock to freedom.

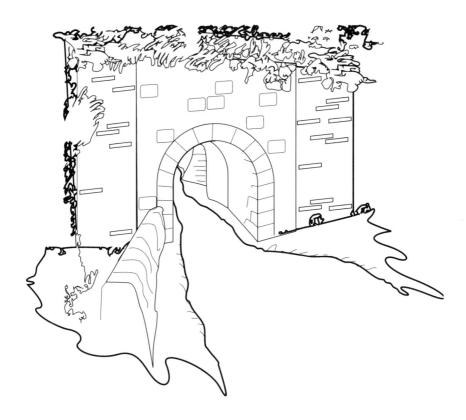

Ruins of former priories dot the landscape between Durham and New-castle upon Tyne. Newcastle was one of the original towns founded by the Romans along Hadrian's Wall. The wall, fifteen feet high and seven-and-a-half feet thick (5 by 2.5 m), ran across the border country for seventy-three miles (117 km). At one-mile intervals small contingents of soldiers who guarded the gatehouses were housed in "mile castles." Roman legions were garrisoned in seventeen forts on or near the wall. The best preserved of these is Housesteads. In the vicinity of the Roman fort Vindolanda, the wall has been reconstructed stone by stone by local schoolchildren from Gateshead. At Chester an excavated Roman bathhouse can be seen.

Henry II began building the castle at Newcastle upon Tyne in 1172. Today Newcastle is an elegant, tree-filled town with graceful curving streets and many impressive Victorian public buildings with colonnaded facades. Lawns, fountains, and pools surround the new Civic Center, opened in 1968. Newcastle University's Department of Antiquities has a museum that con-tains one of the largest and oldest collections of prehistoric, Roman, and Anglo-Saxon relics in Britain. A fortified gate formerly part of the castle, known as Black Gate, houses the world's only bagpipe museum, with a collection of over one hundred bagpipes, and a pipe maker's workshop. Newcastle's inhabitants, for reasons which are not entirely clear, refer to themselves as Geordies. Possibly this is a corruption of the name George, after the numerous kings who have borne that name.

Newcastle upon Tyne is the birthplace of George Stephenson, the inventor of the first locomotive engine for hauling coal. He later astonished the populace with the speed of his engine, the Rocket, which topped thirty miles per hour. Some people warned that it was unnatural for humans to travel at such speeds, and they were afraid the skin on their faces would fly off!

The Venerable Bede's monastery was in this part of the country at Sunderland, twelve miles from Newcastle. This famous Benedictine monk, of the seventh century, was the most learned man in England. He wrote an *Ecclesiastical History of the English People* that today is still an indispensable source of knowledge about people and events during his lifetime. Bede also instituted the chronology terms B.C. and A.D. in use to this day.

Yorkshire's huge county was reconfigured in 1974, causing Yorkshire to lose her North, East, and West Ridings. Yorkshire is now divided into three counties—North Yorkshire, West Yorkshire, and South Yorkshire—and boasts two large national parks—the Dales and the North York Moors. It is customary in the dales to plow one field and leave the one next to it fallow, yielding a patchwork of different shades of yellow and green. As well as the stunningly beautiful hills and dales well known for their peace and solitude, Yorkshire has innumerable castles, fine historic country houses, and the glorious ruins of Fountains Abbey, the best-known Cistercian monastery in England and the wealthiest. Other once-prosperous abbeys nearby are Rievaulx, Jervaulx, Byland, and Selby.

Yorkshire's valleys are lush and extremely fertile. Beneath these rolling hills are rich seams of coal and iron that gave rise to the great industrial cities of Bradford, Sheffield, Barnsley, and Doncaster. Wool—the backbone of Yorkshire's economy—was clipped from thousands upon thousands of sheep that grew fat on the lush grass of the dales. Hundreds of Yorkshire mill towns turned out woolen cloth for clothes stitched in Yorkshire's city Leeds, that were then exported around the world from Yorkshire ports. Before the vast county was subdivided, Yorkshire was big enough and prosperous enough to have been a separate country unto itself. Without question the jewel in Yorkshire's crown is the glorious city of York. The famed city's beginnings go back to A.D. 71, when a legion of Roman soldiers built a fortress at the confluence of two rivers and called it Eburacum. In 866 Vikings captured the city and renamed it Jorvik, and it became one of the greatest trading cities in northern Europe. York's streets still have Viking names—Nessgate, Coppergate, and Michelgate. Vikings created the basic ground plan of modern-day York, laying out the streets, shops, gardens, a religious center, and a military center. Later the Normans pillaged and burned large parts of York. Its famed library and the city records went up in flames. During the melée and confusion as the flames leapt higher, the Normans, to everyone's astonishment, were defeated. William, stunned by this turn of events, began a revengeful campaign to totally subdue northern England. The countryside between Durham and York was laid waste, and 100,000 people died of starvation. Despite this catastrophe, eventually peace was restored and the Normans rebuilt the cities. They also took the precaution of building huge fortresses at Richmond, Skipton, Scarborough, and other strategic points.

York is no stranger to mammoth battles. The War of the Roses (1455–1485) (so named because a white rose was the emblem of the house of York, and a red rose that of the duchy of Lancaster) raged at York for thirty years as the two sides battled for England's throne. After the Battle of Bosworth, they were united by the marriage of Lancaster's Henry Tudor to Margaret of York. Fittingly their emblem became a large red rose with a smaller white rose centered within it.

York's glory is reflected in the many imposing buildings that have survived here for centuries. Medieval banquets can be arranged at St. William's college, a gorgeous half-timbered black and white building near the Minster. The medieval Merchant Adventurers' Hall is also timber framed. One of the most famous and picturesque streets is the cobbled Shambles, which was once a meat market; meat hooks hang there still. The upper stories of the ancient houses overhang narrow streets, where mullioned windows glitter in the sunshine. Quaint painted signs denote the doorways of tiny, medieval shops. Rising above the old section of the city are the tall, golden-hued towers of York Minster, the fourth church to be raised on this Saxon site. In the crypt stands the altar where the baptism of King Edwin took place in 627. York Minster is the biggest Gothic cathedral in England, second only to Canterbury in ecclesiastical importance. Built between 1220 and 1472, the medieval stained glass magnificently depicting each era since the thirteenth century is stupendous. The fabled east window is larger than a tennis court. From the walkway atop the medieval city walls that surround parts of York, a panorama of the Minster, the city, and its gardens unfolds. Every four years, with the ruins of St. Mary's Abbey as a backdrop, York holds a cycle of mystery plays.

A rich cache of recently unearthed Viking artifacts are on display at the new Jorvik Museum. From studies done of these finds, which include dozens of pairs of leather shoes from a leather-worker's shop, archaeologists know that the workshops, market stalls, and one-roomed houses with their central hearths were all roofed in straw. Geese, chickens, pigs, dogs, and cats foraged here at will. Vikings we now know were meat eaters, used wooden bowls at meals, and wore skins, furs, and leather footwear. Combs for grooming were made from deer antlers, and the houses were illuminated with oil lamps. They were skilled boatbuilders and took to the seas to catch herring for food. The new Jorvik Museum has time-car travel that takes you through an amazing reconstruction of the tenth-century city of Jorvik, complete with its ancient sights, sounds, and smells.

At Melton's on Scarcroft Road in York, on a late May evening visit in 1993, excellent smoked chicken and goat cheese on red and frisé lettuce, served as an appetizer, was followed by celery soup flavored with cumin, and pink, succulent roast lamb accompanied by several varieties of crisply cooked vegetables. Desserts are imaginative and delectable. Michael Hjort, chef-owner with his wife, Lucy, is sensitive to Britain's large number of vegetarians. A unique idea at Melton's is to serve specialities of seafood on Tuesday, puddings on Wednesday, and vegetarian food on Thursday. Local supplies add to the fresh flavors of Michael Hjort's "down-to-earth" cooking. The basic menu changes quarterly, supplemented by daily specials, such as Salad of scallops and smoked bacon; Roast fillet of red snapper with a cucumber salad; Stir-fry of Dover sole with bean sprouts, broccoli, leeks, and garlic; Roast duck with honey and black pepper; and Escallop of salmon poached in red wine with smoked eel. Desserts include White chocolate parfait with lime syrup; Walnut tart; and Steamed ginger pudding with sherry custard. Michael Hjort has contributed two recipes for you to try at home—one interesting lamb dish and one chicken dish.

Lamb Marinated as Game

Marinade

1	bottle of dry red wine
3 T.	red wine vinegar
2 T.	olive oil
10	crushed juniper berries
1	handful black peppercorns, crushed, not ground
1	head of garlic, unpeeled and halved horizontally
	root vegetables, roughly chopped to include one onion, some celery, a few carrots and leeks
1	sprig of thyme
1	strip of orange peel
1	bay leaf
	a few parsley stalks

Lamb and sauce

1   leg of lamb, either whole or boned and rolled
2 T.   butter and flour, combined
        additional butter, if necessary
1   thimbleful of gin

1. Use a container that will allow the marinade to cover the meat. If there is none suitable, you will need to remember to turn the meat periodically so that it marinates evenly.

2. Mix the marinade ingredients and pour over the leg of lamb. Leave to marinate for between 3 and 7 days.

3. Preheat the oven to 350°F (or gas mark 4). Remove leg of lamb from marinade and dry it, saving the marinade.

4. Roast the lamb in the oven for 2 hours or until pink or well-done as you prefer. Let rest.

5. Meanwhile strain the marinade. Set aside the liquid and sweat the vegetables until softened. Pour the marinade over the vegetables and simmer gently for about 20 minutes.

6. Strain the marinade once more, squeezing the vegetables to extract juices before discarding them.

7. Boil the liquid ferociously until reduced to one-third.

8. Add degreased pan juices, and any meat stock you have on hand, and reduce further—unless you feel further reduction will leave you short of gravy, in which case thicken sauce with the butter and flour mixture.

9.   Taste sauce. If it is too sharp add more butter until it tastes right to you. Add the gin and keep warm until ready to serve the lamb.   *Serves 6–8*

Braised Chicken with Garlic and Aromatics

1 lg.   chicken, preferably corn-fed
3   celery sticks with leaves, roughly chopped
2   heads of garlic, peeled
6 T.   virgin olive oil
2 T.   balsamic vinegar (optional)
1   bunch mixed herbs—rosemary or basil, thyme, and parsley
        freshly ground black pepper and salt, to taste

1. Remove fat from inside the chicken carcass.

2. Preheat oven to 300°F (or gas mark 2), and place all ingredients in a large casserole with a tight-fitting lid.*

3. Cook chicken in the oven for around 3 hours. This dish is impossible to overcook and will hold warm if you turn the oven down and leave it.

4. Serve the cooked garlic, which will be soft and fairly mild, the celery, and chicken with plenty of bread to soak up the juices.

*If you seal the pot lid with a paste made of flour and water, all of the scent from the garlic will be trapped inside the pot. You can then break open the seal at the table, releasing all the aroma in front of your guests.   *Serves* 3–4

About fifty miles west of York, near Bradford, is Haworth, home to the Brontë sisters, Charlotte, Emily, and Anne, and their dissolute brother, Bramwell. The Black Bull Hotel where Bramwell spent more of his time than he did on his writing is still there. The Brontë Parsonage Museum holds family memorabilia and manuscripts, and a marble stone in the Brontë chapel is inscribed with the names of family members. Charlotte's *Jane Eyre* is the prototype for all Gothic romances since its publication in 1848.

Southern and western regions of the north country are rich in beautiful country estates built on the proceeds of great industrial achievements. Fine houses, such as Harewood near Leeds, are open to visitors. Castle Howard, well known as the mansion that furnished the background for the television adaptation of Evelyn Waugh's *Brideshead Revisited*, stands in 10,000 acres of parkland, filled with lakes and fountains. This is the most fabulous and the biggest country house in Yorkshire. Its huge dome was rebuilt after a fire. The interior is a treasure-house. The land has been in the Howard family since 1571, and the house is open to visitors from spring until autumn each year.

Medicinal spas at Harrogate and Scarborough have for centuries attracted wealthy visitors to their splendid Victorian hotels. Lord Byron wrote "The Ode to a Beautiful Quaker" while staying at the lavish Crown Hotel, situated near Harrogate's famous sulphur springs. Betty's Tearooms were first opened in Harrogate by a Swiss chef and have expanded and multiplied from the original site to York and other towns in Yorkshire. Betty's is famous for traditional Yorkshire pastries served at breakfast and afternoon tea, such as Fat Rascals—a plump, fruit-filled pastry with spices, citrus peels, almonds, and cherries—and pikelettes, a flat toasted teacake soaked with butter. Luncheon dishes feature rösti and raclette, betraying the shop's Swiss origins. Betty's is a perfect place to stop for a respite from sight-seeing, shopping, or just when clouds threaten.

Ripon in North Yorkshire has an ancient cathedral with a rare Saxon crypt dating from the seventh century. Saint Wilfred, a scholar of repute, was consecrated bishop of Ripon in 669. Since the fourteenth century, Ripon's town wakeman, garbed in a long frock coat, tricorn hat, and buckled shoes, has blown his horn at nine o'clock each night at all four corners of the market square to reassure the populace that all is well. Once upon a time the gates to the town were locked when the horn sounded, and the only people abroad were villains and constables. Wilfra cakes, tarts filled with lemon curd or jam, are named for St. Wilfred of Ripon Cathedral fame.

Richmond is a charming town with a weekly flower market in its wide cobbled square. The ruins of a great Norman castle overlook the town and the gentle River Swale. Near the marketplace is a Georgian theater dating to 1788 that has recently been restored by a group of enterprising townspeople.

At Kirkby Malzeard is the Henry Jenkins pub, a good lunchtime stop named for a man reputed to have lived for 162 years. According to literature available in the pub, his age had been authenticated up to the age of 140 by reliable people who remember Henry Jenkins being present on important family occasions and at memorable community events. It is not hard to believe the tale, sitting on a bench in the fresh country air, after a pub lunch washed down with a pint of Yorkshire ale!

In September the village of Sowerby holds an ancient rush-bearing ceremony commemorating the days when rushes were collected to cover church floors. This practice gave us the word "threshold"—the piece of raised board placed in front of the door to keep the rushes (or threshes) inside the room.

In Middleham in West Yorkshire is the romantic ruin of a feudal castle, which in the thirteenth century belonged to Richard III. It is an impressive reminder of royal might even though it stands roofless with purple wild flowers growing from its ramparts. Middleham is dedicated to the breeding and training of race horses. Racing, the sport of kings, is highly regarded in Britain. It first came into prominence in 1619 when James I attended a race meet at Newmarket. At dawn every morning in Middleham, stable lads and lassies (mostly lassies) exercise the animals on "The Gallops," a long stretch of moorland in the hills above the town. Early risers go up to the Gallops to watch this fine spectacle as, outlined against the morning sky, groups of beautiful racehorses, with their jockeys upright in the stirrups, thunder by. If you close your eyes you can feel the earth tremble ever so slightly as they pass.

Pool-in-Wharfdale, near Otley, West Yorkshire, is lucky enough to have in its midst the Pool Court Restaurant, situated in a fine Georgian mansion, approximately nine miles from Harrogate, Leeds, and Bradford. Their reputation for fine food has been recognized by the leading guides of Egon Ronay, AA, and Michelin, and with a top rating from the *Good Food Guide*. During the summer months all produce is available locally. Having access to both coasts means the fish and shellfish are top quality and spanking fresh. Most of the game used in the kitchen at Pool Court is from Yorkshire. Four miles from the restaurant is Harewood House, a country house that belongs to Lord Harewood, cousin of Her Majesty the Queen. In the summer months a farm at Harewood provides Pool Court with salad vegetables and fresh herbs. David Watson is the head chef, and his cooking has flair and imagination. He trained at two well-known restaurants in London, and his dedication is such that they are both still trying to persuade him to return. The six bedrooms at Pool Court are immaculate, with great care taken by Michael and Hanni Gill, the owners, that every detail should be executed perfectly, from the monogrammed sheets to the thick bathrobes. Breakfasts are served only in the room. David Watson's menu features Roast quail on a potato cake with grapes; Potted lamb with olives wrapped in Parma ham; Hot Sole mousse; Smoked chicken and avocado with lemon mayonnaise; Breast of wood pigeon with puréed parsnip and juniper sauce; Creamed wild mushrooms in a puff pastry case with Madeira; Braised beef and oxtail wrapped in puff pastry; Saddle of Hare with celeriac croutons with a game sauce; and the Vegetarian speciality, which includes four dishes. Desserts command attention with White and dark chocolate terrine, and Hot cherry sponge with kirsch ice cream and hot rum sauce. David Watson's delicate and delicious recipe which he has contributed to this book follows.

Hot Sole Mousse with Vermouth and Chive Sauce

1	lb.	lemon sole, filleted and skinned
		salt and pepper, to taste
24	fl.oz.	whipping cream (3 C.)
2	T.	chopped shallot
1		bunch chives
2	t.	olive oil
5	fl.oz.	Noilly Pratt vermouth (scant ⅔ C.)
10	fl.oz.	fish stock (1¼ C.)
		knob of butter

Equipment
electric food processor
handheld electric beater
fine mesh sieves
8 molds measuring about 3 inches square

1. Purée fish in a food processor with pepper and a good pinch of salt to bring the gelatin out of the fish.
2. Leave fish to cool for 30 minutes.
3. Put half the fish in the processor with half the cream, and purée for about one minute until the mixture is smooth. Repeat process with the other half of the fish and cream.

4. Pass mousse through fine sieve, check seasoning, place in molds, and refrigerate.

5. Heat oven to 375°F (or gas mark 5). Place a water bath in the oven and then cook mousses for approximately 20 minutes.

6. Meanwhile separately chop shallots and chives, finely.

7. Sweat shallots in a little oil, cook without coloring, add Noilly and fish stock, and reduce by half.

8. Leave the stock to simmer. Dice butter and add to the stock. Blend with the electric beater, then keep the sauce warm.

9. Remove mousse from oven and let rest 5 minutes.

10. Reheat the sauce—do not boil—and add the chives. Unmold the mousse and serve with the sauce and vegetables of your choice.

Note: The mousse may take a little more cream before you finish stage four. If it seems too thick, test the mousse in a little boiling water.

Humberside, to the east, is almost bisected by its own mighty River Humber. Happily the world's longest suspension bridge connects the two banks. The famous fishing port of Grimsby, close to the mouth of the Humber estuary, is in operation twenty-four hours a day. Its huge trawler fleet, dragging bag-shaped nets along the ocean floor, first set out to sea from Grimsby and Hull in 1882. Here many busy fish markets auction fresh fish almost round the clock, supplied by over two hundred fishing boats from Denmark as well as from Britain. At nearby Cleethorpes, a three-hundred-foot (91-meter) pier juts out to sea from the golden beach. Farther north along the shore is Withernsea, a resort that has lost two churches to the encroaching ocean. Hornsea, a small resort between the sea and a huge lake, its curious old houses set among a maze of tiny picturesque streets, is also a bird sanctuary.

Yorkshire regional foods are legion. Savory regional dishes include pickled beef, pickled pork, goose pie, bacon and egg pie, Good Friday fish pie, and Collop Monday—a dish of eggs and meat. Sweet pies, cakes, tarts, puddings, pancakes, breads, and fritters abound. Yorkshire is the place to go if you have a sweet tooth! Yorkshire curd tarts are filled with a batter of butter, eggs, sugar, and fine curds, flavored with nutmeg, grated lemon rind, and a teaspoon of brandy. Small quantities of currants, sultanas, and chopped peel can be added to this batter. Regional dishes have quaint names centuries old—Moggy, Nodden cake, and Mell cake, which is eaten on pig-killing day. One form of gingerbread is called peppercake in Yorkshire. Another, called Parkin, is eaten in Yorkshire on Guy Fawkes' night. Parkin is rather dense and is best stored in an airtight container for a few days before eating. This is a good stick-to-the-ribs snack for a nippy November night around the bonfire.

Parkin

6 fl.oz.   milk (²⁄₃ C.)
6 oz.   golden syrup (²⁄₃ C.)
2 oz.   molasses (¹⁄₄ C.)
2 oz.   butter (¹⁄₂ stick)
4 oz.   quick-cooking oats (1 C.)
10 oz.   sifted flour (2 C.)
¹⁄₂ t.   baking soda
2 T.   ground ginger
2 oz.   brown sugar (¹⁄₄ C.)
      pinch of salt
3   eggs

1. Preheat oven to 350°F (or gas mark 4).

2. In a small saucepan, gently heat the milk, syrup, molasses, and butter until melted. Set aside to cool.

3. Using an electric blender, grind the oats to a fine flour and mix with the sifted flour, baking soda, ground ginger, sugar, and salt.

4. Beat the eggs one at a time into the cooled milk mixture.

5. Make a well in the center of the dry ingredients and pour in milk mixture and stir briskly until smooth.

6. Pour into a greased, shallow heat-proof baking dish (10 inch by 6 inch) and bake for 40–45 minutes or until a tester comes out clean.

7. Loosen edges and invert onto a rack to cool. Cut in squares and keep for 2 days in an airtight container—traditionally of wood—before serving.   *Yields* 18 *squares*

Without doubt the most famous dish from Yorkshire, known wherever roast beef is eaten, is Yorkshire pudding. This was usually served as the first course, accompanied by hot, savory gravy, to allay hunger's first pangs, and then followed by the more expensive beef. A homemade Yorkshire pudding is a delight. Institution-made Yorkshire pudding, however, can be absolutely dreadful. In earlier times, when beef was roasted on a spit in the fireplace, the pudding was set beneath the sizzling meat to catch the drippings, producing a soft pudding rich with meat juices. Nowadays the beef is removed from the oven and set aside to rest, the heat raised to very hot, and the pudding, whisked at the last minute to incorporate as much air as possible, is poured over a spoonful or two of smoking hot pan drippings in a preheated very hot dish. The pudding rises in crisp golden peaks, lighter than a soufflé, and is served immediately. The family waits at the table, knife and fork poised, for the pudding's emergence from the kitchen. York-shire pudding accompanies the roast beef at Sunday lunch throughout the length and breadth of Britain today.

Yorkshire Pudding

5	oz.	flour (1 C.)
½	t.	baking powder
½	t.	salt
2	lg	eggs
8	fl.oz.	milk (1 C.)
2	T.	hot fat from roasting pan

1. Sift together the flour, baking powder, and salt.

2. Beat by hand or whirl in the blender the eggs and milk. Add the flour mixture and blend for one full minute. Let stand at least one hour.

3. While the roasted beef is resting, preheat the oven to 450°F (or gas mark 8). Put heat-proof shallow pan with 2 tablespoons of hot fat in it into oven for a few minutes to get really hot. Remove from oven.

4. Whirl the batter briefly and pour over fat in pan. Cook for 10 minutes, then reduce heat to 350°F (or gas mark 4) and continue to cook for 10 minutes longer. Serve immediately with the roast beef.

Serves 6

Shortbread was used in ancient times in Yorkshire as the bride's cake (a successor to oatmeal cake) and was broken above the bride's head. The marriage was sealed when both bride and groom ate a piece of the rich, crumbly confection. Shortbread should always be broken, never cut.

Shortbread

4	oz.	unsalted butter (1 stick)
3	oz.	sugar (⅓ C.)
½	t.	vanilla essence or orange flower water
5	oz.	flour (1 C.)
1	t.	baking powder
		pinch of salt

1. Cream butter and sugar by hand, until light colored and fluffy. Beat in vanilla essence or orange flower water.
2. Sift together the flour, baking powder, and salt, and gradually knead into the butter mixture.
3. Pat into a round, crimping edges to prevent cracking during the baking period.
4. Prick the shortbread decoratively with the tines of a fork. Place on an ungreased baking sheet and let rest for 20 minutes. Meanwhile preheat oven to 325°F (or gas mark 3).
5. Bake for 35 minutes, watching carefully to see that the shortbread does not color too much. *Serves 8–12*

Yorkshire is also famous for Stingo, a good strong beer. Masham, in Yorkshire, has housed breweries behind its public houses since the thirteenth century. Paul Theakston, the owner of the small Black Sheep brewery in Masham, says his company got the name Black Sheep when his family sold their brewery to a larger concern, and Paul refused to leave Yorkshire to manage the Scottish branch of the business. "Theakstons have owned breweries in Masham for 700 years," said Paul, and opened his own Black Sheep brewery directly behind the original and now competing brewery. He says he is proud that his small brewery makes traditional beers using time-honored methods. He explained that 90 percent of the grist for beer making is malted barley—barley that has been forced to germinate. The malted barley is then crisped at 190 degrees Fahrenheit. A little wheat is added to help develop a good head on the beer. A good head is very important to the brew made at the Black Sheep. The malted barley is first crushed in a mill, then slid into the hopper to be mixed with hops grown in Kent. Boiled water from the Yorkshire dales is mixed with the malted barley, and it is mashed to a porridge consistency, the starch in the grain turning to sugar in the process. The sugar solution is extracted from the wort—a name used since Anglo-Saxon days—then the spent grain is used as cattle feed. Yeast is added to the sugar mixture and after five to six days of fermentation sixteen-thousand pints of beer are ready to be barreled or bottled. Paul is especially pleased with the head on his beer; he explained that a truly good beer has a head that will stick to the glass, leaving a ring on the inside after each swallow. Pumps that fill beer glasses in some public houses have holes at the end which help stimulate a foaming head.

Wensleydale cheese, made in the lovely countryside made famous by James Herriot's veterinary tales, has a subtle flavor with a honeyed aftertaste. Traditionally, Wensleydale cheese is eaten by Yorkshire folk with apple pie and also with Christmas cake. There are two kinds of Wensleydale cheese. One is a flat white disk of crumbly cheese that is best eaten fresh.

The other is made with double cream, shaped like a Stilton, and under the right conditions it will develop mold that turns the cheese into the luscious Blue Wensleydale, which was regularly made by the lay brothers of Jervaulx and Fountains Abbeys from a Norman recipe. After the Dissolution of the Monasteries by Henry VIII, Blue Wensleydale cheese continued to be made at local farmhouses. Most farmers at that time kept a pig or two about the place and fattened them up with barley meal, food scraps from the kitchen, leftovers from the table, turnips, potatoes, and windfall fruits from the orchard. The English cured the pig's carcass by packing it in salt to make bacon, unlike their continental cousins who preferred to eat the carcass fresh. Ham, the cured hind leg, was either packed in salt for a few days or pickled in salty brine flavored with juniper berries, sugar, and spices before being smoked. York receives the highest accolades in Britain for its smoked ham; its flavor is incomparable. Legend has it that during the building of York Minster, which took 250 years to complete, the sawdust from all the oak needed in the construction of the church was used to smoke York hams. Several areas in England produce excellent hams using brine recipes that vary according to the districts they hail from, and which have been handed down from generation to generation.

The sparkling rivers of the Yorkshire dales, such as the Nid, the Ure, and the Swale, are famous for trout which makes a fine meal simply pan-fried or grilled. Shrimp too is plentiful in Yorkshire most of it trawled in from the North Sea close by.

Trout with Herbed Butter Sauce and Pine Nuts

2		medium-sized trout, boned
		white pepper, to taste
4		oz. unsalted butter (1 stick)
2½	oz.	pine nuts (½ C.), toasted
2	T.	fresh lemon juice
1	T.	minced parsley
1	T.	minced chives
½	t.	fresh thyme leaves
		pinch of salt

1. Preheat broiler. Place trout skin side down on broiler pan. Season with pepper and broil until trout is just cooked through—3 to 4 minutes, depending on thickness.

2. Meanwhile melt butter in a saucepan, add pine nuts, and continue to heat until butter turns golden brown. Immediately pour into small bowl and stir in lemon juice, herbs, and pinch of salt.

3. Remove trout to heated plates and pour over butter sauce. Serve immediately. *Serves* 2

West of Yorkshire is Cumbria, whose beautiful Lake District National Park makes Cumbria the most popular county in England for holidaymakers from all over the world. The only way to truly experience the Lake District is by foot. A multitude of tourists do so every year, so many that access may be restricted in some areas to allow the terrain—packed hard by thousands of hiking boots—to rest and revitalize itself. In high summer over a thousand visitors a day come through Brockhole, the Visitor Centre in the Lake District National Park. Happily the park authorities remain unfazed and cope remarkably well with the increasing numbers. The park is only thirty miles wide, but it contains some of England's most dramatic scenery. Here England's tallest mountains, lit by innumerable waterfalls, tower above dozens of pristine lakes. The rugged beauty of Scafell Pike, its sheer flank jutting from lake level into the mist, is impressive. Climbers are cautioned to wear appropriate clothing as the Lake District's weather is notoriously fickle from one minute to the next.

Hundreds of miles of paths around the lakes lead walkers and hikers into delightful wooded areas beside rock-strewn streams; other paths circle a lake, and some lead to mountaintops with unbelievable views. Wordsworth, Coleridge, Shelley, and Mary Wollstonecraft, Shelley's wife, tramped these paths and hills. As he strode along, Wordsworth dictated his poems to his sister, Dorothy. Born at Cockermouth in 1770, Wordsworth was the first poet to make the beauty he saw around him the subject of his poems. Poets took their inspiration from classical themes prior to Wordsworth's rapturous poems extolling the natural world at his feet. Wordsworth was also England's first conservationist, campaigning to halt the new railway line from being built beyond his beloved Lake Windermere. He lived most of his life in the Lake District, and his earliest years were spent in Wordsworth House in Cockermouth. Most popular with sightseers is Dove Cottage, the home he shared with Dorothy. Dove Cottage is included in the Grasmere and Wordsworth Museum tour where his manuscripts and portraits of the Wordsworth family are on display. Spring is the time to come to the Lake District when Wordsworth's "host of golden daffodils" are in bloom.

At 13 Castlegate, Cockermouth, is a fine vegetarian restaurant called the Quince and Medlar, owned and run by Louisa and Colin Le-Voi. The food entices customers to travel hundreds of miles to eat here. The elegant restaurant, in a hundred-year-old historic Georgian house, is next to Cockermouth Castle. The Le-Vois have been awarded "Vegetarian Restaurant of the Year" twice since opening. Though this is strictly a vegetarian restaurant right down to the farmhouse cheese from Cockermouth, which has no calf's rennet in it, 70 percent of their customers are not vegetarian. Colin and

Louisa both cook and delight in creating new recipes from their ample supply of fresh local ingredients, and although they only use vegetarian products they don't really think of the Quince and Medlar as being a vegetarian restaurant, but rather as a good restaurant that just happens to be vegetarian. Before opening the Quince and Medlar they both worked at Sharrow Bay Country House Hotel on Lake Ullswater, and Colin says, "Louisa and I both admire Francis Coulson and Brian Sack enormously—they have been a source of inspiration to us and we owe them so much." Some of Colin Le-Voi's dishes on a recent menu are Snowpeas and baby corn on a bed of noodles with a creamy Brie sauce; Avocado and peanut pâté served with homemade oatcakes; Cheese dumplings baked in a Mornay sauce; Butterbean, leek, and courgette casserole in a cider, tomato, and herb sauce; Smoked Westmorland cheese and mushroom roulade; Dried apricots in a Brandy syrup; Almond and raspberry ice meringue; Chocolate terrine with white chocolate sauce; and Warm cinnamon and walnut sponge with coffee cream sauce. Their selection of British cheeses rounds out a great meal. Colin Le-Voi has contributed the following appetizer recipe.

Terrine of Young Vegetables

2	lb.	spinach, blanched and well drained
1	T.	chopped parsley
1	T.	chives
5	fl.oz.	heavy cream
3		eggs
4	oz.	young leek
4	oz.	carrot
4	oz.	young corn
4	oz.	zucchini
1		red pepper
		salt and pepper
		grated nutmeg, to taste

Garnish: salad leaves, blanched sliced tomato, and a tomato rose

    1. Place spinach, herbs, cream, and eggs in a food processor and blend until smooth.

    2. Season to taste. Prepare the vegetables and cut into strips—blanch separately in salted water until tender and drain well.

    3. Line a 2¼-pint (1½-quart) terrine with buttered waxed paper, and alternate layers of spinach mixture and vegetables, ending with spinach. Preheat oven to 350°F (or gas mark 4).

   4. Cover terrine with buttered waxed paper, cover with foil, and cook in a bain-marie for 1 to 1½ hours or until set.
   5. Served chilled with garnish.   *Serves 6*

Motorboats are not allowed on most of the lakes in the region. The refurbished Windermere Iron Steamboat Company Ltd., established in 1848, takes people on lake trips aboard vintage wood-coke, or coal-powered, steam launches. The Windermere Steamboat Museum for boat enthusiasts is a haven on a wet day. Displayed is a 1780 sailing yacht and a forty-foot steam launch, *Dolly*, listed in the *Guinness Book of World Records* as the oldest mechanically powered steamboat in the world.

Nestled on the shores of Lake Windermere is the beautiful Miller Howe Hotel, set amid fells and hills that form a backdrop to the lake. The garden here is pure delight with unexpected graceful statues of nymphs tucked amid trees and flowering shrubs. The view from the window across the secluded garden, which rolls gently down to the lake to the granite mountains beyond, is breathtaking. John Tovey opened the hotel in 1971. His love of British traditional foods, especially steamed puddings, came from his grandmother, who has been a great influence on his life. Travel broadened his palate, and John Tovey's life in the theater cultivated his flair for the dramatic and also introduced him to cooking on a severely restricted budget. For him, each meal is a performance and the chef the star. He creates, experiments, and practices in the kitchen the way an actor studies his part, learns his lines, and improvises with well-honed skills. He is as painstaking in preparing a simple vegetable dish as he is in orchestrating his most complicated creation. John Tovey is backed by a wonderful, committed, and loyal staff. His more than capable head chef, Christopher Blaydes, is second to none. Breakfast is as inventive as dinner, and everything is done with panache and precision. The day starts with John Tovey's famous Buck Fizz (iced champagne and orange juice), followed by porridge that tastes like no porridge you ever had before. The Lakeland platter is a full English breakfast, and the warm breads and homemade preserves are out of this world. At dinner everyone is seated at the same time for a set menu of five courses, finishing with a choice from a panoply of puddings or the simple cheese platter. John Tovey's March menus include Miller Howe Aubergine red pepper cumin terrine served on Fresh tomato basil sauce; Cream of courgette and fennel soup with deep-fried parsley and natural yogurt; Baked marinated salmon cubes (soy orange garlic ginger) on Noilly Prat cream sauce with panfried wild mushrooms; and Roast loin of pork stuffed with onion Dijon hazelnut rosemary and watercress, served on pear mango purée with rich Madeira sauce. Among the seven accompanying vegetable dishes were White cabbage with garlic and sesame, and Mashed Swede with Pommery. The following recipes are reprinted with kind permission from *John Tovey's Entertaining on a Plate!*

Lamb Fillet with Water Chestnuts, Orange Segments, and Watercress

While the lamb fillet, water chestnuts, oranges, and watercress may be prepared the evening before a lunch (or the morning before a dinner), this is a last-moment stir-fry recipe which may seem labor-intensive but which in fact is done very quickly indeed.

2	T.	olive oil
2	oz.	soft butter (½ stick)
2	oz.	onions (scant ½ C.), peeled and finely chopped
1	lb. 2 oz.	lamb fillet, trimmed and cut into ½-inch cubes
		salt and freshly ground black pepper
12		canned water chestnuts, drained and coarsely chopped
3		oranges, peeled and segmented (see below)
1		bunch of watercress, leaves only, washed and dried

1. Heat the oil and butter in a frying pan and fry the onions until golden, about 10 minutes. Turn up the heat and put in the lamb fillet while the heat is very high. Stir and sear, and stir-fry for 4 minutes. Season lightly.

2. Add the water chestnuts and stir until warmed through and lightly brown. Fold in the orange segments, cook until just warm, then turn the whole thing out onto warmed individual serving plates.

3. Garnish with the washed and dried watercress. *Serves 2*

Segmenting oranges

Top and tail the fruit with a sharp knife. Cut down on a board to remove skin and pith completely. (Remember to squeeze the juice from the fleshy bits of peel.) Over a sieve over a bowl, cut down into the orange toward the center, between flesh and membrane—*along* one side of the white line marking the segment divisions. Do this along the *next* line, and a membrane-free segment will fall into the sieve (and the juice into the bowl).

Raspberry Syllabub

If you have an old-fashioned gill measure, the 7½ fl.oz. of booze is easy to measure. Use a good, but not frightfully expensive, dessert wine, or, if you can get it, the Italian Fra Angelico.

2   lemons
1   orange
7½ fl.oz. booze of your choice (scant 1 C.) (see above)
15 fl.oz. heavy cream (scant 2 C.)
2 oz.   soft brown sugar (¼ C.)

Raspberry purée

4 oz. fresh raspberries (¾ C.)
2 T.   icing sugar

Garnish

   a few fresh raspberries
6 sprigs of mint

1. Wipe the lemons and orange clean with a damp cloth and dry. Finely grate the rind from them, and then cut them in half and squeeze out the juice. Transfer the rind and juice to a bowl and mix in the booze. Cover and leave in the fridge for at least 4 hours.

2. Meanwhile, mash the raspberries for the purée with the icing sugar, using a silver fork. Pass through a sieve. Have at hand the six glasses you have selected to serve this dessert in and divide the raspberry purée between them.

3. In your mixer put the heavy cream and soft brown sugar and beat until the mixture starts to become stiff. Then, tablespoon by tablespoon, add the booze mix, still beating. This takes time and patience, but the cream *will* take up all the liquid.

4. Spoon this wonderfully flavored cream on top of the raspberry purée in the glasses, then cover each glass with cling film. Put in the fridge for up to 6 hours. Take out of the fridge about 30 minutes before serving and garnish with fresh raspberries and mint.   *Serves* 6

On Coniston Water the beautiful Victorian steam-powered yacht *Gondola* is running again. Coniston Water is where John Ruskin, the art critic and historian, is buried. Ruskin spent a great part of his life in the Lake District. His home, Brantwood, on the northeastern shore, displays his paintings and memorabilia of his life and work. Brantwood is open to the public.

The storybook scenery of the Lake District seems a particularly appropriate setting for Beatrix Potter, who lived here from about the year 1900. She purchased a farm in Near Sawrey, called Hill Top Farm. *The Tales of Peter Rabbit*, *The Tale of the Tailor of Gloucester*, *The Tale of Squirrel Nutkin*, *The Tale of Tom Kitten*, *The Tale of Samuel Whiskers*, and *The Tale of Jemima Puddle-Duck* were all published while she was living at Near Sawrey. Her cottage stands as she left it, her leather boots still drying on the hearth.

The Lake District has many wonderful treasures, not the least of which is Sharrow Bay Country House Hotel, whose terrace wall is lapped by Lake Ullswater. The hotel stands at the extreme edge of the lake on a wooded promontory backed by Barton Fells, situated six miles from the M6 and twenty-five miles from Carlisle. Sharrow Bay Country House was built in 1840 of soft gray stone, and in 1949 it was a private house when Francis Coulson bought it. He opened in the same year with just a few bedrooms despite many post–World War II problems, such as food and petrol rationing, no motorways, and no tourists to speak of. Fortunately through his enthusiasm and creativity he soon became well known for his wonderful cooking and his gift for making people feel at home. Through a great and lasting partnership with Brian Sack, Sharrow Bay prospered from twelve bedrooms to twenty-nine, and from a modest staff of six to its present staff of fifty. With their loyal and enduring support, Sharrow Bay will continue to maintain the standard that people have come to expect. All the rooms here are luxuriously furnished with antiques, porcelain, and pictures. Views from the front windows are of lake, woods, and mountains, with the Helvellyn range filling the far distance. Beside the house are a private jetty and boathouse. There are twelve acres of gardens and woodlands and half a mile of lake shore, where guests may wander at will. Sharrow is a haven for those who wish to relax completely in peaceful and beautiful surroundings. Guests can enjoy boating, swimming, fishing, and walking or climbing. The area around Sharrow Bay is rich in archaeological sites and towns and villages steeped in history. The internationally renowned cooking emphasizes traditional British dishes, created with care and imagination by chefs Johnnie Martin, Colin Akrigg, and Chris Bond. Francis Coulson says, "I am a staunch believer in truly traditional British recipes. These dishes we must be proud of. . . . They are a part of our heritage." With his customary generosity, Francis Coulson has provided us with four recipes.

Cream of Stilton and Cider Soup

2	oz.	butter (½ stick)
1		onion, finely chopped
1		leek, cleaned and chopped
1	lg.	potato, diced
1	T.	(heaping) plain flour
5	fl.oz.	dry cider (scant ⅔ C.)
20	fl.oz.	chicken stock (2½ C.)
10	fl.oz.	milk (1¼ C.)
4	oz.	Stilton cheese (1 C.), grated or finely chopped
1	T.	heavy cream, approximately
		salt and freshly milled pepper

Parmesan croutons

8 oz. stale bread (2¼ C.), cut into small cubes
4 T. oil
8 T. freshly grated Parmesan cheese

1. Melt butter in a large heavy-bottomed saucepan and add prepared vegetables and a little salt. Cook gently with the lid on for 5 to 10 minutes to draw out the juices.

2. Stir in flour and when smooth, pour in cider, still stirring. Add the chicken stock, cover the pan, and simmer gently for 30 minutes.

3. Add milk and Stilton, and reheat, stirring, until the cheese is melted and the soup is just below the boiling point. Taste and season and stir in the cream, adding a little more cream if the soup is too heavy.

4. At this stage you can purée the soup in a food processor or press through a sieve.

5. Reheat soup but do not boil, and serve with Parmesan croutons. *Serves 6*

Note: The croutons can be made well in advance and stored in an airtight container.

6. Place the bread cubes in a bowl, sprinkle in the oil, and stir until the oil has been absorbed.

7. Add the freshly grated Parmesan and stir until all the cubes are well coated. Preheat the oven to 400°F (or gas mark 6).

8. Place croutons in a single layer on a baking sheet, and heat in the oven for 10 minutes, or if you prefer, place under a grill, turning as necessary.

Parsley Pie

Short crust pastry

4 oz. flour (¾ C.)
1 t. icing sugar
2 oz. butter (½ stick)
1 beaten egg, to mix

1. Sift together flour and icing sugar. Cut in the butter until the mixture resembles coarse bread crumbs. Pour beaten egg into center of flour mixture and mix in until it forms a ball. Place in refrigerator to rest for 15 minutes. Then use pastry to line a fluted or plain flan tin, approximately 9½ inches in diameter with a removable base.

Filling

3 oz.	butter (¾ C.)
½ lb.	onions (1⅔ C.), chopped
10 fl.oz.	heavy cream (1¼ C.)
2	eggs, beaten
3–4 T.	chopped parsley
1 T.	chives (dried or fresh)
1 T.	tarragon, finely chopped
1 T.	watercress, finely chopped
2	spring onions, finely chopped

2. Melt butter in a heavy pan and sweat onions until they are transparent. Cool.

3. Beat cream, eggs, and herbs together and season well. Preheat oven to 350°F (or gas mark 3–4).

4. Add spring onions to cream mixture and pour into pastry case. Bake for about 40 minutes. Serve hot or warm.   *Serves 6*

Gnocchi à la Parisienne

Mornay sauce

2 T.	butter
2 T.	flour
5 fl.oz.	hot milk (scant ⅔ C.)
	salt and pepper
	nutmeg
2 T.	cream
2 T.	Gruyère cheese, grated

1. Melt butter, add flour, stir until smooth, and add hot milk. Cook stirring until thickened and smooth.

2. Season with salt, pepper, and nutmeg. Stir in cream and cheese. Set aside.

Gnocchi

5 fl.oz.	milk (scant ⅔ C.)
1½ oz.	butter (3 T.)
2½ oz.	flour (½ C.), sifted
2	eggs
2 oz.	Gruyère cheese (½ C.), grated
	salt and pepper

nutmeg, grated

10 fl.oz. Mornay sauce (1¼ C.), not too thick

Garnish: Trail a line of hot tomato sauce, with a slight flavor of garlic and plenty of fresh basil, across the gnocchi.

3. Bring milk and butter almost to a boil, remove from heat, and add the flour. Beat until smooth. Preheat oven to 350°F (or gas mark 4).

4. Beat in the eggs one at a time. Add one ounce (¼ C.) of grated cheese, salt, pepper, and nutmeg, to taste.

5. Prepare a wide saucepan of boiling salted water and remove from heat. Using two large spoons, drop small balls of paste into the water and poach for 7 to 8 minutes or until firm. Remove with a perforated spoon, drain on a folded clean tea towel, and arrange in a buttered shallow heat-proof dish.

6. Coat well with Mornay sauce—if it seems too thick add more cream—and sprinkle with the remaining grated cheese.

7. Bake for about 15 minutes. Garnish and serve immediately while the gnocchi are puffed up and light—if left too long they subside.   *Serves 6–8*

Asparagus and Green Onion Timbale

2		bunches of spring onions
1	lb.	thin asparagus
2	T.	butter
1	sm.	garlic clove, finely chopped
½	t.	salt and white pepper, to taste
4	T.	white wine or water
4–5		eggs
16	fl.oz.	milk or cream (2 C.), heated
3	oz.	Gruyère cheese (¾ C.), grated
1–2	oz.	Parmesan cheese (¼–½ C.), finely grated
		nutmeg
4	oz.	bread crumbs (1 C.), toasted
		béchamel sauce*
		tomato sauce (optional)

* Béchamel sauce—follow directions for Mornay sauce above but omit the cheese.

1. Cut off the root ends of the spring onions and an inch from the asparagus. Wash well and chop finely.

2. Melt butter in a saucepan and add the onions, asparagus, garlic, seasonings, and white wine or water. Cook over medium heat until the asparagus is nearly done, stirring continuously—about 3 minutes. Set aside.

3. Beat the eggs well, gradually whisk in the warmed milk or cream, then stir in the cheeses, asparagus, and onions. Season with nutmeg and taste for salt and pepper. Preheat oven to 325°F (or gas mark 3).

4. Generously butter 8-oz capacity ramekins and line them with bread crumbs. Put any extra bread crumbs into the mixture. Divide the custard among the ramekins and cook them in a bath of hot water. Bake until the tops are well colored and firm—about one hour.

5. Meanwhile make béchamel sauce and flavor it with lemon or lemon thyme. Set aside.

6. When ramekins are done, remove from oven and let them rest for a few moments until they are set. Slide a knife around the edge, turn them out onto your hand, and then turn them topside up onto the serving plate.

7. Serve with the béchamel spooned attractively around ramekins, and if desired trail them with a little tomato sauce.

Note: Creamed potato and a green salad go well with this dish.

Serves 8–10

Carlisle, the biggest town in Cumbria and its county seat, is built on the site of a Roman fort near the Scottish border. Rising steeply above the River Eden, Carlisle has a twelfth-century cathedral and an even earlier castle dating from 1092. In 1568 Mary Queen of Scots lived for a time in Carlisle Castle. The dungeon walls are carved by prisoners who were incarcerated here in the sixteenth and seventeenth centuries. Hadrian's Wall is nearby, and artifacts found at the wall are on display at Tullie House—a museum and art gallery. The valley of the River Eden is a serene and lovely area of attractive villages and unspoiled scenery. Appleby, situated on the river, is a good place to stay while exploring the valley. The market square and the main street are lined with splendid buildings, many of them over two hundred years old. A Norman castle, rebuilt in the seventeenth century by Lady Anne Clifford, still stands. Her tomb is in the parish church. Appleby holds the largest horse fair in Britain in June every year. Many of the folk interested in buying and selling horses are gypsies, who gather from all over the country to attend. The Pennine Chain lies to the east of Appleby, and the rigorous Pennine Way footpath can be joined nearby at Dufton. Easier walking can be had on Dufton Pike.

Today several of Cumbria's regional foods are flavored with spices or rum. Merchant venturers returning from the West Indies to the ports of Whitehaven, Cumbria, and Bristol, Avon, brought back rum, ginger, and other spices. Rum punches caught on quickly, and rum was served at many a festive occasion, especially during the Christmas season. Cumberland Rum Butter is esteemed all over Britain. It is simply made with rum, beaten with butter and sugar, and refrigerated until very firm. Wonderful with hot mince pies straight from the oven or Christmas pudding, it really should be eaten more than once a year, since it is a great accompaniment to any sweet suet pudding or steamed sponge and is a pleasant change from the ubiquitous custard.

Indian spices such as cumin, coriander, cardamom, chili peppers, and turmeric were brought back by returning colonists and warriors fresh from Indian campaigns. Many of the steak sauces commonly used to enliven cooked foods in English homes and restaurants have their origins in the strong spices of India and Burma. Ready-prepared curry powders are also staples in most British kitchens.

Cumberland Sauce is fruity and teams perfectly with the robust flavor of game or venison. Most game, venison included, needs to be hung for a few days both to improve its taste and to make it tender enough to be palatable. It is usually hung in a cool place, such as a cellar, where it will be safe from flies. At one time game would be hung in the rafters where it would pick up a smoky taste from the fire that burned below. Game can still be smoked if need be, but the rafters would have to be pretty high not to mention well-ventilated for most folk to put up with the odor while the meat "ripened." Cranberry sauce would also be a good adjunct to the flavor of well-hung game.

Cumberland Sauce

1		orange
1		lemon
4	T.	red currant jelly
2	fl.oz.	port wine (¼ C.)
2	t.	cornstarch
2	T.	water
2	T.	rum

1. Using a swivel peeler or zester, remove zest from orange and lemon. In a small saucepan over medium heat, simmer the zest in a little water for a few minutes. Drain, pat dry, and reserve.

2. Juice the orange and lemon and heat gently in same saucepan, then stir in the red currant jelly until completely dissolved. Stir in the port wine and remove from heat.

3. Blend the cornstarch and water until smooth and whisk into the juice mixture. Heat, stirring, until the sauce is thickened and smooth. Stir in the zest and the rum and remove from heat. Serve with game or strongly flavored fish such as mackerel.

Off Cumbria's northwest coast in the Irish Sea is the Isle of Man, named for Manannan Mac Lir, Celtic god of the sea. Manannan is still well respected, and ragwort sprigs are worn by many islanders to keep evil spirits at bay. The Isle is a self-governing crown dependency and therefore not part of the United Kingdom. Never conquered by the Romans, the island has both history and language that are largely Celtic. Here are Celtic roundhouses (they are also found in Celtic Cornwall), sixth-century Christian Celtic chapels, called keeills, and many neolithic monuments. Norsemen conquered the island about A.D. 798. In time they organized a parliament, called Tynwald, that still operates in the original Norse manner today. The Isle of Man has its own laws, passports, police force, currency, and health and education facilities, all paid for out of their own revenues and taxes. About half of the population on the island today are retired English people, lured here by a temperate climate and by lenient tax laws that are not only a bonus for immigrants to the Isle of Man but a boon to the travel industry. Numerous visitors come every year expressly to gamble in Manx casinos. A further attraction is the two-week-long Tourist Trophy races that take place in June. Native Manx appreciate this extra revenue more than retired newcomers, who complain that the Tourist Trophy turns the island into a deafening motorcycle racetrack.

The Isle of Man is famous for its huge, sparkling-fresh scallops and also for tiny scallops, called Queenies. Fat herrings caught in local waters are smoked over oak fires. No dyes are used to make these kippered herrings; their golden, appetizing glow comes from smoking oak chips.

Scallops in Chili Lime Butter

Chili lime butter

1	sm.	red chili, seeded and sliced thinly
½	t.	sea salt
4	T.	unsalted butter, softened
1	t.	grated fresh ginger
2	t.	grated lime zest

1. Using a mortar and pestle pound chili and sea salt until amalgamated and add to the remaining ingredients. Blend well and refrigerate until needed.

1½ lb. fresh scallops
  1 T. butter
  1 T. olive oil
  3 T. fresh lime juice
         small whole fresh cilantro leaves

2. Wash scallops, pat dry with paper towels, and if very thick slice horizontally in two.

3. Heat butter and oil in a wide skillet over high heat; add scallops and sauté for 2 to 3 minutes or until opaque. Splash with lime juice and continue to cook for one more minute.

4. Add chili lime butter a knob at a time, stirring briskly. Remove to a warm dish and decorate with whole cilantro leaves. *Serves* 4

The Manx Electric Railway takes passengers for a 30-mile run along the eastern seaboard and also climbs to the top of Snaefell, where tremendous views of the surrounding counties can be had. Castletown is named for Castle Rushen, A.D. 1200. The original castle was the home of the last Norse king and Castletown was his ancient capital.

Douglas is a tourist mecca with a two-mile-long beach promenade boasting a host of entertainments, including several dance halls and a theater. Another sand beach with safe swimming is at Peel, a working fishing port where boats bring in fresh fish each day, including herring and the famous Isle of Man scallops. Here too is an archaeological site. On the road that leads from Peel to Ramsey, a town on the north shore of the island, is Curraghs Wildlife Park—a natural habitat for birds and animals, especially deer. Ramsey is a pleasant town with miles of sandy beaches, two long piers, a lake, and a golf course.

South of Cumbria is the county of Lancashire, a striking contrast with its southern towns and cities filled with closely packed houses and streets, that came to prominence during the Industrial Revolution. Perhaps the most densely populated area of Britain are the two huge urban areas of Greater Manchester and Liverpool, once cloth manufacturers to the world. Before 1770 and the invention of the "spinning jenny," Manchester was a simple market town. The spinning jenny made it possible to turn several spindles at one time. This invention and the opening of the first artificial canal, linking Manchester with the port of Liverpool and its River Mersey, caused the cotton trade to burgeon at a tremendous rate. Canals were to change the face of Britain. Packhorses were slow in hauling heavy goods, and roads were still too primitive to transport fragile articles safely. Canals solved both these problems, and soon canals crisscrossed the country, bringing water to some places for the first time and changing both plant life and wildlife. The last canal built to benefit Manchester was deep enough to allow large ships to sail inland right to the city docks. Future inventions brought steam power to the cloth mills, and dozens of factories sprang up near the Lancashire coal mines—the source of power. The rapid pace of steam-powered cloth production lowered prices, and soon England was exporting cotton cloth to Europe, America, Africa, and even to India, which in earlier days had exported pre-spun cotton to England. In 1830 the Liverpool–Manchester railway opened, and steam locomotives eventually replaced horse-drawn barges on canals. Today canals are used for recreation and have become an important component of the tourist industry.

Greater Manchester is a lively city. Its nightclubs and restaurants thrive. Culturally it boasts museums and galleries to rival those in London. Despite its industrial history, the countryside is easy to reach from Manchester. Moors and valleys, woods and rivers, fertile pastureland, and long sandy beaches are all close by. The area is rich in prehistoric and Roman sites, and many splendid mansions sit in large manicured parklands—a testament to Manchester's wealthy history.

Liverpool's shipping industry kept pace with the burgeoning cotton trade. Cargo ships that left Liverpool laden with coal and cloth returned with holds packed with sugar. The sugar business boomed and was followed by an even bigger moneymaking commodity, tobacco. Within a hundred years, the number of docks in Liverpool grew from five to ninety-eight. Now everything is changing again in Liverpool. Though many impressive buildings and lovely Georgian streets remain, Liverpool has built a new center. Warehouses have become elegant boutiques, and the King Albert Dock area is now a rejuvenated village of shops and restaurants. The Maritime Museum has fascinating old sailing vessels and exhibitions. The Liverpool Museum, the Walker Art Gallery, and the Lady Lever Museum, endowed by the wife of Lord Leverhulme, a wealthy manufacturer, are attracting visitors to see their splendid collections. Many important churches were built in Liverpool, among them the magnificent Anglican Cathedral and the equally impressive Roman Catholic Cathedral.

Lancashire's long coast has many resort towns, both lively and sedate. Much of the northern part of the county has lovely countryside—high moorlands and quiet villages—and Morecambe Bay on the coast is close to the county seat of Lancaster. This historic city has Roman, Saxon, and medieval remains. Built on the River Lune estuary, its imposing castle, on Castle Hill, towers above the city. St. Mary's Church—once part of a Benedictine Priory dating to the eleventh century—is also in this part of the city. The church was largely rebuilt in the fourteenth century. Splendid views over the city and the river below can be seen from Castle Hill. It is probable that a Roman encampment stood on this site, since "caster" at the end of place names, i.e., Lancaster and Doncaster, is the Roman word for camp. Lancaster has a fine university and many well-endowed museums.

A regional specialty of Lancashire is Eccles cakes, eaten usually for afternoon tea but also good for breakfast.

Lancashire Eccles Cakes

		puff pastry, either homemade or store-bought
3	T.	butter
2–3	T.	light brown sugar
3	oz.	currants (⅔ C.), washed and patted dry
3	T.	candied orange peel, chopped
		pinch each cinnamon, allspice, and nutmeg
		finely grated zest of one lemon
1		egg white, beaten until frothy
1	T.	superfine or castor sugar

1. Preheat oven to 375°F (or gas mark 5).

2. Roll out pastry to ⅛ inch on lightly floured board, following package directions if applicable. Using a 4-inch cutter, or a similar-sized wine glass rim dipped in flour, cut the pastry into rounds.

3. Melt butter in a small pan, and mix in the sugar, currants, orange peel, spices, and lemon zest.

4. Into the center of each pastry circle place a heaping teaspoon of the fruit mixture. Moisten edges of pastry and pull the edges up around the filling to seal.

5. Turn pastry over and flatten slightly into an oval. With a sharp knife, cut three small slits in the top. Place Eccles cakes on a greased baking sheet.

6. Brush with egg white, sprinkle lightly with sugar, and bake for 12–15 minutes or until puffed and golden. Remove to rack to cool.

Yields 12–15 cakes

Note: These are best served warm. Leftovers can be kept in an airtight container and reheated in the oven.

A village a few miles northeast of Preston seems an unlikely place to find a restaurant of the caliber of Heathcote's, where the service is impeccable and the creative food a delight, but at 104/106 Higher Road, Longridge, in three pretty, unpretentious yet warm and comfortable cottages you will find this treasure of a restaurant. Paul Heathcote has won so many awards lately that he says, "Things have happened so quickly that it's very difficult to appreciate it all and still believe that in spite of all the awards you are only as good as the last meal you served." His cooking has been honored in the guides of Egon Ronay, Michelin, AA, Catey, and in the *Good Food Guide*. Eighty percent of his ingredients are garnered locally, and 20 percent from other sources. Paul says he would not rule out the wonderful products available to us all year round from other countries. Most chefs would agree that sun-dried tomatoes, olives, and Parmesan would be sorely missed. His preferred dishes are fresh skate with a simple sauce made from mussel juices and an infusion of herbs, but Paul also loves to cook robust dishes like the recipe he has kindly contributed to this book, so it really depends on who he is cooking for, the time, and the place.

Pot-roasted Rump of Beef and Oxtail with Root Vegetables, Mashed Potatoes, and "Ale" Sauce

2		carrots
3		celery sticks
		olive oil, or vegetable oil
1	lg.	oxtail, cut into 6 pieces
1		onion
2		garlic cloves
		sprig of thyme
2		bay leaves
12		crushed black peppercorns
1		bottle of Guinness stout
60	fl.oz.	chicken stock (7½ C.)
3	lb.	rump of beef, preferably larded with fat and tied

1. Neatly dice one carrot and one stick of celery into ¼-inch dice. Set aside and keep the trimmings.

2. Coarsely chop the remaining carrot and celery and add to the trimmings.

3. In a hot pan and a little oil fry the oxtail until golden brown on all sides. Add the chopped vegetables and continue to cook until light brown. Drain off the fat by placing the oxtail and vegetables in a colander. Preheat oven to 350°F (or gas mark 4).

4. Place in a casserole dish with all the other ingredients except the beef and cook in the oven for 2 hours.

5. After 2 hours, add the rump and cook for a further hour. During the last half-hour of cooking, remove the casserole lid to brown the beef.

6. Meanwhile boil the diced vegetables until just cooked.

7. Take out the oxtail and beef and keep warm, pass the pan juices through a sieve into a saucepan, skim off the fat, and simmer until it reaches sauce consistency.

Mashed Potatoes

4	baking potatoes, preferably Pentland squires (approx. 2 lb.)
7 fl.oz.	milk (scant 1 C.)
2 oz.	unsalted butter (½ stick)
	salt and pepper, to taste

1. Boil potatoes in their skins in simmering salted water until cooked; avoid overcooking and splitting the skin.

2. Drain in a colander and peel while still warm. Then pass through a sieve or ricer into a bowl.

3. Boil milk and beat vigorously into the potato a little at a time.

4. Beat in butter and adjust seasoning with salt and pepper. The mashed potatoes should be slightly runny.

5. To serve, place oxtail in a bowl, slice some beef over the oxtail, spoon on some mashed potatoes and ale sauce, then scatter the diced vegetables around the bowl.   *Serves 6*

Lancashire's famous cheese is harder than Cheshire cheese but has a similar flavor, and both go equally well with a crusty loaf. Lancashire cheese is excellent for grating into sauces, soufflés, and gratins. Fig pie is also attributed to Lancashire. Figs were eaten traditionally on Mothering Sunday. Prunes too are a favorite here and are one of the ingredients in an unusually elaborate regional dish with the odd name Hindle Wakes—a decorative and delicious cold chicken dish.

Lancashire Hindle Wakes (Cold Chicken with Lemon Sauce)

6–7	lb.	roasting chicken
1		stick celery, cut in two
1		thickly sliced onion
40	fl.oz.	light chicken stock (5 C.), possibly more if needed
2	T.	malt vinegar
		bay leaf
4		sprigs of fresh thyme
1	T.	light brown sugar

For the stuffing

½	lb.	pitted soft prunes; reserve 6 for garnish, chop remainder
6	oz.	stuffing mix (1¼ C.), preferably Pepperidge Farm
		OR
6	oz.	stale bread crumbs (1¼ C.)
2–3	oz.	suet, (½ – ⅔ C.) grated
3	T.	almonds, chopped
1	t.	fresh sage, chopped
1	t.	fresh parsley, chopped
1	t.	fresh thyme leaves
8	fl.oz.	hot water (1 C.)
2	T.	malt vinegar

Sauce

2	T.	unsalted butter
2	T.	flour
16	fl.oz.	stock from cooking chicken (2 C.)
4	fl.oz.	milk (½ C.)
1		lemon, rind and juice
8	fl.oz.	whipping cream (1 C.)
		pepper to taste
2	lg.	egg yolks

Garnish

6 oz.	thinly sliced prosciutto or Bradenham ham
1	bunch parsley, washed and dried
6	prunes
1	lemon, sliced

1. Using a fork, lightly mix together the stuffing ingredients in the order listed.

2. Stuff the chicken and thoroughly secure the opening with skewers.

3. In a heavy-bottomed saucepan with a closely fitting lid, just large enough to hold chicken, place celery and onion slices. Put chicken on top of vegetables, and pour in enough stock to barely cover bird. Add vinegar, bay leaf, thyme, and sugar. Cover closely, bring to a simmer, and cook until chicken is done—approximately 1½ hours.

4. Remove chicken to a platter to cool, then refrigerate. Reduce cooking liquid by about one-third.

5. In a heavy-bottomed medium saucepan, melt butter and stir in flour. Pour in 16 fl.oz. (2 C.) of reduced cooking liquid and continue to cook until smooth.

6. Add milk and cook, barely simmering, for 15 minutes. Stir in lemon juice and cook for another few minutes. Cool.

7. Meanwhile, to complete sauce, pour heavy cream into top half of a double boiler with the grated lemon rind and fresh ground pepper. Simmer over boiling water, stirring, for about 5 minutes. Cool slightly and beat in egg yolks one at a time. Stir until thickened.

8. Place a sieve over the saucepan of lemon and stock sauce, and push the thickened cream and egg yolk mixture through into the sauce. Stir and heat gently—do not boil. Cool sauce, taste for seasoning, and refrigerate.

9. To serve, place chicken on a rack over waxed paper and coat completely with lemon sauce.

10. Remove to large platter, decorate edges of platter with prosciutto or ham, place small bunches of parsley at each end of bird, slice prunes lengthwise, and decorate chicken and platter. Carve chicken and serve with lemon slices, passing the remaining sauce separately.   *Serves* 8

Near the seven-mile-long beach resort of Lytham St. Annes in Kirkham, a Lancashire town of long heritage, is the Cromwellian Restaurant. On Kirkham's main street, in a historic narrow seventeenth-century house with beamed ceilings, Peter and Josie Fawcett have created a very pleasant, cozy restaurant with a reputation for excellent food. Josie Fawcett continues to create new dishes for the monthly changing menu and recently held a Washington State Wine Promotion at the restaurant that has augmented their wine list to well over one hundred selections. Josie Fawcett likes to cook seafood with light herb sauces, and traditional British bread and butter pudding, as well as game. But she says that a prerequisite of happy cooking is a happy eater, and vegetarians are not forgotten at the Cromwellian. All the restaurant's game, fish, and poultry come from Lytham St. Annes; the meat comes from a local Kirkham butcher who slaughters his own livestock; and produce comes from local growers. Selections from a recent menu include Koulibiac of Salmon in phyllo served with an herb cream sauce; Breast of Pheasant served with sage and onion stuffing and a rich gravy; and Fillet of trout lightly poached with a spicy pilaf and a ginger and orange sauce.

Josie Fawcett has given her permission to print the following recipe in this book.

Panfried Breast of Wood Pigeon
Served Cassoulet Style on a Bean Ragout
with Smoked Sausage and Crispy Bacon

4		fresh wood pigeons
1	lg.	smoked pork sausage, approximately 6 oz.
6	oz.	smoked bacon
2	T.	unsalted butter
1	lg.	onion, finely chopped
2		garlic cloves, crushed
2	oz.	haricot beans, soaked overnight
1	lb.	fresh tomatoes (3 C.), peeled and seeded
1	T.	tomato purée
1	t.	chili powder
1	t.	ground coriander
1	t.	paprika
1	t.	Tabasco sauce
10	fl.oz.	strong pigeon stock (1¼ C.)
6	fl.oz.	red wine (⅔ C.)
		salt and pepper to taste
2	T.	unsalted butter

Garnish: fresh herbs and new potatoes

1. Carefully remove the pigeon breasts, using a small sharp knife, keeping as near to the rib cage as possible. Remove the skin; wash and dry breasts.

2. Cut the sausage into thick slices and rind and dice the bacon. Fry the bacon until crispy and drain on kitchen paper. Set aside. Preheat the oven to 425°F (or gas mark 7).

3. Sauté the onion and garlic in butter until soft but not brown. Rinse the beans and add to the onions.

4. Liquidize the tomatoes and add to the pan with the tomato purée, the spices, the stock, and the wine. Simmer for about 40 minutes until the haricot beans are softened but not mushy.

5. Stir in the smoked sausage and bacon to reheat. Season if necessary.

6. Melt the remaining butter until hot and fry the breasts for 2 minutes on each side. Place them on a baking tray and cook in the oven for 6 to 7 minutes, depending on their size.

7. To serve, place 2 tablespoons of cassoulet in the center of a heated dinner plate. Slice each pigeon breast diagonally into four

and arrange eight pieces around the cassoulet on each plate. Serve with new potatoes and garnish with fresh green herbs.   *Serves* 4

Lancashire and Yorkshire both claim the hot pot as their own. It is usually cooked in a tall earthenware pot large enough to accommodate sautéed lamp chops stood on their blunt ends with lamb kidneys between the chops. Traditionally, a layer of oysters, once less expensive than they are today, were placed beneath the potatoes. From Liverpool comes lobscouse, a dish similar to hot pot. Also cooked in an earthenware pot, lobscouse contains no oysters but uses lamb or mutton, vegetables, and barley. Scouse is also the word used to describe a pattern of speech unique to Liverpool.

Lancashire Hot Pot

6		single loin lamb chops, trimmed by your butcher
3	T.	flour, seasoned with salt and pepper
2	lg.	onions, thinly sliced
5		fairly large new potatoes, preferably Yukon gold, sliced
8		young carrots, peeled and halved
4		sprigs of fresh thyme
1	T.	fresh sage leaves
		salt and freshly ground black pepper
40	fl.oz.	hot chicken broth (5 C.)
2	T.	butter

1. Preheat oven to 350°F (or gas mark 4).
2. Flour lamb chops.
3. In a deep, lidded, narrow heat-proof casserole layer half the onions, one-third of the potato slices, half the thyme and sage, and three lamb chops interspersed with half the carrots. Season each layer with a little salt and a good grinding of black pepper, as you proceed.
4. Repeat layers. Finally arrange a decorative layer of potato slices as the last layer.
5. Remove one slice of potato and pour the hot chicken stock through the gap until it just covers the last layer of lamb chops. Replace potato slice and dot potatoes with butter. Place a layer of foil over casserole and then put on the lid.
6. Place casserole in heated oven and immediately reduce heat to 350°F (or gas mark 3). Cook for 2½ hours, removing lid and foil for last half-hour of cooking to lightly brown potatoes.
7. Serve directly from the casserole dish, with a green salad on the side and lots of crusty whole grain bread.   *Serves* 3

9

WALES

The principality of Wales is one of four countries that make up the United Kingdom. Wales is also the smallest country in Britain. It stretches little more than one hundred thirty-five miles from Liverpool's River Dee to Wye on the River Severn. Broad, sandy beaches face the Irish Sea. The Welsh language is used increasingly—especially for place names on road signs that may not be the same as the name on your road map. Welsh is spoken in the north by 61 percent of the people, with English the second language. Closer to the border with England only about 20 percent speak Welsh, but signs welcoming visitors all over the country read "Welcome to Wales: *Croeso i Cymru*" in both languages. Wales's Celtic past goes back a long way. When Saxons invaded England many people fled to the Welsh mountains to join the Celts rather than submit to Anglo-Saxon rule. Wales is a land of legend and myth, and the Welsh people tend to talk of their legends and stories as though they happened yesterday, just down the road a piece.

Two great mountainous areas in Wales are now national parks—the Brecon Beacons in the south, and Snowdonia and Cader Idris in the north. The most breathtaking scenery in the country is in Snowdonia. The northern coastline has popular resort towns, border castles, and the Isle of Anglesey, which is now connected to the mainland by two bridges. The third national park, Pembrokeshire Coast National Park, and the surrounding areas in west Wales are rich in farmlands, coastal resorts with fine beaches, and good fishing grounds.

Castles abound in the Marcher lands along the English border. In all, Edward I built seventeen castles in Wales to bolster his campaigns against the Welsh in the thirteenth century, and the Welsh in turn built a few of their own, so the Welsh countryside is well endowed with wonderful castles to visit. Caerphilly Castle, Mid Glamorgan, is the second biggest castle in Britain. Situated on thirty acres of land in Caerphilly's town center, the castle is the site of medieval banquets and concerts held in the great hall during the summer. The town of Caerphilly is about eight miles from Cardiff. The cheese that bears its name has made Caerphilly world famous.

For visitors to Wales, there are castles, abbeys, cathedrals, and historic houses to explore. The National Museum of Wales has branches throughout the country. And for sports enthusiasts there are championship golf courses, fishing and boating, mountaineering, hiking, and walking in the gorgeous Welsh countryside. Families with children will find the many miniature railways in Wales amusing to travel on. The National Eisteddfod, held annually in the summer, is a week of competitions, concerts, and recitals. The word *Eisteddfod* means a "session," and in Wales it refers to a gathering of poets and musicians that began in the early 1100s.

After the Romans left Britain's shores, Wales was ruled by various princes who fought among themselves constantly, uniting the first time to successfully fight off the Anglo-Saxons around A.D. 600, and the second time, less successfully, to oust the Normans. The word *wallas*, meaning "foreigners" in Anglo-Saxon, gave the feisty folk their English name. *Cymru*, meaning the land of fellow countrymen, is the name they choose to describe themselves.

Roughly following the border between Wales and England is Offa's Dyke—a vast earthwork built in Anglo-Saxon times by Offa to separate his kingdom of Mercia from Wales. How he managed to finish such an enormous enterprise is still a mystery. The 149-mile (240-km) dike runs beside rivers, through thickly forested areas, and over steep hills. About eighty miles of the dike can still be seen today from the Offa's Dyke Path that follows the Welsh border.

The Romans made Cardiff the principal town in Wales, but it was not until 1955 that Queen Elizabeth II officially made Cardiff, South Glamorgan, the capital city. Brilliantly decorated Cardiff Castle is the oldest building in the capital. The town, and its major port at the mouth of the River Taff, grew to prominence during the Industrial Revolution. Here too is the National Museum of Wales, one of the biggest museums in Britain. It has wonderful art and extensive exhibits that strongly emphasize Welsh civilization and history. Cardiff is a cultured city much given to education. Its citizens, who number around three hundred thousand, spend their time in debating societies, theatrical groups, and other cultural forms of self-improvement. Welsh men also raise their voices in dozens of choirs. It seems as though almost every organization has its own choral society; some of these compete with one another in the Royal National Eisteddfod. The festival did not become fully national until the Industrial Revolution brought railways to

Wales and enabled people to travel from anywhere in Wales to attend the Eisteddfod. When the daily competitions are finished, evening concerts, recitals, and so on are held. Since 1950 a strictly enforced rule requires that all Eisteddfod events be performed in the Welsh language.

In the center of Cardiff, in walking distance from Cardiff Castle, is The Town House, 70 Cathedral Road, a beautifully appointed B & B run by Bart and Iris Zuzick. This delightful American couple are experienced hotel keepers, having formerly owned and run the prestigious Egerton Grey Country House Hotel in Porthkerry. They returned to live in Florida after selling the hotel but quickly grew bored and came back to Cardiff to convert their elegant, antique-filled, town house for guests. Breakfasts here are phenomenal. As well as eggs, bacon, and so on, each day there is a different specialty plus all the American extras that will keep you content until teatime. Bart is extraordinarily kind and will go out of his way to make sure that you lack for nothing. The richly decorated dining room, sitting room, and hallway are elegant yet welcoming.

Town House Tatties

6 lg. potatoes
3 lg. leeks, thinly sliced
1 sm. green pepper, diced
1 sm. red pepper, diced
4 oz. butter or margarine (1 stick)
    salt and pepper to taste

1. Peel and boil potatoes until semisoft. Allow to cool, then slice or dice.

2. Sauté leeks in half the butter. Add peppers and continue to sauté until tender.

3. Brown potatoes in remaining butter. Add leeks and peppers to the pan. Season well and combine ingredients gently. Serve piping hot.

Serves 8

North of Cardiff at St. Fagan's is the Welsh Folk Museum. This museum is part of the National Museum of Wales, whose major institutions are the Folk Museum, the Main Building at Cathays Park, Cardiff, and the Welsh Industrial and Maritime Museum in Cardiff Bay. It also has seven specialist museums and galleries around Wales. The land the Folk Museum stands on was donated by the Earl of Plymouth and the museum was modeled on the Uppsala Museum in Sweden. Each year four hundred thousand people come to visit the quaint historic buildings that have been removed from other parts of Wales and brought here for preservation and educational purposes. These include a working water mill that grinds flour daily for the old bakery, where people can watch, touch, and eventually eat the bread, buns, and scones that are baked in the old-fashioned oven. An ancient grocer's shop is manned by a knowledgeable grocer, Mr. Evans, who brings his home-roasted hams and salt-cured bacon, called *Cig moch wedi ei Halltu* in Welsh, to the shop. Mr. Evans also collects wonderful Welsh farmhouse cheeses that he will allow you to taste. On a recent visit most of these were cow's milk cheeses, intensely flavored with additions of white wine, garlic, and herbs. Gyda Hadau was spiked with mustard seed and ale. Particularly delicious was a new and expensive cheese laced with sun-dried tomatoes, wine, and herbs. Cenarth is a crumbly, slightly dry, Caerphilly-type cheese, and another moister version, called Nantybwla, was delicious. A soft, creamy cheese, Caws Llanboidy, is a favorite of Mr. Evans, and a Cheddar-type cheese aged for three years earns accolades. For vegetarians, Penbryn cheeses, made without calf's rennet, and unpasteurized milk from organically reared livestock, is also displayed on Mr. Evans's cooled marble slab.

Painstakingly reerected at the Folk Museum is a Celtic village settlement, with furnishings and household and hunting equipment, that portrays life as it was two thousand years ago. Many workshops are manned by craftspeople working with traditional tools—the Saddler, Tanner, Tailor, Potter, Smithy, Cooper, and Weaver in the working Woollen Mill. Llwynyr-eos is a gaslit farmhouse where outbuildings shelter farm animals and poultry, and the interior is decorated in the Edwardian style. Furnishings and building styles reflect the areas of Wales from which they came, as well as their use, be it St. Fagan's Castle, or the cider mill, boathouse, farmhouse, cottage, workshop, post office, or dairy. Even a thatched circular cockpit is here from the days when cockerels, wearing metal spurs, were trained to fight to the death and people placed bets on the outcome.

The Welsh are very fond of native foods such as seaweed, growing on land washed by the sea. Various sea vegetables, relished here for both flavor and nutrition, grow spontaneously along the coast of Pembrokeshire and the Gower Peninsula. Largely ignored for years, seaweed is now making a comeback as people grow more health conscious. Samphire, or marsh samphire, is being grown today in vegetable gardens under tall clay pots that keep the shoots tender and white. Samphire needs gentle cooking and pairs well with buttery sauces, such as Hollandaise, and is a perfect accompaniment to seafood. Another variety of seaweed, laver, has never been out of fashion in Wales or along the coastal areas of East Anglia. Slowly simmered in seawater until soft, then puréed, in Wales it is bought in cans as laverbread, rather than laver. Mixed with fine oatmeal, laverbread cakes are fried in bacon fat for breakfast all over Wales. Another popular way to serve puréed laverbread is to mix it with orange juice to accompany roast meats.

Seaweed is packed with goodness, and several different varieties of dried seaweeds are sold now in the better grocery stores or in health-food stores. Canned laverbread, available in London, can also be mail-ordered from Wales by contacting Mr. J. Dawson, Welsh Barrow (Draneway Laverbread), P.O. Box 218, Mumbles, Swansea, West Glamorgan SA3 4ZA, Wales. Sun-dried laver is available in the United States through Maine Coast Sea Vegetables, Shore Road, Franklin, Maine. To substitute sun-dried laver for laverbread in recipes it will need to be cooked in boiling water for 25–30 minutes, drained, and puréed with a few tablespoons of the cooking liquid. Three-quarters of an ounce of sun-dried laver will yield six ounces (one cup) of laverbread.

Another gift from the sea that laps the Gower Peninsula at Penclawd is a delicate, tasty mollusk gathered by dozens of people into buckets on the beach when the tide recedes. It has become a thriving cottage industry.

The River Wye and the River Usk are renowned for their salmon and trout fishing. The demand for these fish has always been high. But you do not have to be a fisherman to take home a succulent fish straight from its natural habitat, as fish farms also rear these and other fish on a healthy diet in good fresh water. Wet-fish vans travel inland, selling cod, haddock, plaice, and whichever other fish are available each day to farms and villages in the valleys. A wide selection of the more unusual varieties of fish and shellfish can be found at the Cardiff market. Fish stalls cater to the large, diverse immigrant populations—many of whom run ethnic restaurants—who happily buy singular fish and mollusks, not to mention the more slithery creatures.

Welsh baked goods have always been exceptionally good. Typically Welsh is the superb fruit-filled loaf called *bara brith*. Welsh griddle cakes—small flat cakes filled with dried fruit—served hot with lashings of butter, are simply unbeatable. At the Welsh folk museum at St. Fagan's, you can watch flour being ground from grain in the miller's house, then walk over to the bakery to see the dough being prepared by hand by a wonderful woman called Chris. The bread is then baked in an old-fashioned hot-ember stove. It is not unusual to be offered six or eight different kinds of bread—all fragrant and fresh-baked—in the better restaurants and hotels.

Fruits and vegetables flourish in the fertile soil of the Wye valley and the Vale of Glamorgan. Again the varieties of fruits, vegetables, and herbs have increased recently fourfold. Foreign travel and a liking for Continental, Greek, and Middle Eastern cuisines have created a demand for arugula, coriander, and fresh wild mushrooms, as well as new and different wines. During the summer and early autumn months, market stands spring up overnight like mushrooms selling homegrown fruits and vegetables. They sell not only produce—much of which is organically grown—but honey, preserves, farmhouse cheeses, homemade sausages, and yogurt or fresh cream to dip your strawberries in. If you are lucky you will find homemade ice cream too. Italian families are natural transplants to South Wales and its sweet-toothed folk. Boiled sweets, toffees, and chocolates are well-established industries in this region. Since the milk subsidies have been abolished many Italian café owners are taking advantage of the newly abundant fresh milk in South Wales to open ice cream plants.

Vineyards are relatively new on Wales's southern slopes and until recently have produced only white Germanic wines. Now red wine is being successfully produced on certain sunny slopes. Llanerch Vineyard, making Cariad wines and elderflower cordial, is situated on twenty acres of fertile land, lakes, and woods owned by Peter and Diana Andrews, both from families who for generations have been pharmacologists. Elderflowers have long been believed to be a cold and flu remedy and are known to instill a sense of well-being. Diana Andrews is an award-winning wine maker. The Andrewses have the only vineyard in Wales where the wine is bottled on the estate. They also run a newly built bed and breakfast guesthouse on their estate, with three or four en suite bedrooms of such excellence they have won a Two Crown Highly Commended citation from the Welsh Tourist Board.

Gilli Davies, a longtime promotor of Welsh foods and an accomplished cookbook writer, has done much to persuade the Welsh to value their unique culinary heritage. While cooking lunch in her farmhouse kitchen, Gilli Davies's enthusiasm for each ingredient was delightful and contagious, as she mixed fine oatmeal and laverbread, from the Pembrokeshire coast, to make crisp fritters. On the table were delicious Carmarthen ham that has the taste and texture of prosciutto, and a Welsh cheese with the looks and smoothness of Brie but with an added indefinable lively flavor. Glorious yellow, spanking fresh cockles were tucked into an omelette. Gilli Davies was tremendouly pleased to have found two small round loaves cooked on a griddle that morning in the Swansea market. Cariad elderflower cordial—a light-colored liquid made from steeped elderflowers, lemon, sugar, and mineral spring water—accompanied our lunch. Gilli Davies talked about the wonderful fish, excellent black beef, Welsh mountain lamb, cheeses, cream, and organic produce that appear increasingly in hotel and restaurant kitchens in Wales, attesting to her success as a promoter. She has given us permission to use two recipes from her book *Gilli Davies Taste of Wales*, published by BBC Books, London, England.

Pheasant with Sage and Apples

Game stock

	pheasant carcass
½	onion
6	parsley stalks
1	carrot, diced
1	stalk celery, diced

1. Ask the butcher for any gamy bits and pieces he has suitable for stock—perhaps a pheasant carcass—and add this to a pan of cold water with the above ingredients. Bring to a boil and simmer for no longer than 20 minutes, or it may become bitter. Leave to cool, then strain the game stock.

1	T.	sunflower seed oil
4	T.	butter
2		plump pheasants
1	lg.	onion, chopped
5	fl.oz.	Calvados and dry cider, mixed (scant ⅔ C.)
10	fl.oz.	good game stock (1¼ C.)
4–5		apples, peeled, cored, and sliced, preferably Cox's

1 T.   fresh sage, chopped
1   bay leaf
         salt and freshly ground black pepper
10 fl.oz. thick cream (1¼ C.)

2. Heat the oil and butter in a heavy-based casserole large enough to take both pheasants. Fry the pheasants so that they brown on all sides. Lift them out and fry the onion until soft and golden. Pour in the Calvados and cider. Let it boil until it has reduced by half its volume.

3. Pour in the stock, add the apples, herbs, and seasoning, and bring to a boil. Replace the pheasants, cover tightly, and simmer gently for about 50 minutes. The pheasants will be cooked when the leg feels as though it will come away easily from the body.

4. Remove the pheasants from the casserole, carve, and arrange in a serving dish.

5. Strain the casserole juices, pressing the contents well so that the apples and onions pass through the sieve, and return the sauce to the pan. Add the cream and bring to a boil. Season to taste, adding a little more Calvados or perhaps a squeeze of lemon juice to sharpen, and pour the sauce over the pheasant.

6. Serve with mashed potato that has been cooked with celery.

Serves 4

Plum Pudding

2 oz.   fresh white bread crumbs (⅓ C.)
10 fl.oz. double cream (1¼ C.)
2   egg yolks
1 T.   white wine
¼ t.   cinnamon
1 T.   heaped, castor sugar
12   Victoria plums
1   egg white

1. Preheat the oven to 350°F (or gas mark 4).

2. Put the bread crumbs in a bowl. Heat the cream in a saucepan until almost boiling. Pour over the crumbs and stir to blend. Cover the bowl and leave until cool; then stir in the egg yolks, wine, cinnamon, and sugar.

3. Poach the fruit in a little water until barely tender, then drain. When cool enough to handle, skin the fruit, remove the stones, and purée the flesh. Stir the purée into the cream and bread crumb mixture.

4. Whisk the egg white until stiff and fold into the mixture. Pour into a lightly greased, shallow, ovenproof dish, and bake for about 40 minutes.

5. Serve hot with a bowl of lightly whipped cream or clotted cream.   *Serves 4*

West of Cardiff at Laleston, near Bridgend just off the M4, is a pristine hotel with comfortable and beautifully decorated rooms, called The Great House, owned by Stephen and Norma Bond. Part of the main building began life in 1538 as a yeoman's cottage. Beams supporting the ceilings date from 1066. The stone spanning the fireplace is the longest single span in Wales, and the curiously shaped chimneys were originally built by Flemish people who came as weavers and lace makers to Wales. Two wings were added to the cottage by the local squire in the late 1600s. In the early 1800s the house reverted to a farmhouse and suffered great neglect until the Bonds rescued it. Norma Bond created the elegant, richly colored, decorative bedrooms, all with private bathrooms. Across the courtyard another set of larger rooms is being built, including a bridal suite and a fitness center. Andrew Huddart, the fine chef here, is an enormous asset to The Great House. Local suppliers bring fresh meat, poultry, fish, game, freshly smoked products, dairy foods, herbs, wild mushrooms, vegetables, and fruits from the neighboring farmlands. Even the chocolate for dessert making, the coffee, and the wines come from within the Principality. Frozen products are never, ever used, and all baked goods are cooked in The Great House kitchens. The wide eclectic menu also features "Dishes for the Less Indulgent" and at least four creative and elegant vegetarian dishes.

Welsh Lamb Chops en Croûte, Great House Style

3	premium-quality Welsh lamb chops*
1 T.	butter
1 T.	oil
1	shallot, chopped
	garlic and fresh herbs, to taste
2 oz.	mushrooms (scant ½ C.), chopped
2 oz.	puffed pastry
	beaten egg to glaze
	salt

* Have the butcher trim the lamb chops, removing all excess fat, and leaving only the clean bone and the "eye" of the meat.

1. Seal the chops in butter and oil on both sides in a frying pan. Set aside.

2. Fry the finely chopped shallot, garlic, and mushrooms together, adding a little seasoning to taste. Place a teaspoonful of this mixture onto each chop and keep refrigerated while you roll out the puff pastry to a fairly thin sheet. Meanwhile preheat the oven to 375°F (or gas mark 5).

3. Cut the pastry into circles just big enough to encase each lamb chop, leaving the bone sticking out. Glaze with egg wash and a little salt.

4. Bake until the pastry is golden brown and cooked.

Sauce

6	fl.oz.	dry white wine (⅔ C.)
12	fl.oz.	lamb stock (1½ C.)
		a little red currant jelly
2	oz.	fresh red currants (scant ½ C.)
		fresh rosemary

1. Using the pan in which the lamb chops were sealed, add the wine (we use Cariad, Welsh wine) and stock. Bring to a boil and reduce to a slightly syrupy consistency.

2. Add a little red currant jelly, some fresh red currants, and a few sprigs of rosemary. Season to taste. *Serves 3*

Courgette (Zucchini) Tagliatelle—*a delicious accompaniment to Lamb Chops en Croûte*

1 courgette per person
salted water
butter

1. Soak courgettes in cold, salted water for about 30 minutes to reduce the bitterness.

2. *Very* finely slice the courgette in lengthwise strips and drop into boiling salted water for 30 seconds. Drain and toss in butter to finish.

Traveling up through the Brecon Beacons toward Llyswen, and Llangoed Hall, is exciting with the tall dark mountains lowering over the tiny roads that wind through splendid valleys, among heather-clad hills and forests where wild Welsh ponies live. Black slag heaps until recently marred the valley here. Now that the last coal mine in Wales has shut down, these eyesores have been removed and the meadows reseeded. Light industry is making inroads, and tourism is becoming a major industry. The Welsh wonder why most American visitors go to London, Bath, and the Cotswolds, and then Ireland or Scotland, but rarely come to Wales. This is a great shame because the unspoiled beauty of the Welsh mountains is quite breathtaking, and the coastline is one of long, sheltered, sandy beaches. The food is fresh and delicious and far less expensive than in many other countries, and Wales is well endowed with interesting things to do—championship golf courses abound, as do hang gliding, fishing, hiking, and mountaineering. Many manor houses, set in gorgeous grounds, have been turned into country house hotels, and there are more castles to visit than you can shake a stick at.

William the Conqueror fostered the building of motte and bailey castles in Wales to control his holdings. In 1194 Llewelyn the Great, the powerful Prince of Gwynedd, captured many of the Norman castles and ruled over the greater part of Wales until his death at the monastery he had founded in Aberconwy. Edward I marched relentlessly against the Welsh, cut off their supplies, and finally starved Llewelyn's successor into submission on Anglesey. King Edward speedily built a ring of fortresses at Conwy, Caernarfon, Criccieth, Fflint, Rhuddlan, Harlech, and Beaumaris and bestowed the title Prince of Wales on his son, and for one hundred years there was peace.

Brecon, a market town, rests where two rivers meet—the Usk and the Honddu. Towering above the town are the mountains that bear the same name—Brecon. The Brecon Beacon National Park Information Centre is in Brecon, one of the oldest towns in Wales. Brecon's charter was granted in 1246. Part of a wall and a single tower attest to a former Norman castle. The abbey church of St. John, though built during the thirteenth and early fourteenth centuries, was designated a cathedral only recently in 1923. The Brecknock Museum—Brecon is also known as Brecknock—specializes in Welsh history and local folklore and houses a collection of love spoons. The individual designs of these fanciful spoons have special meanings. Traditionally carved by a swain for his ladylove, they can be found by noncarvers in Welsh craft shops.

A long immaculate driveway leads to Llangoed Hall, set in ten acres of gardens and parkland in the Wye valley, nine miles from Hay-on-Wye. Formerly known as Llangoed Castle, there has been a dwelling on this site since 560. Here the first Welsh Parliament was held, and for several centuries the site housed an Episcopal Grange. It was largely rebuilt in 1632 by

Sir Henry Williams, a gambling man who subsequently lost the property and castle on a bet. Eventually the property was acquired by Mrs. Archibald Christy, wife of a London hatter, who commissioned Sir Clough Williams-Ellis to restore and redesign the house. This was his first major commission, preceding Portmeirion, the famous, fanciful Italianate village he designed in North Wales. Williams-Ellis was an Edwardian architect of the school of Sir Edward Lutyens, and he created a great country house, whose finest interior features are its paneled library and dining room and the carved timber staircase leading to the ninety-five-foot-long pillared gallery, flanked by Llangoed's principal bedrooms. By the 1970s the building had again declined. It was bought in 1987 and restored by Sir Bernard Ashley, whose bright blue helicopter was parked on the lawn outside the dining room.

No reception desk confronts you as you enter Llangoed Hall, which has the feel of a private house. It was surprising not to see huge dogs lounging before the baronial fireplace. The hotel is looked after by Gareth and Helen Pugh—a friendly and efficient young couple dedicated to satisfying your every whim. Bedrooms at Llangoed are beautifully appointed—a decanter of sherry, two bottles of elderflower spritzer, and a bowl of ripe fruit sat on an antique table before the mullioned windows. A huge bathtub took up very little space in the sumptuous bathroom. Windows on two sides of the room looked over immaculate gardens to the mountains beyond. Dinner—served in the pretty yellow and cornflower blue dining room where long windows look across the emerald green Wye valley—was exquisite. A trio of terrines, game, chicken, and salmon, started the splendid meal, then Wye salmon with a rich herb-scented butter sauce, followed by Trelough duck breast, pale pink and tender—the accompanying vegetables were cooked exactly right. Flavorful Welsh cheese and a baked chocolate pudding in a Welsh whisky Anglaise finished the meal. The food, prepared under the direction of Nigel Morris, the head chef, is just about perfect. Nigel Morris won the prestigious Welsh Chef of the Year award for 1994.

Trelough ducks are raised in Hereford apple orchards, which give the ducks their distinctive and delicious taste. Local estates supply wood pigeon, snipe, pheasant, and woodcock. Farmed venison comes from nearby Brecon, and the delicious honey on the breakfast table is from hives right here in Llyswen. Nigel Morris has generously shared several of his recipes with us for this book.

Fillet of Wye Salmon with Roasted Baby Vegetables and a Hermitage and Shallot Jus

3	oz.	baby carrots (½ C.)
3	oz.	baby corn (½ C.)
3	oz.	baby leeks (½ C.)
2	oz.	Grillot onions (⅓ C.)
4		globe artichokes
4		6-oz. fillets Wye salmon
4	T.	butter
2	T.	olive oil
4	oz.	finely chopped shallots (⅔ C.)
10	fl.oz.	Hermitage wine (1¼ C.)
20	fl.oz.	veal stock (2½ C.)
1		pinch of fresh-picked thyme

1. Prepare and wash all the baby vegetables including the onions. Lightly blanch them separately. Refresh in iced water, then drain.

2. Prepare the artichoke and cook in simmering, seasoned water for approximately 12–15 minutes, then leave to cool. Once cool, remove the chokes and slice at an angle.

3. Season the salmon fillets. Heat half the oil and butter in a pan and gently cook the fish for 3 to 4 minutes each side. Be careful not to over-brown.

4. In a saucepan, season and sweat the shallots. Add the Hermitage and cook right down until the pan is nearly dry, then add the veal stock and reduce until you have the correct consistency for sauce.

5. Season the baby vegetables and artichokes. Heat the rest of the oil and butter in a baking tray. Add the vegetables, artichokes, and thyme, and cook in a hot oven for 3 to 4 minutes until lightly colored.

6. Place the roasted vegetables to one side of the plate and the salmon on the other. Pour a small amount of the sauce in the middle, then serve.   *Serves 4*

Whole Roasted Welsh Partridge Served on a Bed of Endive with a Light Ginger and Parsley Jus

2	T.	olive oil
1	T.	unsalted butter
4		whole young partridge*
2	oz.	baby carrots (⅓ C.)
2	oz.	baby leeks (⅓ C.)
4		endive (Belgium)
1	t.	butter
1	t.	sugar
20	fl.oz.	veal stock (2½ C.)
		small knob of butter
2	oz.	oyster mushrooms (⅓ C.)
2	T.	chopped parsley
		pinch of pickled ginger, or to taste

* Buy the partridge already prepared and trussed from your local game dealer or butcher.

1. Preheat the oven to 425°F (or gas mark 7). Heat the oil and butter together in a heavy frying pan. Season the birds inside and out, then lightly brown the birds on all sides. Place the partridge in the oven for 4 minutes on each side, then remove and allow to rest.

2. Trim and clean the baby vegetables. Lightly blanch the carrots and leeks separately. Refresh in iced water, then drain.

3. Cut the endive into strips and cook in a mixture of water, butter, and sugar.

4. Remove the partridge meat from the bone and cover with buttered parchment paper. Add the bones to the veal stock and simmer for 10 minutes. Pass through a fine sieve.

5. In a small frying pan, place a knob of butter and gently fry the mushrooms until the liquid has evaporated.

To serve:

6. Reheat and season the endive, carrots, and leeks, separately. Place the partridge back in a warm oven to heat through.

7. Check seasoning on the sauce and add the parsley and ginger.

8. On heated plates, place a neat pile of endive in the center, and arrange baby vegetables and mushrooms around the edge. Top the endive with the partridge. Coat with sauce and serve.

Serves 4

Jerusalem Artichoke Soup Enriched with Saffron and Thyme

2	lb.	Jerusalem artichokes
5	T.	butter
3	oz.	white mirepoix (⅔ C.) (mixture of leek, garlic, shallot, and thyme)
1		pinch of saffron
4–5		sprigs of fresh thyme
¼		bottle dry white wine
30	fl.oz.	chicken stock (3⅔ C.)
5	fl.oz.	heavy cream (scant ⅔ C.)
		pinch of salt and pepper

1. Peel and dice the artichokes and sweat in the butter with the diced mirepoix, half the saffron, and a sprig of thyme.

2. Add white wine and reduce until almost dry. Add the chicken stock and cook until vegetables are soft.

3. Liquidize, or blend and pass through a fine sieve. Add cream to taste, and lightly whip the remainder of the cream. Check for seasoning.

To serve:

4. Portion the soup among four bowls and garnish with a ribbon of whipped cream, a sprig of thyme, and the remaining saffron.

Serves 4

Salmon and Mussel Sausage on a Fricassée of Leeks Scented with Coriander

6	oz.	salmon
1		egg white
		pinch of salt and pepper
20	fl.oz.	heavy cream (2½ C.)
2	lb.	mussels
3	oz.	white mirepoix (⅔ C.) (a mixture of leek, garlic, shallot, and thyme)
¼		bottle white wine
1		bunch chives, chopped

10 oz.	leeks (2 C.)
8 oz.	tomatoes (1½ C.), peeled, seeded, and diced
1	bunch coriander, chopped
½	bunch dill, chopped

1. In a food processor, purée the salmon with one egg white and salt and pepper. Pass through a fine sieve over ice. Gradually beat in enough cream to make a mousse. Leave to rest.

2. Clean mussels well. Place in a heated saucepan with white mirepoix and wine. Cover and cook until mussel shells open. Remove mussels from shells, reserve one-quarter, and chop the rest. Mix chopped mussels and chopped chives with salmon mousse.

3. Mold the mousse in cling film to form a sausage and poach for 8 minutes. Refresh with cold water. Set aside.

4. Chop the leeks into small dice and sweat in a saucepan. Add remaining cream and seasoning. Bring to the boil and finish with diced tomato and chopped coriander.

To serve:

5. Divide the leek mixture between four plates. Then gently pan-fry the sausage and place on leeks.

6. Arrange mussels around edge of plate and garnish with chopped dill. *Serves* 2

Baked Chocolate Pudding in a Welsh Whisky Anglaise

3½ oz.	bitter Couverture chocolate (½ C.)
3½ oz.	butter (scant ½ stick)
5½ oz.	castor sugar (scant ⅔ C.)
2	eggs
2	egg yolks
4 T.	flour
	butter for ramekins

1. Preheat oven to 375°F (or gas mark 5.) Butter individual ramekins.

2. In a small saucepan, melt chocolate and butter together.

3. In a mixing bowl, mix together sugar, eggs, and egg yolks. Stir in the melted chocolate and butter and gradually mix in the flour.

4. Pour mixture into buttered ramekins and bake for 15–17 minutes.

Welsh Whisky Anglaise

4	egg yolks
3 oz.	castor sugar (⅓ C.)
5 fl.oz.	milk (scant ⅔ C.)
5 fl.oz.	heavy cream (scant ⅔ C.)
½	vanilla pod, about 2 inches long
4 T.	Welsh whisky
2 t.	confectioners sugar
	sprigs of fresh mint

1. Beat the egg yolks and sugar together until the sugar dissolves.

2. In a saucepan, heat the milk, cream, and vanilla pod until it reaches a boil. Gradually beat the hot milk mixture into the yolks and return to saucepan. Cook gently, stirring, until the sauce is thickened and smooth. Remove and discard pod.

3. Remove from heat and stir in whisky.

To serve:

4. Place a ladle of whisky cream sauce into a soup plate. Unmold the chocolate pudding into the center of the plate; garnish with a dusting of confectioners sugar and a mint sprig.

A lavish way to start the day is breakfast at Llangoed Hall. Start with a compote of fruit and follow that with a fat, golden smoked haddock cake, set on a bed of slivered green beans in a pool of beurre blanc sauce, and freshly brewed coffee. Sir Bernard Ashley's bright blue helicopter took off from a side lawn during the meal, its whirling blades scattering cherry blossoms as it wobbled up and over the mountains.

Mid Wales is very mountainous. Ranges tower above two thousand feet (610 meters), and the rainfall can be considerable. Giant reservoirs supply water to the big industrial towns to the east. Hardy Welsh lamb graze the open moorland. Farmers, through the new grading of cuts of lamb by Welsh Lamb Enterprise, are paid handsomely for top-quality meat. This in turn goes to local butchers, who label it as such for discerning customers. Organically grown produce is in full swing in mid Wales, as are organically reared Guernsey cows. Cheeses made from Guernsey milk and ewe's and goat's milk are superb. Welsh cheese is quality controlled by the Agricultural Development and Advisory Service.

Farther east, nestled on the south bank of the River Wye, at the foot of the Black Mountains in lovely rural countryside, is Hay-on-Wye, which is the market town for the region's farmers and holds important livestock auctions during the year. But the village, crammed to the gills with secondhand bookstores, is acclaimed as the used-book capital of the world. An estimate of the number of books overflowing shops at every turn is anywhere between one and two million. Most shops adopt the system of categorizing books by countries—Welsh literature, English literature, Irish literature, American literature, and so on—although you can also find shops that devote all their space to one subject. The Hay Cinema bookshop is devoted to books on cinema and actors. It is the only store in the village to have a parking lot in the rear. Another shop has an enormous collection of adventure storybooks for children. Huge stuffed animals and teddy bears as tall as many adults greet you as you enter. Glimpsed through a heavy wooden doorway set in a thick stone wall on a recent visit were dozens of ratty bookcases standing exposed to the elements in what must once have been the castle's moat and is now a dense moist circle of greensward. The area was deserted. Books overflowed the cases and tumbled from a large table that had an honor-system money box. In various nooks and crannies in the castle's interior were more small bookshops, all of these owned by Richard Booth, the man who made Hay-on-Wye a center for secondhand books in the first place. He opened his earliest one in 1962 in the old fire station. Booth is dedicated to the simplicity and integrity of country life as it once was. He has a healthy disrespect for bureaucracy, and "progress" when its comes to automation is anathema. A great writer of polemics on pet subjects, he once declared Hay-on-Wye an independent nation, proclaimed himself king, and sells passports and knighthoods in one room of the castle. As no bookshop owner knows with any certainty what he has in stock, it is possible in Hay-on-Wye to come across an unnoticed bargain-priced rare edition. In any event, all books are a bargain when compared with prices for secondhand books in London or Oxford. Reached by a narrow road four miles to the south of Hay-on-Wye that twists and turns through hilly, forested terrain is an area of flat moorland with splendid views, walking trails, and a spot where hang-gliders take to the airwaves. Offa's Dyke crosses the moor at this point.

Seven miles from Hay-on-Wye on the Builth Wells Road is Llyswen's charming Griffin Inn, festooned with flowery window boxes. This old and long-established sporting inn continues a tradition of warm hospitality, good food, and comfortable accommodation. Richard and Di Stockton took over the inn in 1984 and soon earned many accolades, including "Pub of the Year" in 1989. The guest bedrooms accommodate sixteen people, and there is a comfortable residents' lounge and a separate room for television viewing. The inn has a full-time ghillie and keeper, as shooting and fishing are the two main sporting pursuits. The Stocktons are happy to arrange demonstrations and gun-dog training for all breeds of gun dog at a nearby training center. Di Stockton says that they now have the facilities for oak-smoking fish, so any caught by residents can be smoked and safely taken with them when they leave. The style of the food at the Griffin Inn has developed over the years to include more sophisticaed dishes such as tournedos Rossini, pâté, and terrines, but the real heart of their cooking is still native game—everything from rabbit to venison and snipe to pheasant. Local suppliers bring fresh farm produce, free-range chicken, duck, and eggs to their door every day. Fish, particularly trout and salmon, are from the Wye River. Welsh lamb and Herefordshire beef come from the local butcher in Talgarth, augmented by supplies from Vin Sullivan and coastal fishermen. As well as all this, Di Stockton, who is an avid gardener, grows flowers and vegetables to supplement supplies at the Griffin. Eileen Harvard, a farmer's daughter, runs the kitchen and not only cooks wonderful game dishes, such as pheasant pie with red currant jelly, but a whole raft of honest to goodness puddings and crumbles for dessert. The menus at the Griffin Inn feature Homemade pâtés, Jugged hare, Poached salmon with Glanwye Sauce, Sirloin steak with French onions, Fresh brook trout, and Roast duckling with apple sauce—among other dishes. Here is one of the Griffin Inn's game dishes for you to try.

Civet of Rabbit in Cider

1	lg.	rabbit
4	T.	flour
		oil for frying
2		sticks celery, sliced
6	oz.	carrots (1¼ C.), diced
12		button mushrooms
6		slices bacon, cut into strips
2		cloves garlic, finely chopped
2		bouquet garni
12		pitted dried prunes, soaked in 10 fl.oz.(1¼ C.) tea
12		black or green olives, pitted
2	T.	concentrated tomato purée
10	fl.oz.	cider (1¼ C.)
2	T.	cornstarch, optional

1. Preheat oven to 350°F (or gas mark 4).

2. Cut rabbit into eight serving portions and toss lightly in flour.

3. Heat oil in large frying pan and fry meat, turning pieces until golden brown. Remove rabbit to heat-proof casserole. Add vegetables, bacon, and garlic to frying pan and fry until slightly browned.

4. Add vegetable mixture to the rabbit with liquid, bouquet garni, prunes, olives, tomato purée, and cider. Cover with tight-fitting lid and bake for about 90 minutes or until rabbit is tender.

5. Correct seasoning, and if necessary thicken sauce with corn-starch mixed with a little cold water. *Serves* 8

The mild climate and fertile soil of West Wales grow exceptional fruits and vegetables. Dairy farmers thrive too on the verdant pastureland of Carmarthenshire and southern Pembrokeshire with a great deal of the milk going into making distinctive farmhouse cheeses, yogurt, butter, buttermilk, and rich cream. Cereal for cattle feed is grown in the central part of the west coast region, and the northern plateau is home to flocks of fine Welsh mountain sheep.

With the increased demand for healthy fresh fish, recent innovations within the fishing industry have helped meet this challenge. For example, in Cardigan bay lobster beds are being reseeded, and mussels are again becoming plentiful in the Menai Straits. Oyster farming is in full swing in Carew. Increasingly people buy their fresh fish from small trawlers that pull in at docks along the coast. Most ports have a fish stall or two that cater to the general public. Enterprising fishermen have built saltwater pens off the dock to farm fish in their own salty habitat. If you decide to buy at Pembroke Dock, do not forget Pembrokeshire is renowned for the great flavor of its potatoes, and nothing goes as well with fish as buttery, new potatoes sprinkled liberally with parsley.

Leek and Potato Frittata

2	leeks, white and some green part too, thoroughly washed
2 T.	unsalted butter
6 oz.	new potatoes
4 lg.	eggs
1 T.	minced tarragon
1 T.	minced parsley
2 T.	olive oil
4 T.	Parmesan cheese, grated
4 T.	Gruyère cheese, grated

1. Slice leeks. Melt butter in small frying pan over moderate heat, stir in sliced leeks, and cook until tender—approximately 10 minutes. Set aside.

2. Steam potatoes until tender. When cool enough to handle, peel and slice. While potatoes and leeks are cooking, beat together eggs and herbs in a large bowl.

3. Carefully add sliced potatoes and sliced leeks to egg mixture. Preheat broiler.

4. Heat olive oil over medium heat in a medium-sized nonstick frying pan with metal handle. Pour in egg mixture and allow to cook without stirring until almost set—about 4 minutes. Center will still be loose.

5. Sprinkle with cheeses and place under broiler until cheese is beginning to bubble and the edges are golden brown.

6. To serve, loosen edges of frittata with a spatula, slide onto a warm serving plate, and cut into four wedges; accompany with green salad.   *Serves 4*

Pembroke has a fortified castle, towering above the river, built on rock. Here the town encircled by massive stone walls grew up around the castle. Today some of Pembroke's streets have a Georgian look to them, but the main part of the town near Pembroke Dock is thoroughly Victorian. Coracle fishing boats can be seen at Cenarth and Carmarthen. These small boats, light enough to carry down to the sea, have not changed their design in two thousand years. The frame of the little boat is made from intertwined laths of ash, covered with tarred calico to make it watertight. Ancient Britons used similar craft covered in hide. Being so lightweight, they can be maneuvered with astonishing speed. On the River Towey at Carmarthen in Dyfed, coracles fish in pairs for salmon with a net strung between the two boats. Carmarthen and Caerleon share the title of the oldest town in Wales. In the mid-1400s, an Eisteddfod of Welsh poets was held in Carmarthen. A Celtic settlement was here before the Romans replaced it with a fort in A.D. 75. A Roman amphitheater discovered below ground was capable of seating five thousand people. Relics from this find can be seen in the National Library, Aberystwyth. A little later in A.D. 480, Merlin, King Arthur's wizard, is said to have been born near Carmarthen. Carmarthen produces a wonderful deep ruby red cured ham that is very similar in taste and appearance to prosciutto and equally delicious. Swirl strips of it into a creamy pasta sauce or use some diced to give added flavor to meat pies.

The road north from Llyswen goes to Builth Wells, home to the Royal Welsh Agricultural Show, and bearing right leads to Llandrindod Wells. Spa waters can still be sampled at Rock Park Pavilion. Elegant architecture and verdant parks grace this Edwardian spa town. A ruined castle from the eleventh century still stands at New Radnor just east of Llandrindod Wells. Hikers can take forested paths through the mountainous area of Radnor Forest. Old Radnor has an ancient church that has used a megalith as a font for the last twelve hundred years.

Continuing north to Llangurig, you can take the A44 west toward the university town of Aberystwyth, a popular resort town overlooking Cardigan Bay. The street plan here follows the original medieval grid plan. Or you can travel further north, passing the A44 junction on to Llanidloes—a pretty town with some half-timbered black and white buildings and a half-timbered covered market in the town center. The countryside in this part of Wales is spectacular. Impressive black mountains brood over the valleys, and every now and again a break in the clouds shows a tantalizing glimpse of sunny slopes of higher mountains behind the first range. If the weather is clear, and you are so inclined, take the small B4518 road up into the mountains, skirting the edge of Hafren Forest and going on to the market town of Machynlleth.

Every Wednesday Machynlleth, dominated by the enormous Castle-reagh clock tower, holds a large outdoor market on its streets. In earlier days Romans settled here. Later, in 1404, Machynlleth was the seat of parliament for Prince Owain Glyndwr—the last leader to hold out against the encroaching English. The carefully restored granite and slate Old Parliament Building is beautiful, and it still draws visitors today. North of the town is the Centre for Alternative Technology, where there are demonstrations and interesting designs for the use of solar, wind, and water power. There are also a fascinating energy-conservation house to marvel at, craftshops, and a farm where everything is organically grown. The farm supplies the Centre with free-range hens, goats, fish, beef, lamb, and pork.

A few miles south of Machynlleth on the A487 at Hen Efail is the Furnace Restaurant, highly recommended for lunch or afternoon tea. The spotlessly clean café/restaurant has a superb array of homemade cheesecakes, pies, chocolate desserts, and homemade ice cream, all of which contain only natural ingredients. Other baked goods include scones to be eaten with strawberry jam and clotted cream, spiced syrup cake, chocolate toffee shortbread, toasted teacakes, Danish pastries, and *bara brith*, the traditional Welsh fruit loaf. Also on the property is a shop filled with Welsh crafts. Across the road from the restaurant is a working watermill built high on a steep bank. Hiking trails follow the river that powers the mill and lead to a misty waterfall set amid pine trees. Should you see swift streams or waterfalls in West Wales, water-powered mills will not be far behind. Many of these have been refurbished and restored to working order, grinding fresh flour on a daily basis, and some of them sell delectable baked goods.

Poached Peaches Filled with Soft Cheese

4	lg.	peaches, peeled, pitted, and halved
16	fl.oz.	white wine (2 C.)
2	oz.	castor sugar (¼ C.)
1		2-inch strips of lemon zest
10	oz.	fresh raspberries (2 C.)

4 oz.	mild goat cheese (½ C.)
4–6 T.	crème fraîche
1 t.	honey
¼ t.	almond essence
1 oz.	crumbled amaretti cookies (¼ C.)
	amaretti cookies

1. In a saucepan large enough to hold peaches in a single layer, place peaches, wine, castor sugar, lemon zest, and enough water to barely cover fruit. Bring to a boil, reduce heat, cover, and simmer for 15 minutes.

2. Remove peaches with a slotted spoon and set aside to cool completely. Meanwhile reduce syrup to 4 fluid ounces (or half a cup) and set aside.

3. Purée raspberries in food processor, then force through a sieve to remove seeds. Stir in reduced wine syrup to taste.

4. For filling, cream together mild goat's cheese, crème fraîche, honey, and almond essence. Pipe filling into peach cavity. Sprinkle with amaretti crumbs and refrigerate until serving time.

5. Swirl a spoonful or two of raspberry sauce on each dessert plate and top with a peach half. Pass additional amaretti cookies separately. *Serves 8*

Just a few steps south is Ynyshir Hall, a Georgian Manor house that sits in fourteen acres of glorious gardens, containing many rare varieties of unusual trees and shrubs. April and May bring a blaze of vibrant azaleas and rhododendrons. Since the sixteenth century the house has been cherished by a succession of eminent owners, including Queen Victoria. Now it is owned by a professional artist, Rob Reen, and Joan Reen, his wife, who with flair and skill have created one of Wales's finest privately owned hotels. Antiques, Welsh pottery, and carefully chosen color schemes enhance the interiors of Ynyshir Hall that glow with Rob Reen's paintings. The bedrooms, named for famous artists, are all different, with sumptuous fabric accessories hand sewn by Joan Reen. The dining room is full of light and color with views over the fourteen-acre manicured grounds. Joan Reen is so pleased to have chef Tony Pierce as part of their team. She claims he is able to turn his hand to anything. His expertise has been gleaned from many special hotels, including Gleneagles and Llangoed Hall. His cooking has freshness and lightness, coupled with intense flavors. Seafood from Cardigan Bay is plentiful. Here crabs, lobsters, cockles, mussels, fine wild salmon, and sea trout are caught in the Dovey estuary directly behind the hotel. The Welsh mountain lamb and farmhouse cheeses available close at hand are second to none. From the hotel's kitchen garden come fresh-picked herbs, salad vegetables, gooseberries, and black currants. Apple, pear, and plum trees flourish here too. Specialty items come from Vin Sullivan at Abergavenny. Some of the dishes on the menu are Rillette of confit duck leg with black olives, shallots, and red chicory salad; Delicate sausage of smoked salmon and trout mousse with lemon dressing; Paupiettes of guinea fowl with poached apricots, bacon, and thyme; and Roast loin of Welsh lamb with Puy lentils, confit of shallots, and a light rosemary jus. One of their famous desserts is sticky toffee pudding with butterscotch sauce. Tony Pierce's favorite recipe is a sea bass and scallop mousse.

Sea Bass Filled with a Scallop Mousse with Squid Ink Noodles and Coriander Butter Sauce

Preparation time 1¼ hrs; cooking time 15 minutes

Nage de légumes (vegetable stock)

1		carrot, diced
1		stick celery, diced
1		leek, diced
1		onion, diced
2		lemon slices
5	fl.oz.	water (scant ⅔ C.)
2	oz.	fresh basil (⅓ C.)
2	oz.	fresh chervil (⅓ C.)
2	oz.	fresh parsley (⅓ C.)
4		pink peppercorns
6		white peppercorns
8	fl.oz.	white wine (1 C.)

1. Place diced vegetables, lemon slices, and water in a saucepan and boil for 8 minutes. Add herbs and peppercorns and boil for one minute more.

2. Add wine and leave to infuse for 30 minutes, then strain. Set aside.

Squid ink noodles

½	lb	plain flour (scant 1½ C.)
4	t.	squid ink—2 packets
2		whole eggs
5		egg yolks

few drops of olive oil
seasoning

3. Add all ingredients to mixing bowl and mix for 10 minutes. Let the dough rest for one hour.
4. Roll dough thinly, or use pasta machine, to make noodles. Blanch 2 minutes in boiling water.

Scallop mousse

4	plump fresh scallops
3½ fl.oz.	heavy cream (scant ½ C.)
	cayenne pepper
	salt to taste
	squeeze of fresh lemon juice
2-lb.	sea bass, whole

5. Using a food processor, purée scallops for one minute. Slowly add cream until well mixed, then add cayenne, salt, and lemon juice.
6. Prepare sea bass by removing scales and bones, make a small incision on flesh side, and carefully fill with scallop mousse. Wrap fish in buttered cling film.

Sauce

5 fl.oz.	nage de légumes (scant ⅔ C.)
2 oz.	cold diced butter (½ stick)
	coriander leaves
	tomato concassée

Garnish

4	plumb fresh scallops
4 sm.	dollops of caviar (optional)

To serve:

7. To make the sauce, boil down the nage de légumes liquid, whisk in butter, and add coriander and tomato at last minute.
8. Sear scallops for garnish.
9. Place bass in steamer for 7 minutes. Set aside in warm place.
10. Warm noodles on stove and divide among four heated plates.
11. Unwrap and slice bass, placing a portion on top of noodles.
12. Garnish with seared scallops and caviar, if using, and dress with sauce. Serve with Gewürztraminer wine. *Serves 4*

At one time, the only Welsh cheese that came to mind was Caerphilly, an unripened cheese, which actually is a relative newcomer as British cheeses go, being little more than one hundred fifty years old. Easily digestible, it was quickly adopted by Welsh miners and others who have to work in cramped quarters. Lunch for these hardworking men was generally nothing more than a slice of Caerphilly and a piece of cake, called teisen lap. The sweet, moist cake went well with the slightly sharp taste of Caerphilly. More Caerphilly is produced now in Somerset and Wiltshire than in Caerphilly. But this should surprise nobody in a land where Stilton cheese has never been made in the village of Stilton, and Cheddar cheese is made at Chewton Mendip. Nowadays fresh farmhouse cheeses by the dozens are being made all over Wales. At one time these delectable, dewy cheeses were sold only locally, but with enterprise and better distribution, farmhouse cheeses are appearing in specialty shops and good supermarkets throughout the principality. Made from top-quality cow's, goat's, or ewe's milk, much of it from organically reared livestock, some of these cheeses can be found flavored with fresh herbs or a hint of garlic. Some favorites are Merlin, a semi-hard full fat goat's milk cheese wrapped in a shiny jet-black rind; Pencarreg, a soft full fat cheese made from organic cow's milk, with a white mould-ripened crust; Pant-ys-gawn farm goat's cheese, soft, white, and perfect with an aperitif; Acorn farmhouse ewe's milk cheese, firm white with an ideal texture for cooked dishes; Plas Dairy farm cheese, made from low-fat goat's milk and available plain or flavored with herbs or garlic; and Llanboidy cheese, full fat and hard pressed, made from a special breed of cattle called Red Poll. Traditional Cheddar or Lancashire cheeses are also being handmade in farmhouses, as is Caerphilly, naturally.

Return by the road to Machynlleth and go west to Aberdyfi, or Aberdovey, as it is called in English, to the Penhelig Arms Hotel and Restaurant, which stands beside Penhelig harbor. Oceangoing schooners were built here many years ago. Robert and Sally Hughes have turned this old inn, which was originally built in the 1700s, into a charming retreat. Robert Hughes is an energetic, efficient, and humorous person, who will look after you well. Wine is a consuming interest, and Robert Hughes's cellar shows depth and range. There is also a fine selection of half bottles. The hotel is on the edge of the Snowdonia National Park and is ideally situated for exploring mid Wales. There are stunning views from the bedroom and restaurant windows across the estuary to the mountains beyond. Sally Hughes no longer does the cooking, but she is very much in evidence in the hotel as well as looking after their two children, aged three and seven. The head chef is Jane Howkins, and she is assisted in the kitchen by Jean Bowen. Great fresh ingredients from local suppliers assure excellent eating that attracts legions of repeat customers. On a recent visit the menu featured seven starters, including

Pâté, a Roulade with prawns, Pancakes filled with mushrooms and cheese, Home-cured salmon, and Tomatoes filled with smoked trout. Among the main courses were Fillet of turbot baked with prawns, Roast breast of duck, Roast sirloin of beef with bearnaise, and Char-grilled escallop of lamb with garlic hollandaise. Desserts are luscious. The chocolate ones were rich and smooth, the Lemon soufflé rose like a trumpet note, the Bread and butter pudding managed to be creamy all the way through, and the Brandy snap baskets filled with fresh fruit and raspberry sauce were mouthwatering. Farmhouse cheeses finished the meal with panache. Sally Hughes has given us a recipe for Spicy Chicken which follows.

Spicy Chicken

1-in.	cube fresh ginger, peeled and chopped
4	garlic cloves, crushed
3 T.	water
4 T.	peanut oil
3 lb.	chicken pieces, skinned
2 t.	cumin seeds, freshly ground
5	cardamom pods, hulls removed and seeds ground
8 oz.	onion (1½ C.), chopped
2–3 oz.	tender celery (¼–½ C.), chopped
8 fl.oz.	yogurt (1 C.)
2 T.	sultanas
	salt and pepper
	lemon juice, to taste

1. Place ginger, garlic, and water in the container of an electric blender and whirl to a paste. Remove and set aside.

2. Heat oil in a large frying pan and sauté chicken pieces until brown. Remove to a warm place.

3. In the same pan stir the cumin and cardamom until fragrant. Stir in the paste from the blender, add the onion and celery, and stir until softened.

4. Remove pan from heat and bit by bit add the yogurt to the pan, stirring constantly to make a sauce. Heat gently.

5. Return chicken to the pan, cover, and simmer for 20 minutes. Stir in the sultanas and simmer for 10 minutes more. Season with salt and pepper.

6. Remove from heat, stir in the lemon juice, and serve hot with raita.

Cucumber raita

1 lg.   cucumber, peeled, seeded, and sliced
1 T.   salt
8 fl.oz. plain yogurt (1 C.)
1 t.   cumin seeds, toasted and ground
1 T.   fresh cilantro, minced

7. Toss cucumber and salt together, and let rest for 10 minutes. Squeeze out excess moisture from cucumber.

8. In a medium-sized bowl, mix yogurt and ground cumin until smooth.

9. Stir in cucumber and cilantro. Cover bowl and refrigerate for at least an hour. Serve chilled.   *Serves 6*

Aberdyfi is a pretty, unspoiled village, and there is much to do here. From the wharf, fishing trips and a variety of watersports, including canoeing, waterskiing, and windsurfing, can be arranged. Just beyond the quaint shops is an 18-hole championship golf course situated right on the sand dunes. Nearby are the little Tal-y-Llyn Railway and the massive Cader Idris. Don't miss visiting the Old Coffee Shop, 13 New Street, Aberdyfi, for a cup of steaming freshly brewed morning coffee. Allan and Sue Griffiths own this delightful shop, which brims with their collection of china teapots.

From Llanegryn, a little farther north along the coast, there is a narrow road no wider than a driveway that snakes up through the foothills of the Cader Idris, climbing higher and higher, among rushing streams and an occasional waterfall. This enchanting little road eventually leads to Castell-y-Bere, the remains of a granite castle built by Llewelyn the Great in 1221. Baby lambs, no bigger than house cats, dot the hillsides and will come running to greet you, bleating joyfully through the fence if you stop nearby. Turn right at the first turning and then left onto a somewhat larger road that skirts the massive Cader Idris and on down to the town of Dollgellau. This pretty town to the south of the great Cader Idris range is a perfect base for walkers and hikers. Footpaths and trails lead to splendid views.

Near Dolgellau is a beautiful country house, Penmaenuchaf Hall, owned and managed by Lorraine Fielding and Mark Watson. Nestling peacefully in the foothills of the Cader Idris mountains, its position is enviable. The hotel windows overlook the lovely Mawddach Estuary, one of the finest in Europe, and the hills beyond. The house was built roughly 135 years ago by a Victorian cotton merchant named James Lee Taylor—his initials can still be seen in the sea-green glass panel at the end of the entrance hall—and the lion above the front door was once part of his coat of arms. More pretty stained glass tops the door lintels. One wall of the entrance hall is dominated by a huge, floor-to-ceiling, carved, black wooden fireplace. Curly pillars support the deep recessed mantle. The light-filled morning room has wide windows opening on beautiful views of the Rhinog mountains. There are fourteen delightful en suite bedrooms, each decorated differently, but all furnished with antiques, deep armchairs or comfortable sofas, and many have king-sized beds. Pairs of cherubs grace the walls. A well-stocked library or the snooker table beckon when the day is not conducive to outdoor activity; otherwise, country pursuits abound. Penmaenuchaf Hall has thirteen miles of fishing on the Rivers Mawddach and Union. Sailing, canoeing, pony trekking, clay pigeon shooting, golf, and walking in the mountains are some of the activities open to you here.

Nic Walton is the head chef at Penmaenuchaf Hall. His favorite dishes include loin of Welsh lamb wrapped in a coriander mousse; home-smoked rosette of salmon on an apple and cider cream; and grenadine of veal filled with game mousseline, roasted on a cassoulet of lentils and a confit of onions. Desserts are marvelous; try the whole poached apple in wine set on a bed of marshmallow with a lime syrup. Supplies are mostly local, and game is obtained from nearby shoots. All the baked goods are homemade, and Nic Walton smokes his own meat and fish. The sea is only five miles away, and fishermen deliver freshly caught lobster, crab, prawns, bass, and many other seasonal fish. Penmaenuchaf Hall is renowned for the quality of the lamb, venison, and beef served in its pretty dining room. Mark Watson receives fresh herbs, beautifully wrapped and boxed, from a local nursery. Acres of grounds surround this historic manor house. During a spring visit, two gardeners were busy setting out plants in the enclosed formal garden, reached by stone steps from the terrace in front of Penmaenuchaf Hall's main entrance. Nic Walton's recipe for poached leg of lamb in hay follows.

Poached Leg of Lamb in Hay

hay		enough to line a large casserole—cut in the fields and rinsed or bought from a supplier
		salt and pepper
1½		onions, diced
1		carrot, diced
2		sticks celery, diced
6-lb.		leg of lamb
20	fl.oz.	lamb stock (2½ C.)
2		chicken breasts, boned
		tarragon, bay leaf, rosemary to taste

2		cloves of garlic
2		egg whites and one yolk
2	fl.oz.	cream (¼ C.)
1	T.	neutral-tasting oil
2	T.	white wine vinegar
2	t.	tomato purée
2	fl.oz.	Madeira (¼ C.)
2	fl.oz.	sherry (¼ C.)
2	T.	cornstarch

1. Place hay, seasoning, one-third of the diced onion, the carrot, and celery in a deep casserole, cover with lamb stock, and bring to a boil.

2. Meanwhile, place chicken breasts, one-third of the onion, and the herbs and garlic in the food processor and purée until smooth, add the eggs and cream, and pulse to blend.

3. Lay out the lamb and spread with the chicken mousse, roll, and tie. Refrigerate for 30 minutes. Meanwhile preheat oven to 400–425°F (or gas mark 6–7).

4. Sear the lamb and chicken roll in a dry sauté pan, and place in the hay and lamb stock. Cover and roast for 45–50 minutes, then allow to rest for 10 minutes.

5. Remove the lamb from the casserole and sauté the remaining onion in oil until transparent, deglaze with the white wine vinegar, and reduce until nearly all has disappeared, then take four ladles of the stock, tomato purée, Madeira, and sherry and add to the pan. Reduce further by half, then thicken with cornstarch.

6. To serve, carve the lamb, place onto a warmed plate, and surround with the sauce.   *Serves 6*

Baked Pencarreg Cheesecake Flavored with Honey and Cardamom, Served with a Tuile Basket of Mead Ice Cream and Red Wine Syrup

Pencarreg is a full-fat, soft creamy cheese.

The dessert

1	T.	butter
2	oz.	digestive biscuits (scant ½ C.) (substitute graham crackers), broken into crumbs
4	oz.	Pencarreg cheese (⅔ C.) (rind removed)

3	T.	clear Welsh honey
1	T.	cardamom, ground
2	oz.	castor sugar (¼ C.)
1	lg.	egg
2	fl.oz.	double cream (¼ C.)

1. Melt butter and add the biscuit crumbs. Press the mixture into a large bottomless cookie cutter on a highly greased tray. Preheat oven to 300–325°F (or gas mark 2–3).

2. In a blender, place the cheese, honey, cardamom, sugar, and egg, then blend until smooth. Fold in the cream.

3. Pour onto the biscuit crumbs and bake for 10 minutes.

The syrup

5	fl.oz.	red wine (scant ⅔ C.)
4	T.	soft brown sugar
1		bay leaf

4. Place red wine, soft brown sugar, and bay leaf in a pan and reduce to a syrupy consistency. Set aside.

The ice cream

6	T.	heavy cream
2	T.	golden syrup (light corn syrup)
4	fl.oz.	mead (½ C.)
20	fl.oz.	crème anglaise (2½ C.) (vanilla custard sauce)

5. Add the cream, syrup, and mead to the crème anglaise and place in an ice-cream machine. Churn until ice cream is stiff, and keep in freezer until ready to serve.

Tuile basket

4	oz.	butter (1 stick)
4	oz.	sugar (½ C.)
3		eggs
4	oz.	plain flour (¾ C.)
		sprigs of mint

6. Cream the butter and sugar for the tuiles. Preheat oven to 425°F (or gas mark 7).

7. Add the eggs one by one, stirring, then fold in the flour.

8. Spread a circle of mixture on a baking sheet and cook until golden brown.

9. Press the tuile over a muffin mold, and when set fill with a small scoop of ice cream and garnish with a sprig of mint.

To serve:

10. Turn a cheesecake out onto each plate and pour a pool of red wine syrup next to it. Serve with tuile basket of mead ice cream.

Serves 4

Following the Mawddach River estuary down to Barmouth, where the road turns north toward Portmeirion, a twenty-mile (32-km) drive along the pretty coastline will bring you to Harlech Castle.

Harlech is one of the group of castles built by Edward I in 1283 along the north Wales border, following his defeat of Llewelyn, the first and last Welsh prince to rule the entire country. Though surrounded by land on three sides, it was thought to be impossible to effectively lay siege to Harlech Castle because its fourth side was lapped by the Irish Sea, giving access to supplies of food and munitions from the water. The castle is almost square, with huge strong towers at each corner and a vast gatehouse centered in its eastern wall. It is situated on a rugged rocky promontory of hard gritstone that drops steeply from the castle walls. Its north side is protected by a treacherous rocky ravine and a waterfall, and on the west the headland drops steeply to sea level and the castle's water gate.

However, Owain Glyndwr, in about 1400, led an uprising backed by the whole nation that captured Harlech and also the castle of Aberystwyth further south. Owain was crowned prince of Wales, probably at Harlech where he lived with his court and family. His parliament was summoned to Harlech and also convened at the Old Parliament building at Machynlleth. Harlech was eventually recaptured by the English and later played a part in the Wars of the Roses. Harlech was the last castle to fall to Cromwell's forces at the end of the Civil War, and they took their revenge by stripping the castle of its roof and floors and removing its glass and lead. Nevertheless, it still stands a proud and impressive reminder of its former strength and glory.

The castle towers above four miles of uncrowded, sandy beach adjacent to a championship golf course. North from Harlech, close to the village of Talsarnau on the B4573, is the Hotel Maes-y-Neuadd, which means "house in a meadow." The leafy drive leading to Maes-y-Neuadd seems to go on forever, and when you finally reach the hotel the peace and quiet is phenomenal. The beautiful stone house was bought in 1981 by two couples, Olive and Malcolm Horsfall and June and Michael Slatter. Since then they have restored the house, parts of which date to the fourteenth century, and the eight-acre beautifully landscaped gardens. Personal service and a dedicated staff create a peaceful, relaxing atmosphere. Sixteen bedrooms offer panoramic views of the Snowdonia Mountains or Tremadoc Bay and the distant Lleyn Peninsula. Each room is individually designed and comfortably furnished. Relaxing among the flowering trees will perhaps be all you will want to do when you come to Maes-y-Neuadd. But for the more energetic, there is much to do in the area from golf at Royal St. David's to visiting historic sites and castles, riding the Great Little Trains of Wales, and taking quiet walks in the mountains. Peter Jackson, the talented and highly experienced head chef here, creates wonderful dishes from superb local ingredients and the fresh produce grown on the property. Menus change frequently; fresh fish, Welsh baby lamb, and local game are often featured. Since choosing a dessert can be a difficult task, at Maes-y-Neuadd you get to taste all of them, plus a wide selection of Welsh farmhouse cheeses. Dinner on a recent visit was a wonderfully seasoned hot leek and potato soup; a fish cake on a bed of slivered green beans, with diced tomatoes and crisped fennel leaves on a sorrel coulis; and milk-fed lamb stuffed with nuts and served with pastry. Pant-ys-gawn, a soft full-fat creamy goat cheese, flavored with Welsh laverbread, and a Scottish blue cheese were accompanied by an astonishing selection of home-baked bread. The basket was filled with *bara brith*, fluffy brioche, a granary loaf with cheese, another with poppyseed, and a soft-textured loaf with tomato swirled through the dough. The trio of desserts were a heavenly fruit compote, strawberry and almond crème brulée, and a choice of ice creams or sorbets.

Much of Maes-y-Neuadd's produce is grown in the extensive kitchen gardens and greenhouses adjacent to the lane that leads to the old schoolhouse on the property. It was delightful to accompany Peter early one morning on a stroll among the beds of herbs, vegetables, and soft fruits that were just beginning to poke above ground. Peter Jackson has given permission for us to include his recipes for a potage of Welsh seafood, and sea trout with laverbread*, both delicious and typically Welsh.

Potage de Fruits de Mer Pays de Galles (Welsh Seafood Soup)

2	lb.	lobster, cooked and shelled
24		Dublin Bay prawns, cooked and peeled
2	lb.	grey mullet, filleted
48		mussels
8		King scallops
2		baby squid, cleaned and sliced

Soup ingredients

17	fl.oz.	fish stock (2 C. + 2 T.)
1		shallot, chopped
1	T.	unsalted butter
4		leeks, cut julienne
4	oz.	dry vermouth (½ C.)
3½	oz.	crème fraîche (scant ½ C.)
		chervil for garnish

1. Poach all the fish separately in the fish stock. Keep warm.

2. Sweat the shallot in butter until soft. Add the leeks and cook until they are soft. Deglaze pan with vermouth, reduce by half.

3. Strain the cooking liquid, and again reduce by half. Add crème fraîche. Reduce again and check seasoning.

4. Add the fish. Check seasoning. Serve in a tureen or divide between plates and garnish with chervil.

Recommended wine: Puligny Montrachet   *Serves 8*

Sea Trout with Laverbread*

4	lb.	sea trout

Court bouillon

1		bay leaf
1		carrot, chopped
8		peppercorns
2		shallots, chopped
4	fl.oz.	white wine vinegar (½ C.)
1		bunch fennel

1. Simmer all court bouillon ingredients for 20 minutes. Press through a sieve, discarding solids, and set aside.

Sauce

2		shallots, chopped
2	T.	unsalted butter
4	fl.oz.	white wine (½ C.)
17	fl.oz.	fish stock (2 C. + 2 T.)
4	fl.oz.	heavy cream (½ C.)
4	oz.	laverbread (⅔ C.)

2. Bring the court bouillon to a boil, pour over fish, and simmer for 3 to 4 minutes. Remove the fish and keep warm.

3. Sweat the shallots in half the butter until soft. Deglaze with wine. Reduce by half, add fish stock, and again reduce by half, then add the cream and reduce to sauce consistency.

4. Add the laverbread. Check seasoning, and finish with remaining butter.

5. Coat the fish with sauce.   *Serves 8*

*Sun-dried laver is available in America from Mr. Shep Erhart, Maine Coast Sea Vegetables, Shore Road, Franklin, Maine 04634. See p. 260.

Recommended wine: Crémant d'Alsace

The road passes through the village of Talsarnau on the way north to Portmeirion where, in 1926, the architect Sir Clough Williams-Ellis completed his fanciful Italianate village. In 1954, following the end of postwar restrictions, the village was extensively rebuilt and strengthened, without marring its original design. The government considers it of architectural and historic importance and therefore immune to interference or alteration. Over one hundred thousand people a year come to walk around this unexpected site. The village has a central piazza with gift shops, a pillared colonnade, a triumphal archway, a campanile, a domed pantheon, a balconied Town Hall, parts of the twelfth-century Norman Castell Deudraeth, and a statue of Hercules holding up the world.

In the Town Hall a barrel-vaulted seventeenth-century ceiling sculptured in high relief comes from a former ballroom that Sir Clough bought at the auction of a mansion in the north of England. The leaded-glass mullioned windows and the fireplace come from the same mansion. The ballroom has wonderful acoustics and is used frequently for concerts, dances, plays, and conferences. The Town Hall also boasts a supper room, gallery, kitchen, and other ancillary rooms. An oval grille in the Town Hall basement came from the Old Bank of England. Several romantic features of the village are the rescued parts of other Renaissance-Gothic mansions, brought to Portmeirion by Sir Clough. The huge Ionic columns of the colonnade came from Hooton Hall in Cheshire. Another major rescue and restructuring resulted in the "Gloriette," named for the classical confection at Schonbrunn Palace near Vienna. Decorative steps lead from the balcony of the Gloriette down to a pool and fountain. From Siam came the gilded dancing statues atop the piazza columns. Surrounding the village on three sides are seventy acres of subtropical woodland gardens known as the "Gwyllt." Miles of paths crisscross the woods, leading to rocky coves and sandy beaches along the headland.

In 1966 the trustees of the Italianate village gave a fortieth birthday garden party for the village, attended by high government officials. A military parade marched to its own band. Many eminent architects gave speeches from the balcony of the Gloriette. The new fountain was officially turned on, and a bust of Sir Clough Williams-Ellis was unveiled. The garden party was followed by a grand ball and fireworks. Sir Clough, who lived happily into his nineties, was also present at the fiftieth village birthday party. He restored the original house on the estate and converted it into the top-notch Portmeirion Hotel, well known for its decor, service, and Craig Hindley's fine cooking. The Italianate village towers above the hotel on the clifftop. In the evening, when the sightseers have left and darkness falls, soft lights come on in the cottages, and the peaceful village is a place of enchantment. Suites and rooms in these cottages are part of the hotel, and guests can elect to stay in the village. The writers George Bernard Shaw, H. G. Wells, and Bertrand Russell were habitués of the hotel. Noel Coward wrote his best-known comedy, *Blythe Spirit*, during a two-week stay here. The hotel is superbly situated right at the end of the peninsula, affording a 180-degree view over the tidal estuary to the foothills and mountains beyond. The large curving glass-walled dining room takes full advantage of the magnificent view. Some of the dishes on the menu are Loin of Welsh lamb with tagliatelle of creamed leeks and roast garlic; Roast Trelough duck with caramelized apple and ginger; Monkfish wrapped in bacon with eggplant and sun-dried tomatoes; Creamy flan of oyster mushrooms, asparagus, and truffle; Terrine of chocolates with a caramel sauce; and Lemon tart. Craig Hindley, who is head chef at the Portmeirion Hotel, has given us three of his recipes for this book.

Timbale of Lobster

7	oz.	tomato (1¼ C.), peeled, seeded, and finely chopped
1	t.	olive oil
8		carrot ribbons
1	t.	vinegar
2	T.	basil-flavored dressing
7	oz.	lobster, diced (save claws for garnish)
2	oz.	French beans, (scant ½ C.) cut julienne
2	oz.	cucumber (scant ½ C.), cut julienne
1½	oz.	curly endive (scant ¼ C.)
		chervil

Garnish

crème fraîche flavored with pesto
lamb's lettuce

1. Mix the chopped tomato with the olive oil.

2. Blanch the carrot ribbons in boiling salted water to which a spoonful of vinegar has been added. Refresh and dip into the dressing.

3. Line the inside of a 3-inch cutter with two pieces of carrot.

4. Place the lobster, beans, cucumber, and endive in a bowl and season with the remaining dressing.

5. Pack this salad into the carrot-lined cutter until it reaches ¼ inch from the top edge.

6. Spoon the tomato on top and smooth with a warm knife. Top with a piece of the lobster claw and a sprig of chervil.

7. Place the cutter in the center of a plate and carefully remove the cutter from the timbale.

8. Garnish with crème fraîche and lamb's lettuce.   *Serves 4*

Loin of Lamb with a Tagliatelle of Leek and Roast Garlic

12	garlic cloves
	milk
5 oz.	leeks (1 C.), cut into thin strips
	knob of duck fat or butter
4	5–6 oz. loin of Welsh lamb cutlets
2 T.	vermouth
3 fl.oz.	heavy cream (⅓ C.)
3 oz.	spinach (generous ½ C.)
3 t.	butter
	pinch sugar
2 T.	balsamic vinegar
4 T.	white wine
8 fl.oz.	veal stock (1 C.)
6 T	unsalted butter
2 T.	parsley, chopped
3 oz.	tomato (generous ½ C.), diced

1. Place the garlic in a saucepan and cover with milk. Bring to a boil and simmer for 5 minutes. Strain and reserve.

2. Blanch the leeks in boiling salted water for 8 minutes. Refresh. Preheat oven to 400°F (or gas mark 6).

3. Heat a heavy-bottomed pan and add a knob of duck fat or butter. Sear the lamb on all sides and place in a hot oven for 4 to 5 minutes. Remove and keep warm.

4. While the lamb is cooking, roast the garlic in the same pan. Cook the leeks in the vermouth over a high heat until the liquid has turned syrupy. Add the cream and cook until it has reduced by half, or until sauce consistency is reached.

5. Cook the spinach in 1½ tablespoons of butter, season, and keep warm.

6. When the lamb is cooked, remove from pan, and use the same pan to make sauce.

7. Sprinkle in a pinch of sugar and the vinegar and caramelize. Add the wine and reduce by half. Add the stock and reduce by one-third. Whisk in the butter a little at a time. Correct seasoning. Add parsley and tomato.

8. Twist the creamed leeks around a roasting fork and stand in the middle of the plate. Slice each piece of lamb into three and place around the leeks. Garnish with spinach and garlic, add sauce, and serve.   *Serves* 4

Honey Mousse with Orange and Almond Biscuit Cones

1¼		gelatin leaf
4	T.	honey
1		egg yolk
4	fl.oz.	milk (½ C.)
4	fl.oz.	heavy cream (½ C.)

Garnish

4 orange and almond biscuit cones
crème Chantilly
toasted flaked almonds

1. Soften gelatin leaf in cold water.
2. Place honey and egg yolk in a bowl and beat together.
3. Bring the milk to a boil and pour onto the honey. Mix well. Return to a medium heat and cook for 2 minutes, stirring all the time. Strain into a bowl.
4. Drain the gelatin and squeeze out the excess water. Dissolve gelatin in milk and place over ice to cool.

5. Whisk the cream to soft peaks and fold into the cooled milk. Pour into four molds and refrigerate for a minimum of 2 hours.

6. Remove from molds and center each honey mousse on a plate, garnish with crème Chantilly and almonds, and top with the biscuit cone.   *Serves 4*

Biscuit cones

2 oz.	plain flour (scant ½ C.)	
9 oz.	castor sugar (⅓ C.)	
4 oz.	ground almonds (¾ C.)	
	zest of one orange	
4 fl.oz.	orange juice (½ C.)	
3½ oz.	butter (scant stick), melted	

1. Mix together all ingredients and chill for one hour. Preheat oven to 375°F (or gas mark 5).

2. Spoon a small ball of the mixture onto a greased baking sheet and bake until golden brown. Allow to cool a little and make a slit from the center to the outer edge. Lift from sheet and fold biscuit, overlapping the cut edges to form a cone.

Following the road toward the end of the peninsula, passing the strong-hold, Criccieth Castle, and on through the village of Pwllheli, brings you to the charming Georgian Manor House of Chris and Gunna Chown, Plas Bode-groes. It sits in perfect seclusion in a garden filled with wisteria, rhododen-dron, and roses. An avenue of two-hundred-year-old beeches fronts the house, and on a recent visit the pathway between the trees was awash in bluebells. The Chowns describe their establishment as a restaurant with rooms, since there is so much emphasis here on the food. Needless to say, the eight bedrooms in the house are charming and well appointed. Plas Bodegroes is the perfect place to stay while exploring the rugged seacliffs and secluded sandy coves of the Lleyn Peninsula. The mountains of Snow-donia, castles, famous gardens, and historic houses are all within easy reach. Their location on the wild Lleyn Peninsula, which thrusts into the sea above Cardigan Bay, gives Plas Bodegroes easy access to wonderfully fresh seafood—lobsters, crab, sea trout, bass, and turbot. Welsh lamb is also on their doorstep, and the beef here is second to none. Free-range chickens and ducks supply succulent meat and eggs, and some of the fresh produce is grown right here in the garden. Chris Chown's cooking is acclaimed in all leading guides as one of the best in Britain. He has recently won the County Restaurant of the Year Award. One of his most famous dishes is a warm salad of monkfish, Carmarthen ham, and mushrooms. A few of the other dishes from the menu are a Roulade of sea bass and smoked salmon with dill and sour cream; a Terrine of guinea fowl and pigeon with blackberry sauce; Roast fillet of salmon with spinach and chive sauce; a Mousseline of scallops, crab, and laverbread; Grilled local seafood with lime hollandaise; Char-grilled fillet of Welsh beef with fried shallots and potatoes in a rich mustard sauce; Saddle of lamb in puff pastry with mushrooms on ratatouille and red wine sauce; a Grilled goat's cheese salad; Summer pudding with elderflower sauce; and Trio of Chocolate with mango coulis.

Chris Chown has given his permission for us to include the following sea trout recipe in this book, which he says is based on the traditional Welsh dish trout wrapped in bacon. Carmarthen ham is a salted, wind-dried raw ham like Parma (which could be used instead). Laverbread is not a bread at all but puréed stewed seaweed.

Sea Trout Wrapped in Carmarthen Ham, with Leeks, Laverbread,* and Mustard Sauce

1¼	lb.	sea trout fillet
6		thin slices of Carmarthen ham
8	oz.	sliced leeks (1⅔ C.)
4	oz.	laverbread* (½ C.)
2	oz.	butter (½ stick)
8	fl.oz.	fish stock (1 C.)
8	fl.oz.	white wine (1 C.)
4	fl.oz.	cream (½ C.)
4	T.	dry vermouth
4	T.	grainy mustard

1. Cut the fillet into six equal pieces. Wrap each one in a slice of ham.

2. Sear on each side in a hot pan, then grill for one to 2 minutes until not quite firm.

3. Toss the leeks with the butter and a splash of water in a hot pan for 2 to 3 minutes until soft. Remove from the heat and stir in the laverbread.

4. Reduce the fish stock and white wine until you have 4 fluid ounces (½ C.) left. Add the cream and vermouth and boil until thickened. Stir in the mustard.

5. Divide the leeks between six hot plates, top each with a sea trout fillet, pour the sauce round, and serve.

*Sun-dried laver is available in America from Mr. Shep Erhart, Maine Coast Sea Vegetables, Shore Road, Franklin, Maine 04634. See page 260.   *Serves 6*

The food in north Wales is superb. North Wales has plenty of arable land, and the sea off the coast teems with fish and shellfish. The mountain slopes provide good pasture for sheep and cattle. Dairy farmers today are using their delicious milk to make farmhouse cheeses, cream, yogurt, and ice cream. Market gardeners are branching out and producing the more unusual fruits and vegetables, and enthusiasm for pick-your-own outlets is burgeoning here. They are also blessed with the most important factor—many talented and inventive chefs. Healthy organic food and prepared dishes using health foods, such as pâté, quiche, mustards, cheesecake, and nondairy-based dishes, can be bought in many areas of north Wales. Honey, preserves, and sugar-free items are also readily available. Good bread is more and more popular, and bakers are keeping up with this trend, baking traditional as well as new goodies. Llandudno makes scrumptious toffee, Anglesey makes a divine fudge, Wrexham brews fine beer, and Trofarth bottles its own pure natural springwater to quench your thirst.

Shellfish is plentiful in north Wales. Reseeded oyster beds on the Isle of Anglesey and in the Menai Strait have regenerated the delicate mollusk. Mussels abound, and both the larger king scallop and the small queen scallop flourish in the waters off Holyhead. Holyhead is a thriving deepwater port that is in full swing twenty-four hours a day. It affords trawlers from the Irish Sea a place to dock and unload their catch. Lobster beds are being reseeded off Cardigan Bay, and crabs are plentiful. The catch of fresh sole, cod, plaice, bass, brill, hake, whiting, turbot, and monkfish off the Welsh coast is considerable. Unfortunately for the restaurant and hotel trade in Wales, fresh fish command higher prices at Grimsby in Humberside, at Fleetwood in Lancashire, and at fish markets in London, so it takes effort on the part of the restaurant trade to keep Welsh fish in Wales. Small fish farms inland welcome fishermen who want to catch trout or salmon, and it can be cleaned on the spot and smoked too, if you wish. Salmon and trout is there for the asking, ready prepared if you did not bring your fishing rod.

Welsh lamb has also been given a new image in tune with the creative new cooking. Lamb, fed on the lower slopes of the mountains, have an additive-free diet and are no longer allowed to get fat. Fatty lamb is spurned by the housewife and therefore of little use to the butcher. Milk-fed baby lamb is ready for the table by Easter. Butchers, trying to get housewives to look further than the Sunday roast, are butchering lamb in new ways to provide a wider range of lean top-quality cuts, from lamb steaks to boned, rolled lamb that cooks evenly and is so easy to slice.

Returning to Pwllheli, pick up the coast road north via Penygroes toward Caernarfon—whose name means "fort by the shore." Caernarfon Castle was one of the strongholds King Edward I began building in 1283 to secure north Wales. The castle was completed in 1330. The walls are constructed in layers of two colors, giving it a decidedly different look than other castles built at that time. Inside the walls are sixteenth- and nineteenth-century houses. Perhaps the largest tower to have been erected in the Middle Ages is the Eagle Tower of Caernarfon Castle. The future Edward II was created Prince of Wales at Caernarfon Castle in 1284. Since then two more future kings have been invested with the principality at Caernarfon—Edward VIII in 1911 and Prince Charles in 1969.

From the town of Caernarfon traveling east on B4366 take the turn signposted Seion and you will come to Ty'n Rhos Country House, an immaculate farmhouse owned and run by Nigel and Lynda Kettle. When they bought the 72-acre farmhouse in 1972 the Kettles ran it solely as a farm, but over the years Ty'n Rhos, "the house in the vale," has been transformed into a country house of great charm and comfort. One major travel award deemed it "the best in Wales." You will still find sheep, cattle, and a flock or two of ducks on the farm, as well as the Kettles' friendly sheepdog, Moss. Lynda Kettle is a talented chef who uses seasonal foods and the best quality local ingredients. All herbs and many vegetables are grown on the farm. The restaurant has lovely views over Ty'n Rhos's rolling farmland to the Isle of Anglesey. The location of this charming country house is a definite plus. Not only are you in the part of Wales where Welsh is the first language, but nearby are the historic castles of Caernarfon, Beaumaris, and Conwy, the Isle of Anglesey's sandy coves and beaches, and the mountains of Snowdonia. Lynda Kettle shares with you some of her favorite recipes.

Irresistible Nutty Banana Flan

Pastry for tart shell

- 3 oz. butter (¾ stick)
- 5 oz. plain flour (1 C.)
- 2–3 T. cold water

    1. Have all pastry ingredients at room temperature. Rub butter into flour until it resembles fine bread crumbs. Leave to rest for half an hour, then roll out and line an 8-inch fluted flan dish.

    2. Refrigerate for 30 minutes. Preheat oven to 400°F (or gas mark 7), foil line crust and bake for 10 minutes. Allow to cool.

Banana flan

- 3 bananas, finely sliced
  rind and juice of ½ lemon
- 3 oz. whole blanched almonds (generous ½ C.)
- 4 T. soft brown sugar
- 6 T. heavy cream

1. Toss banana slices with grated lemon rind and juice. Layer into pastry case. Preheat oven to 325°F (or gas mark 3).

2. In a food processor, whirl together nuts, sugar, and cream. Spread over bananas and bake for approximately 25 minutes until lightly browned and set. *Serves 4–6*

Lemon Chiffon Tart

1. Prepare partially baked pastry case, as in preceding recipe.

Lemon curd filling

	juice and rind of three lemons
4 oz.	butter (1 stick)
8 oz.	sugar (1 C.)
3	whole eggs
1	egg yolk

2. In a double boiler, over simmering water, beat filling ingredients until thickened and smooth. Allow to cool and spread in pastry case.

Topping

3	egg whites
4 oz.	castor sugar (½ C.)

3. Preheat oven to 325 °F (or gas mark 3). Whisk egg whites until stiff, whisk in 2 tablespoons sugar, then fold in 4 tablepoons more. Pile meringue on top of the filling and sprinkle over the remaining 2 tablespoons castor sugar.

4. Bake for 10 minutes and then reduce heat to 275°F (or gas mark 1) and bake for 25 minutes.

Baked Cabbage and Cheese

1	savoy cabbage (or similar type of cabbage)
20 fl.oz.	milk (2½ C.)
4 oz.	mixed Gruyère and Cheddar cheeses (¾ C.), grated
4 oz.	cream (½ C.)

1. Preheat oven to 325°F (or gas mark 3). Finely shred cabbage. Boil for approximately 5 minutes in the milk.

2. Drain, but not completely—cabbage should be moist—and place in serving dish.

3. Season well and scatter with cheeses. Drizzle heavy cream over cabbage and bake for 20 minutes, until bubbly and golden brown. This lifts humble cabbage into the luxury class! *Serves 4*

Creamed Celeriac

2 med. celeriac
      juice of ½ lemon
2   eggs
5 fl.oz. heavy cream (scant ⅔ C.)
      salt and pepper to taste
      grated nutmeg to taste

1. Preheat oven to 350°F (or gas mark 4). Peel celeriac and cut into chunks. Place in water and lemon juice.

2. Bring a pan of salted water to a boil; simmer drained celeriac until cooked through. Drain and return to saucepan. Over low heat, dry out the celeriac for approximately 5 minutes.

3. Place in food processor, with the eggs, cream, seasoning, and nutmeg. Process to a thick purée. Pile into an ovenproof serving dish and bake for about 15 minutes. Serve hot. *Serves 3–4*

Breast of Trelough Duck with Herb and Reduced Stock Sauce

1   Trelough duck (a hybrid specialty from Hereford Duck Co.)
2   sticks celery
2   carrots
1   onion
6   parsley stalks
2 T. fruity red wine
2 T. corn oil
2 T. olive oil
4–6 T. unsalted butter
1 T. each chervil, parsley, tarragon, chopped watercress sprigs, for garnish

1. Cut the breast and legs off of the duck, reserving legs for another recipe (e.g., cassoulet).

2. Chop carcass and brown in the oven. Add vegetables and allow to color in duck juices.

3. Put browned carcass and vegetables in stock pot, cover with water, and simmer for 4 hours. Allow to cool, skim off the fat, and reduce stock to 10 fl.oz. (1¼ cups) over high heat.

4. Slash duck breast skin, and marinate in wine and oil for 6 to 8 hours.

5. When ready to serve, heat a heavy frying pan until very hot and fry the duck breast skin side down until almost black—approximately 10 minutes—tipping off the fat as it accumulates. Turn breast over and fry for a further 5 minutes. Allow to rest in a warm oven.

6. Bring reduced stock to a boil and whisk in butter and herbs.

7. Thinly slice duck breasts, arrange on heated plates, and surround with sauce. Garnish with watercress sprigs.   *Serves 2*

Fillet of Gray Mullet
with Saffron and Tomato Sauce

Gray mullet is frequently landed by local fisherman and is superb when very fresh, much cheaper and a good substitute for sea bass.

1 lg.	very fresh gray mullet
10 fl.oz.	fish stock (1¼ C.)
6 oz.	unsalted butter (1½ sticks)
	pinch of saffron
1	glass white wine
	juice of ½ lemon
1	shallot, finely chopped
2	tomatoes, peeled, seeded, and chopped

1. Fillet, skin, and debone mullet. Cut into four portions.

2. Make a fish stock with the trimmings.

3. Place mullet in buttered foil, season, and brush with a little clarified butter. Fold foil to completely enclose fish.

4. Infuse saffron in a little water for half an hour. Meanwhile preheat oven to 350°F (or gas mark 4).

5. Pour saffron and water through a fine sieve into a saucepan. Add wine, lemon juice, and shallots to pan and reduce until most of the liquid has evaporated. Whisk in the remaining butter a knob at a time.

6. Bake mullet until just cooked, 10–15 minutes. Stir chopped tomatoes into the sauce. Serve mullet on heated plates surrounded with sauce.   *Serves 4*

Return to the coast road and continue north, taking the Menai Bridge over to the Isle of Anglesey, and head for Beaumaris. Edward I built Beaumaris Castle here in the thirteenth century. Beaumaris means "fair marsh." The town has many half-timbered houses and terraced housing dating from the Victorian era. About two hundred yards from the castle on Castle Street is Ye Olde Bulls Head Inn, which belongs to Keith Rothwell and his partner David Robertson. The original inn dates to 1472 when it was a busy stopping place for travelers taking the most direct route between Holyhead, Ireland, and London. Rebuilt in 1617, the inn has an entry in the *Guinness Book of Records* for having the largest simple-hinged door in Britain—thirteen feet high and eleven feet wide—through which coaching horses entered the courtyard. Among its many famous visitors is Charles Dickens who stayed here when he was a young reporter for a London newspaper. The restaurant, which seats about forty-eight people, was once the tack room. Keith Rothwell says, "The Inn is what you would expect for such an old building, with beams everywhere, not a right angle in sight, and full of antique weaponry, crockery, brassware and furniture." The bedrooms, of course, are all refurbished and offer all modern creature comforts.

The restaurant's à la carte menu has eight starters and eight main courses and changes daily. There is also a single-choice fixed-price menu. Some of the dishes on an April menu were Arbroath Smokies—smoked baby haddock in a rich cream sauce; Homecured Bresoala with rocket and shaved Parmesan; Parcels of smoked salmon and fresh crab; Steamed fillets of salmon and sea bass on a sauce of freshwater prawns and chervil; and Medallions of venison saddle with oyster mushrooms. The inn's location affords the freshest of seafood—some of it still flapping on delivery. Anglesey is so fertile it was known as the "Mother of Wales" to the invading British, and it still produces strawberries, raspberries, new potatoes, and leeks, as well as the finest Welsh beef, lamb, venison, and cream. Keith Rothwell loves to cook dishes with local foods in ways that enhance their natural flavors. At Ye Olde Bulls Head Inn, and at their former restaurant near Caernarfon, accolades and enthusiastic reviews have poured in from all the major food guides, rating the inn as having some of the finest food and wine in Wales. Keith Rothwell's recipes are for a terrine of chicken and ham, and an accompanying peach and chili salsa; and parcels of salmon with laverbread, served with a smoked prawn sauce.

Terrine of Chicken and Ham

Quantities can be easily varied.

	bacon to line the terrine
3	chicken breasts or legs
5 fl.oz.	heavy cream (scant ⅔ C.)

2	oz.	pistachio nuts (scant ½ C.), peeled
1	med.	carrot, cooked then diced
1	t.	pink peppercorns
2	T.	fresh herbs
2		chicken breasts, diced
8	oz.	ham, cut in large cubes
2		garlic cloves, chopped

1. Line a terrine or bread tin with bacon, leaving an overlap to fold over the top. Preheat oven to 350°F (or gas mark 4).

2. Mince the chicken breasts or legs and season with the cream. Add the remaining ingredients, mix all together, and place into mold.

3. Wrap in foil and place in a baking dish of water that comes halfway up the sides of the mold. Bake for about 1½ hours.

4. Cool overnight in refrigerator before using.

Peach and Chili Salsa
(to accompany cold meats and terrines)

4	lg.	peaches, peeled and finely diced
2	T.	currants, soaked in 1 T. rum
4	T.	red pepper, finely diced
4	T.	red onion, finely diced
4	T.	raspberry vinegar
2	T.	grape seed oil
1–2	T.	chili pepper, finely chopped
3–4	T.	basil, shredded
3		garlic cloves, chopped

Mix all ingredients and leave for at least 6 hours before using. The salsa will keep for 1 or 2 weeks in the refrigerator.

Parcels of Salmon with Laverbread

4		escallops of salmon, 4–5-inch squares, less than 1/4" thick
8		escallops of white fish
4	oz.	laverbread* (⅔ C.)

1. Lay the four escallops of salmon on a flat surface and place an escallop of white fish on top of each one.

2. Now divide the laverbread by four and spread on top, then cover with a second escallop of white fish.

3. Finally wrap the outer salmon escallops around the fillings to form four parcels.

4. Steam or cook in a covered dish with a little fish stock until parcels are just cooked through.

* Sun-dried laver is available in America from Mr. Shep Erhart, Maine Coast Sea Vegetables, Shore Road, Franklin, Maine 04634. See page 260.

Smoked Prawn Sauce

4	oz.	smoked prawns
2	T.	butter
1		shallot or small onion
5	fl.oz.	white wine (scant ⅔ C.)
1	T.	brandy
10	fl.oz.	good fish stock (1¼ C.)
5	fl.oz.	cream (scant ⅔ C.)
1	T.	chopped chervil

Garnish

potatoes
small pinch of saffron
2 sprigs of chervil

1. Shell the prawns, and using the shells make a stock by sweating the shells in a little butter with chopped shallot or onion.

2. Add the wine and reduce, then add the brandy and flame. Reduce again.

3. Add the fish stock and cook for another 10 minutes, then strain the stock.

4. Reduce the stock to a syrup before adding the cream, chervil, and, at the last minute, the prawns.

5. Pour around or over the salmon and garnish with nicely shaped potatoes cooked in saffron water with sprigs of chervil.

Bodysgallen Hall stands high on a hillside in two hundred acres of wooded parkland and beautiful gardens, with magnificent views of the mountains of Snowdonia and majestic Conwy Castle. For centuries Bodysgallen Hall was the home of the Mostyn family who have featured prominently in Welsh history. Edward Mostyn and Owen Williams decided in 1849 to transform the little fishing and mining village of Llandudno into a major seaside resort. The location was perfect for such a task, as Llandudno is situated on a curving bay, flanked in the west by the Great Orme headland, which rises to seven hundred feet, and to the east by the Little Orme, a somewhat less strenuous climb. Today the longest cable-car ride in Britain—five thousand three hundred and twenty feet—takes passengers in its gently swaying cars to the top of the Great Orme. From here are views of Snowdonia, and on a clear day the Isle of Man and the Lake District. Atop Great Orme is St. Tudno's church—parts of which date to the twelfth century or perhaps earlier. If cable cars do not appeal, there is a railway that goes to the top. The two men designed wide main streets and spacious promenades to grace Llandudno. It is possibly one of the most frequented resort towns in Britain. In 1862 Alice Liddell stayed at Llandudno and so loved the tales told her by a family friend, don and mathematician Charles Lutwidge Dodgson, that he wrote one out for her. From this grew *Alice in Wonderland* and *Alice Through the Looking-Glass* under his pen name, Lewis Carroll.

Richard Broyd, chairman of Historic House Hotels, bought Bodysgallen Hall in 1979—his goal the conservation and restoration of buildings of architectural and historical interest—and rebuilt it as a first-class hotel. At Bodysgallen Hall delightful reception rooms with huge fireplaces greet the traveler. There are nineteen spacious, comfortable bedrooms in the house and nine cottage suites dotted around the gardens. Andrew Bridgford runs the superb Bodysgallen Hall, and the service is truly exceptional. Mair Lewis is head chef at Bodysgallen—there are six chefs in the kitchens,

which provide splendid dishes made from top-quality ingredients. Long windows on two sides of the dining room overlook the exquisite gardens. The delicately colored glass in some of the windows is embellished with the coats of arms of the two families whose history is interwoven with the house—Mostyn and Wynn. A severe baronial fireplace dominates one end of the dining room. Dinner was superb, the finale of white chocolate and whisky bread and butter pudding was preceded by some marvelous aromatic Welsh cheeses. A soft goat's cheese with chives was named Melin, Teifi was a smoked Caerphilly, and Llanboidy cheese came speckled with that most Welsh of all ingredients, laverbread. Mair Lewis has contributed three wonderful recipes for this book.

Smoked Caerphilly and Leek Soufflé

12	fl.oz.	milk (1½ C.)
6	oz.	finely chopped leeks (1¼ C.) (without deep green leaves)
3	oz.	butter (¾ stick)
3	oz.	flour (½ C.)
8	fl.oz.	approximately (scant cup) heavy cream
5		egg yolks
6	oz.	smoked Caerphilly cheese (1½ C.), grated
		seasoning
		nutmeg
		cayenne pepper
6		egg whites
		butter and flour to coat ramekins

1. Preheat oven to 400°F (or gas mark 8).

2. Bring the milk to a boil and add the leeks. Cook to soften the leeks, about 3 minutes. Drain through a sieve, reserving both commodities.

3. Make a béchamel sauce with the butter, flour, and reserved milk. Add the cream and cook over low heat for 20 minutes, making sure that the sauce does not boil. Cool slightly.

4. Butter the ramekin molds and dust lightly with flour, making sure that the lips of the molds are free from any butter or flour.

5. Add the egg yolks to the sauce and beat well, followed by the cheese, leeks, and seasoning. Whisk the egg whites until light and firm, fold in one-third to loosen the sauce, and gently fold in the remaining two-thirds.

6. Carefully spoon the soufflé mixture into the molds, keeping the lips free from the mixture. Continue to pile the mixture into the

center of the ramekins so that the rims are untouched and the soufflé stands about half an inch higher than the rim. Carefully level the top and bake in a hot oven on a hot baking sheet for 10 to 12 minutes or until the top and sides are golden brown.

7. Serve immediately with a small tossed green salad.

Makes 6 individual ramekins

Platter of Anglesey Seafood
with a Spinach Mousse and a Laverbread Butter

The platter

6	oz.	salmon fillet
6	oz.	lemon sole (2 fillets)
2	oz.	smoked salmon
4	lg.	scallops with their coral
12		mussels (cooked) reserving 4 shells
8	fl.oz.	fish stock (1 C.)
		sprig of fennel
16		prawns—large shrimp
		seasoning
		lemon juice
		chervil for garnish

Spinach mousse

2–3	lb.	spinach
4	T.	butter
3		egg whites
		seasoning

Prepare the spinach mousse

1. Remove the stalks from the spinach and wash roughly. Drain well.

2. Grease four deep individual molds (dariole) with butter and chill. Melt the butter in a large saucepan, add all the spinach, stir, cover with a lid, and cook to a purée. Cool slightly. Drain in a colander to remove the liquid. Transfer the spinach to a blender or liquidizer and purée further, add the egg whites, and blend again. Remove spinach from blender to a bowl and season lightly with salt and pepper. Mix well.

3. Fill each mold with the spinach mixture and cover each with buttered foil.

Prepare the fish

    4. Cut the salmon fillet into four equal portions.

    5. Skin the lemon sole, cover with cling film, and flatten slightly with the flat of a large knife, being very gentle so as not to damage the flesh. Cover the fillets with a thin layer of smoked salmon and roll up like a Swiss roll. Cut each fillet in half.

    6. Remove any sand from the scallops and mussels and refrigerate.

Laverbread butter

1	oz.	shallots (2 T.), peeled and finely chopped
1	T.	white white vinegar
2	T.	dry white wine
2	fl.oz.	cream (¼ C.)
½	lb.	unsalted butter (2 sticks)
2	t.	laverbread*
		seasoning

    7. In a small heavy-bottomed saucepan combine the shallots, vinegar, and wine and boil until you have about one tablespoon of syrupy liquid. Then add the cream and reduce the syrupy liquid again.

    8. Over gentle heat whisk in the cold diced butter, a little at a time, until completely amalgamated.

    9. Whisk in the laverbread and correct the seasoning to taste. Keep warm but do not let it boil.

    10. Prepare a steamer for the fish. Preheat the oven to 350°F (or gas mark 4).

    11. Place the spinach mousse in a shallow pan or roasting pan and half fill with hot water to come three-quarters of the way up the molds. Place in the oven for 30–40 minutes or until the mousse feels quite firm and set.

    12. Reheat the fish stock, add a sprig of fennel, and simmer gently for about 5 minutes. Keep warm.

    13. Place the salmon pieces and lemon sole in a shallow dish, season lightly, and steam in the steamer for about 3 minutes. Then add the scallops, season, and steam for a further 2 minutes. Add the mussels and prawns next and steam yet again for one to 2 minutes. Test to make sure the fish is cooked and the mussels and prawns are hot.

    14. Warm four large dinner plates. Spoon a ladle of laverbread butter onto the center of each plate. Remove the fish from the steamer and the spinach mousse from the oven. Turn the mousse out onto the middle of each plate. (You may need to loosen the edges of the mousse with a small knife.)

15. Place a selection of seafood around each mousse, i.e., piece of salmon, cluster of mussels, piece of lemon sole in half on an angle to reveal the pink smoked salmon, cluster of prawns, and a scallop.

16. Strain the warm fish stock once again through a fine sieve. Add a dash of lemon juice for flavor. Pour a little onto each plate.

17. Garnish each platter with a sprig of chervil and a mussel shell. Serve immediately.

Note: If desired, the scallops may be crisscrossed with a red hot skewer before steaming for extra effect on the finished dish.   *Serves 4*

*Sun-dried laver is available in America from Mr. Shep Erhart, Maine Coast Sea Vegetables, Shore Road, Franklin, Maine 04634. See page 260.

Welsh Rarebit

1 lb. 2 oz.	grated cheese (4½ C.)
	Pommery mustard and Worcestershire sauce
6 fl.oz.	light ale (⅔ C.)
6 T.	flour and 6 T. butter, mixed together until smooth
6	egg yolks
5 fl.oz.	cream (scant ⅔ C.)
	toast and lettuce leaves for garnish

1. Melt the cheese, mustard, and Worcestershire sauce.
2. Add ale and boil.
3. Whisk in enough flour and butter mixture to thicken. Remove from heat and cool.
4. Beat in egg yolks and whisk in the cream.
5. Spread on toast and grill until glazed. Cut out with a round pastry cutter about 4 inches in diameter. Serve decorated with a few lettuce leaves.   *Serves 6–8*

From Bodysgallen it is a short trip to visit the historic Conwy Castle, Caernarfon Castle, scene of the investiture of the Prince of Wales, historic houses such as Plas Newydd on the Isle of Anglesey, and the world-famous gardens at Bodnant.

Traveling south on the A470 brings you to the Old Rectory, owned by Michael and Wendy Vaughan. The house sits at the top of three levels of immaculate gardens reached by stone steps, which grace the hillside in front of the Old Rectory. From these fragrant gardens there are panoramic views over the estuary to Conwy Castle and the mountains of Snowdonia. Hospitality and the comfort of its guests are the main considerations of the Vaughans, and they have won a Michelin Double Award for both cuisine and accommodation. Wendy Vaughan's cooking is meticulous in every detail. She says, "I derive my enjoyment of food from its color, texture, and the combination on the plate, so these are the things that I concentrate on when cooking for guests." Fish is strongly represented on Wendy Vaughan's menu. Her fish merchant's family are trawler owners, and as Wendy always pays cash on delivery, she has first pick of the fresh turbot, bass, brill, salmon, plaice, and shellfish. Her butcher, who lives just down the road, sells only hormone-free meat and has won awards for his excellent sausages. Wendy cooks with assurance and great creativity and has earned many accolades in food and restaurant guides. Residents are served a set dinner and can choose to eat together around one large communal table or to dine at separate tables grouped around the antique-filled dining room. Everything served is homemade by Wendy Vaughan from the soup to the petits fours, and she does it all without kitchen help. Wendy feels that with a set menu, when choosing what to cook, she has the advantage of being able to substitute the freshest and best at the last moment. Her starters include Warm smoked sea trout garnished with a tartlet of quail's egg and asparagus; Turbot in Phyllo pastry with mustard and tarragon; and main courses such as Roast fillet of Welsh mountain lamb with a leek and laverbread timbale and tarragon jus; and Stuffed fillet of Welsh black beef with a balsamic vinegar sauce. A no-smoking rule applies to the house but not to the separate Coach House bedrooms. The Old Rectory is close to the castles of Conwy, Caernarfon, Beaumaris, and others, and to the narrow-gauge railways of Ffestinog, Llanberis, and Snowdon. A short distance down the road is the turning for the world-renowned Bodnant Gardens, whose eighty acres of floral beauty are among the highlights of a stay in the Conwy Valley. Wendy Vaughan has contributed the following recipe to this book.

Chicken Maesmawr (Welsh for "big field")

2	oz.	butter (½ stick)
4		chicken breasts or a 3-lb. chicken, jointed and floured
½		bottle of dry white wine
1		lettuce
1		handful of fresh spinach leaves
1	T.	thyme, finely chopped
1		handful of lemon balm, shredded
5	fl.oz.	chicken stock (scant ⅔ C.)
		salt, pepper, and nutmeg to taste
5	fl.oz.	crème fraîche (scant ⅔ C.)
4	T.	chopped fresh parsley
		garnish with crisp lettuce or endive

1. Melt the butter, add the chicken pieces, and sauté until brown.
2. Add the wine to the pan, cover, and simmer gently until cooked through.
3. Remove the chicken from the pan and keep warm.
4. Turn up the heat under the pan and simmer until the wine is reduced by half.
5. Add the lettuce, spinach, thyme, and lemon balm, and stew for a few minutes until wilted.
6. Put into a food processor or liquidizer and blend until smooth, then put through a sieve into a clean pan.
7. Add the chicken stock, reduce slightly, stir in the salt, pepper, and nutmeg to taste, add the crème fraîche, and blend to a smooth green sauce.
8. Arrange the chicken on a serving dish, top with green sauce, and sprinkle with fresh parsley. Surround with crisp lettuce or endive.

Serves 4

Continuing south toward Betws-y-Coed, just off the main highway at Llanrwst is the Chandler's Brasserie, run by Adam and Penny Rattenbury and their partner Tim Kirton. Their aim, says Adam Rattenbury, is to do away with the pretentious side of eating out and to concentrate on the food and wine without airs and graces. Comfortably cushioned school benches provide seating on the locally hewn slate floor. In winter a log fire burns in the fireplace near the bar, and with luck you may even get to sit in Tim's grandmother's original Orkney chair. Smoking is not permitted in the restaurant.

All three partners are accomplished cooks, and they amicably divide the work. Penny Rattenbury bakes a variety of breads every day and makes the majority of the puddings, as well as cooking vegetarian dishes and starters. Tim Kirton too can turn his hand to puddings and vegetables, but his main job is looking after the restaurant and bar and buying wines from as far away as California. Adam Rattenbury concentrates on cooked-to-order dishes. His preference is for cooking with locally caught fish—turbot, brill, sea bass, lobster, salmon, sea trout, and mullet—or game—pheasant, hare, pigeon, and venison—and with specialty meats (offal) such as lamb's sweetbreads, kidneys, and chicken livers. Friends in the village grow most of the salad vegetables and herbs for Chandler's Brasserie in their gardens.

Some of the dishes on the menu are Whole prawns with garlic mayonnaise; Hot goat's cheese salad with sage dressing; Roast rack of glazed Welsh lamb with onion sauce; Panfried breast of pheasant with apples and Calvados; Steamed fillet of sea bass with ginger, garlic, spring onions, and soy sauce; and several vegetarian dishes, such as Celery, apple, and roquefort phyllo pastry parcels with roast red pepper sauce. Not to be missed are Penny's Pear and almond tart with praline ice cream; Coffee and ginger parfait with chocolate sauce; Queen of puddings; and a Trio of yogurt ice creams in a Brandy snap case with butterscotch sauce. Adam Rattenbury shares his sea bass recipe with us.

Roast Fillet of Sea Bass with Herb and Cream Sauce

2–3 lb.   sea bass, scaled and filleted (save bones)
10 fl.oz. heavy cream (1¼ C.)
         fresh herbs of your choice, minced

Make a fish stock from the sea bass bones with

20 fl.oz. white wine (2½ C.)
1   onion, chopped
1   carrot, chopped
2   celery sticks, chopped
2   bay leaves
12   peppercorns

1. Cover bones with white wine and water; add chopped vegetables, bay leaves, and peppercorns. Bring to a boil, skim off the foam, and simmer for 30 minutes.

2. Strain stock and taste for seasoning. Return to saucepan and reduce stock until strong and flavorful. Meanwhile preheat oven to 425°F (or gas mark 7).

3. Place fish fillets, skin side up, on a flat, oiled ovenproof dish, and roast them at the top of a very hot oven for 10 minutes. Skin should be crisp. Remove fillets and keep warm.

4. Pour reduced stock and cream into pan and boil to thicken sauce, then stir in as much or as little as you like of the minced, mixed herbs.

5. Coat warmed plates with sauce and arrange fish fillets on sauce. Serve immediately.   *Serves 4*

Betws-y-Coed, situated at the eastern edge of Snowdonia National Park, grew into a resort town to serve the influx of tourists to this particularly beautiful area of Snowdonia. Three river valleys meet at Betsw-y-Coed, which means "chapel in the woods." The waters from these rivers—the Lledr, Llugwy, and Conwy—plunge into the village over two spectacular waterfalls—Swallow Falls two miles to the west and Conwy Falls two miles to the south. Conwy Falls are arguably the most dramatic in the principality.

The Llugwy is spanned by a romantic fifteenth-century stone bridge, and crossing the Conwy is a graceful iron bridge built by Thomas Telford, who built one of two bridges connecting the Isle of Anglesey to the mainland. Small shops selling Welsh crafts line Betws-y-Coed's pretty village streets, often crowded with tourists in the summer months.

Tan-y-Foel Country House at Capel Garmon, just east of Betws-y-Coed, is set high in the hills overlooking the Conwy valley and the peaks of Snowdonia. Tan-y-Foel, "the little house under the hill side," is peacefulness itself. The house, surrounded in spectacular scenery, accommodates only a few couples at one time in superb en suite bedrooms, each furnished in its own individual style. Some of these have king size and super king-size beds. Two spacious sitting rooms afford retreats for guests—one in the conservatory on the sunny southern side of the house, and the other in the former library, where log fires burn in the cooler months. The house is owned and run by Peter and Janet Pitman, and the tranquil atmosphere makes guests feel as though they are staying in a home rather than a hotel. Certain areas of the residence were once parts of a sixteenth-century manor house. Roman legions maintained a small lookout here, Saxon colonists worked the forested slopes, and Tudor yeomen erected the timber framework of the long barn. Nestled in the grounds is a heated swimming pool for summer afternoons. Tan-y-Foel is a nonsmoking establishment, and the Pitmans regret that they cannot accommodate pets. Janet Pitman is a fine cook, preferring to base her dishes on quality local produce. There are two choices of starter, main course, and dessert offered at dinner. Some of the dishes on the menu are Roses local smoked salmon laced with lemon juice and black pepper; Oyster mushrooms panfried on a light coconut curry-flavored sauce; Panfried breast of Hereford duck on a port wine and ginger sauce; and Poached Conwy trout on a sharp beurre blanc sauce. Menus are changed daily, desserts are scrumptious, and one of Peter Pitman's special interests is Welsh farmhouse cheese, so whatever you do, do not miss the cheeseboard. Janet Pitman has kindly contributed this recipe for use in this book.

Mediterranean Melin-y-Coed

20		black olives, pitted
6	T.	olive oil
1	lg.	garlic clove, crushed
1	T.	white wine vinegar
1	T.	chopped parsley or chives

2   tins anchovy fillets
6   firm tomatoes, seeded and finely diced
4 sm. Melin-y-Coed goat's cheese with chives, thinly sliced through
       the round into approx. 5 slices

1. Finely chop black olives, or put into grinder for a few seconds so that they are coarsely ground.

2. Mix olives, olive oil, garlic, white wine vinegar, parsley or chives, one tin anchovy fillets, and half of the diced tomatoes. Season.

3. Using an 8-inch plate, reassemble the cheese, place the first layer of Melin-y-Coed into center of plate, top with olive and tomato mix, continue layering alternately, and finish with top slice of Melin-y-Coed.

4. Sprinkle the remaining diced tomato around the plates. Drizzle the remaining oil mixture over tomato, and top with the remaining anchovy fillets.

5. Serve with warm malt bread.   *Serves 4*

10

SCOTLAND

Scotland's many regional foods reflect her climate and geography. Endowed with deep lochs, swift rivers filled with salmon and trout, and far-flung islands where sea fishing is a thriving industry, Scotland has some of the best fish in the world. Scottish smoked salmon has no peer. Most counties in these islands have a wealth of baked sweet regional specialties, similar in execution but known by various regional names that go back centuries.

Scotland's bannocks are well known, and depending where you are, the grain these flat, round griddle cakes are made from will change from oat to rye to barley meal. Bannocks' rise to fame began in Robbie Douglas's bakery in Selkirk in 1859, when the first bannock was made, and their renown spread when Queen Victoria, while visiting Sir Walter Scott's grandaughter at Abbotsford, would eat only a piece of Selkirk bannock for her tea. Parkin is a biscuit or cookie made with syrup and oatmeal, soda scones are to be eaten hot, and baps are big soft rolls served at breakfast.

Griddles, heated over peat fires, were used to bake cakes, breads, and scones in both Scotland and Ireland before the closed oven came into use. Many baked goods were flat and round to follow the shape of the griddle or hot stone used for baking. Even today there are people in Scotland, Ireland, and Wales who prefer the griddle for making oatcakes and soda bread.

Scottish Oatcakes

8 oz.   rolled oats (2 C.) (not quick cooking)
4 oz.   regular flour (¾ C.)
1 t.   baking powder
         pinch of salt
4 fl.oz. approximately, buttermilk or regular milk (½ C.)

1. Whirl oats in a food processor until fine. Place in a mixing bowl and stir in flour, baking powder, and salt.

2. Make a well in the center and add buttermilk a little at a time until you have a fairly stiff dough. Let rest in the refrigerator for 30 minutes.

3. Preheat oven to 350°F (or gas mark 4). Flour a board and roll out the dough to ⅛-inch thickness. Dip biscuit cutter in flour and cut dough into rounds. Place on an ungreased baking sheet. The oatcakes will not spread, so you can place them close together. Bake for 20 minutes. Move to a rack to cool.   *Makes about* 20

One of Napoleon's generals reported that the Scottish regiments had a great advantage over the French troops because the Scots carried a small iron griddle and a bag of oats, and wherever a campfire was ablaze they made fresh oatcakes. These the general said strengthened them for battle and helped them beat the French. Oatmeal is popular all over the world, though it is still associated mostly with the Scots. Scotland's oatcakes were traditionally formed by hand, while Wales preferred a rolling pin; both were baked on a griddle and served with butter.

Crowdie, a cottage cheese known here for millennia, is traditionally eaten in summer—the only time of year when cream is rich and plentiful. Crowdie is made with milk taken directly from the cow and a drop or two of rennet, added to make the curds separate from the whey. Once drained, the curds are mixed with a little heavy cream and eaten with oatcakes and raspberries. Another version has the cream whisked curds stirred into toasted oatmeal with a dash of whisky and honey. Raspberries, strawberries, and tomatoes ripen slowly in Scotland's cooler climate, and when they do they are superb.

Cock-a-leekie, a regional dish, is a warming soup made from a flavorful hen and tender leeks. Scotch broth is another, consisting of a steaming pot that holds mutton, vegetables, and barley.

One other succulent item that is superlative here is Loch Fyne oysters. Eat them on the half shell with or without lemon, roll them in cornmeal and fry them, tuck them into a warm, hollowed-out bread roll with some sauce, or make a creamy oyster stew. Whatever, just do not pass them by. Loch Fyne's juicy kippers (smoked herrings) are also acclaimed around the globe.

Steak and Oyster Pie

1½	lb.	beef sirloin
½	oz.	dried porcini mushrooms
		salt and pepper
2	T.	flour
3	T.	butter
2½	oz.	chopped onion (½ C.)
1		slender carrot, diced
4	fl.oz.	beef stock (½ C.)
4	fl.oz.	red wine (½ C.)
		puff pastry for one-crust pie
6		oysters on the half shell
2–3	T.	milk or cream

1. Trim steak and cut in medium-sized cubes.

2. Place dried mushrooms in a heat-proof bowl and cover with boiling water. Soak for 30 minutes, drain reserving liquid, and wash any sand off mushrooms—halve if very large.

3. Mix salt, pepper, and flour and toss with the steak cubes.

4. In a large saucepan, melt the butter and sauté the onion and carrot until beginning to soften. Remove vegetables with a slotted spoon and set aside. Sauté the steak cubes until brown.

5. Return the cooked vegetables to the pan with the mushrooms, stock, wine, and strained mushroom liquid. Simmer for 2 hours, partially covered, or until steak is tender.

6. Preheat oven to 375°F (or gas mark 5). Roll out the pastry and cut a thin strip to fit rim of deep pie dish and a crust to fit the dish.

7. Put half the steak filling in the dish. Pry oysters from their shells and place with their liquid evenly over steak filling. Cover with remaining filling.

8. Position strip around edge of dish, moisten, position pie bird to prevent pastry from falling, and top with the pastry crust. Seal and crimp edges. Use remaining pastry to cut out leaves or other decoration for crust, then brush entire crust with milk or cream.

9. Bake pie for about 40 minutes. If the crust browns too quickly, tent with foil to prevent burning. Serve piping hot.   *Serves* 4

Samuel Johnson said, "The way to eat well in Scotland is to eat breakfast three times a day." To be fair, the same remark is made when the breakfast referred to is English, but there really is something wonderful about a Scottish breakfast. Perhaps it is the oatmeal eaten with cream and brown sugar or the black pudding that is known to be addictive. Perhaps it is wonderful backgammon bacon, the golden kippers, or the marvelous marmalade, not to mention eggs, and that overflowing basket of warm breads straight from the oven with a slab of creamy butter. Or perhaps it is a hearty appetite sharpened by Scotland's clean air.

Scotland has been inhabited since the Ice Age, first by a tribe the Romans called Picts, who liked to paint themselves blue. These original Scots were joined by members of the Scotti tribe from Ireland and Welsh folk, all of whom thought Scotland's land was more fertile, and the climate milder, than it really is, but who decided to stay anyway. Vikings tried to do the same thing but were thrown out by the fledgling nation. Over time the nation separated into two distinct parts—the Highlands inhabited by Celtic people with their own language, and the Lowlands where a mixture of Scots and English spoke a language of their own indecipherable to people from the "sooth."

The Borders area of southern Scotland has been the site of continual battles and skirmishes throughout its history. The Romans tried to conquer it and failed, and the English waged war there for over a thousand years. Even after King James VI of Scotland became James I of England, uniting the two feisty countries, fighting continued for another one hundred fifty years. Much of this dreadful period of Scottish history has been immortalized in the novels of Sir Walter Scott. His home, Abbotsford House, near the beautiful ruins of Melrose Abbey, is open to visitors. The area along the border between the two countries is rich in history and ruined castles and abbeys, among them Dryburgh, Jedburgh, and Kelso, testament to its turbulent history. The Border country has some of Scotland's finest scenery and splendid houses, open to the public, such as Mellerstain, north of Kelso. Mellerstain was designed and built by William Adam and his son Robert for Lord Binning, son of the earl of Haddington. This Georgian masterpiece is possibly Scotland's most exquisite house. Its terraces and famous rose gardens have breathtaking views over the lake to the Cheviot Hills. Ornate Adam plasterwork ceilings grace the interior. The library is a striking room, noted for its antique Queen Anne, Sheraton, Chippendale, and Hepplewhite furniture. Paintings through the lovely house are by artists such as Constable, Gainsborough, and Ramsay, as well as many that represent the Italian and Dutch schools.

The Borders region is the center for woolen goods of every kind—woolen mills and knit shops are all over the place. The mills offer a bonanza of goods in different styles, textures, and colors, from kilts to cashmeres. Another specialty well represented in the Border region is candy; sweet shops dot the area, selling local fudge, caramel, and quaintly named Berwick Cockles, Hawick Balls, Soor Plums, and Jethart Snails. Peebles, an ancient and peaceful town, is situated on the banks of the River Tweed. Spanning the river is the fifteenth-century Tweed Bridge with five graceful arches and splendid ornate lamps. Trout and salmon fishing by permit is available to fishermen. Peebles was not always so peaceful; remnants of the town walls built to keep the maurading English at bay still remain. St. Mungo came to Peebles in the sixth century and baptized newly converted Christians in the town well that today carries his name. In June Peebles is abuzz with people here to attend the sheepdog trials, an event that always arouses pride and enthusiasm. In September the crowd returns to admire feats of strength and skill at the Peebles Highland Games. A grant from Andrew Carnegie helped to enlarge a town house, donated to the citizens by William Chambers, to hold two museums, an art gallery, libraries, and a reading room. Peebles is surrounded by a wealth of smooth, green golf courses.

A short distance north of Peebles off the A703 before Eddleston is the grand and glorious Cringletie House Hotel. Set in twenty-eight acres of gardens and woodland, this Scottish baronial turreted mansion with crow-stepped gables was built for the Wolfe Murray family in 1861. The reception rooms and bedrooms are beautifully decorated and furnished with comfort and grace. The lovely dining room with its snowy linens and elegant upholstered chairs is on the second floor of the house, as is the drawing room, to take advantage of the magnificent views of the Moorfoot Hills and the valley that runs down to Peebles. A two-acre walled kitchen garden provides fruit, vegetables, and herbs. Since 1971 Aileen Maguire and her kitchen team have provided imaginative, always freshly cooked, dishes using impeccable local ingredients. The menu changes daily and is complemented by a well-chosen wine list. Aileen Maguire's cooking has been recognized by all the leading hotel and restaurant guides. She says she is delighted that the range of foods people will eat has widened so much in the last few years, as this gives free rein to her imagination when preparing her menus. Among the dishes on the menu are old favorites such as Aberdeen Ramekin—smoked haddock in a creamy cheese and tomato sauce; Roast duckling with white wine, rosemary, and honey; and the wonderful dessert Cringletie Mist—a green ginger wine and lemon syllabub served with pears. More recent favorites include Smoked trout mousse with horseradish cream; Grilled marinated salmon with tarragon and walnut dressing; Casseroled haunch of venison with prunes and Guinness; Spinach, mushroom, and sunflower seed phyllo parcel; and a rich chocolate amaretto truffle.

Aileen Maguire has given us her recipe for Border tart to use in this book. Border tart is a local tart served warm or cold with cream.

Border Tart

---

shortcrust pastry to line 8-inch flan tin
6 oz.   mixed dried fruit (1¼ C.) (golden raisins, currants, and mixed peel)

2 fl.oz. whisky (¼ C.)
4 oz. butter (1 stick)
4 oz. brown sugar (½ C.)
4 eggs, beaten
  lemon juice or rind (optional)

1. Soak the dried fruit and peel for several hours in the whisky.

2. Line the flan tin with pastry and prick lightly. Preheat oven to 350°F (or gas mark 4).

3. Cream together butter and brown sugar and beat in eggs.

4. Stir in fruit and, if a less sweet taste is desired, the lemon juice or rind. Pour mixture into pastry shell and bake until golden brown and filling is set, about 30–40 minutes.   *Serves 6–8*

The Border region is rich in trout and salmon streams and fertile farmland. Borders farmers make superb farmhouse cheeses such as Bonchester, a full-fat mold-ripened strong flavored cheese, and Teviotdale, a full-fat semi-hard vegetarian cheese, both made near Hawick. Three out of four Scots live in the Lowlands, most of them on the peninsula formed by the Firths of Forth and Tay to the east and the River Clyde to the west. Glasgow sprawls around the Clyde estuary, Edinburgh hugs the southern bank of the Firth of Forth, and Dundee and Perth share the long narrow Firth of Tay.

The shallow, narrow River Clyde flows down to meet the sea at the Firth of Clyde, passing the towering Dumbarton Rock—its ancient castle once a lookout for dreaded Vikings. The river's wide estuary harbors resort towns and small islands. To the south stretch Ayrshire's beaches and gentle farmlands. Near the town of Ayr is Castle Culzean, the seat of a Kennedy Clan since the 1400s. Most of the castle was rebuilt in the eighteenth century though some fifteenth-century parts remain, including the tower. More recent restoration has been undertaken, and now Castle Culzean is open to the public. Nearby is the sumptuous Edwardian Turnberry Hotel, set in magnificent grounds. The view from almost every room in the long, low, beautifully appointed hotel overlooks the hotel's two golf courses, the Ailsa and the Arran, and beyond across the Firth of Clyde to the Isle of Arran. The cooking here is top-notch with impeccable ingredients, and the style is French Scottish. Breakfasts would delight Samuel Johnson—wonderful porridge and cream, fresh raspberries, and all the substantial cooked dishes of eggs, sausage, bacon, black and white pudding, and tomatoes, not to mention bannocks, scones, and Dundee marmalade.

The bustling resort town of Ayr was immortalized by Robert Burns who praised its "honest men and bonnie lasses." One of seven children born in 1759 to a poor farmer in the village of Alloway near Ayr, he became Scotland's national poet. His birthday, Burns Night, is celebrated each year by Scots all over the world. Robert Burns died in Dumfries in July 1796 at the very young age of thirty-seven from a heart defect caused by rheumatic fever. His heart had been weakened by too little food and far too much hard physical work as a child. At Alloway there is a shrine to Robert Burns built by his father—a thatched whitewashed cottage and a museum. The Burns Memorial and Gardens with fine shrubbery, trees, and well-kept borders is also in Alloway.

Ayr's rich farmland and excellent milk cows produce a superb cheese, Dunlop, that tastes a bit like a young Cheddar. Farmhouses produce many cheeses that are called by their original regional name though they are made in other parts of Scotland. For example, a Lanark blue cheese from ewe's milk is made in Ayrshire. It is well worth keeping an eye open for these dewy-fresh cheeses—either from the farmers themselves or in shops or restaurants—as their tastes are superlative.

Caraway and Dunlop Cheese Spread

2 T.	caraway seeds
4 fl.oz.	Scottish ale such as McEwans (½ C.)
1 lb.	grated Dunlop cheese (3 C.)
1 t.	Worcestershire sauce
1	garlic clove, pressed
½ t.	salt

1. Toast caraway seeds over medium heat in a heavy skillet, shaking pan to prevent scorching. Set aside.

2. In a double boiler over simmering water, heat ale. Stir in cheese, and as soon as it begins to melt, remove from heat and beat in Worcestershire sauce, garlic, salt, and toasted caraway seeds until completely blended.

3. Refrigerate until ready to use. Serve with crackers or toast points. *Yield: approx. 2½ C.*

The Isles of Islay and Jura off the Ayrshire coast are known for their malt whisky. Many other Highland products have won acclaim beyond the Scottish borders. Islay's lobsters are flown to Michelin-starred restaurants in London, Paris, and Brussels. Crabs from the Orkneys go by air to Scandinavia. Scottish venison is much in demand in Germany and Belgium, and since the Middle Ages Scotland and England have sent their herring to grace the tables of Europe. Scottish smoked salmon is prized in much of the hemisphere and rightly so. The techniques for smoking salmon in Scotland traditionally have been passed down from father to son, or mother to daughter, using various combinations of salt, sugar, herbs, and whisky. Prior to smoking, the sides of salmon lie in the cure for a day, absorbing the special flavors that give the salmon its worldwide reputation. The slow charring of oak shavings in the kiln completes the preservation cycle and adds its own unique flavor and succulence to this noble fish.

Fillets of Trout with Smoked Salmon

4	trout fillets
3 oz.	smoked salmon
3 T.	strongly flavored fish stock or white wine
	homemade pasta
	knob of butter
	freshly ground pepper
2 T.	cream

Garnish

smoked salmon
tomatoes, diced
parsley

1. Preheat oven to 425°F (or gas mark 7).
2. Wash trout fillets and pat dry.
3. Cut smoked salmon into thin strips and reserve one-third for garnish.
4. Lay fillets insides up and divide remaining salmon into four. Place on fillets and roll up or fold over.
5. Place in buttered ovenproof dish. Pour over fish stock or white wine and bake for 8 to 10 minutes.
6. Meanwhile cook pasta in boiling water for 2 to 3 minutes. Drain and toss with a knob of butter and keep warm.
7. Remove trout to serving platter and keep warm.
8. Pour liquid from baking dish into a small saucepan and boil down to 4 tablespoons. Stir in freshly ground pepper and the heavy cream. Bring to the boil and spoon over trout.
9. Serve trout with pasta and garnish plate with salmon slivers, diced tomatoes, and parsley.   *Serves* 4

South of Ayrshire in Dumfries and Galloway is the lively market town of Dumfries. The town is situated on the estuary of the River Nith that empties into the Solway Firth. Some elegant eighteenth-century houses, built of red sandstone, grace the streets. The pretty waterfront area has a medieval stone bridge spanning the river. Dumfries and Galloway's farms produce rich milk, cream, and splendid cheeses. One is called Barac—a full-fat, semi-hard cheese with a gentle flavor and a waxed crust; another is Corban—a soft ricotta cheese with a variation of the same ricotta cheese mixed with chives.

Syllabub

---

4 fl.oz. Madeira wine (½ C.)
6 T.   fresh lemon juice
1 T.   brandy
3 oz.   castor sugar (⅓ C.)
12 fl.oz. heavy cream (1½ C.)
          grating of nutmeg

1. Mix the Madeira wine, lemon juice, and brandy and let sit overnight or all day, covered.

2. An hour or two before serving, stir in the sugar until it is completely dissolved. Refrigerate. At the same time put four wine glasses or individual serving dishes in the refrigerator to chill.

3. Pour the Madeira mixture into a bowl large enough to hold the cream when whipped, then pour in the heavy cream and whip with an electric beater until stiff enough to hold its own shape. Do not overbeat.

4. Stir in the nutmeg and spoon into the chilled wine glasses. Serve with thin sugar cookies, preferably homemade.

Serves 4 or more

History is everywhere in Scotland and nowhere more so than in the city of Edinburgh. Much of Edinburgh's history has been violent. Attesting to this is the massive Edinburgh Castle, standing on Castle Rock, that has been razed and rebuilt many times. From the high craggy ridge a panoramic view gives the lookouts on duty plenty of warning of invaders from any direction. Below the castle the river leads to the Firth of Forth and quick access to the south. The castle rock has seen many invaders. Picts had fortifications on the rock in the third century B.C. Over its 1,300-year history, it has been besieged by Romans, Angles, and Saxons. The castle has been held at some periods of its history by the English crown.

The town grew up around the castle in the eleventh century during the reign of Malcolm Canmore when he and his queen, Margaret, made the castle their home. King Malcolm killed Macbeth to avenge his father's murder. His youngest son, David I, built Holyrood Abbey in Edinburgh in 1128. Sixty-six years later the ineffective ruler John Balliol, a lackey of Edward I, turned tail and formed an alliance with France. Known as the Auld Alliance, it continued until the late 1500s when France remained Roman Catholic and Scotland became Protestant. The city walls, built in 1436, were no deterrent to the avenging Henry VIII's forces when marriage plans for his son, Edward, and Mary Queen of Scots were foiled. The Scots prudently sent Mary to live in France, and Henry's wrath was great. He had the castle and town pounded to the ground twice. In 1566, Mary Queen of Scots, then married to the feckless Lord Darnley, gave birth to the future King James VI of Scotland at Edinburgh Castle. Queen Mary's apartments survive and are open to visitors. The enormous esplanade in front of the castle was built in the eighteenth century and is a splendid sight when the Tattoo takes place during the Edinburgh Festival.

The castle stands at one end of the Royal Mile, and at the other end is the Palace of Holyroodhouse, reached through spectacular wrought-iron gates. The palace is Queen Elizabeth's official residence when she is in the city. Originally on this site was a guesthouse of Holyrood Abbey that gradually fell into disrepair. The palace as it is today was completely rebuilt in the French style by Charles II when he took the throne in 1660. Queen Victoria, who loved Scotland dearly, refurbished it again during her reign. Behind the palace are Holyrood Park and the remains of the original Abbey. A line of S's mark the pavement of the Royal Mile at Canongate. These denote the limit of the Abbey's sanctuary, which continued to be given to those who needed it until 1880.

Until the late 1700s Edinburgh was a noxious place of tenements, rats, and disease, so much so that James Boswell was embarrassed to have his friend, Samuel Johnson, see and smell Edinburgh. A competition held to find the best plan for redesigning the city was won by James Craig, a relatively unknown architect. His ideas for parallel streets ending in wide squares, sweeping crescents, and gardens beautified the city. Edinburgh's inhabitants are busy beautifying their city today by cleaning the soot from old buildings to reveal the original creamy sandstone.

Edinburgh's restaurants get better and better with each visit. In light of Scotland's French heritage—Mary Queen of Scots's mother, Mary of Guise, was a Frenchwoman, and Scotland maintained close ties with France for three hundred years—many of Edinburgh's restaurants are French. But even here French-trained chefs happily experiment with homegrown, farm-fresh ingredients, and the trend is toward lighter and simpler dishes.

The Dubh Prais Restaurant at 123b High Street in Edinburgh is situated on the Royal Mile. James McWilliams is the chef and proprietor of this small cellar restaurant. He is the winner of three gold, two silver, and one bronze medal in National Food Competitions. "All my dishes are cooked with fresh wholesome ingredients," says James McWilliams, "and I have no deep-fat fryer, microwave, or freezer in my kitchen." Seafood is from the West Coast; venison, hare, and pheasant come from the Highlands; Aberdeen Angus beef and lamb are from the Borders; and all of it is personally selected by James McWilliams. Some of the dishes on his current menu are

Rabbit and Ayrshire bacon terrine with mustard sauce; Smoked venison Cumberland with salad; Scottish smoked salmon; Fillets of sole Islay served with a cheddar mustard sauce; Supreme of chicken Munro with hillside mushrooms; Veal Glenfalloch topped with smoked pheasant, served with sherry sauce; and Saddle of hare Melrose stuffed with chestnut and thyme pâté, coated with a Drambuie and port sauce. Desserts are great—Chocolate and pistachio parfait and Butterscotch terrine, to name but two. James McWilliams has given us permission to use his recipe that follows.

West Coast Broth

20 fl.oz.	fish stock (2½ C.)
2 oz.	finely chopped tomatoes (⅓ C.)
1	garlic clove, crushed
2 oz.	smoked haddock

4 oz.   fresh Scottish salmon
2 oz.   squid
4 oz.   scallops
16   mussels, shelled
10 fl.oz. heavy cream (1¼ C.)
1 t.   Tabasco sauce
            salt and pepper
            parsley, minced

1. In a heavy-bottomed saucepan, bring to a boil the fish stock, chopped tomatoes, and garlic.

2. Carefully add the smoked haddock, Scottish salmon, squid, scallops, and mussels, and cook until the fish is just opaque—a few minutes.

3. Remove from heat and stir in the heavy cream, Tabasco, salt, pepper, and parsley. Gently return to the boil and serve straightaway in heated soup bowls.   *Serves* 4

L'Auberge, 56 St. Mary's Street, is conveniently located close to the Royal Mile. Fabrice Bresulier is the chef here, and his cooking makes good use of all things Scottish while cooking French regional food. The menu changes frequently and portions are generous.

The Vintners Rooms, 87 Giles Street, Leith, is a converted wine warehouse with ceilings decorated in seventeenth-century plasterwork. The chef is Tim Cummings, and his cooking deserves all the praise he receives. His dishes are inventive and packed with fresh flavors.

Martin's, 70 Rose Street, North Lane, is owned by Martin Irons. The chef is Forbes Stott, who cooks some of the best food in Edinburgh. His dishes are exquisitely presented and tend to be modern and light. Vegetables, breads, and cheese receive as many accolades as his superbly cooked main dishes.

Kelly's, 46 West Richmond Street, lists French and Scottish dishes on the menu. Jacquie Kelly owns this restaurant with her husband, Jeff Kelly. Jacquie Kelly and Nicholas Carnegie do the cooking for this tiny restaurant serving beautifully prepared, succulent Scottish lamb and game in season, as well as simply cooked, delicious fish dishes. Jeff Kelly's expertise is his wine list.

The Waterfront Wine Bar at the Quayside Dock is acclaimed for its food, its wine list, and Edinburgh's justly renowned ales.

The Edinburgh Festival of Music and Drama takes place in summer, as it has since its inception in 1947. A different theme is chosen for the Festival each year. For three weeks in August and September the town is abuzz as within the same time period the Edinburgh International Film Festival and, in alternate years, the Edinburgh Book Festival take place. McEwan's Edinburgh International Jazz Festival plays jazz concerts daily throughout the festivals. Edinburgh has always been a place where education, literature, and art were highly respected. Sir Walter Scott was raised in Edinburgh and practiced law before devoting himself to his writing. Glimpses of famous Scots can be seen through a collection of their personal effects housed in the National Museum of Antiquities. Here too are the Royal Scottish Academy, the National Gallery of Scotland, and the Scottish National Portrait Gallery.

Edinburgh's regional foods are numerous. Perhaps the most famous is the rather unusual Black Bun. This consists of a rich, dark fruit cake, spiced with cinnamon, cloves, and black pepper, completely encased in pastry and baked in a loaf pan. Definitely not a dish for every day. Black Bun is traditionally eaten thinly sliced on New Year's Day. The farmers in Lothian, the county surrounding Edinburgh, make farmhouse cheeses that include a low-fat Crowdie, a pressed gouda-type cheese called Langskaill, Lothian cheese that resembles Camembert, Smallholder that resembles a crumbly Cheddar, and delicately flavored, peat-smoked cheese, as well as cream cheese, goat cheese, and yogurt cheese. West Lothian also produces haggis, that most Scottish of sausages. Made from chopped sheep's heart, liver, and lungs, mixed with toasted oatmeal, finely chopped suet, and onion, it is sewn into a sheep's stomach, boiled for four or five hours, and served piping hot with potatoes and bashed neeps (mashed turnips). The preferred drink to wash it down is malt whisky.

Following the Firth of Forth farther inland from Edinburgh is Linlithgow, a peaceful town surrounded by lovely countryside, rich in farmland. Linlithgow's fame and fortune has had links with royalty since the twelfth century. Edward I's army was headquartered here, and David II built a manor house retreat at Linlithgow. A huge fire leveled the town in the fifteenth century, and the present graceful Linlithgow Palace was begun after the fire. Mary Queen of Scots was born here, and it is reputed that when James V gave Linlithgow Palace to her mother, Mary of Guise, the fountain in the courtyard gushed wine instead of water. Though parts of the elegant structure are crumbling, Linlithgow Palace stands five stories high. Many of the well-preserved rooms are evocative of its former glorious days. Near the palace is St. Michael's Church, whose history is closely entwined with the royal palace. Both suffered devastation under Cromwell, who stabled his horses in St. Michael's and shot muskets into the walls.

Champany's restaurant off the M9 specializes in well-hung beef, glistening salmon, and lobsters swimming in their tank. The bounty is set out before you to make your choice. Steaks are cut to order and can be marinated in the house marinade and char-broiled, if you wish. Everything is cooked to perfection by Clive Davidson, the chef proprietor with his wife, Anne Davidson. Plenty of fresh vegetables will accompany your choice. The Champany's standards are high, and it is deservedly famous for its great traditional food.

Southwest of Linlithgow is the teeming city of Glasgow, which in recent years has washed off the grime that clung to its beautiful buildings and refurbished the Merchant area and others with new shopping malls and

apartment buildings. Domestic coal fires were prohibited in the United Kingdom in 1950. No longer are there pea-souper fogs that necessitate keeping one hand on the wall or fence in order to find your way along the sidewalk. Fog deadens sound, and it is heart-stopping when a face looms out of the fog a foot from your own. Bus drivers would ask a volunteer to walk in front of the bus swinging a warning as the bus inched through the fog. Pea-soupers are a thing of the past, the weather is a hundred percent better, the sky is blue instead of gray, and as someone recently remarked, "We can plan picnics ahead of time now, as you do in America." Beautiful old town houses line many city streets, and Glasgow's spacious squares and grand public buildings are very striking. The pre-Reformation Gothic Cathedral was built in the 1100s in the same place as the former church of St. Mungo, traces of which are still visible. St. Mungo was buried here in 603, and the site has become a place of pilgrimage.

George Square, filled with trees and flowers, is possibly Glasgow's most beautiful square. The Italian Renaissance city chambers, thoroughly ornate inside and out, grace the eastern side of the square. People stroll here on a sunny day, and tourists slung with cameras photograph the buildings and statues. Sir Walter Scott on an eighty-foot-high column is somewhat out of the camera's eye—at least for close-ups. Sir Walter Scott is beloved by Scots everywhere, just as he was beloved during his lifetime by his countless friends. His talent for writing stories and ballads about historical events that he brought to life by intertwining them with the stories in the present was remarkable. He laid the foundations for all historical novels that have been written since.

Glaswegians have a fatalistic streak and a wry sense of the absurd. Though Glasgow had many slums during the Industrial Revolution, with several families crowded into one apartment with few, if any, conveniences, they are a resilient people and have cheerfully pulled their city up by its bootstraps. In 1990 Glasgow reigned as the Cultural Capital of Europe. The city throbs with energy and enterprise, and there is much to see and do. The Scottish Opera, National Orchestra, and Ballet are all here. Crowds throng Glasgow's Folk Festival and Jazz Festival in June and July, not to mention the World Pipe Band Championships in August. Two kinds of bagpipes are played in Scotland—the Highland pipe, at one time suitable only for playing out of doors, and the Lowland bagpipe, which is operated with the right elbow squeezing the bellows—known as warm-wind and cold-wind pipes. Both instruments are beloved of Scots and defended with more than just fierce pride. The Lowland bagpipe is heard increasingly with the folk music groups, ballads, songs, and jigs. Historical scores that date back to the fifteenth century and tell of great Highland events are called Pibroch, and they should be listened to with respect and attention.

Rich in works of art, museums, and galleries, Glasgow has the world-renowned Burrell Collection housed in a fantastic building in Pollock Park, especially built for its needs and integrated with its environment. This treasure house is located three miles (4.8 km) southwest of the city. Glasgow is surrounded by green and beautiful mountains, boasts the oldest city park in the United Kingdom, and has some of the finest examples of Victorian architecture in Britain.

Glasgow has plenty of good restaurants. Among the best are the Buttery at 652 Argyle Street, where elaborate well-wrought dishes are cooked by Stephen Johnson and served in a gentlemen's club atmosphere.

One Devonshire Gardens at 1 Devonshire Gardens—the restaurant occupies three houses—is a place where you will dine luxuriously in spacious rooms. Andrew Fleming is the chef, and he cooks traditional as well as modern dishes with enthusiasm, using impeccable ingredients.

Crannog Scottish Seafoods have opened a sister restaurant to their first one in Fort William at 28 Cheapside Street, Glasgow. This Seafood Restaurant also brings fish directly from the fisherman to the table, and the result is delicious and the cooking very good indeed.

The Poachers Restaurant at Ruthven Lane, Byres Road, is a diminutive restaurant in a 1870 farmhouse. The food is cooked to order, using excellent meat, game, and fish.

The Ubiquitous Chip sounds like a fish and chip shop but is actually a very pretty restaurant with a waterfall, lots of plants, and pretty wall murals at 12 Ashton Lane. The staff here are friendly and helpful and Ron Clydesdale, the chef proprietor, is an exceptional cook. He cooks traditional as well as highly original dishes using fresh Scottish ingredients, and he is also much appreciated among well-satisfied vegetarians.

Glasgow is famous for its tripe, and for fresh lactic goat's curd cheese, called Ledlewan. Endrickvale is a soft Coulommiers type of cheese sometimes available rolled in herbs. Southeast of Glasgow, Lanarkshire makes a close-textured Dunsyre Blue and Lanark Blue, a full-fat, mold-ripened ewe's milk cheese that resembles Roquefort.

Only a few miles northwest of Glasgow is Loch Lomond, rimmed with mountains and dotted with tiny islands. Another scenic expanse is the wooded valley called the Trossachs, which can be seen in all its glory from a Loch Katrine steamer in the summer months. The mountains are reflected in the sparkling, pure water of the Loch. Sir Walter Scott's *The Lady of the Lake* and *Rob Roy* brought fame to this lovely region. Wordsworth and Coleridge also visited the Trossachs, and Wordworth was inspired to write "To a Highland Girl."

Centered on the peninsula between the Firth of Forth and the Firth of Tay is St. Andrews, for many people the absolute shrine of golf. The first golf association was actually located in Edinburgh, but St. Andrews, with its Royal and Ancient Club and the revered Old Course along the seashore, has become the mecca of all things relating to golf. Not that St. Andrews has no other claim to fame. The Celtic church was founded in Scotland when St. Rule or Regulus was shipwrecked on the coast here carrying relics of St. Andrew. The tower that bears his name has wonderful views over the town. Construction began on St. Andrews Cathedral, Scotland's largest cathedral, in 1161. In 1200 work was started on the Bishop's Residence overlooking the North Sea that eventually became St. Andrews Castle. St. Mary's College has a tree in the grounds that was planted by Mary Queen of Scots. St. Andrews University is the oldest university in Scotland. The town has some medieval buildings built on the original medieval pattern of parallel streets. St. Andrews is also a seaside resort of considerable bracing charm. Salmon fishing thrives in Fife in its many lochs and rivers, which provide ample irrigation for its agricultural lands.

Smoked Salmon Pâté

½ lb.   smoked Nova Scotia salmon
1 T.   fresh lemon juice
4 oz.   unsalted butter (1 stick)
6 fl.oz.   heavy cream (⅔ C.)
   freshly ground white pepper

Garnish: dill sprigs, minced red onion, and tiny capers

1. Slice salmon into strips and toss with lemon juice. Place in a blender jar.
2. Melt butter, cool slightly, and pour over salmon. Add cream and white pepper and blend until smooth.
3. Wet eight small molds that are just large enough to hold salmon pâté. Pack salmon into molds, smooth tops, and cover with cling wrap. Refrigerate for at least 6 hours.
4. To serve, dip mold briefly in hot water. Place small serving plate on top of mold and invert onto plate. Garnish with dill sprigs and serve with minced red onion, tiny capers, and crackers.

Serves 8

Fife's long coastline, though wind-prone, is good for vacationers as it is one of the sunnier parts of Britain. The B9131 runs directly south of St. Andrews to Anstruther on the north shoreline of the Firth of Forth. The Cellar Restaurant at 24 East Green, Anstruther, is where Peter Jukes cooks perfectly executed, marvelous seafood—lobster, scallops, halibut, and smoked haddock. The restaurant is definitely worth a detour.

Six miles (9.6 km) from St. Andrews is the Peat Inn, at Peat Inn by Cupar, Fife. The Peat Inn was originally an old coaching stop at the crossroads of a tiny village named after the inn. David and Patricia Wilson bought the Peat Inn in 1972, and since then his cooking has earned him an international reputation and a Michelin Star. In 1986 he was made a chef laureate by the British Gastronomic Academy. David Wilson's expertise has consistently been rated among Britain's best by the major food guides, including stars from Egon Ronay. In 1989 he was the first restaurateur outside of London to win the Restaurateur of the Year Award. The wine list has also won awards over the years. Wine is a hobby of David Wilson's, and he says his list is "consumer friendly" as far as the prices go. The restaurant is formal yet friendly, and the staff discreet and attentive. The reception room has an open log fire. Three separate dining rooms provide facilities for private parties. In 1987 the Residence was built in the grounds behind the inn to accommodate people wishing to stay the night. The Residence has eight luxury suites—seven are split level—with double, king, or twin beds. Patricia Wilson, a design graduate, has furnished these rooms with gorgeous fabrics and period French furniture. David Wilson says that over the years cooking has become lighter and healthier, and he has discovered that olive oil enhances flavors more accurately than butter or cream. In the summer months locally grown soft fruits and produce are used in the kitchens, and at other seasons of the year they come from the Glasgow market. David says that if he had to choose a favorite three-course meal in late August, he would have lobster and crab salad, roast young grouse, and mille-feuille of raspberries with vanilla cream. Dishes on a recent menu included Peat Inn fish soup, Lobster salad with a citrus vinaigrette, Roast salmon with Thai spices, Ragout of pigeon breast with wild mushrooms and truffle sauce, Medallions of venison saddle in a red wine sauce, Grilled fillet of beef with roasted shallots, Roast breast of Gressingham duck in a rich sauce with honey and orange, and Whole local lobster poached in a vegetable and herb broth. Desserts are a magnificent Caramelized apple pastry with a caramel sauce, a Trio of nut desserts, a Trio of caramel desserts, and David Wilson's famous Little pot of chocolate and rosemary followed by the cheese tray. He has given us permission to use the following recipe.

Ragout of Scallops, Monkfish, and Pork with Spiced Apple

12	lb.	pork belly
		chicken stock
4	oz.	monkfish fillet
8		scallops with roes, if possible
1		Granny Smith apple
1		level t. mixed spices, including coriander, cumin, cinnamon, nutmeg, allspice, caraway, ginger, cloves, and cardamom
1	T.	sunflower oil

Vinaigrette sauce

4	T.	virgin olive oil
2	T.	red wine vinegar
1	t.	soy sauce
2	T.	walnut oil
		salt and pepper

1. Dice pork belly into pieces about ½-inch square, then precook in a little stock until very tender—about 45 minutes.

2. Slice monkfish fillet into thin slices and the scallops in half. Reserve roes of scallops, if available.

3. Strain pork, then place on flat tray and grill under preheated grill until crisp.

4. Peel and core apple. Using size 10 or 12 parisienne scoop, make apple balls, or dice into 1/4-inch dice.

5. Add apple balls to pork, sprinkle the spices over pork and apple, then reheat under grill.

6. Put some sunflower oil in sauté pan and heat until it begins to smoke. Fry monkfish slices for about 2 minutes each side. Keep hot. Then in same pan fry scallops and roes about one minute each side.

7. Spoon pork and apple onto center of warm plate and place scallops and monkfish on top.

8. Spoon warm vinaigrette over the food and around the plate.

Serves 4 as a starter

Cupar, once the administrative capital of Fife, has many fine eighteenth-century stone houses built with the same golden-toned limestone as the Cotswold villages. Nearby is the Scottish Deer Center with a restaurant, nature trail, and farm walk beloved by children who love to pet the deer. The Visitor Center here is particularly interesting and informative. The Ostlers Close, 25 Bonnygate, Cupar, is a jewel of a restaurant, owned and managed by James and Amanda Graham. The small space is informally decorated with beechwood tables, a stunning collection of plates, and bowls of fresh flowers. The atmosphere is relaxed and happy, and candlelight adds romance at dinner. Each of the eight tables has one booking each evening, so diners are encouraged to stay all evening long if they wish, without fear that other people are waiting for them to finish their meal. James Graham is the chef, and he and Amanda Graham rely heavily on local smallholdings for their organic vegetables. On the outskirts of Cupar an excellent soft fruit farm grows raspberries and tayberries that thrive until at least mid-October. The Grahams pick their own wild mushrooms, grow their own herbs and salad leaves, and receive a steady seasonal supply of river salmon, pheasant, partridge, pigeon, wild duck, and venison. The majority of their seafood comes from a local supplier who goes to a boat dock some twenty minutes away for fresh fish and lobster. Butcher meat comes from a butcher in Cupar, and it is all Scottish. The menus change daily depending on the local bounty, and an assortment of starters include Baked mussels Hollandaise, Compote of fruits in sweet muscat with a strawberry and champagne sorbet, Terrine of seafood on a herb vinaigrette, and Panfried duck livers on a bed of Puy lentils in a Madeira sauce. Main courses include Fillet of turbot with East Neck lobster on a champagne sauce, Roast saddle of venison with wild mushroom in a game sauce, Fillet of salmon, and Pot roast breast of wood pigeon with wild mushrooms. The dessert menu offers a Trio of chocolate desserts, Thin shortcakes filled with raspberries on a cream of passion fruit, and Local strawberry Romanoff. James Graham has given us the following recipe to include in this book.

Fillets of Monkfish in a Light Cheese Herb Batter on a Red Pepper Sauce

Batter

1	oz.	each (¼ C.) finely grated fresh Parmesan, Jarlsberg, and Pecorino cheeses
2		eggs
2	oz.	flour (scant ½ C.)
5	fl.oz.	milk (scant ⅔ C.)
2	oz.	mixed chopped fresh herbs (¼ C.)—basil, chives, parsley, dill, and chervil
		seasoning

1. Whisk together batter ingredients until smooth and allow to rest. This can be made in advance and refrigerated.

Red pepper sauce

1	lb.	red peppers (3 C.), chopped
1		onion, chopped
2		carrots, chopped
1		stick celery, chopped
½		head of fennel, chopped
1		garlic clove, minced
1		bay leaf
1		star anise
1	T.	tomato purée
		olive oil
1	T.	paprika
20	fl.oz.	fish stock (2½ C.)
10	fl.oz.	white wine (1¼ C.)
2	oz.	butter (½ stick)

2. Sweat the vegetables, garlic, bay leaf, anise, and tomato purée in olive oil until softened. Add stock, wine, and paprika and bring to a boil. Simmer until vegetables are tender and reduce by half.

3. Cut butter into pieces and, taking pan off the heat, whisk each piece into cooled sauce. Liquidize or blend and put through a sieve. Return to pan for reheating.

1 lb. monkfish fillets
     seasoned flour for dredging
     olive oil for frying

4. Dip slices of monkfish into seasoned flour, then into batter.

5. Fry in hot pan with coating of olive oil. If pan is not big enough to hold all the monkfish, cook in batches and keep in warm oven.

6. Coat plates with sauce and divide monkfish between plates.

Serves 4

The A913 road will take you through Newburgh on the Firth of Tay to Perth, situated at the mouth of the River Tay. Perth is an attractive town, made famous by Sir Walter Scott in his *Fair Maid of Perth*. The home of the Fair Maid—Catherine Glover—can be visited on Charlotte Street in North Port. Scottish exhibits of paintings and crafts are held here, and Perth is also known for its wonderful scones. In the western suburbs of Perth is the huge Dewars Whisky works.

Scottish Scones

½ lb.   flour (1⅔ C.)
1 T.   baking powder
1 t.   salt
         generous pinch of sugar
1   egg
1 T.   melted butter
5 fl.oz. buttermilk or milk (scant ⅔ C.)

1. Preheat oven to 425°F (or gas mark 7).

2. Sift the dry ingredients into a medium-sized mixing bowl.

3. Beat together the remaining ingredients and add all at once to the flour mixture.

4. Stir just enough to form a soft dough. Invert bowl onto a floured surface and lightly roll the dough, or pat with your palms, until it is about ¾ inch thick.

5. Cut as many scones as you can from the dough using a well-floured cookie cutter about 2 inches wide. Gather scraps, pat together, and cut out the remaining scones.

6. Bake for 10 to 15 minutes on a greased baking sheet. Serve warm with butter or clotted cream and raspberry preserves.

Makes about 6 scones

Carole and Athole Laing own and manage the restaurant Timothy's, 24 St. John Street, Perth. The Laings are very well respected in the community, and the restaurant on occasion is used as a social or community center. Almost all foods used in the kitchen are local, and the flavors are fresh and clean.

Restaurant Number Thirty Three, at 33 George Street, Perth, owned by Gavin and Mary Billinghurst, serves sophisticated dishes that are well executed and much appreciated by their clientele. Mary Billingshurst is in charge of the kitchen, and her fish dishes particularly draw accolades. The restaurant is attractive, and good use is made of the oyster bar by oyster enthusiasts.

In the countryside around Perth farmers make delicious Drumturk double cream goat's milk cheese, crusted with peppercorns, and another Drumturk White, which is a soft curd cheese. Two miles (3.2 km) north of Perth is Scone Palace, a nineteenth-century restoration of a sixteenth-century dwelling, owned and still lived in by the earl of Mansfield. Open to the public, it has plenty to see, including Marie Antoinette's writing desk. Edward I stole the Stone of Scone, on which Scottish kings were crowned, and took it to London where it has been part of the coronation chair in Westminster Abbey. In 1950 it was stolen and stashed at Arbroath by Scottish nationalists, who kept it for three months before it was returned. Many Scots believe that the stone in Westminster Abbey for all these years is not the original carved stone but a replica.

North of Perth on the Perth/Inverness Road is Blair Castle, bristling with turrets, gables, chimneys, and parapets. Blair Castle has commanded the main route through the Central Scottish Highlands for over 700 years. The formidable stronghold has been the home of the earls and dukes of Atholl for centuries. There are thirty-two rooms, including a ballroom and a dining room with exquisitely wrought plaster ceilings. The collection of paintings, lovely furniture, porcelain, and a great deal of armor present a stirring picture of Scottish life from the sixteenth to the twentieth century. The privately owned castle is surrounded by magnificent grounds, which include a deer park, and there are picnic areas and nature trails.

A mile or two south of Blair Castle, north of Pitlochry, is the Killiecrankie Hotel, where very good food can be had in the restaurant and in the bar. The proprietors are Colin and Carole Anderson, who go out of their way to be helpful and friendly. The chef, Paul Booth, earns lots of accolades for his excellent beef dishes, and his menu also caters well to vegetarians.

In a spectacular situation at the end of the Firth of Tay is Dundee. A bridge spans the Firth linking Dundee with Fife. Dundee has two excellent regional specialties: Dundee marmalade and ginger preserves made by the Keiller family for generations, and the rich, fruit-filled Dundee cake, which has slivered almonds pressed into its dark, glossy top. Both of these specialties are world renowned and with good reason. The original white stone jars of

Keiller's famous marmalade are sold as collector's items, and Keiller preserves are still packed in white stone jars today. Dundee is home to Captain Scott's royal research ship, *Discovery*, that carried him on his polar expeditions. The ship was built here and is now on permanent exhibit. Jute was for centuries a mainstay of Dundee's economy, and some jute is still worked today. Dundee has few architectural treasures as the city was thoroughly modernized in the 1950s and 1960s. However, the highest point of the city is a hill with the remains of a Roman fort on top, where the views alone are worth the climb.

Steamed Ginger Pudding

4 oz.	chunky Scottish ginger preserves (½ C.)
3 oz.	unsalted butter (¾ stick), softened, plus enough to butter pudding basin
5 T.	castor sugar
2 med.	eggs
3 oz.	flour (generous ½ C.)
1 t.	baking powder
½ t.	ground ginger
3 oz.	crystallized ginger (⅔ C.), chopped
	milk

Accompany with crème fraîche or English custard

1. Butter the pudding basin well. Heat the preserves slightly and put through a sieve or whirl in the blender until smooth. Coat the bottom of the pudding basin with the ginger preserves.

2. Cream butter and sugar together until light and fluffy.

3. Beat the eggs and add them slowly to the creamed ingredients. Sift together the flour, baking powder, and ground ginger, and beat into the creamed ingredients bit by bit.

4. Stir in the crystallized ginger and enough milk to make a cake batter.

5. Spoon batter into pudding basin, tapping basin to eliminate air bubbles. Cover surface of pudding with buttered waxed paper.

6. Cover basin with aluminum foil, leaving enough space for the pudding to rise. Secure with kitchen string and carefully lower pudding basin into a saucepan containing enough *boiling* water to reach halfway up the sides of the basin. Cover and boil for 2 hours. If the water gets too low, replenish with more *boiling* water.

7. When pudding is cooked, remove foil and waxed paper and invert pudding into a warm serving dish. Serve immediately with crème fraîche or English custard.   *Serves 6*

Farther along the Angus coast from Dundee is Arbroath, Tayside. Here the famed Arbroath Smokies—juicy young haddock smoked to a deep golden color—are made. The best smoked haddocks in Scotland come from Arbroath, and from Findon in Kincardine. Arbroath is both a fishing port and a holiday resort. In Arbroath is The Abbey built in 1178 by William the Lion in memory of his friend, Thomas à Becket.

Kedgeree

1	lb.	smoked haddock fillets (absolutely not frozen)*
4	oz.	long grain rice
6	T.	butter
3		eggs, hard-boiled, roughly chopped
2	T.	lemon juice
		pinch of cayenne
		grated nutmeg
4	fl.oz.	whipping cream (½ C.)
		salt and pepper
2	T.	minced dill
		parsley or dill sprigs for garnish

1. Poach the smoked haddock in just enough water to cover fish in a shallow pan for 10–20 minutes, depending on thickness. It will flake easily when ready. Drain and when the fish is cool, flake into the top part of a double boiler. Set aside.
2. Meanwhile, cook the rice in boiling salted water for 15 minutes. Drain, if necessary, and add to the flaked fish, along with the butter, chopped egg, lemon juice, cayenne, nutmeg, and cream. Stir very gently with a fork to mix ingredients. Season to taste.
3. Bring the double boiler to a simmer and heat the kedgeree until steaming hot. Stir in the minced dill.
4. Serve garnished with parsley or dill sprigs.   *Serves 3–4*

---

* If unfrozen smoked haddock is not available, this dish can be made with fresh or canned salmon or fresh shrimp.

North along the coast is the pretty resort town of Montrose, which sits between the sea and a tidal basin. Miles of sandy beach, an excellent golf course, and the surrounding lovely countryside make this a popular place with holidaymakers.

Farther north Aberdeen, called the granite city as it was built predominately from this local stone, sits on the North Sea coast. The older part of this very upright town holds the Cathedral of St. Machar, dating to the fourteenth and fifteenth centuries. Its twin spires are an Aberdeen landmark. The cathedral, also built in granite, which glitters when the sun touches it, was erected on the site of the original Celtic settlement established by St. Machar. Aberdeen's long silvery sand beach stretches for two miles (3.2 km) north of the port. Aberdeen has the lowest crime rate in Britain and the lowest unemployment rate. Scotland's largest fishing port brings in cod, whiting, haddock, and especially herring, all destined to be smoked in the processing plant here over damp wood chips before being shipped south to market. Aberdeen's kippers are famous, and almost equally so are Aberdeen's sausages. Aberdeen Angus prizewinning cattle provide some of Britain's best beef. Aberdeen's fish market has been modernized fairly recently, and it is a fascinating sight when buyers crowd the harbor going through stacked boxes of fish with an eye to a bargain. Aberdeen is the main market town for most of the products grown or raised in the Highlands, and it is also the center of the North Sea oil boom. Though fortunately no oil comes through the town, offshore oil rigs, supply ships, and aircraft are much in evidence. However, the townspeople go calmly about their business as they always have. The advent of free-spending oilmen has improved the restaurant scene in Aberdeen, and the nightlife too is lively with several discos and a casino. Situated smack on Pocra Quay, Footdee, is the Silver Darling Restaurant, which specializes in barbecued fish dishes.

Faraday's, at 2–4 Kirk Brae, Cults Aberdeen, has a menu that gleans dishes from all over the world, including Thai, Moroccan, Italian, French, and Scottish. John Inches' cooking is very good, and people come from afar to eat at his table.

Ardoe House Hotel is a massive Scottish baronial mansion on a large estate on the River Dee. The hotel has its own restaurant and two bars. Fresh fish and Aberdeen Angus beef are the delicious mainstays in this part of Scotland.

Grampian produces Aberdeenshire Farmhouse—a hard, sweet milk cheese—some are clothbound, some have their natural crust, and some are flavored with caraway. Another hard, traditional cheese is Banffshire Farmhouse.

Fifty miles (80.4 km) inland from Aberdeen is Balmoral Castle—the retreat of the royal family who arrive in September to attend the Royal Highland Gathering held at Braemar at the foot of the Cairngorm Mountains. Queen Victoria loved Scotland, calling it her "dear Paradise." Prince Albert bought the land in 1852 and had Balmoral, a Scottish baronial-style castle, built in white granite as a winter retreat for his growing family. Between

Braemar and the Spey valley the Cairngorms provide some of the wildest and most dramatic scenery in Scotland. No roads cross these formidable peaks. Hikers and walkers should be well equipped before venturing forth. For skiers and nonwalkers a chairlift in two stages goes to the 3,600-foot peak and the wide-ranging views to the west of the Spey valley and Loch Morlich. A panorama of the whole area can be had by taking the path that leads upward for an additional 500 feet (152 meters).

The Grampian Mountains have many castles built in differing styles that are well worth a visit, and most of them are within easy reach of Aberdeen. These include Craigievar Castle, Crathes Castle, Dunnottar Castle, and Castle Fraser. From Aberdeen the A96 will take you to the Spey Valley, noted for its fine whisky. The earliest whisky was single malt, distilled since the 1400s in small pot stills, all over Ireland and Scotland. Whisky in both countries is dubbed "the water of life" from the Gaelic. Though not the refined whisky we know today, nevertheless, each wee dram cheered the heart during the long, rugged winters. Ripe barley, the main ingredient in whisky, thrives in the cool climate of the Highlands, Lowlands, and rugged Islands of Scotland. The barley is germinated or malted, dried over burning peat, then left to ferment before being distilled twice in onion-shaped, handbeaten copper stills. The precious, smoky-tasting liquor is aged until smooth in oak casks. It was not until the early 1800s that the patent still, which produces a continuous stream of whisky, was invented. Developed further later in the century, this still yields a milder whisky distilled from grain. Today there are at least a hundred varieties of malt whisky distilled in Scotland, each with its own taste that varies from rough and peaty to silky smooth. The length of maturation time, and the kind of cask the whisky is matured in, will produce different tastes. There are half a dozen grain distilleries, all located in the Lowlands, and their whisky differs in the percentage of barley used in the mash and the variations in water. Today's blended Scotch is made from as many as forty differently flavored grain and malt whiskies.

Irish whiskey has its own distinctive taste, which is fuller, slightly sweeter, and without the smoky taste. Irish whiskey uses no peat in the curing process. Note the different spelling of the name. The Irish claim they invented whiskey, and Celts fleeing over the water to Scotland took their recipe with them and introduced the Scots to whiskey distillation.

Continuing on the A96, one comes to the town of Elgin, situated in rich agricultural land on the banks of the River Lossie. The main street in Elgin links what once was Scotland's most beautiful cathedral, Elgin Cathedral, and the site of the former castle. Restoration began on the cathedral in the nineteenth century. Elgin has preserved its medieval street plan.

Parsnip and Apple Soup

2	T.	butter
1	t.	oil
1	sm.	onion, or two shallots, finely chopped
1	sm.	garlic clove, crushed
1	t.	fresh ginger root, peeled and minced
2		slender carrots, thinly sliced
1–2		tender stalks of celery, thinly sliced
40	fl.oz.	chicken broth (5 C.)
1	lb.	sliced parsnips (3 C.)
1	med.	tart apple, thinly sliced
2	t.	minced fresh sage
		light cream (optional)
		salt, pepper, and freshly grated nutmeg to taste

1. Melt butter in a large heavy-bottomed saucepan over medium heat with the oil.

2. Stir in all the vegetables, with the exception of the parsnips, and cook until they begin to color lightly and soften.

3. Add broth, parsnips, apples, and sage, and continue to cook until tender.

4. Cool soup, then purée in a blender or food processor. Thin the soup with either additional chicken broth or light cream.

5. Season to taste, stir in the nutmeg, and serve in warm soup bowls.   *Serves 6–8*

Farther on is the once prosperous fishing village of Nairn on the Moray Firth. Nairn today is famous for its single malt whisky. Southwest of here is Cawdor Castle, built by the Thanes of Cawdor, and the Cawdor family lives here still. Shakespeare's Macbeth was Thane of Cawdor, and the castle is reputed to be the place where Duncan was murdered. The earliest part of the structure, the central tower, dates to the fourteenth century. The castle is protected by a dry moat, and the entrance to the castle is over a drawbridge. Beautiful rooms display porcelain, tapestries, fine furniture, and family portraits. The castle has a walled garden that is a delight in summer.

A short distance from here is the city of Inverness, the capital of the Highlands. The city stands astride the River Ness, which empties Loch Ness into the sea, at the northern end of the Great Glen. The Great Glen is the geologic fault that runs from Loch Linnhe to the Moray Firth and divides the Central and Northern Highlands. The Caledonia Canal, constructed by Thomas Telford in 1803–1821, links the deep, freshwater lochs and rivers to form a natural waterway across the Highlands.

Inverness's importance as a strategic site is attested to by the wealth of prehistoric burial cairns, carved stones, and monuments found here. St. Columba visited Brude, king of the Picts, at his capital beside the Ness. Inverness has been fought over by so many tempestuous Highland clans and warring kingdoms that there are precious few buildings of any age left standing. Most of the architecture in Inverness is of the nineteenth century. The Inverness Museum contains many relics of the famous and powerful Highland clans. The nineteenth-century castle stands on the site of several former castles, and its esplanade bears a statue of Flora MacDonald, the woman who helped Bonnie Prince Charlie to safety on the Isle of Skye before he fled to permanent exile in France. Six miles (9.6 km) east of Inverness is the Culloden Battlefield, where the final Jacobite uprising led by the Bonnie Prince's army was cruelly defeated by the Duke of Cumberland's forces. The duke has gone down in history as "Butcher Cumberland" because of his brutality toward prisoners and the injured. A Visitor Center on the site has maps and information detailing the events of this horrendous battle.

Loch Ness is world famous for Nessie, the monster who reputedly resides in the incredibly deep loch. Some lochs in this area are deeper than the North Sea. The first sighting of the monster was reported in the eighth century by St. Adamnan in his biography of St. Columba. Since then Nessie has been seen by many people, including thirty people in a hotel by the Loch, but all the latest equipment and sonar cameras have not been able to detect sight nor sound of the creature. Cruises on the lochs are popular, but not many people would want to spend a night on Loch Ness!

Culloden House Hotel, outside the city, is extremely elegant with a beautiful drawing room to the right of the entrance with huge log fires, deeply cushioned furniture, and splendid carpets. Ian Mackenzie, the owner, with his wife, Marjory, is usually on hand to see that one is comfortable. Windows from this lovely room overlook the very wide stretch of lawn that fronts the house with driveways on each side. Here at six in the evening every evening a kilted Highlander playing his bagpipe marches back and forth across the grass to the delight of the guests. Bedrooms are spacious and well appointed. Michael Simpson is the head chef, and meals are luxurious, beautifully presented, and delicious.

Durain Park, one mile (1.6 km) outside the city, owned and managed by Ann and Edward Nicoll, is a relaxing place to stay. There are a sauna and swimming pool to ease you into an evening in which the main feature is Ann Nicoll's wonderful inventive cooking. Ingredients are impeccable, and she loves nothing better than to juxtapose different flavors and textures to create delicious and unique dishes. Not suprisingly, the menu changes daily, and you could probably stay here for months without getting the same dish twice. Desserts are traditional, on the other hand, all the wonderful steamed puds, to be followed later, if you wish, with a single malt from Edward Nicoll's enormous collection.

Ivy Cottage restaurant a few minutes from the city center at Muirtown Locks has excellent unpretentious food cooked by Paul Whitecross in a pretty and rather quaint attic dining room.

The Dower House at Highfield, Muir of Ord, is situated close to the end of Beauty Firth on A862. As you would expect, the Dower House is an ancient house set in a beautiful garden with spacious, old-fashioned rooms. The atmosphere is restful and the food well cooked and imaginatively spiced by Robyn Aitchison.

The A82 will take you the length of the lochs and rivers that connect Loch Ness to Loch Linnhe across the Highlands. About sixteen miles (25.7 km) outside Inverness at Drumnadrochit is the Loch Ness Monster Exhibition Centre with information and photographs that tell all there is to know about Nessie. Here too is Urquhart Castle, once one of the largest castles in Scotland and now a romantic ruin against the hills overlooking Loch Ness. Farther on is Neptune's Staircase—eight lochs linked by the Caledonian Canal—that lowers the water level by ninety feet (27 meters) in the two miles (3.2 km) between Loch Lochy and Loch Linnhe. The canal links the North Sea to the Atlantic.

At the conjunction of Loch Linnhe and Loch Eil is Fort William, named for William III, who built a fort here in 1690 to keep the rebellious Scots in order. It featured in the Jacobite uprisings in 1715 and 1745 and was finally dismantled in 1855. Fort William is a tourist base for climbers of Ben Nevis, Britain's highest mountain. A footpath outside the town leads to the summit, and a race is held annually up to the summit and back. Ben Nevis is not an easy climb; the sheer north face of the mountain challenges the most experienced rock climbers. Skiing on Ben Nevis is increasingly popular. Four miles (6.4 km) north of Fort William there is a new skiing center and a gondola system for taking skiers, and people who just want to see the glorious views, up to the slopes. The Glen Nevis river race also takes place here. Fort William is ideal as a base for touring the region as several roads, as well as two lochs, converge here. In the countryside near Fort William farmers make dewy fresh handmade cheeses. Glencoe is a full-fat, mild, soft goat's cheese, and Caledonia is a semi-hard goat's cheese that is sometimes mixed with chives, pepper, or garlic.

With water everywhere you look from lochs, rivers, streams, and the canal, this is an area exceedingly rich in fish and shellfish. Fat langoustine prawns are available all along the west coast of Scotland and also in Loch Linnhe. Oysters cluster at Oban where Loch Linnhe meets the Firth of Lorn, scallops are bountiful at the Kyle of Lochalsh near the Isle of Skye, and mussels and surf clams come from Argyll. All of this wonderful fresh seafood is taken splendid advantage of by the Crannog Seafood Restaurant on the town pier at Fort William. Crannog means fortified island, often man-made, on which dwelt a self-contained community whose livelihood was almost always fishing. The Crannog Scottish Seafoods concept was started by Finlay Finlayson, initially as a way for fishermen to sell their fish directly to major towns and cities in Scotland. The fledgling company moved to Fort William in 1981. As the business expanded, with enthusiastic support from buyers and chefs throughout the United Kingdom, a smokehouse was established on Blar Mohr, Fort William, to produce smoked salmon, gravadlax, smoked trout, smoked trout pâté, smoked mussels, and fresh-cooked langoustine. These are marketed to restaurants and stores such as Harrods. In 1989 Crannog Limited converted the bait store on Fort William town pier to a restaurant, making possible a food chain that goes from the source—fishermen—to processing when needed, and then directly to the customer. In 1991 a second restaurant was opened in Glasgow, and now Crannog's sights are set on Edinburgh. This all boils down to but one point, that Fort William Town Pier Seafood Restaurant is the place to go for fabulous seafood. If you are lucky enough to get a table by the window, you can eat the specialty of the house—steaming garlicky langoustine—while looking at the long and glorious view down Loch Linnhe. As you would expect, salmon is strongly featured on the menus, either as gravadlax or smoked, and there are almost a dozen different varieties of white fish served in ways that make the most of their good fresh flavors. Susan Trowbridge is the talented chef. The following recipe has been contributed to the book by Crannog Scottish Seafood.

Hake in a Fresh Herb Crust

3 T. chopped fresh herbs—dill, chives, basil, tarragon, or parsley
6 oz. bread crumbs (1⅔ C.), slightly dried
1½ t. crushed garlic
2–4 T. olive oil
1½ lb. hake fillets
 tomato or parsley sauce

1. Preheat oven to 375°F (or gas mark 5).
2. Mix the herbs, bread crumbs, and garlic together. Season.
3. Pour on the olive oil a little at a time until you get a moist, but not soggy, consistency.
4. Spread the mixture over the fish fillets and bake on a lightly oiled shallow dish for 12–15 minutes.
5. Serve with a tomato or parsley sauce. *Serves 3*

Approximately ten miles (16 km) south of Fort William, on what is now the A828, the road turns inland to Glencoe. Glencoe means Glen of Weeping and it is an appropriate name, for here, on February 13, 1692, the Macdonalds of Glencoe were slaughtered as they slept by their guests, Campbell of Glenlyon and his 128 soldiers, who for several days had accepted the Macdonalds' hospitality. In the village of Glencoe a tall slender cross—the Massacre Memorial—is a poignant reminder of this dishonorable act. The Glencoe and North Lorne Folk Museum consists of a group of thatched cottages filled to the brim with Jacobite and other historic exhibits, as well as domestic implements, dolls, dollhouses, costumes, photographs, and much besides. Rannoch Moor stretches beyond Glencoe, a wild and desolate area of swamp and wasteland inhabited only by birds.

Farther down Loch Linnhe in Port Appin is the Airds Hotel, which in the sixteenth century was a ferry inn and is now a charming, white stucco hotel with a wide conservatory that takes in the wonderful views over the gardens and the loch. The vibrant, flower-filled Airds Hotel is run by the Allen family. Two sitting rooms are prettily furnished in flowery prints with comfortable places to relax beside the fire, which is always brightly burning. Aperitifs and after-dinner coffee are generally served in the sitting rooms. Bedrooms are similarly furnished with comfortable chairs and ample bathrooms. The dining room has pristine white linen tied with tartan ribbon. Betty Allen has won the Chef Laureate Award from the British Academy of Gastronomes, and the food here is excellent in every way. The cooking looks simple, but this is deceptive—food that zings with flavor such as this is only achieved with consummate skill. Fish and shellfish are fresher than fresh, admirably and lightly sauced with intense herbal oils or smidgeons of ginger or coriander. Betty Allen is assisted in the kitchen by son Graeme, and the great good food is complemented by Eric Allen's long and wide-ranging wine list.

Oban, a fishing port protected by the island of Kerrera, provides a safe haven for the fishing boats, cruisers, and ferries that ply the waters. Most of the hustle and bustle in the town is around the harbor, which is lined with hotels and boarding houses. The town is built on Oban Bay and is backed by a range of hills. Though Oban is the livestock market town for the surrounding area and the islands, the town's mainstay now is tourism. Ferries leave frequently for the Isle of Mull and the Inner and Outer Hebrides. Dominating the skyline of Oban is McCaig's Tower, financed by a banker, John Stuart McCaig, to employ some of the townspeople who were out of work. When he died the construction halted, and the remains look like a towering unfinished Roman Colosseum.

South of Oban is the Knipoch Hotel, owned by the Craig family. The hotel has views overlooking Loch Feochan. Award-winning cooking here is achieved through the Craigs' passion for exemplary ingredients—freshly gathered wild mushrooms, home-smoked salmon and trout, and home-baked breads—and attention to all the details that make up a satisfying dining experience. Colin and Jenny Craig are the cooking team responsible for the wonders performed in the kitchen.

The Manor House on Gallanach Road, Oban, offers great Scottish-French food, specializing in fish dishes. The house was built by the duke of Argyll in 1780 and later became a dower house. The views here are splendid, and the Manor House is a very comfortable place to stay.

Highland farmhouses produce many variations of Crowdie cottage cheese. Among them is Highland Crowdie low-fat and high-protein, Hramsa Crowdie mixed with chopped wild garlic leaves in cream, and a similar low-fat version without the cream and Grun Dhu—Crowdie and cream cheese mixed and rolled in crushed peppercorns. Galic is soft, full-fat with chopped wild garlic leaves rolled in oats, almonds, and hazelnuts. Caboc is a buttery curd, double cream with a toasted pinhead oatmeal crust.

Potatoes and barley grow in the Highlands—it is too cool for wheat. Potatoes are a nourishing and therefore important part of the Highland diet. Clapshot is a favorite specialty of Scotland traditionally served very hot with haggis.

Clapshot

1 lb. potatoes
1 lb. rutabagas (Swedes)
2   heaped T. butter
4 t.   chopped chives or shallots
2 t.   salt
       freshly ground black pepper, to taste

Garnish: additional melted butter

1. Peel potatoes and rutabagas and cut into chunks.
2. Cook vegetables separately in boiling salted water until completely cooked through.
3. Drain and return to their respective pots and dry vegetables out.
4. Mash potatoes and rutabagas to a smooth purée—use a ricer if you wish but not a food processor.
5. Stir in the two tablespoons of butter and the chopped chives and season with the salt and black pepper, to taste.
6. Serve clapshot very hot with additional melted butter.

Serves 4–6

The Isle of Skye in the Inner Hebrides is an enchanting place associated with legends and folklore. The scenery changes with the rapidly shifting light—one minute misty with cloud and the next shot through with brilliant sunshine. Dramatic mountains over 3,000 feet (914 meters) high, called the Black Cuillins, present a challenge to the most intrepid climbers. Encircling Loch Coruisk, these mountains are interspersed with steep ravines and topped with sharp, craggy peaks. Across the glen facing the Black Cuillins are the Red Cuillins, whose rounded peaks of rose granite, though more benign, should also be climbed with caution. Almost 60 percent of the people of Skye speak Gaelic—there is even a Gaelic University here. Most people earn their livelihood by crofting, forestry, or tourism. Traditionally crofters live on small-holdings with a few sheep, cattle, and poultry. If the land is fertile, crofters grow potatoes and hay for their cattle. Sheepshearing, peat cutting, and such like are often performed communally. As the holdings are so small, it is virtually impossible to make a living from crofting, and to earn extra funds many crofters will plant in the spring, fish or do construction work in summer, and return to help with the communal harvesting in autumn. Young people leave for periods to work on the coasts in hotels or as domestics during high tourist seasons, or take seasonal work in fish-processing plants. Though some croft houses have electricity and gas, peat is still burned for heat. At one time in far-flung islands, livestock shared the dwelling with the crofters.

At Isleornsay in Sleat on the Isle of Skye is Kinloch Lodge, once a shooting lodge on the vast Macdonald estates, and now a ten-room hotel beautifully managed by Lord and Lady Macdonald. Claire Macdonald, the author of at least ten cookery books, needs no introduction here. The atmosphere in the lodge is like that of a private country house, which, as it is also home to the Macdonalds and their four children, is not surprising. Views are breathtaking whichever way you look. Some of the comfortable, pretty bedrooms look over Loch Na Dal. Food here is marvelous with all those well-thought-out touches that one would expect from such an accomplished cook as Lady Macdonald. Four-course menus change daily with a choice between two or three dishes at each course. Cheeses, many of them from unpasteurized milk, are an important part of the meal and feature in soup as well on occasion. Desserts are absolutely divine—especially the chocolate profiteroles. The dining room at Kinloch is spacious and quite splendid, lined as it is with portraits of members of the Macdonald clan, and furnished with lovely antiques, silver, and crystal. Breakfast begins with a wide selection of dishes set out on the deep sideboard, and the choices are difficult to make among the juice, various stewed fruits, yogurts, and cereals. Freshly made scones are served with homemade marmalade, followed by hot porridge with cream and a plethora of eggs, bacon, black and white puddings, tomatoes, and sausage, or a dish of buttery plump kippers. After all this the pretty flowery walks through the grounds offer gentle but welcome exercise.

Not far from the lodge is Armadale Castle, built by Gillespie Graham in 1815 and owned by the Macdonalds. Part of the castle is crumbling, and another part has been restored and holds the Clan Macdonald Centre and Museum that tell of the Lords of the Isles and Clan Macdonald. A forty-acre woodland nature preserve has nature walks, gardens, and an arboretum. There are a children's play area and a well-stocked gift shop and restaurant in the restored coach house and stables.

The seat of Clan Macdonald since at least the 1200s is Dunvegan Castle, set on a rocky ledge overlooking Loch Dunvegan. At one time the only access was by sea, but now a bridge spans the dry moat bed. The castle has many interesting things to see including the Fairy Flag—reputedly a parting gift to the fourth chief of the clan from his fairy wife after they had been man and wife for twenty years. The Fairy Flag has powers to ward off disaster—but apparently not marital disaster!

At Colbost, Dunvegan, is the Three Chimneys Restaurant, owned by Eddie and Shirley Spear. The chef here is Shirley Spear, who is staunch in her loyalty to fresh, wholesome ingredients from the Isle of Skye. Fish and shellfish dishes are stupendous, featuring crab, lobster, clams, mussels, oysters, and prawns all topped with delightful sauces. Soups are terrific, and if meat is preferred there is a wide choice from succulent baby lamb to well-hung game.

The history of many of the Highland clans goes back to the Viking era. Each member of a clan took the surname of the clan chief—through loyalty if not by blood. Clan members were committed to one another and devoted to their chief, who ruled over them, meted out justice, and could call on the members of the clan to fight beside him at a moment's notice. The prefix "mac" means "son of." The wearing of the tartan dates to the thirteenth century, though the bright, colorful patterns worn then may not have looked the way tartans look today. After the Battle of Culloden in 1746, the Suppression of the Highlands broke up the clans and forbade the wearing of tartan to civilians. Tartans survived through the Scottish Regiments, who wore different patterns to distinguish one regiment from another. They became popular once more after royalty began wearing them about seventy-five years later on their visits to Scotland. Clan feelings can still run strong on occasion, and many Highlanders still have a yearning for the old days. Highland gatherings and Games are held not only in Scotland but in America, Canada, Australia, and New Zealand. Scots attend in their clan tartans to watch their fellow Scots perform feats requiring great strength. Lads and lassies dance Scottish reels to the music of a piper, and colorful woolen tam-o'-shanters are the order of the day. Due to the twenty million American and Canadian Scots, who are fiercely proud of their heritage, there is now a worldwide renewal of the great clan spirit. The majority of clan chiefs in Scotland are large landowners and farmers and feel it their responsibility to maintain the land and preserve their heritage for clansmen all over the world. The chiefs of the clans and their families still occupy their baronial castles in many parts of Scotland. Some of these are Inveraray Castle in the West Highland county of Argyll, Invercauld

Castle in Aberdeenshire, Broomhall in Dumferline, Achnacarry Castle in Inverness-shire, and Duntrune Castle on the Isle of Jura, which has recently been renovated and is the oldest continuously inhabited castle in Scotland.

During the Suppression of the Highlands in the mid-1700s, it was expedient for various Highland chieftains to leave the Highlands. Some were taken into custody and transported, and others, parted from their clans and their way of life, went to live in cities abroad to wait out the difficult situation. Eventually, deprived of their livelihood, some of them were pressed into renting their lands in the Highlands to sheep farmers from southern counties who needed more pasturage but did not want smallholders on the land. Many Highland chiefs paid the crofters' travel expenses to emigrate, others helped them move to coastal areas and started them off in fishing businesses, and some simply evicted the crofters with the help of agents. This dreadful period of history is known as the Highland Clearances. Many families scattered and ended up swelling city populations already looking for work. For awhile kelp farming on the islands was a way to stay afloat—the seaweed was turned into fertilizer—but the bottom dropped out of this market in the early 1800s due to cheap foreign competition. The Highlands were depopulated further by the same virulent potato famine that decimated Ireland. Spores from the potato blight borne on the wind wiped out the Scottish potato crops that sustained half the population. Thousands starved, and those who could emigrated to the former colonies. Since this heartbreaking period, the rights of crofters are strictly upheld by the Crofting Commission. Though the Highlands and the Islands have been an official economic district since 1965, covering one-sixth of the entire landmass of Britain, a scant 7 percent of Scotland's population live here now.

The Inner and Outer Hebrides, Orkney, and Shetland Isles are slowly losing their young people, who emigrate to make their way in less harsh climates. Winds in the winter months are fierce, scouring the land with pitiless force. In summer, when the days are very long, the grass grows well and nourishes Highland livestock. Crops of potatoes and barley thrive, but it is too cold for wheat. Scotland's fierce clansmen and inhospitable climate even deterred the Romans, who retreated to Hadrian's Wall. Vikings from the north fought and subdued the islands from the Shetlands down to the Isle of Man. Christianity came to the Hebrides with St. Columba, and pilgrims today still sail to Iona to visit the Benedictine Priory he founded. The Scotti tribe from Ireland helped spread Catholicism, and many parts of Scotland are staunchly Roman Catholic. Some of the southern islands are almost solidly Catholic—Eriskay, for example—and the northern islands around the Isle of Lewis and Harris are mainly Protestant. Around these lochs and islands shellfish such as clams and mussels are very plentiful.

Seafood Soup

2	pints mussels
3	garlic cloves, coarsely chopped
16 fl.oz.	white wine (2 C.)
	salt and freshly ground black pepper
½ lb.	swordfish steak or monkfish, cut into strips
½ lb.	fresh shrimp, shelled and deveined
2 T.	unsalted butter
3	shallots, thinly sliced
4 fl.oz.	heavy cream
2 t.	minced parsley

1. Scrub mussels and remove beards, if any, discarding mussels that do not close tightly when tapped, or any broken-shelled mussels.

2. Place mussels, garlic, white wine, and salt and pepper in a deep, lidded saucepan. Cover and set over medium high heat. Remove mussels as they open to a large bowl, and when cool enough to handle take mussels out of their shells and keep warm. Pour any mussel liquid back into saucepan with cooking liquid. Discard shells.

3. Strain cooking liquid through a sieve lined with cheesecloth and set aside.

4. Melt butter in a heavy frying pan, add shallots, and soften over medium heat. Add to the shallots the swordfish strips and the shrimp—cut in half if large. Stir for 2 or 3 minutes or until just cooked and transfer with a slotted spoon to a warm place.

5. Pour reserved mussel liquid into frying pan with juices from seafood and boil briskly to reduce a little.

6. Whisk in cream and cook for one minute, stirring. Remove from heat.

7. To serve, divide seafood between four wide warmed soup bowls, pour an equal amount of soup into each bowl, sprinkle with parsley, and serve with salad and crusty granary bread.   *Serves 4*

Not all of the Highlands by any means have fierce wind and cold temperatures. An ocean current, the North Atlantic Drift, combines with prevailing winds along the west coast that enable palm trees and semitropical plants to flourish alongside hardy oaks and maples. Inverewe Garden at Inverewe, near Poolewe, was started by Osgood Mackenzie, son of the laird of Gairloch, on a peninsula of land given to him in 1862, barren save for heather.

Though soil had to be brought in by basket, this persevering man built first a windbreak of pine trees and then set about collecting plants from all over the globe. Today the garden is set on a steep incline, sheltered by hills at the top and projecting into the loch at the bottom, with over 2,500 plant species. Rock gardens, palm trees, ornamental pools, meandering woodland paths, and an extensive collection of flowering species make it hard to remember you are in the northern reaches of Scotland. Interesting gardens are abundant in Scotland; wherever you are, there will be one within an hour's drive at most. Some of these are Broderick Castle on the Isle of Arran; Arduaine, in Argyll on the west coast of Scotland; Crarae on Loch Fyne, belonging to Sir Ilay and Lady Campbell; the Royal Botanic Garden, Edinburgh; and Logan Botanic Garden, near Stranraer.

The Highlands of Scotland are scented with heather and pine trees and contain some of Britain's most fascinating scenery. By the late 1800s they had become fashionable among wealthy sports enthusiasts from as far away as Brazil for the hunting seasons. From August 12 the hills are alive with the sound of gunfire, and peers of the realm, rich industrialists, and their entourages sweep through the gorse and heather accompanied by hounds and ghillies. Castles and manor houses in some places have been converted into luxury hotels.

A pleasant fifty-mile (80.4-km) drive will take you from Inverewe Gardens to Ullapool on the northern shore of Loch Broom. On the opposite bank of the loch is the Altnaharrie Inn, where if you telephone someone will send a launch to pick you up at the pier. Ten minutes by launch will save you a long, rough ride to the inn by car. Altnaharrie, owned and managed by Fred Brown and Gunn Eriksen, was an eighteenth-century drovers' inn when they bought it, and now it is possibly Scotland's most acclaimed inn, primarily for Gunn Eriksen's cooking, which has won her two Michelin Stars. The sparkling whitewashed inn stands right on the shingle that is lapped by the waters of the loch just outside their garden gate. The flower-filled dining room is also whitewashed and looks out to the pretty garden and over Loch Broom. Polished tables are adorned with Norwegian silver and glassware. Gunn Eriksen is from Norway, and her cooking is a lively blend of fresh flavors and different textures, which add intrigue and anticipation to the elegant meal. Except for desserts, a set menu is offered, which changes daily depending on the availability of ingredients. The Highlands' abundant game, local lamb, or marvelous fresh fish and shellfish, sometimes tucked inside buttery pastry cases, are some of the main dishes, and everything is served with Gunn Eriksen's imaginative sauces. Dessert is a difficult choice between featherlight cakes, crumbly fruit tarts—perhaps rhubarb, apple, pear, or cherry—or luscious chocolate and creamy confections. Coffee is served in one of the two attractive sitting rooms, and sometimes petits fours include chocolate truffles. The bedrooms are pretty and comfortable, and though you might find a flashlight beside your bed, you will not find a television set or a telephone. The total peace here is as welcome as Gunn Eriksen's sublime food, and the heather-clad hills have trails for both exercise and fine views.

Once back on dry land in Ullapool, take the A835 to Drumrunie and then a left onto a small road that goes around a tiny peninsula until you reach Achiltibuie and the Summer Isles Hotel. The village street is lined with croft houses, and spectacular views over the water on a clear day take in the Isles for which the hotel is named and the Hebrides beyond, though in fact summery scarcely describes the Isles, as in reality they are rather forbidding. Mark and Geraldine Irvine own and manage the hotel and have since the 1960s. Chris Firth-Bernard cooks with flair and finesse, and the fresh tastes are truly wonderful. He takes advantage of fish straight from the bay's sparkling clean waters, and everything else is grown or raised on the spot. The hotel has a hydroponicum that provides fresh vegetables and fruits, a dairy, a poultry yard, its own smokehouse, and solar panels. All this makes the hotel practically self-sufficient. This is a perfect place to get away from it all, and the peace here is profound.

Crab Tart

---

		shortcrust pastry for 9-inch tart shell
1	lb.	lump crabmeat
3		eggs
¼	t.	salt and freshly ground pepper, to taste
6	fl.oz.	whipping cream (¾ C.)
2	fl.oz.	buttermilk (¼ C.)
1	T.	grated Parmesan
1	T.	grated Dunlop
1	t.	minced dill
1		slice day-old bread, toasted

1. Preheat oven to 425°F (or gas mark 7).
2. Roll out pastry, position evenly inside 9-inch pie plate, and flute edges. Line with foil to cover rim and add pie wieghts or dried beans.
3. Bake for 9 minutes. Remove from oven and discard foil and beans. Cool.
4. Meanwhile pick over crabmeat and discard any cartilage. Separate eggs, reserving whites, and beat yolks with salt, pepper, cream, buttermilk, cheeses, and dill.
5. Break the toasted bread into pieces and whirl in a food processor to make fine bread crumbs.
6. Using a teaspoon or two of egg white, paint the inside of the tart shell, then sprinkle bottom of tart shell with bread crumbs.
7. Add crab to egg yolk mixture and fold in gently without breaking up the lumps.

8. Whisk remaining egg whites until stiff, fold into crab mixture, and immediately pour into tart shell, making sure crab is evenly distributed.

9. Put tart in oven and reduce heat to 375°F (or gas mark 5). Bake for 35 minutes or until filling is just set. Serve straightaway with a green salad. *Serves 6*

A ferry from Ullapool chugs through the loch and on to the Outer Hebrides. On Lewis and Harris weaving is part of the crofter's life, especially in winter months when there is less to do on the land. To qualify for the Harris Tweed Association's orb stamp of approval, three-yard lengths of handwoven cloth must be made from pure Scottish virgin wool, spun, dyed, and finished in the Outer Hebrides. Some weavers still make natural dyes using the colors from ragwort, buttercups, bracken, and moss. The big island has a dish similar to Ireland's colcannon called kailkenny—both are made with potatoes, cabbage, and onions, sometimes kale, and on Lewis they add a carrot or two.

The seas around these islands are rich in salmon—always one of Scotland's most prized foods. Today not only fish are winning accolades but homemade cheeses are becoming much sought after—particularly those from Orkney, which are perfectly delicious, whether the hard cheese that is great for snacking and cooking or the luscious soft cheeses that are so versatile they even fill sweet pastries. Kirkwall, the capital of Orkney, is one of the oldest towns and at one time was a Norse trading post. The remains of the Bishop's Palace and the ancient St. Magnus cathedral form the nucleus of the town. Ten miles (16 km) west is Maes Howe—the finest Stone Age burial cairn in Britain. Its huge buttressed chamber is lit from a beam of sunlight on the winter solstice that reaches the chamber through a perfectly aligned stone passageway. Burial cells are to be found directly off the chamber. A leisurely twenty-minute drive from Kirkwall along the historic Churchill Barriers will take you to St. Margaret's Hope, the principal village on the island of South Ronaldsay, joined to Lamb Holm by four miles (6.4 km) of causeway. The village is named for Princess Margaret of Norway. During the voyage taking her to England to marry Prince Edward, the seven-year-old Maid of Norway died of seasickness. The ship that bore the tiny body put in at South Ronaldsay.

On Front Road in St. Margaret's Hope is the Creel Restaurant and Rooms owned by Joyce and Alan Craigie. Opened in May 1985, the restaurant, due to the excellent cooking of Alan Craigie, has won numerous awards including an A. A. Rosette and Taste of Britain Scotland Winner 1986 and Scottish Tourist Board 3 Crown Commended. There are three spacious bedrooms, all with private facilities and fantastic views over the sea. Nearby are a tennis court and bowling green. Alan Craigie takes full advantage of the quality of local produce and seafood. He says his favorite dishes are mussels cooked in cider, tomatoes, garlic, and onion; or perhaps grilled filet steak with whisky sauce; or maybe scallops sautéed in garlic butter. He admits that his favorite list could possibly be endless, as he genuinely loves good and well-prepared food. All his suppliers are located on the Orkney Islands. Dishes on his menu include Cullen Skink—a typically Scottish creamy smoked haddock soup; Fresh crab with salad; Braised Cockie chicken, on a bed of root vegetables with mustard sauce; Scallops seared on a hot charcoal grill, with lentil and coriander sauce; Roast monkfish tails with fresh herb butter, garnished with rhubarb; Baked salmon wrapped in puff pastry with ginger and currants and tarragon sauce; and Lemon sole stuffed and garnished with Scapa Flow prawns. Desserts are luscious Chocolate mousse, meringues, and crème caramel served in a brandy snap basket with butterscotch sauce, Echna Loch Swan—pastry swan floated on a loch of raspberry and drambuie coulis—and homemade Strawberry shortcake. Alan Craigie has kindly given us three recipes for this book.

Clootie Dumpling

6 oz. self-raising flour (1 C. + 2 T.) (if using plain flour, add a half
        teaspoon of baking powder)
6 oz. brown bread crumbs (1½ C.)
6 oz. suet (1½ C.)
4 oz. currants (½ C.)
6 oz. raisins (¾ C.)
6 oz. sultanas (¾ C.)
1 t.   baking soda
       dash of ginger, nutmeg, cinnamon
4 oz. soft dark brown sugar (½ C.)
2 T.   syrup
1 C.   milk

1. Mix all ingredients.
2. Boil pudding cloth and coat with flour.
3. Put mixture in cloth and tie with string.
4. Boil for 2 to 3 hours.   *Serves* 10–12

Beremeal Bannocks

4 oz.   plain flour (¾ C.)
1 t.   salt
2   heaped t. baking soda
1   heaped t. cream of tartar
12 oz. beremeal (3 C.) (barley flour)

2 oz.   butter (½ stick)
20 fl.oz. buttermilk (2½ C.)

1. Sieve flour, salt, soda, and tartar, then add beremeal.
2. Rub in butter, then mix in enough buttermilk to form a soft dough.
3. Shape into flat cakes and cook on a hot griddle for 2 to 3 minutes each side, approximately.   *Makes 12 bannocks*

Roast Pears with Honey Baskets and Coffee Bean Sauce

Honey baskets

4 oz. butter (1 stick)
4 oz. castor sugar (½ C.)
4 oz. honey or syrup (½ C.)
4 oz. plain flour (¾ C.)

1. Preheat oven to 400°F (or gas mark 4–5).
2. Melt the butter in a pan, add the castor sugar and honey, and mix well.
3. Blend in the flour and allow to cool.
4. Roll out into small balls and place on baking sheet.
5. Bake for 5 to 10 minutes.
6. Remove from baking sheet while still warm and carefully place over a small inverted muffin tin to form baskets.

Coffee bean sauce

10 fl.oz. milk (1¼ C.)
6 T.   castor sugar
1 t.   ground coffee
3   egg yolks

7. Bring the milk to a gentle simmer with half the sugar, then remove from heat.
8. Add the ground coffee and leave to infuse for about 15 minutes.
9. In a bowl whip the egg yolks and remaining sugar until light and creamy.
10. In a heavy-bottomed pan gently heat the sauce until it thickens, stirring all the time. (Be very careful not to overheat the sauce as it *will* curdle.)

Roast pears

4		pears
4	oz.	sugar (½ C.)

11. Peel and core the pears, being careful to retain the stems.

12. Poach the pears in 20 fluid ounces of water with 2 ounces (¼ C.) of sugar until tender.

13. Slice pears into five pieces.

14. Sprinkle with remaining sugar and roast with blowtorch, or place under preheated broiler to brown.

15. Place pears on warmed plate, garnish with honey basket, and spoon coffee bean sauce over pears and around plate.   *Serves* 4

Sixty miles (96.5 km) north of Orkney are the Shetland Isles with a surprisingly mild climate, considering that they are halfway to Norway. Only fifteen isles in the hundred-island archipelago are inhabited. People on these far-flung islands speak Gaelic, which is quite distinct from the Gaelic spoken in Ireland, and English as a second language. In Scotland, Gaelic is taught in schools, and there are numerous Gaelic publications available. Recently modern Gaelic music has increased dramatically in popularity through Scottish music groups who perform both live and on radio and television.

Dairy farming and vegetables thrive on the main island. Shetland ponies roam the hills, and sheep farming is important. Shetland sheep have very fine wool, and a true Shetland shawl is fine enough to pull through a wedding ring. Shetland sweaters are world renowned, and before the oil boom crofters lived by crofting, fishing, and knitting. Life has been made easier lately by the oil, while fortunately supply ships and offshore oil rigs affect only a part of one island.

The old way of pickling foods to preserve them is still being taught to young housewives by their mothers and grandmothers. Despite the use of refrigerator and freezer, the cured meat is not only a long-standing tradition but the flavor is a welcome change and can be delicious. The meat is pickled in a brine of salt and water for three or four weeks, depending on the size, then hung to dry over burning peat until it is as hard as a rock.

The Shetland Islanders are not given to waste of any kind—as well as making good use of the regular cuts of meat, on the Shetland Islands the insides of an animal are made to yield many delicacies. Tripe has always been a favorite here, stuffed with savory bread, onions, and dried fruit, or with spiced fillings sweetened with treacle. Blood puddings, both red and white, are boiled and served hot. Cold pudding is delicious sliced and fried or grilled for breakfast. Haggis is probably the most famous dish in Scotland, and it is traditionally eaten on Hogmanay (New Year's Eve), or on Burns Night, the world over.

11

NORTHERN IRELAND

Northern Ireland, part of the United Kingdom, comprises six of the nine counties of Ulster—Antrim, Armagh, Down, Fermanagh, Londonderry, and Tyrone. The other three—Cavan, Donegal, and Monaghan—are part of the Republic of Ireland, which gained its independence from Britain in 1921. Northern Ireland does have a heritage of good peasant cooking. Two Northern Irish regional dishes, made from superb potatoes grown in Ireland's uncontaminated soil, are champ (floury mashed potatoes mixed with chopped scallions softened in hot milk, served in a healthy-sized mound with a well of melted butter in the top) and fadge (a flat, golden potato cake, cooked on a griddle and served in wedges slathered with butter). Soft rather than crusty soda bread is also associated with the north. Butter is superb in Northern Ireland, as are all dairy products. However, following World War II, when the United Kingdom oversaw the distribution of food, and most of it cheaper foods, Northern Ireland adopted a policy of convenience and speed. Supermarkets were the preferred places to shop, and the honest to goodness homegrown fresh foods sometimes seem to have been bypassed. In the capital, Belfast, there are a great many cafés and restaurants that don't seem to have been influenced a great deal by the movement toward fresh foods that has swept the southern counties, but there are always exceptions. In the Lisburn Road area are several good places to buy superior quality olive oils, pasta, Irish farmhouse cheeses, organic yogurt and vegetables, well-butchered meats, fresh fish, good breads, and excellent prepared foods.

Champ Irish Potato and Scallion Purée

2	lb.	floury potatoes—not suitable for new potatoes
4		bunches of scallions
2	fl.oz.	milk (¼ C.)
3	T.	butter
5	fl.oz.	single cream or milk (½ C. + 2 T.)
		salt and pepper, to taste
		pinch of nutmeg
		additional melted butter

1. Peel and cut the potatoes into quarters. Place in a saucepan of salted water, bring to a boil, and cook until potatoes are tender, about 25 minutes. Drain.

2. Meanwhile, thoroughly wash the scallions and trim the root end and any coarse leaves. Slice scallions, including some of the pale green part. Place in a saucepan with the milk and simmer gently for 3 or 4 minutes, stirring. Set aside.

3. Rice the potatoes with a handheld food mill or press through a sieve. Return to saucepan and dry over low heat for a second or two before beating in the scallion mixture and the butter and cream. Season to taste with salt, pepper, and nutmeg.

4. Serve piping hot with additional butter. *Serves 4*

Note: Traditionally, champ is mounded on the plate, and a depression is made in the top that is filled with melted butter. Each forkful of champ is dipped in the butter before eating.

Some of the most beautiful, rugged scenery on the island is found in the north, particularly along the splendid Antrim coast. The tourist boards of Northern Ireland and the Republic have produced one map for the spectacular coast of the nine counties of Ulster. From Larne above Belfast Lough to Portrush in the north, the sixty-mile road hugs the shore as it dips and soars, revealing a breathtaking coastline of churning sea or tranquil bay on the one hand, and on the other sweeping glens where rivers rush through green sloped valleys down to meet the sea. South in County Down the varied granites of the Mourne Mountains, catching the evening light, sparkle in a rainbow of color. Northern Ireland comprises 5,000 square miles of the most spectacular scenery and geologic wonders to be seen in Great Britain. The Giant's Causeway is believed to have been flung down by the legendary giant Finn MacCool, who crossed the sea to Scotland on its basalt columns, returning the same way. Broad sandy beaches line the shore. The Antrim Mountains swoop down to deep lakes (loughs), and form

the scenic Glens of Antrim. Mountains near the shore tower over narrow inlets very like Norway's fjords. Pristine lakes, rivers, and streams make this a fisherman's paradise. The largest lough in Northern Ireland is Lough Neagh, which gives rise to the River Blackwater that flows the length of Ireland, finally crossing County Cork on its way to the sea.

The Northern Irish are united in a deep and abiding love of their country. Nowhere is this more apparent than in Belfast, the capital of Northern Ireland. Belfast is situated on the mouth of the River Lagan at the head of Belfast Lough. Green, unspoiled mountains encircle the city to the north and west. Belfast's wealth was founded on tobacco and flax, from which linen and linseed oil are made. Other towns in the area also prospered on the flax trade, notably Derry, which today is still a busy shirt-making center. Many industries in the region are still involved in cloth, through dying, bleaching, or fabric printing. In 1859 shipyards were constructed at Belfast. The Harland and Wolff shipyard grew famous as the biggest in the world—the *Titanic* was built here. During World War II aircraft carriers came from Belfast's shipyards. The city's former affluence shows in its many architectural treasures. The Renaissance-style City Hall in Donegall Square, with its copper domes outside, Italian marble and stained glass within, is splendid. It was designed by Brumwell Thomas in 1903. Overlooking Donegall Quay is the fine Customs House. Other buildings of historic and architectural interest are Belfast's graceful churches, St. Anne's Cathedral which has mosaics inside by Gertrude Stein, and the Grand Opera House, bedazzling in its newly restored gilt interior. Local granite from the Mountains of Mourne and Portland stone were used to build the Parliament Buildings east of the city center at Stormont.

Belfast is home to a third of Northern Ireland's subjects. The city claims at least 400,000 lively, hospitable people and is packed with wonderful old pubs, pedestrian shopping streets, theaters, and restaurants, many of which are located on or near the Golden Mile, as one restaurant area is called. Belfast's most famous place to dine is Roscoff's on Shaftesbury Square. This is the only restaurant in Northern Ireland to win a Michelin rosette. The spare, stark white and chromed-steel decor offers a subtle contrast to the luxurious ingredients in the dishes at Roscoff's. Owners Paul and Jeanne Rankin have traveled far and wide—Greece, Asia, Australia, Canada, and California—and the eclectic menu reflects their globe-trotting experiences. Paul Rankin insists that the dishes he cooks are simply foods that he and his wife love to eat. Coriander, ginger, and sesame oil add an Asian touch to many dishes, truffles and foie gras reveal the cooking of France, risotto and pesto bring Italy to mind, and California's happy knack with fresh organic vegetables finds a home here, but through it all shine the fresh, impeccable ingredients that are typical of Ireland.

Nick's Warehouse, 35–39 Hill Street, behind St. Anne's Cathedral, is run by Nick and Cathy Price. Nick Price cooks excellent food, using fresh fish, superb shellfish, and sweet, succulent Ulster meats. Some of the vegetables here are organically grown. Local game is featured in the autumn and winter months. Nick Price uses exotic Southeast Asian seasonings with flair—ginger, soy, lemongrass, and chili—yet also with restraint so that the fresh flavors are enhanced rather than masked. Simple foods such as sausages are beautifully cooked, sometimes embellished with a fruit sauce, and dessert leaves you wishing you had room for more.

Restaurant 44 at 44 Bedford Street offers a menu that gleans dishes from around the world. This is a very pleasant place to dine. Fresh fish and crustaceans feature imaginatively in many dishes as well as in mousses and in delicious lobster sauce. Vegetarians are made very welcome with superb vegetarian dishes starring in every course.

Beyond the Golden Mile is the university area. Considered the safest area in Belfast, it boasts many small hotels and bed and breakfast establishments. In the north potato bread, fadge, fried with bacon is often eaten for breakfast, accompanied by the traditional "fry."

Fadge

2	lb.	freshly mashed potatoes
4	T.	butter or bacon fat
4–8	T.	flour—depending on the texture of the potatoes

salt, to taste
additional bacon fat

1. Lightly mix together the mashed potatoes, butter or bacon fat, and flour. Taste for salt.
2. On a floured surface roll out the potato dough to a thickness of ½ inch. Either cut into rounds using a large cookie cutter or slice the dough crosswise into triangles. Prick the dough to release steam during cooking.
3. Grease a griddle with additional bacon fat and fry the potato cakes for 3 to 4 minutes on each side.
4. Serve hot with plenty of creamy butter.   *Makes 8–9 cakes*

Good food and watering holes abound in the university area. One of these is a wine bar cum bistro called the Strand at 12 Stranmillis Street. Michael MacAuley and Donna Donaldson's cooking is very good—fresh flavors speak out—and the wine list features every wine-producing country in the western world. Desserts are absolutely not to be missed.

Belfast's great old Victorian pubs are more than just wateringholes; they are part of the very fabric of the city. People come to spend an evening with friends in a congenial atmosphere. Often there is good bar food, as well as everyman's favorite brew, Guinness stout, Bushmill's excellent whiskey, a wide selections of malt whiskies, and if you are lucky there will be music played and sung by young talented musicians. Some of the best food can be found at the Morning Star at 17 Pottinger's Entry, off Anne Street.

Leaving Belfast and traveling along the southern side of Belfast Lough toward Bangor, on the coast of County Down, are several unexpectly good eating places. Holywood, the town closest to Belfast, has one or two good restaurants. Santé, at 30 High Street, is a friendly spot with good food that is well cooked by Bartjan Brave. Sauces are based on excellent stocks of chicken and fish, farmhouse cheeses are delightful and find their way into tempting salads, some dishes reflect France's beloved bistro cooking with lardoons and cream, flavors are fresh, and an assortment of menus give a very wide selection of dishes. At 27 Church Street is Iona Bistro. Choices are picked from a blackboard, and checkered tablecloths and candles stuck in a wine bottle give ambience. But the cooking says "Ireland" with the best of local lamb spiked with rosemary, lightly grilled spanking fresh fish, and several interesting and delicious vegetarian dishes.

A little further along the Lough is Helen's Bay. Here in the old station building on Station Square is Deane's on the Square. Michael Deane's cooking is innovative, bursting with flavor, and makes good use of local ingredients. You will not be disappointed here.

Risotto with Shellfish and Lemon Butter Sauce

Sauce

8	fl.oz.	dry white wine (1 C.)
2	T.	chopped shallot
1	T.	minced fresh chervil
1	T.	minced fresh tarragon
1	T.	minced fresh parsley
4		white peppercorns
4	oz.	unsalted butter (1 stick), cut in pieces
3	T.	fresh lemon juice

1. Pour the wine into a small pan and add the shallot, chervil, tarragon, parsley, and peppercorns. Simmer until wine is reduce to a few tablespoons. Cool and purée in a food processor. With motor running, add the butter a little at a time to make a thick sauce.

2. Scrape butter sauce into a small dish, beat in the lemon juice drop by drop, and set aside in a cool place.

Risotto

1	oz.	butter (2 T.)
3	T.	olive oil
3		shallots, minced
12	oz.	long grain rice (1½ C.)
24	fl.oz.	chicken broth (3 C.), heated
		freshly ground white pepper, to taste
1½	lb.	fresh shrimp, shelled and deveined
½	lb.	lobster meat, cooked

3. In a heavy-bottomed pan with a well-fitting lid, heat butter and oil and soften shallots for 1 to 2 minutes.

4. Add rice and stir for 2 minutes. Reduce heat a little, then begin adding the hot liquid a little at a time, stirring constantly. After each addition continue stirring until liquid is absorbed before adding more liquid. This should take about 20 minutes. The rice should be creamy and still have a little "bite" to it.

5. Stir in the white pepper, place rice in a buttered ring mold, and keep warm.

6. Briefly warm shellfish and butter sauce. Mix in enough lemon butter sauce to coat shellfish.

7. Unmold rice on a hot platter and place shellfish in center of ring. Serve immediately, passing rest of sauce separately.   *Serves 6*

Bangor, County Down, is situated at the end of the Belfast Lough on the coast. At 14 Queen's Parade is the Back-Street Café—ignore the unprepossessing outside—where Peter Barfoot cooks magnificent food. You can watch him cooking in the open-plan kitchen while you wait for your dinner. Superb ingredients from local sources coupled with the skill of a well-trained and imaginative chef and the delightful relaxed, happy atmosphere will give you an evening to remember as well as an excellent meal. East of Bangor is Groomsport on the Lough, and just outside Groomsport on the Donaghadee Road is the Adelbogen Lodge. This bustling restaurant is open for twelve hours at a stretch, serving lunch, afternoon tea, light early evening meals, and later dinner. Margaret Waterworth's cooking caters to simple and sophisticated tastes, and vegetarians are by no means neglected. The food is fresh, wholesome, and very well cooked.

On the western edge of Belfast Lough is Carrickfergus Castle, built in 1180 on a sturdy rock ledge in typical Norman fashion by John de Courcy. The walls of the keep are eight feet thick (2.5 meters), and the castle with its fine Great Hall is very well preserved. Up until 1928 an English regiment was garrisoned here. During the summer months medieval banquets are held. In the medieval walled town on the shore of the lake is Dobbins Inn, whose popularity stretches back for three hundred years. Just outside the town is the Andrew Jackson Centre, dedicated to America's president, whose parents emigrated from Carrickfergus in 1765. West of Carrickfergus is the resort town of Whitehead at the foot of the Island Magee Peninsula.

North alongside Larne Lough is the town of Larne, a good base for exploring the nine tranquil and beautiful Glens of Antrim. Here are found ancient castles, waterfalls, forests, trails for vigorous walkers, boating, fishing, and grouped around pretty harbors and pebbly beaches resort villages such as Carnlough, built of white limestone, overlooking an attractive walled harbor. The Londonderry Arms, a traditional ivy-covered hotel on the harbor, was once owned by Sir Winston Churchill. Run today by the O'Neill family, the hotel has bedrooms ranging from spacious with fantastic views, and Georgian with antique furnishings, to rooms with a decidedly contemporary decor. Food here is delicious. Baked goods are all homemade, and the main meal of the day often features freshly caught fish. In the grounds of this former coaching inn is a lovely garden with views over the sea. Farther north on the winding two-lane road are Glenariff—one of the prettiest glens—and Glenariff village on Red Bay. At the foot of Glendun is Cushenden, a charming resort village protected by the National Trust. The precipitous cliffs along the Antrim Coast road are called the Gobbins, and the terrain becomes even more rugged farther north. At the most northeasterly tip of the country Scotland is only thirteen miles away. The Scots-Irish fled Ireland in droves during the eighteenth century—about a quarter of a million in all—and many descendants of these stalwart Ulster folk became famous. Among these Scots-Irish Americans are ten American presidents, as well as Sam Houston, Edgar Allen Poe, and F. Scott Fitzgerald.

On the northern coast is Ballycastle, the main resort town of the Glens, which continues to attract golfers and fishermen. The remains of a sixteenth-century Franciscan priory are near the links. The ancient Celtic festival Lughnasa, celebrated in many places, is a two-day event here called Oul' Lammas Fair. Ireland's oldest fair has been held yearly in August since 1606. Sheep and sheep's wool are sold at the fair, as are two unusual regional foods—dulse, a salty, blackish seaweed that northerners chew on with relish, and yellow man, a hard, very sticky, yellow toffee which is even more of an acquired taste. Wysner Meats at 18 Ann Street is a butcher's shop and restaurant that, not suprisingly, offers superlative sausages and blood puddings, cooked to perfection.

Across the sound on Rathlin Ireland is the cave where Robert Bruce is believed to have watched a persevering spider spin its web. Inspired by the spider's patience, Robert Bruce went on to further successful endeavors against England's military might.

Staying with the shore road west along the splendid rugged Antrim Coast from Ballycastle, you will come to the renowned Giant's Causeway. Here 37,000 hexagonal columns were formed when hot lava bursting from the seabed cooled into these curious basalt formations. The astonishing size of the Causeway brings to mind the sweep of the Grand Canyon. Tall columns lean against the sides of mountains; others lie flat and gleaming in the sand and disappear into the foam. The Causeway continues out to sea toward the coast of Scotland and does not stop there. More basalt columns—the end of the Giant's Causeway—can be seen on the Scottish coast where the stones march right out of the waves.

A stone's throw from the Causeway is Bushmills, reputedly the place where the very best Irish whiskeys are made. Bushmills is the oldest licensed distillery in the world, and it is worthwhile to take a guided tour of the place and have a nip of Irish whiskey on the way out. Three miles (5 km) farther on brings into view the romantic ruin of Dunluce Castle perched on a rock jutting out to sea. This Norman fortress, built in the thirteenth century, was captured some four hundred years later by the clan MacDonnell— a powerful force in this neighborhood. In 1639 part of the castle that held the kitchens and also the cooks dropped into the sea.

The Ramore Restaurant and Wine Bar is also close to the water, located in the Harbour at Portrush. George McAlpin loves to turn out spectacular-looking food in his upstairs dining room. His dishes can be quite intricate but the fresh tastes of his well-chosen ingredients come through loud and clear. The restaurant is very chic. Downstairs is a wine bar with a blackboard showing specials for the day. The food here is also bright and clever and the atmosphere congenial.

Just a bit inland from Portrush is the historic town of Coleraine, in County Londonderry, known for its excellent Cheddar cheese and also for its famous and witty resident, Jonathan Swift, clergyman, journalist, and author of *Gulliver's Travels*. Swift became dean of St. Patrick's in Dublin. Reprimanded for preaching a sermon of inordinate length for a charitable cause, he determined his next sermon to raise money for charity would be short. Dean Swift took his text from Proverbs and said, " 'He that hath pity upon the poor lendeth unto the Lord; and that which he hath given will he pay him again.' You have heard the terms of the loan, and if you like the security, put down your money." Many amused and approving listeners did just that.

The bridge over the River Bann on the road to Derry City passes through Limavady, home to the family of the American president James Monroe, and also to the young woman who copied down the tune played by a passing musician that became the much-loved song, "Danny Boy." The name "London" was affixed to Derry in the seventeenth century when the city was given to colonists and planters—mostly Scottish Protestant settlers—financed by the guilds of London. Derry City's fortified center is within 30-foot (9-meter) walls that offer splendid views from a walkway of the city that has spread far beyond the original ramparts. The name *Derry* derives from *oak grove*, and it was in an oak grove in the sixth century that St. Columba founded a monastery. Directly south of Derry is Strabane, in County Fermanagh. In this area are many reminders of men who emigrated to America and whose descendants became famous. President Woodrow Wilson's grandfather, James Wilson, was one of these men. The original Wilson farm, still with much of its eighteenth-century furniture, can be visited at Dergalt near Strabane on the Plumbridge road. Farther south on the road to Gortin is the Ulster-American Folk Park, where there are re-creations of an eighteenth-century Tyrone village and an American log-cabin settlement, plus docks and ships that emigrés of the period might have used. Here too is the old whitewashed cottage and ancestral home of Andrew Mellon, the American banker and treasurer who died in 1937, and the former home of Archbishop John Hughes, founder of St. Patrick's Cathedral in New York. Derry City's most prestigeous restaurant is Beech Hill Country House Hotel at 32 Ardmore Road. Noel McMeel has worked with master chefs Paul Rankin and Ian McAndrew, as his love of bright, clear flavors attests. Noel McMeel has been working independently for a few years now and his own signature on his food comes through loud and clear. His dedication to finding the best of organically reared and nurtured ingredients and his consummate skill at the stove produce food that is exceptional, light, flavorful, and deeply satisfying.

South and west of Derry City is County Fermanagh, where Upper and Lower Lough Erne spread their pristine waters almost the entire length of the county. Well known to boating enthusiasts and fishermen, Lough Erne is rich in perch, bream, roach, and eels. Dotted with hundreds of islands, these quiet lakes are ringed with enchanting scenery and many relics of early Christian times. Boats can be rented, and along the way there are many intriguing places to moor a boat, and many little jetties and marinas served by shops next to the water. Devenish Island in Lower Lough Erne is the site of numerous early Christian remains, including an extensive monastic house dating to the sixth century, which the Danes sacked several times. Also of great interest is a well-preserved round tower with sculpted decoration and a handsomely carved cross. At the foot of Lower Lough Erne is Enniskillen, one of the two predominately Catholic towns in Northern Ireland. The other is Tyrone. Enniskillen is built on an island that divides two branches of the River Erne, and the town is connected to the mainland by bridges. Near the West Bridge is Portora School, whose pupils include Oscar Wilde and Samuel Beckett. This part of Ireland was at one time dominated by the Maguire clan, but Maguire Castle is presently a British barracks. East from Enniskillen is Castle Coole, one of the most handsome of the Anglo-Irish mansions, built in the Palladian style with wide wings spreading on either side of the central dwelling. Owned and lived in still by the earl of Belmore, this neoclassical eighteenth-century house has elaborate plasterwork and splendid period furniture.

From Castle Coole the road east leads to Dungannon, seat of the O'Neill clan until 1607. Today Dungannon is both a market town selling pigs and cattle and home to many industries producing linen goods, glassware, firebricks, and tiles. A stone's throw from here is Britain's largest lake—Lough Neagh. These large bodies of water can run like a sea in bad weather and produce rough waves five feet high or more. People who stay at Grange Lodge on Grange Road, Dungannon, are in for a treat. Norah Brown is a natural cook and knows by instinct which ingredients complement one another and exactly what fillip a dish needs to bring it from being merely good to absolutely marvelous. Ralph Brown is also good at adding that extra touch of brilliance—if you haven't tried his hot oatmeal spiked with Bushmills fabled whiskey, you should. Dinner guests are welcomed on Friday and Saturday; during the rest of the week Norah Brown cooks only for guests at the Grange.

South of Dungannon is Armagh—the metropolitan see of Ireland, originally founded by St. Patrick around 457. Ecclesiastical titles have been bitterly fought over since the Anglo-Norman invasions. During one of these battles the Catholic cathedral was taken over by the Protestants and has never been relinquished, forcing the Catholics to build another cathedral on the opposite side of town. One of Armagh's most interesting places to visit is the Astronomy Centre, originally founded in 1791, housing a planetarium and observatory with models of spacecraft and videos showing the night sky in all its glory. Armagh has many splendid Georgian houses. Three miles west of the city of Armagh is the site of the palace of the kings of Ulster from 300 B.C. to A.D. 332. Still to be seen today are the remains of this huge residence, which include ramparts enclosing two smaller forts. In the first century A.D. the Navan center trained the Red Branch knights, whose exploits are part of Ireland's literary history, notably in the works of W. B. Yeats.

From Armagh the drumlin- (hillock-) filled countryside leads south to Newry, a market town beloved of shoppers from across the border who stream in on market days to take advantage of lower prices. Farther south Carlingford Lough leads to the Irish Sea, its length bordered by the famous Mountains of Mourne. An attractive base for exploring the mountains of Mourne is Newcastle, a resort town with five miles of sandy beach situated at the foot of Slieve Donard's towering peak.

The Buck's Head Inn in Dundrum village is a pub and a restaurant ably looked after by Craig and Maureen Griffith. Their clientele—lots of happy family groups—attests that the Buck's Head is more a restaurant than a pub. There are three menus chalked up on separate blackboards—a sandwich menu, a vegetarian menu, and a fish menu. Choice is wide and food very good. There is also a pretty flowery garden at the back where you can enjoy your meal.

Held in County Down is the Castleward Opera Festival, Ireland's version of England's Glyndebourne, which is held in a massive Georgian House on the shore of Strangford Lough. Between acts dinner is served on the lawns under a huge white tent. A butler from a nearby country house serves good Irish cooking, using exquisite ingredients, accompanied by fine champagne in fluted crystal. It is an experience not to be missed.

12

THE REPUBLIC OF IRELAND

O nce upon a time in Ireland humble cottage fare, eaten most days of the year, was boiled potatoes, onions, and perhaps a bit of bacon or sausage, called coddle. Chopped kale or cabbage and floury potatoes mashed with milk and parsley (colcannon) was eaten traditionally on Halloween. Meat was a rare treat, and when it was available it was layered with potatoes, onions, and parsley and simmered in water to stretch the meat as far as it could reasonably be expected to go, and about fifty years ago this dish became known as Irish stew. Nowadays skilled chefs in sophisticated restaurants appreciate these staple dishes for what they are—good, simple, flavorful food—and make them using superlative ingredients.

Irish Stew

2	lb.	potatoes—6 medium-sized
3	lg.	onions
2½	lb.	lamb leg or breast, fat removed
3		sprigs of fresh thyme
2	T.	minced parsley
		salt and freshly ground pepper

    1. Preheat oven to 275°F (or gas mark 1). Slice potatoes and onions into ¼-inch-thick slices.

2. Cut lamb into medium-sized cubes.

3. Layer potatoes, onions, and lamb in a lidded flameproof casserole, sprinkling each layer with salt, pepper, and parsley. Tuck the sprigs of thyme in among the lamb cubes and finish with a layer of potatoes.

4. Pour in enough water to just reach the top layer, and bring to a boil over medium heat. Cover and cook in the oven for 1½ to 2 hours, replenishing the liquid only if it appears in danger of burning. Remove lid for last 20 minutes of cooking if potatoes are not browned.

5. Serve from the casserole with an assortment of steamed vegetables. *Serves 4–6*

Steaks and chops in Ireland are superb, and today's excellent cuts of meat and gleaming fish need only the lightest saucing. Irish stew is made in hotel and restaurant kitchens with the finest lamb and vegetables available and cooked with care in a slow oven. The top layer of potatoes forms a golden brown crisp crust. Ireland has the best natural ingredients anywhere in the world. Sauces are no longer complex and smothering but instead are made with lemon juice or wine with an infusion of herbs and sparingly embellished with cream or butter. Food enthusiasts in the last decade or two have realized the changing tastes in Ireland and are promoting the fact to a wider audience. Country house hotels and restaurants have multiplied, manned by chefs who demand only the freshest and best of seasonal foods—succulent tender lamb from March through the summer, oysters in autumn and winter starting in September, and fish plucked from sea, stream, or lake, delivered and cooked on the same day. Market gardeners aware of the great potential to be found in pristine fruits, vegetables, herbs, and edible flowers also deliver right to the kitchen door. No place in Ireland is more than an hour and a half's journey from the sea, and inland the country is alive with loughs, rivers, and streams, bursting with trout, salmon, and other freshwater delicacies. Enthusiastic fishermen take great pride in providing impeccable fish and shellfish. The range of fish caught off the coasts of Ireland is wide. There are at least two dozen kinds—lemon and Dover sole, turbot, brill, monkfish, mackerel, herring, haddock, shad, John Dory, grey mullet, and tench, called coarse fish, to name a few. Shellfish abound—lobster, langoustine, crayfish, crab, giant scallops, clams, sea urchins, mussels, cockles, and absolutely superb briny oysters. Fishermen, delighted at the increasing demand, now work happily hand in glove with skillful chefs to bring the freshest and best to Irish tables. Esteemed everywhere are salmon and trout, caught locally, and oysters and lobsters from the coast. To fill the chefs' requirements fish is delivered throughout the day as it becomes available. Game teems in wood, forest, field, and mountaintop and starting in October is seen on restaurant tables braised, roasted, jugged, or in temptingly rich pâtés, terrines, and game pies. Lush pasturage, sheep, goats, and contented cows, coupled with the skill and dedication of farmers—both male and female—produce rich milk, cream, heavenly butter, and award-winning farmhouse cheeses. French cheese makers are finding the Irish farmhouse cheese to be stiff competition. Increasingly in Britain and Ireland cities are losing their charm. More and more people literally seeking pastures new and green opt for life on a farm or become market gardeners as an alternative to grime and crime. Produce, poultry, dairy foods, and meat from small holdings with land that is pesticide-free, and chemical fertilizer-free, are much in demand.

Apple Rhubarb Crisp

1	lb.	rhubarb
8	oz.	brown sugar (1 C.)
½	t.	ground cinnamon
3		pieces of crystallized ginger, minced
1¼	oz.	coarsely ground almonds (¼ C.)
12	oz.	fresh pumpernickel bread crumbs (2¼ C.)
6	T.	unsalted butter, melted
3	lg.	tart apples, peeled and sliced thinly
3	fl.oz.	sparkling cider (⅓ C.)

1. Trim rhubarb and slice into one-inch pieces. Mix sugar and cinnamon.

2. In a medium-sized bowl, mix 2 tablespoons sugar mixture, ginger, almonds, and bread crumbs. Pour in melted butter and stir to coat crumbs.

3. Toss the rhubarb and apple slices with remaining sugar. Preheat oven to 350°F (or gas mark 4).

4. In a 1½-quart souffle dish, layer half the crumbs, cover with the fruit, drizzle over the cider, and top with the remaining crumbs.

5. Partially cover and bake for 40 minutes. Remove cover and bake 30 minutes longer.

6. Serve hot or warm with vanilla ice cream or whipped cream.

Serves 6–8

Irish hospitality springs straight from the heart. The legendary open-handedness is evident today in the generous portions served in Ireland's restaurants. Breakfasts are ample affairs starting with juice and cereal or porridge, followed by eggs, bacon, sausage, tomato, mushrooms, and regional specialties such as fadge or black pudding, generous plates of Irish soda bread, slabs of golden Irish butter, marmalade, or jam, and endless pots of tea "strong enough to trot a mouse." Irish soda bread is found in every cottage or mansion in the country, not to mention every hotel and restaurant. It would be hard to find a kitchen that did not bake its own bread, and served right alongside will be a dish of creamy, incomparable Irish butter.

Lunch in Ireland is quite often the main meal of the day, especially in the countryside where all restaurants are open at lunchtime. Though restaurants are found in most towns and villages, in some places meals will be available only in the local hotel. Irish hotels are social places where people while away hours of time together, as Europeans are apt to do in cafés and coffee shops. During the day pubs serve the same function as hotels, offering sandwiches, cakes, pots of tea, and light meals. In the evening children, and women in some places, are frowned upon in pubs when masculine conviviality and earnest drinking is the rule.

Wild Mushroom and Asparagus Salad

3	T.	unsalted butter
3		minced shallots
10	oz.	mixed fresh wild mushrooms (2 C.), sliced (discard stems)
5	oz.	button mushrooms (1 C.), sliced
6–8		thin asparagus spears, cut in bite-sized pieces
		pinch saffron soaked in 2 T. hot water
½	t.	paprika
6	T.	extra dry vermouth
1	T.	fresh lemon juice
		salt and freshly ground black pepper, to taste
5		butter lettuces, washed and dried
2	oz.	Parmesan cheese curls (½ C.)

1. Using a large skillet, melt butter and soften shallots for 2 minutes.

2. Add mushrooms and asparagus and cook, stirring gently, until mushrooms are wilted.

3. Stir in saffron, paprika, vermouth, lemon juice, salt, and pepper and simmer until liquid is reduced to about 8 tablespoons.

4. Line four salad plates with lettuce leaves, then divide hot mushroom and asparagus mixture attractively over the lettuce.

5. Decorate with cheese curls and serve immediately.   *Serves 4*

Ireland is possibly the least populated country in the west, with the exception of Iceland. Ireland's population is less than four million people.

New York has close to 24,000 people per square mile, as opposed to Ireland's 160. Traffic in Ireland is minimal, and even the largest city, Dublin, is within easy reach of green countryside. And green it truly is—from the pale apple green of new shoots in field and hedgerow to the dark forest green of the pines. Frequent soft rain showers that come and go during the day help to keep Ireland green. Though the climate on a daily basis is not really predictable, being subject to the vagaries of the seas surrounding the island, the temperature stays mild all year and extremes are rare. Ireland in spring is a delight. May trees blossom in the hedgerows, cottage gardens are a riot of color, and the air is so filled with scents of flowers and new greenery it almost obscures the wintery smell of burning peat. The worst month is February, mainly because everyone is heartily sick of leafless trees, soggy fields, and rivers too high for good fishing.

Fishing is important both for the Irish themselves who are fanatics about the sport and for the tourists who come to Ireland regularly to catch trout and salmon. Fishing is also a major industry. Oyster producers abound in County Galway, County Cork, County Donegal, County Mayo, and County Kerry and are also to be found in the counties of Antrim, Clare, Down, Limerick, Louth, Sligo, Waterford, and Wexford.

Warmed Oysters with Carrot Chive Sauce

24		oysters on the half shell, juices reserved
		rock salt
1½	oz.	unsalted butter (3 T.)
2		slender young carrots, cut in thin slivers
4	T.	malt vinegar or white wine vinegar
		half a bunch of chives, minced
1½	T.	fresh lemon juice
		minced fresh parsley leaves

1. Place oysters on the half shell on a bed of rock salt in a heat-proof shallow dish. Refrigerate until ready to cook.

2. Melt butter and gently stir in carrot slivers, then cook over medium heat for 2 minutes.

3. Add vinegar and reduce until the sauce is syrupy. Preheat broiler.

4. Stir in minced chives, lemon juice, and oyster juices and heat through.

5. Divide mixture between oysters and place dish under broiler for 2 minutes.

6. Scatter minced parsley over oysters and serve immediately.

Serves 4

The Irish love of words is well documented. A little blarney is appreciated at any time of day, but especially it seems in a pub of an evening—talk there is nonstop, often brilliant, almost always hilarious. Though given to teasing, the Irish are courteous, friendly, and welcoming. The high regard in which they hold each individual is very noticeable. They are curious to know all there is to know about one another, and all about you too if you turn up in their midst, though they are too polite to pry. If you stop to ask directions while on the road, people will drive miles out of their way to show you the lane or road you should be on. The crime rate in Ireland is exceedingly low.

The counties above Dublin closest to the border with Northern Ireland are Monaghan, tiny Louth, and Meath. Though hilly, Monaghan has good agricultural land and plenty of pasturage for sheep, cows, and goats, but much of its industry centers around poultry—ducks, chickens, and turkey yards are dotted throughout the county. Carrickmacross is renowned for its exquisite lace. Near Clones on the border with Fermanagh is a stately Palladian-style country house hotel called Hilton Park. A working farm that has been in the same family since the early 1900s, when Hilton Park was bought by Samuel Madden, the owners now are John and Lucy Madden. Lucy is responsible for the delicious food, served in the princely dining room, and her well-thought-out beautiful dishes make Hilton Park a wonderful place to stay. Here too is a lake for fishing and boating, and golf and croquet are near at hand.

Louth is the county just north of the city of Dublin, where Boyne Valley Honey is produced at New Mellifont Abbey, Collon, by Cistercian monks. Old Mellifont Abbey stands beside the River Boyne. It is a particularly beautiful ruin, with a Romanesque lavabo that originally was octagonal but now has missing walls and is open to the skies. Parts of the Abbey building are still standing, as are some of the cloister's arches. Possibly the best preserved is the twelfth-century two-story Chapter House that is used now to store medieval tiles. Drogheda is an extremely interesting town historically. Set on the banks of the River Boyne, heavily fortified Drogheda was one of the most important towns in Ireland in the 1500s. In 1609 the "Plantation" of Ulster with Protestant people was instituted by James I. Most of these people came from Scotland ostensibly to take the place of Irish nobles who had fled into exile on the Continent. Soon Protestants owned most of the land in Ireland, and the Irish peasants had no recourse but to toil for the newcomers. Four miles (6.5 km) west of Drogheda on the northern bank of the Boyne is King William's Glen, the site where Protestant militia hid before the Battle of the Boyne in 1690. The Protestant William of Orange defeated Catholic James II, winning the "War of the Two Kings." Now every year in Northern Ireland, Protestant Orangemen exuberantly celebrate the Battle of the Boyne with marches, parades, and deafening drums.

Farther west in the County of Meath are the fantastic prehistoric sites of Dowth, Knowth, and Newgrange. Excavations at these sites have been going

on at Dowth and Knowth since 1962, and parts of the site are off limits. Knowth is extensive, more so than Newgrange, with some areas dating to 3000 B.C., although the site was still in use in the fourth to eighth centuries A.D. as the seat of the High Kings of Ireland. It is interesting to watch the archaeologists at work. Now seven of Knowth's tombs have been completed and are open to the public. Newgrange also dates to the Stone Age, and the enormous effort it must have taken to move and install 250,000 tons of stone continues to baffle. When the sun's rays strike the entrance to the tomb at dawn on the winter solstice, they illuminate sixty-two feet of passageway and flood the burial chamber with light that lasts about twenty minutes.

Dublin

The city of Dublin, sliced in two by the River Liffey, is built on a wide plain, edged by the headlands that overlook a broad bay and sheltered from the boisterous Irish Sea. This beautiful setting is further enhanced by the glorious green Wicklow Mountains south of the city. Dublin is graced with elegant Georgian terraces and squares, graceful public buildings, art galleries, parks, pubs, and bookshops galore.

Dublin is famous for the writers who have lived and worked in this capital city—Jonathan Swift, Oliver Goldsmith, William Butler Yeats, Brendan Behan, Sean O'Casey, Thomas Moore, Oscar Wilde, and, perhaps the most famous of all, James Joyce. James Joyce's tragicomic work *Ulysses* is the story of two men, Stephen Dedalus and Leopold Bloom, who walked the streets of Dublin on the same day, Thursday, June 16, 1904. Eventually their paths cross. The book chronicles the lives of the Dubliners each man meets on his walk. The Dublin locations Joyce wrote about in *Ulysses* have become places of annual pilgrimage for faithful Joyceans who walk in the footsteps of Dedalus and Bloom on Bloomsday, June 16. The Martello Tower mentioned in Joyce's book is now a museum displaying James Joyce memorabilia. Books, words, and writers are all special to the people of Ireland. In fact, fiction writers working independently are not subject to taxes in Ireland. In Trinity College, east of College Green, the Colonnade's Gallery beside the Old Library houses the beautifully illuminated Book of Durrow, created by monks at the Durrow monastery, now a ruin, in the seventh century, and also the Book of Kells, dating to the ninth century, that contains the four Gospels. The college has a collection of over three million books. Trinity is the college of Dublin University that was founded by Elizabeth I in 1592. Rigidly Protestant when it was founded, in the last thirty years it has been open to all denominations.

In the heart of Dublin is Phoenix Park, one of the biggest urban parks in Europe and five times the size of Hyde Park in London. Herds of red deer inhabit its vast acreage. The Irish are sports fanatics, and you will see polo players, mounted on bicycles instead of horses, crashing into one another as they slice at the ball. Phoenix Park has football and cricket pitches, bridle paths, walking trails, and a zoo. Ireland is united when it comes to sport, and Ireland's Olympic Council chooses athletes from both Northern Ireland and the Republic of Ireland.

Pubs are the mainstays of Dublin life, and Ireland's favorite brew is undoubtedly Guinness stout, a full-bodied, dark, and somewhat bitter draught that is very dependable. It goes famously with all things Irish, from simple brown soda bread and butter, to seawashed Irish oysters, and the renowned Irish stew. Guinness stout can be mixed with English bitter ale to make a mixture called Black and Tan. Mixed with champagne it has the elegant name Black Velvet. In the heart of the city you can catch a whiff of toasted hops from across the River Liffey where the great Dublin brewery produces the delicious black brew. The first Arthur Guinness founded the brewery in 1759 at St. James's Gate with a nine-thousand-year lease. Now the biggest brewery in Europe, Guinness is sold today to 120 countries around the globe. Made from hops, yeast, roasted barley, and pure Dublin water, seven million pints of the robust brew are downed each day throughout the world. Guinness's head is so thick and creamy a foamy ring is left around the inside of the glass with each satisfying swallow.

Irish whiskey is made from malted barley, fermented into pot ale—a pale, cloudy liquid which is 8 percent proof. This is distilled three times, then syphoned into wooden casks and left to rest for at least seven years. During this incubation it develops its rich taste and tawny coloring. It is then graded and bottled. Another fiery, but colorless, liquid is poteen (pronounced po-cheen) which is illegal to make and lethal if made improperly. Poteen is also illegal to sell, though stills are found that make it in various parts of the countryside. The first Irishmen to flee to Scotland took their poteen along, and the Irish believe that their potent liquid provided the Scots with a base from which all Scottish whiskies evolved.

Here is a list of some restaurants to try in Dublin.

The Commons in Newman House on St. Stephen's Green is an extremely elegant restaurant offering intricate, complex dishes that lean toward the cooking of France, such as squash blossoms stuffed with mousse or sweetbreads. Gerard Kirwan is the chef here. Ireland's straightforward and succulent steaks and chops are also on the menu. Dubliners head for the Commons when they have something to celebrate and want to go all out. Do not miss out on the cheese tray—the Commons has a good selection of perfect, dewy, farmhouse cheeses culled from most of the southern counties.

Cooke's Café, 14 South William Street, is an up-to-the-minute restaurant serving great food cooked with flair and imagination by John Cooke. A particular favorite in season is spanking fresh clams with a tomato sauce touched with chili, served over linguine. The tastes and vibrant color of California's food, as well as the pastas and risottos of Italy, find their way onto the menu here. This is a lively and fun place to eat, and Mary Gill's freshly baked interesting breads are worth the journey—try her wonderful brown rosemary bread.

The National Museum Café is located in a lovely room within the museum on Kildare Street. Joe Kerrigan's dishes are fresh, pleasing, and full of flavor. His cooking method is to do as little as possible to detract from the goodness of his carefully chosen ingredients, although he is not above cooking some of the early regional favorites such as Dublin Coddle.

Blazing Salads II in the Powerscourt Townhouse Centre, Clarenden Street, is a vegetarian restaurant with a difference. It is, of course, gluten-free, dairy-free, yeast-free, and sugar-free, but the difference lies in the imaginative cooking. Here vegetarian dishes are spiked with wonderful fiery ingredients, vegetables or tofu come wrapped in flavor-packed seaweed or bitter greens, and unexpected flavors enliven the soups. As well as a plethora of juices and herbal teas, there are a few organic wines to add interest. The cakes and puddings are delicious.

For a respite in the afternoon try Bewley's on Grafton Street. This is a much-loved restaurant, designed in the decor of another age, that has become so popular in Dublin that now branches have opened in other locations. Soda bread, sweet butter, and strong tea are offered in the afternoons along with a panoply of luscious pastries and cakes.

About twenty minutes' drive north of the city in County Dublin is the small village of Skerries situated right on the seashore. The old village and

its harbor form the heart of a modern town. Wide tree-lined streets and parks give this pretty resort town a spacious and tranquil air. Historically Skerries is associated with the return of St. Patrick to Ireland. The Saint landed on Inish Patrick in the year 432 and from there came to the mainland to proselytize among the people. This island was one of the first to be raided by the Vikings, and the name Skerries is derived from the Old Norse word for rocky islands. Nowadays the offshore islands are home to a wide range of seabirds—Shenick Island is a wild bird reserve. It is also not unusual to see seals swimming in the harbor. The area around Skerries is known as Fingal, and it is an enviable place to live, especially if you happen to be a chef, for farmers hereabouts grow most of the excellent produce for the Dublin vegetable markets, and here too are all the ports that bring fresh fish and shellfish into the city. Skerries has an active seafishing fleet, and the village is famous—even world-famous—for its Dublin Bay prawns. In the seventeenth century sailors who manned the fishing fleet routinely brought their wives with them when they set sail. While their vessels lay off Dublin Port, the wives caught and sold prawns in the streets of the city, helping to spread word of the excellence of Dublin Bay prawns all over the world. Happily ensconced in the Red Bank Restaurant, once the Munster and Leinster Bank, at 7 Church Street, Skerries, are chef proprietor Terry

McCoy and his family. Terry McCoy specializes in cooking seafood, and you can rest assured it is the freshest and best. His love of the sea is second only to his love of cooking. And most of his extensive chef training seems to have been in places near or on large bodies of water, such as the Lausanne Palace Hotel on Lake Leman. Some of Terry McCoy's fish and shellfish dishes on the menu are Baked crab Loughshinny—brown and white crab meat blended with dry sherry and cream; Hot smoked Irish salmon with tarragon sauce; Seafood dumplings in a pastry shell; Cockles and oysters "Molly Malone" in a creamy wine sauce; Haddock Louisiana Creole style; Black sole on the bone with lemon butter; Dublin Bay prawns "Ogen" with melon; and Sea trout "Carpetbagger"—stuffed sea trout fillets cooked in a foil bag with dry sherry and fresh herbs.

Terry McCoy has contributed two recipes to this book, one of which is Dublin Bay Prawn Bisque, and he suggests you try a good dry Chardonnay or champagne with this one. However, he loyally concedes that "a glass of Guinness is equally good." His other contribution is Fillet of Hake "Kenure House." Kenure House, unfortunately now demolished, was a Palladian mansion in the next parish of Rush that had a fine kitchen garden which still pushes up wonderful wild horseradish root.

Dublin Bay Prawn Bisque

8	fl.oz.	olive oil (1 C.)
½		head of celery, chopped
2		carrots, chopped
1		onion, chopped
¼	lb.	mushrooms (¾ C.), chopped
3		garlic cloves, crushed
4		sprigs of tarragon
4		sprigs of parsley
3		bay leaves
3		whole cloves
8	fl.oz.	dry white wine (1 C.)
4	lb.	whole Dublin Bay prawns
		a knob of butter
1	T.	flour
1	T.	tomato purée
1	lb.	fresh tomatoes
8	fl.oz.	brandy (1 C.)
10	fl.oz.	fresh cream (1¼ C.)
3		egg yolks

1. In a very large pot, heat the olive oil, then add the chopped vegetables, garlic, herbs, bay leaves, cloves, and white wine. Sweat the vegetables to increase the flavor of the stock. Preheat oven to 425°F (or gas mark 7).

2. Add 4 to 6 pints (10–15 cups) of cold water to the vegetables and bring almost to boiling point. Plunge in the whole prawns and bring the pot just to a boil. Remove prawns immediately, and let cool.

3. Remove prawn heads and shells and place them on a baking sheet in the oven until they are sizzling hot and beginning to color. Set aside the prawns.

4. Meanwhile, in another large saucepan melt the butter, add the flour, and cook gently. Stir in the tomato purée, the tomatoes, and the baked prawn heads and shells. Add this to the vegetable stock and simmer for one hour.

5. Stir in the brandy and cook for another 10 minutes. Strain the stock.

6. Beat together the cream and egg yolk and add to the bisque. Heat gently—do not allow to boil or it will curdle.

7. To serve, place prawns in bowls or soup plates and pour the bisque over the prawns. Serves 8

Note: With a side dish of boiled potatoes, this will serve as a luncheon dish.

Fillet of Hake "Kenure House"

1	3–4 lb. hake on the bone
sm.	jar of horseradish relish
8 fl.oz.	whipped cream (1 C.)
	salt and pepper
4 T.	butter
2 fl.oz.	heavy cream (¼ C.)

1. Skin and bone the hake (or have your fishmonger do this for you) and reserve the skin and bones to make 3 cups of fish stock.

2. Cut the two fillets in half and remove any pinbones—these are quite large and easy to remove.

3. Fold the horseradish relish into the whipped cream and divide among the four pieces of fish, slathering it onto the underside of the fish. Season lightly with salt and pepper. Fold the fillets in two to enclose the filling.

4. In a steamer place the 3 cups of fish stock, arrange the fish on the rack above the boiling stock with any quick-cooking vegetable, such as snow peas, and steam for 5 to 10 minutes or until the fish is just cooked through. Remove fish and accompanying vegetable to a warm platter and pour the fish stock into a saucepan.

5. Add the heavy cream and reduce over high heat until one-quarter of the original volume remains. Add the butter and stir until melted.

6. To serve, pour the sauce around the hake and vegetable and pass a side dish of boiled potatoes.   *Serves 4*

Southeast of Dublin on Dublin Bay in Dun Laoghaire is the Restaurant Na Mara where Derek Dunne cooks all things from the sea with a consummate hand. Fish straight from the sea zings with flavor. For a change of pace try the crab mousse or the perfectly prepared seafood sausage.

County Wicklow

Close to Dublin are the wildly beautiful Wicklow Mountains; their rounded tops and deep valleys, filled with shining lakes and rivers, were carved during the Ice Age. In one valley is the reservoir that supplies Dublin with water, in another the Palladian mansion built in the 1700s to house the earl of Miltown and now home to the Alfred Biet art collection. In yet another valley, in deep seclusion, are the ruins of a great monastic settlement, Glendalough, complete with disintegrating churches and a cathedral that was once known as the "Rome of the Western World." Glendalough was founded in 545 by St. Kevin, whose vision of sanctity encompassed both solitude and peace. Here Irish clansmen buried their kings. Though Vikings frequently raided this peaceful settlement, it held fast until the thirteenth century. Charles Stuart Parnell's Georgian home at Avondale is now a museum set in a park that is open to the public. Close by is the Vale of Avoca, where the Avoca handweavers make beautiful soft woolens that capture the colors of Ireland's misty countryside. Woolen goods have been woven hereabouts since the 1700s. The success of the operation today is due to the help and advice given Avoca by the Kilkenny Design Centre. In Wicklow Town the harbor is an attractive and interesting place to explore. There is a pier at the end of Harbour Road and lots of alleyways to poke about in. A bridge across the River Vartry leads to another smaller pier. Follow the beach at the northern end to the wide Lough which is well known for its wildfowl. Nearby on a promontory is the ruin of Black Castle built in 1169.

In Wicklow Town is the Old Rectory Country House, owned and run by Linda and Paul Saunders. The Old Rectory's main claim to fame is its exceptional food. The acclaim is due in large part to delectable vegetables, herbs, salad leaves, and edible flowers that are specially grown for the Saunders by a friend in an organic garden. The "Garden of Ireland Salad" on the menu is composed of organic radicchio, frisée, rocket, summer purslane, lambs lettuce, borage flowers, mallow, marigold petals, and pansies. Linda Saunders is a keen gardener with a special interest in edible flowers, and she has created a menu for a floral dinner event using honeysuckle, elderflowers, marigolds, roses, and the blossoms of sage and chives. The meal, which is served with hot marigold muffins and chive flower butter, ends with spiced elderflower fritters. It smells gorgeous. Linda Saunders says, "A guest favorite is cheese fondue with nasturtium flowers," but she is quick to point out that flowers should never be allowed to dominate a dish, as most people are happier with them as decoration. Linda and Paul Saunders have great sources for their locally caught fish that includes salmon, sea trout, herrings, lobster, prawns, and crabs. Their meat is delivered from a prizewinning local butcher given to making such specialties as traditional spiced beef for pot-roasting at Christmas. Linda Saunders is happy to share her recipe for Spiced Apple Sorbet in a Biscuit Tuile, which she says "is really a redesigned 1990's version of traditional apple pie and cream." It also demonstrates the light and decorative approach to food at the Old Rectory.

Old Rectory Spiced Apple Sorbet in a Biscuit Tuile

3 lb. cooking apples
½ t. cinnamon
½ t. ginger
½ t. mixed spice
     juice of 1 lemon

1. Peel and chop the apples, put all ingredients in a mixing bowl, and microwave until a smooth pulp is obtained. Sieve if necessary. Cool.

2. Add an equal quantity of apple pulp to basic sorbet syrup recipe below. Mix well and freeze.

3. When softly frozen, put the mixture in a food processor and break up the crystals to make the sorbet white and frothy. Refreeze.

Basic sorbet syrup

1 lb. white sugar
3 oz. powdered glucose (⅓ C.)
40 fl.oz. water (5 C.)
     juice of 1 lemon

4. In a large pan bring ingredients to a boil and boil briskly for 10 minutes. Allow to cool. (You can combine this syrup with an equal quantity of any fresh fruit juice or liquidized fruit pulp to create other fruit sorbets, adding lemon juice to taste.)

Biscuit tuile

4 oz. butter (1 stick), softened
4 oz. castor sugar (½ C.)
2   eggs
2 t.   lemon juice
4 oz. flour (¾ C.), sifted

5. Cream butter and sugar together; mix eggs in thoroughly, then the lemon juice, and lastly the flour.

6. Place teaspoons of the mixture on 5-inch squares of cooking parchment. Spread mixture with a knife to a 3-inch disc. Cook at 180°F (or gas mark ¼) for 7 minutes or until golden at edges.

7. To make the bowl-shaped tuiles: While still hot and flexible, very carefully drape each biscuit over an upturned small bowl, peeling off the parchment as you go. When cool they will be crisp and will keep their shape. Store very carefully in an airtight box.

Frosted flowers

24   perfect rose petals
1 lg. egg white
2 oz. castor sugar (¼ C.)

8. Take perfect rose petals and cut off the white base. Brush lightly with diluted egg white. Shake castor sugar over and leave to dry. Other suitable flowers to use are whole primroses and pansies.

9. To serve, put a scoop of spiced apple sorbet with a scoop of rich vanilla ice cream in a biscuit tuile. Decorate with sugar-frosted rose petals. If a more dramatic presentation is desired, set the tuile on top of a circle of sweetened fresh raspberry purée decorated with a few whole berries.   *Serves 8 or more*

Rathsallagh House near Dunlavin is a country house hotel set in 500 acres of particularly beautiful parkland. This comfortable, charming house is owned and run by Joe and Kay O'Flynn. Though the atmosphere is relaxed and low key, the O'Flynns' standards are both professional and high. Kay O'Flynn is justly renowned for her cooking. Good Irish joints of beef and lamb are cooked to perfection, and much of the produce is grown in the kitchen garden. Recourse to the tennis court or the golf course will enliven your appetite, and if the weather is not conducive to outdoor activities the Flynns have a heated swimming pool and sauna indoors.

West of the Wickow Mountains, on the Central Plain near the town of Kildare, is Ireland's famous racetrack, the Curragh—a Gaelic word meaning racecourse. Many of Ireland's famous horses are trained here. Curragh is also the home of a government-owned farm, the Irish National Stud, where breeding horses are stabled. Breeding thoroughbreds, show jumpers, and hunters is Ireland's national passion. Annual auctions, private sales, and fees for breeding these beautiful animals come to over 140 million dollars and keep roughly 15,000 people gainfully employed. Steeplechasing was started in 1752 when two men—possibly for a wager—decided to race one another on horseback from Buttevant Church to St. Leger's Church in County Cork, leaping stonewalls, streams, and anything else that got in their way. Steeplechasing, as it was dubbed, became instantly popular, as it was great fun.

Kildare Town, about three miles (5 km) from the Curragh, is a town with a central market square. In the vicinity of the square are the remains of a fifth-century monastery founded by St. Bridget, a saint held in high esteem, second only to Saint Patrick. The ancient cathedral complex here has been rebuilt and reinforced several times since its inception in 1229 and is worth a detour if only for its stained glass windows. One of the most serene and beautiful sights you will encounter close to Kildare Town is the Japanese Garden that was founded in 1906 by a brewing millionaire with the input of famous Japanese gardener Tassa Eida. The garden is beautifully kept up, and it is delightful to walk among the lakes and over the graceful bridges that are a core part of Japanese gardens. Naturally there is a Japanese teahouse tucked away within the garden for refreshments. The county town of Naas is a lively market town believed to have been visited on several occasions by St. Patrick. Naas is well situated for touring the sights of Kildare. Nearby is the beautiful Palladian mansion, Castletown House, which, when it was built in 1722 for the speaker of the Irish House of Commons, was the biggest private house in Ireland. Now it is the home of the Irish Georgian Society, which is responsible for the extensive refurbishment of both the elegant house and its formal garden.

Kilkea Castle at Castledermont, near Athy, has a reputation for good, fresh, seasonal dishes, much of it based on produce grown in the kitchen garden. Amenities for guests, apart from luxurious bedrooms in the castle with en suite bathrooms, are a gymnasium with pool and sauna, tennis, fishing, bowls, riding, and archery. Built in the twelfth century for the Fitzgerald clan, the castle is said to be haunted.

County Wexford

County Wexford's spectacular golden beaches rim the southeastern shore of Ireland. The quaint coastal town of Wexford was settled by Vikings in the ninth century, as were many eastern towns. Tall blonde blue-eyed Irishmen on the streets of Wexford attest to this heritage. Dark-haired descendants of Norman invaders are also easy to spot. The Normans ousted the Vikings, but no conqueror was ever more cruel than Oliver Cromwell. His brutal armies slaughtered thousands of Irish people in the mid-1600s, including 300 of Wexford's inhabitants who had gathered to pray in the Wexford Bull Ring. Wexford's High Street runs beside the quays on the waterfront. Here are a small fishing fleet and the Wexford Wildfowl Reserve. Wexford is a charming town with narrow streets leading up from the quay, lined with intriguing shops and congenial pubs. The people here are friendly and helpful, and the town boasts many nineteenth-century buildings, fine churches, and remnants of the original town walls. The Granary is a very good choice for dinner here. Owned by Paddy and Mary Hatton, the Granary has excellent local fish and shellfish in summer and a wealth of game in winter, cooked to perfection by Mary Hatton, who was trained at Ballymaloe.

The John F. Kennedy Memorial Park, located at Slieve Coilte in County Wexford, is planted with row upon row of trees, many of them donated from around the world. The late president's great-grandfather was born at nearby Dunganstown, which still houses Kennedy relations.

Kilkenny

Nineteen thousand lively folk make Kilkenny their home. Independence is a proud part of their nature. Kilkenny declared itself the capital of an independent Irish Confederacy in scornful defiance of Oliver Cromwell. In retribution the roundhead stabled his horses in the cathedral and smashed all its glorious stained glass windows. The church of St. Canice was built on the site of a monastic settlement founded by a medieval saint in the sixth century, long before Vikings came to Ireland. Now the cathedral dominates the medieval city of Kilkenny, once the capital of Ireland, that spreads over both banks of the River Nore. Originally Roman Catholic, the cathedral changed to the Protestant faith during the Reformation. Now, though still Protestant, people of both faiths revere the beauty of this historic edifice. In times of war, people used the tall tower of St. Canice as a place of refuge, fleeing up the stairs en masse. Views over the city are superb from this aerie. In the vicinity of the cathedral are narrow lanes with down-to-earth names, such as Pudding and Gooseberry. Many of these winding alleys were once secret "Mass paths" used by faithful Catholics on their way to celebrate the forbidden Mass. The city is an architectural gem from huge Kilkenny Castle at one end of the city to St. Canice Cathedral at the other. Between them lie a treasury of medieval buildings, most of which have been beautifully restored. The twelfth-century castle, built by the Normans, was once the home of the Butler family—elevated to the earls of Ormonde.

Now Butler House, built in the eighteenth century, is a hotel on Patrick Street at the side of Castle Yard. Opposite the castle is the Kilkenny Design Centre, where talented craftspeople produce spectacular gold and silver jewelry, linens, woolens, crisp crystal, and ceramics with softly glowing glazes. Well-designed, high-quality Irish goods are available in Design Centre shops in Kilkenny and Dublin. If you visit Ireland in August, time your stay in Kilkenny to coincide with their famous annual arts festival. Some craft studios are located in Castle Yard. Kilkenny has been busy restoring its ancient monuments in the last few years, as well as sprucing up the town in general. Bright new paint adorns doors and windowsills, and older cottages have been re-whitewashed, some in delicate pastel shades. Shops are forbidden to use neon lighting to advertise their premises as it is not in keeping with Kilkenny's "medieval" image. On the High Street is the Kilkenny Herb Shop, from which Joe Kiely sends herbs, edible flowers, wild mushrooms, foie gras, and Barbary ducks to restaurants all over the country and also to the better supermarkets for gourmet home cooks. Ireland's pubs are legendary and nowhere more so than in Kilkenny. After all, the good monks of this fine city started brewing alcohol here in 1234, so it is no wonder that Kilkenny has at least seventy, possibly eighty, places to satisfy thirst. The Edward Langton award-winning pub is known throughout the Isle, and the Marble Bar also has its devotees.

For the best food in town, go to Lacken House Restaurant and Guesthouse on Dublin Road. Eugene and Breda MacSweeney bought Lacken House in 1983 and built for themselves a solid reputation for warm hospitality, creative and excellent cuisine, and professional service. Eugene MacSweeney creates menus for Lacken House based on the best of Irish foodstuffs and his own distinctive cookery style. Breda MacSweeney set out to learn all there was to know about wine and has become an expert. Her skills as a sommelier are widely recognized. Both of them have won awards in their fields. Eugene and Breda have lovingly restored Lacken House room by room as funds became available, starting with the elegant relaxing restaurant and reception rooms and then moving on to the eight en suite bedrooms, not to mention bringing up three children at the same time. It was only a year or two ago that the kitchens were equipped the way Eugene MacSweeney had envisioned them. Lacken means a high area above a river. This beautiful Victorian house was originally built as a dower house in 1847 for the Lord Viscount Montmorency. A dower house, by the way, is the house where the widowed, or dowager, duchess goes to live when her son, who has inherited his father's title, brings his wife, now the duchess, to live in the main house. Since its establishment Lacken House has become one of Ireland's leading restaurants and has received awards from all major food guides, including the Irish Tourist Board's Award of Excellence and Galtee Irish Breakfast Award. Eugene MacSweeney has represented Ireland in culinary competitions far and wide, giving Breda MacSweeney the opportunity to learn about wines local to the area. There is plenty to do at Lacken House. The lovely countryside is perfect for walking, riding, or driving, the River Nore and the River Barrow for fishing, the Jack Nicklaus-designed Irish Open golf course is just ten miles away, and there are golf, swimming, and horse racing near historic Kilkenny city, which is a five-minute stroll from Lacken House. Eugene MacSweeney has contributed several recipes for us to use in this book.

Celery and Apple Soup

2	oz.	butter (½ stick)
10	oz.	celery (2 C.), finely sliced
2	oz.	leeks (½ C.), finely chopped
2		apples, peeled and diced
1	sm.	potato, peeled and diced
10	fl.oz.	chicken stock (1¼ C.)
5	fl.oz.	fresh cream (scant ⅔ C.)
		salt and pepper, to taste

1. Melt the butter in a saucepan, add the celery and leeks, cover, and sweat for 5 minutes over gentle heat.
2. Add the apple and cook for 2 minutes.
3. Add the potato and chicken stock, bring to a boil, and skim, then simmer for 15 minutes.
4. Liquidize or whirl in the food processor, and strain the soup.
5. Stir in the cream and check the seasoning.   *Serves 4*

Smoked Haddock and Leek Chowder

1	t.	oil
3	med.	leeks, thinly sliced
3	med.	celery sticks, sliced
10	fl.oz.	fish stock (1¼ C.)
20	fl.oz.	milk (2½ C.)
2	sm.	bay leaves
3		potatoes, peeled and cut in chunks
1	lb.	smoked haddock, skinned, boned, and cut into pieces
		juice of ½ lemon
		salt and pepper

1. Heat the oil in a large pan and cook the leeks and celery until just softened.

2. Pour the fish stock and milk into the pan and bring to a gentle simmer. Add the bay leaves and potatoes and cook for 8 minutes.

3. Stir in the smoked haddock and lemon juice and season to taste. Cook for 8 minutes. Remove bay leaves.

4. Serve the chowder at once with warm crusty bread.

Serves 4–6

Roast Glazed Goose

1 8–10 lb. goose
   seasoning

Marinade

3 T. clear honey
1 t. chopped thyme
4 T. soy sauce
3   garlic cloves
1 t. grated ginger root

1. Rinse the goose inside and out and dry with kitchen paper. Remove wing tips and reserve with the neck and gizzard for the stock.

2. Mix marinade ingredients and pour them over the goose. Cover and leave to marinate overnight.

3. Preheat oven to 425°F (or gas mark 7). Remove the goose from the marinade to a roasting pan and cover with foil.

4. Roast for 20 minutes, then reduce the temperature to 400°F (or gas mark 6), and roast for 15 minutes per pound.

5. When cooked, transfer to a serving dish and let rest before serving.

Eugene MacSweeney's favorite accompaniments to roast goose are roasted turnips, parsnips, and potatoes.

Roast Leg of Venison with Elderberry Sauce

1½ lb. joint, cut from the leg
3 T.   butter
2 t.   oil

3 T.   mixed fresh herbs—parsley, tarragon, and coriander—
         minced
         salt and pepper
3 fl.oz. red wine (⅓ C.)
10 fl.oz. brown sauce (1¼ C.)
3 oz.   elderberries, crushed (⅓ C.)
2 fl.oz. cream (¼ C.)

1. Preheat the oven to 375°F (or gas mark 5). Rub the venison with butter, oil, herbs, and seasoning and sear the meat in a hot roasting pan.

2. Cook venison for 25 minutes.

3. Pour off the fat from the roasting pan; pour in the red wine and then the brown sauce. Let reduce.

4. Add any juices to the pan that have accumulated around the venison while resting.

5. Add the crushed elderberries. Boil for 5 minutes, then strain the sauce.

6. Add the cream.

7. Slice the venison and serve with the sauce.

This dish is usually served at Lacken House with red cabbage and roast potatoes.

Potato and Beetroot Cake

2 oz. butter (¼ C.)
1 lb. potatoes, peeled and grated
1 lb. beetroot, cooked, peeled, and grated
1 t.   grated orange rind
        salt and pepper

1. Melt half the butter in a pan and fry the potatoes for 10 minutes, stirring well. Season, set aside, and keep warm.

2. Melt the rest of the butter and add the beetroot and orange rind. Fry for 2 minutes, season, and keep warm.

3. Place a heaped tablespoon of potato into a 2½-inch round plain pastry cutter and press down. Top with one-fourth of the beetroot and then a final layer of potato. Press well and reheat in a hot oven.

4. To serve, place on a warm plate and remove cutter.

Serves 4

Outside the town is a former Cistercian monastery, Druiske Abbey, that has been restored with funds and volunteer labor by the people of Kilkenny. Pretty villages dot the banks of the River Nore, which runs through Kilkenny. Near the town of Thomastown are the starkly beautiful ruins of Jerpoint Abbey. Nearby is Mount Juliet, set in over a thousand acres of parkland. Originally built for the earl of Carrick, the impressive mansion has been converted into a splendid, supremely elegant, and richly furnished country house hotel with its own golf course, its own hunting, shooting, and fishing—salmon from the River Nore that runs through the estate—and here too is plenty of countryside within the parkland where anyone can ride to his heart's content. A great part of the pleasure in the evening comes from the imaginative cooking of Chris Farrell, who was lucky enough to train with both Gerry Galvin of Drimcong (see Galway) and Hans Peter Mattia of Chez Hans, a French restaurant in Cashel.

Waterford County

Waterford City was founded by Viking invaders, and the older walled part of the city has a solid round tower—Reginald's Tower—with walls ten feet (3 m) thick and a stairway leading to the top. The tower, once used by Norman kings, now holds the Civic Museum. Another legacy of the Vikings is the site of St. Olaf's church, but all that remains of the church today is the door. The Vikings in turn were ousted by the Normans, and then in the seventeenth century Waterford was decimated by Cromwell's men and its prosperity remained tenuous until the founding of the Waterford Glass Factory in the eighteenth century. This newfound affluence produced many fine Georgian buildings including the City Hall, which has a massive early nineteenth-century Waterford glass chandelier hanging in the Council Chamber. In America, Independence Hall in Philadelphia has a replica of this chandelier. Next to City Hall is the Bishop's Palace, another splendid example of Georgian architecture. Waterford is known the world over for its crystal, and the Irish are immensely proud of their elegant and world-coveted product. The Glass Factory, a mile or two outside the city, is well worth a visit to see the huge fiery furnaces and to watch craftsmen blowing the glass, then cutting and polishing the gorgeous, intricate designs.

Dwyers of Mary Street, situated in the Royal Irish Constabulary barracks, has original paintings on the walls and a mixture of antique and ultramodern furnishings. This pretty restaurant serves regional as well as French-influenced foods, using local Irish ingredients. Don't miss Martin Dwyer's Brown Bread ice cream.

Waterford Castle, located on three hundred acres on an island in the River Suir, can be reached by car ferry. The guest rooms are magnificent, as are the Great Hall and reception rooms filled with antiques, tapestries, baronial fireplaces, and paneling. Ireland's great traditional dishes are cooked with flair and imagination at Waterford Castle.

From Waterford follow the River Suir west to Clonmel and the mountains of Comeragh. Nestled at the foot of Comeragh Mountains is the Cistercian monastery of Melleray, founded in the nineteenth century by French monks, and now housing Trappist monks. The road north runs straight to the Rock of Cashel. *Cashel* means "stone fort" in Gaelic. Atop the massive circular mound that towers two hundred feet (60 m) above the Tipperary plain are several monastic buildings and an ancient cross. This cross is believed to be where St. Patrick baptized King Aengus, Ireland's first Christian monarch, and used the shamrock's three leaves on a single stem to illustrate the concept of the Trinity. The original Coronation Stone of the kings of Munster at the Rock of Cashel is housed in the museum at the entrance to the site, but a replica of the stone stands on the spot where the kings were crowned. Among the ruined buildings are part of St. Patrick's Cathedral and remains from both pagan and early Christian times. There are lovely views over the Tipperary countryside from the Rock of Cashel and places of interest to see in Cashel town, including the Cashel Folk Village.

At the foot of the Rock is Chez Hans, where chef Hans Peter Mattias uses Clonmel cider, apples, free-range chicken, gleaming fresh fish, spring lamb, and local produce to make his French-inspired dishes. Nearby is the Cashel Palace Hotel, once a Bishops Palace and a favorite watering hole of Elizabeth Taylor and Richard Burton. The place is sumptuous and exquisitely furnished. Rooms at the rear of the palace look up at the Rock of Cashel. The kitchen here, run by the Four Seasons, relies on wonderful roasts, steaks, and chops and serves them in its elegant dining room resplendent with Waterford crystal and gorgeous linens. The Spearman Restaurant, 97 Main Street, Cashel, has been pleasingly decorated, and the two chefs provide excellent modern dishes using the freshest and best of local ingredients.

Between Cashel and Tipperary Town is the Golden Vale, where some of Ireland's richest farmland is to be found—so rich it is said that a stick thrown into a field at night would grow so tall as to be out of sight by morning. Rich pastures, dairy farms with fat livestock, meandering rivers bursting with salmon, shade trees, and mountain slopes so gentle they are cultivated almost to their summits—unlike the rugged granite peaks of Connemara. Between County Waterford and County Cork the flat coastal area is dotted with farmhouses and laced with pretty country roads. Cork is Ireland's biggest and most southerly county. It is also enjoys some of the best weather in the country, especially in western Cork, warmed as it is by the Gulf Stream. Wild fruits and wild flowers crowd the hedgerows, and everywhere you look you see the ruins of a castle or gatehouse, a monastery or abbey, or a crumbling Georgian pile. Cork has at least four hundred castles, many of them in ruins but some refurbished and safe enough to wander about in and some positively glorious where you can spend a night of two. Many of Cork's castles are along the banks of the Blackwater River, which runs west to east across County Cork, joining the Celtic Sea at Youghal. Parts of Youghal's medieval city walls are still intact, and they encircle the marvelous St. Mary's Collegiate Church built by the Normans in the thirteenth century. Youghal's medieval past is apparent in its ancient Benedictine priory and the crumbling thirteenth-century abbey, but Youghal's life is very much in the present. This busy market town is also a resort with beach, boardwalk, and a wealth of shops and fine places to eat.

Sitting peacefully on the Blackwater River in Youghal is Aherne's Seafood Bar, 163 North Main Street. This well-known and much-loved bar and restaurant was started in 1924 by Jimmy Aherne and is now run by the Fitzgibbon families. This remarkable peaceful, low-key establishment is known by seafood lovers far and wide for its excellent food. David Fitzgibbon trained with the fabulous Roux brothers and also at Arbutus Lodge in Cork City. Prawns are the specialty of the house, and they can be had smothered in garlic butter in an escargot dish. The wine list is well stocked, and it is a comfort to know that Aherne's also has accommodations for people who can't bear to leave.

Walter Raleigh sailed into the harbor at Youghal with the first potatoes and tobacco to be seen in Ireland. An annual potato festival takes place in July at Raleigh's home, Myrtle Grove, which is open to the public. The Blackwater River is a major waterway through the counties and is famed for its succulent salmon and trout that weigh far more than their counterparts in European waterways. The Blackwater is also known as the Irish Rhine, because its southerly location makes it warm enough—in a good year—to grow the white grapes necessary for dry German-type white wine. If you follow the lovely serene Blackwater you will come first to the town of Fermoy, where a little farther north near Mitchelstown at the foot of the Gaulty Mountains a signpost points to the village of Ballyporeen. President Ronald Reagan's forebears lived at Ballyporeen, and some members of his family still call this small village home. Souvenirs are sold here commemorating the president's visit in 1984, and the local watering hole has been renamed Reagan's Bar. Farther along the Blackwater is Mallow. Mallow Racecourse is a great place to attend a meet in the summer months—it is subject to floods in the winter. Mallow's famous literary connection is to Anthony Trollope (1815–1852), who worked at Mallow post office. Trollope wrote his great novels and political books between half-past-five in the morning and breakfast before leaving for the post office. He worked for most of his life for the post office in various places, including the West Indies.

Three miles west is Mallow's other claim to fame, Longueville House. This spectacular white Georgian mansion is built on an eminence overlooking the Blackwater valley. Longueville House sits at the center of a 500-acre wooded estate. These lands were originally owned by Donough O'Callaghan before being appropriated by a Cromwellian supporter, Longfield. Longfield was made Baron Longueville and changed the name of the house from Garamaconey to Longueville. The two wings of the house date from this period—circa 1795. A fine conservatory of curved ironwork was added in 1866—now used as an additional dining room—that adds greatly to the beauty of the facade. The ancestral home of the O'Callaghan clan, historic Dromineen Castle, reduced to ruins by Cromwell's forces, is perched on cliffs overlooking the Blackwater and can be seen from Longueville House. The drawing room has been described as one of Ireland's grandest rooms, and a welcoming fire always burns here. The red-walled dining room—the Presidents' Restaurant—has a lovely ceiling executed by Italian craftsmen two centuries ago and a graceful Adam fireplace. The walls are hung with portraits of former Irish presidents, many of whom have been visitors to Longueville. A door from this room slides open to reveal the romantic conservatory. An extensive library has among its collection books that relate the history of Ireland and its association with Longueville House. Sixteen supremely comfortable bedrooms grace the upper floors, many with antique furnishings. Longueville House is a working farm with a flock of Suffolk sheep that provide milk-fed lamb for the restaurant. The owner, Michael O'-Callaghan, has three acres of the garden planted with grapevines and manages to produce a light and flavorful white German-style wine that he proudly serves to Longueville guests. Freshly picked salad greens, vegetables, and fruits from the farm are brought to the kitchen every day. All breads and pastries are baked daily in the kitchens. William O'Callaghan, the superb chef, trained with Raymond Blanc. Guests are free to fish in the Blackwater for salmon, and William O'Callaghan says he will either prepare it for them for dinner or smoke it so that they can take it away with them. Smoked salmon and gravadlax appear on the menu at Longueville House, as does fresh seafood delivered from the nearby port. Some of the dishes on the dinner menu are Ravioli of Castletownbere prawns; Salad of panfried scallops with gravadlax and oysters; Noisettes of Longueville lamb with tarragon mousse; Rack of roast suckling pig with apple and truffle sauce; Brill with sorrel sauce; and Seasonal vegetables in a light puff pastry. Irish farmhouse cheeses and delectable desserts include Pyramid of chocolate and praline with a crème anglaise sauce; Lemon pudding; and Puff pastry filled with garden rhubarb and apples with caramel sauce. William O'Callaghan has given us one of his favorite recipes for mussels to include in this book.

Mussels Gratinated with Herb Bread Crumbs in Aromatic Tomato Sauce

7 lb.	mussels
½	onion
1	carrot
1	sprig of parsley
1	sprig of thyme
1	knob of butter
1	glass of white wine

Bread crumbs

4	stale bread slices, crumbled
1	sprig of thyme
2 T.	chopped parsley
1	sprig of rosemary
1	sprig of fennel
1½ T.	olive oil

Tomato sauce

6	tomatoes
1	onion, chopped
½	fennel bulb
1	sprig of thyme
1	star anise

1. Wash all the dirt off the mussels and remove the "beard."

2. Sweat the vegetables and herbs in the butter, add mussels and white wine, and cover with a lid. Shake the pan occasionally. When all the shells have opened, remove from the heat. Strain mussels, reserving cooking liquid.

3. Remove mussels from the shells and set aside.

4. Blend the bread crumbs with the herbs and olive oil and set aside.

5. Remove seeds from the tomatoes. Sweat the chopped onion and fennel over low heat until beginning to soften. Add tomatoes, thyme, star anise, and mussel liquid. Simmer for 15 minutes, then season to taste.

6. On a shallow baking dish, place a greased mold 2 inches high and 3 inches wide. Season the warm mussels and press into the mold, leaving space at the top for the layer of bread crumbs.

7. Gratinate under the broiler until well colored.

8. Unmold in the center of a warmed plate and surround with the sauce. *Serves 8–10*

Cork city center sits on an island formed by two branches of the River Lee. This part is known as the "flat of the city" in contrast to the hilly northern part where St. Patrick's Hill is so steep steps are cut in the pavement. Beautiful Georgian houses here attest to Cork city's former affluence during its days as the butter capital. Cork was an important port for the British when Irish butter and beef were shipped to England before Ireland's War of Independence. St. Mary's Cathedral and St. Anne's Church steeple dominate the skyline. The two branches of the river flow through the city so that wherever you look are waterways and graceful bridges that add a great deal of charm. Near Oliver Plunkett street is the old ironwork English Market selling country produce and Cork meat specialties such as Drisheen sausages. The Regency Market or Grand Parade Market is held inside, and the aisles are bursting with fine Irish products—fish from rivers and sea, free-range chickens and eggs, organically reared beef and lamb, fine fruits and vegetables, and a wealth of Ireland's prestigious farmhouse cheeses. Cork is a beautiful city of pastel-colored houses with narrow hilly streets that climb steeply to the top of a range of hills in the east, reminding visitors of hill towns in Provence. Cork is second only to Dublin in size, but the pace here is slower than in Dublin. Cork's 140,000 inhabitants take great pride in their pretty, well-kept city. Patrick Street is the main city street, and lining its pavements are many interesting shops to browse, including some fine places to buy antiques. Cork city has newly pedestrianized streets full of boutiques, cafés, and coffeeshops.

Much of Cork's affluence today comes from its tourist trade, and an important feature for the tourist is Cork's wonderful restaurants. One of the very best is the Ivory Tower Restaurant in the Exchange Buildings at 35 Princes Street, where the chef proprietor, Seamus O'Connell, makes practically everything from scratch. This means each dish is unique as the homemade sausages, preserves, mustards, and vinegars used as components of his dishes are never exactly the same from one season to the next. Seamus O'Connell's dishes can be wild and seasonal, filled with the flavors of jasmine, honeysuckle, and orange blossoms. "Local foods are of supreme importance," he says, "for reasons of health and economy as well as for the perpetuation of culture and identity." Gathering ingredients from forest and foothill is one of his passions. Seamus O'Connell has generously contributed four recipes for this book.

Wild Herb Spring Tonic Soup

l	onion
l	potato
l	leek
2 T.	butter or oil
10	wild garlic stems, finely chopped
20	nettle tops—only the top four leaves
l	leaf comfrey—young and small
	parsley
2	handfuls watercress
5–10	sorrel leaves

1. Dice onion, potato, and leek and sweat, covered, in oil or butter for 3 to 5 minutes. Add wild garlic and 24 fluid ounces (3 C.) of water. Bring to a boil and simmer for 5 minutes.

2. Chop nettle, comfrey, parsley, and watercress and add to the soup. Simmer for 5 minutes. Add sorrel leaves and cook for one minute more.

3. Blend soup and season.

4. Serve with cream, chopped chives, and brown soda bread.

Serves 4

Smoked Fish and Potato Cake

l T.	oil or butter
6 lg.	potatoes, peeled and sliced ¼ inch thick
l	onion
l	leek
l	handful of mushrooms
½ lb.	smoked mackerel, herring, and salmon (or any one by itself)
6 fl.oz.	cream (⅔ C.)
l T.	whole-grain prepared mustard
l	tomato, chopped

1. Heat heavy 10–12-inch frying pan, cover bottom with oil or butter or both, and gently fry half of the potatoes in an even layer.

2. Layer half the sliced onion and half the leek on the layer of potatoes, then add mushrooms and smoked fish, followed by the remaining onion and leek.

3. Cook very gently, covered, until the potatoes are tender. Invert onto a plate, set aside, and keep warm.

4. Reheat pan with oil and fry the rest of the potatoes, covering the bottom completely. When almost tender, slide rest of half-cooked cake onto the potatoes, add cream and mustard, and simmer gently for 10 minutes, or put in a medium hot preheated oven at 325–350°F (or gas mark 3–4) for 10 to 15 minutes.

5. Serve with salad for a great winter dish.   *Serves 4*

Venison with Blackberries and Mint

2	lb.	haunch of venison—hung for 10–15 days—cut into 1½-inch cubes
10	fl.oz.	red wine (1¼ C.)
2		carrots, peeled and cut in 1½-inch chunks
1	lb.	shallots, peeled and left whole or cut in half if large
5		garlic cloves, unskinned
		flour to dredge meat cubes, plus 2 optional T.
		salt and pepper
2–3	T.	duck fat or oil
18	fl.oz.	chicken stock (2¼ C.) or dark venison stock
20		coriander seeds, crushed
10		peppercorns, ground
2	T.	honey
2		tomatoes, peeled, seeded, and diced
1	lb.	blackberries (3 C.)
3		sprigs of mint, julienned
2	t.	red wine or balsamic vinegar
2	T.	butter, optional

1. Marinate venison overnight in wine, carrots, shallots, and garlic.

2. Drain meat and reserve marinade. Dredge meat cubes in flour, season lightly with salt and pepper, and brown gently in duck fat or oil. Add marinade and all ingredients except blackberries and mint.

3. Cook covered at a gentle simmer for one hour or until tender. Remove solids with strainer and keep warm in covered crock.

4. Add blackberries and 16 fluid ounces (2 C.) water. Cook for a further 10 minutes. Add mint and a dash of red wine or balsamic vinegar, and thicken with a little roux (flour and butter mixed together), if needed.

5. Strain sauce over meat and reheat. Adjust seasonings and serve.   *Serves 4*

Pears Poached in Elderflower Wine
with Geranium Sorbet

8	lg.	pears, Concord or d'Anjou
32	fl.oz.	elderflower wine (4 C.)
		OR
24	fl.oz.	dry white wine (3 C.)
4		umbrellas or elderflower or honeysuckle or camomile flowers
4	oz.	honey (½ C.)
		zest of one orange
		zest of ½ lemon
4		peppercorns, crushed
10		coriander seeds, crushed
¼		vanilla pod
		OR
5		drops vanilla essence
2		lemon geranium leaves
1		lemon, juiced

1. Peel and core pears. Halve pears and place in a stainless steel saucepan. Cover with remaining ingredients, except geranium leaves and lemon juice, and poach gently until just tender. Let cool in liquid.

2. Pour half of poaching liquid into a clean saucepan, add geranium leaves, and reduce over medium heat.

3. Purée four pears with this liquid, add juice of one lemon, and freeze in ice cream maker*.

4. Reheat remaining pears in their liquid and serve with sorbet.

Serves 4

---

*If no ice cream maker is available, freeze in shallow trays and every hour whisk to break up crystals, until frothy and set.

Arbutus Lodge has a reputation for some of the finest cooking in Cork city, understandably, as Declan Ryan's cooking is out of this world. He uses top-quality Irish ingredients, such as superb meats and fish, and sauces them with delicacy to bring out their splendid flavors. The flower-filled dining room is small with high ceilings and large windows. Paintings by Irish artists decorate the walls.

Clifford's, 18 Dyke Parade, is a restaurant owned and run by Deirdre and Michael Clifford. His training includes stints at Claridges, the Connaught, and Arbutus Lodge. Clifford's is in the beautifully renovated County

Library building; the atmosphere is warm and friendly and the cooking top-notch Irish. Michael Clifford finds time on occasion to go out and fish for the salmon on his menu himself. He believes that the true flavors of food, be it fish, meat, or vegetable, should be allowed to come through and that anything less than this destroys the food.

Cork's harbor, Cobh, faces the open sea. From here hundreds of emigrants left Ireland for America during the potato famine that decimated the county. A new Heritage Center, the Queenstown Project, re-creates the experience of people who left their homeland from the bleak eighteenth to the twentieth century. North of Cork city is Blarney Castle, where hundreds of people climb the 128-step spiral stairway to the top of the castle to lie on their backs, clutching two handles, and reach up to kiss the Blarney Stone. Reputedly the stone bestows the gift of eloquence on whoever is lithe enough to kiss it. Even more people rifle through the gift shops and take tea and scones in the tearooms.

East of Cork city and southeast of Midleton at Shanagarry on the Youghal Road is Ballymaloe House, owned by Myrtle and Ivan Allen. Myrtle Allen is chairman of Euro-Toque for the whole of Europe and has done an enormous amount to promote Ireland's splendid foods. This is what Eugene MacSweeney of Lacken House has to say about Myrtle Allen: "In recent years I have been strongly influenced by the ideas and the cooking of Myrtle Allen of Ballymaloe House. When I first met Myrtle I was spellbound by her enthusiasm, her vast knowledge of Irish foods and her dedication to advancing Irish traditions of cooking. I have remained spellbound ever since for I believe that she has had an outstanding positive influence on Irish cuisine."

Ballymaloe House first opened its doors in 1964. The atmosphere is relaxed and informal. The lovely wisteria-covered farmhouse is set on a wide green meadow, amid fertile farmland, and the rooms are pretty and comfortable. Myrtle Allen is executive chef, orchestrating the menus, and the cooking is simply incredible. Since many of the dishes rely solely on produce, it is perfect for vegetarians too, with dishes such as squash blossoms filled with a delectable mousse or cheese soufflé, or a roulade or strudel packed with vegetables that taste as vegetables are supposed to taste. Local butchers, fishermen, and oystermen have been patronized from the beginning, and a tremendous variety of produce, including radicchio, garden peas, broad beans, sweet corn, Jerusalem artichokes, globe artichokes, and soft fruits such as loganberries are grown on the four-hundred-acre holding for the restaurant and for the adjacent Ballymaloe Cookery School. Sea kale is forced under tall pots that keep it white. There are also greenhouses for growing early vegetables and herbs. Anything else comes from local farmers and housewives. Ballymaloe Cookery School has a formal herb garden with geometric beds nearby. At the end of the kitchen garden behind the school is a framework house with views of the sea. The Cookery School is run by daughter-in-law Darina Allen, who also writes cookbooks. The full course at the cookery school is twelve weeks, but visitors to Ballymaloe House can take some lessons while there if they wish. The building where students stay has roses blooming over the door. The Allen family is extensive, and Allens of all ages will be found in kitchen, house, school, or garden.

Roughly eighteen miles to the southeast of Cork city is Kinsale, a town where in 1601 the people were defeated by the British and banned for centuries from their own hometown. In 1941 when the British finally departed, Kinsale was derelict and decaying. In the last thirty years Kinsale has known an incredible revival, largely due to a trio of pioneers, Heidli Mac-Neice, Peter Barry, and Gino Gaio, brave souls who decided together that they would open restaurants different enough from each other not to compete but rather to support one another. It worked. Soon they were joined by other chefs, including Gerry Galvin and his wife, Marie, who started the Vintage—Gerry Galvin is now at Drimcong House in Galway—and Brian Conin, who redid the Blue Haven. These restaurants' owners worked as a team—even to the point of staggering their vacation times. As more and equally diverse restaurants opened they set up the Kinsale Good Food Circle together. At the same time improvements were made to the town, and soon there was a new marina with sailing and angling clubs—you can rent a sailing boat for your vacation that comes with its own chef. The culminating event that attracts tourists to Kinsale, and also brings people interested in food and wine from all over the world, was the creation of the Kinsale Gourmet Festival, held annually at the end of October. Restaurants not to be missed in Kinsale are the Blue Haven with chef Stanley Matthews, the Vintage with chef-owner Michael Reiss, and Philip Horgan's Man Friday.

Directly south of Kinsale on the edge of the next bay to the east, Summercove, at Oysterhaven is the Oystercatcher Restaurant owned and managed by Sylvia and Bill Patterson. On the bay side of the street are oyster beds; on the other is the stone and stucco restaurant where the Pattersons now have a regular clientele from both local people and people who visit from all over the world. Sylvia's flair for design has created an atmosphere of warmth and intimacy, and Bill's career in several excellent hotels and restaurants has made him an expert in the kitchen. The menu at the Oystercatcher changes about five times a year so that full use can be made of seasonal produce. Local markets supply the majority of the ingredients used, except for wild mushrooms and herbs that are gathered in the surrounding countryside or from their own garden. Dales of Cork offer a splendid variety of fine fresh produce—organic produce is preferred—lamb comes from a neighboring farmer, and fish, of course, is right on the doorstep. The Pattersons' wine list has won a number of awards. Bill Patterson says his selection of favorite dishes—hot smoked salmon on blinis served with a sauce of leeks and saffron, roasted lobster with a lobster and truffle ravioli in a light tomato coulis and chili sauce, and Landes duck steak with garlic, lemon, and herb sauce have been "selected for their flavor, use of local produce and the added attraction that they allow me to use what I hope to be my flair for presentation. For example the Wild Mushroom Brioche is presented as a Penny Bun (a mushroom from the Bolitus family) with a tossed green leaf salad." Other superb dishes to try are the Oyster sausage on a saffron sauce, a Quartet of rock oysters simmering in garlic butter with almond, Fillet of lamb with a tapenade-flavored juice, and Breast of pheasant with walnuts and wild mushrooms. Desserts, and surprisingly savories, are superb—try the Chocolate profiteroles or the Angels on horseback. Bill Patterson's kind contribution to this book follows.

Filet Mignon with Cashel Blue Cheese and Port Wine as Prepared at the Oystercatcher

4	filet steaks, fully trimmed and weighing about 8 ounces each
	olive oil
2	shallots, finely chopped
	salt and pepper
2½ oz.	sultanas (½ C.), soaked overnight in
6–8 fl.oz.	port (⅔–1 C.)
4 oz.	roasted pine nuts (⅔ C.)
5 T.	unsalted butter
1 t.	Dijon mustard
2 T.	cream
4 oz.	Cashel Blue (1 C.), or any good creamy blue cheese

1. Brush the steaks with olive oil and cook to your liking in a good thick-based frying pan.

2. Remove from the pan and sprinkle with the shallots, season with salt and freshly ground black pepper, cover, and keep warm.

3. Using the same pan, add the sultanas and port, stirring to dissolve the caramelized meat juices. Add the pine nuts.

4. Thicken the sauce by shaking knobs of butter into the pan. Add the Dijon mustard, cream, and any juices accumulated from the steak.

5. Top the steaks with the cheese and pop under the grill to brown. Place on warm plates and surround steaks with the sauce.

6. Serve immediately with a crisp green salad.   *Serves 4*

If you hug the scenic road along the coast west of Kinsale you will come to Timoleague. South from here is Butlerstown, and continuing down to the coast you will find Dunworley Cottage Restaurant, owned and managed by a wonderful Swedish cook, Kathleen Norén. This restaurant has some of the best cooking of any kitchen in County Cork, much of which will satisfy vegetarians. Kathleen Norén uses no canned or frozen foods, and each dish is prepared to order, which sometimes means a wait, but you won't be sorry for the food has taste and freshness in every bite. She has a small smoker, and some of the fish is home smoked and served with a salmon roe and cream sauce that is simply blissful. Icy glasses of aquavit are a fitting accompaniment to the smoked fish. Smoked mussels are prepared in a vinaigrette dressing. In summer there is a gourmet menu for a cost of £20, offering four choices and ending with homemade petits fours and coffee or tea. Gratinated crab is popular all summer, and nettle soup is a springtime treat and very good for you. Though meat is beautifully cooked in many different ways, Kathleen Norén's favorite food is spanking fresh fish straight from the sea. She feels that cod is underrated by many people and says that, properly prepared, cod can be turned into superlative gravadlax. She also says that when visiting Europe she makes a point of taking farmhouse cheeses to her friends, who are always surprised at the superb quality of the cheeses made here. Her favorite cheeses "are a young Durrus, or a young Gubbeen, or maybe a goat's cheese from Cape Clear—but it's not easy to choose." All the vegetables here are grown in the cottage garden. Kathleen Norén bakes two to three different kinds of bread that are served with each meal, and keeps hens, ducks, and pigs—the latter providing the meat for the salami and sausages she makes herself in her old farm kitchen. The house used to be a farm long ago, parts of it are three hundred years old, and it is situated about three minutes from the sea and a beach with wonderful walks along the shore. Kathleen Norén shares her recipe for a vegetarian gratin with us.

Vegetarian Gratin

1½ lb.	potatoes, peeled and cubed
1½ lb.	onions, sliced
	butter for frying
1½ lb.	mixed vegetables, cut in pieces, such as carrots, leeks, summer squash, beans, or your choice
2	garlic cloves, or more to taste, minced
3	eggs
12 fl.oz.	cream (1½ C.)
3 T.	minced parsley

```
     salt and pepper, to taste
4  oz.  grated cheese (1 C.)
```

1. Preheat oven to 350°F (or gas mark 4).

2. In a large frying pan, quickly fry the potatoes and onions in some of the butter. Put them in a shallow ovenproof dish and finish cooking them in the oven until almost tender, about 10 minutes.

3. Quickly fry the mixed vegetables in the remaining butter for 4 to 5 minutes—no longer. Remove from heat and stir in the minced garlic.

4. Beat together the eggs, cream, parsley, salt, pepper, and grated cheese in a large bowl. Stir in the potato mixture and the mixed vegetables and pour into an ovenproof baking dish—or individual ramekins if you prefer—return to the oven and bake until puffed, golden, and just set, checking occasionally—approximately 45 minutes.

5. Serve hot with a salad, or as a side dish with cold, sliced, smoked ham or roast beef.   *Serves 4–6*

Freshly baked Irish brown bread and Irish soda bread smell fantastic and taste even better. Irish soda bread can be made with whole wheat flour, but in Ireland it is generally made with wholemeal, which is richer, heavier, and difficult to find in the United States. Yeast is not used; instead the raising agent is soda and salt, and thick, fresh buttermilk quickly binds the dough. A cross is traditionally slashed into the top and the dough cooked directly on a baking sheet, which makes a crusty free-form shape. When the dough is placed in a shallow, round, eight-inch cake tin it yields a higher loaf. The following recipes for Brown Bread and Barm Brack are reproduced with permission from Eugene MacSweeney of Lacken House Restaurant on Dublin Road, Kilkenny.

Brown Bread

```
1½  lb.   whole wheat flour
14  oz.   plain flour (scant 3 C.)
 2  oz.   bran (scant ½ C.)
 2  t.    bread soda (baking soda)
 2  t.    salt
 2  T.    brown sugar
16-20 fl.oz. buttermilk (2–2½ C.)
```

1. Preheat oven to 325°F (or gas mark 3).
2. Sieve the white flour, soda, and salt into the wheat flour.
3. Add the bran and brown sugar.

4. Mix the ingredients thoroughly and quickly stir in the buttermilk to form a soft dough.

5. Divide in two and place in greased baking tins. Bake for 80 minutes. *Makes 2 loaves*

Barm Brack

1	lb.	strong (bakers) flour
1	t.	salt
10	fl.oz.	tepid milk (1¼ C.)
1	t.	castor sugar
1½	oz.	dried yeast (or 3 oz. fresh)
4	T.	butter
5	T.	castor sugar
8	oz.	sultanas (1⅓ C.)
3	T.	chopped mixed peel
3	T.	sliced glacé cherries
1		egg, beaten
		honey or marmalade

1. Sieve flour and salt into a bowl and leave in a warm place.

2. Cream the yeast by warming the milk, dissolving one teaspoon of sugar in the milk, and sprinkling the yeast over the surface of the milk. Leave in a warm place for about 10 minutes to activate the yeast.

3. Rub the butter into the flour and add the sugar. Stir in the fruit. Line the bottom of a 2-pound loaf pan with buttered waxed paper.

4. Add the creamed yeast and the beaten egg to the flour mixture and work to a stiff dough. Knead well for 10 minutes to develop the gluten. The stronger gluten the higher the brack will rise. Fold dough and place in the loaf pan. Cover and leave in a warm place for one hour to double in bulk. Preheat oven to 425°F (or gas mark 7).

5. Remove cover and bake for 5 minutes in the hot oven, then reduce the heat 375°F (or gas mark 5) and continue to bake for another 45 minutes. When the brack is cooked it will have a golden crust and sound hollow when the bottom of the loaf is tapped with the knuckles.

6. Cool on a wire rack and brush with warm honey or marmalade to give a shine. A sugar and water glaze may be used instead, if you wish. *Makes one 2-pound loaf*

On the Main Street in Schull on Roaringwater Bay is a delicatessen and bakery called the Courtyard, owned by Dennis and Finola Quinlan. The delicatessen is packed to the rafters with good things to eat, most of them local, but nothing quite as local as the wonderful bread made by Jackie Bennett across the courtyard. Interestingly the bread is baked in an ancient bread oven, using the original bread pans. The only other oven like it in Ireland is in a Cistercian monastery.

Follow the road to Bantry, set on glorious Bantry Bay. Bantry House, which overlooks the water, was built for Richard White, the first earl of Bantry, in 1739 and is still occupied by the same family. The beautiful, aging mansion is open to the public and has lovely tapestries and furnishings as well as a large collection of paintings. Fantastic views over Bantry Bay can be seen from the upper floors, and when you descend you can wander outside to stroll in the famous Italian gardens. The Bantry 1796 French Armada Exhibition Center, next to the house, details France's aborted attempt to liberate the Irish people from the clutches of the English. Further north is Ballylickey, where Kathleen O'Sullivan is the chef proprietor at Sea View House Hotel and Restaurant. Here too are fabulous views over the bay. In 1993 Kathleen O'Sullivan won the coveted Gilbeys Gold Medal Award for catering excellence. County Cork has won this award for the third year in a row. Seaview House dates back to 1890 and was bought by Kathleen O'Sullivan's father as a family home. In the 1970s, after her parents had built another home nearby, Kathleen O'Sullivan began to develop Sea View House as a hotel. Menus are based firmly on food products from West Cork. Seafood is on the doorstep, meat is organically reared in the Lee River valley, and organically grown herbs and produce are grown in the hills between Bantry and Dunmanway. Cork has a wealth of small suppliers, growing unusual and delicious foods in their gardens, such as ripe wood strawberries, and they love nothing better than to bring them right to the door of local restaurants where their labors are so appreciated by eager and talented chefs. Kathleen O'Sullivan is especially talented in preparing and developing seafood and dessert recipes. A sampling of dishes from recent menus are Cocottes of smoked haddock Mornay, Crêpe fruits de mer au gratin, Roast stuffed loin of pork, Roast rack of lamb with rosemary, Poached supreme of fresh salmon, Fillets of John Dory with mussel sauce, Dover sole, and Grilled sirloin steak. Desserts are an interesting assortment of crêpes, a Grand Marnier soufflé, Cream meringues with butterscotch sauce, and Profiteroles with chocolate sauce. Menus change substantially every evening, and if you stay here you will be treated to the largest breakfast of your life. Clonakilty's famous black and white puddings will surely be part of the fare, along with fluffy eggs, potato bread, kippers, pancakes, and more. Kathleen O'Sullivan has given us her recipe for Bailey's Mousse for this book.

Bailey's Mousse

4		leaves of gelatin
4		eggs
4	oz.	sugar (½ C.)
15	fl.oz.	heavy cream (scant 2 C.)
4	T.	Bailey's Irish Cream liqueur

1. Soak gelatin in a little water.

2. Meanwhile separate eggs and beat the yolks and sugar until they are light and fluffy.

3. Beat egg whites until stiff but not dry and fold into the yolks.

4. Whip cream and fold into the egg mixture. Carefully add Bailey's and gelatin.

5. Pour into small ramekins—sometimes soufflé collars are used for a taller dessert, and when the collar is removed the sides can be dusted with toasted almonds. Another presentation could be inverting the dessert onto a plate and decorating it with coffee cream or chocolate sauce; and a third presentation could be the addition of a tiny tuile basket of fruits.   *Serves 4–6*

Glengarriff's sheltered position on Bantry Bay, surrounded as it is with a ring of mountains, provides the gentlest of climates where subtropical plants thrive. Just offshore is Garnish Island, whose lovely garden is filled with a great variety of subtropical vegetation. Fishermen nearby will be glad to take you across to the island.

Fresh Salmon Salt-cured with Dill

2	lb.	fresh salmon, center cut in one piece (have your fishmonger take out the bone for you)
4	T.	white peppercorns
4	T.	black peppercorns
4	T.	sea salt
4	T.	sugar
3		bunches of fresh dill

1. Wash salmon inside and out and pat dry with kitchen towel.

2. Using a blender, or spice grinder, coarsely grind the peppercorns and toss with sea salt and sugar. Rub this mixture all over

salmon, inside and out. It is important to use up the entire amount, so press it into the salmon with the flat of your hand if necessary.

3. Wash and spin dry the dill, and spread one bunch in the bottom of a nonreactive dish that will hold the salmon in one piece.

4. Put salmon on top of dill, and tuck the second bunch on the inside of the salmon. Arrange the third bunch over the top.

5. Cover salmon, not the dish, with cling film and weight it with a plate slightly smaller than the circumference of the dish. Place a heavy object on the plate—such as a quart-sized can of tomatoes or a foil-wrapped brick.

6. Refrigerate for a full 5 days, turning once a day and replacing weight. Juices will accumulate in the bottom of the dish. Leave these as they help to marinate the fish.

7. When the time has elapsed, scrape all the spices and dill off the salmon with the back of a knife and discard. Return to the refrigerator until ready to serve.

8. Thinly slice salmon and serve chilled with lemon wedges and tiny capers, or whisk together some prepared mustard, minced dill, lemon juice, and a little oil to make a sauce.   *Serves 8*

County Kerry

Kerry is known to have some of the most beautiful scenery in all of Ireland on the Ring of Kerry—a 110-mile circular drive on dizzying mountain roads around the Iveragh peninsula. As the road dips and rises, it affords spectacular views of serene offshore islands, chains of lakes, steep mountain passes, and fertile valleys where chattering streams plunge over rocks and disappear under humpbacked bridges. Wooded areas clinging to the lake shores are home to herds of red deer. From the Oisin Pass you will see the highest peak in Ireland, Carrantuohill. Oisin, the son of Finn MacCool of Giant's Causeway fame, is reputed to have left Ireland to dwell in Tir na nóg, the land of eternal youth. Lush gorges are graced with wild orchids, and the hedgerows are bedecked with wild fuschia. Ancient monastic ruins on the shore near Ballinskelligs are washed by the sea, and on Great Skellig the remains of beehive cells, tombs, and moss-covered crosses from a ruined thousand-year-old hermitage are to be found. The Skellig Heritage Centre has a very worthwhile exhibition detailing the area's fascinating history. The people of Kerry are known for their love of humor, their quick wit, and their passion for Gaelic football. Red sandstone mountains, cleft with steep gorges where salmon go to spawn, delight stalwart fishermen. Vistas that shift and glimmer are part of

Kerry's magic—the magic that breeds tales of giants. Kenmare, one of Kerry's most important towns, is close to the mountains called the MacGillycuddy Reeks. Kenmare is a great base for walkers and hikers. In fact an annual walking festival is held each June in the town. Here the Michelin-starred Park Hotel sits in a lovely wooded garden. It was originally a railway hotel, the Great Southern built in 1897, and it continued to operate into the late 1970s. Francis Brennan bought it in 1984 and turned it into the special place it is today. Elegantly furnished with super antiques, the service is faultless yet not in the least fussy or obtrusive. Perhaps this is because everyone who works here is quite young and filled with energy and enthusiasm. Chef Brian Cleere is a talented, creative chef, and the food is impeccable in both the choice of fine ingredients and its exemplary execution.

Following the coast road you will come to Parknasilla—the Irish riviera—made famous by Victorians in search of summer retreats. This sheltered bay has waters warmed all year long by the Gulf Stream, and the prolific vegetation, surprisingly, includes flowering mimosa and eucalyptus trees. The little town of Sneem relies on tourists for its prosperity. It is very attractive with pastel-colored houses and tidy streets.

Caherdaniel, near Sheehans Point, has the Michelin-listed restaurant Loaves and Fishes, owned and managed by Helen Mullane and Armel Whyte. Armel Whyte's cooking could well be some of the best you will eat anywhere. His creativity is in finding unusual ingredients that pair so well together that the dish zings with flavor. Accompanied by a colorful platter of perfectly cooked vegetables and followed by meltingly delicious desserts, the food served at this restaurant is supremely satisfying.

At Waterville, Llough Carrane's ample supply of trout and salmon attract fishermen, golfers come for the championship course, and archaeologists flock to the many standing stones, beehive cells, and hill forts this area is blessed with. Waterville's Fisherman's Bar, part of the respected Butlers Arms Hotel, is a great place to catch your breath and tuck into your choice from a menu of fresh and appealing dishes cooked by chef Robert O'Mahoney.

Killorglin is a quaint pretty village beside the River Luane, where in early August the annual Puck Fair is held. Men go to the hills, capture a wild male goat, place a crown on its reluctant head, drape its horns with ribbons and flowers, and set it to rule over the proceedings that unfold during this three-day event. The roots of this festival go back to pagan time, but today its major attractions, aside from merrymaking, are livestock and horse shows. Lughnasa, named for the Celtic god Lugh, but also meaning "August" in Gaelic, is another pagan festival held cheerfully in the month of August. Traditional foods served at the Puck Fair are Kerry Pies—made with mutton, onions, and parsley, tucked into a mutton fat pie crust firm enough to be transportable. At the feast of Lughnasa the appropriate food is wild blueberry—either eaten simply with sugar or made into that most delightful of desserts, a fruit fool.

Wild Blueberry Fool

16 oz.   blueberries (2 C.), wild if available
3 T.   sugar
¼ t.   vanilla essence
8 fl.oz.   heavy cream (1 C.)

1. Crush blueberries and mix with sugar and vanilla, stirring gently until the sugar is dissolved.
2. Whip cream and fold into the blueberry mixture.
3. Spoon blueberry fool into wine glasses.
4. Chill until needed and serve with thin, warm shortbread biscuits.

Dingle, a tiny, charming town on the coast directly below Connor Pass on the Dingle Peninsula, is acclaimed for its wonderful fish, supplied daily from its own fishing fleet. Restaurants, taking advantage of the abundance of glistening mouthwateringly fresh seafood, flourish. Doyle's Seafood Restaurant has an international reputation despite its simple decor, lack of pretension, and breezy atmosphere. This is the perfect place to relax with a pint of Guinness and a plate of spanking fresh crustaceans. Next door in John and Stella Doyle's house are six well-appointed comfortable rooms, and breakfasts here are copious.

Accolades are also heard for John and Pat Moore's restaurant on Green Street called Beginish. Pat Moore has a master's hand in the kitchen, and her seafood dishes are full of fresh flavor, lightly sauced, and leave one feeling happy and content. Missing Pat Moore's dessert soufflés, however, would be a grave mistake—they are out of this world. There are stunning views all around over Dingle Bay.

Tralee is Kerry's largest town. Wide streets and elegant houses lend an air of prosperity to Tralee. The National Folk Theatre makes its home here, and it is worth a detour to attend one of their fine performances.

County Limerick

Fishing has its devotees all over Ireland, and it is no wonder for the whole country seems to be as much water as land, but particularly so in the northern regions. The River Shannon, which is neither polluted nor heavily trafficked, flows in and out of pristine lakes all the way down to Killaloe, fourteen miles from Limerick. The river has three great lakes, Lough Ree, Lough Derg, and Lough Allen. The latter is three miles (5 km) wide and six miles (10 km) long. Completely encircled in inhospitable-looking mountains,

Lough Allen is a fisherman's paradise. Cabin cruisers can be rented for the trip down the river from Carrick-on-Shannon, and it is possible to moor at one of the little islands that dot the lakes, or put in at one of the villages for a meal or to restock your boat. Cruising the River Shannon and its lakes is astonishing for Europeans whose own inland waterways have become polluted and terribly overcrowded because of their enormous popularity. Limerick is the largest city on the River Shannon. King John's Castle, dating to 1210, can be visited. Before flowing out to sea, the river passes its namesake the town of Shannon where a tourist attraction—Bunratty Castle and Folk Park—offers "medieval" banquets, three redecorated castles, thatched cottages, and a restored village street with pubs and shops near the airport. Shannon was the world's first airport to offer duty-free goods. This part of Ireland is rich in prehistoric remains and ruined, mostly Norman, castles.

County Clare

County Clare is rich in traditional music, dancing, and folklore. Musicians will come to a pub of an evening and play their music without any reward save the respectful attention of the patrons as they play. In the summer months, the tiny village of Doolin on the coast teems with folk music collectors, ethnic musical groups, and troupes of dancers from all over the world. The overflow is housed under canvas, and the sounds of pipes, concertinas, fiddles, and whistles rend the air. For five miles (8 km) south of Doolin to Liscannor Bay the Cliffs of Moher tower over the seashore, reaching a height of seven hundred feet (200 m). Sheer and stark, they are an impressive sight. Lisdoonvarna, a quiet resort town, holds Ireland's only spa. Its restful atmosphere and healing waters attract many visitors, particularly when the annual matchmaking festival is in full swing in September. From here a treeless terrain of rounded hills and bare rocks with not a drop of water in sight form the oddest landscape in the country. Called the Burren, it covers an area of approximately one hundred square miles (260 sq km) in northern County Clare. The underlying terrain is composed of porous limestone known as karst, and it is pockmarked and pitted with holes. Water flows beneath the surface, nourishing the uncharacteristic plant life that is more reminiscent of flora in the Arctic than in Ireland. In the spring sky blue alpine gentians push their way through clefts in the rock. Caves, lakes, and streams underlie the surface of the Burren. One cave stumbled upon by a local farmer has been open to the public since 1978. Its entrance can be found near Ballyvaughan. At Kilfenora the Burren Display Centre interprets the geology and the unusual plant life.

Aran Islands

Lying off the coast, directly opposite this geologic anomaly, are the Aran Islands formed by the same limestone ridge that creates the Burren in County Clare. These three islands, lapped by the waters of Galway Bay, are roughly thirty miles from Galway city. When settlers first came to live here, the rugged Aran Islands were devoid of soil. Slowly and laboriously, in order to grow potatoes and cereal for food and grass for their livestock, these stout-hearted folk made their own soil by mixing seaweed and sand from the coast with soil found in deep crevices between the rocks. The Aran Islands are crisscrossed with serene gray stone walls, built laboriously one by one to create a foil against the steady winds that buffet the headlands. The islanders live by fishing, especially lobster, their livestock, and tourism. Currachs, small boats used for fishing, made from tarred canvas stretched over a frame of wooden laths, are light enough for a man to carry on his back. These hand-formed crafts can also be seen near the island of Inishmaan, which has no deepwater port, ferrying livestock and passengers from ships to the island. Inishmaan is renowned for its beautifully woven colorful belts and shawls. Homespun flannel is also made here, and fairly recently Inishmaan craftspeople are using their traditional fabrics to fashion clothes for export. Here too you will see the traditional rawhide shoes that when worn for a while conform to the feet and protect them from the craggy rocks that form much of the island's surface. The largest of the three islands, Inishmore, boasts the finest prehistoric hill fort in Europe, Dun Aengus. Built on a cliff top that towers two hundred feet (61 meters) above the shore, the site offers fantastic views from Connemara in the north to Kerry in the south.

County Galway

Galway city is home to fifty thousand happy souls and is a lively busy place both in winter and summer. It started as a fishing village on the most sheltered part of Galway Bay and progressed to a fortified walled city by the thirteenth century. It prospered under the management of several prominent families, collectively known as the tribes, and today Galway is still referred to as the city of the tribes. Remnants of the imposing houses built as family homes by members of the tribes can be seen today; one of these houses a bank. The Church of St. Nicholas, the parish church, is the finest medieval cathedral in Ireland and since the Reformation has been Protestant. Christopher Columbus is reputed to have attended Mass in this most spectacular edifice. Unfortunately there is not a lot left of Galway's former architectural glories, as Cromwell showed no mercy, burning, razing, and looting in retaliation for Galway city's support of the monarchy over the roundheads. Part of the medieval wall called the Spanish Arch remains. Miraculously the maze of tiny streets that form Galway's inner city has been preserved. Here on the streets you will hear Gaelic and English spoken, as Galway is part of the Gaeltacht—parts of Ireland where Gaelic is spoken as the first language. Gaelic has been the official language of the country since independence, but it has never succeeded in totally replacing English, even though it is a required subject in schools. Many Irish people are fluent in the language, and about a third of the population have a working knowledge of Gaelic. Education is compulsory for children between the ages of six and fifteen. The school budgets come from public funds, but schools are run on religious lines. The Catholic Church manages the primary grades, and Catholic religious orders direct the secondary grades.

Galway city is a great place to be on a Saturday when the Galway Saturday market is held, and farmers and their wives along with myriad stall holders come to sell their glorious homemade cheeses, breads, cakes, home-grown fruits, wild mushrooms gathered in the forests, vegetables, bedding plants, flowers, and local shellfish—especially oysters in the winter months. The whole town smells of fresh baked bread, and people stand on the street with a pint in one hand and a slab of farmhouse cheese, a hunk of salami, or a briny Galway oyster in the other and shoot the breeze. Oysters, available the world over, seem to taste better in Galway, and they go down well with a crusty slice of fresh brown soda bread and a glass of Guinness. September is the month for the Galway Oyster Festival, when everyone turns out to watch the parades, listen to the bands thumping out their boisterous music, and eat their fill of cool, succulent Galway oysters. Perhaps the biggest collective get-together for the people of Galway city is Race Week, when the shops and offices shut their doors so everyone can attend. Held at Ballybrit outside the city, the course is so situated that you can look over the bay to the Aran Islands. Everyone in Ireland who can get there attends, and the entire week is one huge carnival.

Just fifteen minutes west of Galway city, and one mile west of Moycullen on the main Galway–Clifden road, is Drimcong House and Restaurant, a seventeenth-century house set in twenty-five acres of lake and woodland, owned and managed by chef Gerry Galvin and Marie Galvin, his wife, who bought the property in the early 1980s and have worked phenomenally hard to make it what it is today. Gerry says, "We cherish every acre." Marie Galvin started a garden within minutes and grows vegetables, soft fruits, and a wealth of herbs. She also keeps a chicken or two to provide free-range eggs for the kitchen, and Gerry Galvin says she has designs on sheep next! Drimcong House has been the recipient on more than one occasion of the Supreme Award of Excellence for Restaurants from Bord Fáilte, the Irish Tourist Board. Here in their lovely lakeland home they have created an exceptional restaurant. Turf fires in winter and polished oak tables set the scene for memorable meals. Menus change weekly, influenced by what is best in the garden, the lake, and Galway Bay. Gerry Galvin says, "Our fish is unsurpassed, organic growers abound locally and their repertoire increases all the time; lamb from County Galway is still special and reliable butchers provide well-hung beef." Starters from their summer menu include Grilled oysters and smoked salmon in a lovage cream, Black pudding with sweetbread mousse, and Fresh salmon tartare with potato cake. A main course selection from a winter menu includes a wealth of fresh fish dishes that change daily, and also Grilled loin of lamb; Duck confit with orange and ginger; Aromatic venison with beetroot, juniper, and pepper sauce; and for dessert Strawberry and banana duet with ice cream and sabayon sauce, Seasonal fruit tart, and a luscious chocolate confection. The following recipes are reprinted from *The Drimcong Food Affair* by Gerry Galvin, with his permission.

Melon and Avocado in Green Sauce

1	ripe honeydew melon
1	ripe avocado
10 fl.oz.	green sauce (1¼ C.)

    1. Cut melon in two, scoop out seeds, and slice each half into four sections.

    2. Cut avocado in two and, having discarded the stone and outer skin, slice each half in two.

    3. Arrange the melon and avocado in an attractive fan shape on each serving plate, accompanied by some green sauce.

Note: Include a slice of watermelon, when available.   *Serves 4*

Green sauce

    juice of 3 lemons and 2 oranges
½   ripe avocado, chopped
    a 20-ounce (2½ C.) measure full of fresh herbs such as mint, lemon balm, parsley, chervil, fennel, chives
2 t. honey
    salt and pepper

    4. Liquidize, or whirl in a blender, all ingredients except salt and pepper to a smooth sauce.

    5. Season.   *Makes about 20 fl.oz. (2½ cups)*

Note: When ripe, melons and avocados will have an obvious "give" to a gentle touch. An unripe avocado can be ripened over a few days, wrapped in newspaper in a dark place.

Shiitake Mushroom and Prawn Lasagne

4	oz.	pasta (see recipe below)
12		medium-sized prawns, shelled
4	oz.	shiitake mushrooms (¾ C.), chopped
6	fl.oz.	cheese sauce (⅔ C.) (see recipe below)
2	T.	butter

Pasta

7	oz.	strong flour (bread flour) (1⅓ C.)
2	T.	semolina
½	T.	olive oil
1		egg
4	T.	warm water
		salt

1. Mix together flour and semolina and make a well in center.
2. Put all other ingredients into the well and work to a smooth dough.
3. Wrap in cling film and cool.

Cheese sauce

20	fl.oz.	milk (2½ C.)
2	fl.oz.	cream (¼ C.)
1	t.	dry English mustard
2	T.	flour
3	T.	butter
3	oz.	Gruyère cheese (¾ C.), grated
		salt and pepper
		pinch of cayenne pepper
½	t.	lemon juice

4. Over medium heat whisk together the milk and cream, mustard, flour, and butter until smooth. Cook gently for 5 minutes.
5. Add Gruyère and simmer for another 3 minutes, stirring all the time.
6. Whisk in seasoning, cayenne, and lemon juice.

Note: If necessary, cheese sauce can be diluted with fish stock or more milk.

7. To prepare lasagne: Roll out pasta thinly. Cut into 12 two-and-a-half-inch circles (three per portion) and poach for one minute.

8. Preheat oven to 400°F (or gas mark 6). Fry mushrooms in butter for a minute. Season.

9. Assemble lasagne portions in layers as follows: Pasta, prawns, a teaspoon sauce, pasta, mushrooms, a teaspoon sauce, pasta again, 3 teaspoons sauce over the top.

10. Bake for 12–15 minutes.

11. Before serving, brown under hot grill.

12. Serve extra sauce in a sauceboat.   *Serves 4 as appetizer*

Drive west on the same road from Drimcong House, and the road will skirt the enormous Lough Carrib, where you will have splendid views of the islands in the Lough and fine mountain vistas of the Maumturk Mountains rising to the right of the road on its way to Clifden. In Clifden, a resort town on beautiful Clifden Bay famous for its elegant tweed, you will find on the Square, Destry Rides Again, a lively restaurant owned and run by Julie Foyle and chef proprietor Paddy Foyle. The food here is very good indeed, as you would expect from a chef who cooked at the splendid Rosleague Manor at Letterfrack. Though the menu is simple, Paddy Foyle's inventiveness lifts whatever he cooks to new heights. His forte is an unusual but judicious blending of ingredients that enhances the flavor of the food.

Following the road around toward Leenane you will come to Letterfrack, home of Connemara Handcrafts, who sell well-made Irish china, pottery, and other fine crafts. Farther on is the exquisite Klyemore Abbey, now a boarding school run by Benedictine nuns. From Leenane, situated at the head of the incredibly deep fjord, Killary Harbour, the only one in Ireland, you will pass into County Mayo.

County Mayo

County Mayo is the third largest county in Ireland and encompasses much of the rugged beauty of Connemara, a wild area rich in lakes awash in wild trout and rushing rivers thrashing with wild salmon. In southern Connemara deep bays indent the shoreline, and broad beaches sprout many colored seaweeds. Connemara is a barren, beautiful part of the country, composed of rugged marshland and sea. It is a watery world, cut through with range after range of mountains. Whitewashed cottages and farmhouses gleam through the gloom on a cloudy day, clinging to the sides of mountains, dotted through valleys, nestled close to the seashore, and clustered near towns like beacons in a storm. The resilient, resourceful folk living in barren areas of County Mayo have learned to augment their income any way they can. One of these is by distilling in hidden stills here and there the potent spirit poteen from barley, yeast, sugar, and water. Poteen is illegal to make and can be dangerous to your health if not correctly made.

Connemara, and also Kerry and Wicklow, are three mountain areas where tender, succulent mountain lamb thrive. No pesticides or fertilizers have ever been used on these high peaks, so the tiny lambs are organically reared. Some people say this delicacy has the same peerless flavor as the best veal. You will find lamb from these three areas in some butchers' shops by the middle of August, and the supply generally continues until the last days of October. If the label mentions both mountain lamb and the name of the area it hailed from, then you have found the very best there is.

On the southern shore of Clew Bay looms the Holy Mountain Croagh Patrick, from whose summit glorious views can be seen over the surrounding counties and the Atlantic Ocean. Every year thousands of pilgrims—some of them barefoot—climb the stony incline to the little oratory on the top of Croagh Patrick on the last Sunday in July, when they honor the spirit of St. Patrick with penitential prayers. The seeds of Christianity were planted in Ireland by St. Patrick in the fifth century. Many early monasteries which sprang from his teachings were destroyed by the invading Vikings two hundred years later. New religious orders founded during the Middle Ages by Cistercians, Augustinians, Dominicans, and Franciscans thrived and grew rich until Henry VIII broke with the Church of Rome and sacked the monasteries throughout his realm. Scattered all over Ireland, England, and parts of Scotland, the beautiful ruins of these monasteries attract many visitors today, particularly Jerpoint Abbey and Holy Cross Abbey, which has been restored, in the south of Ireland; Dryburgh Abbey in Scotland; and Fountains Abbey and Glastonbury in England. St. Patrick continues to exert a strong influence on the faithful. St. Patrick's Day, March 17, falls during Lent, and people having given up something for Lent—usually candy for children and perhaps alcohol for the men—are ready for a break. The feast on St. Patrick's Day is the most important in all of Ireland and is celebrated with traditional foods of corned beef and cabbage or boiled bacon and cabbage. A little celebratory drink of the Pota Padraig is also in order on that welcome day.

Corned Beef and Cabbage

3–4 lb.	corned beef, soaked overnight
2	onions—one stuck with whole cloves
2	carrots
1	medium-sized cabbage, cut in quarters

1. Place corned beef, onions, and carrots in large saucepan and fill with water to barely cover meat.

2. Put the lid on and cook for about 2 hours. Add cabbage quarters and cook for about 20 minutes longer.

3. Remove meat to a warm platter in a warm place. Reduce cooking liquid by half.

4. Surround corned beef with the well-drained cabbage and some boiled potatoes. Pass the reduced liquid and hot mustard separately.   *Serves 6*

Irish monks, who adapted the Celtic beliefs of the Irish to Christianity, transcribed many Irish legends into Gaelic prose. These sagas furnish a rich account of the Celtic way of life. Brave and zealous warriors, Celtic women were equal in stature to Celtic men. The Celtic ruler of the Iceni tribe in Britain, Queen Boudicca, burned Roman London in A.D. 60. The Gaelic language of the Celts is in everyday use in parts of western Ireland. Ancient and beautiful works of art in gold, silver, bronze, iron, and stone are rooted in Ireland's Celtic tradition. Celtic culture throve throughout the Middle Ages in Ireland while most of Britain was under the heel of the Roman Empire. About one hundred fifty early Celtic High Crosses, based on a circular design, still survive. Possibly the circle typifies sun worship.

On the southern part of Clew Bay is the graceful town of Westport, designed by the architect William Wyatt. Near the Octagon in Westport is the Cork restaurant, owned and managed by Willie and Jutta Kirkham, who cater to vegetarians and vegans with specially prepared, interesting dishes and do not neglect people who like a little meat or fish. From Westport to Newport, Clew Bay has a fantastic coastline filled with inlets and islands. Its northern shore sweeps round to Achill Island, which is joined to the mainland now by a bridge over Achill Sound. At Newport is the historic Newport Country House and Restaurant, a grand, luxurious Georgian dwelling that looks over the Newport River and its quay. The interior is gorgeous—decorative, creamy plasterwork embellishes ceilings and walls, and the staircase is magnificent, sweeping gracefully aloft and lit by lovely windows set high in the walls. The house is loved and lovingly run by Thelma and Kieran Thompson. Their smoked salmon and cured fish are legendary, vegetables, salads, and herbs come from the kitchen garden, fish leaps from river and bay to the table, and the desserts are out of this world.

Inland from the Bay is Castlebar, the county's most important town, and a stone's throw from here is the village of Knock, where in 1879 several people saw the silhouette of the Virgin Mary on the gable of the church. Now a fifteen-thousand-seat basilica has been built in the village of Knock in honor of the Virgin Mary, and pilgrims by hundreds of thousands, many of them invalids, visit the village annually.

County Sligo

County Sligo is one of the loveliest counties in Ireland and perhaps the least traveled. William Butler Yeats lived here, and many places in Sligo are mentioned in his plays. He is is Sligo's most famous son. Students flock to Sligo every August to attent the annual Yeats Summer School. His wonderful poem "The Lake Isle of Inishfree" was inspired by the island in Lough Gill. Yeats is buried in Drumcliff churchyard on Drumcliff Bay, overlooked by the dramatic Benbulben. Resorts, some with championship golf courses, ring Sligo Bay. A curious mountain here, Knocknarea, is really just an enormous pile of loose rocks that are reputed to hold the grave of Queen Maeve of Connaught, whose life history is related in Ireland's most famous narrative, *Táin Bó Cuailnge*. Sligo is rich in antiquities, many of which are located on the islands off Sligo's curling coastline. The largest of these is Coney Island, and all of these islands are easily accessible by boat.

County Donegal

County Donegal is famous for its great-tasting potatoes and for the plethora of lobsters caught in the raging Atlantic Ocean away from the protected waters of its fishing ports. These lobsters are very like American lobsters trapped off the coast of Maine. The greater part of Ireland's lobster catch goes to the better restaurants in France. A rather down-putting phrase is used in Donegal to characterize a person who lets you down and cannot be found when you need them. They say he or she "did the turn of the lobster," as these wily creatures do when they back out of a trap and slide quietly out of view. An activity traditional to the northwestern areas of Ireland is turf-cutting in boggy areas in the early summer when the land is still moist from the long winter rains, making it easy to slice. Men, often in groups, work with long shovels to cut the dark brown peat. Left to dry in stacks that are a familiar sight in County Donegal, the peat will be moved later to cottages and farmhouses to store for use in the winter months. On Donegal's western shore, The Rosses (meaning islands) peninsula is a very popular vacation spot and in the summer can be packed with holidaymakers and tourists. As its name implies, its shoreline is studded with dozens of islands. The Rosses is equally popular with "weekenders," and cottages and bungalows proliferate. The northwestern counties are deservedly popular. The hills are clad in purple heather, the views are dramatic, and the long coastline, indented with innumerable narrow remote peninsulas, promises peace and relaxation.

County Donegal has the largest Gaeltacht (Gaelic-speaking region) in Ireland. Unless you have a map that gives place names in both languages, it is very easy to get lost—though in Ireland people are so gracious and friendly, you will not be lost for long.

Donegal town in the mountainous southern region of the county is renowned the world over for its beautiful soft, handwoven tweed. At one time all the cloth was woven by villagers in their homes. Suit lengths of fabric were taken to market in baskets, called creels, and sold to middlemen. Now that the demand has increased for this lovely cloth, woven in the muted colors that can be found in the winter landscapes of Donegal, larger concerns are weaving their own cloth and then selling it on the spot or making custom-made suits on their premises. Many cottagers continue to weave tweed at home but mostly now on a part-time rather than full-time basis. Kilcar is another town where cloth is woven.

West from Donegal town on Donegal Bay is the busy, thriving fishing port Killebegs, where the dock is smack in the middle of town, and people crowd around to watch the catch being unloaded. The water here is deep enough for large fishing trawlers to dock from France and other Mediterranean countries. Farther around the headland is the little village of Glencolumbkille, revered for its association with St. Columba. Many prehistoric cairns can be visited in this village. On the cliffs north of the village is the House of Columba, a small oratory where the saint is reputed to have stayed. Barefoot local pilgrims walk the two miles to visit the shrine on June 9 each year. Near the seashore is a folk village with exhibits and crafts. Further north is Ardara—a village that holds a Weaving Fair each year—and where the Lobster Pot restaurant sells wonderful fresh seafood dishes as well as the ubiquitous hamburger and fries. Straw, not reed, is the roofing material for cottages in County Donegal, often held down with colorful ropes tied to wooden pegs protruding from the white walls. The next large peninsula has dramatic rocky headlands and masses of islands off shore. The largest island is Aranmore. On the coast directly opposite Aranmore is Burtonport, possibly the busiest fishing port in Ireland, where more lobsters, salmon, and other fish are landed than anywhere else. The land here is an unending vista of rocks and boulders, stretching for over 60,000 acres crisscrossed with streams and lakes. At Gweedore, thrusting out to sea is the headland known as Bloody Foreland Head for the dramatic red color of its rocks. The Derryveagh Mountains farther inland shelter the Glenveagh National Park, a twenty-four-thousand-acre wilderness area with a lake, and a castle built by a despot called John Adair. He emigrated to the United States, and after his death, his wife, Cornelia Adair, made Glenveagh Castle her home. She greatly improved the splendid gardens that surround the dwelling today. The property was given to Ireland for use as a national park by the last owner, Henry P. McIlhenny, in 1984. From here the road runs south to the county town of Letterkenny, situated on the River Swilly. On Ramelton Road, one and a half miles (2.5 km) outside of town is Carolina House Restaurant, owned by Charles and Mary Prendergast. Mary Prendergast trained at the famous Ballymaloe Cookery School, so you can expect to eat dishes made of the finest and freshest ingredients possible. Fresh fish and local meat are beautifully cooked, and desserts are scrumptious.

Rathmullan House, built in the late eighteenth century, is situated on the shore of Lough Swilly, a totally unpolluted, sparkling body of water that empties into the ocean at Fanad Head. This lovely house, owned by Robin and Bob Wheeler, is a great place to stay with the lake literally on the doorstep, and between the house and the lake are a sweep of gorgeous award-winning gardens. A walkway, called Batt's Walk for a previous owner, follows the shoreline to the village of Ramelton. If the lake is too cool for swimming, there is a modern saltwater swimming pool inside where the temperature is kept at 70 degrees Fahrenheit. Beautiful detailing around the doors and windows, and lovely wooden floors graced with antiques, make this hospitable house a wonderful place to stay. Local meats, particularly baby lamb, and spanking fresh fish are superb. Whatever you do, do not miss breakfast.

If you decide to return to Letterkenny and drive along the eastern side of Lough Swilly, to explore the Inishowen peninsula and visit Ireland's most northerly point, Malin Head, there is a signposted route you can follow. This is a desolate mountain area but very beautiful. Before you get to the broader reaches of the Lough, about twenty-nine miles past Letterkenny is a small road signposted to Grianán Aileach that winds for about a mile to the top of an eight-hundred-ten-foot (250-m) mountain. Here is a fascinating circular fort that possibly dates back to the Iron Age. It was mentioned by Ptolemy, the Greco-Egyptian astronomer, geographer, and mathematician, in the second century A.D. It became the seat of the O'Neill clan and remained so for hundreds of years. The circular fort spans a seventy-six-foot area. Inside are other circular walls interlaced with passageways around a central edifice.

A few miles before you reach Buncrana—the main town in this area and another spot very popular with holidaymakers—you will reach Fahan. On the lake in a restored Georgian house is the Restaurant St. John. Here in a pretty dining room with open fires, Reg Owen and Phil McAfee serve delicious pâtés, homemade soups, crusty warm bread, and succulent meat and fish dishes, using impeccable Irish ingredients and seasonal organic produce. Their love of foods grown without pesticides and fertilizers extends to seaweeds, such as carrageen moss, that fringes some beaches nearby. This typically Irish ingredient is made into a delectable soufflé.

Malin Head is a tiny fishing port that over the years has become possibly the crab-fishing capital of Ireland, most of which is processed here in the local factory. The pier was originally built in 1884 for cargo boats. Recently the village of Malin became the proud winner of the Tidy Towns competition.

The eastern edge of County Donegal below the Inishowen peninsula is flat and fertile. Quite a few Protestant farmers live and work in this productive region of Donegal close to the border with Northern Ireland.

Geographical List of Contributing Restaurants and Hotels in *The New Cooking of Britain and Ireland*

London

The Lexington
45 Lexington Street
London W1R 3LG
England

The Dorchester
Park Lane
London W1A 2HJ
England

Waltons Restaurant
121 Walton Street
London, SW3 2HP
England

The Ivy
1 West Street
London WC2H 9NE
England

Leith's Restaurant
92 Kensington Park Road
London W11
England

Southeast

Read's Restaurant
Painter's Forstal
near Faversham
Kent ME13 0EE
England

Spencers Restaurant
36 North Street
Emsworth
Hampshire PO10 7DG
England

Gravetye Manor
Vowels Lane
East Grinstead
West Sussex RH19 4LJ
England

The Wife of Bath Restaurant
4 Upper Bridge Street
Wye, Ashford
Kent TN25 5AW
England

West Country

The Castle Hotel
Castle Green
Taunton
Somerset TA1 1NF
England

Gidleigh Park Hotel
Chagford
Devon TQ13 8HH
England

The Mulberry Room Restaurant
1 Scarborough Road
Torquay
Devon TQ2 5UJ
England

Popham's
Castle Street
Winkleigh
Devon EX19 8HQ
England

Lower Pitt Restaurant
East Buckland
North Devon EX32 0TD
England

Heartland

The Beetle and Wedge Hotel
Moulsford-on-Thames
Oxfordshire OX10 9JF
England

Wickens
Market Place
Northleach
Gloucestershire GL54 3EJ
England

Midlands

The Merchant House
Lower Corve Street
Ludlow SY8 1DU
Shropshire
England

Vine House Hotel and Restaurant
High Street
Paulersbury, Towcester
Northamptonshire NN12 7NA
England

The Evesham Hotel
Cooper's Lane, off Waterside
Evesham, WR11 6DA
Worcestershire
England

East Anglia

Adlard's Restaurant
79 Upper St. Giles Street
Norwich NR2 1AB
Norfolk
England

North Country

Sharrow Bay Hotel
Lake Ullswater
Penrith CA10 2LZ
Cumbria
England

Miller Howe
Rayrigg Road
Windermere LA23 1EY
Cumbria
England

Pool Court Restaurant
Pool-in-Wharfedae
Otley LS21 7EH
West Yorkshire
England

Quince and Medlar
13 Castlegate
Cockermouth CA13 9EU
Cumbria
England

The Cromwellian Restaurant
16 Poulton Street
Kirkham PR4 2AB
Lancashire
England

Heathcote's
104/106 Higher Road
Longridge
Preston PR3 3SY
Lancashire
England

Melton's Restaurant
7 Scarcraft Road
York YO2 1ND
N. Yorkshire
England

Wales

Penhelig Arms Hotel
Aberdovey
Gwynedd LL35 0LT
Wales

The Town House
70 Cathedral Road
Cardiff
South Glamorgan CF1 9LL
Wales

Portmeirion Hotel
Portmeirion
Gwynedd LL48 6ER
Wales

Bodysgallen Hall
Llandudno

Gwynedd LL30 1RS
Wales

The Old Rectory
Llansanffraid Glan Conwy
Colwyn Bay
Clwyd LL28 5LF
Wales

Hotel Maes-y-Neuadd
Talsarnau, near Harlech
Gwynedd LL47 6YA
North Wales

Chandler's Brasserie
Trefriw
Gwynedd LL27 0JH
Wales

Penmaenuchaf Hall
Penmaenpool Dolgellau
Gwynedd LL40 1YB
Wales

Ye Olde Bulls Head Inn
Castle Street
Beaumaris, Isle of Anglesey
Gwynedd LL58 8AP
Wales

The Great House
High Street
Laleston, near Bridgend
Mid Glamorgan CF32 OHP
Wales

Plas Bodegroes
Pwllheli
Gwynedd LL53 5TH
Wales

Tan-y-Foel Country House
Capel Garmon, near Betws-y-coed
Gwynedd LL26 0RE
Wales

Llangoed Hall
Llyswen, Brecon
Powys LD3 0YP
Wales

Ynyshir Hall
Eglwysfach
Machynlleth
Powys SY20 8TA
Wales

The Griffin Inn
Llsywen, Brecon
Powys LD3 0UR
Wales

Ty'n Rhos Country House
Llanddeiniolen
Caernarfon
Gwynedd LL55 3AE
Wales

Ireland

Ivory Tower Restaurant
The Exchange Building
35 Princes Street
Cork
County Cork
Ireland

The Oystercatcher
Oysterhaven
Kinsale

County Cork
Ireland

Dunworley Cottage
Dunworley
Butlerstown
County Cork
Ireland

The Redbank Restaurant
7 Church Street
Skerries
County Dublin
Ireland

Lacken House Restaurant
Dublin Road
Kilkenny
County Kilkenny
Ireland

Drimcong Restaurant
Moycullen
County Galway
Ireland

The Old Rectory
Wicklow
County Wicklow
Ireland

Longueville House
    and Presidents' Restaurant
Mallow
County Cork
Ireland

Sea View House Hotel and Rest
Ballylickey
Bantry
County Cork
Ireland

Scotland

Creel Restaurant
Front Road
St. Margarets Hope
Orkney Islands KW17 2SL
Scotland

Seafood Restaurant
Town Pier
Fort William PH33 7NG
Scotland

Cringletie House Hotel
Peebles EH45 8PL
Scotland

Ostlers Close Restaurant
Bonnygate
Cupar
Fife KY15 5LH
Scotland

The Peat Inn Restaurant
and Residence
Cupar
Fife KY15 5LH
Scotland

Dubh Prais Restaurant
123b High Street
Edinburgh EH1 18G
Scotland

BIBLIOGRAPHY

Ashton, Amanda, *Suffolk Home Cooking* (Stowmarket, England: Blackthorn Press, 1985).

Beeton's Book of Household Management, first edition facsimile (New York: Farrar, Straus and Giroux, 1969).

Bunn, Mike, *Ireland: The Taste and the Country* (London: Anaya Publishers Ltd., 1991).

Chapman, Kit, *Great British Chefs* (London: Octopus Books, 1989).

Davies, Gilli, *Lamb, Leeks and Laverbread: The Best of Welsh Cookery* (London: Collins Publishing Company, 1989).

Davies, Gilli, *Taste of Wales* (London: BBC Books, 1990).

Davies, Gilli, *The Down to Earth Cookbook* (Cardiff: British Gas plc Wales, 1993).

Dixon, G.M., *Traditional Recipes of East Anglia* (Peterborough, England: Broadgate House, 1987).

Fitzgibbon, Theodora, *Irish Traditional Food* (New York: St. Martin's Press, 1983).

Fitzgibbon, Theodora, *A Taste of Scotland in Food and in Pictures* (London: J.M. Dent & Sons Ltd., 1970).

Fodor's Great Britain 1993 (New York: Random House, Inc., 1993).

Fodor's Ireland 1994 (New York: Random House, Inc., 1994).

Fodor's Scotland 1994 (New York: Random House, Inc., 1993).

Fry, Plantagenet Somerset, *The Kings and Queens of England and Scotland* (London: Dorling Kindersley, 1990).

Galvin, *The Drimcong Food Affair* (Dublin: Colour Books Ltd., 1992).

Garmey, Jane, *Great New British Cooking* (New York: Simon & Schuster, 1981).

Grigson, Jane, *Good Things* (New York: Alfred A. Knopf, Inc., 1971).

Grigson, Jane, *English Food*, revised edition (London: Ebury Press/Random House UK Ltd, 1992).

Hachette Guide to Great Britain (New York: Random House, Inc., 1988).

Hartley, Dorothy, *Food in England* (London: Futura Publications, 1954).

Hill, Shaun, *Shaun Hill's Gidleigh Park Cookery Book* (London: Random Century Group Ltd., 1990).

Insight Guide: Great Britain (Hong Kong: APA Publications Ltd., 1993).

Insight Guide: Ireland (Hong Kong: APA Publications Ltd., 1993).

Jaine, Tom, *The Good Food Guide* (London: Hodder and Stoughton, 1992).

Mann, Gladys, *Good Food from Old England* (London: Frederick Muller Ltd., 1956).

McKenna, John, and Sally McKenna, *Bridgestone Irish Food Guide* (Durrus, County Cork: Estragon Press, 1993).

McKenna, John, and Sally McKenna, *The Bridgestone 100 Best Restaurants in Ireland* 1992 (Dublin: Estragon Press, 1992).

Miers, Richenda, *Scotland* (London: Cadogan Books plc, 1987, 1989, 1991, 1994).

National Geographic Society, *Discovering Britain and Ireland* (Washington, D.C.: National Geographic Society, 1985).

Nicholson, Nigel, ed., V. *Sackville-West's Garden Book* (London: Michael Joseph, 1968).

Norwalk, Mary, *A Taste of Norfolk* (Norwich, England: Jarrold & Sons Ltd., 1988).

Rance, Patrick, *The Great British Cheese Book* (London: Macmillan Ltd., 1988).

Spurling, Hilary, *Elinor Fettiplace's Receipt Book: Elizabethan Country House Cooking* (London: Salamander Press, 1986).

Sylvester-Carr, Denise, *London* (London: Collins & Brown, 1991).

Tannahill, Reay, *Food History* (New York: Stein and Day Publishers, 1973).

Tovey, John, *John Tovey's Entertaining on a Plate!* (London: Macdonald & Company Publishing Ltd., 1981).

Tovey, John, *John Tovey's Feast of Vegetables* (London: Century Hutchinson Ltd., 1985).

Whipple, Andy, and Rob Anderson, *The English Pub* (New York: Viking, 1985).

White, Florence, ed., *Good Things in England* (London: Futura Publications, Limited, 1974).

Wilson, C. Anne, *Food and Drink in Britain: From the Stone Age to the 19th Century* (Chicago: Academy Chicago Publishers, 1973).

RECIPE INDEX

Appetizers

Chicken:
  and Ham Terrine, 301
  and Stilton Terrine with Walnuts, 103
Cheese:
  Cheddar Soufflé, Hot Montgomery, 87
  Dunlop and Caraway Spread, 320
  Mediterranean Melin-y-Coed (goat's
    cheese), 312
  Welsh Rarebit, 308
Crab Dip, Hot, with Toast Points, 79
Fish, Smoked, and Potato Cake, 394
Melon and Avocado in Green Sauce, 411
Mushroom(s):
  Caps with Cashews and Double
    Gloucester Cheese, 152
  in Garlicky Tomato Sauce, 62
  Shiitake and Prawn Lasagne, 412
  Wild, Ragout with Toast Points, 35
Mussels with Creamy Herb Sauce, 99
Oysters:
  with Dill Butter Sauce, 86
  Warmed with Carrot Chive Sauce, 371
Salmon:
  Marinated Scotch Salad, 106
  Salt-cured with Dill, 404
  Smoked Pâté, 330
Scallops, Ragout of, with Monkfish, Pork,
    and Spiced Apple, 331
Vegetables, Terrine of Young, 461

Soups

Broth, West Coast, 324
Celery and Apple, 385
Haddock, Smoked, and Leek Chowder, 385
Jerusalem Artichoke Enriched with Saffron
    and Thyme, 270
Kentish Cob Nut (hazelnut) and Artichoke,
    84
Oyster Stew, 201
Parsnip and Apple, 340
Prawn, Dublin Bay Bisque, 377
Seafood:
  Scottish, 349
  Welsh (Potage de Fruit de Mer Pays de
    Galles), 288
Spring Tonic (Wild Herb), 394
Stilton and Cider Cream with Croutons, 240

Main Dishes

Bacon, Boiled, with Mashed Potatoes and
    Mushy Peas, 57
Beef:
  Essex Boiled with Carrots and Dumplings,
    204
  Filet Mignon with Cashel Blue Cheese and
    Port Wine, 399
  Medallions of Scottish with Wild
    Mushrooms and Whisky Sauce, 42
  Pot-roasted Rump and Oxtail with Ale
    Sauce, 250

Roast with Green Peppercorn Sauce, 53
Steak and Oyster Pie, 316
Cheese Smoked Caerphilly and Leek
    Soufflé, 305
Chicken:
    Braised with Garlic and Aromatics, 226
    Cold with Lemon Sauce (Lancashire
        Hindle Wakes), 251
    Maesmawr, 309
    Poached:
        with Creamy Mashed Potatoes, 158
        with Sun-dried Tomato Sauce, 186
    Spicy, 282
Crab:
    Ravioli, 122
    Salad, 211
    Tart, 351
Duck:
    Aylesbury, Steamed and Crisp-fried, 160
    Breast Marinated with Plum Sauce, 128
    Breast of Trelough with Herb Sauce, 299
    Crepinette, 83
Fennel Soufflé, 47
Fettucine with Mussels and Anchovies, 212
Goose, Roast Glazed, 386
Grey Mullet, Fillet with a Saffron and
    Tomato Sauce, 300
Haddock, smoked with rice (Kedgeree), 337
Hake:
    Filet Kenure House, 378
    in a Fresh Herb Crust, 343
Halibut, Steaks with Mustard Dill Sauce, 152
Herring, Grilled with Rhubarb and Allspice,
    118
Lamb:
    Chops Grilled with Shiitake Mushrooms,
        72
    Fillet with Water Chestnuts, Orange
        Segments, and Watercress, 238
    Lancashire Hot Pot, 255
    Loin with Tagliatelle of Leek and Roast
        Garlic, 292
    Marinated:
        as Game, 225
        and Roasted with Rosemary and Red
            Wine Sauce, 102
    Parcels:
        with Laverbread, 302
        of New Season Lamb Stuffed with
            Chicken Mousse, 88
    Poached Leg in Hay, 284

Rack of, with Parsley, 177
Welsh Chops en Croûte, 264
Lobster:
    Cornish Thermador, 114–115
    Timbale, 291
Monkfish, Fillets in Cheese Batter with Red
    Pepper Sauce, 333
Mussels:
    in Creamy Herb Sauce, 78
    Gratinated with Herb Bread Crumbs in
        Tomato Sauce, 392
Partridge, Roasted with Endive and Ginger
    and Parsley Jus, 269
Pheasant:
    Norfolk in Cider, 213
    with Sage and Apples, 262
Pork, Roast Loin with Apple Stuffing, 155
Rabbit:
    Civet in Cider, 274
    Cotswold in Yogurt, 147
Salmon:
    and Mussel Sausage on a Fricassée of
        Leeks Scented with Coriander, 270
    Parcels with Laverbread and Smoked
        Prawn Sauce, 302
    Steaks Baked with Dill and Cashew Nuts,
        220
    Wye with Roasted Vegetables and
        Hermitage Shallot Jus, 268
Scallops, in Chili Lime Butter, 246
Sea Bass:
    Filled with a Scallop Mousse with Squid
        Ink Noodles, 279
    Roast Fillet with Herb and Cream Sauce,
        311
    with Saffron Potato and Roast Garlic, 133
    with Tomatoes, Saffron Sauce, and
        Spinach Mousse, 205
Seafood:
    Anglesey with Spinach Mousse and
        Laverbread Butter, 306
    with Sauce Bourguignonne and Winter
        Vegetables, 209
    Terrine with Salmon Caviar Sauce, 73
Sea Trout:
    with Laverbread, 289
    Wrapped in Carmarthen Ham, with Leeks,
        Laverbread, and Mustard Sauce, 295
Shellfish Risotto with Lemon Butter Sauce,
    361
Shrimp, Spiced with Coriander, 193

Sole:
  Fillets with Apple Cider and Cream Sauce,
    119
  Mousse with Vermouth and Chive Sauce,
    229
Spinach and Blue Cheshire Cheese Tart, 181
Stew, Irish, 367
Stilton, and Potato Tart, 44
Tripe and Onions, 63
Trout:
  with Asparagus, Lemon, and Capers, 105
  Fillets with Smoked Salmon, 321
  with Herbed Butter Sauce and Pine Nuts,
    234
Veal, Chicken, and Ham Pie, 185
Venison:
  Aunt Holda's Rissoles with Potatoes and
    Red Wine Sauce, 195
  Beer-Braised Casserole with Cabbage and
    Bacon Dumplings, 36
  with Blackberries and Mint, 395
  Roast Leg with Elderberry Sauce, 386
  Steaks in Cumberland Sauce, 129
Wood Pigeon, Pan-fried Breast of, Served
    Cassoulet Style, 254

Vegetable and Side Dishes

Asparagus:
  and Green Onion Timbale, 243
  and Stilton Crèpes with Hollandaise
    Sauce, 173
Avocado, Salad with Hot Smoked Bacon,
    127
Cabbage:
  and Bell Pepper Salad with Almonds and
    Asian Noodles, 40
  and Cheese Baked, 298
Celeriac, Creamed, 299
Fennel, Carrots, and Snow Peas in Lemon
    Sauce, 163
Leek and Potato Frittata, 275
Mushroom, Wild, and Asparagus Salad, 370
Parsley, Pie, 241
Potato:
  and Beetroot Cake, 387
  cakes (Fadge), 359
  Gnocchi à la Parisienne, 242
  Gratin de Jabron, 178
  Harmer Galette, 174
  and Scallion Purée (Champ), 357
  and Swedes mashed (Clapshot), 345

Town House Tatties, 258
Ratatouille with Parmesan Shavings and
    Pine Nuts, 157
Spinach Timbales with Red Bell Pepper
    Sauce, 65
Vegetable Marinated Salad with Goat's
    Cheese, 49
Vegetarian Gratin, 400
Yorkshire Pudding, 232

Desserts

Almond, Apricot Bars, 60
Apple:
  Fenland Dumplings, 214
  Rhubarb Crisp, 369
  Sorbet in a Biscuit Tuile, 380
Banana, Irresistible Nutty Flan, 297
Blueberry, Wild, Fool, 407
Brandy Snaps, 191
Cake:
  Coventry Godcakes, 183
  Devon or Cornish Saffron, 125
  Dorset Apple Tea, 137
  Eccles, 249
  Norfolk Harvest, 200
Cheesecake, Honey, with Mead Ice Cream
    and Red Wine Syrup, 285
Cranberry Apple Pie, 175
Cream Burnt with Raspberries, 143
Fruit, Marinated in Rose Petal Syrup with
    Melon Sorbet, 197
Mousse:
  Bailey's Irish Cream, 404
  Honey with Orange and Almond Biscuit
    Cones, 293
Pancakes, Shrove Tuesday, 166
Parkin (gingerbread), 231
Peaches, Poached and Filled with Soft
    Cheese, 277
Pears:
  in Elderflower Wine with Geranium
    Sorbet, 396
  Poached in Red Sweet Wine, 162
  Roast with Coffee Bean Sauce, 354
Pudding:
  Cherry Chocolate, Baked, 81
  Chocolate, Baked in a Welsh Whisky
    Anglaise, 271
  Christmas, 90
  Clootie Dumpling (dried fruit), 353
  Ginger, Steamed, 336

Orange with Caramel, 34
Plum (fresh), 263
Sticky Toffee, 54
Summer, with Clotted Cream, 120
Sussex Pond, 93
Raspberry:
　Savarins with Eau-de-Vie Cream, 89
　Syllabub, 238
Syllabub, 238, 322
Tart:
　Almond, 189
　Border (custard and dried fruit), 318
　Custard with Nutmeg Ice Cream, 134
　Lemon Chiffon, 298

Breads
Barm Brack (fruit bread), 402
Beremeal Bannocks, 353
Brown, 401
Oatcakes, Scottish, 315
Scones, Scottish, 334

Sauces
Cumberland, 245
Peach and Chili Salsa, 302
Prawn, Smoked, 303

Drinks
Champagne Cocktail, 169

Subject Index

Akrigg, Colin, 240
Allen, Myrtle, 397

Blaydes, Christopher, 237
Bond, Chris, 240
Brawn, 13

Chapman, Kit, 131
Cheese:
  Blue Vinney, 137
  Blue Wensleydale, 234
  Caerphilly, 257, 281
  Cheddar, 130
    Irish, 364
  Cornish Yarg, 39
  crowdie (cottage cheese), 315
  Double Gloucester, 151
  Dunlop, 320
  Dunsyre blue, 329
  farmhouse:
    English, 7–8, 63, 168, 181
    Irish, 369, 400
    Scottish, 319, 321–322, 326, 335, 338,
      342, 345
    Welsh, 259, 281
  Lanark blue, 320
  Lancashire cheese, 251
  Leicester cheese, 192
  sage Derby cheese, 186
  Stilton, 28, 184, 186
  Wensleydale cheese, 233

Coulson, Francis, 5, 54, 236

Fortnum & Mason, 46
Frumenty, 14

Harrods, 2, 39–40
Henderson, Paul, 121
Hill, Shaun, 2, 159
Hjort, Michael, 6
Hotels and Restaurants:
  Adlard's Restaurant, Norfolk, 208–210
  Beetle and Wedge Hotel, Oxon., 156–159
  Bodysgallen Hall, Gwynedd, 303–308
  Castle Hotel, Somerset, 5, 13, 131–134
  Chandler's Brasserie, Gwynedd, 310–311
  Creel Restaurant, Orkney, 352–355
  Cringletie House Hotel, Peebles, 318–319
  Cromwellian Restaurant, Lancs., 253–255
  Dorchester Hotel, Mayfair, 47–50
  Drimcong Restaurant, County Galway,
    410–413
  Dubh Prais Restaurant, Edinburgh,
    323–325
  Dunworley Cottage, County Cork, 400–401
  Evesham Hotel, Worcs., 174–175
  Gidleigh Park Hotel, Devon, 5, 121–125
  Gravetye Manor, W. Sussex, 103–104
  Great House, Mid Glamorgan, 264–265
  Griffin Inn, Gwynedd, 273–275
  Heathcote's, Lancs., 249–251
  Hotel Maes-y-Neuadd, Gwynedd, 287–290

431

Ivory Tower Restaurant, County Cork, 393–396
Ivy, Covent Garden, 63–64
Lacken House Restaurant, County Kilkenny, 384–387, 401
Leith's Restaurant, Kensington, 36–37
Lexington, Soho, 57
Llangoed Hall, Brecon, 266–272
Longueville House, County Cork, 391–393
Lower Pitt Restaurant, Devon, 128–130
Melton's, North Yorkshire, 6, 225–227
Merchant House, Salop., 2, 177–179
Miller Howe, Cumbria, 5, 13, 237–239
Mulberry Room Restaurant, Devon, 117–118
Old Rectory, Clywd, 308–310
Old Rectory, County Wicklow, 379–381
Ostlers Close Restaurant, Fife, 332–333
Oystercatcher, County Cork, 398–399
Peat Inn Restaurant, Fife, 330–332
Penhelig Arms Hotel, Gwynedd, 281–283
Penmaenuchaf Hall, Gwynedd, 283–287
Plas Bodegros, Gwynedd, 294–295
Pool Court Restaurant, West Yorkshire, 228–230
Popham's, Devon, 126–128
Portmeirion Hotel, Gwynedd, 291–294
Quince and Medlar, Cumbria, 235–236
Read's Restaurant, Kent, 86–90
Red Bank Restaurant, County Dublin, 376–379
Seafood Restaurant, Fort William, 342–343
Sea View House Hotel and Restaurant, County Cork, 403–405
Sharrow Bay, Cumbria, 5, 13, 240–244
Spencers Restaurant, Hants., 105–106
Tan-y-Foel Country House, Gwynedd, 312–313
Town House, Cardiff, S. Glamorgan, 258
Ty'n Rhos, Country House, Gwynedd, 297–300
Vine House Hotel and Restaurant, Salop., 194–198
Waltons Restaurant, Kensington, 41–42
Wickens, Gloucs., 146–147
Wife of Bath Restaurant, Kent, 82–83
Ye Olde Bulls Head Inn, Gwynedd, 301–303
Ynyshir Hall, Powys, 278–280

Influence on British food:
New world, 40–41
Norman, 26
Roman, 21–23
Saxon, 23–25
Viking, 25–26

Kedgeree, 3
Kippers, 3

Laver, 11

Markets:
Billingsgate fish, 23, 73
Cardiff, 261
Galway Saturday, 410
Leadenhall, 69
Machynlleth, 277
Oxford, 155
Regency, 393
Smithfield meat, 68–69
Martin, Johnnie, 240

Perry-Smith, George, 29, 117

Rance, Hugh, 7
Rance, Patrick, 7, 168
Regional foods:
East Anglia:
apple dumplings, 214
Colchester oysters, 201
crab, Norfolk, 212
Essex boiled beef with dumplings, 203
harvest cakes, 200
jugged rabbit, 206
saffron, 204–205
Heartland:
Banbury cakes, 154
whigs, 162
Isle of Man:
herrings, oak smoked, 246
London:
jellied eels, 69
Midlands:
Bakewell tart, 189
brandy snaps, 190
cider, 175
fidget pie, 175
Melton Mowbray pie, 184
Pax cakes, 175

Shrewsbury cakes, 179
Shrewsbury biscuits, 180
simnel cake, 179
soul cakes, 180
Worcestershire sauce, 172
yeomanry pudding, 182
North Country:
  collop Monday (eggs and meat), 230
  Cumberland rum butter, 245
  Cumberland sauce, 245
  curd tarts, 230
  Eccles cakes, 249
  fat rascals, 227
  hindle wakes (cold chicken with
    prunes), 251
  hot pot, 255
  May Day milk dishes, 221
  parkin (gingerbread), 230
  pikelettes, 227
  scouse, 255
  shortbread, 232
  singin' hinny, 221
  Stingo beer, 233
  Wilfra cakes, 228
  York ham, 234
  Yorkshire pudding, 231
Northern Ireland:
  champ, 356
  fadge, 356
  soda bread, 356
Republic of Ireland:
  barm brack (fruit bread), 401
  brown bread, 401
  coddle (potato dish), 367
  colcannon (kale and potato dish), 367
  Irish stew, 367–368
  soda bread, 401
  stout, Guinness, 374
  whiskey, Irish, 339, 374
Scotland:
  Arbroath smokies, 337
  bannock (griddle cake), 314

bap (roll), 314
black bun, 326
Border tart, 318
clapshot (potato dish), 345
cock-a-leekie (soup), 315
Dundee cake, 335
Dundee marmalade, 335
Dundee ginger preserves, 335
Finnan haddie (smoked haddock), 3, 337
haggis, 326, 355
Kippers:
  Aberdeen, 338
  Loch Fyne, 315
oatcakes, 315
parkin, 314
Scotch broth, 315
Scotch pancakes, 3
smoked salmon, 320
soda scone, 314
Whisky:
  malt, 320–321
  Scotch, 339
Southeast:
  maids of honor, 110
  puddings, savory and sweet, 94
Wales
  bara brith (fruit bread), 261
  Carmarthen ham, 262, 276
  laverbread cakes, 259–260
West Country:
  Bath buns, 138
  cider, 130
  clotted cream, 120
  Devon or Cornish saffron cake, 125
  Dorset apple tea cake, 137
  Sally Lunn bread, 138

Sack, Brian, 236, 240

Tovey, John, 5, 237

Vickery, Philip, 1, 132